HISTORY

An introduction to theory, method and practice

Most students of history still see in Historiography a long and forbidding word, best avoided. Here is a book which will change all that. In their timely textbook Peter Claus and John Marriott invite readers to join the many – past and present – who have taken history seriously and have contributed to its making. *History: An introduction to theory, method and practice* is accessible, interesting and inclusive. At a time when history has come to include so many approaches and sources, this is also a welcome guide to how historians understand their traditions and their roles in contemporary culture.

Professor Miri Rubin, Queen Mary, University of London

This is a comprehensive introductory guide to the nature of historiography which examines the history of historical writing from Herodotus to post-modernism, discusses the nature of historical knowledge and examines a wide range of perspectives with which historians have made sense of the past. It is clearly written and set out, includes extracts from the works of many of the historians whom it discusses and suggests ways in which students can develop the subject for themselves. It will be welcomed both by teachers and by their students.

Steve Rigby, Emeritus Professor of Medieval Social and Economic History, University of Manchester

Students (and their teachers) will be grateful for this book. From Herodotus to postmodernism and internet ·istory, Peter Claus and John Marriott's survey of how the human past has been studied and written about is essive in both its range and its clarity. It can be dipped into when needed, while its totality provides a did overview of the richness and diversity that exist within the writing of History.

Dr Bryan Ward-Perkins, Trinity College Oxford

systematic and well-structured assessment of modern historical writing. Students will find that nade of such approaches as psychohistory, Marxism and postmodernism, that each is illustrated ete and lively examples, and that potential pitfalls and further reading are identified. Some may hole book; far more will draw on the chapters most useful to themselves.

Professor Michael Hicks, University of Winchester

Marriott introduce students to different aspects of historiography and methodology in a simple, ınd engaging manner. Using interesting methods and examples to explore historical and theoretical this is a good book to support the study of history at university level.

Dr Xavier Guégan, School of Historical Studies, Newcastle University

HISTORY

An introduction to theory, method and practice

Peter Claus and John Marriott

Harlow, England • London • New York • Boston • San Francisco • Toronto • Sydney
Auckland • Singapore • Hong Kong • Tokyo • Seoul • Taipei • New Delhi
Cape Town • São Paulo • Mexico City • Madrid • Amsterdam • Munich • Paris • Milan

Pearson Education Limited
Edinburgh Gate
Harlow
Essex CM20 2JE
England

and Associated Companies throughout the world

Visit us on the World Wide Web at:
www.pearson.com/uk

First published 2012

ISBN: 978-1-4058-1254-2

British Library Cataloguing-in-Publication Data
A catalogue record for this book is available from the British Library

Library of Congress Cataloging-in-Publication Data
A catalog record for this book is available from the Library of Congress

10 9 8 7 6 5 4 3 2 1
15 14 13 12 11

Typeset in 9.5/13pt ITC Charter by 35
Printed by Ashford Colour Press Ltd., Gosport

Contents

Preface

While there may have been a perceptible shift away from the further reaches of linguistic theory, where postmodernism and 'deconstruction' methodologies have sought to convince us that there is no such thing as historical truth, and where history is merely a 'text' that can be read in endless different ways, historians continue to reflect on their craft. This book seeks to be part of that reflection but is written unapologetically for real tutors, real students and relates to courses actually being taught in colleges and universities today. In fact, with an increasing emphasis on interdisciplinary approaches, as well as a greater focus on the processes of historical study and writing, courses on theory, method and historiographical practice seem to grow in number and significance. Even in those history departments that attempt to integrate the teaching of historiography into thematic- and period-based courses, a book such as this which discusses the main issues presented by history as a discipline outside the context of the topic, or else uses an historical era or topic as a dynamic example of how a core idea of history works, might prove to be a useful teaching and learning aid.

In this sense, our ambition is to be part of a debate about historiography but also to provide a resource to students working at both an introductory and an advanced level. In doing this, the book enthusiastically engages with theoretical disciplines and perspectives forged in areas such as literature, sociology, geography, and anthropology, and the rest of the arts or social sciences. It draws distinctions between history as a method in the humanities and the practice of historians engaged in the production of history, both in the academy but also those working outside the profession.

Theories of history, historical methodologies and historiography sometimes present themselves as distinct and problematic areas in the life of the historian. While studying history at university, however, rarely are they encountered as discrete spheres. Each topic or problem comes with its theoretical and methodological components which suggest in the strongest possible terms how history should be done. These elements are so completely intertwined that it takes conscious and informed deliberation to tease them apart. This is a problem that *History* aims to help the student solve. Each chapter, theme and case study pays particular attention to each of these elements but also recognises their profound interrelationship. Drawing on the experiences of historians working in every historical period makes this an academically rigorous, yet intellectually accessible and transparent exercise: from those beavering away at the shape and significance of field systems in the Middle Ages; those building an expertise in palaeography as a vital tool of translation; to historians of visual culture of the Renaissance; or those peeling away the layered meanings of Tudor state papers; or even to contemporary political or cultural histories thrown up by more immediate concerns of politics or locality.

At the heart of the book is an analytical narrative that carries forward the main description and discussion of the topic or theme of each chapter. All of the supporting material relates to a greater or lesser extent to this core text. Effective pedagogy is the main concern of every part of the book and this is as true of the continuous text as of any of its parts. However, where many points have required particular illustration, explanation and elaboration, further pedagogical support is provided alongside or within the narrative.

At certain points it has been necessary to acknowledge the difficult and problematic nature of the material under review in the main narrative and that this material needs special treatment. Particular elements of theoretical and methodological problems or historical debates are discussed in this way. Some historiographical debates stand out not just because of their importance for how we understand and interpret the past but because they cut to the heart of the methods by which we actually study and write history. These debates are often complex, however, and their importance in terms of theory and method are rarely spelt out in history books whose main concern, not unreasonably, is to tell a story, but in the telling of that story historical theory tends rather to be encrypted within the historical argument of the books and articles themselves. Consequently, it is very difficult for students to come to terms with the underlying elements of these debates, something that the structure of this book is at pains to address. A jargon-busting attempt to define difficult and unfamiliar concepts is provided as the text unfolds as are brief biographical introductions to the major figures that have made the discipline of history a solid and verifiable branch of human knowledge.

Finally, at its best the existing literature on applied historiography (for use in the seminar room) offers the views of experienced professional historians on the theory and practice of history and there is an inescapable tendency for them to be more or less subjective and reflexive in their surveys of themes and problems. For a number of reasons this book attempts to step beyond this, featuring as it does a wide variety of explanatory devices, where clarity and accessibility of information is of vital concern.

This volume is an extension of our experiences as working historians and teachers, and is driven by our own capabilities and thoughts about the subject picked up over years and across a number of diverse institutions. We hope that what follows itself reflects those valuable experiences and our knowledge of the discipline garnered in some small measure since our own days as students, days that now seem lost in the mists of time.

Peter Claus (Oxford)
John Marriott (Yorkshire)

Acknowledgements

It would seem an act of madness in this age of research assessment exercises, focused subject specialisms and narrow periodisations to embark on a textbook that roams across periods, disciplines and geographical boundaries with little apparent regard for the particular expertise of its authors. Hence our thanks are due to those colleagues and readers of the book who have helped us enormously to convey historical ideas and concepts familiar to us as experienced tutors, but often through the use of examples less familiar, say from the early modern or medieval periods or from the ancient world. If we have not always pulled this off it is our responsibility and not theirs.

Colleagues include Paul Sinclair at St Clare's College in Oxford, Dr Roy Edwards, University of Southampton, Avichag Valk in Tel Aviv, Dr Emma Cavell, University of Exeter, Dr Abigail Green, Brasenose College, Oxford, Dr Bernard Gowers, Kings, London. The Master and Fellows of Pembroke College, Oxford provided Peter Claus with an academic home while Dr Adrian Gregory (Charlton Athletic) and Dr Stephen Tuck (Wolverhampton Wanderers) at Pembroke have been a constant source of strength and humour. John Marriott has equally found colleagues and students at the University of East London to be creative sources for ideas and approaches that have now crystallised in the chapters of this book. The late Raphael Samuel and now the Raphael Samuel History Centre has been a point of contact for both Peter and John. While Raph may have resisted the notion of a textbook, seemingly fixed in a point of time, he may well have appreciated the attempt to create a cross-disciplinary narrative that falls outside any special focus on period or subject and which may have utility for students of history.

To those who were professionally employed by the publishers to read chapters we extend both sympathies and profound gratitude. Their comments were invariably useful and we have done our best to incorporate their suggestions. These include Dr Amanda Power, University of Sheffield, Dr Xavier Guégan, Newcastle University, Dr Alan Marshall, Bath Spa University, Dr T. J. Hochstrasser, London School of Economics, Professor Steve Hindle, Huntington Library, San Marino, California, Professor Michael Hicks, Head of History, University of Winchester, Professor Philip Williamson, University of Durham, Dr Stephen Caunce, University of Central Lancashire, Professor Diana Jeater, University of the West of England, Bristol and Dr Martin Johnes, Swansea University.

Above all we want to put on record our thanks to Stuart Hay from Pearson Longman who read chapter drafts from the point of view of a student from hell but who has helped to bring clarity (if clarity there is) to the book, and to John Shaw, the original co-author alongside Peter Claus, who shaped the architecture of the book and who will recognise much in its final structure.

Finally we thank our families to whom we dedicate the book: Xavière Hassan, Avichag Valk, Samuel Claus (L'Chaim) and June and Malcolm Claus on behalf of Peter, and for John, Kanta and the twins Kabir and Karishma.

Publisher's Acknowledgements

We are grateful to the following for permission to reproduce copyright material:

Figures

Figure on page 374 from http://www.nationalarchives.gov.uk/Palaeography/where_to_start.htm#abbreviations, and contains public sector information licensed under the Open Government Licence v1.0.

Text

Extract on pages 72–3 from *The Secret of World History: Selected Writings on the Art and Science of History*, edited and translated by Roger Wines, New York: Fordham University Press (von Ranke, L. 1981) pp. 56–59; Extract on pages 104–5 from Reprinted by permission of the publisher from 'Historical emplotment and the problem of truth' by Hayden White in, *Probing the Limits of Representation: Nazism and the 'Final Solution'*, edited by Saul Friedlander, pp. 37–40, Cambridge, Mass.: Harvard University Press (1992), Copyright © 1992 by the President and Fellows of Harvard College; Extract on pages 251–2 from *Imperial Meridian. The British Empire and the World, 1780–1830*, Longman (Bayly, C. A. 1989) pp. 98–99; Exhibit on page 130 from Herodotus, *The History of Herodotus*, translated by George Rawlinson, http://classics.mit.edu//Herodotus/history.html, with permission from The Internet Classics Archive; Extract on page 166 from British values, whatever they are, won't hold us together by Linda Colley, *The Guardian*, 18 May 2006, Copyright Guardian News & Media Ltd 2006; Extract on pages 170–1 from Polydore Vergil, *To Henry V111, Invincible King of England, France, and Ireland, Defender of the Faith, the Poem of the English History*, http://www.philological.bham.ac.uk/polverg/1e.html#letter (taken 19 Dec. 2010), edited and translated by Dana Sutton, Copyright the University of Birmingham; Extract on page 231 from Review by Patrick Wright of 'Shadow Sites: Photography, Archaeology and the British Landscape 1927–1955' by Kitty Hauser (Oxford University Press, 2007), *Twentieth Century British History*, 19 (2), 2008, pp. 239–242, by permission of Oxford University Press; Extract on page 341 from *The Pub and the People by Mass-Observation*, Faber & Faber (Smith, G. 1987) pp. 46–47; Extract on page 348 from *Economic History of Medieval Europe*, Longman (Pounds, N. J. G. 1994) p. 37; Extract on pages 360–1 from *Economic History of Medieval Europe*, Longman (Pounds, N. J. G. 1994) pp. 91–92; Extract on page 384 from Understanding the Cap of Liberty: symbolic practice and social conflict in early nineteenth century England, *Past and Present*, Oxford University Press, 122 (1), pp. 75–119 (Epstein, J. A. 1989), by permission of The Past and Present Society; Extract on pages 368–70 from *The Jew in the Medieval World: A Sourcebook*, Cincinnati: Hebrew Union College Press (1938), with permission from HUC Press; Extract on page 390 from On the methods of History Workshop: A Reply, *History Workshop Journal*, 9, 1, pp. 162–175 (Samuel, R. 1980), by permission of Oxford University Press; Extract on page 406 from Archives of American History, http://americanhistory.si.edu/september11/ September 30 2007, Smithsonian Institution; Extract on page 408 from Barbara Hughes, King's Cross Voices 2004, http://www.kingscrossvoices.org.uk, Camden Local Studies and Archives; Extract on page 409 from Norma Steel, King's Cross Voices, 2004, http://www.kingscrossvoices.org.uk, Camden Local Studies and Archives; Extract on pages 406–7 from Helena Wright, a Curator at the Smithsonian Institution at Washington, Archives of American History, http://americanhistory.si.edu/september11/ September 30 2007, Smithsonian Institution; Extract on pages 408–9 from Reg Hopkins, King's Cross Voices, 2004, http://www.kingscrossvoices.org.uk, Camden Local Studies and Archives; Exhibit on pages 409–11 from East Midlands Oral History Archive, transcripts from, http://www.le.ac.uk/emoha/community/resources/county/newton/describe.html, East Midlands Oral History Archive; Extracts on pages 411–12, page 412 from http://www.southafrica.info/public_services/citizens/education/sahistoryonline.htm.

Photos

The publisher would like to thank the following for their kind permission to reproduce their photographs:

(Key: b-bottom; c-centre; l-left; r-right; t-top)

278 Bridgeman Art Library Ltd: Ashmolean Museum, University of Oxford, UK; 283 Pitt Rivers Museum, University of Oxford; 333 Bruce Hoffman courtesy of crimetheory.com; Plate 1 Bridgeman Art Library Ltd: Metropolitan Museum of Art, New York, USA / Photo © Boltin Picture Library; Plate 3 English Heritage Photo Library; Plate 4 Alamy Images: David Hoffman (b). Mary Evans Picture Library: (t); Plate 5 © The British Library Board; Plate 6 Guildhall Art Gallery; Plate 7 The Library of The London School of Economics and Political Science; Plate 8 The Open University; Plate 9 Mary Evans Picture Library.

All other images © Pearson Education

In some instances we have been unable to trace the owners of copyright material, and we would appreciate any information that would enable us to do so.

Introduction: history matters

In the sense of both the past and the study of the past, history matters. At a personal level, history offers us an unrivalled means of making sense of where we have come from, and therefore where we are in the modern world. In this respect, we are all historians by instinct for, when faced with a personal problem, we look to the past in order to trace its origins and from this hopefully work toward a resolution. The extraordinary popularity of history programmes, costume dramas, documentaries, historical novels and heritage sites testify to the enduring importance of history in the lives of non-historians. At a wider level, different interpretations of the past have provoked, and continue to provoke conflict between peoples. When this escalates into war, opposing sides justify their action by appealing to the historical record. Past grievances – real or imaginary – have therefore served as a powerful stimulus to action. Finally, although it is fashionable to bemoan the failure of contemporary politicians to learn from the mistakes of the past, it is clear that in some dramatic instances such as the dropping of atomic bombs on civilian populations, lessons have been learnt.

This book is not intended, however, to persuade anyone of the importance of history. We anticipate that by the time it is read by a prospective historian or enthusiastic amateur, the case would already have been made in their minds. Rather, we wish to provide an accessible introduction to some of the concerns that have preoccupied historians over time. Instinctive though we may be as historians, we can become better historians if we take the trouble to learn something about the discipline of historiography, that is, how historians go about the task of exploring the past. For this seemingly simple project is fraught with difficulties. From the time of Herodotus and Thucydides in the ancient world, the role of the historian and the very nature of history have been contested. For the past two thousand years, therefore, the boundaries of history have been fluid. Even now, some hundred or so years after the establishment of history as an academic discipline, we are not entirely sure what 'proper' history is, or where the line separating history from say sociology or geography runs.

The difficulties are further compounded when we broach the question of historical truth. At school we were inclined to believe the claims that history books told us about the past as it actually happened. Much of this derives from the moment in the late nineteenth century when the discipline of history emerged, and embarked on what was considered as a realistic mission to retrieve the truth from the past. Prior to this, people who wrote about the past had other objectives in mind, most notably the political imperative to consolidate the authority of the state or peoples they represented. Many historians today are also committed to historical truth, but despite the various methods used to retrieve it, historical truth remains an elusive goal. Some critics go as far as to suggest that the promise is entirely false for the historical record is always open to different interpretations, and who is in a position to decide which one is the truth?

These are the matters we intend to explore in the course of the book. Its publication is timely. Some of the classic introductory texts which opened up debates within historiography, such as E. H. Carr's *What is History?* (1961) and G. E. R. Elton's *The Practice of History* (1967), now look decidedly dated in that they do not address the important developments of recent years. John Tosh's popular and admirable *The Pursuit of History* (2009) claims to be an introduction to modern history, but is not for the person coming to history for the first time. We felt the need for a textbook which encompassed the broad range of historical inquiry in ways which were accessible to the non-specialist. We have assumed no previous knowledge of the discipline, eliminated as far as possible the use of jargon, and drawn upon historical examples which we anticipate will be of interest to a modern readership. Above all, in writing the book we had in mind a person who was about to embark on a serious study of history, and therefore needed to know more about the nature of the discipline from examples of studies undertaken by some of its leading figures. We hope too that it may be of interest in some of the areas it touches upon to postgraduates eager to consolidate their knowledge and to take that knowledge up to another level. Although this is indisputably a textbook we are anxious not to imply that closure is either likely or desirable in history; in all areas of our discipline we would want to treat history as very much open to dispute. Indeed, we would like to encourage debate and dispute among students and general readers alike.

The book is not designed to be read sequentially; rather, we consider it as a handbook, and prefer that you simply dip into individual chapters when the need arises to know more about particular aspects of the discipline. The book is, however, organised in a way to help you make sense of the material. Here we have adopted the three broad themes of the title – Theory, Method and Practice – which are addressed in turn. Theory is divided into three parts. In Part One, Perspectives and themes, we begin by talking through two issues which have been seen as the defining elements of history, namely, the pursuit of historical truth and the ordering of time. It will come as no comfort to know that these fundamental features of historical inquiry raise complex issues which continue to be hotly debated, but we take you carefully on the first steps of the journey.

Part 2, Philosophies, examines the theoretical precepts of modern historical practice which arose out of the Enlightenment, but which were developed in the course of the nineteenth and twentieth centuries, and came in recent years under challenges mounted to this paradigm by perspectives from postmodernism and postcolonialism. Part 3, Histories surveys the broad trajectory of historical inquiry from ancient times, through the work of Christian, Jewish and Islamic scholars of the middle ages and Renaissance periods, to the emergence in Britain in the aftermath of the seventeenth-century Civil War, of Whig interpretations of history, and so on to the work of our best known contemporary historians.

Reaching the 'Method' theme in Part 4, Varieties, we describe some of the more influential strands of history which have emerged in the postwar period as a challenge to traditional approaches. The boundaries of cultural, feminist, public and global histories may be defined imprecisely, but historians working in these fields have greatly extended the scope of historical inquiry, and at the same time placed on the agenda new ways of thinking about who and what are legitimate subjects and objects of study and, indeed, who might be regarded as a bona fide historian. Part 5, Approaches & disciplines looks at the often troubled relationships between history and disciplines within the social sciences, including geography and anthropology. Given that the boundaries of history are fluid and permeable, it comes as no surprise to learn that historians have tended to borrow freely from other disciplines. By breaking down what are often artificially constructed barriers between disciplines, this too has opened up exciting new avenues of historical inquiry. Finally, in 'Practice', Part Six, Skills and techniques, we provide more practical guidance on some of the problems encountered by an historian embarking on an exciting venture of research. The focus is on evidence – what forms it takes, how it is gathered and stored, and some of the problems it presents for us.

We have attempted to make the material accessible not only by avoiding overly complex theoretical discussion but also through various pedagogical devices. Each chapter therefore begins with a short introduction which elaborates on the themes in the context of the study of history. At the end of the chapters, there is a brief section entitled 'In Practice' which explains why the issues raised remain important to the study of history, and why they should be taken seriously by practising historians. The Summary brings all the arguments of the chapter together while the 'Discussion document' feature at the end takes the form of brief extracts from primary or secondary sources which touch directly on these issues and provide useful starting points for further reflection, particularly in seminar discussions. Finally, the 'Further reading' section provides guidance on material which we have found useful and hope will extend and deepen student awareness of the overarching themes.

Both of us are modern historians. Peter Claus has researched histories of the metropolis and has been committed to widening participation and the democratisation of the archive, while John Marriott is a cultural and intellectual historian with a long-standing interest in London and Empire during the nineteenth and twentieth centuries. In writing this book we have understandably drawn upon knowledge of our particular specialisms, but at the same time we have attempted to widen the geographical and temporal scope of the book by including discussions of historical episodes in ancient and medieval periods, from both European and non-European worlds. While the authorship has been shared, the large bulk of the writing has been done by Peter. John joined the project when the original co-author was forced to pull out through ill health, by which time the book had already taken shape, and several of the chapters had been completed in draft form.

We stated at the outset that our primary intent was not to persuade anyone of the relevance and excitement of history, but we share a passion for the subject which we hope comes over in the writing. If some of this happens to rub off onto potential historians then perhaps that is no bad thing for at least one of our unstated goals will have been met.

Part 1

PERSPECTIVES AND THEMES

1 Proof and the problem of objectivity

1 History: a science or an art?
2 History and the status of knowledge
3 Choosing evidence, challenging interpretations

Introduction

This chapter introduces history as a discipline and as an approach to historical knowledge. While it cannot be comprehensive, its aim nevertheless is to explore problems faced by historians as they seek to understand past societies. How they do this depends on many factors. At its simplest, however, it largely depends on whether history is regarded as a science which has the historian as objective fact finder and analyst. Or whether, alternatively, history is treated as an art in which the historian presents an interpretation of the past that is a result of either personal experience or the social and cultural milieu in which the historian is located. The first section introduces these issues by looking afresh at the argument first raised in the 1960s between historians E. H. Carr and Geoffrey Elton but in the newer context of postmodernism. It sets out the varying ways in which each of these prominent historians approached the discipline and dealt with historical evidence in all its varied forms. Section 2 uses historical writing concerned with the events of 1857, the Indian Mutiny, in order to discuss whether history is truly a dependable basis of knowledge that can provide a comprehensive and reliable explanation of how past societies change. The third and final section will focus on another dispute between historians, that of Chartism. We shall see how historical facts are generated but also how historians select evidence and then use innovative techniques to inform our historical understanding. This section will explain how historical explanations for a single historical event or period can change radically over time, either by the discovery of new evidence or, more likely, the altering approach to evidence by historians influenced by developing methodologies.

Section 1

History: a science or an art?

Why bother? Why study history? Why does history matter? For professionals who teach and research history it provides, let it be said, a source of income and occasionally a very pleasing one at that. But it is more than that. Most historians are deeply engaged in trying to uncover the past, not only because there are fascinating stories to be told, but also because the telling of the past has enormous contemporary importance. Our understanding of the present relies in large part upon how we view the past, and this vital issue is of concern to us all, whether or not we are trained historians. This recognition lies at the very heart of what we would describe as historical imagination – an imagination possessed by all those who look to the past as a means of understanding their place in the contemporary world. Something of this spirit is captured by the comic writer and raconteur, Stephen Fry:

> **Great and good men and women stirred sugar into their coffees knowing that it had been picked by slaves. Kind good ancestors of all of us in this room never questioned hangings, burnings, tortures, inequality, suffering and injustice that today revolts us. If we dare to presume to damn them with our fleeting ideas of morality then we risk damnation from our descendants for whatever it is that we are doing that future history will judge as intolerable and wicked: eating meat, driving cars, appearing on TV, visiting zoos, who knows? We haven't arrived at our own moral and ethical imperatives by each of us working them out from first principles, we have inherited them and they were born out of blood and suffering – as all human things, and human beings are. This does not stop us from admiring and praising the progressive heroes who got there early and risked their lives to advance causes we now take for granted. In the end, I suppose my point is that history is all about imagination rather than facts. If you cannot imagine yourself wanting to riot against catholic emancipation say, or becoming an early Tory and signing up to fight with the Old Pretender, or cheering on Prynne as the theatres are closed and Puritanism holds sway . . . knowing is not enough – if you cannot feel what our ancestors felt when they cried 'Wilkes and Liberty!' or indeed cried 'Death to Wilkes!' if you cannot feel with them, then all you can do is judge them and condemn them, or praise them and over-adulate them. History is not the story of strangers, aliens from another realm, it is the story of us had we been born a little earlier. History is memory, we have to remember what it is like to be a Roman, or a Jacobite or a Chartist or even – if we dare, and we should dare – a Nazi. History is not an abstraction, it is the enemy of abstraction.** (*The Observer*, 9 July 2006)

This does not address the question of precisely *what* history is. Put simply, history is the study of the past, but as you make your way through this chapter, indeed this book, you will realise such simplicities mask some complex issues. Note, for example, that there is ambiguity in the term 'history'. When we talk of 'history', do we mean the past? Or do we mean what is written and taught about the past – historiography? It is usually clear from the context which meaning we are using, but the very fact that we have the same term to describe both meanings says something rather important. Studying history at a more advanced level should make us become a little more circumspect about the nature of the relationship between the past and what is written and taught about the past. Fry defines history and historians in a promiscuous way (as writers about the past) and that too will be the approach of this chapter as we seek to get at the essence of our subject and why we are or why we want to be historians. In particular we shall examine the extent to which history as a discipline can be seen, crudely put, as either a science or an art and the implications for taking one view over the other.

The former Regius Professor of Modern History at the University of Cambridge, the late Sir Geoffrey Elton (1921–94), put it succinctly: history is at once interesting and exciting, amusing and instructive. Yet Elton was against historians having empathy for the past, for such an emotional engagement displaces what should be the object of the historian, namely, rational enquiry into past events. As a traditional historian, he believed very much in the possibilities of history as an exercise in empirical or fact-based truth and the ability of the historian to analyse objectively the results of research with a high degree of precision.

These ideas were expressed in Elton's *The Practice of History* (1967), which remains a useful elaboration of how history is conventionally viewed. It is a book, however, which was written consciously as a rejoinder to E. H. Carr (1892–1982) and his *What is History?* (1961), which had argued for a rather more sensitive approach to historical evidence. For Carr, history is subjective because historians are recognised as part of the process of doing history, unable to separate prejudices and presuppositions from conclusions drawn solely from evidence. It is this factor above all others that has secured Carrs' reputation as a radical in his approach to history, while Elton is seen as a defender of the conservative approach to history. If both views are caricatures, arch conservative and historiographical radical, each historian has left us with a legacy upon which we can build.

This spat between Elton and Carr on the status of historical knowledge is by common consent the defining debate about how the study of the past should be approached. While Elton was unquestionably suspicious of history's ability to predict the future, he nonetheless understood the role of the historian and saw history as 'scientific', that is, a method of rational inquiry. By approaching evidence critically, he argued, historical truth can be revealed. 'Hard work' and 'clear thinking' would promote a healthy scepticism as the historian investigates the primary sources or considers the views of other historians.

According to Elton, the successful resolution of all historical problems depends upon the appropriate use of evidence. To this end three main stages of reading evidence are required: a review of the available evidence (what sources exist?), the informed criticism of that evidence (what exactly does it testify to?), and from that evidence the framing of answers (what actually happened in the past?). Historical research must therefore 'arise from the evidence not from the mind of the enquirer', thereby avoiding the 'preconceived notions' of the historian. By following these guidelines, the historian 'well trained in the principles of scholarship' can reveal the truth, or 'as near to the truth of the past as he has any hope of getting' (Elton, 2002, pp. 46–80). In his *Return to Essentials: Some Reflections on the Present State of Historical Study* (1991), Elton develops these arguments by rejecting theory, 'theory mongers' and the abstraction of history because theory imposes ideas upon the evidence in ways which compromise its objectivity or distort its use. Elton was thus adamant that the involvement of the historian as a subjective individual, the 'infiltration of historiographical methods' and the 'problem of historical reconstruction' should be 'reduced to a minimum.

The historian must act only as a conduit through which the experiences of the past travel while a relationship with the dead provides the thrill and the challenge of history. If nothing else, for the 'honest historian', as Elton put it, just doing history allows 'the enormous enlargement of one's acquaintances', a list that is renewed and refreshed with every visit to the archive (Elton, 2002, pp. 83, 79, 142).

Yet historians, like anyone else, are social and cultural animals, prompting the suggestion that history is less a science and more an art: it is made through the imagination of a particular moment rather than discovered or applied by objective methodology. The past can reveal truths which are part of our personal and collective lives. If, for example, we consider a landscape beautiful, it is because we have absorbed historical assumptions which influence how we understand that landscape. Mountains were seen only as obstacles to easy travel before the eighteenth century, and then subsequently regarded as glorious monuments to nature; these changing views were not based on objective approaches to the evidence but in sensibilities that emerged from the Enlightenment; that is, notions of the sublime majesty of nature that quite simply changed dramatically with the influence of Romanticism (see Chapter 3). In this context, we may have an idea of the English village that is bucolic, charming and seemingly unchanging, the epitome of Englishness. It may consist in our mind's eye of a church, a duck pond, a war memorial, a cricket pitch or village green and a public house or 'pub', a sense of England as a pastoral idyll symbolised by the thatched roofed house or, perhaps, the 'babbling brook' or haystack, even if this particular feature of the countryside actually disappeared from English fields almost half a century ago (Samuel, 1994, p. 107). It is an image that contrasts with landscapes of smoking chimneys or rows of terraced houses that make up the 'pit' village of the former mining communities, the 'dark satanic mills' demonised by writers such as Blake, Dickens and Arnold Bennett who are all evoked when scholars of the Victorian period write the history of industrialisation or, with contemporaries of that time, they examine the 'condition of England'.

People outside this European sensibility may never know this aesthetic, and instead may see the thatched roof in an English village as a sign of poverty. People of earlier periods might read the picture differently not because they lacked humanity, sensibilities, taste, or should somehow be considered inferior to us, but because the historical milieus in which they lived were simply different. William Cobbett (1763–1835), pamphleteer and social commentator, recalled in his *Rural Rides*, sometime in the 1820s, travelling through the rolling hills of the Cotswolds in England. He hated the picturesque scenery: to him the livestock that populated its gentle hills and slopes would feed the 'Great Wen' or large drain; the teeming multitudes of London. Before Cobbett, or certainly in the century before he was born, the argument that the Cotswolds was a storehouse for the industrial masses could not have been made or would have been made in a quite different way.

It could be argued then that whatever period or era of history we live in is steeped with sensibilities and dominant ascetics that colour our lives and shade how we learn or write history, challenging our efforts to be dispassionate in the way we read evidence. Although the ancients, it should be noted, could not have known they were ancient and could not in some way live out ancient lives any more than we can know precisely that we are somehow 'postmodern'. Johan Huizinga's highly speculative but extremely stimulating *The Waning of the Middle Ages* (2001), first published in 1924, looked at the culture of fourteenth and fifteenth century France and the Low Countries and concluded that artists, as well as theologians, poets, chroniclers, princes and statesmen should be treated 'not as the harbingers of a coming culture, but as perfecting and concluding the old' (Huizinga, Preface to Doubleday Anchor edition). Chivalry, hierarchy, gothic forms and symbolism that were so important to medieval architecture, art and life were not the rotten remains of a stagnant, 'dark' or 'middle' age in history whose only real purpose was to stand in contrast to the bright, humanist 'Renaissance period' that was about to be born. If we were alive then, unknowingly on the cusp of the medieval and early-modern eras, we would surely have a maelstrom of influences that dictated our attitudes to what might be uniquely considered *at this moment* to be pleasing in appearance.

If the contemporary observer can therefore differentiate between beauty and ugliness and make historical judgements about what they represent or how they have changed, it is because our experiences in the present are altogether more encompassing than attempts to recapture the past through the acquisition of analytical skills or training for historians proposed by Elton. As children we are not aware of ideas of beauty or what is culturally significant, but soon learn to understand what is beautiful, and what we are attracted to and what repels our sensibilities, as we are shown, for instance, a vista and told emphatically that it is pleasing or important.

These examples from the history of landscape, aesthetics or the competing ideas of the English village, serve to illustrate the message at the heart of this section: that history does indeed matter in a way that would find agreement between both Carr and Elton, if in differing ways. If we are to understand our ancestors, as Fry says, and the real importance of history, then we must learn about the human condition, a condition that after all is both individually *and* socially constructed. To see such a construction, however, is to assert that what influences historians are situated primarily in the present. Accordingly, this present-minded approach to history and historical evidence does not speak for those historians who legitimately, and often in ways that are very productive, believe that 'the past is another country' which should be treated entirely in its own terms.

'The past is a foreign country' is the opening line to the novel by L. P. Hartley called *The Go-Between*, and is a place where 'they do things differently.' This articulates how from the perspective of Elton and others, the present is indeed separated from the past: 'they' are separated from 'us'. And yet as David Lowenthal noted in his 1985 book *The Past is a Foreign Country*:

> **During most of history men scarcely differentiated past from present, referring even to remote events, if at all, as though they were then occurring. Up to the nineteenth century those that gave any thought to the historical past supposed it much like the present. To be sure, the drama of history recorded major changes of life and landscape, but human nature supposedly remained constant, events always actuated by the same passions and prejudices. Even when ennobled by nostalgia or depreciated by partisans of progress, the past seemed not a foreign country but a part of their own. And chroniclers portrayed bygone times with an immediacy and intimacy that reflected the supposed likeness.**
>
> (Lowenthal, 1985, p. xvi)

Only with the rise of scientific-type methodology and the importance placed on ways of gathering evidence could distinctions be made between 'then' and 'now', and by so doing demonstrate that objectivity could find historical proof and that history could tell an unfolding and coherent story that was plausibly true.

Some commentators interested in questions that arise from the quest for historical objectivity and coherent narratives, such as the historian Gertrude Himmelfarb, articulate an overwhelming need to revive histories that promote synthesised or unified themes concerned with class, nation, ideas and so forth. However universal or 'whole' narratives such as the story of nation or class have been, efforts to foster and promote a single, coherent and integrated history have become increasingly difficult precisely because of renewed efforts to write histories of gender, race and so on that speak to our lives in the here and now.

Like Elton, Himmelfarb has argued that a downplaying of political history over a number of years has encouraged historical knowledge to be treated in isolation with each topic treated like a piece of a jigsaw but where seldom a complete picture comes into view. The real distinction that Himmelfarb makes, however, is between an 'old' history that attempts to understand contemporaries in their own terms and the 'new' history that, while laudable in taking notice of say the historical role of women or black people, tends to interpret the past solely through the optic of the present (Himmelfarb, 2004). The fragmentation of historical narratives into stories about 'identities' has been influenced by literary theory that deconstructs the language used in historical sources to the point where the voice of the author of a document is given no authority and whose meaning can never be truly known. The text and the language of the text, from this perspective, have no context besides the preoccupations and concerns of the historian in the present day (see Chapter 5).

We are presented then with a serious choice about how history as a discipline works, what it can reasonably do and how it is approached. Taking our cue from historians such as Elton or Himmelfarb, is the objectivity of history something we strive for? Or is the subjectivity and (to an extent) present mindedness of Carr and others more convincing? What are the pressures and influences bearing down on us as we 'do' history, and can we resist these pressures to the extent that we can really know things about the past by using objective methods? To address these questions and to introduce others, we shall need to take a trip to India and the British Raj.

Section 2

History and the status of knowledge

The Indian Mutiny began in the summer of 1857 and was finally crushed nearly a year later. It has entered into our popular imagination, but just note how. The use of the term 'mutiny', rather than, say, revolt, suggests that this was a traitorous act perpetrated by subjects of the British crown. This was how it was seen at the time, and helps to explain why the retribution of the British was so brutal. A memorial in Delhi remembers the mutiny. Built by the British in 1863, it takes the form of an octagonal shaped tower and ornamental facade in the gothic style. It is dedicated to the memory of those soldiers and loyal Indians of the Delhi Field Force who were killed or died of disease during what now might be considered as the initial war for Indian independence. In 1972 a new plaque was added, correcting any impression given on the original memorial that the 'enemy' were anything else but, as it is inscribed, 'freedom fighters and martyrs of India'. And so this history of the Mutiny is first built, then reconstructed.

The clash was ostensibly sparked by the replacement of standard issue Minie rifles with Pattern Enfield's rifle-muskets. As a result, both Hindu and Muslim soldiers were required to bite off the end of the cartridge that was thought to be caked with cow or pig fat, thus in one stroke causing offence to each religious group that made up the Indian ranks of the East India Company's Bengal Army. The origins and complexities of the war are more complicated of course, but they have provided evocative reading for generations, giving us pause to consider, as we shall throughout this section, what it is that we can actually know, truly *know*, about the past and how precisely our subjectivism affects our understanding and writing of history. In making this consideration, there will be cause to visit once again the approaches of Elton and Carr, this time with a more jaundiced eye.

Many of our generation learnt nothing about the Indian Mutiny of 1857/8 at school. Parents, no doubt as part of the general reassessment of the empire that took place in the midst of post-war decolonisation, may have told stories about the cruelty of the British as they took revenge on the hacking to death of 260 women and children in the massacre of Cawnpore in July 1857 by tying the mutineers to the mouths of cannon and blasting them to oblivion – a form of execution that the British reasoned was quick, yet spectacular, giving fair warning to would-be protesters who harboured any lingering doubts about the wisdom of British rule. These were acts of particular cruelty as – the British knew full well – Hindus believed that the body needed to be intact in order to be reincarnated.

These stories and others like it – the attacks by white settlers on American 'red' Indians in countless Westerns ('Got him' we shouted as they were shot from their horses), ruthless Nazis in comics, forever exclaiming *Achtung* – takes us to questions about the nature of history and our understanding of the past. Bearing in mind as we established in the last section that many of us don't come to these subjects without prejudice, what is it that we can really know about the past?

The rather comfortable view held by Elton that the past is there and all we have to do is record it in a logical and coherent way is one which formed the cornerstone of the discipline of history when it emerged in the nineteenth century, largely with the life and work of the German historian, Leopold von Ranke (1795–1886). Von Ranke, who we meet again in Chapter 4, lived by his famous maxim that the job of the historian was to show the past as it really was. Since then, this is precisely what many important historians have attempted to do and with Elton-like rational justification. From the perspective of Carr-like subjectivists, however, the whole edifice of that particular maxim is built on the mistaken premise that the past is out there just waiting to be discovered and then recovered by professionals trained in all the appropriate skills of gathering evidence and putting the fragments together again to form a whole picture true to its original likeness. This is what Elton meant when he said '. . . the reality – yes, the truth – of the past exists in materials of various kinds, produced by the past at the time that it occurred and left behind by it as testimony' (Elton, 1994, p.).

What Elton is claiming here is that evidence is the basis of proper History with a capital 'H'. Historians are firmly bound by its authority, and must not use fiction to fill in the gaps that inevitably exist. It is in the sources – the evidential facts – that Elton's 'truth' can be found. But of course from this perspective it is only the skilled, the professionally trained historian, who is able to do the proper work with such sources – only he or she who with an objective and open mind can select, evaluate and arrange them into a meaningful account of the past. These then are questions that take us to the heart of what it means to be objective in our approach to history; that is, how we can be free of bias or prejudice caused by personal feelings or memory and who it is that we can regard as a *bone fide* historian.

Now there are elements of this argument with which no historian, professional or otherwise, could quarrel. Elton recognises that history is not the study of the past (we have no time machine to allow us to travel back), but the study of what remains of the past in the present. Clearly we must take evidence seriously: approach it with honesty and a degree of integrity; even it if we find it does not accord with an argument we are trying to make. Historical facts found in the evidence cannot under any circumstances be squeezed into preconceived notions of what it is that we wish to argue and made to fit a pre-existing theory. Similarly, evidence ought not to be disregarded if we find it does not accord with our argument, no matter how beautifully designed that argument may be. We certainly should not make up evidence; making doubtful causal links between persons and events that strengthen that argument. Even with these basic provisos, there remain real problems in relying purely on evidence as the necessary basis of an historical account.

Elton suggests that somehow the process of research and writing can be undertaken in an objective way by the historian. All of us, suggest those who argue that subjectivity is unavoidable, are creatures profoundly influenced by both the past and by history, a point introduced in the previous section. Perhaps what Elton fails to recognise is the sheer impossibility of being neutral with evidence. Not that all historians have a particular axe to grind – most are not engaged in propaganda work which blatantly sets out to assassinate historical characters or causes. Nor are we especially motivated by emotions such as anger, love or contempt, but more that we all inhabit particular social and political milieus that will inevitably influence how we put together our histories. For the new social historians of the 1960s and 1970s, as we shall find in Chapter 9, the necessity of subjectivity was turned into a virtue when certain historians were encouraged to use their own experiences in the present to shape their reading of historical evidence. This was true of feminist histories in particular and was also true of socialist and feminist historians who encouraged a dialogue between workers and historians.

To illustrate these points developed from the opening section, we want to use the extract about the Indian Mutiny from Percival Spear's 1990 book *A History of India*. Looking at this secondary source by a noted, if traditional, historian of India, we should try to highlight the salient points of the argument as it is presented. So, if we were researching the cause and effects of the Mutiny of 1857 from which we began this section, and particularly its effect on British colonial authority, we may note the following evidential facts:

1. The Indian Mutiny ended in the summer of 1858.
2. Most of the rebel leaders were killed, executed or disappeared.
3. Clamour for vengeance against the Indians was tempered by the Viceroy Lord Canning and the Governor of the Punjab, Sir John Lawrence.
4. Delhi lost its independence and was incorporated within the Punjab.

5 The East India Company lost its colonial authority, the Indian army was reorganised and Indians began to be incorporated into the apparatus of government.
6 Queen Victoria issued a proclamation in November 1858 which outlined new policies toward India.

In order to save time, these 'facts' are listed in a rough chronological order. They are all evidential facts which cannot seriously be disputed, at least not without some difficulty. But in themselves – even when arranged in the order that they happened – they say nothing about the nature, causes or effects of the Indian Mutiny. These facts of themselves do not constitute history; that is, they are of the past but beyond their mere selection by us as historians, they are not yet part of historiography. They are like a catalogue of information, and so only become history when they are linked one to another as part of a narrative framework.

Spear has done precisely this. Let us, however, look in a little more detail at what is going on in the passage. What he does here is to use the chronicle of events as building blocks of a particular story with a beginning (the end of the Mutiny) and an end (the subsequent 50 years of British rule). A number of important points follow from this:

1 The story is put together by linking the various chronological elements in causal relationships. The Indian Mutiny resulted in the death or disappearance of many of the rebel leaders. In the immediate aftermath there were demands for vengeance but these were silenced by the British authorities. Lessons were learnt from the Mutiny. Measures were introduced to heal the wounds. The separation between Briton and Indian which had caused the Mutiny were mitigated by the Queen's proclamation, the end of the reign of the East India Company and the introduction of Indians in colonial administration.
2 The story thus unfolds as a secondary elaboration of a narrative of British colonial authority in India. Britain ruled with humanity and harmony until events forced a separation, resulting in the Mutiny, the defeat of which left India devastated and humiliated. But although the Mutiny was a tragedy, in the longer term it promoted progressive forces of cooperation and hope which once again led to a happy and benign colonial relationship. Just consider how the language in the passage reinforces this narrative. India was 'inert' and 'lacerated'; the 'wisdom' of Canning, the 'strength' of Lawrence muting the cries for vengeance; 'good came out of the evil of the mutiny'.

This narrative is part of a larger narrative that Spear inhabits. Here colonial rule is exercised by the British as progressive and benign and operates for the benefit of both colonisers and colonised. The story, however, is only one of many that can be constructed using this chronicle. Another, from the perspective of an Indian rebel could certainly be imagined or even retrieved from exactly the same evidence but is not given a voice by Spear. As an alternative history, then, we could interpret the evidence as follows:

- After years of suppression large sections of the Indian population decided to take matters in their own hands and drive the British out of India.
- The revolt was nearly successful, but because of the military superiority of the British and their access to technology such as the telegraph, the nationalist struggle was defeated.

- The British press cried out for vengeance against those who had been responsible for the atrocities. Many of the rebels were executed, but not on the scale that some had wished for.
- The British government now recognised that their rule could no longer be based on military power alone, and therefore decided to take due account of India's religion and customs in order not to cause offence, and assimilate influential sections into the British ruling elite as a means of diverting them from future nationalist struggle.

What this example illustrates is that seemingly objective accounts based on hard factual evidence are deeply riven by ideological influences, such as the historian's feelings about the nature of British rule in India. Here there is a critical difference between historical and evidential truth. There are certain truths in history – interpretations which cannot easily be refuted – although, as Carr argued, through a dialogue between theory and evidence we can only approach historical truth but never truly arrive there.

It is the increasing recognition of the importance of historical truth that has given rise to something of a transformation in historical thought over the last 20 years. Such has been this transformation that there are now currents in the philosophy of history which almost completely invert the relationship between evidence and interpretation. For Elton, evidence is the origin and basis of all historical knowledge (again as we saw in the last section) whereas more recent interventions point to the critical importance of the interpretation of evidence and indeed the status of evidence.

As we introduced the term postmodern in the opening section, it is enough to reiterate now that postmodern historiography denies that historical truth is possible (see Chapter 5). The past is not out there simply to be grasped, but is actively created by historians working with particular values, ideologies and interpretations. The task, then, is not only to scrutinise the evidence, but to reveal the processes through which that evidence is used to create interpretations in historical accounts. This in many ways can be seen as a healthy development. Unfortunately, as in all such movements when established orthodoxies are being challenged, an awful lot of heat is wasted in vituperative debate, insult and misrepresentation.

Both these positions are unfair and untenable. We cannot dismiss the whole corpus of previous historiography as theoretically naive simply because emphasis is given to this evidence rather than to the problem of interpretation. Many historians working within this tradition have provided us with rich, sophisticated accounts of historical events and change. If we subsequently wish to read them with due recognition of the moment they were produced and the framework they inhabited, then they must retain their value. Yet, equally, we cannot dismiss postmodern history as a mere figment of their imaginations. To my knowledge, no historian working within this tradition would dismiss evidence as inconsequential – that, for example, the Holocaust had no material reality; all take it seriously. Postmodern historians, however, argue that for it to be understood, that materiality has to be appropriated by ideas and theories about the nature of historical change, of the lives and rituals of human behaviour and the very status or form of writing itself. Historians, needless to say, are not neatly divided between 'empiricists' and 'postmodernists'. All historians, however, are cognisant of the need to explore the limits of historical knowledge and the place of the historian in the creation and transformation of knowledge as they encounter the fragments of the past in the present. To do this well, something must be known about choosing and interpreting evidence – the very issues confronted in the next section with a survey of the historiography of Chartism.

Section 3

Choosing evidence, challenging interpretations

Monday was a traditional day of riot and protest in Britain and derives from a traditional holiday called St Maundy. Probably because of this reason, on Monday, 25 September 1838, the Manchester Political Union organised a rally at Kersal Moor, Salford, where an estimated 300,000 people marched from the Manchester factories to the moors accompanied by bands and carrying banners rescued from the 'massacre' at Peterloo in 1819. 'More pigs less parsons' or 'For children and wife, we war to the knife' were carried that day by the so-called Chartists demanding the 'six points' of political reform: universal male suffrage, annual parliaments, vote by secret ballot, abolition of the property qualification for members of parliament, payment of MPs and equal electoral constituencies, all of which were subsequently granted save, mercifully, annual parliaments. Chartist activity however, intense though it was, had all but ceased by the final National Convention in 1858. The questions that historians have asked about Chartism's rise and fall do not change: was it economic, social or political in nature; was it a national movement; was it well or badly led; was it revolutionary; and did it succeed or fail? Nor has what we know about Chartism from the evidence altered in any considerable way, although how the evidence is approached has. The purpose of this section is to use Chartism as a case study to demonstrate how historians build knowledge through research, innovative approaches to research and the deployment of evidence and in so doing transform our historical understanding.

Some historians have located Chartism in the long history of radicalism beginning with the seventeenth century agitation by the Levellers and their 'People's Agreement' which included demands for popular sovereignty and the extension of suffrage or the dissenting, agrarian communism of the Diggers. Alternatively, the election of the radical John Wilkes in the Middlesex elections of the 1760s and 1770s is sometimes regarded as the beginning of the democratic impulse in Britain. Whatever its origins radicalism in Britain got a boost from the American and French Revolutions and the radical pamphleteering of such activists as Obadiah Hulme, James Burgh and Major John Cartwright in the 1770s, which acted as counterweights to popular loyalism and led to the state suppression of radical agitation in the mid-1790s. Radicalism revived at the end of the French wars or else went underground during this time, with Luddism, political radicalism such as that of the Tory William Cobbett (he from the first section who despised the Costwolds because it fed the industrial masses in London), taking us down to Peterloo in 1819 and beyond. Next, we saw the rise of philosophical radicalism and those associated with political economy, for example the Benthamite assault on public policy towards the poor, and subsequently the heightened interest in parliamentary reform. Quiescence of the state in the mid-1820s, during a period of relative prosperity, was followed by revival of activity over religious disabilities in 1828–9, which informed middle class agitation down to 1832 and the First Reform Act through to the repeal of the Anti-Corn Law in 1846 and working class agitation that fed Chartism until (and beyond) the year of European revolutions in 1848.

This working class agitation demanded land nationalisation and legislative change to free workers from 'industrial slavery'. Reforms to the poor law, support for the unemployed and calls for the disestablishment of the Church of England as administrators of relief to the poor, and for a system of free education, including the establishment of industrial schools, anticipated the rise of the welfare state of the early twentieth century. Likewise, the reforms to the state anticipated an inclusive pluralism that brought nonconformists (non-Anglican Protestants), Catholics, Jews and atheists into the 'pale of the constitution' in advance of universal suffrage and the rise of mass class politics.

Given this narrative, how has Chartism been treated by historians? How have they chosen which evidence to highlight and how have they interpreted that evidence? What, more generally, has characterised the changing approaches to these questions? Early histories of radicalism made an explicit link between the political and social motivations for Chartism – 'the knife and fork question'. Both Fabian (the intellectual arm of the British labour movement that argued for the evolutionary transformation of capitalism) and Marxist histories regarded Chartism as the forerunners of the modern Labour movement. For example, Graham Wallas (1858–1932), was a Fabian and arch rationalist, a figure somewhat remote from many of those Chartists who were overtly religious in outlook. His *The Life of Francis Place* (1898) told the story of Francis Place (1771–1854), who was a follower of the radical William Godwin (1756–1836) and a member of the London Corresponding Society, which boasted of its unlimited membership sympathetic to the egalitarian aims of the French Revolution. Place had made his name in the Westminster elections with Francis Burdett. He also, in 1838, with the London Working Men's Association, helped to draft the People's Charter; only thereafter becoming disillusioned with Chartism and its rainbow coalition of currency reformers, socialist followers of Robert Owen and local heroes with their almost infinite variety of colourful views. After opposing factory reform and supporting the Anti-Corn Law League, he retired to write the voluminous account of his times which Wallas and countless scholars have drawn upon since.

The Place collection held in the British Library has been known about and used by historians since at least the 1890s. The 'facts' associated with the Chartist experience were not yet fully known by the 1940s, however, and the interpretation of Chartism had advanced little. Marxist histories highlighted 'physical force' Chartism as part of a heritage of revolutionary politics and this too was of a piece with contemporary Communist politics. Likewise, both Theodore Rothstein (*From Chartism to Labourism*) in 1929 and Reg Groves (*But We Shall Rise Again*) in 1938 emphasised the evolutionary and revolutionary strands within Chartism but did so with a Popular Front agenda in mind – the touchstone of radical politics and historiography in the 1930s that argued for a united force on the left to counter right-wing and reactionary politics.

Fabian historiography (in which for these purposes we can count G. D. H. Cole's 1941 *Chartist Portraits* which continued the biographical tradition begun by Gammage), tended towards framing the 'moral force' element of Chartism as part of a constitutional and gradualist politics that he largely supported in his own day. Cole and then the historian George Kitson Clark (1900–75), in a 1953 book, were keen to emphasise how 'rational Chartism' or 'hungry Chartism' was a movement broken by working class divisions of the sort which wrecked the 1950s Labour party, then out of power, and which served as a warning to internal dissidents of the danger of division. The concern was with contemporary working class unity as much as it was with the objective truths thrown up by historical research.

Whether Fabian or Marxist in approach, the Place collection proved to be the primary source. Chartism, now a hundred years old, had become a plaything of the present. Cole, for instance, in his *Portraits* had underlined the importance of leadership, surely a wartime preoccupation that reflected a major issue of his day. All this seems to make the case for the present-minded subjectivity that we outlined in the first section and which was championed by Carr.

Chartism as a cautionary tale for those on the Left facing a formidable foe was emphasised less by the Liberal historians J. L. (1872–1949) and Barbara Hammond (1873–1961) who in their very popular 1930 book, *The Age of the Chartists, 1832–1852*, did something to address the confusion Liberals had hitherto felt towards Chartism. Likewise, Asa Briggs wrote his *Chartist Studies* in 1959 and opened up a social democratic commentary. Questions were asked about the effect of the trade cycle on the ebb and flow of Chartist militancy. His was a narrative that continued a biographical approach but one that very much saw Chartism as a local and regional phenomenon. By now, histories of the Labour party or of the labour movement put class at the centre of their considerations. Francis Williams, a journalist and Labour party activist, wrote *Fifty Years' March: The Rise of the Labour Party* (1949) and *The Magnificent Journey: The Rise of the Trade Unions* (1954) as celebrations of the radical tradition but did so in a way that presented the history of radicalism as the history of class.

Class then had become a shared determinant among historians of various political traditions. Enter Dorothy Thompson who was perhaps the most influential historian of Chartism. Her students and followers – James Epstein, Neville Kirk, John Saville and Geoff Eley – together transformed Chartist studies, emphasising the national characteristics of Chartism as the culmination of a 'literate and sophisticated' working class radicalism which simultaneously renewed Chartism as a political, rather than an economic movement. The intervention by Thompson in her book *Chartism: Popular Politics in the Industrial Revolution* (1984):

- saw a need for a general survey of what we thought we knew about Chartism;
- rejected local studies which suggested that Chartism was simply a series of protest movements;
- introduced a longer timeline for Chartism (back to 1832);
- placed less emphasis on the heterogeneity of Chartist support, rethinking the occupations of Chartists;
- detected a common language based on what was now believed to be a coherent political and social programme.

Chartism is thus an example of an historical question that had been through several phases of historiography, its parameters set firm by both the establishment of historical facts and the conceptual boundaries of the discipline. Biographical accounts focused on leadership, placing emphasis on 'moral force' or 'physical force' Chartism, the political or social aspects of their demands, Chartism as a series of local protests versus Chartism as a systematic national movement – all at one time or the other came to prominence. The archive, such as the Place papers, had been all but exhausted but still historians found ways of reading evidence in new and interesting ways; this leads us to the most important intervention in our understanding of Chartism by Gareth Stedman Jones.

Stedman Jones in an essay called 'Rethinking chartism', published in *Languages of Class* in 1983, transformed our knowledge of Chartism and simultaneously the methodology of modern historical studies. Stedman Jones adopted the notion that language – how we describe the world – is prior to our experience of it, insisting that the movement was not a perfect contemporary reflection of a revolutionary class-consciousness in the 1840s but instead, by studying the language used by Chartists, an opposition to the 'Old Corruption' of land, church and aristocracy in the period before 1832 could be detected. This language belonged to the eighteenth century, not the 1840s, the decade in which Chartism ostensibly thrived. It was language used by Wilkes in the 1770s and by other radicals in the 1790s following the French Revolution, not a language that could possibly be used to critique a new industrial order. Thus the banners carried onto Kersal Moor in 1838 with which we began the section – 'More pigs less parsons' – was indeed a political language but one aimed at the church not the poverty induced by industrialisation, nor could Chartism be a mirror held up to Peel's 1841–6 government measures. In short, for Stedman Jones, social being could not be reflected simply in consciousness and then be revealed through what he thought were the simple empirical procedures of Marxism (Stedman Jones, 1983).

As suggested by Miles Taylor (1996), the historian of nineteenth-century popular politics, Thompson and Stedman Jones had much in common:

- both were sceptical about Chartism as a local phenomenon;
- both said Chartism was not simply a protest movement but had greater coherence;
- both wanted to emphasise the political elements of Chartism;
- both recognised the rational nature of Chartist arguments;
- both located Chartism within a longer chronology of radicalism.

They disagreed profoundly, however, about why Chartism collapsed and they did so not because new evidence had become known but because new interpretations were now available. For Thompson it was because the working class lost the collective belief that they could reform politics in the conditions thrown up by mid-century capitalism; for Stedman Jones it was the collapse of the Chartist critique of the state, a critique inherited from a pre-reform politics. This disagreement was as much a disagreement of approach to the relevant facts: for Stedman Jones, Chartism could not respond to the limited nature of factory reform – new policing legislation, reform of local government and the New Poor Law; for Thompson, the state restricted newspapers and trade unions, crushing class consciousness, which in turn led to the collapse of Chartism.

The result of this debate about what we consider to be an historical fact and how we approach the analysis of historical evidence, has led to fresh strands of enquiry; especially the systematic study of language and symbols; what one early historian of Chartism Robert Gammage once called the 'gaudy trappings' of Chartism: poetry, ballads, hymns, banners and flags. Thompson was always inclined to seek out the expressive aspects of the movement, but this and revisions based on the languages of what the historian Edward Royle has called 'Chartist culture', have seen some rich work undertaken in popular politics more generally. Patrick Joyce in his *Democratic Subjects* (1994) has attacked class as a universal category and looks instead for 'other discourses of "the People"' that are not confined to Chartist agitation. Margot Finn (1993) takes Chartism beyond its usual periodisation, connecting it to European nationalism and socialism of the 1860s, while Eugenio Biagini and Alistair Reid take up Chartism, like Stedman Jones, as one part of a radical tradition that stretches forward to influence both Gladstonian Liberalism and a nascent Labour movement.

The most recent contributions to Chartist scholarship have not successfully challenged the approach of Stedman Jones, although Ariane Schnepf's *Our Original Rights as a People* (2006) has attempted just that. Instead there are studies which take the reader across the whole narrative of Chartism, such as Malcolm Chase's *Chartism: A New History* (2007), and W. Hamish Fraser's *Chartism in Scotland* (2010). There is even a turn back to the biography that had originally characterised historical writing about the Chartists from the 1850s with Stephen Roberts looking at the career histories of Chartist figures Thomas Cooper and Arthur O'Neill in his *The Chartist Prisoners* (2008). Yet none of these worthwhile additions to the genre do much more than make do with accepted 'facts' but instead do what historians ought to do – concentrate equally on both the choice and selection of evidence and balance theory and evidence.

By focusing on this one area of historiography we should be in a position to pull together some of the themes of the chapter. Whether the historian is objective or subjective about the Chartist phenomenon ought not to matter if it is believed that historical evidence remains unsullied, as it were, by the unreasonable prejudice of the historian or even influenced by the time in which the history is researched and written. Nor should an approach that regards the historian as objective, treating the past as quite unconnected to the present, necessarily be a right-wing or conservative idea. To take one further example, the husband of Dorothy Thompson, E. P. Thompson (1924–93), raised wife sales (like his essays on 'rough music' in 1972 or the 'moral economy' in 1971) as an example of a 'rebellious traditional culture' among the masses against a background of industrialisation, an illustration of 'the dis-association between patrician and plebeian cultures'. This suggested a concern for radical and class-based experiences but these historical experiences were, Thompson maintained, first revealed to him through primary sources.

Thompson as a Marxist did not collapse into a subjective empathy – the historical imagination that Fry invited us to apply to the past may well have been far too soft focused and woolly for Thompson. He used the archive in order to glimpse social relations among a strata of society previously treated with condescension: an attempt by the mainly rural poor to claim rights in the face of a rapidly changing economy and a plebeian culture that was separate from its patrician counterpart. In using that archive he applied method just as surely as Elton. Indeed, in an argument with Raphael Samuel in the pages of the *History Workshop Journal* in the 1990s, Thompson railed against the 'modish subjectivism now so current' and argued that the evidence of the archive was not 'silent and inert to be manipulated into any form the questioner proposed. Nor can the choice of context or setting be decided by the flip of a coin.' When Samuel suggested that the idea of wife sales as an unofficial form of divorce was 'like any piece of historical reasoning and research, it was a child or creature of its time', Thompson insisted that his argument derived 'from the instances which kept popping up in the newspapers when I was researching' (*History Workshop Journal*, 1992, issue 34). From this debate alone we can see that if reliable knowledge about the past is possible, it depends upon the judgments and disagreements of historians.

In practice

Many of us were encouraged to believe at school that since history books recorded events as they happened they were reliable and truthful statements about the past. Hopefully, anyone who has continued an interest in history – whether an established researcher or someone reading a history book or watching a television documentary as a source of relaxation and entertainment – has had the resourcefulness to develop a more critical awareness of such accounts, and therefore should be sufficiently aware of the need to ask probing questions about the nature of the evidence presented and how it has been used by the writers.

What is clear from the consideration in this chapter of how historians have approached the past is that there is no consensus; indeed the topic has remained a contentious one. In the course of the nineteenth century when history emerged as a discipline in its own right, the task of the historian was seen to be that of recording things as they actually happened. This seemed obvious enough. Under appropriate circumstances, any historian trained in the techniques of working with evidence could produce a solid picture of the past. This vision of the role of the historian has proved to be remarkably enduring; indeed, many historians today would accept in large measure that this is what they strive for.

Recent scholarship, however, has begun to unsettle this rather too convenient approach. Until we have a time machine, it is argued, historians cannot work in the past, but examine in the present what evidence has survived from the past. Even historians are creatures of their time, and so are in some ways influenced by the spirit of the age no matter how much they may wish to rise above such mundane considerations. The debate between Geoffrey Elton, in the blue corner, representing the traditional historian, and E. H. Carr, in the red corner (no necessary significance here in the colour coding), representing a more critical approach to evidence, addresses directly these sorts of concerns. Unlike Elton, Carr contends that since we are all unable to divorce ourselves from contemporary political and social concerns, our approach to historical evidence can never be objective or dispassionate. This challenges the idea of the potential neutrality of the historian as recorder and questions whether we can ever gain access to historical truth.

In certain respects, we can. We know beyond reasonable doubt, for example, that Earl Cornwallis surrendered to the combined forces of North America and France on 19 October 1781, that a Bosnian nationalist assassinated Archduke Franz Ferdinand on 28 June 1914, and that Jawaharlal Nehru declared Indian independence from British rule at midnight, 17 August 1947. Yet historical debates still rage on the historical significances of these events. Thus although we have access to what might be described as evidential truth, that same evidence can be used in very different ways by historians to construct a narrative and hence interpret the historical significance of the episode. When Percival

▶

Spear wrote of the aftermath of the Indian Mutiny, he used limited evidential truths to forge a distinct account that in many respects is open to challenge by historians who have less sympathy for British rule. Theories on nationalist struggles, the role of the individual in historical processes, the nature of imperial power and so on will thus shape how historians view evidence.

Carr concluded that evidence and theory must be in continual dialogue, that is, theories must be tested against evidence, and evidence viewed through the lens of theory. The theory in question can be that suggested by Gareth Stedman Jones to historians of Chartism. Without digging up a single new fact, Stedman Jones has suggested an approach to existing evidence that has utterly transformed the way modern historians think about both Chartism as a movement and popular politics more generally.

These, then, are the sorts of questions we should bear in mind when approaching the past. The past is gone – we can never gain access to it except through the evidence which has survived to the present. What we do with that evidence determines the sort of accounts which are written.

Summary

The three sections of this chapter have said three things:

- Historians, certainly English-speaking historians, quite often protest that they would prefer to get on with the business of researching and writing history than concentrating on that theory that serves this evidence. Despite this, a surprising number are happy to engage in discussing the boundaries of history, in particular, the extent to which the discipline has a history, and the interaction of the historian. In order to illustrate this simple problem, this section has explored the debate as to what history is about and how it is (or should be) practiced. Nowhere has the important question about the objectivity or subjectivity of the historian been more comprehensively debated than in the argument between E. H. Carr and Geoffrey Elton. We tend not to take sides in this debate but recognise that the notion of history as a verifiable 'science' or an art where the subjectivity or imagination of the historian is taken into account has been one of the most enduring problems in historiography. It does argue, however, that as the historian is part of history, subjectivity may be impossible and may even be an advantage, once admitted and in some circumstances.

- Questions regarding objectivity and subjectivity are highlighted by looking at the way in which the Indian Mutiny in the nineteenth century has bequeathed us both 'hard' empirical evidence and received ideas about the role of the British during the imperialist experience. Here by looking how one historian has used evidence, and through the application of a simple exercise, it was demonstrated how a perfectly respectable history of India can be written using certain historical and linguistic assumptions held by the author. This then, allows us to reconsider afresh the view of Geoffrey Elton that history should be evidence led with the historian decentred from the application of clear historical method applied to the evidence.

- Since the decline of Chartism in the 1850s, historians have sought to explain its demise. Biographical approaches that examine the expressive aspects of Chartism have all been used at one time or other. Chartism has also been the source of present day tussles that have emphasised the political nature of the movement, its national or local character, its economic basis and so on. Choosing evidence to support this or that viewpoint has differed, while the interpretation of that evidence has often depended on the preoccupations of the here and now. The section emphasises, however, that the most significant breakthrough in this field was prompted by the work of Dorothy Thompson and then Gareth Stedman Jones. They agreed on much but the use by Stedman Jones of linguistic theory succeeded in transforming our knowledge of Chartism without the addition of a single new fact.

Discussion document 1

These extracts from both Elton and Carr ought to illustrate their essential argument and disagreements; with Elton focusing on the rational, scientific and objective approach to history as a discipline and Carr who at least accepts (if not values) subjective approaches to evidence.

> The study of history is an intellectual pursuit, an activity of the reasoning mind, and, as one should expect, its main service lies in its essence. Like all sciences, history, to be worthy to itself and beyond itself, must concentrate on one thing: the search for truth. Its real value as a social activity lies in the training it provides, the standards it sets, in this singularly human concern. Reason distinguishes man from the rest of creation, and the study of history justifies itself in so far as it assists reason to work and improve itself. Like all rational activities, the study of history, regarded as an autonomous enterprise, contributes to the improvement of man, and it does so by seeking the truth within the confines of its particular province, which happens to be the rational reconstruction of the past . . . The quality of an historian's work must . . . be judged purely by intellectual standards; the same is true of his contribution to society . . . It is not the problems they study or the lessons they teach that distinguish the historical sheep from the goats, but only the manner of their study, the precision of their minds, and the degree to which they approximate to the ultimate standards of intellectual honesty and intellectual penetration. *Omnia Veritas* [Truth Conquers All].

Geoffrey Elton, *The Practice of History* (1967), pp. 49–50.

> Let us take a look at the process by which a mere fact about the past is transformed into a fact of history. At Stalybridge Wakes in 1850, a vendor of ginger-bread, as the result of some petty dispute, was deliberately kicked to death by an angry mob. Is this a fact of history? A year ago I should have said 'no'. It was recorded by an eye-witness in some little known memoirs; but I had never seen it judged worthy mention by any historian. A year ago Dr. Kitson Clark [the historian George Kitson Clark, 1900–75] cited it in his Ford lectures in Oxford. Does this make it into a historical fact? Not, I think, yet. Its present status, I suggest, is that it has been proposed for membership of the select club of historical facts. It now awaits a seconder and sponsors. It may be that in the course of the next few years we shall see this fact appearing first in footnotes, then in the text, of articles and books about nineteenth century England, and that in twenty or thirty years' time it may well be established historical fact. Alternatively, nobody may take it up, in which case it will relapse into the limbo of unhistorical facts about the past from which Dr. Kitson Clark has gallantly attempted to rescue it.

E. H. Carr, *What is History?* (1961), pp. 6–7.

Discussion document 2

This is a passage from a standard work by an historian of India. Spear for many years taught in Cambridge and at St Stephen's College in Delhi, India. He was a trained historian using all the appropriate techniques of historical writing – a clear presentation of the facts, a scrupulous regard for the evidence and objectivity. It may be, however, that he was himself locked into a particular narrative of the Indian Mutiny from which he never quite escaped.

In the summer of 1858 northern India lay inert and lacerated. The wisdom of Canning and strength of men like Sir John Lawrence restrained and soon ended the punitive measures and clamours for vengeance which followed the wake of the armies. But much remained to be done. Most of the rebel leaders were killed in battle like the Rani of Jhansi, or disappreared like the Nana and Bakht Khan of Delhi, or were executed like Tantia Topi. The Emperor Bahadur Shah had been promised his life. After a trial of doubtful legality he was exiled to Rangoon where he died in 1862 at the age of eighty-seven. The Mughal family lost its royal status. Delhi and Locknow slowly returned to normal life, but Delhi with its territory lost its semi-independent position and was attached to the Punjab. A number of implicated princelings lost their states and their lives. In Oudh Canning's confiscatory proclamation was not withdrawn, but its application was left to the discretion of the new Chief Commissioner Montgomery, and its rigour mitigated by a system of regrants.

These were the immediate and local results; there followed a number of measures of great importance. The East India Company ended its long career as the ruling power in India; a new attitude was adopted toward the princes; the army was reorganised; a new beginning was made in associating Indians with the supreme of their country. The new age was ushered in and its intended spirit defined in the Queen's proclamation of 1 November 1858. If good can come out of the evil the mutiny can claim the credit for most of these measures. There remained the psychological gulf between the peoples of India and Britain. This gulf was not created by the Mutiny as we have seen. The forces of separation had outstripped that of cooperation and the hope of self-government. This spirit was reinforced by that of fear on the British side and the resentment which it aroused was deepened by the memory of defeat and vengeance on the Indian. In this sense the Mutiny was a calamity whose effects only time could heal. Happily the progressive forces of reform and cooperation were not consumed but only consumed by the smoke of passion. They had received a severe set-back, but the next fifty years showed that it was a check rather than a halt.

Percival Spear, *A History of India, 1740–1975* (1990), pp. 227–8. (Originally published 1965.)

Further reading

* *essential*

* **www.history.ac.uk/ihr/Focus/Whatishistory/carr1.html.**
Here the historian Alan Munslow examines the importance of the seminal work of both E. H. Carr and Geoffrey Elton in the light of historiographical advances since the 1960s and, in particular, the way in which postmodernists have cast doubt on history as a dependable basis of knowledge.

Geoffrey Elton, *The Practice of History* (1967, 1994, 2002).
The standard case for history as an objective science. The 2002 Blackwell edition is introduced by Richard Evans.

E. H. Carr, *What is History?* (1961).
The standard case for history as a subjective art.

Dorothy Thompson, *Chartism: Popular Politics in the Industrial Revolution* (1984).
The emphasis here is on the national characteristics of Chartism and the culmination of working class radicalism. The renewed focus is on the political, rather than the economic roots of Chartism and the occupations of those that became Chartists.

* **Gareth Stedman Jones**, 'Rethinking chartism', in *The Languages of Class* (1983).
Probably the most controversial and influential account of Chartism, which asks questions about the significance and role of language and its relation to class consciousness; finally suggesting that Peel's reforms in the 1840s rendered the Chartist critique of the state as out of date.

* **Miles Taylor**, 'Rethinking the Chartists: searching for synthesis in the historiography of Chartism', *Historical Journal*, 39 (1996).
A wonderful overview of the historiography by an historian who really understands nineteenth-century popular politics.

2 The ordering of time

1 Time, history, modernity
2 Newton and the 'time reckoner'
3 Time, history and the shape of things to come
4 Events, people and periods: what is Victorian, when were the 'sixties'?

Introduction

This chapter explores the connection between history and time. The very idea of time, its relationship to human history and our understanding of it as either circular, coming back on itself, linear where it moves inextricably forward or as existing in isolated pockets of experience, differs within *and* across cultures. Time then relates to the type of past society under review, specifically whether the society is primitive, pre-literary, agrarian, advanced or industrial. Time is also a site of struggle; the modern world is the outcome of a reordering of time impelled by capitalist rationalisation. Historians tend to order past time by slicing it up into epochs and periods, but there are incongruities in so doing. The decade that we call the 1960s is not necessary congruent with 'the sixties' as an historical period. Where the 1960s is measurable as a block of time, not so the cultural phenomena that we associate with 'the sixties'. And as a distinct period which, for example, was detectable in the United States, France, Britain and Italy, it may have passed almost without trace in, say, South America or the Soviet Union. Questions follow from this. What are the elements that might be associated with historical periods? To be a Victorian, for example, is to be associated with a particular time but also with an historical style. Think Victorian and, more likely than not, we can conjure up a world of extreme richness and extreme poverty – shoeless children working in chimneys and gentlemen in top hats making their way through the London fog carrying silver-topped canes. Sex and hypocrisy sleep together. When do historical periods begin and end? Is the decade we call the 'the sixties' actually a discrete period with its own associations of free love and counter-cultural protest, quite unlike the period that came before it, the 'age of austerity' characterised by war, food shortages and drabness? Answers to questions such as these and to others like it, must always be given in the knowledge that historians impose 'periods', 'eras', 'epochs' and 'ages' on time.

Section 1

Time, history, modernity

To live in any modern western society is to be a narrative junkie. We crave stories (in whatever medium) that have a beginning, middle and end. History is no exception. Primarily these narratives relate to an understanding of time that we think we know best – our own lives. Time is projected towards an end-point, moving forward in stages, which Shakespeare in *As You Like It* identifies succinctly as infant, schoolchild, lover, soldier, wise man or woman ('justice'), and old age ('pantaloon'). Finally there is second childhood – 'sans teeth, sans eyes, sans taste, sans everything' – and then death. Time in our own personal 'life cycle' is circular. From the writer of the book of *Ecclesiastes*, however, we learn there is a 'season set for everything, a time for every experience under heaven'. Yet:

> **Only that will happen**
> **Which has happened,**
> **Only that occurs**
> **Which has occurred;**
> **There is nothing new**
> **Beneath the sun!**

Time in an advanced, industrial society is conceived, not as cyclical, but progressive – it runs in a forward direction. It is linear. It has a beginning, middle and end with the next age seemingly improving on the last. Although personal cyclical time and public linear time cannot be reconciled, an important question nonetheless should be asked: where does this sense of time as progressive and linear come from and why is it important for historians?

Understandings of the passing of time are dependent on social factors such as age and gender as well as culture. Educationalists and psychologists have suggested, for example, that children understand the passing of time in wholly different ways from that of adults. They soon learn that the day is broken down, seemingly for the convenience of grown-ups. There is a time to get up, a time to work and a time to play and, most certainly, a time to go to bed. With the onset of industrialisation came differing understandings of time in the experiences of women, men and children depending on the work that they did and the roles that they performed. In this respect, some feminist historians regard time as socially constructed through the domestic or private sphere. For women there was the experience of so-called 'maternal' or 'family' time in the private sphere. For men there was the experience of work and decision-making in the public sphere, influenced by other factors such as social class.

Social historian Tamara Hareven (1937–2002) examined the question of 'family time' compared to 'historical time' in a New England industrial community and emphasised how time, that is, 'social age' can vary in different places and cultures:

> **Historical time is generally defined as a linear chronological movement of changes in a society over decades or centuries, while individual lifetime is measured according to age. But age and chronology both need social contexts to be meaningful. Social age is different from chronological age: in certain societies, a twelve-year-old is an adolescent; in others, he is old. How were typical lives 'timed' in the past, and how did these life-course patterns fit into their economic, institutional, and demographical setting?** (Hareven, 1983, p. 59)

While industrial or 'historical time' is the linear movement of change in the public sphere and is measured conventionally over years, decades and centuries, individual lifetimes are measured according to the particular social context of age and gender. Time works differently for adults and children. As the male experience of time has been dominant over female experiences of time in modern or industrial societies, it is the 'chronological' and linear understanding of time that dominates history as both a process and as a discipline. To answer fully the question of why this should be so, however, we have to move beyond understanding time through personal experience and the narratives of our own existences. To do so is critically important for historians regardless of their level of learning or their particular specialist area of interest.

Attitudes to time in the West are tied to the industrial process of the last couple of hundred years or so. In the phenomenon of industrialisation and all that accompanied it, we find a critical divide between cultures. According to Peter Laslett's *The World We Have Lost* (1965), time before industrialisation was located in the rhythm, not of the machine, but of the natural seasons and with it the organisation of pre-industrial family life. As the first industrial nation, Britain was at the apogee of much that was to develop elsewhere. Rural time had a different shape from what was to become 'urban time'; time measured not by clock but by season. Weather, the movements of the moon and sun, sowing and harvesting, dictated the cycles of rural life, while feast days, fast days, and days dedicated to the saints, maintained religion at the centre of rural life.

'Time-discipline' imposed on workers newly arrived from the countryside, according to the historian E. P. Thompson in his path breaking 'Time, Work, Discipline and Industrial Capitalism', published in the journal *Past and Present* in 1967, ensnared the industrial proletariat, chaining them to the incessant and remorseless rhythm of the machine. Like labour itself, time had a value and a price. Time was money. Taking a place on a production line of a factory or workshop, 'clocking out' eventually became the lot of the industrial working class. Only the pursuits of popular culture, association football and the like provided a respite, although with commercialisation even the football match had a regular kick-off time and a measurable length of season and therefore it too relied on a secular, civil calendar.

With industrialisation came urbanisation. Then came the railway and the usurpation of local time by national time. In order to have a national railway timetable, each major town and city conformed to a nationally agreed time, where once localities had kept their own, and railway journeys from, say, London to Bristol took longer according to these clocks than journeys from Bristol to London. Industrialisation generally heralded the introduction of both national and international time – Greenwich Mean Time – and the notion of linear progression in time. This notion had profound consequences for the understanding and writing of history; whether or not 'progress' or 'decline' can be determined in the present by knowing what happened to civilisations in the past. For Victorians, history worked in the knowledge of the fate that once befell Greece and imperial Rome. As empires rise (such as the British Empire) so too could they fall. In other words, history could run backwards as well as forwards. Herbert Spencer, philosopher, sociologist and social Darwinist, announced in 1851, the same year as the erection of that beacon of Victorian optimism, the Crystal Palace, that progress was evolutionary but that evolution could also run backwards. Like so many others, Spencer was devastated when he learnt that the second law of thermodynamics meant that the world had from its very creation begun to grow cold and become more chaotic: to degenerate; a notion connected to what natural scientists now call entropy (Spencer, 1862).

With this realisation (at least in the West) came both a different understanding of the mechanics of time, a changing idea of progress, and with it changing ideas of how history worked. It is this that provides late-Victorian Britain with its most pervasive dialectic, that of progress and degeneration. If 1851 marked the highpoint of the 'age of equipoise' or the 'age of improvement', by the 1890s notions of degeneration overtook or challenged these ideas of progress. Even Charles Darwin, while optimistic in his *On the Origin of Species* (1859), could offer no guarantee of human progress by the publication of his *Descent of Man* in 1871.

Pre-industrial societies or pre-literate societies had no such idea of time running either forwards or backwards. Without an agreed method of measuring and keeping time, these societies could not conceive of 'eras', 'ages' or 'periods', anymore than they would measure in objective terms the age of an individual within a group. Subjectively they could measure the *relative* ages of say the elder, the novice, or, indeed, the *relative* importance of an event compared to another event: one year becomes the year of the drought, another the year of the exploding volcano. As there was no established chronology, there could be no agreed calendar. It was impossible to conceive history as either linear or progressive. The chronology of past events could not, therefore, be determined by objective criteria. In pre-industrial societies there could be no assumption that any event had any universal significance, not least because of the absence in these societies of a recognised dating system. Nor could it be assessed for its significance or be seen objectively as part of an historical pattern or trend. Divisions between pre-industrial and industrial approaches to time and history are thus profound.

Sociologists and anthropologists have revealed something of the comprehension of time in different parts of the world. When the anthropologist, Pierre Bourdieu (1930–2002) studied Algerian peasants in the late 1950s and early 1960s, painstakingly retrieving the social and economic world of the indigenous Kabyle Berbers, he observed that time in this society was understood as 'so many experiences' that existed in 'self-enclosed units', usually with some social, political or religious significance, but not at any rate as industrial society assumed time to work, as part of a continuous line leading to an endpoint in history:

> **[E]vents in the past are located by reference to memorable occurrences: one speaks of 'the year in which there was misery', 'the year in which there was a plague', 'in which there was snow for many years', or, in Algiers, 'the year when the ship burned in the harbour'. Temporal points of reference are just so many experiences. One must avoid seeing here points of division, which would presuppose the notion of regular measured intervals, that is to say, a special conception of the temporal. The islands of time which are defined by these landmarks are not apprehended as segments of a continuous line, but rather so many self-enclosed units.** (Bourdieu, 1963, p. 59)

Any reckoning of the relationship between history and an understanding of time must take in religious sensibilities. Islam, for example, is one such tradition where an idea of linear history or history as progressive is quite absent. There is, however, a definite chronology at work, a need to measure time for profound reasons attached to religious law but where there appears to be a real difference between western and eastern conceptions of time, or at least between Islam and Judeo-Christianity:

> **The Qur'anic vision of history rests upon a certain conception of time and space and a certain style to express that conception. Islam and history are coeval: 'It was God who called you Muslims from days of old' (22:78). A community or *umma*, of God has from time immemorial been the 'witnesses of God on earth, aligning to virtue and forbidding evil'. It is a 'community of the centre' which came into being with Adam. Thereafter, the Qur'an pans over a landscape where time is less a chronology than a continuum, where Abraham, Moses, Jesus and Mohammed are all described in a grammatical tense which one is tempted to call the eternal present. The whole of history is present at once to God. Within this design, events are arranged in clusters repetitive in form. This means that a Qur'anic *quissa* or tale, is closer in function and meaning to a 'case in point', an 'affair' or even a 'parable' than it is to a story or narrative.** (Khaldi, 1994, p. 8)

Instead of the industrial model of time first conceived in the West, history is a 'continuum' or an 'eternal present'. In the concept of Islamic time and its expression through Arabic, there is no sense at all of past, present or future, nor yet of a 'continuum', but rather time is 'complete or incomplete' depending on whether or not an action willed by Allah has been fulfilled:

> **The link of causality that appears to rule the world and human life becomes subordinate to Allah, and natural causes give way to divine will. As a rule, God does not interrupt the continuity of events . . . though He is able to intervene at any moment by what is commonly termed a miracle but simply means an interruption of His customary activity. Atomism was not only most congenial to a vision of God acting instantaneously in the world as the sole true cause, it also proved most closely akin to Arabic grammar, which lacks genuine verbs for 'to be' and 'to become'. Neither does Arabic employ the tenses of past, present and future. Instead, it uses verbal aspects of complete and incomplete, marking the degree to which an action has been realized or is yet to be realized without distinguishing precisely between present and future.** (Bowering, 1997, p. 60)

Other, if different, understandings of time can be taken from Judaism, Buddhism or even Aboriginal Dreamtime. The sociologist Emile Durkheim in 1903 and 1912 noted how time is divided technically between seconds, minutes, days, months and years but could also be understood through public events such as feasts, rites, public ceremonies that are particular and peculiar to different cultures. Durkheim had in mind, however, the processes of modernity and the differences apparent between mechanical societies that are pre-industrial and organic societies; and how in these advanced, industrial societies, time was just another form of globalised commercial property to be bought, sold, bartered or negotiated.

Thus far we have examined the cultural and ideological dimensions of time, but in many respects the political has been the most important in world history. In general, political authority has been exercised in part through an ability to control time. Consider, for example, the fascinating story of how western global hegemony in the modern period was secured by the imposition of a world system of time. In 1714 the British parliament instituted a prize of £20,000. They wanted urgently to locate longitude at sea. For centuries, sailors had employed various celestial methods in order to find the vertical lines that circle the globe. The need to measure longitude accurately was urgent for a number of reasons. Latitude, or the horizontal lines on the globe, was well known; so well known in fact that the sea lanes were dangerously crowded with ships, including pirate ships, sticking to these narrow routes. Without longitude, the ability to trade across unknown seas, to discover, to conquer, would be quite impossible or would remain (like the discovery of America by Columbus) a matter of luck.

Astronomers, from the German Johannes Werner in 1514 to the genius of the Italian Galileo in 1610, and before them some of the greatest figures from the classical world, had attempted to find the position of a ship by variations of a single method. This method in some way involved mapping the skies, sun, planets and stars and then, in a hideously complex process, measuring the relation of the moon to a point fixed in time and space. Galileo, more simply, even hit on the idea of fixing longitude by measuring the ellipses of the moons of Jupiter. All of this could work, except it was extremely time consuming, not particularly accurate, and impossible when skies were cloudy.

The problem of finding longitude, however, was solved by a working-class clockmaker who happened to be a genius, not an astronomer. Between 1737 and 1760, John Harrison built four clocks for use on board the British fleet, each an improvement on the last. The fourth was able to overcome the problems of the destabilising conditions found on board ship to keep time with astonishing accuracy and hence allow the navigator to calculate the ship's longitude at any time of the day or night, and whatever the weather. Harrison was eventually awarded the prize, but it caused more than a ripple of disquiet on otherwise calm naval waters. Although resistant to his method and the very fact of his being a mere maker of mechanical devises, not a 'scientist' steeped in the mysteries of astronomy, the authorities abandoned celestial approaches – that is, those approaches that looked to the sky for a fixed longitudinal point – but decided to retain the convention of using the Observatory at Greenwich as 'Mean Time'. Greenwich, at '0' degrees latitude and longitude, thus became the centre of the world and ships could traverse the seas quicker than ever before. Now Britain controlled both time and space and because of it Britannia ruled the waves. This invention, although unbelievably difficult in conception, long in gestation and painfully drawn out in its delivery, was to have momentous repercussions in the understanding of time in relation to history. Above all, it was to have long-term consequences for western hegemony, for it can be argued that to control time and space is to control history and the writing of histories.

David Harvey in his book *The Condition of Postmodernity* (1990) argues that money, power and capital combine to ensure that the conquest and control of time and space was never independent of social relations anymore than history, and history writing, it might be argued, could be anything else but part of the society from which it emanates, although in the last chapter we found many historians who would disagree. As the enclosure movements transformed the landscape of eighteenth and nineteenth century Britain, for instance, so imperialism empowered a new mercantile class. Turnpikes, canals and trains changed special relations (bringing hitherto remote areas 'nearer' to London) and in so doing led to a redistribution of wealth and power. This 'pulverisation of space', Harvey tells us, meant also that capital could move faster along lines of communication than ever before, via say the network established by the Rothschild family that spread over Europe in the early part of the nineteenth century. Specifically during the changes evoked by industrialisation, time and space compressed as technological changes increased speeds of travel and communication, transforming relations of distance.

Stephen Kern in his *The Culture of Time and Space 1880–1918* (2003) investigated the apogee of this process at the *fin de siècle* through the fields of physics, philosophy, psychiatry, sociology, art and literature. He labelled Harvey's description of this process of 'space-time compression' as 'one-sided', arguing that new transportation and communication technologies expanded as well as compressed space-time. Taking the newly invented telephone as an example, he suggested that telephones 'compressed space in that they reduced lived distances' but also expanded space 'by extending the special reach of an individual from one place to another' (cf. xii). This 'space-time' relationship is experienced in a variety of ways, according to Kern: in cultural forms such as art, distance and direction and by speed. This is especially highlighted between 1880 and 1918 through changing modes of production (Taylorian time management systems in Ford factories, for instance), diplomacy and perceived abilities to communicate quickly across geographical boundaries, cinema and the phonograph which modified perceptions of the past, luxury liners such as the Titanic, and military endeavours like the Schlieffen Plan, that relied on speed. Or take the synchronised wristwatches that were distributed from headquarters and passed along the trenches at the Somme. At precisely 7.30 a.m. on the morning of 1 July 1916, the whistles blew and the greatest loss of life ever experienced by the British army began. Without the concept of standard time and without the technical means of measuring time, events could not have happened as they did. In any case, war had made time homogeneous once again, experienced not as James Joyce had described it in *Ulysses* (1922) as flowing or broken consciousness, nor as Marcel Proust in his *Remembrance of Things Past* (1913–27) had conceived it through memory and private reflection: vague, arbitrary and inexact. Capitalism had rationalised time in a number of areas that would affect the writing and popular understanding of the past. A need to understand the past and to locate the present, however, was not, as we are about to find out, exclusively a product of modernity.

Section 2

Newton and the 'time reckoner'

It was essential for Christendom in the Middle Ages to record with accuracy the birth and death of Christ, to know precisely when Christmas and more critically Easter should be marked in relation to the solar and lunar calendars. The overall purpose was to use astronomy and mathematics to confirm that biblical sources could support an agreed chronology and to allow Christians to celebrate Easter (and other moveable feasts) together and at the same time. Theologically speaking, this was vital, as without this precise ability to build a Christian chronology that could pinpoint the Creation and the Incarnation, it would be impossible to calculate the End of Days. One such 'time reckoner' was the historian we know as the Venerable Bede (672–735 CE). We shall hear more from Bede in Chapter 7. He argued for the concept of a leap year as a way of catching up on a calendar which was losing days in relation to the really quite advanced calculations about the motion of the Sun around the Earth and the measurements of equinoxes. In doing this, he used a specially designed sundial and observed the tides around Northumbria in northern England. By the time he had finished, the word 'calculator' had entered the language.

Bede took much of his chronology from Dionysius Exiguus (d. *c.*544), agreeing with his dating of the birth of Christ and designating this year as 'year one'. He also shared with Dionysius a concern to properly date Easter. As an abbot (some say monk), Dionysius was summoned to Rome to catalogue the pontifical archives and by 525, at the bequest of Pope St John I, he created a chronology that is to some extent in use still today, introducing the term Christian Era. The origin of the 'Christian Era' was argued to be the Incarnation. What had previously been known as the 'Era of Martyrs', became known in Italy and Spain (in the eighth and ninth centuries) and in England (in the tenth century) as 'Era of Incarnation' (Stiglmayr, 1909). There had been earlier attempts to date the Creation of the world. In the third century, Julius Africanus (*c.*160–*c.*240) had established a Christian chronology that predicted the Second Coming of Christ (it would be around 500 CE). What were known as Pauline divisions of time (named after Paul the Apostle) charted a journey between Creation and Apocalypse: the age before Mosaic Law (the state of nature), the Mosaic Law (erroneously, it was thought, still accepted by the Jews) and the age of grace under Christ. This age would conclude with the Second Coming. Where precisely the present was located in the Christian chronology, however, was something that Calabrian Abbot Joachim of Fiore (1135–1202) elucidated with his proposal for history and time to be understood through a trinity of ages: Father (before Christ), Son (the time of Christ) and the age of the Holy Ghost (the future). His was an apocalyptic vision which assumed that eschatology – the study of church doctrine – would reveal a divine plan that could chart all human experience to the End of Days, or at least this is how it looks to the eyes of most modern historians.

Bernard McGinn's book *The Calabrian Abbot: Joachim of Fiore in the History of Western Thought* (1985) argued that his 'theology of history' was similar in range and method to the better known St Augustine of Hippo (354–430 CE). Works by Augustine such as *De Civitate Dei*, or the City of God, posited ages starting with Adam and Noah and which finished with Christ and the present. Before the Christian era, however, historians such as Herodotus (*c.*490 BCE) had said little about chronology, with dating deduced by using the reigns of Emperors and Kings. Indeed, much of classical scholarship, as we shall see in Chapter 6, was concerned with locating golden ages and to a limited extent at least, as in the example from Shakespeare and *Ecclesiastes* from which we started the chapter, recurrent cycles of ages.

Mathematical exactitude united attempts by medieval scholars such as Bede to establish a Christian chronology and the chronology drawn up by the natural philosopher and mathematician, Sir Isaac Newton (1642–1727). The need to establish both religious and civil calendars coincided in the seventeenth century. It became vital to know where humanity was in the journey to judgement and redemption and to have a chronology that would allow 'epochs' and 'eras' to be identified and examined for the purpose of charting the rational progress of time passing. Time, the measuring of time and the theological need to agree a calendar, therefore, simultaneously emerged out of the European Enlightenment – a movement that will be explained in detail in the next chapter. This is critically important for historians because they, uniquely perhaps, work with time and chronologies in order to make sense of the world.

Newton's chronology provided a new basis for measuring time, conforming to laws of motion that he argued governed the entire universe. The *Chronology of Ancient Kingdoms Amended*, published a year after his death in 1728, included a preface of 'the first memory of things in Europe'. In other words, a chronology of what he regarded as significant historical events that demonstrated how history moves forward. Yet it was one also deeply influenced by Christianity. Taking his dating system from the French Jesuit scholar, Dionysius Petavius (1583–1652), who had first set out the BC/AD categories in 1627 and who wrote *The History of the World or, an Account of Time*, which was published posthumously in 1659, Newtonian time was absolute time in the sense that it removed anomalies associated with cultural and religious differences inherent in religious conceptions of time.

Newton's assumptions, however, remained those of the Christian narrative of Creation (birth of Jesus), death (Crucifixion) and Resurrection (second coming). The story of Jesus in the New Testament is an account of man and God, an account of the ages of man, and the fate and redemption of humanity. After all, this was a religious man who dedicated much of his time trying to turn base metals into gold, proving the existence of fairies or determining the best theological course for rebuilding the Second Jewish Temple destroyed in 70 CE. The time Newton spent, however, on cosmology, or what we might construe as modern physics, turned out to be significant, not least for the writing of history. As the historian William Gallois goes on to say, time from the perspective of the Enlightenment is 'neutral and progressive':

> **History is therefore utterly dependent upon a new means of picturing time which emerges in western Europe at a distinct moment. It conceives of itself as neutral and progressive because it is self-evidently different from earlier conceptions of time, and because it is part of a complex of ideas about space and time which enabled huge advances in productivity, in making histories as much as in making paintings or machines. As a human creation, this idea of historical time is just as subject to critique and innovation as any other invention.**
>
> (Gallois, 2007, p. 46)

Yet Newtonian ideas of time then were born from Christianity, and nurtured in western European society as a continuation of a specifically Christian attempt to understand time. In this sense, however, historians owe Newton a debt for another reason that will now be outlined.

Simply measuring time was once *the* basic task of the historian; to chronicle all that has been and to use prophecy to reveal all that might yet be. Now there was also an attempt to construct a narrative of progress via Enlightenment science and rationality. The need to establish a chronology was essential in order for historians to lay the foundations from objective historical reasoning. Future historians could identify specific eras, periods or epochs, or 'timeframes' within which events could be organised, analysed and understood. No longer could the 'year in which there was a plague', as Bordieu's Algerian peasants might have put it, be understood in isolation or the origins of history dated arbitrarily from the Creation or the Incarnation.

Newton's 'general laws' of the universe applied to the writing of history, an 'absolute' chronology that was true in all times and all places – it was constant. As the time of an historical event could be known precisely, it can also be compared to an event on another part of the timeline. An explosion of European writings and works of art in the fourteenth, fifteenth and sixteenth centuries, for instance, could suggest when taken together a new sense of individualism – a Renaissance.

Equally, a rational chronology could look critically at seemingly unimportant historical events such as the incarceration of two, apparently harmless, old ladies. A Scottish grandmother named Helen Duncan was arrested under the 1735 Witchcraft Act, along with a 72-year old Londoner, Jane Yorke. The year was 1944. By consulting a linear timeline or chronology, it can surely be deduced very quickly that these arrests were not prompted by a society that believed they were actually witches, nor was there a general belief in witchcraft. Thus without knowing much about their cases but because we have an agreed chronology of events, it can be said emphatically that the witch craze belongs to an earlier period and that these women could not represent a continuity from the fifteenth and sixteenth centuries. It turns out, instead, that both women were seen as security risks in wartime Britain. Séances held by each of the women, at the bequest of the apparently grieving relatives of serving seamen, had inadvertently revealed the names of torpedoed ships but whose fate had not yet been announced by the British authorities. As survivors of these vessels had fed details to the women contrary to the best interests of the war effort, the Witchcraft Act became the most convenient way to bring these apparent fraudsters to trial and to shut them up. The Act was not abolished until 1951.

Because of Enlightenment-inspired approaches to chronology, historians can make comparisons over time and analyse the meaning of events. As Wilcox puts it, following this western innovation in history writing and historical knowledge, 'judgement follows measurement' and not the other way around:

> **The dating systems in use before Newton were not absolute and did not contain the implications about absolute time that characterize the BC/AD system. Pre-Newtonian time had no conceptual grid to give universal applicability to numbers. Dates in that time were tied to specific themes, events and moral lessons, and they gave a meaning and shape of their own to the events they dated. Without the conceptual grid the fundamental sequence/measurement and judgement was radically different from our own. Whatever our attitude towards the function of history and the possibility of objectivity, we assume that an historian answers the question of when an event occurred before determining its meaning; judgement follows measurement . . . Historians writing before Newton reversed this order. Events created their own time frames. Before locating an event in time, the histories had to make judgements about its meaning and its thematic relation to other events. New insights, synthesis, or major events, such as the rise of Rome, the coming of Christianity, the development of modern nations, or the revival of culture in the Renaissance all created their own time frames . . . the time frame did not include a group of events; a group of events contained the time frame.**
>
> (Wilcox, 1987, p. 9)

Post-Newtonian historians could now judge and measure events against an agreed and 'rational' timeline in order to determine both the existence and importance of distinct historical periods: the 'antique' period, the 'Middle Ages', the Reformation and counter Reformation, Renaissance, Enlightenment and so on. This timeline has become difficult to defend from a postmodernist perspective, however, as will be outlined in Chapter 5, with history seemingly unfolding in a progressive direction that relentlessly moves forward. Nevertheless, a judgment about the importance of an historic event within a chronology was easier to agree when the whole of Europe went over to the Gregorian calendar. It is worth recounting this story briefly because it was to have consequences for western historical practice.

In western Europe, the Gregorian reforms introduced an arithmetical system that counted days in a similar way as the previous Julian calendar, a product of Pagan Rome. It allowed for the drift caused by previously incorrect calculations of the year's length in relation to the vernal equinox. As the Gregorian dropped ten days to correct this error and brought the calendar back into line with the seasons, historians could agree a chronology of events from mainland Catholic Europe to its Protestant fringes which in turn required general agreement based on simple, verifiable and agreed historical facts. How, for instance, could two people die on the same date but not on the same day? The explanation could be that one died in Spain, which had been one of the first countries to adopt the Gregorian calendar, while the other person died in Protestant England which was among the last. (Scotland had made the change in 1600.) Understanding the precise occurrence of battles, enthronements, peace treaties and plagues, dating for tombstones, all recorded by contemporaries either according to the Julian or to the Gregorian calendars, still today creates enormous difficulties for historians. Even the relatively straightforward business of dating a birth is contentious: certificates often append both the Old Style (OS) and New Style (NS), expressed as (for example) 1752/53. The first date denotes OS, the second NS. Both are correct.

Such difficulties were overshadowed in the early twentieth century with the revolutionary transformation in the measurement and concept of time brought about by the work of Albert Einstein. Contrary to Newton, Einstein established that time was subjective, not absolute. This theory suggested that there could no longer be a single 'objective' clock but many clocks spread across the Universe, 'each telling a different correct time'. Einstein used his now famous metaphor of the moving train to argue that while space was a fixed and absolute concept, time was relative. Placing a clock at either end of a moving train, Einstein imagined a flash of light that illuminated each clock face. Sitting in the middle of the moving train, the clocks told exactly the same time. When a stationary person observed the moving train from a platform, however, the flash lit up the clocks at what appeared to be very slightly different times. The work of Einstein has had little direct impact on historians, not least because the changes in time he talked of occur under exceptional circumstances. However, the principles which arose from this work suggested two things. The first was that time is not absolute and unchanging but relative. The second is important for historians because it suggests that the observation of time changes time itself. That is, time is not a Newtonian constant only to be measured objectively from the outside but is something that can be experienced subjectively.

Section 3

Time, history and the shape of things to come

Futurology is no longer a respectable form of history. It aims to predict the future by understanding historical trends in the present. Very often the suggestion that history has predictive qualities is to be found among previous generations of historians but also with non-academic commentaries on the past and particularly, perhaps, in science fiction. Tales such as *The Time Machine* (1895) and *The War in the Air* (1908) that came from the pen of H. G. Wells (1866–1946) more often than not saw the positive benefits of science to human development. By the time of his death, however, Wells, autodidact, author and socialist, was pessimistic about the direction of history. His *Outline of History*, published in 24 fortnightly parts from November 1919 until November the following year, sold 2 million copies and was translated into many languages. Running to 780 pages this was no sketch, nor could we describe it as an outline. Nor, indeed, was his *Short History* – published in 1922 and revised constantly until 1945 – actually short. Its range, however, was simply breathtaking. The opening chapter begins with 'The world in space', where Wells described the Earth as 'a spheroid, a sphere slightly compressed, orange fashion'. By locating the origins of time in space, not with Creation, the birth of Jesus or the Council of Nicaea, he immediately took issue with the Christian account of human origins and traditional Christian chronology.

Changes in understandings of time that led to ideas of history as linear and forward-looking were histories heavily influenced by both Christianity and the Enlightenment. In the shadow of the two world wars of the twentieth century, however, popular histories such as those by Oswald Spengler, Arnold Toynbee and H. G. Wells did not necessarily or inevitably point forward. Indeed, in the fictional *Shape of Things to Come* (1933) he makes sneering reference to the 'Chronological Institute', a band of enthusiastic amateurs who from at least the mid-1850s produced transactions of their deliberations and who were undergoing a review of 'the cardinal dates in our social evolution':

> **Until the Chronological Institute has completed its present labours of revision and defined the cardinal dates in our social evolution, it is best to refer our account of the development of man's mind and will throughout this hectic period of human experience to the clumsy and irrelevant computation by centuries before and after the Christian Era, that is still current. As we have explained more fully in a previous book . . . we inherit this system of historical pigeonholes from Christendom; that arbitrary chequerwork of hundred-year blocks was imposed upon the entire Mediterranean and Atlantic literatures for two thousand years, and it still distorts the views of history of all but the alertest minds. The young student needs to be constantly on his guard against its false divisions. . . . we talk of the 'eighteenth century', and we think of fashions and customs and attitudes that are characteristic of a period extending from the Treaty of Westphalia in C.E. 1642 [was actually 1648] to the Napoleonic collapse in C.E. 1815; we talk of the 'nineteenth century', and the pictures and images evoked are those**

> **of the gas-lighting and steam-transport era, from after the distressful years of post-Napoleonic recovery to the immense shock of the World War in C.E. 1914. The phase 'twentieth century', again, calls forth images of the aeroplane, the electrification of the world and so forth; but an aeroplane was an extremely rare object in the air until 1914 (the first got up in 1905), and the replacement of the last steam railway train and the last steamship was not completed until the nineteen-forties. It is a tiresome waste of energy to oblige each generation of young minds to learn first of all in any unmeaning pattern of centuries and then to correct that first crude arrangement, so that this long-needed revision of our chronology is one that will be very welcome to every teacher. Then from the very outset he or she will be able to block out the story of our race in significant masses.** (Wells, 2005, pp. 25–6)

This section dwells on the problems posed by notions of 'progress' and its relation to the non-linear development of history to the writing of history itself. To be able to identify histories that are implicitly either linear or non-linear in their methodological prejudices is an essential skill for the historian. Difficulties remain of defining periods or even the problems involved in establishing the appropriate timeframe to be studied, from geological time which moves at a glacial pace and begins before human beings occupied the planet, to spans of time that cover mere decades or even a single year. William Fishman's *East End 1888: Life in a London Borough Among the Labouring Poor* is a good example of a study of a single year – admittedly an eventful one – in the history of the old East End.

In the world in which Wells wrote and worked, it was quite natural for historians to ascribe periods with certain characteristics and attribute to them moral values. It was also quite normal, increasingly so between the First and Second World Wars, to be pessimistic about the forward trajectory of history. Both popular and professional histories, however, are now built on timelines which break time down into stages of development with 'civilisation' as the most advanced stage of history. Amongst eminent writers of the past who identified stages of development were Adam Smith (1723–90) with his unfolding economic-based model (the Age of Hunters, the Age of Shepherds, the Age of Agriculture, the Age of Commerce), Auguste Comte (1798–1857) who attempted to theorise social progress through a philosophy of science and came up with three stages (Theological, Metaphysical, Positive), and Karl Marx who also had used historical stages as a way of explaining scientific historical movement (see Chapter 4). Astonishingly, as late as the 1980s, archaeological survey courses at reputable universities in the United Kingdom maintained the three stages of 'Civilisation', 'Barbarism' and 'Savagery' model of time that had been established by the anthropologist and social evolutionist Lewis Henry Morgan (1815–81) in his *Ancient Society* (1877). By presenting history in stages and attributing to them certain properties and characteristics, historians of very early societies could make value judgements, which if applied to the contemporary world would label say the Aborigines in Australia as barbaric or savage.

Equally, historians while influenced by science (Newton and Einstein are obvious examples) remain ignorant of the methods and approaches with which scientists would measure change and locate the origins of life. Here time is measured as geological time or as 'deep time' where physical factors such as destruction of rock formations or the onset of an ice age act as 'turning points' or 'watersheds' in history but which nevertheless remain evolutionary. Modern historians envisage time differently, but they nonetheless sometimes connect time with stage theories. Jacques Le Goff, including in his book on *The Birth of*

Europe (2005) on the one hand, identifies 'antique', 'medieval' and 'modern' as the dominant divisions in Western historiography, while R. G. Collingwood (1889–1943), on the other, wondered what determined an age as 'modern' especially when contemporaries would never had recognised it as such, and how might boundaries between these artificial periods be decided. These are legitimate questions for historians. How then do we understand the relationship between history and time after Newton and Einstein and after the discredited futurology of Wells and others? After all, Greeks and Romans would not consider themselves to be ancient and if we think of ourselves as historical beings we may think of ourselves as 'modern', perhaps, but only in comparison with them.

The historian, Penelope J. Corfield in her *Time and the Shape of History* (2007), has called for a return to 'big histories' and an end to histories that are so narrow and particular that they have the tendency to disconnect one 'period' from another. The trend for historians to research, write and teach according to these confined periods prevents consideration of *longue durée* narratives of the type now routinely written, for example, by geologists. Cornfield's is an important work in the philosophy of history and in some senses takes us back to histories pioneered by Wells and those popular historians of that period who underlined the big picture and the long term, stressing continuity over change in history writing. It also recalls the *Annales* approach to history which will be outlined in Chapter 5.

Corfield was a prominent figure in 1970s historiography, part of a generation that, unwittingly perhaps, became ever more specialised and narrow in their concerns but which has now emerged from the wreckage of 1960s feminist and Marxist historiography. She sought histories that confronted 'diachronic change', that is, change which looks over the long term, even the deep geological past of millennia – historical change which is not simply determined by considerations of gender or class. From this perspective, micro change prompted by changes to the environment, shifts in religious or secular movements or natural environmental disasters like the Lisbon earthquake of 1755, produce 'turning points' as important as the more conventional ones such as political revolution, invasion or war. This diachronic approach is, she tells us, in sharp contrast to the 'synchronic immersion' of specialised periods and histories focusing on a fairly specific moment in time that in recent decades has seen the kind of narrow history inevitably produced by professional historians addressing narrow subject communities (Corfield, 2007, pp. 14–15).

In whichever way historians (professional or otherwise) define historical periods, great and momentous events are made important by the writing of history. These 'watersheds' can define a generation or even a century. Yet, these watersheds do not always survive as seminal events. The attacks on Washington and New York in September 2001, or the so-called Arab Spring of 2011, seem destined to define our own age, and the surprise attack on Pearl Harbor in December 1941 is clearly of enormous importance to the development of the twentieth century. But who now remembers the Papal Aggression of 1850? This attempt to reintroduce a Catholic hierarchy of bishops into Britain for the first time since the Reformation is a moment when anti-Catholicism in England bubbled violently to the surface, only to submerge just as quickly. Look through the records of the period, almost any record, and we find priests attacked in the street, churches burnt to the ground, *Times* editorials that are equally inflammatory in tone as intention. This so-called 'watershed' in British religious and political life, the entry of the post-Reformation Catholic Church into mainstream British social and ecclesiastical life, iconically every bit as large and important as an aircraft hitting the Twin Towers of the World Trade Center, in the end produced relatively minor aftershocks and has all but disappeared from view.

These watersheds or 'turning points' are constructed by historians but historians can also suggest counterfactual histories that work along different timelines. What would have happened, for instance, if the British had prevailed at the battle of Saratoga in 1777 and the American colonists failed to raise a coalition of major European powers against the colonial power? Not only would this momentous event have failed to constitute part of the American War of Independence – known universally as the American Revolution – but also the course of modern history would have been radically different. Counterfactual history is useful as a questioning device and allows history to be imagined along different imaginative tramways. Niall Ferguson in his *Virtual History: Alternatives and Counterfactuals* (1997) described these 'what if' histories as an exercise in 'imaginary time'. In any case these scenarios are sparingly used among historians and probably rightly so. Ferguson's target was the Christian determinism that so troubled Wells and the seemingly inevitable progress of history (Creation, the Fall, the election of Israel, the Age of Prophets, exile and the rise of Rome, the Incarnation, the Crucifixion, the Resurrection and promise of return). He was offended too by the determinism of other grand theories but most particularly Marxism (the stages of primitive Communism, Feudalism, Capitalism and back to Communism) and their apparent sense of progressive history as inevitable. To this extent, he had a serious point to make.

Yet still the need for narratives in the West remains. To tell or listen to a story is one very powerful way of being human, although these narratives differ radically from East to West with the 'shape of things to come' imagined in spectacularly different terms across societies and at different moments in history. It also true that periods are still attributed characteristics. To be a Victorian, as we shall see in the next section of this chapter, is to be associated with a particular time but also with an historical style. The question is why we associate these characteristics (and others) to this particular period. Likewise, how do we determine when a period begins and ends? When, for example, did the 1960s or 'the sixties' happen? Dating, chronology and periodisation present profound theoretical problems for history as a discipline. How do we decide on periods as worthy of research and study? By looking at very definite and readily identifiable periods, we shall now attempt to answer that question but also examine how we establish the terminal dates of any given period.

Section 4

Events, people and periods: what is 'Victorian', when was 'the sixties'?

It is New Year's Eve, 1959. As the chimes of midnight sound, party revellers throw off their stiff suits and wool skirts, changing into Afghan coats and the horribly bright hippie gear that is to become a motif of 'the sixties'. Haircuts become a remarkable sight. 'Teenagers' suddenly look less like their parents: a subspecies has evolved; although there had been earlier sightings with Teddy Boys, Rockers and Beatniks. Someone changes the vinyl record from jitterbug, skittle or plain 'rock n roll' to Eastern-influenced music that tears conventional orchestration to shreds (Marwick, 2005). Dancing stops and, sitting cross-legged on the floor, partygoers actually listen to the 'composition' as if it were a work of art: not a conventional work of art but one that is innovative and experimental. Out goes the canon of accepted art, in comes the psychedelic. Men can dress like women; women like 'chicks'. They all fervently hope they die before they get old. Guilty sex becomes open sex and even public sex. With the introduction of the contraceptive pill, love becomes 'free' while abortion is available on demand. There is no church next Sunday, just a drug-fuelled spiritualism heralding a sudden and catastrophic secularisation (Brown, 2009). Rigid social hierarchies, repressive sexuality, respect for all forms of authority – from the park keeper to the family doctor – dissolve. Racism slowly becomes unacceptable and a plethora of opposition to conventional politics through civil disobedience is born with the Civil Rights Movement and violent opposition to the American war in Vietnam. Counter-cultural movements seemingly transform every area of life and every institution, including the university, much to the disgust and puzzlement of establishment figures such as the respected and vastly influential Cold War diplomat, the American George F. Kennan (1904–2005). Kennan is instructive because he represents an older generation, marked by the rise of Communism (to which he became an implacable foe) and Fascism (to which he became briefly attached) and the duty or disciple of war and public service. He represents everything that 'the sixties' did not.

> **And one would like to warn these young people that in distancing themselves so recklessly not only from the wisdom but from the feelings of parents, they are hacking at their own underpinnings – and even those of people as yet unborn. There can be no greater illusion than the belief that one can treat one's parents unfeelingly and with contempt and yet expect that their own children will some day treat one otherwise; for such people break the golden chain of affection that binds the generations and gives continuity and meaning to life.**
>
> (Kennan, 1968, p. 14)

What a party. 'Turn on, tune in, drop out.' Then in 1979 with the election of Margaret Thatcher in Britain and in 1980 with Ronald Reagan in the United States, the final nail is driven in the coffin. The hangover begins.

Thus 'the sixties' is a period labelled as such by historians – not simply a decade measured on a timeline. Whatever constitutes this period had, in fact, started well before New Year's Eve 1959 and ended just a few years before the election of Thatcher and Reagan. But then historians select aspects of history such as these as worthy of particular attention. They construct chronologies *through* their narratives, in the stories they tell, breaking down time into comprehensible chunks that they define as 'periods', 'ages' or 'eras'. Their description of a period eventually becomes illustrative of that period. Of course, historical periods rarely, if ever, fit the exact contours of a decade or century. Arthur Marwick (1936–2006) in his comprehensive work on 'the sixties' – *Cultural Revolution in Britain, France, Italy and the United States* (1998) – sees the period as beginning in 1957/58 with various cultural changes and ending in 1974 with the results of a massive oil price hike in 1973, brought on by the Yom Kippur war and a crisis in the Middle East that is with us still. From this came mass unemployment and a more conservative politics. Marwick also made clear the difference between a period and a decade, between history and time:

> **Is it legitimate to make contrasts and comparisons between the 'fifties', the 'sixties', the 'seventies'? We readily think in decades, but that is only because we count the years as we would our fingers or our toes. In historical study we do need a concept of periods, or eras, or ages, though such periods do not automatically coincide with decades or with centuries, nor do they have any imminent or natural existence, independent of the analytical needs of historians. Periodisation, the chopping up of the past into chunks or periods, is essential because the past in its entirety is so extensive and complex; but different historians will identify different chunks, depending upon their interests and the countries they are dealing with – a periodisation which suits the study of Western Europe will not suit the study of Africa or Japan. The implication of periodisation is that particular chunks of time contain a certain unity, in that events, attitudes, values, social hierarchies within the chosen 'period' seem to be closely integrated with each other, to share common features, and in that there are identifiable points of change when a 'period' defined in this way gives way to a new period.**
>
> (Marwick, 1998, p. 5)

In the same way as the 1960s as a decade is identified with 'the sixties' as a singular period, the Victorian period is also discernible by the way that the nineteenth century is understood by historians. The project of 'inventing the Victorians', for example, can be traced back to an immensely influential single source. Lytton Strachey published *Eminent Victorians* in 1918. By demolishing great Victorian figures such as Cardinal Manning, Florence Nightingale, General Gordon of Khartoum and Thomas Arnold, the Bloomsbury set, of which Strachey was a prominent member, he consigned a whole age as excessively religious, sexually repressed, jingoistic and moralistic. The Bloomsbury set, as a group of notable and enlightened artists and writers, had almost alone hastened the modern age. At least, so they believed. It has taken the concerted effort and scholarship of subsequent historians to give greater balance to this rather skewed picture.

If the 1960s added up to the revolutionary ideals of discernible and clearly identified counter-cultural movements, quite opposed to the world of the previous generation, then the Victorian period ended, not with a great event or the end of a reign, but a conversation. Uttering the word 'semen' hastened another age, a period when 'the word bugger was never far from our lips', heralding what Frank Mort has called 'a new modernist chronology of sex'. Modernity, according to Virginia Woolf began at this very moment in 1910:

> **[One] scene has always lived in my memory . . . It was a spring evening. Vanessa and I were sitting in the drawing room . . . Suddenly the door opened and the long sinister figure of Mr Lytton Strachey stood on the threshhold. He pointed his finger at a stain on Vanessa's white dress.**
>
> **'Semen?' he said.**
>
> **Can one really say it? I thought and we burst out laughing. With that one word all barriers of reticence and reserve went down. A flood of the sacred fluid seemed to overwhelm us. Sex permeated our conversation. The word bugger was never far from our lips. We discussed copulation with the same excitement and openness that we had discussed the nature of good. It is strange to think how reticent, how reserved we had been and for how long. It was, I think, a great advance in civilization. When all intellectual questions had been debated so freely, sex was ignored. Now a flood of light poured in upon that department too. We had known everything but had never talked. Now we talked nothing else.**
>
> (Woolf, 1985, pp. 195–6)

While it is clearly ludicrous to say that an historical epoch could begin or end with a conversation, equally it would be folly to suggest that there is no such thing as a Victorian period at all. Even at its most basic, the Victorian period must begin with the ascent to the throne of a monarch and end with the death of a long-reigning Queen. It could also be argued that the 1960s as a decade (as opposed to 'the sixties' as a period) cannot be detached from the context of a century. Eric Hobsbawm did just that by identifying a short twentieth century that stretches from the end of the First World War to the destruction of the Berlin Wall and the end of Communism in 1989. Within this 'age of extremes', to use the title of his 1994 book, Hobsbawm situates a 'golden age' of prosperity, with terminal dates from 1945 to 1973. The 'sixties' from this angle is not a separate period but a time of profound social, cultural, political and economic change that begins, not in 1957/8, as Marwick suggested, but with the reforming governments established after the Second World War in 1945. Unlike Marwick, there is also an assumption by Hobsbawm that 'the sixties' is the result of freedoms won after the experience of global conflict. This is as may be. The point that needs to be understood is that history and historians impose a narrative on time; that the Renaissance is a period identified by historians, as is the 'short eighteenth century' (1789–1832), the 'long nineteenth century' (1815–1914) and the 'short twentieth century' (1914–1991). Each period or date has significance, chosen precisely because it is deemed to constitute a fundamental watershed. Periods can only be successfully identified if the relationship between time and history and the ways in which historians construct chronologies and analyse historical periods is given due consideration. This chapter has sought to do just that.

In practice

If geographers are interested primarily in space, then it could well be argued that time is the province of the historian. The study of history is, after all, concerned with change over time – how episodes took place, how we passed from one age to another – and in order to provide a semblance of order to the record of human activity, historians have found it convenient to divide it up into periods of manageable duration. These periods have become the great building blocks of the past. Although there are squabbles over the precise dates, we have an almost taken-for-granted understanding of when and what was, say, the medieval and Victorian eras, the ages of discovery and imperial expansion, the seventeenth century, even the 1960s.

In constructing these blocks or slicing up the past in this way, time is taken as a given, a constant which somehow is just there as a backdrop. The notion of time we tend to work with is that inherited from Newton, and it is one which pervades the western world. This has set a set a precedent with very real and damaging consequences, not least in asserting the dominance of the West. When historians talk of the age of empire or the feudal era, for example, it is the western experience that is being referred to. For one thing, it masks the extent to which time is not only uneven and changing, but is subject to contestation. Our sense of time, and how it impacts on our lives is constantly changing. Thus although most in the West, including historians, see history changing linearly and progressively, in other parts of the world change is thought to be cyclical or even regressive. It is on the basis of such conceptions of time that particular teleological narratives are constructed. If, for example, time is linked to progress, as it is in Whig interpretations, then historical change is thought to be the gradual unfolding of events toward a better (more liberal, more democratic, more equal) world. History is replete, however, with struggles over time. The introduction of more precise measurements of time in the early phases of industrial capitalism was part of an attempt, it could be argued, to control the working lives of people in ways which led to longer and more intense forms of labour. At a broader level, the general acceptance of Greenwich Mean Time as the absolute standard with which to divide up the world into time zones was a triumph of western hegemony. Such episodes are of fundamental importance not only in themselves but also by virtue of the fact that they signal radical shifts in the way that the world is organised.

David Harvey has persuasively argued that all significant historical change is accompanied and characterised by a reordering of time and space. Arguably, we are now in the middle of such a change. The development of the Internet has transformed the transmission of messages, which can now be performed almost instantaneously. It is perhaps too early to assess the nature of this phenomenon or its longer-term impact, but historians of the future will look back on these years as decisive in redefining our sense of time, and hence the course of history and its interpretation.

Summary

The four sections of this chapter have said four things:

- Time and its relation to contemporary forms of history is inextricably bound up with modernity and notions of time that historians tend to associate with advanced, industrial countries. Whether that results in ideas of time that are culturally contingent is explored as 'family time', 'industrial time' and time that became linked with the western imperial project, such as the struggle to locate longitude at sea or the commodification and rationalisation of time by a dynamic, rapacious, capitalist system.
- History writing also depends on an understanding of time developed by Christian chronologies and chronologies informed by other religious traditions. Yet the exact dating of events, for example, between the Julian and Gregorian calendars, has remained a problem for Christian historiography. This is a model of time and history that has been at the core of developmental theories of history treated elsewhere in this book but not necessarily in non-linear histories that regard the narrow periods adopted by historians as stifling and pessimistic about the trajectory of history.

- These chronologies, however, have often been conceived as linear and progressive, pointing history forward but have also led to a scepticism about the ability of history to anticipate the future. The process of industrialisation has been influenced by conceptions of time, but religious ideas of time remain important to the seventeenth and eighteenth century English, Scottish and European Enlightenments. While the notion of 'absolute' time developed by Sir Isaac Newton in the eighteenth century established the first widely accepted chronology, free of religious influence, time/space and 'time compression', it made possible profound political and cultural relationships of power and hegemony in the West.
- 'Watersheds' and 'periods' imposed by historians, such as the Victorian period and 'the sixties', depend on a particular understanding of time developed in the West in the period since the eighteenth century. The imposition by historians of 'periods', 'eras' and 'ages' on time is a product of an understanding which is historically influenced.

Discussion document

Most of this chapter has been concerned with the way historians deal with time in all its differing cultural settings and in relation to its very complexity. This document, however, shows how historical figures such as the commentator Thomas Carlyle influenced how we now think of his age. Whether the Victorian period can be said to be 'The Mechanical Age' and whether historians can employ labels such as these is, of course, a matter of debate.

Were we required to characterise this age of ours by any single epithet, we should be tempted to call it, not an Heroical, Devotional, Philosophical, or Moral Age, but, above all others, the Mechanical Age. It is the Age of Machinery, in every outward and inward sense of that word; the age which, with its whole undivided might, forwards, teaches and practises the great art of adapting means to ends. Nothing is now done directly, or by hand; all is by rule and calculated contrivance. For the simplest operation, some helps and accompaniments, some cunning abbreviating process is in readiness. Our old modes of exertion are all discredited, and thrown aside. On every hand, the living artisan is driven from his workshop, to make room for a speedier, inanimate one. The shuttle drops from the fingers of the weaver, and falls into iron fingers that ply it faster. The sailor furls his sail, and lays down his oar; and bids a strong, unwearied servant, on vaporous wings, bear him through the waters. Men have crossed oceans by steam; the Birmingham Fire-king has visited the fabulous East; and the genius of the Cape were there any Camoens now to sing it, has again been alarmed, and with far stranger thunders than Gamas. There is no end to machinery. Even the horse is stripped of his harness, and finds a fleet fire-horse invoked in his stead. Nay, we have an artist that hatches chickens by steam; the very brood-hen is to be superseded! For all earthly, and for some unearthly purposes, we have machines and mechanic furtherances; for mincing our cabbages; for casting us into magnetic sleep. We remove mountains, and make seas our smooth highways; nothing can resist us. We war with rude Nature; and, by our resistless engines, come off always victorious, and loaded with spoils.

What wonderful accessions have thus been made, and are still making, to the physical power of mankind; how much better fed, clothed, lodged and, in all outward respects, accommodated men now are, or might be, by a given quantity of labour, is a grateful reflection which forces itself on every one. What changes, too, this addition of power is introducing into the Social System; how wealth has more and more increased, and at the same time gathered itself more and more into masses, strangely altering the old relations, and increasing the distance between the rich and the poor, will be a question for Political Economists, and a much more complex and important one than any they have yet engaged with.

But leaving these matters for the present, let us observe how the mechanical genius of our time has diffused itself into quite other provinces. Not the external and physical alone is now managed by machinery, but the internal and spiritual also. Here too nothing follows its spontaneous course, nothing is left to be accomplished by old natural methods. Everything has its cunningly devised implements, its preestablished apparatus; it is not done by hand, but by machinery. Thus we have machines for Education: Lancastrian machines; Hamiltonian machines; monitors, maps and emblems. Instruction, that mysterious communing of Wisdom with Ignorance, is no longer an indefinable tentative process, requiring a study of individual aptitudes, and a perpetual variation of means and methods, to attain the same end; but a secure, universal, straightforward business, to be conducted in the gross, by proper mechanism, with such intellect as comes to hand. Then, we have Religious machines, of all imaginable varieties; the Bible-Society, professing a far higher and heavenly structure, is found, on inquiry, to be altogether an earthly contrivance: supported by collection of moneys, by fomenting of vanities, by puffing, intrigue and chicane; a machine for converting the Heathen. It is the same in all other departments. Has any man, or any society of men, a truth to speak, a piece of spiritual work to do; they can nowise proceed at once and with the mere natural organs, but must first call a public meeting, appoint committees, issue prospectuses, eat a public dinner; in a word, construct or borrow machinery, wherewith to speak it and do it. Without machinery, they were hopeless, helpless; a colony of Hindoo weavers squatting in the heart of Lancashire. Mark, too, how every machine must have its moving power, in some of the great currents of society; every little sect among us, Unitarians, Utilitarians, Anabaptists, Phrenologists, must have its Periodical, its monthly or quarterly Magazine; – hanging out, like its windmill, into the *popularis aura*, to grind meal for the society.

Thomas Carlyle, 'Signs of the times', originally published in the *Edinburgh Review* in 1829. This text comes from Volume 3 of *The Collected Works of Thomas Carlyle*, 16 volumes (1858).

Further reading

* *essential*

* **Penelope J. Corfield**, *Time and the Shape of History* (2007).
Provides a useful and comprehensive review of the literature but more than this is a major intervention into this important area of historiography. Conceptually complex and difficult in places it nevertheless succeeds in prompting careful thought about the temporal nature of history and history writing.

Niall Ferguson (ed.), *Virtual History: Alternatives and Counterfactuals* (1997).
A flawed but intellectually brave attempt to prompt debate about the way that historians adopt chronologies and timelines. By inviting us to think about these chronologies and timelines in a counterfactual way, we also think about the relationship between time itself and how historians use time in their periodisation.

William Gallois, *Religion, Time and History* (2007).
Complex and sometimes allusive as an introductory text, it nonetheless provides an intelligent and wide-ranging coverage of time/history as a cultural construction and which in turn can define our very humanity.

* **Stephen Kern**, *The Culture of Time and Space 1880–1914* (2003).
A tremendously detailed and ambitious account of changes in technology and culture in the period between the end of the nineteenth century and the outbreak of the First World War, and our modern understanding of how space and time work in the light of these fundamental changes and how, indeed, these changes may impact on history.

D. J. Wilcox, *The Measure of Times Past: Pre-Newtonian Chronologies and the Rhetoric of Relative Time* (1987).
A fine and comprehensive commentary on how time was measured before 'absolute time' and 'objectivity' associated with Newton and the eighteenth century. This book is difficult but rewarding as it takes us back to pre-modern ideas of discontinuous, relative time in the late-Middle Ages.

Part 2

PHILOSOPHIES

3 Enlightenment and romanticism

1 Secular histories: Hume, Gibbon and Robertson
2 Romanticism, national histories and the hero in history: Sir Walter Scott and Thomas Carlyle
3 The legacies of Enlightenment and Romanticism

Introduction

This chapter is concerned with history writing and how the Enlightenment and Romantic movements affected an understanding of the past. New methods of observing phenomena emerged from the seventeenth century in England and in eighteenth century Scotland and Europe. Enlightenment thinkers attacked the beliefs and assumptions of organised religion. In this respect, the philosopher historians in the eighteenth century – Hume and Gibbon – were the most important while the more modern methods of the Scot, William Robertson, pointed us towards historiography as it develops in the nineteenth century. Also a product of the Scottish Enlightenment, Adam Smith both constructed a blueprint for capitalist economics and described how societies change and develop. In Section 2, we look at how Romantic notions of nationalism and heroism impacted on the writing of history in the modern period. In contrast to the reason, order, symmetry and harmony that are associated with the Enlightenment, we will explore the significance of freethinking, emotionalism, mystery and a profound engagement with nature to the growth in the nineteenth century of Romanticism. Both the Enlightenment and Romanticism gave rise to some extraordinary histories but, as we shall see, were most significant for providing a backdrop or setting that reconstituted ways of looking at the past. The final section of the chapter will consider the legacy of the great shifts in intellectual currents that produced the German Herder, the Italian Vico and the Frenchman Michelet and how historicism became embedded in America and mainland European society, culture and historical practice.

Section 1

Secular histories: Hume, Gibbon, Smith and Robertson

After a night of whoring in July 1776, James Boswell, the diarist, paid his friend David Hume (1711–76) a morning visit. Hume, author of the six volumes of the constitutional *History of England* published between 1754 and 1756, an implacable foe of revealed religion, was dying. Hume shaped the growing secularity of the eighteenth century and he knew now with an apparent certainly that he was eyeball to eyeball with infinity. According to an account of this meeting between Boswell and Hume in an essay by the political theorist Michael Ignatieff in his *The Needs of Strangers* (1984), Boswell was horrified that Hume had not recanted his atheism when faced with imminent and certain death. And indeed Boswell's diary tells us that upon witnessing Hume's nonchalance he was gripped 'with a degree of horror . . . mixed with a sort of wild, strange, hurrying recollection of my mother's pious instructions, of Dr Johnson's noble lessons, and of my religious sentiments and affections during the course of my life' (McC. Weis and Pottle, 1970). This does not begin, however, to express the conflict Boswell experienced between a rationality of the mind and a spirituality that was not based in reason but which he felt – that was emotional. Admittedly, he had long rejected the strict piety of his Calvinist mother yet still clung to the promise of an afterlife. Hume would have none of it, of course, and was content to give an account of his life and conduct, not to God, but to his fellow man. As such, he very much belonged to the Enlightenment.

We associate the Enlightenment with some key words such as reason, order, harmony, symmetry and the restraint of emotion. These words come up repeatedly as the world of science, art, literature, music and architecture changed in a way that reflected Hume's scepticism, but it is change that is also regretted; a regret that we see in the shock expressed by Boswell at Hume's atheism. Make no mistake that Boswell admired the great rationalists of his day. Nevertheless, his urge to embrace reason and discard superstition was in constant battle with an inner life that seemingly pulled him in an opposite direction. Thus like many contemporaries he was far from reconciled with what the great figures of the Enlightenment were truly saying. Hume's scepticism set down in print was one thing; to see the great man facing death without expectation of an afterlife was quite another. After all, it was only in 1764 that Boswell had engaged in a debate over two days about the truth of Christianity with the French philosopher, poet and sometime historian Voltaire (1694–1778), and he had left his native Edinburgh in March 1760 for the express purpose of converting to Roman Catholicism and becoming a monk.

In the persons of Hume and Boswell then, we can discern countervailing forces – religious sentiment and rational calculation – with each unleashed by a revolution in politics, science and historical thinking. The Enlightenment eventually emancipated women, blacks and religious minorities such as the Jews; letting loose historical writing in the Romantic tradition which focused on national sentiment, the role of the hero, a focus on the universal attributes of human beings and their soluble differences. Forces that ran counter to the Enlightenment, on the other hand, articulated a deep-seated regret for a world lost to the machine amid a voracious commercialism: a revolution in thought that affected the credibility of Christian schemes of a teleological history that has as its end or purpose the Kingdom of Christ. We shall deal with these themes across this chapter.

Before exploring the intellectual tensions thrown up by the Enlightenment and their consequences for the researching and writing of history, however, we should ask, as did the German philosopher Immanuel Kant in 1784, 'What is Enlightenment?' While this is a complex, messy and sometimes contradictory historical movement, the term itself suggests a number of things:

- a sense that natural and universal laws, the laws of physics, govern both human beings and nature;
- the use of reason and the ability of human enquiry to penetrate the mysteries of the world and by so doing control it;
- a conviction that the external and physical world could be known by reason and reason alone.

Similarly, the origin of the Enlightenment as a movement or even as a set of ideas is not easy to date or define. There is not a single Enlightenment nor are its central figures necessarily in agreement with each other. Some historians see fundamental change occurring in the years 1720–80, mostly in France and Germany, but also in Scotland. The historian Peter Jones (2004) selects 1759 as a signal year and concentrates on the 'philosophes' and other figures prominent in Continental Europe. In that year Handel, the composer, died and the Seven Years War (1756–63) was at its height. Voltaire published *Candide*, Samuel Johnson *Rasselas* and Adam Smith his *Theory of Moral Sentiments*. The French philosopher Diderot was stifled by King Louis XV as he was about to publish the eighth volume of his *Encyclopedie*. In 1759, according to Jones, 'no one can be said, in a defensible modern sense', to have known:

- anything about forms of energy other than light and heat;
- anything about the composition of air or water;
- anything about the nature of fire, breathing or procreation;
- anything about the age of the Earth or the size of the universe;
- anything about the nature of stars or the origins of life;
- anything about the evolution of animals or genetic inheritance.

Nor could they have known much about history, except as a branch of literature and certainly not as a science.

Yet the Enlightenment was to transform history writing. As history stopped being a literary endeavour, it began to resemble a science, embracing a framework of natural laws that were thought to govern the universe. As science determined, for example, how gravity works, so history could determine how societal transformation came about. As French ideas of the laws of motion rested on principles borrowed from the philosopher René Decartes (1696–1750), on Greco-Roman assumptions that the universe is made up of immovable atoms, so history could begin to comment on the mechanics of change, whereupon all physical phenomena could be explained in terms of momentum and velocity, all motion, including historical motion, was thought to work according to *specific* laws.

Cartesian mechanical philosophy (theories taken from the philosophy of Descartes) thought that motion was restricted as there was no space between particles and thus no vacuum. The universe was full-up and (accordingly) in stasis; precisely because there was no apparent motion, there could be neither historical movement nor progress. As a result, societies themselves stood still, not changing with any rapidity. This 'law', it was hypothesised, governed the natural world but extended to consider the 'motion' of societies over time. Only when this stasis became dynamic could the study of history (or the study of change) become a distinct discipline and a credible basis of knowledge, plausibly able to explain everything. Only when the laws of motion were seen to work on universal principles, could a universal history of the world be contemplated.

The historian Roy Porter (1946–2002) in his *Enlightenment: Britain and the Creation of the Modern World* suggests that the conditions for enlightened thought based on reason were already apparent in seventeenth-century England with the work of Sir Francis Bacon (1561–1626) and Sir Isaac Newton – in particular, the insistence by Bacon that knowledge should be rooted in observable fact and not in 'untestable speculation'. We could even look to the earlier work of William Harvey (1578–1657), who transported Renaissance science from Italy to the University of Cambridge, describing how circulation in the body worked. From this perspective, the Enlightenment is something made in Britain, not France or Germany, with its origins found in the seventeenth century, not the eighteenth. Let us run with this supposition for a moment.

English or British empiricism – the understanding of the world through experience rather than abstract theory – informed the methodology of natural science: the observation of phenomena, not the construction of untested paradigms based in philosophic speculation. History was seen as a philosophy through much of the eighteenth century, only morphing into a science in the nineteenth century with the word 'scientist' not coined until the 1830s.

Newton was arguably at the origin of this process. Influenced by the work of Bacon and Robert Boyle, he created a methodology that would focus on the creation of a hypothesis and the testing of that hypothesis through observation. His *Principia Mathematica* (1687) was based on observation, not speculation, arguing that the universe conformed to general or universal laws not partial or specific laws:

> **I have not as yet been able to deduce from phenomena the reason for these properties of gravity, and I do not feign hypotheses. For whatever is not deduced from the phenomena must be called a hypothesis; and hypotheses, whether metaphysical or physical, or based on occult qualities, or mechanical, have no place in experimental philosophy.**
>
> (quoted in Achinstein, 2004, pp. 87–88)

Newton then was not content to speculate in the abstract, a hypothesis must be tested and observed by our God-given senses; hence his story about the apple falling on his head. He hypothesised that the gravity of the Earth must alter the path of the moon, he could not prove it; thus, when the apple fell, it accelerated using the same force that curved the path of the Moon. No doubt, this story got better in the telling – it is not documented and so we are unable to tell – but a bump on the head from a falling projectile would be, for

Newton, adequate empirical proof of gravity. In addition, this empirical phenomenon could be repeated; it was true at all times and in all places. This approach had a massive impact on the way evidence, including historical evidence, is observed and tested. Directly or indirectly, it was Newton then that had such an influence on historians and 'philosophers' such as David Hume.

Newton's laws of motion and gravity attempted to explain the world as a whole by suggesting that the universe is in balance. His science then had a tremendous affect on almost all facets of human existence. Too often, historical figures are labelled geniuses. In this case, Alexander Pope in his elegy to Newton in 1723 was incisive

Nature and Nature's laws lay hid in night
God said, 'let Newton be' and all was light.

More importantly for historians, perhaps, certainly in the long term, is the development by Newton of his theories of force and inertia. These laws of motion – in contrast to Descartes' – envisaged a universe in flux. This allowed change to occur; a discovery that is crucial for our understanding of the impact of Enlightenment thought on historical practice.

The notion that individual interests and social interests might coalesce and balance, a balance which was thought to occur in natural phenomenon, affected Adam Smith's *An Inquiry Into the Nature and Causes of Wealth of Nations* (1776). Smith, like his friend Hume, was also concerned with change. As we saw in Chapter 2, he sketched four phases of development, from the 'lowest and rudest' society based on hunting, without property or government, to the fourth stage that is a commercial, exchange economy. Smith had three motives:

- To explain Britain's commercial success
- To explain the relative poverty of Scotland as compared to England
- To conduct a general enquiry into trade and economic phenomena (Brown, 1980)

In doing so, he argued against monopolies in home and colonial markets; the restraint in the import of foreign goods caused by the Navigation Acts which protected the markets of sugar, tobacco and cotton/wool. He also argued, unlike the so-called physiocrats of the Enlightment, that wealth was not necessarily wholly derived from agriculture but that precious metals and bullion, as well as money, can be the basis of an exchange economy. Indeed this exchange economy and the wealth it created would obviate the views of Thomas Malthus, who argues in his *An Essay on the Principles of Population* in 1798 that agricultural production could not keep up with population increases without restraining marriage and procreation, war and natural disasters: both checks to population which would lead to human misery. Malthus is discussed again in Chapter 17.

In his 'scientific system' Smith had the following in mind (Brown *et al.*, 1983):

- like Voltaire's attack on the church in France, he argued against existing privileges but also argued against anomalies in the mercantile system;
- man can imagine or reason his self from one kind of society to another, for example, by the construction of a 'system';
- although he did not advocate power in the hands of one particular social or economic power – that would be monopoly – but instead argued for a balance of power between the monarchy, the nobility, the landed gentry, merchants, manufacturers, clergy and labouring poor.

Smith's universalism was of a piece with Enlightenment thinking: trade should be in balance with the removal of tariffs and protectionism; taxes should be kept low with a commercial system having a moral advantage over the old mercantilism that had used naval and military might to maintain markets. 'Classical' economics would encourage free trade; prosperity along with peace between nations would grow. Using the manufacture of pins, he highlighted the advantages of the division of labour where every selfish instinct and act had a social consequence:

> **If the produce of domestic industry can be bought as cheap as that of foreign industry the regulation is evidently useless. If it cannot it must generally be hurtful. It is the maxim of every prudent master of a family never attempt to make at home what it will cost him more to make than to buy. The tailor does not attempt to make his own shoes, but buys them off the shoemaker. The shoemaker does not attempt to make his own clothes but employs a tailor . . . What is prudence in the conduct of every private family can scarce be folly in that of a great family. If a foreign country can supply us with a commodity cheaper than we ourselves can make it, better buy of them with some part of the produce of our own industry employed in a way which we have some advantage.** (Smith, vol. 1, 1977, p. 401)

This level of specialisation and the 'separation' between trades will lead, Smith argued, to the further growth of towns and to social intercourse that would in and of itself promote peace. There was then a moral dimension to his plan. Behaviour would inevitably change when individuals were encouraged to make rational economic choices. A complex society would be a consequence of a sophisticated division of labour, leading to a limited, perhaps reduced, benevolence among members of society. Yet, and this is important if we are to understand Smith's contribution to Enlightenment thinking, the self-regarding behaviour apparent in the new capitalist economy meant that self-interest, not mutual sympathy, would promote the common good.

In order to illustrate this, Smith used the metaphor of an 'invisible hand' of individual selfishness as the unwitting cause of social benefit when production was organised through a division of labour. This is not to say that reason triumphed totally over religious sentiment. As was stated at the beginning, the Enlightenment is messy, complex and contradictory. Hume, for example, pleaded with his friend Adam Smith to become his literary executor upon his death. For all his championing of rational economic man in his new, anti-mercantile, capitalist economy, Smith refused. As a clergyman he was unable in conscience to fulfil the dying wish of his atheist friend.

The historian Edward Gibbon (1737–94) at first reflected a similar ambiguity about religion, converting to Roman Catholicism which he later recanted. Yet his magnificent account of the Roman Empire, *The History of the Decline and Fall of the Roman Empire*, betrays a deep-seated and emphatic scepticism towards religion, especially Christianity. To this extent, he had much in common with Hume who had written 'Of superstition and enthusiasm' in 1741, pejoratively linking religion with priestly power and undue emotional fervour. Gibbon is known as an Augustan historian; that is, an historian that looked back with admiration to a golden age of Roman literature: the poet Virgil and the historian Livy, and this can be seen in Gibbon's treatment of Christianity. Gibbon presented history 'candidly' and 'rationally' while writing prose as if it was to be spoken or performed (Lentin, pp. vii–xv). This, along with his attack on Christianity as an organised religion, is what makes Gibbon an

Enlightenment historian. It may also be instructive that *The Rise and Fall* was published in 1776 – the fateful year when Boswell called upon Hume on his deathbed, when Hume's friend Adam Smith published his *Wealth of Nations*, when Thomas Paine published *Common Sense* and when, as we shall see in Section 3, American colonialists embarked on their revolution that was to push so much of the world towards democracy.

Above all else, the Enlightenment and Enlightenment histories changed Christianity from within, particularly the Protestant strand of Christianity, questioning the truth of the Bible and the interrogation of the scriptures in the light of new discoveries made by natural science. As the nineteenth century progressed science became a credible alternative to traditional religious explanations of natural phenomena. Studies in geology, for instance, demonstrated that fossils could date the age of the world, while theories of natural selection and the descent of human beings from primates, outlined by Charles Darwin and others, confounded the Biblical story of creation. German theorists or the 'Higher Critics' such as Friedrich Schleiermacher (1768–1834), David Friedrich Strauss (1808–74) and Ludwig Feuerbach (1804–72) ensured that religion was seen merely as a projection of human frailties while Jesus was turned back from a God into a man. The *Critical Essay Upon the Gospel of St Luke* by Schleiermacher in 1825, for example, established that scripture should be considered part of human history and not as a divine text.

Friend and confidant of the poet William Wordsworth (1770–1850), Samuel Taylor Coleridge (1772–1834), helped to bring these ideas to a British public. Inspired by Coleridge, the Young Reformers (notably the novelist George Eliot) led 'Broad Church' opinion by translating into English Strauss' *The Life of Jesus* in 1846 and, in 1854, Feuerbachs' *The Essence of Christianity*. Religious doubt filled the pages of the *Westminster Review*, spilling over to a wider public when a religious census in 1851 identified the 'unconscious secularist' and 'fireside heathen' as chief villains in declining attendance at church. Meanwhile criticism from within the church itself continued to acknowledge the passing of religious certainties. *Essays and Reviews*, published in 1860, recalls this moment precisely when, in his essay on the interpretation of scripture, Benjamin Jowett, later Master of Balliol College, Oxford, famously said that the Bible should be read like any other book. From at least the revolution in France in 1789 to the rise of Marxism as a secular creed in the twentieth century, the Enlightenment as a popular and intellectual movement has transformed the world and transformed the way historians write about the world. As historians we must unavoidably take it seriously.

Perhaps more than Hume or Gibbon, the real historian of modernity (considered by historian John Burrow (1935–2009) to be the first modern historian) is another figure of the eighteenth century Scottish Enlightenment, William Robertson (1721–93). His *History of America* was published in 1777 and used modern methods of research and scholarship, comparing what we would now call the American or native Indian with the 'tribes' of Germany, while his accounts of King Charles V in 1769 and his history of Scotland were cosmopolitan in ways quite unprecedented. Robertson was anxious to contextualise the history of Scotland by comparing the national experience of the Scots with the experiences of other nations in Europe. He even widened his frame beyond Continental Europe and America to India, coming close to taking in a global perspective. Robertson was an unapologetic Presbyterian, in fact like Smith a clergyman. With his emphasis on the importance of religion and spirituality, he gained fame and fortune from his work and was briefly the official historian of Scotland while his histories have some claim to be counted in the Romantic tradition of history writing. It is to Romanticism and national histories that we now turn.

Section 2

Romanticism, national histories and the hero in history: Sir Walter Scott and Thomas Carlyle

Tourists to the Highlands of Scotland in the eighteenth century could only truly appreciate the beauty of its landscape by turning their backs on it. Pitching around a tortuous pass, scrabbling to the summit of a grand peak, they would come across a pre-built booth with a convex, tinted mirror. Walking into the booth, they would view the vista behind them by looking into a mirror or 'Claude glass'. The purpose of turning their backs on nature and looking at it in a manufactured booth was to reproduce the works of the popular landscape painter, Claude Lorrain (1600–82) who, using a subtle graduation of tones in his paint, lent nature a soft, mellow tinge. Claude glasses suggested that the only way to appreciate the natural world was mechanically; an idea derived from Enlightenment ideas of the subservient relationship of nature to man. Romanticism would change all that. Aesthetic tastes began to extend to scenery that was wild and unrestrained, not mastered and controlled, one that did not have to be literally 'framed', transformed for our pleasure. Nature itself became sublime, evoking fear in its vastness and mystery and could inspire terror; its colours imagined not in the pastoral tones of Lorrain but rather in gloom and darkness. *Sturm* and *Drang* (storm and stress), as an expression of extreme emotionalism, is associated with Romanticism or the counter-Enlightenment, giving vent to unbridled emotion in the teeth of stifling rationality.

Romanticism then appeared to set its face against objective rationalism. It emphasised instead (Table 3.1), subjectivity, the use of imagination, freethinking, emotionalism over logic, spirituality and the naturalness and wildness of nature:

Table 3.1 Key words and concepts of Enlightenment and Romanticism

Enlightenment	*Romanticism*
Reason	Freethinking, spirituality, passion
Thinking	Feeling
Objectivity	Subjectivity, imagination
Order, symmetry, balance (like classical architecture)	Irregular and mysterious (like gothic architecture)
Harmony	Discord
Restraint of emotion	Emotionalism, wildness
Mechanistic	Nature and naturalism

One of Romanticisms' greatest proponents, Jean Jacques Rousseau (1712–78), famously said that 'I felt before I thought'. In a sense, this summarises Romanticism. This is not to say Romantics somehow abandoned reason. Johann Wolfgang Von Goethe (1749–1832), who had an enormous influence on eighteenth- and nineteenth-century European thought, was as competent in natural science as he was in poetry and literature. Equally, the Romantic poet Percy Bysshe Shelly (1792–1822) was expelled from University College, Oxford in 1811 for refusing to disavow a notorious book he had co-written with Thomas Jefferson Hogg called *The Necessity of Atheism*. Yet when his room was cleared scientific equipment was found – strongly suggesting that the young Shelley was continuing with his scientific experiments. Romanticism then did not somehow replace Enlightenment thought but as often ran parallel to it. Romantic poetry for instance, in these stanzas from 'Turning the tables' as part of William Wordsworth's *Lyrical Ballads* (1798), celebrated the intrinsic wisdom of nature and urged the reader to abandon 'our meddling intellect' and the 'full and endless strife' of book learning as impediments to real knowledge:

Books! 'tis a dull and endless strife:
Come, hear the woodland linnet,
How sweet his music! on my life,
There's more of wisdom in it.
Sweet is the lore which Nature brings;
Our meddling intellect
Mis-shapes the beauteous forms of things:–
We murder to dissect.

What else stands out in this extract of the poem is the pinnacle of Romantic sensibility, that is, the emphasis placed on the individual and the sensory perceptions of the individual rather than reason which would 'murder to dissect' knowledge and then still not truly gain it. Whether it is, as we shall see with Thomas Carlyle, the importance of the individual in historical representations of the hero, or Sir Walter Scott's reaction to nature or the gloom, darkness and grotesque mystery of the gothic, Romanticism remained central to narrative writing in the decades after the 1790s.

Sir Walter Scott (1771–1832), the novelist who did so much to reinvent Scottish history in the reflection of the Romantic light of the early-nineteenth century, grew up between Edinburgh and the Scottish borders in a society increasingly aware of its own changing nature. He had an acute notion of the sublime in nature that was both awe-inspiring and spiritual, applying these ideas to his historical fiction. In the 'Waverley' series of novels, he evoked the past by capturing the wildness and beauty of his native Scottish borders. *The Antiquity*, published in 1816, featured the antiquarian Jonathan Oldbuck and used a great many devices that we would associate with the gothic genre, such as the almost overwhelming force and power of weather (that is, nature) and corrupted family lineage or 'bad blood'.

The first gothic novel and one that established these themes was probably the *Castle of Orantro* (1764) by Horace Walpole. Later we have Mary Shelley's *Frankenstein*, subtitled the *Modern Prometheus* (1818), which confronts the power of the forces let loose by industrialisation, while a high point in the genre came, arguably, with Bram Stoker's *Dracula* in 1897. Often the gothic dwelt on the fear apparent at the time of French invasion (or the fear, perhaps, of Jewish immigration in the 1880s, or the rise of the 1890s New Woman in the case of Stoker), a dread of the transformative power of science and an older fear of Republican revolution after the political disruption caused by 1789. Everywhere the untamed landscape, the barbarities of the past (the 'darkness' of Catholicism with its secretive orders a favourite target among artists) was overwhelming.

In *The Antiquary*, however, Scott conflates the sublime wildness of nature with the horrors meted out to the lost innocents of early, pre-Church, Christianity:

> **It was indeed a dreadful evening. The howling of the storm mingled with the shrieks of the sea fowl, and sounded like the dirge of the three devoted beings who, pent between two of the most magnificent yet most dreadful objects of nature – a raging tide and an insurmountable precipice – toiled along their painful and dangerous path, often lashed by the spray of some giant billow which threw itself higher on the beach than those that had preceded it . . . Here, then, they were to await the sure though slow progress of the raging element, something in the situation of the martyrs of the early church, who, exposed by heathen tyrants to be slain by wild beasts, were compelled for a time to witness the impatience and rage by which the animals were agitated, while awaiting the signal for undoing their grates, and letting them loose upon the victims.** (Scott, 1834, p. 76)

Besides relating the wildness of nature to the wild primitiveness of man's religious past, another element in the relationship between man and his environment was the relationship noted by Scott between life in the new urban core and the equally changing rural periphery. Edinburgh as the capital city of Scotland, a financial centre, a hub of the European Enlightenment and the metropolitan core is just to the north of the still remote and rugged hills of the borderlands. It was this relationship, this proximity, the difference between the city as the heart of commercial and political modernity and the vastnesses of surrounding rural regions, which provide the dynamic context for the emergence of a way of thinking about the past. A part of this process depended on an emerging identification of the urban with modernity and the rural with tradition, folk-life, superstition and eternal and unchanging values, which are both virtuous and wicked. In this context, the countryside, country people, and country folkways and practices, could be seen as a world where the past ways still survived and, in a time of great change caused by commerce, industry and urbanisation, it was a past that was in danger of disappearing forever.

Scott's view of the past contributed to a growing sense of the need to retrieve and record for posterity important aspects of Scottish life. In most of his Waverley novels, starting with *Waverley* (1814), he recounted key moments in Scottish history and thus revealed a central concern of the Romantic imagination: nationalism. Nationalism, however, had developed in historically different ways. Herder, the German Romantic thinker (of which more in the next section), saw nationalism as an extension of feeling or sentiment and consequently as a form of identity. Nationalism as it emerged from the chaos of the French Revolution determined that a *citoyen* or citizen could be created by the suppression of social, regional, sexual and racial difference; although we know from historical research that regional quirks of language, local currency or non-standard systems of weights and measures nevertheless survived into the twentieth century despite all efforts to fashion a national identity (Weber, 1977). After 1789, the state was not a theocracy or a state run on the dynasty of a family but one based on a notion of popular sovereignty.

This form of nationalism was progressive, even liberal. It explains why great Romantic figures such as Lord Byron went to Greece in 1824 to fight for Greek independence where he ultimately lost his life *en route* to defend the principle of national self-determination: 'Your efforts to preserve my life will be vain. Die I must: I feel it. Its loss I do not lament; for to terminate my wearisome existence I came to Greece. – My wealth, my abilities I devote to her cause. – Well: there is my life to her' (Marchand, vol. 3, 1957, p. 1224). It is also the 'feeling' of nationalism that made a hero of Lujos Kossuth in Hungary in the 1850s and Garibaldi in Italy a decade later. Only later would nationalism in places such as Germany become illiberal, when the push for territory and the promotion of race combined with terrifying consequences.

For Scott, however, his concern was with the folk elements of national consciousness, such as language and the myths of national origins. But his vision ran even deeper into the undercurrents of society than this. Before he turned to fiction, his poetry had begun to engage with a more popular sense of the national past. *The Minstrelsy of the Scottish Border* (1802–3) was a three-volume collection of ballads that he had collected in the country around his grandparents' farm at Sandyknowes where he had spent so much of his polio-afflicted childhood. He collected what we would now call folklore both as an end in itself but also as raw material that would not only provide substance for, but also give shape to, his literary endeavours. This is explicit in the case of the *Minstrelsy* and recurs at moments throughout all of the Waverley novels, but is the backbone of books like *Tales of My Landlord* (written variously between 1816 and his death in 1832). What appears to be a literary device, writing fiction as if it were being related by an ancient who is recalling times past, is really a metaphor for the manner by which Scott's fiction grew and also for its relationship with history. And central to this relationship with history was the idea that commerce and the urban world were destroying an older world which had to be recorded soon if it were not to be lost to the world entirely.

Perhaps the most enduring element of Romantic and nationalist histories, however, is the role of the hero. Scott was notable in his depiction of heroism for his popular readership. *Rob Roy* (1817) was written in lieu of a history of Scotland that he had promised his publisher. It is a story set during the time of the Jacobite Rebellion of 1715 that aimed to return the crown to the Catholicism of the Old Pretender and as a novel proved to be a huge commercial success. *Ivanhoe* was published two years later in 1819 but this time Scott turned to medieval England for his subject matter. While obviously fictional, *Ivanhoe* may well have been inspired by an 1818 essay on chivalry or by his own growing collection of antique weaponry from the period. In either case, it is a work that drew the reader into the past through a careful and evocative description of man in nature.

While Scott was very influential, it was left to another Scot from the borders to take forward themes of heroism and national pasts into the modern age and who has influenced historians since. Thomas Carlyle (1795–1881) did much to formulate what became known as the 'condition of England question' in the 1830s and 1840s. He coined the term the 'cash nexus' to describe how social relations had been disastrously transformed by industrialisation. Carlyle hated the narrow calculation of his age. Political economy could 'reason' that a ration of precisely 137 oz of food per inmate of the workhouse per week was enough to feed a human being, dependent on their sex. When the church had administered to the poor then at least part of that calculation involved human passion or feeling. Now while Carlyle had renounced traditional forms of Christianity, somewhere between 1818 and 1822, having experienced a spiritual crisis, he nonetheless believed in human solidarity. Man was born into society, he wrote in his *Characteristics* (1831), and that:

> **To understand man . . . we must look beyond the individual man and his actions or interests, and view him in combination with his fellows. It is in Society than man first feels what he is; first becomes what he can be. In Society an altogether new set of spiritual activities are evolved in him, and the old immeasurably quickened and strengthened. Society is the genial element wherein his nature first lives and grows; the solitary man were but a small portion of himself, and must continue forever folded in, stunted and only half alive.**
>
> (Tennyson, 1984, p. 75)

Carlyle's main objection to modern society was, like many figures of Romanticism, mechanisation, of which the factory system is an obvious but by no means the only example. He extends his critique of the production process to a complaint about the mechanisation of the whole of life. Industrialisation, he believed, is a symptom of an underlying malaise rather than the root cause of human woes, although human beings would now be tied to the ceaseless rhythm of the machine and that beyond doubt this salutary fact threatened our very humanity. 'If we are required to characterise this age of ours', said Carlyle in an essay called *Signs of the Times* in 1829, 'by any single epithet, we should be tempted to call it, not an Historical, Devotional, Philosophical, or Moral Age, but above all others, the Mechanical Age' (Carlyle). The base calculations of the schoolteacher Gradgrind (the character created by Dickens who in *Hard Times* wanted only facts) was itself calculated to infuriate Carlyle – he described economics as the science that could measure any human output and capacity as a 'dismal science' – prompting fresh approaches to history which are important for us to understand.

Given Carlyle's implacable opposition to the mechanised and atomised world caused by industrialisation, he wanted to argue that this age needed great men to lead and to reinstitute individuality. For this, he turned to the importance of biography in history:

> **Social Life is the aggregate of all the individual men's Lives who constitute society; History is the essence of innumerable Biographies, nay, our own Biographies. But if one Biography, study and recapitulate it as we may, remains in so many points unintelligible to us; how much more must these million, the very facts of which, to say nothing of the purport of them, we know not, and cannot know! . . . Praying only that increased division of labour do not here, as elsewhere, aggravate our already strong Mechanical tendencies, so that in the manual dexterity for parts we lose command over the whole, and the hope of any Philosophy of History be farther off than ever, – let us all wish her great and greater success.**
>
> (Tennyson, 1984, p. 66)

Where 'men have become mechanical in head and heart', Carlyle sought to use history as a way of understanding this process and to suggest palliatives. G. B. Tennyson recalls how Carlyle gave a lecture in May 1840 on 'Heroes, hero worship and the heroic in history'. His early heroes are from classical mythology, then there are divine heroes such as Mohammad, then poets such as Dante or Shakespeare, then priestly heroes such as Luther. Then come the heroes nearer to his own time who were 'men of letters' such as Johnson or Rousseau and finally there are heroes who are 'Kings' such as Cromwell or Napoleon. After 1850, his pessimism about the world deepens with his *Latter Day Pamphlets* of that year, *The Life of*

John Sterling in 1851 (a friend who he felt had been thwarted by the vulgarities and cruelty of the age) and most famously, perhaps, his life of *Frederic the Great* published in successive volumes (1858, 1863, 1864 and 1865).

Carlyle's work on Chartism in 1839 registered his opposition to liberalism and democracy; his politics confirmed by his support for the appalling behaviour of General Eyre, the Governor of Jamaica, who used undue force against the local population in the Morant Bay rebellion during October 1865. Carlyle defended Eyre in the subsequent controversy, a moment that divided liberal and conservative opinion in Victorian England. Carlyle had already expressed his racist views on the Irish, who he essentially described as sub-human, and had infamously written in 1853 about slaves in his *Occasional Discourse on the Nigger Question*. Carlyle fell short of despotic but certainly he revered strong men and found these leaders in the pages of history.

We know from his work before 1850 that Thomas Carlyle was a formidable satirist and commentator on his times. But he also understood the discipline of history and never ceased to argue for its importance. In *On History Again*, an 1833 tract, he argues that history 'is the most profitable of all studies', recognising that in the passing of time all other human interests and activities will fall into its purview. He could write history and write it well. His multi-volume *The French Revolution*, published in 1837, was a balanced attempt to access and judge an event that had bitterly divided intellectual and popular opinion. *Sartor Resartus* (1833–34) perhaps contained the ideas that would sustain him until his death. It certainly contained an extraordinary use of language that would be his trademark, not hesitating to make up a word if the existing vocabulary failed him and thus revealing all the subjectivity and creativity we associate with Romanticism as a creative movement. It is this use of prose that reflected his hold on and respect for Romantic literature and German literature in particular; names such as Johann Wolfgang Goethe and Frederich von Schiller who are particularly associated with nationalism, mysticism and spiritual rebirth. Carlyle wanted to make his world (and its past) organic or 'natural' rather than mechanical, moral, hierarchical and certainly not democratic. Duty, work, silence, truth and the hero should be justly revered. In this sense his influences, as we are about to discover, came as much from Continental Europe as his native Scotland.

Section 3

The legacies of Enlightenment and Romanticism

The most prominent member of what became known as the Hudson River School of American artists was Thomas Cole (1801–48). Cole was born in Lancashire in England and had a keen sense of history. His set of paintings called *The Course of Empire* (1833–6) charts the rise and fall of the powerful, warning of the hubris that comes with power and untrammelled expansion. His equally famous series *The Voyage of Life* (1840) is also a set of narrative paintings that this time follows an individual, a pilgrim, through the dangers and perils that accompany him from infancy to old age. In 1836 he painted *The Oxbow* (Plate 1), which, by using conventional European techniques of landscape painting, summed up a vision of man in nature that revealed the influence of European Romanticism. In his depiction of the Connecticut river cutting back upon itself in a horseshoe shape, we find on the right of the canvas a landscape that is flat and controlled; on the left, however, we see the darkness of a sky which is wild and menacing and a brushwood that comes before and bears witness to the taming and perhaps destruction of this 'new' land. In other paintings by him, an American Indian is placed in the scene to suggest unspoilt nobility (the noble savage, perhaps?) or even a train rushing through the wilderness and felled trees, each serving as a warning that America may yet go the way of Europe.

This take on the history of a new nation must be read alongside the influence of transcendentalism – a creed that hit Boston on the east coast of America among New England Congregationalists (a Protestant creed that placed religious authority in the congregation). Prompted by both English and German Romanticism, individuality was important to transcendentalists and so was social transformation. By the mid-century they were part of the movement that opposed slavery. They promoted an ethos of struggle and striving, of fundamental change, a sense of a future for America that attacked Puritan pessimism, for the unity and rationality of God and a belief that a new millennium was to be born through the future actions of this vast continent. This future was soon to be realised where the 'manifest destiny' of a country expanding from Atlantic to Pacific coasts would lead, as the Democrat journalist John L. O'Sullivan said in 1839, to a fresh era in human affairs under one God. We might consider how Europe is understood in the context of this virgin nation and how any discussion about 'manifest destiny' can omit any consideration of the past. Manifest destiny was metaphysical but also it promised a life so utterly different from the European experience. All the more surprising then, that those transcendentalists who were involved in agitation for the abolition of slavery or the promotion of women's rights, could adopt the intellectual basis of the European Enlightenment from the very Continent that they had left. This was to be one legacy of the Enlightenment which was important to historians.

As we have seen, toward the close of the eighteenth century Samuel Taylor Coleridge and Immanuel Kant opened up an intellectual inquiry which helped shape a philosophy independent from conventional Biblical truths and the acceptance of the essential unknowability of God. German critics thus began to cast doubt on the authority of the Bible. As we have seen, Schleiermacher's *Critical Essay Upon the Gospel of St Luke* (1825) regarded the Bible as a result not of divine intervention but as integral to human culture and history. And in 1833, a translation of Johann Gottfried van Herder's *Spirit of Hebrew Poetry* (1782) appeared in America. The Hudson River School asserted this independence through their art, but it was also to state the unyielding progress of 'manifest destiny' that threatened, they feared, to sweep all of nature before it as their new nation claimed land from 'sea to shining sea'. These ideas were to have a profound influence also on American historical scholarship such as that of the Harvard educated, New Englander George Bancroft (1800–91). These developments would change how we think about the past, asking questions that are fundamental about the value of history as a form of knowledge. They also explain why the historical sensibilities of the New World could only be understood by reference to the Old. In order to illustrate this, we need to look briefly at von Herder, Michelet and Vico, the principal theorists who helped to pave the way for this intellectual transformation and at the same time reshaped thinking on approaches to the past.

Johann Gottfried von Herder (1744–1803) was a German philosopher and theologian who exercised a great influence on historiography. He was part of the Romantic revolt against the Enlightenment belief in scientific method that would judge every society by the standards of the most modern. He argued instead that each period, civilisation and historical event was unique, specific to time and place, and should be studied as such. It comprised the special qualities of nationality, national destiny and the life of the *Volksgeist*, or spirit of peoples within that nation. The proper focus of history should be upon the language, folk-law, myth, literary traditions or 'national character' and culture of the group. In this sense, unlike Carlyle, his search was not for individual heroes but the *zeitgeist* or mindset of a whole society. Yet this mindset was not in any way innate or eternal but rather the specific product of social, historical and cultural forces. This may sound straightforward and rather too obvious a point to make. In the eighteenth century, however, it provided history with a definite task: to find the origin of these forces and allow historians to relive, reconstruct and to rethink the past using their own subjectivity, a subjectivity that we have found in the last section was part of the Romantic critique of Enlightenment objectivity.

For the French historian, Jules Michelet (1798–1874), the author of the then definitive history of the French Revolution in seven volumes (1847–1853), the subjectivity associated with Romantic thought allowed an inquiry into the past through popular psychologies and beliefs, but also permitted the historian to understand their own psychologies. To this end, he pioneered histories of mentalities in the areas of witchcraft, children, labour and the family. His work on the Renaissance is of great moment while this concentration on culture and art revealed new ways of understanding the past. Under his scrutiny cathedrals became 'great historical facts' while tombs and gravestones were evidence of changing attitudes to death (Haskell, 1993, p. 262).

We cannot get to the heart of the contributions of Herder and Michelet, or understand why they are important to our own work today, unless we understand the earlier work of Giambattista Vico (1668–1744), in particular his *Principi di Scienza Nouva* (1744). This was designed to be a new science of humanity but one whose laws could be discerned subjectively. It was an unusual, rich and repetitive work, but one which has influenced generations of historians and philosophers, including Herder, Michelet, Benedetta Croce, R. G. Collingwood (1889–1943) and Isaiah Berlin (1909–97).

Berlin saw Vico as an important figure in the so-called 'counter-Enlightenment', linking him to the alternatives features which sprang up to challenge 'Enlightenment dogma'. Perhaps the greatest of these so-called alternatives is Vico's emphasis on imagination, the type of imagination that informed the Hudson School of Art with which we began this section and whose approach may well be ultimately traced back to Vico.

Vico's case against an Enlightenment scepticism which threatened to kill God and raise the study of the natural world – science – to the status of a popular faith, was built on the following premises:

- knowledge of the external world can never be completed;
- the culture and the specific and uniqueness of each society are unique;
- culture can best be understood through the study of language;

- forms of language, therefore, shape the present and are worthy of study, for example, myths;
- history (the study of culture such as customs like burial rituals, language, myth) allows us in turn to understand the laws of social development. (Burke, 1985)

Many of Vico's ideas then were allusive but they did tend towards a historical methodology which could reveal and reconstruct the mentalities of past peoples. To Herder and the German Romantics this revealed a national spirit that transcended all divisions and a consciousness that (according to Georg Wilhelm Friedrich Hegel in the next chapter) also transcended history. It is this 'spirit' that meant for the American historian, George Bancroft, and the Hudson River School democracy, divine providence and the natural desire of all human beings for liberty, and provided examples of the historical culture that was one major element in the legacy of the Enlightenment.

In practice

In order to understand the emergence of history as a discipline it is necessary to locate it within the broad contours of intellectual inquiry. Taking a broad paint brush, it could well be argued that if the seventeenth century was the age of science, and the eighteenth that of philosophy, then the nineteenth belonged to the historian, before the twentieth seemed to forget the lessons from history at precisely that moment when they were needed most. A sense of the past and the emergence of historiography as a discipline in its own right thus came to prominence in the nineteenth century, and suffused virtually all spheres of cultural life. People found that, at a time of unprecedented change, life's complexities could better be understood by thinking back to the past, or, if that failed, by seeking refuge therein.

But there was more to it. Historians had a new confidence in what they were doing, and for that they had to thank some of the great thinkers of previous ages, in particular English, French, German and Scottish philosophers of the seventeenth and eighteenth centuries. Whether or not the origins of the intellectual revolution known as the Enlightenment can be traced back to seventeenth-century England, it was the work of Roger Bacon, Robert Boyle, William Harvey and Isaac Newton that laid the foundation for an innovative approach to knowledge. No longer built from superstition or religious orthodoxy, knowledge now was seen to derive from the application of a rigorous empirical methodology, the results of which were testable by others. For some, by revealing the mathematics underpinning, say, the movements of the planets, there was no longer a need to acknowledge the works of a divine architect, although many (including Newton) still did. In the social sciences (note the significance of the term), the seventeenth-century philosopher John Locke began to reveal the mechanisms of social cohesion, that is, how societies managed to exist without splitting apart.

▶

Enlightenment thinkers paid due regard to this rational epistemology, and considered whether the laws of science could be employed to reveal the hidden structures and processes of human society. This was combined with a powerful desire to know more about the nature of those societies which lay beyond the boundaries of Europe, in particular America, India and China. Limited though this venture was in the hands of writers such as Voltaire and William Robertson, it forced onto the intellectual agenda an appreciation of comparative historical development. Different societies were no longer seen to be simply different, as were botanic species, but different by virtue of the fact that they occupied different positions on the ladder of societal evolution. Elaborate schemes were drawn up to plot the stages of this evolution, which were recognised to operate with a certain inevitable logic, driving the development of primitive societies such as were found in Africa toward the most advanced, i.e., commercial, societies of Europe. Such profound intellectual transformations often experience a backlash, and so it was that a group of influential nineteenth-century writers, who collectively forged Romanticism, viewed the Enlightenment as a dismal science. In their different ways, therefore, Walter Scott and Thomas Carlyle reacted to what they saw as the cold rationality of Enlightenment dogma, and to capitalist industrialisation and urbanisation (yet other manifestations of inexorable laws), by reclaiming a mythical, organic past, untouched by the ravages of 'civilisation'. This required not rational science, but those qualities evident in art and poetry but seemingly abandoned by the Enlightenment: imagination, emotion and spirituality.

From this intellectual milieu emerged three philosopher-historians who exerted a powerful influence on nineteenth-century historiography. Herder, Michelet and Vico in their own ways denied that historical change takes place according to inexorable laws. History is replete with diversity, and so they were therefore rather more interested in trying to understand the contingent nature of change, and mapping the distinct and specific characteristics of peoples in particular ages. This approach to what might be thought of as a microhistory opened up the opportunity to study those aspects of society such as language and ritual which shape the lives of ordinary people but which had been neglected by historians working within the Enlightenment tradition. By these means, they argued, we can reconstruct the sensibilities of past peoples, and thereby the uniqueness of the societies they inhabited.

Most historians working today are heirs to these traditions. The intellectual origins of modern historical inquiry are therefore diverse, and historians tend to draw selectively upon them. This has largely been responsible for the continued tensions which exist among the various approaches to the past, but at the same time this diversity has provided a sense of dynamism to the discipline as a whole which underpins its richness and excitement.

Summary

The three sections of this chapter have said three things:

- The Enlightenment affected the writing and understanding of history. Specifically this is to recall its beginnings in eighteenth century France and Germany or, alternatively, the contribution made through empirical or observational natural science that can be traced back to seventeenth century Britain. The contribution of the Scottish Enlightenment is especially noted. The main aim of the section is to say something about the importance of secular approaches to the past in the work of Hume, Smith and Gibbon. The section concludes with a short discussion of William Robertson – a great figure of his time – who combined Enlightenment rational method with Romantic religiosity and respect for cultural diversity in the past.

- Romanticism as a phenomenon ran counter to the Enlightenment but also grew out of it. In particular, we are keen to establish how a more mystical, spiritual and emotional approach to the world affected historical practice. The fixation of nationalism and national heroes, folklore and the effort to retrieve a world that existed before the voraciousness of industrialisation is discussed by looking closely at the contribution to history of Sir Walter Scott and Thomas Carlyle. Where Scott described the wildness of his native Scots borders in order to allow us to imagine the past, Carlyle fashioned his histories and his approach to the past through biography, both personal and collective. Each viewed the modern world with a certain amount of regret as they each understood that the world that they once knew was slipping beyond memory.

- Continental Enlightenment and Romanticism influenced early attempts to describe and then to claim the new lands of North America, from 'sea to shining sea'. Imagination, culture, language, myth and subjectivity came into historical view with the work of Herder, Michelet and Vico. These were all Europeans who directly influenced approaches to the past in the New World. These departures, from what one contemporary commentator called 'Enlightenment dogma', opened up new historical vistas by beginning the process of distancing history from the natural sciences. From these commentators, moreover, we can see one upshot of the Enlightenment: the American faith in historical or 'manifest destiny' and the supposed universal human longing for democracy and liberty.

Discussion document

What does this extract reveal in respect to the concerns of Romanticism? Why does the original publication of *Ivanhoe* have a historical preface? How are nature and the natural environment represented with trees, hills and streams as unchanging witnesses to historical events? Certainly, the celebration of the Middle Ages and the loss of chivalry in the modern age – both themes for Scott – were to become a staple of romantic sensibilities as the nineteenth century wore on.

> This state of things I have thought it necessary to premise for the information of the general reader, who might be apt to forget, that, although no great historical events, such as war or insurrection, mark the existence of the Anglo-Saxons as a separate people subsequent to the reign of William the Second; yet the great national distinctions betwixt them and their conquerors, the recollection of what they had formerly been, and to what they were now reduced, continued down to the reign of Edward the Third, to keep open the wounds which the Conquest had inflicted, and to maintain a line of separation betwixt the descendants of the victor Normans and the vanquished Saxons.
>
> The sun was setting upon one of the rich grassy glades of that forest, which we have mentioned in the beginning of the chapter. Hundreds of broad-headed, short-stemmed, wide-branched oaks, which had witnessed perhaps the stately march of the Roman soldiery, flung their gnarled arms over a thick carpet of the most delicious green sward; in some places they were intermingled with beeches, hollies, and copsewood of various descriptions, so closely as totally to intercept the level beams of the sinking sun; in others they receded from each other, forming those long sweeping vistas, in the intricacy of which the eye delights to lose itself, while imagination considers them as the paths to yet wilder scenes of silvan solitude. Here the red rays of the sun shot a broken and discoloured light, that partially hung upon the shattered boughs and mossy trunks of the trees, and there they illuminated in brilliant patches the portions of turf to which they made their way. A considerable open space, in the midst of this glade, seemed formerly to have been dedicated to the rites of Druidical superstition; for, on the summit of a hillock, so regular as to seem artificial, there still remained part of a circle of rough unhewn stones, of large dimensions. Seven stood upright; the rest had been dislodged from their places, probably by the zeal of some convert to Christianity, and lay, some prostrate near their former site, and others on the side of the hill. One large stone only had found its way to the bottom, and in stopping the course of a small brook, which glided smoothly round the foot of the eminence, gave, by its opposition, a feeble voice of murmur to the placid and elsewhere silent streamlet.

Sir Walter Scott, *Ivanhoe* (1820), pp. 6–8.

Further reading

* *essential*

* **Isaiah Berlin**, *Vico and Herder* (1976), esp. pp. 3–142.
An innovative approach to the work of two fundamentally important commentators of what Berlin thinks of as the 'counter-Enlightenment'; that is, the movement that ran against some of the dogmas of rationality and science. It is worth reading closely as it is often quoted by historians and philosophers working in this important area.

Martin Fitzpatrick, Peter Jones, Christa Knellwolf and Iain McCalman (eds), *The Enlightenment World* (2004).
A collection of essays that deal with the origins of the Enlightenment, the so-called 'High' Enlightenment, science, popular culture, print culture and so on. Probably the most useful are those dealing with origins and another that deals with historical writing.

Antony Lentin and Brian Norman (ed. and annotated), **Edward Gibbon**, *The Decline and Fall of the Roman Empire* (1998).
The introduction is a useful and close analysis, not just on the contribution of this marvellous historian and commentator of his own time, but on Gibbon's literary and performative style. Gibbon's chapters on Christianity should be read especially carefully, not least because of the impact they made in Gibbon's society.

Cecilia Miller, *Vico's Imagination and Historical Imagination* (1993).
A monograph that, as the title suggests, deals with the importance of Vico to succeeding historians, but also Vico's historical methodology, his approach to cycles and spirals of time, and the impact of Vico's *New Science*.

* **Roy Porter**, *Enlightenment: Britain and the Creation of the Modern World* (1995).
Porter pursues the argument that Britain, not Germany or France, was the cradle of the Enlightenment. His reading of the origins of observational natural science or cosmology is important to the development of history.

Roy Porter, *The Enlightenment* (2nd edition, 2001).
A wonderfully sharp and innovative guide to the parameters and limits of Enlightenment thought.

G. B. Tennyson, *A Carlyle Reader* (1984).
A comprehensive account of Carlyle as social commentator and, more unusually, as historian. Here we can find tracts and speeches by Carlyle which demonstrate history within the context of Romantic notions of nationalism, biography and the hero in history.

Giambattista Vico, *Principi di Scienza Nouva* (1744), trans. David March (1999).
A classic of historiography for this period.

4 From Hegel to von Ranke

1 Hegel and the spirit of history
2 Marx and 'historical materialism'
3 Marxism in the twentieth century

Introduction

German history, German philosophy and German historiography have dominated Europe since the philosopher G. W. F. Hegel became a Professor at the University of Berlin in 1818. The first section of this chapter will examine this dominance and explain how Hegel has become vitally important as a theorist of historical change. With his rejection of philosophical history, Leopold von Ranke was one product of the Hegelian approach to history and embodied a move towards the acceptance (in his own time) of history as a source-based science. Before von Ranke, however, came Hegel's band of followers, which included Karl Marx and his theory of history which offered a comprehensive explanation of how one society becomes another type of society. Marx (with his companion and sponsor Frederick Engels) adapted Hegel to turn philosophy into a revolutionary theory, a revolutionary politics and a science of history. From this theory, historians have focused on class and social stratification in order to understand the past. His followers in turn called his theory of change 'historical materialism', although he himself never used the term, and this is explored in some detail in Section 2. The final section will outline how historical materialism and an approach to class in history has produced a divided Marxist historiography, and how Marxism and Marxist approaches to history have in recent years been reduced in both volume and importance.

Section 1

Hegel and the spirit of history

The Berlin Wall, first built almost overnight in 1961 but rebuilt over decades, symbolised the policies of containment and the threat of mutually assured destruction – nuclear annihilation – that we know today as the Cold War. When it was breached finally in early November 1989, hordes of people streamed from the Communist East to the capitalist West. Removed completely a year later, the wall represented the end of a potentially deadly standoff between the Soviet Union and the United States. It also represented for Francis Fukuyama, in his *The End of History and the Last Man* (1992), a victory for liberal democracy over its totalitarian alternatives. His conclusions are based on the work of Georg Wilhelm Friedrich Hegel (1770–1831), whose philosophy of history saw 'world history as the progress of the consciousness of freedom' through a 'spirit' or 'idea' that governed history. Not that democracy (or freedom) would triumph without setbacks but it would finally triumph. The pulling down of the Berlin Wall on that momentous winter night represented the terminal decline of Marxism as practical (rather than abstracted) politics, a significant moment in the realisation of freedom that Hegel had outlined and which confirmed his prediction that history was heading towards the end of conflict. The West could not have been more self-confident as the 'East' raised the white flag while the Middle East allies of the former Soviet Union sat in malleable compliance.

The year 1989 also represents a significant date in German history, a date that can be understood alongside 1933 (the rise of Nazism), 1918 (the defeat of Germany) and, critically, 1848 – the failure of a bourgeois revolution that would have brought a new class to prominence in German society, replacing the aristocratic, conservative and authoritarian Junkers. (Junkers in Germany and Prussia roughly equated to an aristocratic class.) Some historians have identified a German Sonderweg or 'peculiar path' which defined a German historical experience distinct from that of the rest of Europe. This sense of national difference or peculiarity was acute in 1789 amid reactions to the French Revolution because the pre-unified German states felt keenly their rivalry with France. Conservative reactions to France and its revolution were matched only by conservative reactions to industrialisation. In any case, the reception to the French Revolution in the German states ensured that liberalism in Germany would be stillborn. Accordingly, economic modernisation was not accompanied by social and political development and, indeed, reactions by the bourgeoisie in the face of Junker backwardness was one of unprincipled compromise, even in that year of European revolutions: 1848. Modernisation had to wait for what commentators have called 'unification from above' through the masterful, if constrained, reforms in the late nineteenth century introduced by Otto von Bismarck, the Chancellor of Germany. Not until the rise of Adolf Hitler in 1933, however, did Germany truly modernise in what some imagined was a 'new beginning' when the craven bourgeoisie finally acted in its own interests.

Germany's foremost liberal historian, Friedrich Meinecke (1862–1954) reflected on the unity of the German national spirit as the nation stood together in preparation for the First World War. In doing so he identified special attributes that characterised Germany at this important historical moment:

> **When the First World War broke out, it seemed once more that a kind angel might lead the German people back to the right path. The exaltation of spirit experienced during the August days of 1914, in spite of its ephemeral character, is one of the more precious, unforgettable memories of the highest sort. All the rifts which had hitherto existed in the German people, both within the bourgeoisie and between the bourgeoisie and the working classes, were suddenly closed in the face of the common danger which snatched us out of the security of the material prosperity that we had been enjoying. And more than that, one perceived in all camps that it was not a matter merely of the unity of a gain-seeking partnership, but that an inner renovation of our whole state and culture was needed. We generally believed indeed that this had already commenced and that it would progress further in the common experiences of the war, which was looked upon as a war of defence and self-protection. We underwent a rare disappointment in our hopes. Within a year the unity was shattered and the German people were again separated upon various paths. Was the uplift of August 1914 after all merely the last flickering of older evolutionary forces which were now coming to an end?**
>
> (Meinecke, 1950, pp. 25–7)

Meinecke detailed the rise of Nazism as a phenomenon quite separate from the rest of German history by ultimately denying the Sonderweg. Yet the history of Germany itself represented a 'failed development' that was in itself unique. This peculiar history left Germany, so the argument runs, different from the rest of Europe: authoritarian, militarist and bureaucratic. The defeat of the Fatherland in 1945 broke down this value system and split it in two with the Berlin Wall dividing East and West.

Understanding and writing German history in this way began with Hegel's publication of *Phenomenology of Spirit* in 1807. This book and the work of Hegel more generally had enormous influence on the Enlightenment figures that we met in the last chapter, and contributed to the decline of Christianity as a force in the world. Yet Hegel's approach is metaphysical; that is, it uses explanations that originate outside of the physical world and as such are not open to proof or testing. His argument (and one picked up by Fukuyama as he witnessed the crumbling of the walls that had contained Communist totalitarianism) was that the essence, or spirit, of human existence is freedom. The progress of history is the realisation of that freedom. Thus, his theory of history is one in which peoples and constitutions actualise their national 'spirit'. Accordingly, history unfolds according to predetermined laws and so history is the sum of a people, their consciousness or 'mind' and their national cultures that inform this process. The 'end of history' for Hegel then is the realisation of that idea or spirit in the institutions of the state, and is a perfect manifestation of the human will for freedom, something that was at least symbolised by the end of the Cold War.

These are complicated ideas but vital to grasp if we are fully to understand the contribution of Hegel to the writing of history and the influence of Hegel on Marx and other post-Enlightenment thinkers. To summarise Hegel's model of historical change:

- History evolves an awareness of and then actualisation of the spirit of freedom.
- Each stage of history has a 'world spirit' that is expressed peculiarly in each nation state.

- This spirit has a consciousness that is expressed in the culture of the nation.
- Historical events follow this national consciousness and progress towards the 'absolute idea' or an end state.
- Change occurs in a dialectic with a clash of ideas or consciousness that moves history through stages towards this end state.

For Hegel, the peculiarity and particularity of the nation was wrapped up in the *Beimtenstaat* (civil service) and militarism of the Prussian state, and in this respect is consistent with the Sonderweg thesis with which historians have sometimes viewed German history. German historiography was therefore shaped by both the Sonderweg and German historicism.

The legacy of Hegel was considerable. Most historians today are in his debt. And yet the legacy was diverse and contradictory. One of the most important developments was the founding of history as a practical discipline which had its genesis in a rejection of the philosophical idealism of Hegel. Here the name of Leopold von Ranke (1795–1886) featured prominently. Von Ranke (von after his ennoblement in 1865 by Wilhelm I), was known as the 'father of objectivity' and is well known in our own time for his pursuit of history as a science and for his use of primary sources in his teaching. This teaching, which stretched across the nineteenth century, was marked by the use of sources and was ultimately a dismissal of Hegel's purely 'philosophical school'. Although Ranke had an abiding interest in a world history determined by abstract principles, he forged the 'historical school' and took Hegelian thought away from philosophy, turning it into 'real' history, that is, a history concerned with 'localised memory', 'human language and culture' that was 'particular and changing'. With this came a distinctly 'scientific' approach to evidence as part of an historical methodology which most historians would recognise today as valid:

> **But from what sources can such a new investigation be made? The basis of the present work, the sources of its material, are memoirs, diaries, letters, ambassadors' reports, and original accounts of eyewitnesses. Other writings were used only if they were immediately derived from such as these, or seemed to be equal to them in some original information. These sources will be noted on every page; the method of investigation and the critical conclusions will be presented in a second volume, to be published concurrently.**
>
> **Aim and subject shape the form of a book. We cannot expect from the writing of history the same free development as is, at least in theory, to be expected in works of literature; I am not certain that it was right to ascribe this quality to the work of the Greek and Roman masters. A strict presentation of the facts, contingent and unattractive though they may be, is the highest law. A second, for me, is the development of the unity and the progress of the events. Therefore, instead of starting, as might be expected, with a general account of the political situation of Europe, which would have confused if not distracted our attention, I have preferred to discuss in detail each people, each power, and each individual only at the time when each played an importantly active or leading role. I have not been disturbed by the fact that here and there they have had to be mentioned earlier where their existence could not be ignored. But thereby we are better able to grasp the general line of their development, the paths which they followed, and the ideas by which they were motivated.**
>
> **Finally, what will be said of my treatment of particulars, the essential part of the writing of history? Will it not often seem harsh, disconnected, colorless, and tiring? There exist noble models for this work, ancient and – we should not forget – modern as well. I have not tried to emulate them; theirs was another world. There is an exalted ideal toward which we can reach: the event itself in its human intelligibility, its unity, its diversity. I know how far**

> **from it I have remained. One tries, one strives, but in the end it is not attained. Let none be impatient with this! The important thing, as Jacobi says, is always how we deal with humanity as it is, explicable or inexplicable; the life of the individual, of generations, of nations; and, at times, with the hand of God above them.** (von Ranke, 1981, pp. 56–9)

Von Ranke saw history as part of a divine plan in which the state (and like Hegel he meant the Prussian state) was (again like Hegel) unique with a unique history. As we can see from this extract, Ranke was determined to treat past societies on their own terms. These principles were reflected in his histories of the rivalries of great powers, from the ancient civilisations to the Ottomans.

Save for the works of contemporary political theorists such as Fukuyama, what has really survived in the work of Hegel is the dialectic according to which the process of change or transition occurs when an idea or consciousness is confronted with an opposite consciousness and from that clash comes a third position. Here the work of Karl Marx was of particular significance, and so in the next section we examine his notion of historical materialism which was at the heart of his theory of history.

Section 2

Marx and 'historical materialism'

Marx used Hegel's notion of the dialectic by replacing a 'spirit' running through history with class relations such that the dialectic describes a clash of classes born out of material relations or the forces of production which then produces another kind of class society. Where Hegel in the *Philosophy of Right* (1820) said that 'the owl of Minerva spreads its wings only with the falling of the dusk', that is, philosophy only understands history and historical epochs when they are about to pass on, Marx suggested that history (or at least epochs) could be anticipated, and hence the well-worn phrase contained in his *Thesis on Feuerbach* in 1845: 'philosophers have only understood the world, the point is to change it'. Finally, Hegel's theory of history outlined most comprehensively in his lectures on the *Philosophy of History*, given between 1822 and 1830, concentrates on the political – on constitutions and states that possess national principles. Marx, in contrast, is concerned with economics and the dynamics of capitalist organisation. Without Hegel, there would have been no Marx, nor the theoretical framework for understanding historical change which has been one of the most important influences on history and historiography in the last century or so.

Whether as a correspondent for the *New York Daily Tribune* or scribbler for one of the many penny pamphlets that mushroomed on the left of Continental politics in his lifetime, Marx was forever reading the runes of what he believed to be the immediate and inevitable collapse of capitalism. So too his erstwhile companion, Frederick Engels, the Manchester-based industrialist who maintained his friend financially and even took up patrimony of a child that belonged to Marx. Engels may have been fonder of the finer things of life – champagne, lobster and even foxhunting – but they shared a fundamentalist belief in the dialectic as the scientific means of understanding history. Yet neither Marx nor Engels were historians and little of what Marx wrote can be considered 'real' history. His writings contained no sweeping accounts of historical episodes or movements of the kind we normally think of as history, although his subject is sometimes the role of the individual in the past and the weight of the past on the actions of the living, such as his *Eighteenth Brumaire* published in 1852. In this guise, he tended to use history – often brilliantly – as a means of making sense of current affairs such as the Indian mutiny, the rule of Louis Bonaparte in mid-nineteenth-century France, or indeed capitalism as a mode of production.

There is enough here, however, to help us understand something of his approach to history, and we might well begin this venture with one of the most famous passages in his writings. Published in 1859 as a *Preface to a Contribution to the Critique of Political Economy*, it sketched his ideas on how society is constituted and undergoes transformation. Pitched at a high level of abstraction, the extract has given rise to some very heated discussions on what Marx really meant, and has unsurprisingly been used by many unsympathetic to historical materialism to launch attacks on its foundations. We have neither the will nor space to enter into this debate, but it is necessary to draw out some of the salient points from the passage as a means of illustrating how Marx and his followers thought about historical change. Let us therefore consider the following:

> **Humans in societies enter into relations of production which are independent of their will. The forces and relations of production constitute the economic base upon which the superstructure is erected.**

Societies are structured by their relations of production which therefore largely determine how people behave. Capitalist society, for example, is defined by the fundamental antagonisms between those who own and control the means of production (employers, capitalists, managers – or, in a word, the bourgeoisie) and those who are forced to sell their labour in order to survive (factory workers, plumbers, needlewomen – or, in a word, the proletariat). Such a conflict has nothing to do with how these people think; rather it is the relations of production that determine how people see themselves and their position in society. This emphasis on the material conditions of life goes to the heart of Marx's methodology. We must start, he argued, with material production, and from there reveal how society in its various stages is created by and connected with the mode of production.

This quite deliberate challenge to how Hegel saw the relationship between how people think and live (as outlined in Section 1) created many problems for Marx and his followers, as we might have anticipated. It is perhaps well to confront notions, which give priority to thoughts, or ideas, critics have argued, but to replace them with theories that see productive relations as all-powerful simply substitutes one determining factor with another. In response Marx later claimed that he never meant to suggest that the economic base determines the form of the ideological superstructure, that is, that forms of religion, philosophy and culture in society are mere pale reflections of the economy. (It would be well at this point to remember the base/superstructure metaphor as it will come up again in the third section of this chapter.) Rather, all he suggested was that how people organise themselves to produce in order to survive, conditions how they think; for example, people in capitalist societies have very different ways of thinking than those who lived in feudal times. It was a spirited defence, but to this day, Marxist approaches to history have never been able to shrug off the charge of determinism.

Historical change is driven by the contradictions between *forces* and *relations* of production.

The mode of production comprises the forces, that is, productive power, machinery, skills, technology and use of labour and the social relations within which production is organised. The relations of production therefore support and are broadly consistent with material production, but at definite stages, tensions appear between them which threaten to destabilise the mode of production itself. At a particular moment in the past, feudal relations of production, for example, could no longer contain a productive and potentially fast-developing economy within the structure of feudal society; feudal lords were too concerned to retain the status quo, thereby restricting innovation. Eventually, the feudal order was overthrown, releasing production from its fetters, and paving the way for industrial capitalism. In turn, Marx argued, the productive power of capitalism would be held back by the repressive class system until irreconcilable antagonisms, say, between the bourgeoisie and proletariat, brought down the capitalist mode of production, and a new mode of production within a classless society – socialism – would be introduced, realising the full potential of society's productive capacity.

This schema of historical change has to be understood in a wider context. As with many thinkers of the Enlightenment (Chapter 3), Marx believed that there was a certain inexorable logic to change; that if we looked closely at the historical record we can see that from the earliest forms of human society, change has been progressive and unilinear: that is, history runs in a straight line – forward. He identified the following stages which marked the trajectory of human progress:

(a) *Primitive communism*, in which individuals carried out all types of work. There was no specialisation and no division of labour, humans were in touch with their true nature. With specialisation, for example, the emergence of a labouring population, and the creation of a surplus primitive communism was superseded by slave society.

(b) *Slave society*, in which divisions opened up between those who had property and wealth and those who did not. On the lowest rung of society were slaves who had neither property nor rights. They were treated as domestic animals. Slave society was not efficient, however, so there emerged a new way of production (although slavery did not die out).

(c) *Feudalism* is a system based on land in which peasants work on the land of their masters, the rent for which is paid by expropriation of a proportion of the crops which are harvested. The whole is sustained by a landed aristocracy with the backing of private or state militaries. This too proved inefficient over time, and so was replaced by capitalism.

(d) *Capitalism* is characterised by a system of wage labour, in which the working class is paid only a part of what they produce. The surplus is extracted by the bourgeoisie who come to own most of the property.

(e) *Socialism* is predicated on the overthrow of the class system and the introduction of the rule of the proletariat, and the withering away of the state.

(f) *Communism* is a society of equality and cooperation, in which there are no antagonisms or contradictory interests. Under such circumstances, humans will realise their true nature. There will be no antagonisms between them, or between humans and their work.

Critics have rightly pointed out that this schema is teleological and as such is unacceptable. What Marx has done is to identify a stages theory of societal evolution, one that operates rather like an iron law. It is as if all human societies are on the same progressive path toward the realisation of communism, which becomes the ultimate, necessary and inevitable goal. The historical record suggests otherwise. There is no such law in operation; societal change is not always 'progressive'; as we well know from the experience of the twentieth century alone when, for example, Germany, recognised at the time as the most advanced country in Europe, regressed into a genocidal state with the most horrific powers of destruction. And Marx's notion of change tends to understate the power that individuals have to promote change – Gandhi, in South Africa or India for example – and that accidents can happen with dramatic consequences. What would have happened if Hitler had actually done well at art school, and become an artist? It is as if individuals are simply conduits for the hopes, fears and desires of the population, or accidents have little influence on the broader contours of historical movements.

Marx's theory of history has remained tainted with what critics have seen as tendencies toward economic and teleological determinism, and yet it has attracted some of the most brilliant historical scholars of recent times. It has done so despite flaws which were very much a product of the nineteenth century; yet the theory is an extraordinarily powerful system of understanding the nature of historical change. No other historical theory quite demonstrates the same ability to encompass the economic, cultural, ideological, social and political into an integrated and coherent analytical system, and to take account of the role of ordinary people in making their own history. Thus, for example, C. L. R. James (1901–89), Eric Williams (1911–81) and David Brion Davis (1927–) have effectively redefined the agenda for studying modern slavery, through a detailed understanding of the relationship between capitalism and slavery, and demonstrating the value of a non-reductive and humanitarian approaches to the problem. Through the work of Christopher Hill (1912–2003) and David Underdown (1925–2009) we know much more about the role of culture and ideology in the seismic struggles of seventeenth-century England, in particular the revolutionary impulses of an emergent capitalist society that underpinned religious conflicts. And Sumit Sarkar, Ranajit Guha and Partha Chatterjee have revealed the ways in which the British bourgeoisie developed their thinking about how to govern India, and the nature of the indigenous resistance mounted against this rule. We could go on, but the list is a long one.

Marx has also entered our vocabulary like no other historian: phrases such as 'All history is the history of class struggle', 'Religion is the opiate of the masses' or 'Workers of the world unite, you have nothing to lose but your chains', are freely quoted, often parodied. Such phrases may be great political slogans, but as historical truths they tend to be rather unreliable. Not only do they operate at the highest levels of abstraction, they are in fact virtually impossible to test in meaningful ways from the historical record. Marx himself has to take some responsibility for this state of affairs. Thus, for example, while he devoted much time to an exploration of the workings of capitalism, he said virtually nothing about what would happen when it fell.

So far we have talked of a unified body of Marxist theory, but this idea has been challenged, most notably by the French political philosopher Louis Althusser in *For Marx* (1962). Althusser argued that Marx had discovered in his allegedly scientific model of historical materialism a whole array of possibilities for understanding and changing the world. But that the corpus of Marxist thought was not a unified one for Marx's approach developed and changed over time. Althusser detected in fact an 'epistemological break' in his writings, signalling a shift from the 'early' Marx of philosophical inquiry evident in the *Economic and Philosophic Manuscripts* of 1844, to the more mature Marx of *Das Kapital* where he is concerned to outline a revolutionary economics and a science of history. The debate how Marx should be understood has since raged within Marxist circles with the same fervour that medieval Christian apologetics were once said to have – probably erroneously – disputed the number of angels that could dance on the end of a pinhead, but is no less important for all that.

In recent years, there has been a move away from Marx, in large part because of the problems identified above; many fewer historians would wish to describe themselves as Marxist. Perhaps he is no longer fashionable (we should never understate the role of fashion in historical writing). But it is not necessary to accept all that Marx wrote. If, on the other hand, historians remain who are influenced by his approach to history, and the questions he asks of historical change, or who by rejecting a simple economic determinism have taken Marx in new directions, then Marxist historiography will be with us for many years to come.

With all this conceded, however, what remains if we look back to the influence of Marxism in history is its relation to practical, everyday politics around the world. In many ways if the Berlin Wall crumbled overnight in 1989, its intellectual ramparts were breached decades before. Like the breaching of the Jewish Temple in Jerusalem two millennia ago, it would take time before the citadel would finally fall; and even then, zealots continued to fight among the ruins long after the conquering armies had overrun the city. Marxism, as we are about to discover, has been compared more to an old time religion than a secular theory of history, and its embattled remnants have emerged in different guises, suggesting other ways of understanding the past, in other manifestations – it is these manifestations over recent decades that we shall consider in the next section.

Section 3

Marxism in the twentieth century

G. D. H. Cole and Raymond Postgate first published *The Common People 1746–1938* in 1938. It was written as a rejoinder to the sort of whig history that will be encountered in Chapter 8 and which told the story of nation, constitution and great men. Its opening page took the reader to a remote dirt road east of Inverness, where in 1746 the clans of Scotland were brutally defeated by overwhelming English forces. As socialists, Cole and Postgate presented the Battle of Culloden and the eighteenth century Jacobean uprising as the conflict between an ancient society and a society much more advanced. As socialism would yet triumph, so the English forces had prevailed precisely because England was a class-based society, not a society based on family, tribe or the individual charisma of this or that leader.

In many ways, Cole and Postgate were anticipated by J. L. and Barbara Hammond, pioneers of 'history from below', who believed that one of the lessons from popular history was the need for institutional reform, and by Fabian historians Sidney and Beatrice Webb who felt that 'the people' could be persuaded to forge a socialist commonwealth if only they knew their history. In the first case, 'the people' were invested with liberal sensitivities and in the second, they became historically significant in their collective combinations, especially through their trade unions.

Marxists, such as A. L. Morton and Allen Hutt, took another viewpoint. *A People's History of England* (1938), for example, was written in the belief of the imminent establishment of a workers' state. Here the emphasis was on the economic system, class and historical transition. The Marxist tradition was anxious to establish histories that anticipated the emergence of a class-conscious industrial proletariat; all posited the working class as the unblemished champions of liberty and democracy in line with the principles of historical materialism and all saw 'the people' as the instruments of inevitable social, political and economic transformation.

Cole and Postgate were influenced by all of these strands, but differed from them in subtle ways. They lacked the absolute faith in revolutionary transformation that marked the Marxist school, but this made the moral message of their work all the more urgent. Faced by the persistence of unemployment and social division and the growing menace of fascism in the 1930s, they wrote a tract for their times that emphasised both the failings of capitalist society and the hope that the democratic traditions of the masses could remoralise the British state and build a better future. In this, they represent a remarkable anticipation of the wartime urge for social reform.

Since the 1930s and 1940s, liberal, Fabian and Marxist inspired history 'from below' has blossomed and thrived. The most famous example of this was E. P. Thompson's *The Making of the English Working Class* (1963), which sought to rescue the experiences of ordinary men and women from the 'condescension of posterity'. Like Raymond Williams and Richard Hoggart who contributed to the 'new social history' of the 1960s, Thompson put class – theorised as a set of relationships both political and economic – centre stage in his narrative of English history. He criticised developmental and progressive accounts of history, as they distorted the past and emphasised only those elements they recognised as harbingers of the future. The victors were celebrated in the Whig accounts which adhered to a developmental model of history, as were the prophets of future electoral victory in the Fabian accounts.

For both Fabians and Marxists, the working classes defeated in the period of the Napoleonic wars and the era of the First Reform Act (and beyond that in Chartism which was discussed in Chapter 1) ultimately emerged victorious as the agents of socialist transformation, despite the trade unions and political parties which caged their radicalism. It is clear, however, that Thompson's (and indeed Cole and Postgate's) socialist faith has been sorely challenged in recent years. The industrial working class has declined in numbers, and the socialist revolutionary experiment in the Soviet Union and Eastern Europe has conclusively failed. We know, for example, that far from being a socialist state, the actions of the Soviet Union from Communism's murderous past resulted in famine, purges, war and seventy million unnatural deaths, according to the historian Catherine Merridale in her remarkable book *Night of Stone: Death and Memory in Russia* (2001). Equally significant is the emerging critique of the intellectual roots of socialist historiography. Rather than being understood as an objective and scientific approach to the study of history, Marxism is now being understood as driven by metaphysical and religious concerns. To many, therefore it seems imperative to challenge the theoretical basis of Marxism and its analysis of class conflict as rooted in economic and social contradictions, and to embark on a post-socialist rethinking of a history of 'the people'.

Let us pause here and unpack the origins of this challenge. Mike Savage and Andrew Miles, authors of *The Remaking of the British Working Class 1840–1940* (1994), have a chapter on 'Labour history' that is useful here. They make the point that leftist histories have always been organised around the notion of agency, either from the point of view of the institutions of the working class (as in Fabian histories) or from the experience of the industrial proletariat within a global context (such as the Marxist histories). The first sought to 'service and celebrate' the Labour movement and underlined its evolutionary development while the second described its membership as being invested with revolutionary potential.

The Communist Party Historians Group most notably promoted this approach to histories of class (Kaye, 1982). From a revolutionary politics grew the *Universities and Left Review* and the New Left. Thompson, along with other notable Marxist historians such as Christopher Hill, Rodney Hilton (1916–2002), Eric Hobsbawm, George Rude (1910–93), Dona Torr (1883–1957), Victor Kiernan (1913–2009), John Saville (1916–2009) and a youthful Raphael Samuel (1934–96), had been members. Their founding texts were diverse and included *Studies in the Development of Capitalism* (1946) by Maurice Dobb (1900–76), which inaugurated an important debate on the transition from feudalism to capitalism.

By the 1960s and 1970s, the Communist party was divided along both organisational and ideological lines. After the Soviet invasion of Hungary in 1956, the party lost members. Thompson, disillusioned, founded what was to become an influential journal called the *Reasoner* and then in 1957 the *New Reasoner*. His ill-tempered and ill-judged open letter to Leszek Kolakowski in 1973, published in his *Poverty of Theory* in 1978, sought to expose this former Communist dissident from Poland, who had washed up at All Souls in Oxford, accusing him of succumbing to the hypnotising charms of capitalism, exposing yet more divisions among former comrades.

The biggest chasm was yet to open up; when it did it would scar the leftist landscape for a generation. This chasm was between Thompson and Perry Anderson. Anderson is known best as author of *Lineages of the Absolutist State* in 1979, *Passages from Antiquity to Feudalism* in 1985 and *Origins of the Present Crisis*, written in the apparent shadow of Britain's economic malaise in 1964. Anderson was committed to demonstrating the continued relevance of critical perspectives on classical Marxist theory. He had arrived from France to edit the *New Reasoner* in 1962 (which was to become the *Universities and New Left Review*) and then promptly sacked Thompson and those others who had been authentic Communist dissidents during the 1950s.

Thompson also distanced himself from crude Marxist approaches, which he felt were determinist and anti-historical. Instead, he wrote histories that emphasised class as experience and for the 'peculiarities' of English history. In his work on Blake, William Morris and, indeed, the English working classes, Thompson had argued for a history of England that traced a particular working class history which, independent from European models, was based on the liberty of the 'Free Born Englishman'. One of his early collaborators on this matter at least was the literary critic and Marxist, Raymond Williams, who in his own work opened up the charge of 'cultural nationalism'; a charge Thompson rejected with some justification, pleading his internationalist activity in the peace movement and elsewhere.

Later, the rise of the History Workshop Movement and feminism widened those divisions (see Chapter 10). The new concern was less for nation or constitution (like the whig historians), or even for structures of class power, but for minorities and outsiders. Like Thompson, they were concerned with the poor and the disenfranchised, but they also turned to the historical plight of women, the colonial victims of imperialism and the sexually excluded. The 'people', thereby, were de-coupled from their representative organisations, whether they be trade union or Labour party, and because of the new sensitivity to gender and race in history, were now diverse as well as fragmented.

Sociological studies suggest that the continuing de-radicalisation of the working class and its very existence as a class with 'only its labour to sell' (the classic Marxist formulation), has all but disappeared in the western hemisphere. Culture was no longer thought to have material foundations linked to the rituals of work. Indeed, the view of the primacy of the economic base was replaced by the belief in the autonomy of culture that in turn placed emphasis on discourse or language before experience (associated with postmodern theory, which we examine in Chapter 5). The spotlight now is less on class and more on the competing identities associated with gender, race, sexuality, national and local belonging. Thus, the past, like the present is thought to be socially fragmented, making the idea of a homogeneous working class implausible.

Where liberal and Fabian Labour historians saw the working class as part of Britain's democratic and tolerant traditions, Marxists were left asking why there had not been a revolution. Some argued that the institutions of the working class had betrayed a more radical working class; the development of an elite or patrician culture had thwarted revolution. Others, such as Hobsbawm, identified an 'aristocracy of labour' that by possessing skills that could be sold readily in the marketplace and by their deferent politics, had divided a potentially homogeneous proletariat. Others still, like Perry Anderson and Tom Nairn, argued that as Britain, unlike much of mainland Europe, had never had a bourgeois revolution, it was anti-intellectual and anti-theoretical, and ill-placed to accommodate a workers' state. Its institutions and outlook remained that of an *ancien régime*, which after the First Reform Act in 1832 could accommodate the demands of the industrialist and financial middle class alike. The dialectic of class and the model of historical materialism demanded the movement of history by the contradictory interests of two antagonistic classes – capital and labour. There was little evidence of this in Britain. By maintaining a monarchy and aristocracy, by developing a fluid and open middle class, by its liberal, almost pre-industrial, labour movement that was modest in its demands, by its artisans or labour aristocrats aping their social betters and by the persistence of a lumpen-proletariat or underclass, the country remained stubbornly unwilling to turn to revolution.

In 1993, the *International Review of Social History* asked whether what has been described really amounted to the end of class histories and, by implication, of Marxist history. Contributors suggested a number of problems at the heart of this malaise which has now affected the social history of labour in the same way as it had once dogged older histories of 'the people':

1 Geographical, spatial and environmental circumstances of labour have been neglected. What are the effects of ecological and locational influences on histories of class?

2 How can we bridge the gap between the objective facts of daily life and work (labour processes, wages, housing and so on) and people's subjective experiences of say work, poverty and living in a slum?
3 How can the history of labour admit outside influences, like business, and how can they be treated together?
4 How can we find a consistent approach to the plural identities of the working class? Issues involving gender, race, ethnicity and age are treated as separate sub-disciplines, while labour history research no longer appears to focus implicitly on young white male workers.
5 Why do we continue to concentrate on the 'core' western countries at the expense of comparative histories and the histories of labour in the poorer nations?

In April 1997, the same journal published a few tentative responses by the German historian Jurgen Kocka, suggesting that historians needed to:

- increase efforts to connect gender and class, linking the history of wage labour with the domestic economy of the household;
- look afresh at the language of the labour movement;
- include more politics in historical accounts of labour;
- look again at the relationship between Fabian-style social democracy and Communism, and judge whether the two socialist traditions can be divided;
- ask, not why there was no revolution, but why there was still so much radicalism among labour movements;
- look at trade unions as a part of civil society not as potentially revolutionary state apparatus.

He adds, in hope more than expectation, that as working class and labour history is influenced by present day concerns, that comparative history will increase, that we will, as he puts it, 'get the economy back in' and even that the 'history of work' will gain a new prominence. Perhaps, he goes on, even Marx will gain new credibility.

As a means of better situating Marxism within the development of intellectual thought rather than a body of theory with universal application, Gareth Stedman Jones began to rethink its importance as a post-Enlightenment ideology. Marxism, according to Stedman Jones, originated in Hegel's theory of history, which derived from reactions to the French Revolution in the 1790s and German philosophical debates of the same decade, attributing to nature a special mystery and energy:

> **Where Hegel's theory of history suggested 'innate powers, purposive activity, striving after perfection, a self-sufficient divine impulse at work within man and the world' . . . , Marx by replacing class for Spirit, did not free himself of these elements by focusing in upon the so-called forces of production. The shocking rider to this view, at least for conventional Marxists, was that mankind, whether before or after the revolution would never escape the clutches of ideology.** (Stedman Jones, 1997, p. 165)

Ultimately, Marxist theories were utopian because they were based on metaphysical assumptions about man which are 'scarcely comprehensible outside the quasi-religious context in which they had been conceived'. Marx, it turned out, had not turned Hegel's theory of history on its head by displacing idealism with a materialism rooted in history.

In contrast, Marx's theory of history was subjective, contained a religious element and was far from offering a science of history. The consequences of this are telling. Hitherto it had been assumed that socialism (a term coined in the 1830s) was a product of the economic conditions thrown up by the industrial revolution, and derived from an analysis of, and a solution to the manifest inequalities of, class, social stratification and economic relations. If Stedman Jones was correct, socialism was born in the 1790s out of the politics of the French Revolution as a utopian quasi-religion which argued that an energy in nature propelled history forward and which might offer democratic alternatives to Christianity.

Now Marx could be placed back into a more general consideration of Enlightenment thought. By doing this, socialism is seen, not as a global movement that sought an alternative to existing human relations – a wholly new society, a higher civilisation, a cooperative system based on rationality that promises the end of division at an 'end state' – but as a philosophy bound by time and place. When asked whether he thought that the ideas of Marx are still important today, Stedman Jones responded in a way that nicely summarises what might be described as a consensus among most historians today: class and class struggle is still important and so is its analysis. However, Marx did not intend to construct a new science of history, but to visualise a Communist society as an alternative to capitalism. In this, he failed, as the ruins of the Berlin Wall would suggest. It also suggests, above all else, that Marx has provided historians with some immensely important insights but with the failure of Marxism as practical politics, Marx's theory of history has been fatally damaged. The result is that Marx is no more and no less important than Hume or Machiavelli or, indeed, Hegel – thinkers who once provided us with ways of understanding the world but whose influence has now waned.

In practice

If the centre of advances in historical thinking during the eighteenth century was France, then arguably that of the nineteenth was Germany. This chapter has attempted to chart the significance of Germany philosophy in the post-Enlightenment period by focusing on three key figures – Georg Wilhelm Hegel, Leopold von Ranke and Karl Marx – the contributions of whom shaped the thinking of subsequent historians and hence the course of modern historiography.

Drawing upon many of the fundamental concerns of the Enlightenment, Hegel attempted to show how notions such as reason, spirit, nature and freedom derived their meaning and therefore their significance only within specific historical contexts. He thus addressed himself as an historian rather than a philosopher to the task of making concrete the operation of such abstract notions on the world stage. For him, the past is evidence of the advance of freedom – the realisation of a world spirit – which comes through recognition of systems of values to the essential benefit of the various peoples of the world. History is therefore not a random course of events – it is a rational process which unfolds according to innate laws which shape the actions and behaviours of individuals. And to show this he embarked on a series of ambitious studies of the ancient Asian world, the Greek and Roman empires, and the emergence of modern Germany.

▶

This emphasis on reason and freedom, and the commitment to working concretely with the historical record, was a significant departure, and it came as no surprise that a group of radical scholars, known as the Young Hegelians, came together to take these ideas forward. From their numbers emerged the figure of Karl Marx, a philosopher, but one with a keen sense of history. Marx, however, broke with what he saw as the idealism of Hegel. He argued in contrast that it was not human consciousness which determined the pattern of historical change, but how humans organised themselves to produce and reproduce their lives. Changes in material production therefore provide the key to understanding historical movement and why particular peoples develop distinct ways of thinking. Endemic in all societies was the struggle between the forces and relations of production, and it was this rather than abstract reason which provided the driving force of historical change.

The work of von Ranke can also be seen as a distinct response to Hegelian idealism. Von Ranke was suspicious of the overt philosophical approach of Hegel, and urged a commitment to the study of what really happened in the past. In so doing, he laid the foundation for history as a science. Historical truth is out there, it survives in the evidence which has survived from the past, but it can only be excavated and employed legitimately by historians who are trained in the appropriate techniques. History therefore starts with the evidential record; the task of the historian is to find it, gather it and utilise it objectively (if possible) to put together a picture of the course of events.

In many respects most historians working today owe a debt to at least one of these three German philosophers. Much has been made about their differences – for example, the radicalism of Marxism compared with the innate conservatism of von Ranke – but perhaps there is a case for arguing that what they share is equally important. Recent work by Gareth Stedman Jones has attempted to demonstrate that Marx was a figure of the German Enlightenment and has to be located therein rather than as a suprahistorical talisman of world revolution. Yet, to invert Hegel is to erect class struggle as the driving force of historical change and risks exhibiting similar forms of essentialism.

The increasing criticism faced by Marxist historians in recent years had led to a rather confused picture in which the old divisions between, say, radical and conservative approaches to history are not so clear-cut. Few histories today have class struggle or class consciousness as their organising theme. Instead, race and gender feature more prominently, and for many, as we shall see in the next chapter, language is recognised to be of fundamental importance to historical understanding. These shifts have at the same time signalled a renewed concern with evidence, and how it is to be used. This may be an old problem for historians, but the recent flush of interest has led to challenging developments which may outlast the merely fashionable to take the discipline forward in exciting ways.

Summary

The three sections of this chapter have said three things:

- The philosophy of history as outlined by Hegel is vitally important to understand in its own right. Although Hegel was an immensely important figure as a philosopher, he is now set firmly within the context of the German Enlightenment. Critically, Hegel argued for a view of world history that had the notion of a 'spirit' or 'idea' that ran through history. This spirit was peculiar to the German nation and a specific national development that is known to us as the Sonderweg. This is as may be. Hegel's major gift to Marx (and to both Left Hegelians and Right Hegelians alike) was the idea that history was dialectical; that is, moves forward by the clash of opposing ideas. It is this dialectic that Marx adapted in his own theory of history.

- Historical materialism as set out by Marx was adapted from Hegel. Here we learn how the Hegelian notion of 'spirit' or 'ideas' that run through world history is turned upside down. Instead the material conditions of human existence – the forces and relations of production – can explain historical change. This theory of history has been enormously important to historians and has been used as a framework for many histories. The effectiveness of historical materialism can now be seen clearly in the wake of the terminal decline of Marxism as a practical and actually existing politics and as a theory of history that can offer a comprehensive explanation of the past and the present alike, both explaining the world and simultaneously changing it.

- Arguments within Marxism have affected historiography since the 1960s and 1970s. The crisis in communism forced a reassessment of Marxist approaches to history as evidenced by the Communist Party Historians Group, E. P. Thompson and Perry Anderson. We finish with the historian Gareth Stedman Jones who by emphasising the metaphysical basis of Marxist theories of history has sought to place Marx back into the context of the Enlightenment and its legacy.

Discussion document 1

This statement contains the bare bones of historical materialism as articulated by Marx. The issues it raises is the central topic of Section 2 but essentially addresses questions about the departure of Marx's theory of history in the context of Hegel, the focus Marx makes on economic relationships in society and the problems associated with the adoption of a teleology.

> In the social production of their life, men enter into definite relations that are indispensable and independent of their will, relations of production which correspond to a definite stage of development of their material productive forces. The sum total of these relations of production constitutes the economic structure of society, the real basis on which arises the legal and political superstructure, and to which correspond definite forms of social consciousness. The mode of production of material life conditions the social, political and intellectual life process in general. It is not the consciousness of men that determines their being, but on the contrary, their social being that determines their consciousness. At a certain stage in their development, the material productive forces of society come into conflict with the existing relations of production, or – what is but the legal expression for the same thing – with the property relations within which they have been at work hitherto. From forms of development of the productive forces these relations turn into their fetters. Then begins an epoch of social revolution. With the change of the economic foundation the entire immense superstructure is more or less rapidly transformed. In considering such transformations, a distinction should always be made between the material transformation of the economic conditions of production, which can be determined with the precision of natural science, and the legal, political, religious, aesthetic or philosophic – in short, ideological forms in which men become conscious of this conflict and fight it out. Just as our opinion of an individual is not based on what he thinks of himself, so we cannot judge of such a period of transformation by its own consciousness; on the contrary, this consciousness must be explained rather from the existing conflict between the social productive forces and the relations of production. No social formation ever perishes before all the productive forces for which there is room in it have developed; and new, higher relations of production never appear before the material conditions of their existence have matured in the womb of the old society itself. Therefore mankind always sets itself only such tasks as it can solve; since, looking at the matter more closely, it will always be found that the task itself arises only when the material conditions for its solution already exist or are at least in the process of formation. In broad outlines, Asiatic, ancient, feudal, and modern bourgeois modes of production can be designated as progressive epochs in the economic formation of society. The bourgeois relations of production are the last antagonistic form of the social process of production – antagonistic not in the sense of individual antagonism, but of one arising from the social conditions of life of the individuals; at the same time the productive forces developing in the womb of bourgeois society create the material conditions for the solution of that antagonism. This social formation brings, therefore, the prehistory of human society to a close.

Karl Marx, Preface to *A Contribution to the Critique of Political Economy* (1859).

Discussion document 2

This is an important example of how Marx put into practice the method of historical materialism. Revealingly, it says something about his intellectual debt to Hegel, the role of the individual in history and the role that the past plays in the lives of the living.

Hegel remarks somewhere that all great world-historic facts and personages appear, so to speak, twice. He forgot to add: the first time as tragedy, the second time as farce. Caussidière for Danton, Louis Blanc for Robespierre, the Montagne of 1848 to 1851 for the Montagne of 1793 to 1795, the nephew for the uncle. And the same caricature occurs in the circumstances of the second edition of the Eighteenth Brumaire.

Men make their own history, but they do not make it as they please; they do not make it under self-selected circumstances, but under circumstances existing already, given and transmitted from the past. The tradition of all dead generations weighs like a nightmare on the brains of the living. And just as they seem to be occupied with revolutionizing themselves and things, creating something that did not exist before, precisely in such epochs of revolutionary crisis they anxiously conjure up the spirits of the past to their service, borrowing from them names, battle slogans, and costumes in order to present this new scene in world history in time-honoured disguise and borrowed language. Thus Luther put on the mask of the Apostle Paul, the Revolution of 1789–1814 draped itself alternately in the guise of the Roman Republic and the Roman Empire, and the Revolution of 1848 knew nothing better to do than to parody, now 1789, now the revolutionary tradition of 1793–95. In like manner, the beginner who has learned a new language always translates it back into his mother tongue, but he assimilates the spirit of the new language and expresses himself freely in it only when he moves in it without recalling the old and when he forgets his native tongue.

When we think about this conjuring up of the dead of world history, a salient difference reveals itself. Camille Desmoulins, Danton, Robespierre, St. Just, Napoleon, the heroes as well as the parties and the masses of the old French Revolution, performed the task of their time – that of unchaining and establishing modern bourgeois society – in Roman costumes and with Roman phrases. The first one destroyed the feudal foundation and cut off the feudal heads that had grown on it. The other created inside France the only conditions under which free competition could be developed, parcelled-out land properly used, and the unfettered productive power of the nation employed; and beyond the French borders it swept away feudal institutions everywhere, to provide, as far as necessary, bourgeois society in France with an appropriate up-to-date environment on the European continent. Once the new social formation was established, the antediluvian colossi disappeared and with them also the resurrected Romanism – the Brutuses, the Gracchi, the publicolas, the tribunes, the senators, and Caesar himself. Bourgeois society in its sober reality bred its own true interpreters and spokesmen in the Says, Cousins, Royer-Collards, Benjamin Constants, and Guizots; its real military leaders sat behind the office desk and the hog-headed Louis XVIII was its political chief. Entirely absorbed in the production of wealth and in peaceful competitive struggle, it no longer remembered that the ghosts of the Roman period had watched over its cradle.

But unheroic though bourgeois society is, it nevertheless needed heroism, sacrifice, terror, civil war, and national wars to bring it into being. And in the austere classical traditions of the Roman Republic the bourgeois gladiators found the ideals and the art forms, the self-deceptions, that they needed to conceal from themselves the bourgeois-limited content of their struggles and to keep their passion on the high plain of great historic tragedy. Similarly, at another stage of development a century earlier, Cromwell and the English people had borrowed from the Old Testament the speech, emotions, and illusions for their bourgeois revolution. When the real goal had been achieved and the bourgeois transformation of English society had been accomplished, Locke supplanted Habakkuk.

Thus the awakening of the dead in those revolutions served the purpose of glorifying the new struggles, not of parodying the old; of magnifying the given task in the imagination, not recoiling from its solution in reality; of finding once more the spirit of revolution, not making its ghost walk again.

Karl Marx, *The Eighteenth Brumaire of Louis Bonaparte* (1852).

Further reading

* *essential*

* **Karl Marx and Frederick Engels**, *The Communist Manifesto* (2002).
An excellent edition with a fine introduction by Gareth Stedman Jones. It is to date the most complete statement of Stedman Jones' work on Marx within the context of post-Enlightenment thought.

Louis Althusser, *For Marx* (2005).
An important intervention in radical philosophy, setting out the case for a structuralist approach to Marxist theories of history. It includes the notion of an 'epistemological break' in the collected works of Marx and the idea of a 'mature' Marx.

E. P. Thompson, *The Poverty of Theory and other Essays* (1978).
As an historian associated with humanist Marxism, this collection of Thompson's work reproduces in acerbic and characteristic style a number of essays that argue against the approach to history of the structuralists in general and Perry Anderson in particular. Of especial note are *The Poverty of Theory or An Orrery of Errors* (1978), *The Peculiarities of the English* (1965) and *An Open Letter to Leszek Kolakowski* (1973).

Perry Anderson, 'Origins of the present crisis', *New Left Review*, January–February (1964).
There are other examples between 1962–1982 and 2000–2003, but both these editorials by Anderson for the *New Left Review* and his early commentary on Britain's relative decline reveal the approach to history taken by this important and influential commentator.

Mary Fulbrook (ed.), *German History since 1800* (1997).
The most authoritative and comprehensive volume on the massive subject of German history and the German contribution to history. Wide-ranging essays are devoted to many subjects under this rubric. The introduction should be read carefully, as should the essay by Stefan Berger on 'The German tradition of historiography, 1800–1995'.

5 Postmodernism and postcolonialism

1 Modernity and the Enlightenment
2 Postmodernism
3 Postcolonialism and the West

Introduction

In many respects this chapter carries forward the debate introduced in Chapter 1 on the status of historical knowledge. There we discussed the problem of historical truth, and whether or not it was realisable. In recent years these concerns have intensified, as a result of which the debate has taken some perhaps unexpected twists and turns. The experience of the Second World War and the immediate post-war period in Europe were of such a momentous nature they changed the world order. No longer was this an order of western power underpinned by colonial possessions in the third world; instead we witnessed the rise of new superpowers. This new order, it was argued by theoretically driven historians, could not be interpreted by the conventional methods of history. Not only that, the horrors of the experience threw into crisis any belief that the West – and Enlightenment thought upon which it was built – could claim superiority. Indeed, for some, this particular historical trajectory had come to an end. Simultaneously, this moment witnessed the demise of the imperial order which had been controlled by European powers, as colonies fought successfully for their independence from foreign rule.

These events forced a fundamental re-examination of the historiographical approaches which had sprung from the Enlightenment to create two new fields of intellectual inquiry – postmodernism and postcolonialism. Although addressing different historical concerns they shared certain suspicions of traditional historiography, in particular those related to the operation of specific types of narratives. By abandoning such narratives, it was argued, history would be released from a strait-jacket, but this promise posed its own sets of awkward questions, most of which remain unresolved. It is with this process that this chapter will be concerned.

Section 1

Modernity and the Enlightenment

It took a German of Jewish descent to observe that the progressive aims of the Enlightenment had been stuck in the mud of Auschwitz and that to attempt to write something as creative or beautiful as poetry in the knowledge of this atrocity would be an act of barbarism. Theodor Adorno, of the famous Frankfurt School of philosophy, was not alone in this thought. Many historians and other social theorists have detected a profound transformation around the time of the Second World War and its immediate aftermath. Of course, the war itself effectively defined a new world order in which the old European powers found themselves in a sorry state, in no position to challenge the rising strength of the two new superpowers – the United States and the Soviet Union. Soon thereafter, these same European powers were forced to cede control of their empires, and grant independence to the fledgling nation states of the continents of Asia and Africa. And yet, perhaps, contemporary observers witnessed at the same time a dramatic shift in the trajectory of history itself, more specifically the end of ideas of liberty and reason which had underpinned and protected the rise of the West.

This moment signalled the end of what has been referred to as the Enlightenment project, or the demise of modernity, and our entry into a qualitatively new age. In broad terms it is difficult to distinguish between the two ways of defining this moment. In talking of the Enlightenment project we may well focus on its intellectual formation as outlined in Chapter 3, while modernity is seen to have a wider remit, encompassing as it does the economic, political, cultural and aesthetic, but in practice as modernity was so implicated in the Enlightenment project such a distinction lacks precision. The Enlightenment was modern and to be modern was wrapped up entirely in the Enlightenment.

So let us begin an exploration of these issues by refreshing our thoughts on what the Enlightenment stood for. According to its protagonists, the Enlightenment spread reason like light, so playing a critically important role in the emergence of modern thought. It formed the first stage in the forging of a modern conception of society as an entity amenable to the action of human agency, whose underlying workings were in principle open to scrutiny and revelation. These changes were attendant of certain important historical shifts in the West, among which we can include the following:

1. The increased use of secular forms of political power and authority displacing absolutist forms of authority based on religious ideology, and the rise of nation states underpinned by conceptions of sovereignty and popular legitimacy.
2. Exchange economies based on the large-scale production and consumption of commodities, the extension of private ownership and new ideas on the worth of private property, and the systematic accumulation of capital characteristic of self-sustained growth.

3 A decline in the feudal social order, with its rigid social hierarchies and overlapping allegiances, and the appearance of dynamic social and sexual divisions of labour, which in a capitalist society meant new class formations based on antagonisms between the bourgeoisie and proletariat, and patriarchal relations between men and women.
4 The displacement of a world view which was religious, superstitious and insular by a secular and materialist culture promoting individualism and rationality.

What lay at the heart of the project was a belief that it was possible for the first time to know human society and behaviour rather than see them through the ancient lens of religious orthodoxy and superstition. And by knowing them it was thought possible to change them. Part of this project was clearly historical. Within the Scottish and French Enlightenments there were determined attempts to understand how societies had developed over time – thus there emerged fully fledged ideas about the stages theory of human development, successfully employed to rank the peoples of the world beneath the 'natural' superiority of Europeans.

Also embracing advances in medical, scientific, technological and other innovations, seen to be part of the endeavour to improve human life, the Enlightenment has rightly been seen as one of the starting points for modern thought. It also signalled the appearance of the secular intellectual within western society – a figure whose role was intimately bound up with the analysis and critique of society and history. In no area was this more important than that of political modernity. The Enlightenment laid the foundations for rule by the modern institutions of state – bureaucracy and capitalist enterprise. Concepts such as citizenship, the state, civil society and the maintenance of the public sphere, human rights, equality before the law, the individual, distinctions between the public and the private, democracy and popular sovereignty, all bear the burden of European thought and history, no matter where they are considered or in what context. We simply cannot think of political modernity without these and other related concepts that found their feet precisely because of the Enlightenment and gained momentum during the subsequent developments of the nineteenth century.

Notions of the modern have therefore been around for a long time. Arguably, since the latter stages of the eighteenth century people have been sensitive to the fact that they live in modern times which invariably they find exciting and challenging. It is only in recent years, however, that we have begun to think more carefully about what 'modern' means. There is a danger to think only of the modern in chronological terms, that is, to be modern is to live in the modern world, in which case the argument becomes tautological. More helpful are those approaches which have tried to think through the question of what is distinct about the modern? What are its defining features? Marshal Berman in *All That is Solid Melts into Air* (1983) provides us with an evocative sense of the modern:

> **There is a mode of vital experience – experience of space and time, of the self and others, of life's possibilities and perils – that is shared by men and women all over the world today. I will call this body of experience 'modernity'. To be modern is to find ourselves in an environment that promises adventure, power, joy, growth, transformation of ourselves and the world – and, at the same time, that threatens to destroy everything that we have, everything we know, everything we are. Modern environments and experiences cut across all boundaries of geography and ethnicity, of class and nationality, of religion and ideology; in this case,**

> **modernity can be said to unite all mankind. But it is a paradoxical unity; it pours us all into the maelstrom of perpetual disintegration and renewal, of struggle and contradiction, of ambiguity and anguish. To be modern is to be part of a universe in which, as Marx said, 'all that is solid melts into air'.** (Berman, 1983, p. 15)

This conveys nicely the dual edged nature of modernity. The modern world offers us empowerment and opportunity, but at the same time has developed unprecedented powers of destruction. What changes have brought about this state of affairs? The following are some of the profound events that have brought about the modern world:

- Great discoveries in the physical sciences, changing our images of the universe and our place in it.
- Industrialisation of production, creating new human environments.
- New forms of corporate power.
- Immense demographic upheavals.
- Rapid and often cataclysmic urban growth.
- Systems of mass communications, which are dynamic in their development.
- Increasingly powerful nation states.
- Drastically fluctuating world markets.

The relationship between how people have viewed the Enlightenment and modernity is therefore close, and in practice it is difficult to disentangle them. Enlightenment ideas underscored and promoted the emergence of the modern world. It seems also that both came to a fairly abrupt end at the time of the Second World War and its immediate afermath. As far as modernity is concerned, largely as a result of changes in production, the increasing dominance of the visual in our lives, the loss of faith in the centredness of the western individual, and growing suspicion of grand narratives or descriptions of the world that can explain everything, it was displaced by the condition we know as postmodernity. The Enlightenment project, launched some two hundred years previously to bring rational thought and action to human endeavours and so banish superstition, irrationality, hunger and disease from the face of the globe, now floundered in the Nazi death camps and disappeared amid the mushroom clouds of Hiroshima and Nagasaki. How, people now asked, can we still talk of progress and civilisation when what were considered the most civilised parts of the world were shown capable of such acts? The fact that these acts of supreme destruction were carried out by the two nations thought to be in the forefront of civilisation – Germany and the United States of America – only compounded the sense of a profound rupture between Enlightenment modernity and postmodernity. This was to have profound implications for the writing of history.

The crisis is seen to be one that we associate with the West, but this assumption is based on some awkward presuppositions. When historians talk of modernity and the Enlightenment, they may necessarily privilege the experience of the West in such a way that they become synonymous – the West is modern, and a definition of modern is centred on the West. If we can detect the modern in other parts of the world, then this is probably a result of the effects of colonialism and global capitalism. In response to this narrative, questions have been raised about precisely to whose modernity we are referring? Surely, we can point to modernising tendencies in, say, China and Africa which owe little to the West? Should we therefore not speak of different modernities rather than a single western modernity? We shall have cause to return to these questions later.

Yet it is true to say that it was out of the Enlightenment that the vital notion of human progress emerged and took hold of influential sections of European opinion in the second half of the eighteenth century. For the first time in human history it was possible to think that human societies were on the path of perpetual progress. This is nicely illustrated by the simultaneous transformations which took place in British thought on the issues of slavery, colonialism and poverty toward the end of the century, all of which came to be seen as massive barriers to progress. After centuries when slavery was unquestioned – seen as a natural condition of man – a transformation of dramatic proportions occurred. In the space of a few decades universal acceptance of the slave trade was overturned by opprobrium directed towards it. Much of the impulse for the stirrings of abolition came from Quakers and other non-conformist denominations. But the real driving force was the new breed of political economists such as Adam Smith who argued that slavery confronted the laws of morality, was a barrier to the breaking up of monopoly interests, and imposed restraints on free trade.

Poverty had previously been seen as a state of grace – a condition to be borne with pious fortitude. If relief was offered as it had been since the introduction of Elizabethan poor and vagrancy laws, it was as a last desperate resource. The real solution was to be found in the regulation of employment and prices of staples such as bread, and the provision of alms. Above all, the merits of labour were extolled – the result of the English revolution and the introduction of the Protestant work ethic. But none of these measures had been successful, and toward the end of the eighteenth century, following displacement from the countryside, large numbers of migrants found their way to the urban centres, in particular to London, where desperate masses of poor settled in enclaves seen increasingly to harbour criminal activity, threatening the imperial and commercial future of the nation. Simultaneously, levels of relief were beginning to compromise the actuarial stability of the poor law system, and measures were laid down which culminated in the harsh disciplinary regime of the New Poor Law of 1834.

Anxieties also surfaced over the nature and extent of imperial ambition in India. Following the loss of the American colonies in 1776, Britain turned to India, and there under the aegis of the East India Company emerged as an imperial rather than simply a trading power. The Company, however, proved inefficient and profligate, and had to be saved from bankruptcy by loans from the government. Then 1776 – an *annus horribilis* for the British state if ever there was one – saw the publication of Adam Smith's *Wealth of Nations*, Edward Gibbon's *Decline and Fall of the Roman Empire*, and, critically, Tom Paine's *Common Sense*, which together mounted a devastating attack on the dangers of imperial endeavour and aristocratic profligacy while supporting the American colonists. The British state drew the appropriate lessons, and, determined not to allow the Company a free rein, interceded to take over an increasing responsibility for Indian affairs.

Despite the troubling presence of the poor, and occasional setbacks in imperial advance, the British were able to assume the high moral ground on the abolition of slavery, consolidating authority as an imperial nation (particularly after the demise of the East India Company in 1858) and striding forward in the nineteenth century, confident in the knowledge that progress was an integral part of modernisation. This profound sense of belief in progress also dominated European thought in the nineteenth century, but as we entered the twentieth it began to falter. The mass slaughter of the First World War and the onset of mass culture engendered a profound sense of pessimism among a European intelligentsia worried that elite culture was threatened by the onset of popular forms such as magazines and the cinema, and yet this was a time of revolutionary change in the spheres of science and the arts. All this impacted on the writing and understanding of history.

Yet it was the Second World War that witnessed barbarities that eclipsed anything seen before. If there was one moment that ended the belief in a law of inexorable progress this was it. What followed was the rise of consumer society in which worth and identity came to be measured in terms of material possessions. Whether we see this period as the end of modernity or of the Enlightenment project, the emphasis is on what many have considered to be a profound shift in social thought. This is because the supposed passing of modernity created a crisis not merely in the economic, political and cultural spheres of our lives: it was also a crisis in the whole way of understanding the world; a state of being that challenged previously accepted approaches to the past. We now enter, it is argued, a postmodern condition which requires an entirely different way of reflecting on our experience; and if this means abandoning the basic tenets of intellectual thought that were founded in the Enlightenment, then so be it. What then is this postmodern condition? The next section will address this and other questions.

Section 2

Postmodernism

There is a story about an academic conference in which one speaker announces that the First World War was nothing but a text, a story or a series of stories in which no final truth can ever be discerned, in a 1967 essay called 'Death of the author' by Roland Barthes, the French literary critic, text is separated from the author whose intentions can never be truly understood. The same goes for historical evidence, thus robbing historians of their status and worth as remembrancers of society and interpreters of its past, condemning them to endlessly reread evidence without ever being in a position to know historical truth or to determine the intentions of historical actors. It is as if the all too vivid reality of the killing fields of Ypres and the Somme are reduced to an exercise in the deconstruction of language used to describe the conflict itself, making any judgment, let alone a final judgment regarding its historical significance, simply impossible. That is until another delegate at the same conference reminded his colleagues that his grandfather had lost a leg in this 'text' that had raged between 1914 and 1918, and that its reality can be confirmed by those millions killed or maimed in its 'discourse'. In so doing, he was restating at least some of the certainties that we associate with the Enlightenment project described in the previous section.

Now, despite the obvious diversity within the Enlightenment, there is an underlying cluster of assumptions and expectations about the nature of the modern world. This collectively makes up western knowledge that has come under scrutiny by postmodern theorists. Something more than a reflection on the changing nature of social experience, it is a fundamental reorientation of the categories of western epistemology or the basis of how we understand the world. The postmodern challenge thus involves either rejecting or at least seriously questioning the pillars of Enlightenment thought, which is itself thought to be a metanarrative or a story about a story. More than this, the postmodern position is often seen as 'the death of centres', an explanation given by a variety of theorists and commentators. The historian Keith Jenkins argues that the 'organising frameworks' that describe human phenomenon privilege various centres. We naturally adopt, for example, 'Anglo-centric', 'Euro-centric', or even 'gender-centric' perspectives, but these are what he calls 'temporary fictions' that serve not universal interests (as is implied by the Enlightenment) but instead very particular interests that reinforce western power. Recognition of this has undermined religion, science and reason itself and thus these 'certaintist discourses' have given way to an ethics that is less public – not about the Enlightenment notions of human progress, reform and emancipation – but is personalised. Now, he goes on,

> **The objects of knowledge seem to be constructed arbitrarily, thrown together in a manner of collage, montage and pastiche. . . . The old centres barely hold, and the old metanarratives no longer resonate with actuality and promise, coming to look incredible from late twentieth-century sceptical perspectives. . . . Post-modernism is the general expression of those circumstances.** (Jenkins, 1991, pp. 59–63)

So what insight can we gain from this about the postmodern critique? It seems, crucially, that it denies the following:

1. The view that our knowledge of society over time was cumulative and broadly progressive in character. Such knowledge was in fact built upon certain grand narratives which were highly selective.
2. The premise that we can attain rational knowledge of society.
3. That such knowledge is universal and hence objective.
4. That enlightened knowledge is both different from, and superior to distorted forms of thought such as ideology, religion, common sense, prejudice and superstition.
5. That such knowledge leads to the mental liberation and betterment of humanity.

The challenge to the status of knowledge has been the most important. Because of the emphasis on the objective and scientific basis of knowledge, Enlightenment thinkers believed that it was possible to attain the truth. Historical and social truth, however, was also predicated on the recognition of certain grand or overarching narratives about the development of society, that is, stories of how and why societies rose and fell over time. Thus, for example, European society took the form it did because it was the logical culmination of inevitable processes of historical development.

Critics such as Jean François Lyotard, philosopher and literary theorist and the historian Hayden White, in contrast, argued that historical and social knowledge, even personal knowledge – how we can know ourselves – derives from narratives which, far from being grand, were often an awkward mix of political ideas, moral attitudes, myths and religious sentiment. Modern Britain, for example, was not the child of Enlightenment rationality, but retained a contradictory mix of the modern and the ancient. Just think for a moment of how the present-day Monarchy operates and is seen. The legacy of the Enlightenment, therefore, is deeply suspect for all universal narratives are tainted. Instead, we have to recognise the contingent nature of historical knowledge.

To take a few examples. The West has tended to believe that the drive to industrial and commercial growth was a precondition for human well-being and civilisation. Of course, these processes have led to the improvement of conditions for large numbers of people, but the costs to others have been immense. And here we are talking, it could be argued, not only about the exploitation of large sections of the population, and not merely about the division that created the third world, but also those cataclysmic events such as the Holocaust and the dropping of atomic bombs on civilian populations.

So let us pause at this moment to consider how one of the most influential postmodern historians approached the Holocaust. Hayden White has in his various writings addressed the matter of narrative. He argued persuasively that narrative – basically, the ways in which we tell stories about the past – reflects something deep within human culture. So pervasive is it as a device to endow experience with meaning, and so accepted and understood across cultures, we can think of narrative as a universal language. While some historical forms such as annals and chronicles cannot be considered narratives, most historical accounts rely on an ability to actually tell a story. Stories about events do not tell themselves and so stories are imposed by historians – such as that of the First World War – but which do not imply that the event itself did not happen. Because of their very universality, however, there is a danger of simply taking narratives for granted – as seeing them as neutral conveyors of meaning. White rejected this, and argued that we have to understand how the operation of imaginative narrative fictions such as the epic, the folk tale, myth, romance, farce, tragedy and so on truthfully represents the past.

Of all the narrative genres that are available to historians, humour seems to be singularly inappropriate as an approach to describing the Holocaust. It would be difficult, for example, to apply the comic or pastoral modes to the task since it would be impossible to reconcile them with the factual record. If, however, they are used metaphorically then they may have validity. White mentions Art Spiegelman's *Maus: A Survivor's Tale*, published in 1986, which uses the medium of the comic book, and in true Orwellian fashion depicts Germans as cats, Jews as mice, and Poles as pigs. Not, one might think, the most appropriate means of representing the Holocaust, but for White Spiegelman's satire is one of the most moving narrative accounts. In the same way, some may recall the initial bewilderment which greeted Roberto Benigni's award winning *Life is Beautiful* (1997), a cinematic account of life and death in a concentration camp. What was remarkable about this film was that it used slapstick comedy to convey a sense of profound humanity and resilience. And *Catch 22* (1961), Joseph Heller's masterpiece, will make you laugh out loud as he launches into one of the most devastating critiques of the Second World War ever written.

Given White's arguments that historical writing is shaped profoundly by particular narratives that we have been introduced to since early in our lives, how do we decide on the status of historical knowledge? As far as French postmodern philosopher Lyotard is concerned, this is the job of the philosopher. It is philosophy rather than science which can distinguish between real knowledge and mere narrative. It is philosophy that can inform us of the true story of human progress because it can interrogate all those concepts such as progress, reason, order, civilisation, well-being and freedom that have been the underlying precepts of Enlightenment thought but have too often been simply taken for granted.

We cannot leave postmodernism without discussion of one of its most influential and baffling figures. Michel Foucault (1926–84) was a French philosopher with an abiding interest in systems of thought and how they shape power relations in society. He may have resisted the idea that he was within the pantheon of poststructuralists, but retrospectively he has been seen as such. His rejection of fashionable theories of existentialism in the 1960s, suspicion of the implied certainties of western rationalism, and a commitment to reveal the hidden structures of knowledge meant that he shared many of their concerns. Although a philosopher, Foucault held firmly to the belief that a study of history was essential to an understanding of how power had been and continued to be exercised. Thus, for example, in works such as *Madness and Civilization: A History of Insanity in the Age of Reason* (1965), *The Archaeology of Knowledge* (1972), *The Birth of the Clinic: An Archaeology of Medical Perception* (1973) and *Discipline and Punish: The Birth of the Prison* (1977), he mapped out how the development of the modern practices of dealing with madness, illness and crime were at the same time deeply implicated in their control, and in the subjugation of those affected.

Foucault's approach to history has, however, been a source of some puzzlement. While engaging critically with Marxism, he abandoned any claim to truth in the scientific histories offered by Marx and von Ranke. More telling was the influence of the *Annales* school, in particular Ferdinand Braudel (1902–1985). Like Braudel, Foucault believed that the task of the historian was not to write a total history that sought to bring the economic, social, political and cultural levels into a unified whole according to a grand scheme, but rather to point to the divergences, incongruities, discontinuities and unevenesses which operate among them as part of the historical process. He was interested in the conditions which engendered the development of particular 'archaeologies' of knowledge which came to possess significance. Take, for example, the case of madness. In the medieval period, madness was first identified as a human vice, but it was not outside reason, rather it was part of everyone's imagination. In this sense, madness and reason existed in a state of free exchange. With the 'Age of Reason' beginning in the middle of the seventeenth century, the mad were defined as such by medical discourse, and subjected to confinement in asylums. Madness was thus banished from the public gaze and thereby silenced. *Madness and Civilization* is thus a study of why this epistemological break in approaches to madness and reason took place at that moment, and what is effects were on the relationships between the state and its citizens.

These relationships went to the heart of Foucault's attempts to understand the modern state. In *Birth of the Clinic* he demonstrated that from the very beginning it sought to control and administer not only madness but the health of the nation. The clinic therefore arose out of a need systematically to observe and record people's health, and assigned the task to the enclosed profession of medicine. This surveillance of, and intervention in, the social domain by state agencies was for Foucault a much more fundamental characteristic of modern societies than their economic forms.

By abandoning familiar historical narratives, the field of postmodernism has thus opened up the possibility of multiple narratives of seeming equal validity and worth. Professional histories now vie with popular histories, black histories, women's histories, regional histories, television histories and the historical novel (which we shall discuss in Chapter 13) in providing interpretations of the past. Has postmodernism gone too far? Well, the achievements have been real, particularly in identifying the constructed rather than given nature of historical knowledge. But there is a sense in some circles that it has led to a free-for-all, a relativism in which all forms of historical knowledge are considered legitimate and of equal worth. It is wise under these circumstances to remind ourselves of some of the achievements of the Enlightenment, and perhaps so guard against the chance that in rejecting its fundamental premises we are throwing out the proverbial baby with the equally proverbial bath water.

It is from the work of the German cultural historian Jürgen Habermas that we have seen the stoutest defence of the Enlightenment in recent years. Habermas (1972) shared many of the concerns of postmodern thinkers. He admitted that the Enlightenment project was only ever an ideal because from the start there was never one source of Enlightenment knowledge. Nor did he have any faith in the future of an Enlightenment project – the brutalities of the twentieth century have shattered this bland optimism. On the other hand, we have to recognise the real gains, few of which are really appreciated by postmodern thinkers. The Enlightenment in its various guises was a massive advance of knowledge when seen in the light of the superstition, bigotry and religious orthodoxy of the pre-Enlightenment era. To abandon it completely leads not to the liberation of thought but to retrenchment and disillusionment because of an abandonment in the hope of progress. The search for some degree of universality (truth) is a viable one not least because it remains wedded to the hope that it might promote justice, egalitarianism, rationality and even happiness. And we can hold onto this without falling prey to naïve expectations. In any case, the alternative is despair arising out of nihilism. Many historians today, whilst welcoming the questioning of metanarratives launched by postmodernism, reject the idea that different forms of knowledge have equal status, and instead cling onto objective notions such as justice and historical truth as preconditions for a more equal, fair and just world, a world where, for one thing, the chains of imperialism have worked loose. It is to the loosening of these imperial chains that we now turn.

Section 3

Postcolonialism and the West

Edward Said (1935–2003) was a Palestinian, raised within a comfortable middle-class family in Egypt. He probably could have been a concert pianist (he was co-founder with Daniel Barenboim of the West-Eastern Divan Orchestra, which brings together musicians from Israel and the Arab world) but migrated to the States to take up a position teaching literary studies at Columbia University. In 1978 he published *Orientalism*, which retrospectively came to be seen as one of the founding texts of postcolonialism. Subtitled *Western Conceptions of the Orient*, the book attempted to demonstrate that from the time of Napoleon's invasion of Egypt in the early nineteenth century, a project was launched by European powers to represent the East as possessing a primitive, exotic, despotic and irrational culture as evidenced, for example, in the salacious potentate presiding over his harem. The extent of this enterprise simultaneously helped to valorise the West as being everything that the East was not, and in a very real way the West continues to live with this legacy, as the rhetoric, language and ideology used to think about the East today have powerful continuities with Orientalism. This powerful thesis, as we are about to discover, had a major impact on postcolonialism more generally.

Postcolonialism as a body of work explores the crucial issue of the relationship between the Enlightenment project and the West. For all the claims to reason, civilisation and progress, writers claim, the Enlightenment was the inner conscience and underlying rationale not only of western industrial capitalism, but also of western imperialism. And here the synchronicity between the emergence of postmodernism and postcolonialism is evident, for it was precisely in the immediate aftermath of the Second World War that European imperialism entered into terminal decline as their colonies waged determined struggles against foreign rule, eventually securing independence. During this period many nationalist leaders and intellectuals understandably raised fundamental questions about the 'natural' superiority of European powers, the centredness of western identity, the legitimacy of imperial rule, and the narratives which have justified foreign rule – questions which reach to the very core of postcolonial concerns.

Influential though Said was, he has not been without his critics. Some like the postcolonial theorists Homi Bhabha and Robert Young have argued that Said extrapolated from a limited historical experience, that is, Egypt and India in the nineteenth century, to erect an edifice of Orientalism which is too monolithic and homogeneous – like a giant machine manufacturing images according to a blueprint. In practice Orientalism has a complexity and nuance depending upon discrete historical experiences and regions; indeed it is from this versatility that it derives its continued authority. There may be parallels between, say, representations of India and Egypt, but over time there were crucial differences – for example, in the ways religion was viewed – which informed contrasts in the nature of British interventions. And these cannot necessarily be applied to, say, China and the Arab world. Related to this is the thorny issue of just how powerful this machine was. Was it actually the case that those subjected to Orientalist stereotyping supinely accepted the images manufactured by the West? Well, given the record of anti-colonial struggles this was clearly not the case for these struggles were often waged precisely over issues of who had the right to determine the culture, identity and history of indigenous peoples.

At first sight there appears little in common between postmodernism and postcolonialism. Both have their distinct range of concerns pursued by particular protagonists such as Said. And yet there are affinities arising from a shared concern to problematise the role of the West in world history. Postmodernism questions those grand narratives, explaining the rise of the West by showing the contingent nature of Enlightenment thought upon which its advance was based. In a related way, postcolonialism exposes ways in which Europe's colonial past was underpinned by the uncritical acceptance of ideas of natural superiority and modernity that masked the brutality and exploitation of its rise to imperial pre-eminence.

According to the narrative that has the West marching triumphantly to a position of world power, it also has its advanced and sophisticated civilisation paying testimony to its ascent.

Only the West had the education, skills and authority (both moral and divine) to embark on this task, and did it out of a sense of duty, even altruism, since by taking control of the destinies of 'primitive' peoples it was offering them the opportunity to step into the modern world. Only with the humanist vision of Arnold Toynbee, who we discuss briefly in the next chapter, did historians first become conscious of the extent to which such narratives were a product of views on the supremacy of the West. We know now how flimsy this 'Eurocentrism' is and how this has changed the ways we think about the past.

And yet for those able to read the signs, this critical consciousness was integral to the Enlightenment project itself. Enlightenment thinkers were fascinated by the non-European world, and saw therein lessons about, say, administration and government, that could usefully be learnt by the West. Many were therefore highly critical of European imperial endeavour (Muthu, 2003). They reject imperialism as immoral and unworkable. Jeremy Bentham, Condorcet, Diderot, Herder, Kant and Adam Smith all attacked what they saw as the injustices of European imperialism on the grounds that it was a corrupt and despotic enterprise, that it conflicted with notions of self-determination, and that it stood in the way of free trade. For the most part, however, and in sharp contrast to its assault on slavery, this critique failed to take root in the broader political culture. Smith's strictures on the monopoly privileges of the East India Company, for example, may have hastened the end of its monopoly trading rights to the East, but the Company continued to operate as an imperial power.

While it is the case that postcolonialism as a body of work emerged in the period when colonialism was ending its lineages, it can be traced back rather earlier. The postcolonial moment as generally understood thus actually refers to a distinct experience centred on the loss of the French and British empires. And yet we can point to other 'postcolonial' moments which might well need to be considered. The loss, for example, of the Iberian empire in Latin America in the early nineteenth century, or even the British loss of the thirteen colonies of North America in the late eighteenth century. Here there is a sense in which colonialism has always provoked postcolonial struggle and that if we examine the history of struggle against European rule we can detect important continuities in the way people have struggled against foreign oppression. In this way, ideas from the Enlightenment shaped the ideals of the American Revolution, and underscored the long struggle for Indian independence. For our purpose, however, we intend to follow convention and focus on the important concerns raised principally by intellectuals of the Third World after the Second World War.

At the heart of postcolonialism is a deep commitment to challenge western historiography, which is seen to be complicit in the European colonial experience. This historiography, it is claimed, is a triumphalist narrative of western dynamism in which the role of colonised subjects in making their own history is neglected or deliberately understated. For example, India gained independence because of the generosity of the British rather than through nationalist struggles waged by Indians themselves. Such accounts tend to emphasise the benefits of colonial endeavour – bringing backward indigenous peoples into the modern, civilised world – while dismissing resistance to foreign rule as atavistic treachery and barbarity. Postcolonial theorists have interrogated every detail of such narratives. They have exposed the changing ideological underpinnings of imperial rule, the complex motives of imperial administrators and agents, the quotidian nature of imperial rule in practice, and the diverse and imaginative ways in which indigenous peoples responded to and resisted that rule. The project has attracted a wide range of scholars from disciplines including history, literature, cultural studies, politics, philosophy, psychoanalysis, law and science, some of whom fit a little uncomfortably within the general rubric. Of these, Edward Said (as we have seen), Homi Bhabha, Gayatri Spivak, and the Subaltern Studies Collective, are among the most important in theorising the nature of postcolonialism and through detailed work with the archives in recovering the role of indigenous populations in resisting British rule.

It is this particular aspect of postcolonial studies that has been most vigorously taken up by the Subaltern Studies Collective. Formed in the early 1980s, largely under the inspiration of Ranajit Guha and Partha Chatterjee, Subaltern Studies became best known through a series of edited collections. In the first of these published in 1982, Guha laid out what was effectively a manifesto for rethinking the historiography of India under colonial rule, in particular its conscious neglect of the role of subaltern groups in anti-colonial struggles. The historiography of Indian nationalism, argued Guha, has been dominated by a concern to record the activities of colonial and bourgeois nationalist elites, with the result that the making of the Indian nation and nationalism are seen as elite achievements, many of which were driven by expectations of rewards of high office. These perspectives have their merits in helping us to understand processes of collaboration and contestation between colonial and indigenous elites such as Nehru, Gandhi and the Brahmans who dominated the Indian National Congress, but they are fatally flawed by an inability to interpret the contributions made by the mass of the Indian people independently of elite nationalism. Rather, the involvement of millions in anti-colonial struggle was represented as a diversion from the politics of the state, or worse as a problem of law and order, such as in 1919 when mass mobilisation took place in opposition to the Rowlatt Act, which was designed to repress forms of popular resistance by banning public meetings and allowing incarceration without trial. To redress the balance we need to pay due attention to the politics of the people, namely, those forms of mobilisation which simply cannot be explained by elite accounts. Popular mobilisations were manifest most frequently in peasant uprisings, but included instances when the working people and petty bourgeoisie in urban areas took up the cause of nationalism, such as in the revolt of 1857. Under these circumstances it was apparent that Indian elites were never able to speak for the nation as a whole; there remained vast areas of Indian life which were beyond their influence. Subaltern politics, however, was not powerful enough to organise a struggle for national liberation, nor was it mature enough to assume and complete the mission for independence which elites had failed to bring about. It is this historic failure, Guha concluded, which should constitute the key question to be addressed by the historiography of India under British rule (Guha, 1982, pp. 1–7).

Although lacking a certain cohesion because of the many different approaches (Guha called for a hundred flowers to bloom), the project initially claimed for its intellectual progenitors the humanistic Marxism of the Italian theorist Antonio Gramsci, and the work of the outstanding group of British Marxist historians – Eric Hobsbawm, Christopher Hill and E. P. Thompson – which had influentially captured a history of the people. What followed in the six edited collections were studies of subaltern culture written by members and associates of the Collective. Partha Chatterjee's 'Agrarian relations and communalism in Bengal, 1926–1935', David Arnold's 'Rebellious hillmen: the Gudem-Rampa risings, 1839–1924', Gyan Pandey's 'Peasant revolt and Indian nationalism: the peasant movement in Awadh, 1919–1922' and Gautam Bhadra's 'Four rebels of 1857' give a good idea of their scope and nature. Here were explorations of a diverse range of tribal groups and peasant communities which engaged in struggles determined by their own sense of priorities and dynamics, and which have to be understood in these terms rather than as the expression of a primitive or undeveloped consciousness.

Subaltern Studies has not been without its critics. Gayatri Spivak in particular, writing as an insider (she was loosely a member of the group), has asked pointedly: 'Can the subaltern speak?' By this, she questioned whether it is possible to get access to subaltern consciousness from acts of insurgency that are recorded only in colonial historiography, particularly when all we can expect from such texts are representations of peasant rebels as criminals or mutineers (Spivak, 1993). Under such circumstances we should recognise not a single 'peasant consciousness' but a variety of intersecting identities derived from the economic, social, sexual, historical and political structures that peasant communities inhabit.

Despite such critiques, and the fact that Subaltern Studies no longer operates as a collective, its legacy is still evident in the body of published work and members who have continued to make important contributions.

In practice

This chapter has sought to develop some of the themes introduced in earlier chapters by looking at how postwar historians have approached unresolved issues about the uncertain status of historical knowledge. As we have seen, conventional historiography had inherited a tradition of inquiry from the nineteenth century. This placed emphasis on the gathering and utilisation of evidence – for the most part documentary – as a means of reporting on the past 'as it actually happened'. Implicit in this approach was the idea that historical truth is accessible to those properly trained in the historians' craft. A minority of historians raised dissenting voices, questioned whether it was ever possible to be objective in interpreting the past, but then the Second World War and its aftermath created a climate in which the very foundations of conventional historiography came under close scrutiny.

The horrors experienced during the war persuaded many theorists that narratives of historical change which had emerged from the Enlightenment had no legitimacy. How, for example, could notions of human progress which had underpinned many historical accounts still be retained when the experience of death camps and nuclear bombing of civilian populations seemed to prove that even the most advanced nations were capable of barbarity? When this critique was combined with a sense that the world order was fast changing, that new forms of organising production and communication had emerged which created a new condition – postmodernity – the critique of grand narratives gathered momentum.

In the meantime, the loss of European empires forced a re-examination of the colonial past. So emerged an influential body of work under the umbrella of what came to be known as postcolonialism. Sharing with postmodernity the same suspicion of narratives such as progress, emancipation and liberalisation, postcolonial historians challenged conventional interpretations of imperial rule, and brought into sharper focus the role of popular struggles for independence.

Much of the work of postmodern and postcolonial historians has operated at a high level of abstraction, tilting the balance away from evidence to theoretical inquiry, and creating works which are often not that readily accessible. At the extremes this has had some unfortunate consequences in promoting the idea that history is a text, that is, something that goes on in the head of the historian, or in arguing for a free-for-all in which varieties of narratives flourish, none of which has privilege over others. So while postmodernism and postcolonialism have been of real benefit in exposing the underpinnings of historical interpretation, the solutions they offer have not always been helpful. What is clear is that the debate continues, and will do so for many years to come.

Summary

The three sections of this chapter have said three things:

- The Second World War and its aftermath had a profound impact on the nature of historical thinking. Seen either as the end of the Enlightenment project or the supersession of modernity by postmodernity, what was apparent to contemporary observers was that they had entered into a new historical era, the analysis of which was not necessarily amenable to the tools of conventional analysis. The formal demise of the Enlightenment project was brought about by a loss of confidence in the idea of progress which had been driven and controlled by western civilisation, while postmodernity heralded novel ways of organising production, using space and creating cultural forms increasingly reliant on visual imagery.

- These changes engendered an acute sense that the past could no longer be understood using grand narratives, whether they be of progress, liberalisation, democratisation or empowerment. All historical frameworks which in various ways were framed by such narratives were therefore treated with growing suspicion because they were seen to impose overarching structures on the historical record in order to provide a sense of order. Postmodern historians have therefore argued consistently for the contingent nature of historical knowledge, and a degree of relativism in history is subject to competing accounts, all of which have legitimacy and value.

- This same period witnessed the closure of European empires. In ways that drew upon postmodern thought, historians of empire began seriously to question narratives of the imperial experience which had promoted the agency of Europeans and any idea of progress and Enlightenment which had been seen to accompany imperial endeavour. Postcolonial historians therefore subjected to detailed scrutiny the record of European imperialism as a means of exposing its exploitative and in many ways regressive nature. In order to redress past neglect, they also embarked on a project to write into the imperial experience those colonised subjects – in particular the urban and rural poor – who had been systematically excluded from dominant accounts.

Discussion document 1

This is an extract from an article by Hayden White in which he sees the problem of thinking about the horror of the Holocaust not as one of reconstruction from the evidence, but of deciding what sorts of stories or narratives we choose to make sense of the 'unthinkable'.

The question that arises with respect to 'historical employments' in a study of Nazism and the Final Solution is this: Are there any limits on the *kind* of story that can responsibly be told about these phenomena? *Can* these events be responsibly emplotted in *any* of the modes, symbols, plot types, and genres our culture provides for 'making sense' of such extreme events in our past? Or do Nazism and the Final Solution belong to a special class of events, such as, unlike even the French Revolution, the American Civil War, the Russian Revolution, or the Chinese Great Leap Forward, they must be viewed as manifesting only one story, as being emplottable in one way only, and as signifying only one kind of meaning? In a word, do the natures of Nazism and the Final Solution set absolute limits on the uses that can be made of them by writers of fiction or poetry? Do they lend themselves to emplotment in a set number of ways, or is their specific meaning, like that of other historical events, infinitely interpretable and ultimately undecidable?

. . . Narratives do not consist only of factual statements (singular existential propositions) and arguments; they consist as well of poetic and rhetorical elements by which what would otherwise be a list of facts is transformed into a story. Among these elements are those generic story patterns we recognize as providing the 'plots'. Thus, one narrative account may represent a set of events as having the form and meaning of an epic or tragic story, and another may represent the same set of events – with equal plausibility and without doing any violence to the factual record – as describing a farce. Here the conflict between 'competing narratives' has less to do with the facts of the matter in question than with the different story-meanings with which the facts can be endowed by emplotment. This raises the question of the relation of the various generic plot types that can be used to endow events with different kinds of meaning – tragic, epic, comic, romance, pastoral, farcical, and the like – to the events themselves. Is this relationship between a given story told about a given set of events the same as that obtaining between a factual statement and its referent? Can it be said that sets of real events *are* intrinsically tragic, comic, or epic, such that the representation of those events as tragic, comic, or epic story can be assessed as to its *factual* accuracy? Or does it all have to do with the perspective from which the events are viewed?

Or course, most theorists of narrative history take the view that emplotment produces not so much another, more comprehensive and synthetic factual statement as, rather, an *interpretation* of the facts. But the distinction between factual statements (considered as a product of object-language) and interpretations of them (considered as a product of one or more metalanguages) does not help us when it is a matter of interpretations produced by the modes of emplotment used to represent the facts as displaying the form and meaning of different kinds stories. We are not helped by the suggestion that 'competing narratives' are a result of 'the facts' having been *interpreted* by one historian as a 'tragedy' and *interpreted* by another as a 'farce'. This is especially the case in traditional historical discourse in which 'the facts' are always given precedence over any 'interpretation' of them.

. . . Considerations such as these provide some insight into the problems both of competing narratives and of unacceptable modes of emplotment in considering a period such as the Nazi epoch and events such as the Final Solution. We can confidently presume that the facts of the matter set limits on the *kinds* of stories that can be *properly* (in the sense of veraciously and appropriately) told about them only if we believe that the events themselves possess a 'story' kind of form and a 'plot' kind of meaning. We may then dismiss a 'comic' or 'pastoral' story, with an upbeat 'tone' and humorous 'points of view', from the ranks of competing narratives as manifestly false to the facts – or at least to the facts that *matter* – of the Nazi era. But we could dismiss such a story from the ranks of competing narratives only if (1) it were presented as a *literal* (rather than *figurative*) representation of the events and (2) the plot type used to transform the facts into a specific kind of story were presented as inherent in (rather than imposed upon) the facts. For unless a historical story is presented as a literal representation of real events, we cannot criticize it as being either true or untrue to the facts of the matter. If it were presented as a figurative representation of real events, then the question of its truthfulness would fall under the principles governing our assessment of the truth of fictions.

Hayden White, 'Historical emplotment and the problem of truth', in S. Friedlander (ed.), *Probing the Limits of Representation* (1992), pp. 37–53.

Discussion document 2

Said outlines the pervasive and all-encompassing nature of Orientalist thought. Asking questions about the mainly French and British models of imperialism, this document reveals how Said saw culture (particularly literature) as constructing western viewpoints of the West and to what extent too the West constructed what it was to be modern by placing the East as the archetype of what it was to be backward.

By Orientalism I mean several things, all of them in my opinion, interdependent. The most readily acceptable designation for Orientalism is an academic one, and indeed the label still serves in a number of academic institutions. Anyone who teaches, writes about, or researches the Orient – and this applies whether the person is an anthropologist, sociologist, historian or philologist – either in its specific or its general aspects, is an Orientalist, and what he or she does is Orientalism. . . .

Related to this academic tradition, whose fortunes, transmigrations, specializations, and transmissions are in part the subject of this study, is a more general meaning for Orientalism. Orientalism is a style of thought based upon an ontological and epistemological distinction made between 'the Orient' and (most of the time) 'the Occident'. Thus a very large mass of writers, among whom are poets, novelists, philosophers, political theorists, economists, and imperial administrators, have accepted the basic distinction between East and West as the starting point for elaborate theories, epics, novels, social descriptions, and political accounts concerning the Orient, its people, customs, 'mind', destiny, and so on. . . .

The interchange between the academic and the more or less imaginative meanings of Orientalism is a constant one, and since the late eighteenth century there has been a considerable, quite disciplined – perhaps even regulated – traffic between the two. Here I come to the third meaning of Orientalism, which is something more historically and materially defined than either of the other two. Taking the late eighteenth century as a very roughly defined starting point Orientalism can be discussed and analyzed as the corporate institution for dealing with the Orient – dealing with it by making statements about it, authorizing views of it, describing it, by teaching it, settling it, ruling over it: in short, Orientalism as a Western style for dominating, restructuring, and having authority over the Orient. . . . My contention is that without examining Orientalism as a discourse one cannot possibly understand the enormously systematic discipline by which European culture was able to manage – even produce – the Orient politically, sociologically, militarily, ideologically, scientifically, and imaginatively during the post-Enlightenment period. Moreover, so authoritative a position did Orientalism have that I believe no one writing, thinking, or acting on the Orient could do so without taking account of the limitations on thought and action imposed by Orientalism. In brief, because of Orientalism the Orient was not (and is not) a free subject of thought or action. This is not to say that Orientalism unilaterally determines what can be said about the Orient, but that it is the whole network of interests inevitably brought to bear on (and therefore always involved in) any occasion when that peculiar entity 'the Orient' is in question. How this happens is what this book tries to demonstrate. It also tries to show that European culture gained in strength and identity by setting itself off against the Orient as a sort of surrogate and even underground self.

▶

> Historically and culturally there is a quantitative as well as a qualitative difference between the Franco-British involvement in the Orient and – until the period of American ascendancy after World War II – the involvement of every other European and Atlantic power. To speak of Orientalism is therefore to speak mainly, although not exclusively, of a British and French cultural enterprise, a project whose dimensions take on such disparate realms as the imagination itself, the whole of India and the Levant, the Biblical texts and the Biblical lands, the spice trade, colonial armies, and a long tradition of colonial administrators, a formidable scholarly corpus, innumerable Oriental 'experts' and 'hands', and Oriental professoriate, a complex array of 'Oriental' ideas (Oriental despotism, Oriental splendour, cruelty, sensuality), many Eastern sects, philosophies, and wisdoms domesticated for local European use.

Edward Said, *Orientalism: Western Conceptions of the Orient* (1991), pp. 2–4.

Discussion document 3

Robert Young, one of the most perceptive analysts of postcolonialism, begins with a discussion of how postmodernism first placed onto the agenda the troubled nature of the relationship between the western and the non-western world. Here the comparison with modernist and progressive histories such as Toynbee's work on civilisations is made with postmodernist discourses about the dissolution of the idea of the West. The shifts Young identifies are entirely consistent with a deepening suspicion of one of the grand narratives that has defined Europe's past, namely, the ascent of the West.

Postmodernism can best be defined as European culture's awareness that it is no longer the unquestioned and dominant centre of the world. Significantly enough one of the very earliest uses of the term 'post-modern', dating from the time of the Second World War, was that of Arnold Toynbee in his *A Study of History*. He used it to describe the new age of Western history which, according to Toynbee, began in the 1870s with the simultaneous globalization of Western culture and the re-empowerment of non-Western states. If this new period brought with it a phase of Spenglerian pessimism after the long years of Victorian optimism, Toynbee did not himself assume that the West was in decline as such, but rather than paradoxically the globalization of Western civilization was being accompanied by a self-consciousness of its own cultural relativization, a process to which Toynbee's own equally totalizing and relativizing history was designed to contribute. Reviewing the genesis of his whole project, he recounts that his history was written against a current of Late Modern Western convention of identifying a parvenu and provincial Western Society's history with 'History', writ large, *sans phrase*. In the writer's view this convention was the preposterous off-spring of a distorting egocentric illusion to which the children of a Western Civilisation had succumbed like the children of all other known civilisations and known primitive societies.

Postmodernism, therefore, becomes a certain self-consciousness about a culture's own historical relativity – which begins to explain why, as its critics complain, it also involves the loss of the sense of an absoluteness of any Western account of History. . . . Postmodernism could be said to mark not just the cultural effects of a new stage of 'late' capitalism, but the sense of the loss of European history and culture as History and Culture, the loss of their unquestioned place at the centre of the world. We could say that if, according to Foucault, the centrality of 'Man' dissolved at the end of the eighteenth century as the 'Classical Order' gave way to 'History', today at the end of the twentieth century, as 'History' gives way to the 'Postmodern' we are witnessing the dissolution of 'the West'.

Robert Young, *White Mythologies: Writing History and the West* (1990), p.

Further reading

Homi Bhabha, *The Location of Culture* (1994).
An influential collection of pieces by one of the leading postcolonial thinkers in which he reflects upon the colonial experience. Not for the faint-hearted because it is imbued with difficult theorising.

Vinayak Chaturvedi (ed.), *Mapping Subaltern Studies and the Postcolonial* (2000).
A collection of recent articles which have debated the approaches of Subaltern Studies. Scholarly and provocative, but not easy going.

Peter Childs and Patrick Williams, *An Introduction to Post-Colonial Theory* (1997).
Accessible and knowledgeable, this is probably the best introduction to the topic.

David Harvey, *The Condition of Postmodernity* (1989).
Written by a geographer, this is one of the most insightful analyses of modernity and postmodernity. Harvey successfully takes from postmodernism what he considers useful, but at the same times clings to the radical potential of a more orthodox Marxist historiography.

Keith Jenkins (ed.)., *The Postmodern History Reader* (1997).
The best single collection of articles written by a wide range of interested parties on the question of postmodernism. Some of the most critical perspectives are included; tough at times, but the material is valuable.

Edward Said, *Orientalism: Western Conceptions of the Orient* (1991).
Although flawed, this remains one of the few examples of a book which has founded a new discipline. Surprisingly accessible, always engaging.

Robert Young, *Postcolonialism: An Historical Introduction* (2001).
The definitive study of how postcolonial theory emerged from anticolonial struggles around the world. It is almost a history of the world written around narratives of resistance.

Part 3

HISTORIES

6 Ideas of history: from the ancients to the Christians

1 Herodotus and gold-digging ants
2 Thucydides and reason: an historian for our times?
3 What did the Romans ever do for history?
4 Late antiquity, Christianity and the End of Days

Introduction

This chapter takes us across centuries, explaining the developments in historical writing from the time of the ancient Greeks to late-antiquity or the 'late-antique' period. This timeline covers the decline of the Roman Empire to the rise of Christianity. The opening section, therefore, examines the emergence of historical writing in ancient Greece, and the contributions of Herodotus and Thucydides. A distinction is made between mythical writing about the past (such as *The Iliad* and *The Odyssey*) and the ethnographical histories of Herodotus and the more systematic work of Thucydides. The next section covers the development of historical writing in the Hellenic and Roman periods. Roman historians are seen to be in many ways much less ambitious in approach and scope than the Greeks that they had succeeded. Finally, we explore the differences in approaches to historical theory, method and practice introduced by Christianity in Europe. This shift in power and influence leads directly to histories that not only seek to understand the past in the present but also to suggest a millennial concern with the future. In this narrow sense, these early interventions from Christian historians set up a latter predominance of history writing that (unlike say Thucydides) is concerned with prophecy and portents.

Section 1

Herodotus and gold-digging ants

Why study ancient history and ancient historians? Surely, our approaches and methods of history in the modern period are far superior to the histories that were written in the centuries either side of the Common Era (CE). (BCE and CE are secular terms that indicate the period before or after the birth of Jesus Christ.) And being superior in sophistication, methodology, scope and erudition we can say more about the ancients than they could possibly say about themselves. Perhaps this is broadly true. Perhaps, however, these historians should be studied for two reasons which make them an invaluable resource to historians today. The first is that our political systems, science, medicine, philosophy and political ideas, architecture and built environment would not exist in their current forms if it were not for the influence of the Greeks and Romans. Second, western morals and ethics, our sense that history has a forward trajectory, the impetus to live under a rule of law and to maintain the rights of the human being, are all shaped by the astonishing influence of that other product of the ancient world: Judeo-Christianity.

Every Victorian or Edwardian with or without a 'classical' education could quote at least some of the classics and the scriptures, or else lived unconsciously with their influences. Alfred Williams, for example, a railway worker who taught himself Greek, recalled in his biography *Life in a Railway Factory* (1915) that the graffiti on the walls of the Great Western Railway's Swindon works was in Latin. The classics and the Bible were with us in profound detail until only very recently and so historians neglect them at their peril.

The word 'history' meaning investigation or inquiry comes from the Greek. It is at the moment in the second half of the nineteenth century, according to the philosopher and historian R. G. Collingwood (1889–1943) in his *Idea of History* (1994), that history became scientific, that is, was no longer simply recounting something that was already known to an audience but was based on original research using the tools of intellectual inquiry. This history was humanistic in that it put 'Man' at the centre of its concerns, rational in that it applied enquiring questions to evidence and derived conclusions accordingly, and was 'self-revelatory' in that it defined 'Man' through past actions. So what, by these criteria, are we to make of the Greek Herodotus who first applied the title 'Histories' to a work solely dedicated to verifiable events that occurred in the past?

Before looking at him, we need to go back to the earliest Greek stories to seek out the origins of historical writing. Collingwood saw them as lacking the standards of history because they were theocratic or mythical – theocratic in that they dealt with gods or supernatural rulers of human societies, mythical in that they were predominately located outside human events (such as the Creation story or the story of the Flood) in some dateless time in the past.

The most renowned of these early stories were of course *The Iliad* and *The Odyssey*, written by Homer in the eighth century BCE. *The Iliad* recounted the adventures and tribulations of the hero Achilles against the backdrop of the Trojan Wars between the Athenians and the Persians around 1200 BCE, while *The Odyssey* told of the adventures of the hero Odysseus on his journey home from the war. Given that they recount stories of a war which actually took place, why then do we not assume that they constitute history? The stories unfold in a mythological time rather than the continuous time of human societies. The events, the death of Achilles with his vulnerable heel, or Odysseus's encounter with the one-eyed Cyclops, all happen in an order but there was no clear conception of chronology that related to the rest of the world. The timeframe of the myth pertains only to the myth itself; events were not set against the real world of real people. This is because Homer's aim was not to explain how things became as they are but to elucidate moral lessons from a tale set in the time of gods and heroes. This is a time in which events are moved solely by the passions of heroes and the caprice of the gods: we presume that this was the only kind of causal explanation for change that his society required.

This would not remain so. Between the time of Homer in the eighth century and that of Herodotus in the fifth century BCE, Greek writers began to develop what Collingwood has identified as three elements of a scientific history:

- Understanding the ways and means of signifying the passage of time in relation to human events.
- Finding ways of relating the passage of time in one society to that in another society.
- Developing ways of periodising time that allows eras and epochs to be described.

The first advance comes with the poet Hesiod (of whom very little is known, save that he seems to have been from farming stock) who in his book *Theogony*, written sometime during the 700s BCE, accounted for the creation of the universe out of a primal chaos and then the establishment of the pantheon of Greek gods, sired by Zeus, father of the gods. But then Hesiod gave some account for a sort of societal human past after this period of the gods that offered a rudimentary explanation for why things were. He divided human history into five successive periods, ages, or, as he puts it, 'races' of men. In many ways these 'periods' were not unlike those discussed in Chapter 2 and at any rate were just as valid when we discuss the ancient world as the periodisation that was to come much later:

- A period of rebellion against the gods, characterised by war and cruelty, known as the Silver Age.
- An age when people had amazing physical strength and vitality which ended through incessant warfare, known as the Bronze Age.
- A time filled with heroes when men were half gods, a state destroyed through wars. The Trojan War described by Homer was one such state.
- A contemporary period characterised by suffering, sickness, misery and meanness.

More sophisticated notions of historical time followed. Hecataeus of Miletus (550–*c*.490 BCE) had already produced works of geography that attempted to demarcate the world in spatial terms (Plate 2). In a work known to us as *Genealogies*, he attempted to bridge the centuries between his time and the time of gods and heroes by describing the successive generations of people, tracking a human history back to the mythical age. He even identified himself as a descendant of a god. This chronological method was augmented later in the fifth century by Hellanicus of Lesbos (terminal dates unsure), whose *Attic History* marked the passage of history by compiling lists of state officials and priests recorded by cities and temples.

If Homer had produced myths of gods and heroes because his age needed explanations about origins and the like but was unprepared for a more 'scientific' or systematic approach, what changes had taken place in Greek society which required a new way of thinking about the past? Between *c.*800 and *c.*500 BCE the Greek world altered dramatically. The *polis* emerged: the city-state, governing itself and a rural hinterland, became the characteristic political unit over the area. Cities like Athens and Sparta provided the context for energetic social, economic and political development. Greek traders, adventurers and colonists spread across the Mediterranean world, bringing Greeks into contact with a wide range of non-Greeks, or, to use their term, 'barbarians' (a word that merely meant 'non-Greek speaker' and does not have the pejorative element that it has today). This awareness of others sharpened their own sense of their identity as Greeks, not just as citizens of their particular city-state but as part of a Hellenic, Greek-speaking world. Their awareness of these differences, often coupled with a sense of their own cultural superiority, fed into their art, poetry and, most critically for our purposes, philosophy, thereby encouraging a more critical awareness of historical change.

The reputation of Herodotus (*c.*484–*c.*430 BCE) has varied greatly over the years, but he richly deserved the title first given to him by Marcus Tallius Cicero (106–46 BCE) of 'the Father of History'. In his great work, known simply as *The Histories*, we can find accounts of gold-digging ants bigger then foxes, Indian men who secrete black semen, men with goats' feet and others who can swim ten miles under water, and armies that drink rivers dry and whose soldiers are carried over the sea on the backs of dolphins. All this seems credulous to us but Herodotus' approach to the past was original. Unlike other Greek historians, he was not interested in chronicling local stories and mythologies preserved by the official interpreters of religious orthodoxy, but rather attempted to understand folklores, cultures and mythologies in an historical context as part of a vision of the past which embraced geography, natural history and ethnography.

Herodotus clearly identified a coherent framework within which to describe the relationship between the many events and developments that he described. The affairs of the Lydians under King Croesus, the Persians, the Egyptians and the Greeks were understood in chronological terms, although there was no overall cohesion yet that related the events in each of these societies to each other within a general chronological historical framework. Where societies do come into direct contact, as in the case of the battles between the Persians and Greeks, the historical relationship was clear but otherwise it seemed the result of an *ad hoc* improvisation. However, Herodotus wished to understand histories across a wider geographical landscape and to record the cultural differences of people that occupied these strange and faraway lands, thus providing a range and type of record much broader than anything attempted by earlier writers.

We know little about the life of Herodotus. We do know that he was born around 490 BCE in Halicarnassus, on the north-west coast of Asia Minor. He is said to have given public readings of his work and been friends with the playwright Sophocles. He is also said to have taken part in the founding of the colony of Thurii in Italy in 443 BCE. What set him apart as an historian, however, are his travels throughout the Mediterranean world, including Egypt, Africa, areas around the Black Sea and throughout many Greek city-states. We can imagine the physical and emotional effort and brute hardship that Herodotus must have endured to research *The Histories*. Having won his way across the vastness of the landscape he did not merely tell of the deeds and conquests of the people he found but also of their habits, customs and folklores. Among ancient historians, this level of curiosity is extraordinary. Herodotus had endurance and ingenuity too. Finding his way across the Mediterranean to the mouth of the Nile he not only recounted the glory of the Pharaohs, but also related the natural history of their remarkable river. He stood on the high ground and was amazed by the great flood of the Nile, each year rising, at first gradually and then growing into a succession of torrents one eddying into another as dried up wadis became lakes and then rivers in their own right. Simultaneously a catastrophe and a miracle, the floodwaters had for millennia inundated the landscape, drowning all in its path, but had also left in its wake layer upon layer of fertile silt. Out of this soil grew the origins of a civilisation, already ancient by the time that Herodotus witnessed it. This amazed him and the Greeks and all other societies with an awareness of it. Among other things it was this determination to locate these origins that makes him so important to us. But also his determination to measure his surroundings (taking a tape measure to the pyramids) or as a pioneer in some respects of oral history, to take account of folklore or local mythologies and regarding them as popular evidence to be recorded and examined.

While there is a debate about the real extent of his travels, most historians now agree that Herodotus stood at the edge of his known world and looked beyond. He reported the world of the Scythians and their neighbours the Cimmerians: about the people of whom he could gain information from local sources such as the 'bald men' who lived beyond the Black Sea of whom the Scythians spoke. He not only ventured among the Scythians, he left us detailed accounts of the nature of their society. The Scythians were an ancient nomadic people, living to the north and east of the Black Sea from the third to sixth centuries BCE. As a nomadic culture their society was based on an unstable, powerful and belligerent clan system. Our only knowledge of them comes from Herodotus and subsequent archaeological evidence. He also wrote about people of whom much less information is available, most notably the Hyperboreans. His account of the magical Hyperboreans was one of a number of instances where Herodotus displays a taste for the fantastic. The Hyperboreans were a mythical and magical people mentioned earlier in a mythological context by Homer and Hesiod. According to Herodotus they lived in an ideal society at the edge of the known world to the north of the Greeks. Critics have insisted that he was prepared to accept hearsay and mythology as historical evidence, yet in the case of the Hyperboreans he makes it explicitly clear that he could gather no direct evidence about them and cites only mythological sources. That he was explicit and transparent in this omission ought to persuade us that he considered his own role as an historian and was aware of the need to deploy evidence in a way that was both convincing and plausible. Often when he reported things that might be far-fetched, it was with the caveat that he has been told this and leaves the judgement as to its veracity to the reader. He used indirect speech ('they say') as a device to distance himself from the flimsiness of the evidence to hand, and sometimes offered alternative explanations to those passed on to him:

> **About the feathers which the Scythians say fill the air, and make it impossible to traverse, or even to see, the more northerly parts of the continent – I think myself that it must be always**

snowing in these northerly regions, though less, probably, in summer than in winter. Anyone who has seen heavy snow at close quarters will know what I mean – it is very like feathers; and it is because of the severity of these northern winters that the country is uninhabited. No doubt the Scythians and their neighbours when they talk of the feathers really mean snow – because of the likeness between the two. I have now related the utmost which can be gathered from the report. (Herodotus, 2003, p. 250)

He did not seek then to speculate beyond the limits of the evidence at hand. He did occasionally cite the will of the gods as causal factors in history: more than his successors but much less frequently and with less force than earlier mythologists such as Homer.

We might consider Herodotus less as the 'Father of History' and more as the founding spirit of cultural history. Certainly, he instinctively realised that human beings are 'culture-bound' and act 'in accordance with their traditions and upbringing'. He also, by the way that he reported his travels, believed that histories that come from a particular culture should be considered on their relative merits. And yet it is impossible fully to appreciate the contribution of Herodotus without consideration of the mutual influence which existed with Thucydides, his contemporary, and the other great Greek historian of the age.

Section 2

Thucydides and reason: an historian for our times?

The writings of Thucydides (460–*c*.400 BCE) lacked the diversity and (at least to the present writers) the sheer excitement of Herodotus. Fact-gathering, awareness of change and continuity, causation of factors, thesis, synthesis, summary and conclusion – these are all words associated with Thucydides. Not that Thucydides was entirely stone-cold rational in his approach to history. He was reported to have once witnessed a reading by Herodotus and to have left in tears. Despite this outburst of emotion he has tended to be more attractive than Herodotus to historians in the modern period – historians who prefer their histories without seasoning or spice, wrapped in more insipid flavours of profession-based methodologies. But he also favoured history as performance – both the Greeks and Romans read aloud regardless of whether they were in private or public, alone or in a group – and perhaps this emphasis on performance has also attracted the more thespian-inclined lecturer. It almost certainly influenced later historians such as Gibbon who chronicled the fall of Rome (as we saw in Chapter 3). Certainly, Thucydides for all his reasoned approach to the discipline can be quoted with gusto.

This approach was nurtured by Thucydides' attachment to the Sophistic movement. Sophists were practitioners of rhetoric, argument and debate, and confident in the mental powers of humanity and the effectiveness of the force of persuasion. Every dispute, for instance, was thought to have two viewpoints. This would extend, presumably, to disputes over historical interpretation and this, the argument might run, formed the basis of his historical methodology. Second, he was also attached to the then growing 'science' of medicine, which involved the close observation of symptoms, diagnosis, prognosis, conditions of environment and so on. Thus for Thucydides, truth was a goal of history. While absolute truth was unobtainable and approximate, historical truth could be observed and effectively conveyed. For these reasons, historians today tend to describe the work of Thucydides as 'full', 'perceptive', 'neutral', 'austere' and 'objective'. Herodotus, by comparison, hardly cuts the rational mustard.

Who was Thucydides? Like Herodotus, little is known of his life. He is thought to have been born around 460 BCE to a well-off and aristocratic Greek family. As a general in the Athenian army he was well-placed to write about warfare and political intrigue, and this formed the basis of his great work *The Peloponessian War*. He was out of favour, however, when in 423 he was exiled from Athens as a punishment for losing the strategically important Amphipolis to the Spartans. He died in mysterious circumstances around 400 and many sources suggest that he was murdered. His unfinished *Peloponnesian War* was continued by Xenophon (444–357 BCE) but in a radically different style.

While Thucydides was remembered for his rational approach, especially during the Renaissance (Chapter 7), he was not above piling on the 'literary artistry'. His use of rhetoric in his accounts of political speeches, of the oratory of generals to their soldiers before battles, his coverage of historic debates, and most famously his reproduction of Pericles' Funeral Oration added up to more than minimalist reportage. This use of the speech as a device was explained by Thucydides in the following terms:

> **As to the speeches of the participants, either when they were about to enter the war or after they were already in it, it has been difficult for me and for those who reported to me to remember exactly what was said. I have, therefore, written what I thought the speakers needed to say given the situations they were in, while keeping as close as possible to the gist of what was actually said. As to the events of the war, I have not written them down as I heard them from just anybody, nor as I thought they must have occurred, but have consistently described what I myself have or have been able to learn from others after going over each event in as much detail as possible. I have found this task to be extremely arduous, since those who were present at these actions gave varying reports on the same events, depending on their sympathies and their memories.** (Thucydides, 1998, p. 11)

This was sophisticated stuff. Here we find Thucydides displaying an advanced and acute awareness of the nature of evidence, the vagaries of memory (both that of his witnesses and of his own as an historian), reliability of witnesses, and the need for the historian to make a judgement about such evidence given that it depended upon the 'sympathies and memories' of the reporters. On the other hand, Thucydides took licence with evidence, reporting what the speakers 'needed to say', but he was quite open about his processes and keeps to the 'gist' of the *actualité*.

This sophistication also explains, perhaps, why he has been preferred to Herodotus by historians writing in the last century or so. Thucydides ignored the supernatural, preferring to focus on the earthbound forces of politics. He squeezed the moment for all its dramatic juices but it was still rooted in the notion of historical phenomena as rational and explicable by the human senses. There was not a 'gold-digging ant' in sight and none of his historical players was goat-footed or performed monumental feats of supernatural strength or

Table 6.1 The role of the gods in Greek historiography

Homer History of the gods central in the affairs of mortals (8th century BCE)

Hecataetus Brought the gods down to earth but they remain omnipresent (6th/5th century BCE)

Herodotus The gods begin to retreat from historical life (5th century BCE)

Thucydides The gods tend not to interfere with human events (5th century BCE)

Xenophon Loyalty to the gods is rewarded. Xenophon completed the work of Thucydides (4th century BCE)

Polybius Emphasis placed on evidence-led history with an absence of the gods as a way of explaining historical phenomena (3rd/2nd century BCE)

endurance. At the same time, there were no causal links made between human and natural disasters, man-made war and earthquakes, drought, famines or eclipses – rarely, if at all, are these phenomena raised as a portent of things to come, or seen as a direct consequence or as punishment for human folly.

Most important, the role of supernatural forces was relegated to the mythical. Table 6.1 charts the gradual decline of theology and mythology in Greek historiography. In classical times, gods waged wars of favour, taking the side of this people or that particular City in question. Humans were often at the mercy of gods who ran the affairs of mortals at a collective whim. By the time we get to Thucydides, however, the gods had been more or less expelled from human affairs. Indeed some have suggested that the originality of Thucydides lies in the very fact that he attempts to gather all human action within the realm of what is humanly possible. In this respect, he has been regarded as the first modern, objective, rational historian who has little time for myths, oracles or for gods as prime movers in history.

What then is the final balance sheet when comparing the contributions of Herodotus and Thucydides? Since wars involving Greek states provided the basic theme of the histories of both of them it might well be instructive to consider their different approaches. For Herodotus the war between the Persians and the Greeks provided a starting point and explaining its causes was his main concern. He also provided an explanation for 'why these people fought each other'. The fault, somewhat predictably given that Herodotus was a Greek, lay largely with the Persians who were regarded as mischievous courtiers advising King Xerxes (485–465 BCE) to make war against the Greeks. Xerxes' own sense of responsibility for the existing empire fed his appetite for imperial expansion and naked greed for Greek wealth. The histories of neither Herodotus nor Thucydides could provide lessons for generations yet to be born – not that the idea of history providing lessons for the future occurred to them. Taken together Herodotus and Thucydides had much in common. Both historians were deeply concerned with war and posterity; both have been remembered for the quality, depth and breadth of their histories, although Thucydides always pressed his worth over Herodotus; both contributed hugely to the establishment of history as a genre over say rhetoric or other literary approaches; and both had the good fortune that their manuscripts survive to be appreciated. In a limited way, both used primary sources dug up from the archives and could distinguish primary sources from secondary sources, although naturally enough with less dexterity and accuracy than would be employed in future centuries but with rather more than that to be mustered by some

Roman historians. Both Herodotus and Thucydides, moreover, were well-travelled and used the experience of travel to write their histories, and both could see the viewpoints of those antagonistic to Greece.

Although the work of Herodotus and Thucydides laid the foundations for Greek history, it was not until Polybius (*c.*200–118 BCE) that the tradition reached its climax. Polybius was probably the greatest of the Greek historians and as a military and political figure, hated the idea of history as a branch of entertainment, literary drama or performance. Instead, he emphasised the importance of research in the archives, was very much alive to the basic historical problem of cause and effect, and reflected on the problems of forging a more systematic approach to history. In this he identified the attributes of the ideal historian (Mellor, 1999, p. 9):

1. Political experience to understand the actual practice of politics and to evaluate sources;
2. Geographical knowledge, preferably from personal travel;
3. Reliance not only on earlier historians, but personal examination of archives, inscriptions and treaties.

More than this, when writing about Alexander the Great, Polybius pondered whether under different circumstances the great man might have successfully marched on Rome, indulging in a device much used by subsequent historians: the counterfactual; asking 'what if,' as a way of analysing the many sides of any historical question.

With the supersession of the Greek empire by that of Rome, the writing of history entered a new phase. While Roman historians and historians of Rome were heirs to the Greek tradition, they tended to be rather more polemical and politically motivated as they sought to come to terms with the now enormous wealth and global reach of Imperial Rome.

Section 3

What did the Romans ever do for history?

Roman historians, acutely aware of their Greek predecessors, were concerned to work out the place of morality and ethics, especially in the conduct of public life and in the face of the temptations of overwhelming political power. Where Herodotus, Thucydides, and even Polybius, used philosophy to fathom the moral depths of politics in the past, Roman historians preferred history as a way of testing the ethical dimensions in the present. For the Romans, history had civic, intellectual and, to an extent, theological functions, but the past was not deigned to be a space for rumination or philosophical thought; it was more inclined to instruct its readers and to provide cautionary tales about, for example, the results of excesses of the flesh or the wages of Senatorial corruption, and conduct on the battlefield. We shall look more closely in a moment at the best of the Roman historians, but for now, as an example of Roman history and its use for Romans as a way of measuring morality in politics, we simply glimpse at how Tacitus (55–120 CE) described the licentiousness of Emperor Nero, a bisexual who was thought by his moral life to have lost all political direction. Here Nero's sexuality and a perceived waywardness in leadership conflate:

> **On the banks of the pool stood brothels well filled with women of high rank, while opposite them one could view stark-naked prostitutes. Obscene gestures and motions were under way, and as darkness came on, all of the adjacent grove and surrounding buildings rang with music and blazed with lights. Nero himself, defiled by natural and unnatural pleasures alike, had omitted no vile practice which could add to his depravity, except that he capped all a few days later by actually becoming the bride of one member of that degenerate crew, an individual named Pythagoras, and marrying him in a formal marriage ceremony. The bridal veil was placed over the emperor's head; the regular witnesses were used; the dowry, marriage bed, the nuptial torches were there; in short, they displayed in full view everything which the night conceals even when the bride is a woman.** (Tacitus, 1965, p. 628)

Where the relationship between morality and politics was closely examined by Roman historians, the best tended always to be located in the past. Roman historians or historians of Rome were not concerned (unlike Herodotus) to transport their readers to strange places or to report on exotic cultures. Indeed, the whole business of writing history need not necessarily bother with the palaver of consulting an archive at all. Another of the Roman historians, Titus Livy (*c*.59 BCE–17 CE), unusual because he appears never to have served in public office or even in the military, was infamously rumoured to be singularly unmoved even to travel into the city to consult documents or to interview protagonists in the drama that he was recounting. He certainly failed one of Collingwood's tests for the 'scientific' historian – the need to research an archive.

In examining the importance of morality in public life, the historian had a responsibility to be legalistic and publicly-minded, and meticulous in the recording and preservation of public documents such as decrees, or *annalles* kept by the Chief Priest which listed names of officials, military victories, and so on. These year-by-year accounts of major officials and important events were reported without much analytical framework, although in the spirit of the Greeks there was an attempt at rhetorical liveliness. (Roman history was not without embellishments and historians would read aloud in the theatre or in the public baths.) Even more systematic and analytical works tended to retain an annalist structure which placed great emphasis on chronology and record.

Here there were continuities with Herodotus and Thucydides, not least of which was an emphasis placed on speeches, drama and the skills associated with rhetoric, and apparent in the work of the main historians of the era: Livy, Sallust (86–35 BCE), Seutonius (*c*.70–*c*.160 CE) and Tacitus. These historians were prominent in any consideration of Roman historiography and were in themselves (with apologies to Monty Python) ample evidence of what the Romans did for us. But what precisely was the nature of this shift from Hellenistic to Roman approaches to history? After a brief consideration of Sallust, we shall return to the not inconsiderable talents of Tacitus, thereafter concentrating on alternative ways that the Romans conceptualised the past: in biography and autobiography and in more popular ways such as family stories.

First, however, we turn to the original problematic of Roman historiography – the place of morality in the face of unlimited imperial power. Sallust or C. Sallustius Crispus was a retired general. His description of Rome (particularly after the death of Julius Caesar in 44 BCE) has very much become our idea of the grandeur and corruption of a mighty empire that has been handed down to us in popular culture; political, economic and social intrigue in the context of moral laxness. Certainly Sallust felt the need to excuse his own behaviour, dismissing his own role in the corruption of Rome as a result of youthful exuberance.

Cornelius Tacitus (56–120 CE) had no such need to excuse his own conduct, although he was a Roman senator. It is the methodology of his history that remains outstanding. Most contemporary historians agree that he read very widely indeed: reminiscences, biography, autobiography, correspondence, and speeches were all consulted. At root, he remained an annalist historian but he also reveals his training in rhetoric. Not that he indulged in the type of rhetorical invention that informed the speeches reported by Thucydides. When, for example, he reported the funeral of Claudius he did so by analysing both the funeral itself and by comparing biographical details of former Emperors:

> **On the day of the funeral the Emperor started his eulogy. While he was reviewing the ancient history of the family and the consulships and triumphs of his ancestors, both speaker and audience were serious. His references to the deceased's cultural attainments and to the fact that during his reign the nation had suffered no disaster abroad were listened to with favour; but when he turned to Claudius' statesmanship and wisdom, no one could suppress a smile, although the speech, which had been written by Seneca, displayed considerable literary polish, for that writer had a talent well suited to the taste of his day. It was observed by the older men, who have the leisure time to compare past and present, that Nero was Rome's first ruler to need a ghost writer. Caesar the Dictator had rivalled the greatest orators; Augustus had a spontaneous, fluent speaking style, such as was becoming to an emperor; Tiberius also was expert in the art of weighing his words and, besides, was forceful in expressing in meaning, or else deliberately ambiguous; even Gaius Caesar's muddled mind did not ruin his power as a speaker; and Claudius, when delivering a prepared address, showed no want of elegance. Nero, however, had even from boyhood turned his mental energies to interests of a different sort, such as engraving, painting, music, or horsemanship, and in his occasional attempts at writing poetry he showed some degree of training in the fundamentals.**
>
> (Tacitus, 1965, p. 628)

Emphasis on biography (and autobiography) in the construction of our understanding of the glories of Rome was also very much part of Roman historiography – although the Romans themselves would not have thought this type of literature to be part of the process of recording and understanding history. In any case, this serves to further explore continuities between Greek and Roman historians.

The *Lives of the Twelve Caesars* by Suetonius has probably been the most influential study written by a Roman historian. While Suetonius was an important and influential person in his time (he was imperial secretary under Trajan), his antiquarian fascination with the everyday has left rich pickings for our understanding of the details of life in Rome, such as diet, and provides for the historian raw materials of life in Rome. Here we find him painting a rich portrait of Augustus by pointing out the source of evidence:

> **In this character sketch I need not omit his eating habits. He was frugal and, as a rule, preferred the food of the common people, especially the coarser sort of bread, small fishes, fresh hard-pressed cheese, and green figs of the second crop; and would not wait for dinner, if he felt hungry, but ate anywhere. The following are verbatim quotations from his letters:**

> **I had a snack of bread and dates while out for my drive today . . . On the way back in my litter from the Regia, I munched an ounce of bread and a few hard-skinned grapes.**
>
> (Suetonius, 2003, pp. 90–1)

Indeed, Suetonius had a sophisticated approach to evidence, even material evidence, and the proper limits of speculation:

> **I can prove pretty conclusively that as a child Augustus was called Thurinus ('the Thurian'), perhaps because his ancestors had once lived at Thurii, or because his father had defeated the slaves in that neighbourhood soon after he was born; my evidence is a bronze statuette which I once owned. It shows him as a boy, and a rusty, almost illegible inscription in iron letters gives him this name. I have presented the statuette to the Emperor Hadrian, who has placed it among the Household gods in his bedroom. Moreover, Augustus was often sneeringly called 'The Thurian' in Antony's correspondence. Augustus answered by confessing himself puzzled: why should his former name be thrown in his face as an insult?**
>
> (Suetonius, 2003, p. 47)

To what extent did these histories influence the historical imagination of the Roman people? Romans themselves deliberately included a wide range of materials which made up the raw material of the past, from myth and legend, to poetry and more conventional forms of historical writing, as demonstrated by Table 6.2.

Table 6.2 Types of Roman histories

Types of 'history'	*Functions*	*Examples*
Myth	Explanation of origins	Romulus and Remus suckled by a she-wolf
Legend	Connection with noble antecedents	Exploits attributed to historical figures, like the Tarquin Kings
Language	Preserves otherwise forgotten etymologies	Money, *pecunia* from *pecus*, sheep, showing the early form of wealth
Buildings and urban plans	Civic, military and religious	Etruscan buildings and plans showing previous northern and central Italian civilisation from 700 BCE
Objects	Family and community memory	Funeral masks and portrait busts
Religion	Social solidarity	Preservation of rituals
Lists	Continuities in civic life	Names of magistrates
Oral tradition	Family and community memory	Funeral speeches
Inscriptions	Continuities in civic and political life	Early treaties
Written poetry	Community and cultural memory	Lucan, Ovid, Horace
Historical writing	Morality and ethics of the state	Sallust, Livi, Tacitus

Source: Compiled and adapted from Mellor (1999), p. 2.

Knowledge of the past for the Romans was therefore socially constructed. In other words, the ways that Romans understood their world and how it might be reinterpreted by historians was not simply the sum of individual histories from this or that historian. Instead, we can find popular ideas of what the past meant from a range of sources that were not always considered as sources by historians such as Livi, Sallust or Tacitus. Family records and stories of heroics, architectural traces of the Etruscan people that were the immediate predecessors of the Romans, or inscriptions on religious temples helped to shape popular understanding of the past. In the same way it may be tempting to think that today an understanding of Rome might derive from the novels of Robert Graves, or from the latest soap opera on Rome, seemingly brought alive by the skills of our Shakespearean actors. Equally, Romans, like the Greeks, had their epic poets or those that would write history as prose. Taken together these public or social ideas of the past gave a sense to *them* about their own past and a sense to *us* that we somehow know Rome, with its gladiators and orgies, its great armies and its political intrigues.

The demise of Tacitus marks the end of historians writing in the language of Rome, and the last of the important Pagan historians. (There was, ironically, a return to Greek in history writing after a pause of several hundred years.) Nobody could ever have guessed it, but both the Greeks and the Romans were about to be displaced by Christian inspired histories. This was to introduce a whole new way of thinking about the past.

Section 4

Late antiquity, Christianity and the End of Days

When in October 312 CE Constantine marched on Rome to confront Emperor Maxentius, he was said to have seen a cross in the sky with a message that read 'In this conquer'. After a famous victory, his 'Edict of Milan' announced freedoms to worship across the empire. As a result, Christian churches became wealthier and the clergy of the early Christian church were declared exempt from taxes and duties. Christianity was transformed from the most reviled of religions in the Roman Empire to become the most privileged. It also transformed itself. By the time the Nicene Creed was declared in 325 CE, a meeting or synod of the church that declared the divinity of the Son as well as the Father, enthusiastically attended by Constantine himself, Christianity's Jewish and Pagan roots had become half-buried and half-denied. Pagans and Jews were the new outsiders.

The Christianisation of Rome was to exist in different levels of intensity in subsequent years, with only Julian I, when he became Emperor in 360, reverting back to Paganism in any serious or meaningful way and then only for a very short time. Thereafter Rome tended to favour Christianity while tolerating Paganism – and all because Constantine saw a light in the sky. The process of Christianisation, however, was also helped along by the historians of late antiquity.

Rome fell in 476 CE, or so most textbooks will tell you. Certainly this date marks the end of the Emperors, yet the eastern remnant of this once global empire could be said to have survived until 1453 in one recognisable form as the Byzantine Empire. Many reasons are given for its decline and final destruction: financial mismanagement; invasion by the barbarians in the shape of Vandals, Goths and Huns; civil conflict and war; moral disintegration and so forth – we shall return to the question in Chapter 17. Yet the empire had never been static. Even in the period covered in the previous section, Rome had reinvented itself many times over, not least in the transition of its political systems. There was also the religious crisis that we associate with the early centuries of what today we call the new millennia: the jostle in late antiquity for supremacy between Pagans, Jews and Christians. And here historians played a part.

Most notable in this period was the work of Eusebius of Caesarea (*c.*275–339 CE). His histories of the church, his works on the Bible and dogma, his life of Constantine, his celebration of early saints and martyrs and his demonisation of Jews, became the measure of history writing over the next few centuries – providing a link between ancient historians and the 'age of Bede' that will be considered in the next chapter. Both Jews and Christians sought to date their beginnings to Creation, but Christians laid great store also in histories that emphasised the birth of Jesus and significant moments in his life, ministry and death. It was from this starting point that Eusebius, historian and first bishop of Caesarea in Palestine, wrote his *Ecclesiastical History* (312–324 CE), which dealt in a history of the church that halted on the eve of Nicaea, and in the life of Jesus and his apostles, martyrs and bishops. Time began with Creation and would end at the Last Judgement with promises of triumph and victory.

Eusebius was followed by Socrates (*c.*380 CE), Sozomen (*c.*400–450 CE), and Theodoret (395–437 CE). These figures are not important individually; or their particular histories notable of and for themselves. They are important in so much as together they developed ecclesiastical or church history as a genre, taking their cue from Eusebius, not only as the historian of the early church, but also in his life as a bishop. In the influences they took from Rome and in their living Christianity, they provided as Arthur Marwick said of Eusebius, the 'culmination of the ancient tradition and a link to medieval Christian Europe' (Marwick, 2001, p. 54). Nowhere was this link stronger over the centuries when Christianity dominated Europe than in the reading of the Bible. It is to the importance of the Bible and its interpretation that we now turn.

From the standpoint of modern scholarship, the stories of the Bible fail to meet most if not all of the criteria which would qualify it as history. They were not supported by an archive of primary source material that provided some verification for the claims made in the Old and New Testaments. No web of footnotes takes us back to a point of proof that these things actually happened. More than that, they appear to have grown by a process of accretion and syncretism, adding and combining over centuries and centuries, appearing from the mists of time rather than a known historical moment. Torah (or Old Testament) that is given from heaven and dictated to Moses is a faith, not something that any historian can verify using modern techniques of evidence. The events described were in any case often explicitly magical or miraculous, defying the laws of physics and biology. This said, the Bible was used by ancient historians and archaeologists as a historical chronology to be proved or falsified, and there was other evidence for the existence of at least some Biblical characters or events.

Historical anthropologists saw these stories, and the great narrative that weaves them into a whole, as the foundational myths, or stories of origin and early development, of the religious basis of Jewish, Christian and Muslim societies, which are discussed in the next chapter. Details and interpretations are contested and debated by believers, but to the social scientist it does not amount to historical description in ways that we would apply to any other sphere of the past. Despite this, we can say that the Bible, perhaps the Old Testament in particular, has played a significant part in shaping how western societies have come to view history.

The Old Testament to Christianity shared a great many characteristics with later conceptions of how the process of history has worked. Indeed, even the idea that history somehow 'works'. What does this mean? Let's start by looking at some of the major characteristics of the Old Testament narrative. Its overarching story is that of the historical development of the tribes of the Holy Lands of the ancient Middle East. Wars, mass migrations, epidemics, disasters, miracles, heroism and wickedness add up to a majestic grand design in which we can recognise key aspects of our common beginning. Great cities rise and are smashed; famines bring peoples to the brink of destruction as God's mysterious will is worked out upon the face of a mythical past. And there was enough in this story to suggest that, at least in some of its elements, future histories are mapped out. From this perspective the Bible can be considered also to be the history of the future as well as the past.

This would seem to provide another reason to rule out the Bible from the historical canon: how can we make claims on the future? The idea that history has a direction and a purpose, a *telos* or teleology, has been a powerful force in shaping later ideas of history and how history 'works'. This is true both in the area of the philosophy of history and in relation to particular moments in history where the idea that history has a trajectory, revealed in the Old Testament, has had a decisive influence.

From the perspective of religion and the Christian influence, from late antiquity and beyond, it can be understood in relation to one word: millennium. Around the time of the first millennium CE, a movement grew up across the breadth of Christendom that preached great fear of an impending apocalypse. Based on prophecies, which were in turn rooted in a close study of the Old Testament, they predicted the more or less imminent destruction of the order of things as they then existed and variously predicted the second coming of the Messiah, or damnation for the sinners and salvation for the righteous. These millenarian movements may have been wrong in their interpretation of history and certainly wrong in their prophecies but they were historically influential in their own period and unquestionably saw themselves as trying to interpret the trajectory of history set forth in the Old Testament.

In these ways, the Old Testament structured history and created a sense of history having a direction that might or might not be predictable, and had a huge influence in shaping how history was to be conceived in later times. It was of tremendous importance to history written in the Middle Ages and to those writing in the Renaissance and then among those historians working up to, including and beyond the seventeenth century. The next chapter will deal precisely with this period in Christian historiography.

In practice

In the writings of these early historians we can see the beginnings of what we would today recognise as history. The foremost Greek and Roman historians sought to impose order upon their knowledge of past events using the skills of research and critical inquiry which are part of the make up of the modern historian. By doing so, they distanced themselves from an earlier tradition of storytelling in which myths based largely on the caprices of supernatural beings prevailed. In the best of their writings there is a sophisticated questioning of evidence, use of a variety of written and oral sources of evidence, and a desire to think comparatively about cultures on the edge of their known world. So extensive were the travels of Herodotus, and so serious his commitment to an understanding of different cultures, he could well be considered not only a pioneering historian, but also an anthropologist and archaeologist. Despite the considerable quantity of evidence accumulated, some of which was of questionable value, these historians succeeded in providing a reasonably clear sense of chronology consistent with the historical record.

In other respects, however, their role as historians was compromised by the tasks they set themselves as public figures. Although Herodotus, Thucydides, Suetonius and Tacitus professed a commitment to the truth, they used the past as a vehicle to explore moral and ethical values, or to record historical lineages. Because of a requirement to provide vivid and entertaining accounts – many of which were intended to be read in public – there was also a temptation to embellish what they perceived to be the truth, use anecdotal evidence, and fill in gaps with fictionalised material. None of the historians was averse to the occasional use of folk tales, fables, myths and epic narratives.

The histories of conflict were meant to be instructive, accounts from which lessons could be drawn by present and future generations. In the work of Thucydides we find attempts to formulate from the past fundamental principles of human action which provide guides for the future. None, however, was concerned with the predictive potential of history. That changed with the emergence of Christian history based largely on the Bible. Both the Old and New Testaments were the products of numerous authors over time, and this led to many contradictory accounts. Amid the confusion, however, are details of historical places, events and people whose existence has been supported by other forms of evidence, including archaeological. Above the historical detail stands an overarching narrative which is teleological, and culminates with the realisation of God's mission on Earth. In this important respect, Christian historians do attempt to map out a scheme for the future.

All of the issues addressed by these early historians are still with us today, indeed, they go to the very heart of history as a mode of intellectual inquiry. Perhaps the answers we can provide are more sophisticated, reliable and consistent, but one of the great merits of our ancient forefathers is that they actually did much to establish the historiographical agenda and set the terms of the debates which continue to challenge us.

Summary

The four sections of this chapter have said four things:

- Greek historiography is at the root of both western value systems and structures and the history has proved to be a major element in the development of western civilisation. The section is careful to pay close attention to the work of Herodotus as the so-called 'Father of History'. While much of his work is acknowledged to be gullible and far-fetched, the determination to record ethnographical details of the people and civilisations he studied has left us with valuable evidence of the lives and habits of once great peoples that are now lost to history, save for some contemporary archaeology. While Herodotus refers to gold-digging ants and other (to us) fantastic phenomena, he nevertheless has a real sense of historical method and imagination which remain both interesting and of usefulness to students of history.
- There were continuities within Greek approaches to the past but also distinct differences. In particular, comparisons are made between Herodotus and Thucydides. Using the criteria set out by Collingwood of what constitutes 'scientific' or 'rational' history, it seems that Thucydides was by far the most systematic in both method and approach. Unlike Herodotus, Thucydides was less likely to construct his history within the contemporary conventions of theatre or rhetoric. He was, however, adept at reading evidence and providing reasonable speculation about historical patterns to be found in that evidence. Above all, Thucydides tended to discount the role of the gods, or supernatural phenomena, in the processes of historical change. Finally, we consider the vital role played by Polybius in his more sophisticated approach to the archive.
- The historians of Rome had some similarities. The differences, however, were fairly profound. They tended to be centred on morality and the wielding of power. There was also a tendency for Roman historians to concentrate less than the Greeks on performance. Instead, we find the historians of this great empire concentrating (in addition to politics and morality) on the evidence of history. In particular, this would include the lives of the Emperors which could be retrieved through reminiscences, biography, autobiography, correspondence, and speeches. In this sense at least, historians in Rome could be said to be in the service of the state.
- Both Greek and Roman approaches to history had a lasting effect on future societies and civilisations, especially in what we now think of as the West. In particular, the Greek historians made initial innovations in technique and imagination. Christian approaches to the past particularly introduced the notion that present day society was constantly on the cusp of a new world which was to be announced in a moment of a catastrophic crisis, forcing historians to think differently about the past but in the context of a future now weighed against prophecy.

Discussion document 1

This extract raises questions about the scope and ambition of Herodotus and his *Histories*. Here we have an account of the ancient Babylonians that is as evocative as it is informative. From it we can learn something of their approach to public interaction, in particular to sickness, death and sexuality. Herodotus takes some care to make comparisons across cultures although not without making value judgements.

The following custom seems to me the wisest of their institutions next to the one lately praised. They have no physicians, but when a man is ill, they lay him in the public square, and the passers-by come up to him, and if they have ever had his disease themselves or have known anyone who has suffered from it, they give him advice, recommending him to do whatever they found good in their own case, or in the case known to them; and no one is allowed to pass the sick man in silence without asking him what his ailment is.

They bury their dead in honey, and have funeral lamentations like the Egyptians. When a Babylonian has consorted with his wife, he sits down before a censer of burning incense, and the woman sits opposite to him. At dawn of day they wash; for till they are washed they will not touch any of their common vessels. This practice is observed also by the Arabians.

The Babylonians have one most shameful custom. Every woman born in the country must once in her life go and sit down in the precinct of Venus, and there consort with a stranger. Many of the wealthier sort, who are too proud to mix with the others, drive in covered carriages to the precinct, followed by a goodly train of attendants, and there take their station. But the larger number seat themselves within the holy enclosure with wreaths of string about their heads – and here there is always a great crowd, some coming and others going; lines of cord mark out paths in all directions the women, and the strangers pass along them to make their choice. A woman who has once taken her seat is not allowed to return home till one of the strangers throws a silver coin into her lap, and takes her with him beyond the holy ground. When he throws the coin he says these words – 'The goddess Mylitta prosper thee.' (Venus is called Mylitta by the Assyrians.) The silver coin may be of any size; it cannot be refused, for that is forbidden by the law, since once thrown it is sacred. The woman goes with the first man who throws her money, and rejects no one. When she has gone with him, and so satisfied the goddess, she returns home, and from that time forth no gift however great will prevail with her. Such of the women as are tall and beautiful are soon released, but others who are ugly have to stay a long time before they can fulfil the law. Some have waited three or four years in the precinct. A custom very much like this is found also in certain parts of the island of Cyprus.

Herodotus, *The History of Herodotus* (trans. by George Rawlinson), available online at http://classics.mit.edu//Herodotus/history.html.

Discussion document 2

This, famously, is Thucydides' reproduction of Pericles' Funeral Oration. He tentatively explains how as an historian he has to contend with 'varying reports on the same events' and the vagaries of memory. He is therefore content to record the 'gist' of what was said and what he thought needed to be said in the circumstances.

Most of my predecessors in this place have commended him who made this speech part of the law, telling us that it is well that it should be delivered at the burial of those who fall in battle. For myself, I should have thought that the worth which had displayed itself in deeds would be sufficiently rewarded by honours also shown by deeds; such as you now see in this funeral prepared at the people's cost. And I could have wished that the reputations of many brave men were not to be imperilled in the mouth of a single individual, to stand or fall according as he spoke well or ill. For it is hard to speak properly upon a subject where it is even difficult to convince your hearers that you are speaking the truth. On the one hand, the friend who is familiar with every fact of the story may think that some point has not been set forth with that fullness which he wishes and knows it to deserve; on the other, he who is a stranger to the matter may be led by envy to suspect exaggeration if he hears anything above his own nature. For men can endure to hear others praised only so long as they can severally persuade themselves of their own ability to equal the actions recounted: when this point is passed, envy comes in and with it incredulity. However, since our ancestors have stamped this custom with their approval, it becomes my duty to obey the law and to try to satisfy your several wishes and opinions as best I may.

'I shall begin with our ancestors: it is both just and proper that they should have the honour of the first mention on an occasion like the present. They dwelt in the country without break in the succession from generation to generation, and handed it down free to the present time by their valour. And if our more remote ancestors deserve praise, much more do our own fathers, who added to their inheritance the empire which we now possess, and spared no pains to be able to leave their acquisitions to us of the present generation. Lastly, there are few parts of our dominions that have not been augmented by those of us here, who are still more or less in the vigour of life; while the mother country has been furnished by us with everything that can enable her to depend on her own resources whether for war or for peace. That part of our history which tells of the military achievements which gave us our several possessions, or of the ready valour with which either we or our fathers stemmed the tide of Hellenic or foreign aggression, is a theme too familiar to my hearers for me to dilate on, and I shall therefore pass it by. But what was the road by which we reached our position, what the form of government under which our greatness grew, what the national habits out of which it sprang; these are questions which I may try to solve before I proceed to my panegyric upon these men; since I think this to be a subject upon which on the present occasion a speaker may properly dwell, and to which the whole assemblage, whether citizens or foreigners, may listen with advantage.

Our constitution does not copy the laws of neighbouring states; we are rather a pattern to others than imitators ourselves. Its administration favours the many instead of the few; this is why it is called a democracy. If we look to the laws, they afford equal justice to all in their private differences; if no social standing, advancement in public life falls to reputation for capacity, class considerations not being allowed to interfere with merit; nor again does poverty bar the way, if a man is able to serve the state, he is not hindered by the obscurity of his condition. The freedom which we enjoy in our government extends also to our ordinary life. There, far from exercising a jealous surveillance over each other, we do not feel called upon to be angry with our neighbour for doing what he likes, or even to indulge in those injurious looks which cannot fail to be offensive, although they inflict no positive penalty. But all this ease in our private relations does not make us lawless as citizens. Against this fear is our chief safeguard, teaching us to obey the magistrates and the laws, particularly such as regard the protection of the injured, whether they are actually on the statute book, or belong to that code which, although unwritten, yet cannot be broken without acknowledged disgrace.

Further, we provide plenty of means for the mind to refresh itself from business. We celebrate games and sacrifices all the year round, and the elegance of our private establishments forms a daily source of pleasure and helps to banish the spleen; while the magnitude of our city draws the produce of the world into our harbour, so that to the Athenian the fruits of other countries are as familiar a luxury as those of his own.'

Thucydides, *The History of the Peloponnesian War*, 'Internet Classics Library', available online at http://classics.mit.edu/Thucydides/pelopwar.2.second.html.

Further reading

* *essential*

Simon Hornblower (ed.), *Greek Historiography* (1994).
A standard undergraduate account of Greek historians that is very good at taking the student by the hand, and gives a real sense of the development of the historian across a long period.

* **G. A. Press**, The *Development of the Idea of History in Antiquity* (1982).
Very useful as both an introduction to historiography and as an informed and lively narrative which is very aware of both the classics and the reassessment of the classics in later periods. In this sense, it can also be read with both Chapters 1 and 2 in mind.

John Marincola, revised introduction and notes, *Herodotus, The Histories* (2000).
This Penguin edition is both comprehensive and informative. The introduction gives a good account of the changing reputation of Herodotus with a good bibliography, maps, etc.

Walter Blanco and Jennifer Tolbert Roberts (eds), *Thucydides, The Peloponnesian War* (1998).
Both an annotated edition of *The Peloponnesian War* and a compilation of some of the comments it has attracted from historians in the modern period. This is a very good way of orientating yourself into Thucydides, his work and commentaries about the importance of his work.

* **Stephen Usher**, *The Historians of Greece and Rome* (1985).
A very fine account (especially for the uninitiated) of the importance and elements of both Greek and Roman historiography. Look especially for the interesting take on Thucydides.

* **Ronald Mellor** (ed.) *The Historians of Ancient Rome* (2nd edition, 2004).
Set out clearly and with obvious attractions for a student new to the subject.

Ronald Mellor, *The Roman Historians* (1999).
As informed as Mellor (2004) but probably with less clarity. The section on the origins of Roman historiography is especially useful, as is the section on historical writing.

Suetonius, *The Twelve Caesars* (2003).
For the worth of biography and autobiography in ancient Rome see Mellor (1999) but also this Penguin edition, which is translated by Robert Graves and introduced by Michael Grant.

* **Robert Graves and Barry Unsworth**, *I Claudius* (2006).
Such is the original research and scholarship by Robert Graves, this should be required undergraduate reading in this area, especially when considering the role of biography and autobiography in Roman historiography.

* **David Rohrbacher**, *The Historians of Late Antiquity* (2002).
This deals with both the framework and context of the period and the provenance of ecclesiastical and church history, hagiography and the rest of the Christian canon in historiography. It also surveys the life and works of notable individual historians. It is invaluable as a survey but also pay attention to the bibliography.

7 From the Middle Ages to the Renaissance

Introduction

This chapter will take up the story where the last chapter finished, examining historiographical trends in the period that in the West was known as the Middle Ages. The main focus in the opening section is the Venerable Bede who as a seventh-century Christian historian developed a remarkable technique of reading sources in order to have a better understanding of chronology, and that the End of Days might be calculated according to prophecy. The notion of history leading to the Second Coming at the end of time dominated Christian notions of the past but also introduced an idea of history that moved inextricably forward to a conclusion that was guided by an omnipotent God. This, at least, was what the monotheistic religious traditions had in common. Non-European contributions to medieval historiography came in the form of Judaism and Islam. The first, the Jewish tradition, shared an idea of history having a forward trajectory but also dwelt, it has been argued, in a narrative of their own which was provided by a rich tradition of Talmud and Torah. Thus from the first century to the fifteenth century, Jewish historians remain silent to us in the sense that jews tended not to articulate histories outside of their own communities and the narrow concerns of the Hebrew Bible. Islamic scholarship, in contrast, thrived; was rich in content and voluminous in scale and scope. This innovative tradition in Islam became less dynamic after the end of the Spanish 'Golden Age' in the 1400s and, indeed, gave way to scholarship more conservative and inevitably less self-critical of the ways of reading testimony and evidence, ideas of objectivity and subjectivity. The West ended the so-called 'dark ages' (or so it was thought) by a Renaissance of ideas, art and culture. Its importance to the history of history was the rediscovery of the classics (not that it completely went away) and all that the historiography of the Greeks and Romans was to mean to the history of a discipline in the centuries to follow.

Section 1

European Christendom and the 'age of Bede'

> **And it came to pass, when Moses came down from mount Sinai with the two tables of the testimony . . . that Moses knew not that the skin of his face sent forth beams while he talked with Him.**
> (Exodus. 34:29)

Pope Julius della Rovere commissioned Michelangelo (1475–1564) to build a tomb. It was never finished. Yet we know from surviving written sources that this magnificent structure was designed to represent the Christian world and, through its very iconography, the world yet to come. The lower level was to be dedicated to Man, the middle level was reserved for Prophets and Saints, and at the top was an unearthly level which would come about at the End of Days. Its summit was to be an embodiment of two angels guiding the Pope out of his tomb on that dreadful day of the Last Judgement. Within this elaborately tiered tomb, the Basilica di San Pietro in Vincoli, can be found statues and icons intimately connected to the symbolism of the age. At its centre is the magisterial figure of Moses: a figure common to the three major monotheistic religious traditions of Judaism, Christianity and Islam; a symbol and a figure that straddles ancient and modern times and who has been understood and received by Chroniclers and historians in a multitude of ways in each of these three major religious traditions.

Overall this is a stirring setting to place Moses, chosen by God at the rather advanced age of 120, or so the story goes, because of his humility and kindness to the sheep that he tended. Sculptured in 1513–16, the protruding knee of the statue was damaged slightly by the flying chisel of the frustrated artist and the beard worn thin by the touch of worshippers, apparently in the belief that a statue of Moses could bring relief for their troubles. But what of the horns protruding from his head? As Moses descended from Mount Sinai with the tablets of law, his countenance glowed from a close encounter of the most spiritual kind. He was said to be emitting a 'horn' of light but this can also be interpreted as meaning 'a ray of light'. (The Hebrew for horn/beam/ray (of light) is (in phonetics) *keren*; in the Latin or *versio vulgate* reading of the Bible, however, it is translated literally as 'his face sent out horns of light'.) Thus medieval and Renaissance artists, including Michelangelo, misrepresented Moses with *actual* horns protruding from his forehead. It is this poor translation, and other misunderstandings and misinterpretations, such as the Hebrew word *naara*, which in the context of Mary is translated as virgin (*betulah*) rather than by its truer meaning of girl or young woman, that illustrate how different, separated, yet connected the three mayor monotheistic traditions had become. Difficulties in the transmission of knowledge such as this extend to the understanding of the past and the writing of history in antiquity, the Renaissance and throughout the Middle Ages. This chapter will seek to address these difficulties, explaining why Judeo-Christian and Islamic approaches to the past and the future are so vital to an understanding of historiography throughout the long centuries of the antique and medieval periods.

Each of these monotheistic traditions did have something besides Moses in common. They struggled in differing ways to understand and tell the various stories of Exile (in the case of Judaism), Incarnation and Resurrection (in the case of Christianity), the lives of the Prophets (in the instance of Judaism and Islam), Creation and the End of Days (in all three traditions). Whether we consider Jewish, Christian or Islamic historiography, influenced so overwhelmingly by the Torah or Five Books of Moses (collectively known as the Pentateuch), or the three gospels of Matthew, Mark and Luke (known as the 'synoptic' gospels) of the New Testament, or the Koran, we find a single God who is thought to be moving and controlling time; who is omnipotent and indivisible. The explanations of the past and hopes for the future were, with the rise of Judaism, then Christianity and then Islam, placed in the context of a unitary God that was the explanation of human origins and human destiny: from this universal power came all judgements and the source of a single law that would eventually govern all humanity. For the first time in human experience came the notion of one force that moved history and could not be rivalled or outbid by any rival deity or, as it were, broken down into gods of this tribe or that nation. This universal power could allow, also for the first time, the possibility of a universal history but one focused on the unfolding chronology of scripture or prophesies.

Yet, as with Michelangelo's depiction of Moses, the transmission of an understanding of the past into the present was far from untrammelled or uncontested. Thought to have written the Bible under divine influence, Moses had real authority in the ancient and early medieval world when the *Tanakh*, the collected books of the Jews, were translated into Greek, and as the *Septuagint* was presented to the world as the dominant narrative of the West. Then, in 382 CE, Pope Demascus ordered Jerome to undertake a translation from the Greek. This version of the Bible story was to become the accepted version by the Catholic Church and in subsequent centuries appeared in the vernacular among the reformed or Protestant churches, culminating in the Authorised Version of the Bible prompted by James I in 1611. This is how Moses was taken into the modern (or early-modern) period. It is this issue of transmission or poor transmission of what are in some respects narratives common to each tradition that remains crucial for any adequate understanding of history writing over this long period.

The job of the historian in late antiquity and into the medieval period was to determine providential acts, miracles, portents, prophecies and markers that could reveal where exactly we were on this linear path to the end of history. Thus the Book of Daniel, for example, was rifled for 'signs' and evidence of history's divine stages. Or, according to Eusebius, introduced in the previous chapter, the reader could be orientated to recognise the 'six ages' of Adam, Abraham, Moses, the building of the Temple, the rebuilding of the Temple and the triumphant birth of Christ. Augustine of Hippo (354–430 CE) was to do something similar with his 'Tripartite Scheme' of 'world stages': time consisting of 'periods before the law', 'under the law' and 'under God's glory'. It was through the efforts of historians and early figures of the church such as Eusebius, the scholar Saint Jerome (347–419/420), Saint Ambrose, bishop of Milan (339–397 CE) and the apologist Lactanius (240–320), the 'Christian Cicero' as he was known, who looked to the classical texts as a source of public morality, that allowed Christianity – with the political clout of that most famous of apostates Constantine the Great – to both cast off and then deny its formative Jewish influences.

Christian eschatology (the doctrine of the End of Days) in the Middle Ages, however, looked not only to the past but the future, and so connected both the past and the future through the processes of historical change. The question was how to hasten the end of the days and to bring on the onset of Christ's Kingdom. Premillennialists were notoriously pessimistic about human progress and potential. The only way to hasten Christ's Kingdom was through divine, not human, intervention. History was biblically prophesied and if studied with care and learning would reveal signs of impending judgement and eventually the Second Coming. In order to separate the moral elect from evil, the sacred and the secular were themselves separated: the former venerated; the latter kept at arm's length.

It was from this perspective that early European Christendom understood its history. Through its Chronicles it could chart these signs and portents, celebrate its saints and soothsayers and honour Christ's ministry by honouring God's Holy church, its holy orders and its monasteries or sanctuaries. It is in the most famous and skilled of these Chroniclers and in an important monastery in the north-east of England that we will discover more about the development of Christian historical ideas through the historiography it produced.

Whether the library was concentrated at the monastery of Wearmouth in the far north-east of England, where the Venerable Bede, foremost scholar and historian of the Middle Ages, lived, or at Jarrow, with which he was also associated, is disputed. Equally it is not known whether it was divided between the two monasteries. What we do know is that the library was big. Containing somewhere between 300 and 600 volumes, it was hardly a store of knowledge to equal the library at Alexandria, but by contemporary standards, at least in the West, it was of huge importance. Within these physical and intellectual walls Bede (672/3–735 CE) wrote his magisterial *Ecclesiastical History of the English People* in 731/2, along with voluminous letters, hagiographies, chronologies and essays that provide a precious insight into the period in which he lived, how the past was understood by the early church, and how that understanding was first absorbed by Bede and then utterly transformed. For this unique work, he drew freely upon books and manuscripts retrieved from Rome and the furthest corners of medieval Europe. Visitors to Northumberland came from far and wide, adding yet more to the collection. That much of the library was preserved on vellum (quality parchment made of calf-, kid- or lambskin) gives as a real sense of the wealth of the institution and it also tells us something about the importance of those that worked there as teachers or scribes.

Bede's transmission of the Christian message through the writing of history, and his transmission of oral testimony that told of the conversion of England to Christianity, relied on a robust selection of written texts and the determination of Bede himself to find reliable witnesses. Yet, Bede included 'miracle stories' as part of his account and, like many medieval Christian Chroniclers, he sought to locate the operation of divine providence in events which are themselves given meaning as the fulfilment of God's will. For example, Bede recalled a story of the death of a nun called Hild and the witnesses who anticipated and marked her death in monasteries situated 13 miles apart. The first account is in the monastery placed some distance from the death scene; the second in a remote wing of the monastery where Hild died:

In this monastery there was a nun called Begu who for thirty or more years had been dedicated to the Lord in virginity and had served Him in the monastic life. As she was resting

in the sisters' dormitory, she suddenly heard in the air the well-known sound of the bell with which they used to be aroused to their prayers or called together when one of them had been summoned from the world. On opening her eyes she seemed to see the roof of the house rolled back, while a light which poured in from above filled the whole place. As she watched the light intently, she saw the soul of the handmaiden of the Lord being borne to Heaven in the midst of that light, attended and guided by angels. . . .

It is also related that, on the same night and in the same monastery in which this servant of God died, her death was seen in a vision by one of the devoted virgins of God, who had been deeply attached to her. She saw Hild's soul ascend to heaven in the company of angels. She related this openly to the servants of Christ who were with her at the very hour it happened and aroused them to pray for her soul, and this before the rest of the congregation knew of her death, for it was only made known to them as soon as they met next morning.

(Bede, 1999, pp. 213–14)

This example is a study in how Christian history is approached during this period and it also tells us something valuable about the ways in which the medieval Chronicle was constructed. Definitions of what was true to the Chronicler are closely connected to what they believed to be accurate. Exactitude, therefore, is given great weight in historical accounts during the Middle Ages, as is its moral or universal application as accepted fact. What was considered accurate or factual *then* is, of course, quite different from what is considered accurate or factual *now*. Veracity in history is at least to some extent of itself an historical construct, a creature of the time in which a standard of truth is held and the history researched and written. This could also be said about the plausibility of any account set in the past. It needed only to correspond to comparable truths accepted as such by readers contemporary to Bede. We should not, therefore, be surprised that these accepted truths are not accepted as truths by us. This ought not, however, to cloud our judgement about the ultimate worth of histories set within their context, nor should it make us overly judgemental about medieval historical scholarship more generally.

Bede was like other medieval Chroniclers in that he determined that the task of the historian was to discern God's will; the task of history was to fulfil providence and determine where exactly we were on the divine journey to the End of Days. Three related elements appear common to medieval Chronicles: they seek exactitude, the universal and moral application of a factual account, and plausibility. They are histories that correspond to comparable truths, albeit 'truths' that we would now probably regard as implausible and far-fetched. On the face of it, Bede's description and explanation for the death of Hild and how it was witnessed by a fellow nun, Begu, is quite simply irrational. Visions, dreams, hearsay are adopted as fact without any secure, evidential basis, but it is an explanation that ought to be set firmly within the context in which it was written. First, the story itself would have originated from a trusted source and would be believable to contemporaries in every detail. In this narrow sense it was neither fanciful, exaggerated nor was it made-up in any way. Second, these contrasting accounts taken from different viewpoints verify a single incident: the foreshadowing of the death of a pious abbess. In this respect it was sound scholarship and good history. It was also well written. Perhaps the narrative itself was difficult to credit but this is not the point. It made perfect sense to Bede and most of his contemporaries and as such should be treated on its own terms. To do otherwise would display naivety on our part.

Bede was especially adept at constructing periods; in particular the attempt to date the religious calendar from historical records. In this respect, his work was analogous to attempts within Islamic historiography to lend veracity to the life and ministry of the Prophet. The difference in this case was that Bede was trying to date, for example, Easter in order to calculate (through a comparison of historical events with biblical prophesies) the establishment of the coming of Christ's Kingdom. In doing this it is quite simply breathtaking how closely he stuck to historical methodology, his ample use of documentation as well as oral accounts and the avoidance of invented speeches – all elements that mark him off from classical historians and quite probably from the bulk of Jewish and Islamic historiography in its infancy. As the medieval historian Given-Wilson (2004) has emphasised, Bede and other Chroniclers of the period were seeking to establish continuity of the past to the present. This was because in the scriptures and the prophecies of the past lay the key to the future; understanding the past provided the key to the gates of heaven. This moved Bede to do nothing less than to locate the origins of Christianity in Britain and to recalculate the age of the world.

Whether it was disagreement about law or faith, the authority of the Prophet or the End of Days, Judaism, Christianity and Islam used history in a variety of ways that would raise the collective eyebrows of many modern historians. Hence Moshe, Moses or the Prophet Moses was a composite as well as a contested figure by the time that the tomb of Pope Julius II was constructed in the middle of the Renaissance, but nonetheless he had by this time been effectively claimed by the Catholic Church. Still, Judaism, Christianity and Islam could agree that history was no longer random, a whim of the Almighty. Before we look at how these ideas developed through the writing of history during the period of the Renaissance, we should pause to consider in more detail non-European conceptions of how the past impacted on the present and future, particularly in the traditions of Judaism and Islam.

Section 2

Peoples of the history book: Jewish and Islamic conceptions of history

Switch now from the cold and deserted wastes of north-east England to the warmer lands of Arabia in the East – modern day Saudi Arabia – to enter the library of the Islamic historian al-Waqidi who, according to the Hijri (Muslim) calendar, died in the year 207 H or 823 CE. What we find is not 600 books that made up Bede's store of knowledge but 600 trunks of books which were only removed upon al-Waqidi's death with the help of two burly men hoisting each container. A similar picture emerges with the essayist al-Jahiz (d.868) who in old age was crushed to death by his falling books; quite a fate as they totalled some 400 camel loads of theology titles alone. By the late tenth century a library in Cairo hosted hundreds of thousands of books, including many history books. This was far in excess of anything that could be claimed by Bede around the same time and much more than had been accumulated by the ancients. Only China, which traced a historiographical tradition back to Confucius (d.479 BCE), could rival this burst of historical literature in the Islamic world in the late eighth and early ninth centuries. The age of Bede and the Abbasid period of Islamic growth were contemporaneous to the T'ang dynasty (618–907), by which time the Chinese had already absorbed centuries of bibliomania. The West would have to wait until the invention of the printing press for the experience to be repeated; most notably the push given to history in Renaissance Europe by the polyglot and printer of books, William Caxton (*c.*1422–92).

Arnaldo Momigliano (1908–87) was perhaps the most notable and important commentator on ancient historiographies and their transmission across space and time. In a wide-ranging working life that began in fascist Italy and ended in Chicago, via post-war London, Momigliano became increasingly preoccupied with Persian historiography, Greek historiography (how it impacted on Rome) and Jewish historiography. He helped greatly to establish how these areas related to one another, to a wider antiquarian historical culture, and to the genres of biography and prosopography. (Prosopography was first used in Roman historiography and is a study whereby evidence is presented as a list of individuals whose lives and work could be connected through family ties, career histories, and so on.) He asks three fundamental questions in his *Classical Foundations of Modern Historiography* (1990):

1 What have Greek and biblical historiography in common?
2 What are the main differences between Greek and biblical historiography?
3 Why did Greek historiography prove to be so vital while Jewish historiography halted, rather abruptly, in the first century CE?

The first two questions have been dealt with in the previous chapter and the last section but it is the third question that will be addressed now.

In the early years of the Common Era and before, Jews tended to write in Greek. Craving respectability and acceptance among the majority communities, they had in many cases lost the ability to communicate in Hebrew or Aramaic, a semitic language of the near Middle East which dates from around 300 BCE. Indeed, Jewish Hellenism, we are told by Momigliano, was openly syncretist – freely mixing Pagan and Jewish elements and working these elements into their own culture and histories. Jewish education was based on the Greek *paideia* of self-knowledge and education for citizenship in the city-state and this fed directly into a wider historical culture. Even observant Jews were not unaffected by this wider historical culture which led in turn to increasing levels of assimilation with the wider gentile population.

As part of this assimilative culture in the opening years of the first century CE, Jewish historiography owed much more to classical scholarship and less to visions of the End of Days. Flavius Josephus (b.37 BCE–*c.*101 CE), the first real historian of Judaism and a Jewish historian, drew upon the *Babyloniaca* and the histories of Egypt by Hecataeus of Miletus (who we met in the last chapter) and Manetho (an Egyptian from the 30th dynasty of whom we know very little) for his reconstructions of the 'Jewish War' against the Romans. His first work was written in Aramaic; his subsequent works in line with Jewish assimilation in the Hellenistic world at this time were composed in Greek. Vastly influential, his histories were to stand the test of time: becoming ubiquitous features, for example, in very many Victorian libraries. Making much of their origins and lineage, he put the Jews at the centre of political and social affairs. He also made assumptions about the Divine Providence of God and prophecy, eager to establish the projection of history and the place of the Jews within it. Accordingly, his 20-volume book *Antiquitates Judaicae*, or *Jewish Antiquities*, began at the Garden of Eden, from Adam, and ended its narrative on the eve of the Jewish revolt against the Romans in 66 CE. As a Jew, educated at a rabbinical school, sometime leader of the Galilee division of Jews that had rebelled against the Romans, he was now valued by the Romans as a seer. His rather changed circumstances allowed him a pension in order that he might devote all his time to writing history.

Flavius Josephus used evidence in a way that was somewhat different from those writing history before him. Personal knowledge and special access to commentaries from Tacitus (especially his records of military operations) gave him a head start. No doubt this access was due to his relatively elite situation, and for similar reasons he wrote in the Roman way of establishing annals or yearly accounts. But he also wrote thematically, digressing across pages in the absence of footnotes or appendices, using long speeches and direct quotations from conversations that he could not possibly have been privy to while exaggerating very much in the tradition of the Greeks. Here he is describing the situation in Jerusalem before the destruction of the Second Jewish Temple in Jerusalem:

> **As a procurator of Judaea Tiberius sent Pilate, who during the night, secretly and under cover, conveyed to Jerusalem the images of Caesar known as standards. When day dawned this caused great excitement among the Jews; for those who were near were amazed at the sight, which meant that their laws had been trampled on – they do not permit any craven image to be set up in the City – and the angry City mob was joined by a huge influx of people from the country. They rushed off to Pilate in Caesarea, and begged him to remove the standards from Jerusalem and to respect their ancient customs. When Pilate refused, they fell prone all round his house and remained motionless for five days and nights.**
>
> **The next day Pilate took his seat on the tribunal in the great stadium and summoned the mob on the pretext that he was ready to give them an answer. Instead he gave a pre-arranged signal to the soldiers to surround the Jews in full armour, and the troops formed a ring, three deep. The Jews were dumbfounded at the unexpected sight, but Pilate, declaring that he would cut them to pieces unless they accepted the images of Caesar, nodded to the soldiers to bare their swords. At this the Jews as though by agreement fell to the ground in a body and bent their necks, shouting that they were ready to be killed rather than transgress the Law. Amazed at the intensity of their religious fervour, Pilate ordered the standards to be removed from Jerusalem forthwith.** (Josephus, 1981, p. 138)

Although Josephus used long, verbatim speeches from his leading historical players, again like the Greeks, his history is in keeping with the methods of the Romans who we now know were concerned with morality in politics, especially the role of war in historical change, and used annals as a chronological device. There were elements that singled out Jewish historiography more generally from both its Greek and Roman counterparts: an inclination among Jewish histories to narrate events from the beginning of the world, not simply the beginning of human affairs; the concern with truth, not simply a truth focused on accuracy as we saw with the medieval Chroniclers discussed in the previous section, but a truth that must be told under the direct and searing gaze of the unitary and omnipotent God. Indeed remembrances of God and the miracles purported to have been part of the Hebrew legacy – the escape from Egypt most prominent among them – were (are) ritualistically re-enacted by Jewish families around the *seder* table every Passover. This was only the most famous of remembrances and the religious Jewish year, then and now, recounts and enacts past events with astonishing vividness and monotonous regularity.

Jews perhaps lacked historical method in comparison with the Greeks (or even the Romans) but they did not lack the wherewithal to establish and maintain public records. Some even described the Jewish archive in the antique period as superior to that of the Greeks. But whereas the Greeks maintained an interest in history through national decline and the rise of the Roman Empire, transmitting this interest through their culture, the Jews just switched off and dropped out.

There was, it appears, no lack of respect for the archive or for the enquiring mind – the Talmud (together made up of the Mishnah and the Gemara) is a codification of Jewish oral law that was written down between the second and fifth centuries and is a byword for jurisprudence and disputation. Yet even without the Talmud, Jewish books seemingly contained adequate descriptions of historical and 'contemporary' events, or so it appeared. The *Books of Ezra*, *Nehemiah* and the *First Book of Maccabees*, which told the story of heroic resistance against the Romans and which, according to Arnaldo Momigliano, stands at the 'crossroads between Jewish and Greek thought', were characterised by fierce rabbinical arguments (Momigliano, 1990). Above all, perhaps, the disappearance of the Jewish state in 66 CE (until its re-emergence in 1948) engineered a situation where Diasporic Jews in exile from the Promised Land, without a Temple in which to carry out the statutes and ordinances of the Law, ensured that they retained group solidarity and an historical fascination that centred above all on each other. And in any case, the Jews had a supreme history book – the Torah. No other history mattered, and it was this, according to Momigliano, that led to an indifference towards historical research.

In his *The Jew and his History* (1977), Lionel Kochan (1922–2005) confirmed that Jewish historiography was indeed all but non-existent from the antique period until R. Joseph Ha' Cohen (1496–1578) wrote an account of the kings of France and Ottoman Turkey. He rebutted, however, notions that Jews were simply absorbed by the biblical narrative or that as a people without a state they were less likely to have any kind of conventional historical culture, and that this provided a total explanation for centuries of silence. Likewise, he denied that Jews were overly affected by the Christian idea that Jews as a people, as a redundant covenant, had atrophied after the coming of Jesus and were now no longer relevant – a nation without a future hardly needed a past. Instead, Kochan suggested that the Jews affirmed history by praxis: by 'elaborating the means as opposed to luxuriating in the ends', which he judged to be 'the precise reversal of the utopian thinking common to the Gentile world' (Kochan, 1977, p. 117). While the Talmud does admit to a messianic process in history and even speculates that the world will endure for six thousand years after the End of Days in a series of eras, it rejects predictions of when, how or by what method the Messiah will appear – unlike the view of Christians. To do otherwise would be impious as it would claim to know the mind of God. Indeed, the whole notion of theology (the study of the nature of God) is not a Jewish idea as it can only invite error and credulity. As one Midrash (an ancient rabbinical interpretation of scripture) warned, if you are ploughing your field and someone shouts across that the Messiah has come, then indeed he may have come. But finish your ploughing before checking. In this sense the future in Judaism is as likely to be as practical and as down to earth as the present.

This scepticism about the propriety or efficacy of predicting utopia may explain why the most influential of scholars in the post-biblical era, Rabbi Moses ben Maimon or Maimonides (1138–1204), embraced all other aspects of Aramaic intellectual life such as maths, philosophy, medicine and poetry but declared historical books to be a 'waste of time'. Perhaps, however, as has recently been suggested by the historian Kenneth Seeskin, he did have a sense of the past but one that was perfectly in line with the medieval period in which he lived and focused on the role of the Jews as witnesses to the whole of human history and their solemn duty to survive (Seeskin, 2004). Not that Maimonides (the Rambam as he is commonly called) worked in a cultural vacuum. Indeed this was the 'Golden Age' of toleration between the three traditions, prompted by the Moorish conquest of Spain in 711, and which did not end until the Jews were expelled by the Christians in 1492. Throughout this period, cultural and intellectual cooperation with Islam was commonplace.

Islam appeared as a military force by 700 but Islamic historiography did not appear in any coherent way until 200 years later. Here, as with Christian historiography and the conversion of Constantine, a great break in history comes with the life and teachings of the Prophet Mohammad (569–632 CE). The emphasis, however, was on two things: history of dynasties and nations that impact on the Prophet's genealogy and lineage; and on histories of the future – again we see at work ideas about the end of the world or the Day of Judgement. Coverage of events such as the Creation of the world existed as part of a more general history but remained incidental. Like Christianity, histories of the life of Mohammad and Islamic historiography were fixed on the end of the world and this was anticipated with absolute certainly as if it had already happened.

Beginning in earnest around 600 or 700, Islamic historiography was subservient to Muslim law and religion, which was itself fused with Byzantine and Iranian influences and self-consciously aimed to become a worldly subject. Historians of these trends in Islam have addressed the issues of when exactly this written form of Islamic learning flourished and have sought to assess its effect and impact. The historian Chase Robinson (2003) talked about a formative period of Islamic historiography, which spanned from 600 to 900, and a classical period of output that ran from 950 to 1500. Franz Rosenthal, on the other hand, dated Islamic historiography as an independent force from 700 and as a tradition which simply reflected Muslim ideas and the learned culture of a civilisation that emerged over a very short space of time, coming to prominence in the late eighth and early ninth centuries. Indeed, while historiography provided an important space for individual self-expression it found its critics later as we moved to the fourteenth and fifteenth centuries from the 'harder sciences' such as philosophy or medicine.

Whatever the truth about the chronology and the reception of history as a reliable epistemology (a basis of knowledge) within the Islamic world, it is impossible to escape the sheer size of its production and its advanced state. This is especially true when we consider that the Chinese took 500 years to reach the volume and sophistication achieved by Muslim scholars over a period of just five generations. If this creative energy appears to burn out quicker than the Christian fuse that was lit, or at least rekindled, by the historian monk Bede, it was at least partly because this period of historical production within the Islamic world is all but irretrievable. Where European medieval scholars used parchment and animal skin to record their histories, their Islamic counterparts used paper materials that faded and disintegrated over time; were destroyed easily by foreign invaders; or fell foul of disputes internal to Islam. Consequently, there is a real problem faced by all present-day scholars of Islam that certainties about the 'formative period' of Islam are difficult to establish, while those seeking to recover the history of pre-Islamic society face an impossible task: there are simply no written records to consult.

What we can do is scrutinise the Islamic historiography of the so-called 'classical period' after 950 for its specific assumptions and methodologies and make judgements about its plausibility and effectiveness. Approaches according to current scholarship break down into a three-part typology of chronology, biography and prosopography. These distinct approaches serve to establish the contours and peculiarities of Islamic historiography within the wider contexts of the Arabisation of Islam, as does a quest for the details of the Prophet's life and the attempt to rescue from oblivion pre-Islamic history before written record or memory.

The evocation of memory played a crucial role in Islamic traditions but in different guises to that of Judaism or Christianity. Islamic historians used chronology to prove the veracity of prophetic biography to understand and 'prove' *hadith* or *hadeeth*, the oral tradition within Islam that recounted the teachings and the life of the Prophet. Likewise, *Sunnah* was a method that sought to learn more about the way of life of the Prophet. The 'science' of *hadeeth* criticism lent method to Islamic historiography. This methodology was immensely complex but at least seven categories of classification have been identified. These classifications were designed to test the reliability of the traditions and sayings that were attributed to the Prophet but where the provenance may be doubtful, or where a new issue of jurisprudence has been thrown up by modern circumstances. *Hadeeth* criticism looked first for an authoritative chain of evidence. This was called an *isnad*. *Isnad* asked questions about the reliability of witnesses, their links to one another, the chronological integrity of the evidence given or order of the evidence given. It is doubtful, however, that *hadeeth* as a legal tradition can be traced directly back to the time of the Prophet, probably dating no earlier than from 200 years or so after his death. While this view is largely a view maintained by western scholarship, naturally enough it is disputed by Islamic scholars. In either case what we discover (and what is critical for historians of Islam in the medieval period) is that the criterion of evidence and reliability of evidence is vastly different in eastern and western historiography, with standards of objective judgement and notions of subjectivity wildly different from each other, at least in periods after what the West calls the Middle Ages (Azzam, 1999).

The main priority of Islamic historiography in the past was to conserve the fragments of the past but it never quite managed to free itself from nostalgia for the past, nor did it adequately press the past into the service of the present. On the cusp of modernity in the 'Golden Age' in Spain, when it led the world in science, philosophy and medicine, thereafter Islam was slow to embrace change. Indeed, the end of the 'Golden Age' in the 1400s coincided with a shutting down of criticism of the Koran while, at precisely the same time, western science and then biblical criticism would encourage an increasingly open and secularising society.

That said, histories in the Arab world had existed in a wider cultural framework than the sayings of the Prophet and broke out somewhat from the constraints of the methodology of the *hadeeth*. Ya'qubi (d.*c.*897) made the first attempt in Arabic to write a world history (while including extracts from the Greeks) and others would later attempt histories that took in natural histories, local histories, dynastical histories, biographies of historical figures and so forth. Histories existed (often in Persian) after the Mongol invasions of the Muslim world in 1219 and by the fourteenth century histories were written in North Africa with a universal aspect and with some theoretical sophistication at that. Islamic histories since, however, have had none of the critical power of their counterparts in the secularising West and existed in circumstances where Muslim societies remained relatively backward and relatively repressive.

Section 3

The Renaissance, humanism and the rediscovery of the classics

The preoccupation throughout this chapter has been with the transmission of ideas; particularly, of course, ideas of how to write history. Ideas of what history meant among the ancients did not rest with the Greeks but continued with the Romans. They were more often than not neglected in the Christian years of the Middle Ages until their revival by the Renaissance. There is then an extraordinary transmission of Roman influence. It was at work, for example, in the short-lived medieval Roman republic (1347–54) in Italy which sought to revive the glories of the old Rome, and in the Italian communes of the European Renaissance, plus later in both the architecture and politics of the imperial ambitions of twentieth-century Italian Fascism and German Nazism. Both totalitarian systems were informed generally by the might of Rome and in particular the histories of Cornelius Tacitus (*c.*55–117 CE), especially his *Germania*, which when rediscovered in the fifteenth century was seen by Germans as a celebration of national independence and their racially pure beginnings. It was also used during the Reformation as yet more evidence of the alleged venal corruption of (by now) Papal Rome and by, comparison, the comparative nobility of the Germans in matters of private and public conduct. We also find the influence of Roman historiography at work in the representations of the American and French Revolutions, with figures such as Thomas Jefferson and Napoleon avid readers of the classical masters.

Yet far from the Renaissance signalling the bright new dawn of modernity, a positive gear-shift from the 'dark ages' of the medieval period, it is not entirely clear whether it ought to be regarded as an historical period at all. The provenance of the word Renaissance itself is disputed. It has been suggested that the term was coined first in 1550 by Giorgio Vasari (1511–74) in his *Lives of the Artists*. Others date it much later and credit the French historian Jules Michelet (1798–1874), supporter of the French Revolution and author of the multi-volume *History of France* (1833–62). That we do have a sense of the thirteenth, fourteenth and fifteenth centuries as forming a coherent whole is largely due to the intervention of a Swiss Hegelian scholar, Jacob Burckhardt (1818–97), especially in his *Civilization of the Renaissance in Italy* (2004).

The notion of the Renaissance was in very many ways a product of the nineteenth century. Here it was imagined that the Renaissance set forth the virtues of truth, reason, art and beauty, free from the superstitious and suffocating constraints of medievalism. The individual was given free reign of expression; the modern state (itself conceived as a 'work of art') was found in the Renaissance in a pure condition. Burckhardt even went as far as to suggest that individual self-consciousness was awoken through art and cultural expression and led directly to a new secular morality. Corporate identities of guild or church were laid to one side in favour of individualism, a kind of classlessness where merit was favoured before the accident of birth and where even (again according to Burckhardt) gender equality flourished. In some commentaries this movement has been understood as a 'movement' of 'villa' intellectuals based in southern Italy which eventually spread to the remainder of Italy and then the rest of Europe. Or an age which was not so much imagined as an era but experienced as a 'spirit', in line with Hegelian and German Romanticism (see Chapters 4 and 3).

Historians since Burckhardt have been more circumspect about this humanist moment when the arts and philosophy of the classical world were rediscovered. Burckhardt, though a Hegelian, rejected the Hegelian *telos*. He was also circumspect about ideas of history as a science, preferring instead to see history itself as an artefact, an imaginative exercise that is constructed through the subjective experiences of the individual. Historians have been resistant and rightly so in wholly taking in the picture painted by Burckhardt. A number of serious objections now make his thesis redundant. First, the new individualism that we associate with the Renaissance did not replace the collective solidarities of the medieval world. Both the guilds and the church, for instance, survived well into the modern era proper, as did affinities among a significant body of people to these institutions. Second, the place of Florence or Italy is not given such a prominent place in the history of the Renaissance and historians now are much more likely to consider economic factors that led to the transformation or 'waning' of the Middle Ages, which in turn ultimately led to the 'renaissance' in culture so brilliantly described by Burckhardt. In addition to these serious objections to Burckhardt, many historians now would point to earlier phases of cultural renewal and certainly not reject the Middle Ages as 'dark' and regressive (see Woolfson, 2005).

Only in the sixteenth century, however, do we see the slow rise of humanist approaches to the past; that is, beliefs that the well-being, values and morals of a society were not reliant on the supernatural intervention of God, or on the earth-bound rule of the church, but instead resided in the characteristics and behaviour of humans themselves. Humanism as a secular and cultural movement grew out of the Renaissance and spread across Europe based on the art and philosophy of ancient Greece and Rome. Above all, humanism and humanist histories focused upon the characteristics of human beings free from any mystical influence, an influence that had characterised medieval historiography. This is vital to understand as it represents a dramatic shift in thinking about the world; producing national histories that were very different in tone and approach from those that had preceded the Renaissance and which simultaneously satisfied a new demand to understand history and historical origins.

Present day historians have also made important interventions in the field and been instrumental in improving our understanding of the period. Some have modified Burckhardt and all have said something about the proximity (or otherwise) of the Renaissance to modernity and whether we might place it as a period (if distinct period it is) as part of a grand narrative in the western tradition. Peter Burke in his *European Renaissance* (1998) prefers to decentre the Renaissance experience, making it a global phenomenon involving a discrete network of locales and urban centres that interact – truly a civic humanism with a republican focus.

All commentaries, however, would agree that this period saw a major and sustained rediscovery of the classics, a renewed enthusiasm for antiquity and the classical tradition, including a *rapprochement* and reassessment of the Greek and Roman historians. Between about 1330 and 1370 we saw a successful attempt to recover Latin texts such as those by Cicero and the historian Livy. More than this, knowledge of ancient Greece was introduced into Italy in the last years of the fourteenth century. Above all, however, we saw the first humanist history published by the first of the 'new historians' in Italy, Leonardo Bruni (*c.*1370–1444), in his influential *History of Florence*. In doing so, he acknowledged a debt to Livy but also to Sallust and Tacitus whose *Annals* and *Histories* were also rediscovered in the closing decades of the fourteenth century. He also admitted to being a keen reader of both Thucydides and Polybius, going out of his way to condemn the lack of method and style associated with the medieval Chroniclers. Bruni made sophisticated use of comparative sources and his use of speeches which were more or less constructed were in keeping with the classics. What then had changed between now, the high point of the Renaissance, and the Middle Ages?

It is not as if the Chroniclers of the Middle Ages were unaware of the ancient historians. Or, indeed, that the classics remained unread. It was just that as Christians they did not look outside of their tradition for explanations or insights into method and approaches towards the past, any more than the Jews or Muslims had spent long outside of theirs. Not until, that is, the 'new historians' began to imagine that Florentine's civic virtues were not necessarily specifically derived through Christianity. In response, perhaps, Pope Nicholas V (1447–55) commissioned Latin translations of the Greek historians to allow the church to find reasons to celebrate its role in the history of Rome. The 'new history' of the Renaissance took rhetoric seriously (reintroducing the long verbatim speeches associated with Greek historiography) and became more inclined to reject legend or hearsay as solid historical evidence. We also find national histories treated much more seriously with histories of England, Italy, as well as a continuing civic concern with the history of Florence, by Polydore Virgil (*c.*1470–1555), Francesco Guicciardini (1483–1540) and Niccolo Machiavelli (1469–1527).

Most important among these is Machiavelli who has been viewed most often as the personification of political intrigue and as an exponent of a distinctive humanist tradition of classical republicanism (Skinner, 1981, pp. 78–88). Quentin Skinner in a brief and interesting account of Machiavelli's life and influence had him working against humanist beliefs in ways that remain both innovative and creative. Known chiefly for the publication of *The Prince* (1513) and *The Art of War* (1520), we can be forgiven for thinking that Machiavelli's' legacy was more important to politics than history. Yet he *is* important for any basic understanding of Renaissance historical thought. The *History of Florence* (1525) that he wrote towards the end of his life suggested a knowing of and sympathy with classical historiography, as did his *Discourses Upon the First Ten books of Titus Livy* (1517) with its emphasis on public morality that in itself demonstrated his humanist concerns (Skinner, 1981, p. 78). Machiavelli was also concerned in his histories with, in common with the ancients, rhetoric and the celebration of ancestry. Here we can see the influence of not only Livy, but Sallust and others. His histories (like the classics) were 'dominated by idealized heroes and reprehensible villains' (Bondanella, 1973, p. 17) and more often than not he preferred a character-led narrative that could bend the truth. Francesco Guicciardini (1483–1540), on the other hand, using the tools of family history such as diaries, was not so easily associated with humanism. Nor did he 'follow the humanist rules for historical writing' which have:

- introductions and general reflections.
- speeches.
- omens and 'celestial constellations' that govern the affairs of Man (Gilbert, 1965, p. 230).

Renaissance humanists like these not only labelled the Middle Ages as the 'dark ages' and characterised their own age as immeasurably enlightened by comparison, but also largely celebrated its culture and governance, a new period set apart from the past with any impoverishment in arts and learning thought to have been inflicted by the stagnation of the Middle Ages. Thus, in 1469, Giovanni Andrea Bussi (1414/17–75) began a process of re-periodising the history of the West in a way that was to become immensely influential well into the modern period when Burckhardt and other figures such as Jules Michelet and Walter Pater (1839–94) looked back at the Renaissance as a period of purple and gold at the expense of the Middle Ages and, in the case of Pater, with a deep-seated criticism of Christianity too. This reassessment also had the effect of placing classical antiquity at the foundation of western civilisation, a notion contested by present-day medievalists such as Marcia Colish:

> **the foundations of western intellectual history were laid in the Middle Ages and not in classical Greece and Rome or the Judeo-Christian tradition. In defence of that claim we argue that the thought of Western Europe acquired its particular character not only as a result of the cultural components that flowed into it. Equally important were the attitudes that western thinkers took to their sources and the uses to which they put them. It is certainly true that medieval thinkers expressed concerns, tastes, tolerances, and sensibilities that distinguish this period from other chapters of the western intellectual experience. At the same time, they developed institutions, viewpoints, and methods that mark them as specifically western and that helps to explain why medieval Europe is the only traditional society known to history to modernize itself from within, intellectually no less than economically and technologically, enabling Europe to impose its cultural as well as political stamp on much of the non-European world as the Middle Ages drew to a close.** (Colish, 1997, p. x)

The Renaissance ended, at least according to Peter Burke, in the early seventeenth century and by the affects unleashed by the scientific revolution, although it does seem that Francis Bacon openly accepted the influence of Machiavelli on English historiography. It is in this scientific revolution (as well as the waves caused by civil war) that we can locate early English attempts to write national histories and to make sense of an antiquarian engagement with the past. It is, therefore, to the battle between the 'ancients and the moderns' in revolutionary England that we next turn our attention.

In practice

There is a certain orthodoxy which views the Renaissance as a time when the arts underwent a profound transformation. After the darkness and backwardness of the Middle Ages, the argument goes, European thinkers rediscovered the works of ancient Greeks and Romans, in part through translations made by Islamic scholars, and embarked on a new course of intellectual and artistic inquiry which paved the way for the great tradition of western humanism. The truth behind this rather convenient narrative is more complicated, and we need only to review the fate of historical inquiry to see this was the case.

The legacy of the outstanding classical historians was never lost. Instead, the three traditions of historical inquiry which dominated the medieval period took what lessons they needed about the nature of historical evidence and the ordering of chronological narratives to create new directions for the writing of history. These directions were determined largely by the emergence of the omniscient presence of 'the book', and the perceived need to consolidate its authority by study of the past. Thus, the Christian historians who came to dominate western historiography sought to explain the past and predict the future in ways which were consistent with accounts found in the Bible. Similarly, Jewish historians found inspiration in the Torah, and Islamic scholars looked to the Koran. Despite the differences in emphasis, what united these traditions was a belief in a single God, a universal power which by governing human destiny allowed for the opportunity of a universal history.

In the medieval period, therefore, we find historians such as Bede who drew freely upon classical historiography to write broad historical narratives of events and periods. They used a wide variety of sources, adopted a critical stance to different forms of evidence, and determinedly set about recording plausible chronicles which were consistent with the evidence. Despite such promiscuity, the extent to which these traditions entered into a dialogue with one another was limited. Bede, for example, wrote at a time before Islamic scholarship established itself, and after an early flowering, Jewish historical scholarship entered into a period of protracted silence, only to re-emerge with the Renaissance.

Although the Renaissance was in part made possible by the forgotten works of the classical period newly translated from the Arabic, it signalled a new enthusiasm, particularly among European historians, to look beyond the boundaries of Christian thought, and with a return to the concerns of classical historians to think more seriously at the role of human agency in historical processes. This shift toward humanism in turn paved the way for the scientific revolution of the seventeenth century. And yet it should be remembered that the Renaissance did not necessarily signal a sharp break, rather it brought together the accumulated scholarship of ancient and medieval Europe and the non-European world, and reworked it into a new vision of humanism.

Summary

The three sections of this chapter have said three things:

- Christian approaches to history in the Middle Ages were based on uses of historical evidence that would not be deemed acceptable or robust to modern sensibilities regarding the objectivity of the historian and the subjectivity of the witness. Historians such as Bede in the early medieval world were overwhelmingly concerned to locate the signs and portents inherent in historical events that would help confirm how far humanity was on the timeline towards the End of Days, discerned according to prophecy. In this sense, Bede was concerned to both establish a chronology that could locate the common feasts and festivals on the Christian calendar and to locate the history of Christianity in Britain.

- Non-European ideas of the nature of history were somewhat different from those of Christianity. Jewish historiography had a vivid exponent in the shape of Flavius Josephus who wrote with verve and colour, giving us an extraordinary account of what it was like to live under Roman rule. This was the last heard of Jewish historians, however, until the sixteenth century. Islamic historiography, on the other hand, was enormously rich by the time Bede was writing in the European context and even richer as the European Renaissance approached. Some attention was given to how Islamic historians understood the methodology needed, for example, to determine how the words of the Prophet Muhammad could be verified. This historical culture dissipated after the fifteenth century when movements toward reformation, secularisation and attempts to create a public sphere where the veracity of the Koran could be criticised were thwarted.

- The end of the Middle Ages was greeted, arguably, with a Renaissance of ideas, culture and individuality but also, unarguably, with new approaches to the past. These were characterised by a number of notable scholars but most had in common a certain reverence for the ancients as humanism took a fresh prominence. Once again the methods and concerns of the great classical historians – most Roman but some Greek – were celebrated. So too was the civic virtue of the city state. Florence in particular and Italy in general were soon viewed in a renewed light. The attributes that we associate both with antiquity and again with the Renaissance were to have a profound effect on the historiography that was to come after, not least to the revolutionary creed of seventeenth-century England.

Discussion document 1

This is an account by a notable ninth-century Islamic historian of the seventh-century invasion of Roman-controlled Syria by Islamic forces. It uses the familiar device of recounting verbatim the forms of the main historical actors but admixes these speeches with direct quotations from the Koran and puts into the mouths of these personalities some basic assumptions about Islam and its relations with unbelievers that would instantly be recognised by Muslims at that time.

Abu Bakr said, 'When you leave a place do not cause the men difficulty in marching. Do not punish your men harshly. Consult them in every matter. Do not abandon justice and stay far from injustice and tyranny because no tyrant nation has ever obtained success nor been victorious over another nation. Act upon the Qura n's dictate:

> When you meet those who disbelieve on the battlefield, never turn your backs on them [i.e. flee]. And whoever turns his back on them on such a day – unless it is a strategy of war, or a retreat (to his own) troops – has indeed drawn upon himself the wrath of Allah.
>
> [8:16–17]

That is to say, when you encounter the army of Disbelievers then do not flee for whoever flees, loses the battle. When you have obtained victory do not slay any small children, old people, women or pre-adolescents. Do not approach the harvests or trees. Crops should not be burnt nor fruit trees cut. Do not slaughter any animal which is impermissible. Do not break any agreement which you make with the enemy and after peace do not tear up your treaties. Remember that you will also meet such people who have undertaken monasticism in their monasteries, thinking this to be the sake of Allah. Do not interfere with them for as long as they choose this isolationism – do not destroy their monasteries and do not destroy them.

You will also meet such a Satanic people who worship the Cross. They shave their heads in the middle to expose their skulls. Cut off their heads until they accept Islam or pay Jizyah [the tax levied in Islamic countries on non-Muslims] disgraced. Now I place you in Allah's hands, may he protect you.'

He then shook hands and embraced Yazid and then shook hands with Rabi ah saying, 'Rabi ah bin 'Amir, show your bravery and intelligence in fighting the Romans. May Allah fulfil all your desires and forgive us all'.

Abia Afsar Siddiqui (ed.), Al-Imam al Waqidi, *The Islamic Conquest of Syria: 'Futuhusham' the Inspiring History of the Sahabah's Conquest of Syria*, translated by Sulayman al-Kindi (2005), pp. 12–13. Available at: www.scribd.com/doc/36129626/Futuhusham-The-Islamic-Conquest-of-Syria-Al-Waqidi.

Discussion document 2

Jacob Burckhardt is a powerful and persuasive advocate for the Renaissance who should always be read with caution. However, we find here a neat summary of his view of the importance of humanism and the rediscovery of the classics in fifteenth-century Italy.

Some modern writers deplore the fact that the germs of a far more independent and essentially national culture, such as appeared in Florence about the year 1300, were afterwards so completely swamped by the humanists. There was then, we are told, nobody in Florence who could not read; even the donkeymen sang the verses of Dante; the best Italian manuscripts which we possess belonged originally to Florentine artisans; the publication of a popular encyclopaedia, like the 'Tesoro' of Brunetto Latini, was then possible; and all this was founded on strength and soundness of character due to the universal participation in public affairs, to commerce and travel, and to the systematic reprobation of idleness. The Florentines, it is urged, were at that time respected and influential throughout the whole world, and were called in that year, not without reason, by Pope Boniface VIII, 'the fifth element.' The rapid progress of humanism after the year 1400 paralysed native impulses. Henceforth men looked only to antiquity for the solution of every problem, and consequently allowed literature to turn into mere quotation. Nay, the very fall of civil freedom is partly ascribed to all this, since the new learning rested on obedience to authority, sacrificed municipal rights to Roman law, and thereby both sought and found the favour of the despots.

These charges will occupy us now and then at a later stage of our inquiry, when we shall attempt to reduce them to their true value, and to weigh the losses against the gains of this movement. For the present we must confine ourselves to showing how the civilization even of the vigorous fourteenth century necessarily prepared the way for the complete victory of humanism, and how precisely the greatest representatives of the national Italian spirit were themselves the men who opened wide the gate for the measureless devotion to antiquity in the fifteenth century.

Jacob Burckhardt, *The Civilization of the Renaissance in Italy*, translated by S. G. C. Middlemore (1878).

Further reading

* *essential*

* **Chris Given-Wilson**, *Chronicles: The Writing of History in Medieval Britain* (2004).
Deals with a relatively short time span (*c.*1270–1430), yet gives a sophisticated account of late-medieval or early-modern historiography, asking essential questions about the writing and practicing of history in this period.

Bede, *The Ecclesiastical History of the English*, trans. (1999).
With introduction and notes by Judith McClure this is an invaluable complement to this chapter. It is best read alongside Penguin's *Age of Bede*, reprinted in 2004.

* **Paolo Delogu**, *An Introduction to Medieval History* (2002).
Translated from the Italian, this short volume is fantastically rich both in its treatment of historians and Chroniclers over a long period (longer than that covered by Given-Wilson) and is very comprehensive in its discussion of medieval history across Europe, paying particular attention to developments in individual countries.

* **Arnaldo Momigliano**, *Classical Foundations of Modern Historiography* (1990).
This is the definitive work in the field and should be read at all costs, not least for its treatment of diverse religious traditions that interact over time.

* **Chase F. Robinson**, *Islamic Historiography* (2003).
Comprehensive and provocative, this take on Islamic historiography is well-researched, clear and accessible to the uninitiated.

* **Lucille Kekewich** (ed.), *The Impact of Humanism: A Cultural Enquiry* (2000).
Published to accompany an Open University course and therefore broken down in a way that is easy to understand. It also contains ready-made questions and discussions around the subject area.

Jonathan Woolfson (ed.), *Renaissance Historiography* (2005).
This collection of essays is designed to orientate students in the wake of a good deal of recent work on the Renaissance, self-consciously styling itself as an updating of Ferguson (1948). Essays by Peter Burke, James Hankins, Robert Black and Jonathan Woolfson himself, are the most useful.

8 The English tradition

Introduction

The researching and writing of English history changed fundamentally in the period that we think of as early modern. When exactly it changed is a matter of dispute but sometime in the late sixteenth century or early seventeenth century seems generally agreed by most historians. How it changed is disputed less. The chronicles of the period before about 1580 took their cue from religious concerns and their primary sources from the Bible. The results tended to disregard evidence based in testimony or verifiable fact and instead reproduced narratives of the past that were mythical and fantastic. As we see in the first section, the writing and research of the national story was influenced largely by the Renaissance and Italian commentators (themselves influenced by the classics) and became the preserve not of monks or churchmen but of the new professional classes who used antiquarian evidence drawn from, say, coins, ruins or landscapes to compose humanist histories. The second section outlines the Whig inheritance of this 'revolution' (or otherwise) of history. Whig history is defined as present minded in that it judges the past in the light of the present. From the Magna Carta to the culmination of English liberties in the events of the Glorious Revolution of 1688, the Protestant ascendency resulted, it was thought, in a perfect constitution. Whig history approved those historical players that were allies to the perfecting of this constitution and condemned those that stood in its way. This led to a school of history practice and outlook that the third section argues can be traced via Macaulay and then Trevelyan to his student Jack Plumb and now to a coterie of 'New Whig' Cambridge historians – Linda Colley, David Cannadine, Simon Schama, Roy Porter, and others such as Neil McKendrick and John Vincent – who were taught by or were profoundly influenced by Plumb and who have developed the whig view in that (1) their research is moved by present-day issues; (2) they think that history has a public, social or popular purpose; and (3) they see the story of nation and constitution as their main concerns with good literary prose and the use of visual evidence as important features of their work.

Section 1

The Battle of the Books: Camden, Clarendon and English historical writing

That great satirist of the eighteenth century, Jonathan Swift, portrayed the 'Battle of the Books' in his *Tale of the Tub* in 1703/5 as a war where printed volumes flew across a library in angry pursuit of one another. These were no ordinary books, however, for this was a war between 'ancient' books and 'modern' books. The lines were clearly drawn and the questions stark. Were the Greeks and Romans superior to those that followed them? Or have the 'moderns' equalled or even surpassed them? This battle was a confrontation between those that looked to the ancients for their approach to the writing of history and literature and those that held onto approaches that were nurtured throughout European medieval Christendom, but which, in this dispute at least, we must think of as modern. This dispute of methodology and style, although first mooted in literally circles, was to have a profound influence on future history writing.

Swift worked at the time of the controversy for the great advocate of the ancient position, Sir William Temple (1628–99). Temple had written *An Introduction to the History of England* (1695), which is seen by historians as limited in scope and range, and wildly inaccurate. As Joseph Levine (1991) argued, it was a history very much written in the style of the classics, in that it:

- emphasised a good story and is well written;
- neglected discussion of sources;
- was without footnotes (like a scroll used by the ancients);
- was reliant, like many of the ancient historians, on a 'borrowed' single source (in this case an Elizabethan historian who was not mentioned).

The moderns, by contrast, focused on Anglo-Saxon or biblical narratives about the past, rehabilitating the approach to English history of the medieval Chroniclers. Quite often Chroniclers used the Pentateuch (the five books of Moses in the Bible) as both the foundation of their histories and the fountain of all narratives concerned with nations and national consciousness. Just as the provenance of Israel could be traced to the exodus from Egypt or to the giving of the Torah at Sinai, so the national story of Albion was told by Chroniclers such as the early twelfth-century Benedictine monk, Geoffrey of Monmouth, by reference to an ancient, mythical past. Albion was a place peopled by giants until Brutus and Curiness came to Britain with the Roman Empire and killed Goemigoy and other giants apparently descended from the biblical figures Noah, Ham, Cain and Enoch who had arrived on these shores sometime before the Flood.

Another Benedictine monk from Chester, Ranulf Higden (d.1364), wrote *Polychronicon*. This was said to be the first universal history written in England and outlined the social customs, religion, social geography, natural history and so on of the British Isles but within the context of a world narrative. Its influence was immense and various editions (different in length) appeared well into the fifteenth century. More generally, the function of these types of Chronicles was to narrate the past, present information, commemorate great events, and entertain the reader. Above all else, Chronicles emphasised the mythical only later giving way in the Elizabethan and early Stuart periods to more rational and verifiable histories.

This Battle of the Books fought between the advocates of the ancients and of the 'modern' or Christian-inspired Chroniclers is important to us because it was part of the eighteenth-century debate about how histories of England should be written. It might appear that differences between the types of narrative used to describe England were at the heart of the dispute, but we shall discover that the approach to evidence also became important. Certainly, the Battle of the Books illustrated the state of historiography in England at this time and how it had changed in the century between the death of Elizabeth I (1603) until the mid seventeenth-century civil war. By the seventeenth century observers could appreciate the effects of long-term change, the vital importance of national narratives, and the attendant changes in manners and sensibilities that turned historical writing from a concern of the local monastic chronicler or civic official into the professional or leisurely pursuit of the university student or lay reader (Woolf, 2000). As a result, English histories drew upon the lessons from the classics by using the evidence of English antiquities and the ruins that marked the landscape, as well as coins, genealogies and maps. But above all else there was a fresh approach prompted by the change in how the church exercised its authority, the rise of commercial considerations of how history might be produced, sold and distributed, and the slow growth of a class who had more time and inclination to indulge in historical research which was once the preserve of medieval scribes. So, as it turned out, the ancients were in fact modern, which points to the contradictory nature of these labels.

The timing of this apparent revolution in history writing and historical understanding has been the subject of debate among historians. F. S. Smith Fusser (1962) thought these changes in historiography happened somewhere between 1580 and 1640. Others such as Arthur Ferguson looked less to the literary changes in writing and more to changes in historical method or, according to Woolf, the slow, 'longer lasting' revolution in social mores as interest grew in literary culture and scholarship along with the ascendency of a commercial society. We could date this moment from the time that the Italian-born Polydore Vergil (*c.*1470–1555) wrote *Anglica Historia* as a humanist-style history in 1512–13 but waited until 1534 before publishing. It was probably the first of its type in England; a history that discussed the English from the time of the Romans right through to Henry VIII. What made it a 'humanist' history was his use of Renaissance-inspired methodology but also the questioning of some of the more fantastic accounts of English history offered by Geoffrey of Monmouth and others. Like the Battle of the Books in the early eighteenth century, it sought to revive classical learning at the expense of more modern Christian accounts. Yet in truth, the humanist moment was not to wield influence with anything like full force until about 1580 when medieval historiography was attacked above all else for the sources it used.

That humanist-inspired scholarship was revolutionary has been placed in grave doubt in recent years. F. J. Levy's *Tudor Historical Thought* (2004) made clear that the changes wrought between Polydore Vergil's arrival in England in 1502 and William Camden's death in 1623 amounted to a fundamentally different approach to historical research and writing but in ways that were essentially gradual. Certainly William Camden (1551–1623), historian and herald, is a significant figure but not a revolutionary one. His *Britannia* (1586) stuck to the chronology of the traditional annals but made – like the histories of Francis Bacon before him – a sharp distinction between secular and religious history, although he is keen to place blame on the Papists while at the same time steering away from any criticism of Elizabeth I. His history may have been partial but it was not, however, a history moved by religious sensibilities. (Vergil's history, or at least the first draft, ended at the reign of Henry VIII and was also keen not to offend the monarch.) Considering the use of heraldry and genealogy and the interest this engendered in local as well as national history, Camden's *Britannia* was, in the words of Smith Fussner, 'original, serviceable, and characteristic of the new scholarship' (Smith Fussner, 2010, p. 217).

As historiography was revolutionised (or not) it also fragmented. In addition to antiquarianism we have memoir and autobiography, local propaganda and satire, which were also concerned with the past. Critically, however, while historians would remain deeply religious and traditional in their own affiliations (Camden wrote in Latin and no translations to the vernacular were permitted in his lifetime) the function of history was no longer simply to 'reveal God's purposes and instruct man in his proper behaviour' (Brownley, p. 2). This represents a change from the Chroniclers, such as the martyrologist, John Foxe (1516/17–87), who had all but disappeared during the seventeenth century.

Perhaps the most complete demonstration of a humanist history in the seventeenth century came out of the terrible conflict of 1640–60, which would become a moment when future (Whig) historians thought that England was begun anew. In 1641, Edward Hyde, the First Earl of Clarendon (1609–74), wrote his *The History of the Rebellion and Civil War in England*, which was to attract huge critical and popular acclaim. In fact the book was so popular it was erroneously said to have provided the University of Oxford with the Clarendon Building – certainly it hosts a statue of the author. Beyond dispute is the fact that Hyde was to become Chancellor of the University and a major figure in Restoration politics. His prose suggests a fundamentally different approach to evidence and analysis than the medieval Chronicles that preceded it and as such can be categorised as an advanced humanist approach. Unlike the Chronicle, it drew differences between past and present, identifying historical anachronism and civil (as opposed to purely religious) morality. Equally, while Camden was an astrologist in his youth, there was no longer need for historians to look for omens and portents in history. Power was more inclined to be earth-bound.

Others who were part of this shift to humanism include Sir Walter Raleigh (1554–1618) who wrote his *History of the World* in 1614 and John Dryden (1631–1700) who became Historiographer Royal in 1670. Second cousin to Jonathan Swift, Dryden was known as a literary figure, having become Poet Laureate in 1668. This is critical to note because history in this time was dominated by antiquarians who utilised the relics of history as the mainstay of evidence while never really elevating history as a literary art. The Society of Antiquaries was founded in 1707 and, both then and now, antiquarianism suggests an approach to the material remains of the past that may include archaeology, works of art, manuscripts and books, or the built environment (Sweet, 2004). Indeed one historian

(Brownley, p. 18) speaks of this period as one of 'arid antiquarian compilation' while suggesting that the 'complete integration of literary art and historical method' would have to wait to the end of the eighteenth century and the work of William Robertson, David Hume and, in particular, Edward Gibbon, all historians we associate with the Enlightenment discussed in Chapter 3.

In order to understand the transition from Chronicle to humanist history to whig history it is important to understand how the seventeenth century has been treated by historians. For Clarendon, the conflict that he himself had experienced was a 'Great Rebellion', while for the whig historian Samuel Rawson Gardiner (1829–1902) it was a 'Puritan Revolution'. His *History of England, 1603–1640* (1863) ran to 18 volumes. Between 1886 and 1891 another three volumes entitled *The Great Civil War* appeared, taking the story beyond the regicide or 'execution' of Charles I in 1649. Next came *The History of the Commonwealth and Protectorate*, which he completed in 1902. In this body of work, Gardiner displayed some of the characteristic features of whig history, most notably a narrative approach which prevails over analysis, and an empiricism that encourages the collection of facts and a steadfast adherence to chronology and statecraft.

Later, Marxists such as Christopher Hill (1912–2003) would see the events of 1640–60 as a 'bourgeois' revolution, while later still the so-called 'Revisionists' and then 'Post-Revisionists' would in some measure rehabilitate Charles I. Only with the 'New British History' did the Bishop's Wars in Scotland (1639–41) and the Irish Rebellion (1641) enjoy full coverage, suggesting, not a purely English history at all, but what seventeenth-century scholars today have labelled a 'War in the Three Kingdoms' or the 'British Civil Wars'. The nature of evidence has changed too. Now there is a good deal more emphasis placed on 'the linguistic turn' (Chapter 9) and sources that highlight the politics of discourse, symbols, or representations of the conflict such as the 'print explosion' which led to the production of the Thomason Tracts, a major source for the English Civil War that Gardiner was one of the first to exploit. As historians have developed this historiography it is in the knowledge that Clarendon made the first, all-important, intervention and commented upon the conflict and the political upset while passions were still flaming hot (Walton, 2010, pp. 13–15).

Some see these essentially humanist histories as important moments in the making of the nation and a critical moment too for the fashioning of history in its most up-to-date guise. It was the Exclusion Crisis at the end of the seventeenth century (explaining why Swift made his intervention on the side of the ancients in 1703/05) that gave birth to the current constitutional settlement that balances Parliament with Monarch. It was as important as the signing of the Magna Carta in 1215 or the defeat by the English over the Scots at the Battle of Falkirk in 1298 or the expulsion of the Jews in the 1290s had been or either the Act of Union in 1707 or the Declaration of Independence in the Americas in 1776 would become. History could now tell the story of constitution and country and it was this narrative of unfolding constitutional liberty which defined the Whig interpretation of history.

Section 2

Constitutionalism and the whig interpretation of history

> **With the ascension of Charles I to the throne we come at last to the Central Period of English History (not to be confused with the Middle Ages, of course), consisting in the *utterly memorable struggle between the Cavaliers (Wrong but Wromantic) the Roundheads (Right but Repulsive).* Charles I was a Cavalier King and therefore had a small pointed beard, long flowing curls, a large, flat, flowing hat and *gay attire*. The Roundheads, on the other hand, were clean shaven and wore tall, conical hats, white ties and *sombre garments*. Under these circumstances a Civil War was inevitable.** (Sellar and Yeatman, 1930, p. 75)

This is taken from the spoof history *1066 and All That*. As a send-up of late Victorian and Edwardian 'drum and trumpet' school history it remains quite brilliant; put simply it satirises the tendency for whig history to pick historical winners while telling the story of nation, constitution and great men.

Whig history has been an influential current in English historiography. It origins can be traced to Thomas Babington Macaulay (1800–59) who was to become the first of a dynasty of whig historians. Some clue to his whiggish approach to history was to be employed to such good effect in his own *History of England* in 1848 as he argued that history must recover from the novelist the recording of ordinary lives alongside narratives that deal only with power. His *History* was not a tract for democracy or radical in any conventional sense but his sources reflected the experiences of the common people – routinely using ballads and popular songs as historical evidence. So despite his broadly empirical approach, he and other whigs did not regard history as a science and the historian as a scientist.

In 1904, George Macaulay Trevelyan (1876–1962), a great nephew to Macaulay and a worthy successor in the whig tradition, published his well-received survey called *England under the Stuarts*. In familiar whig style, his focus was the story of the civil war and the settlement of 1688 where he located the victory of Protestant religious toleration winning over Catholic absolutism in a climate of parliamentary freedom which, critically, signalled the beginning of the modern empire. This was accomplished but unremarkable as an argument, as was that in his *Lord Grey of the Reform Bill* (1920). The reforms of the whig ascendency of the 1820s and 1830s were, after all, the origins of the wider franchise. His *History of England* in 1926 did something similar: it was concerned with the national story, the development of parliament and the evolution of independent systems of law, freedom and the singularity of empire.

Whig history attracted its critics, the most influential being Herbert Butterfield (1900–79), who in his *The Whig Interpretation of History* (1931) launched an assault on an approach to the past which had been dominant – or at least so it was argued – from the seventeenth century to the early twentieth. Butterfield argued that the whig interpretation carried a number of mistaken assumptions. Perhaps the most prominent of these is the present-minded nature of whiggish historical enquiry:

> **Real historical understanding is not achieved by the subordination of the past to the present, but rather by our making the past our present and attempting to see life with the eyes of another century than our own. It is not reached by assuming that our own age is the absolute to which Luther and Calvin and their generation are only relative; it is only reached by fully accepting the fact that their generation was as valid as our generation, their issues as momentous as our issues and their day as full and vital to them as our day is to us . . . for both the method and the kind of history that results from it would be impossible if all the facts were told in all their fullness. The theory that is behind the whig interpretation – the theory that we study the past for the sake of the present – is one that is really introduced for the purpose of facilitating the abridgement of history; and its effect is to provide us with a handy rule of thumb by which we can easily discover what was important in the past.**
>
> (Butterfield, 1931, p. 13)

According to the whig view of history, the constitutional settlement established in England in the seventeenth century – the Glorious Revolution – was the zenith of political governance (the 'Central Period' as Sellar and Yeatman put it) and followed from the establishment of the Magna Carta. From that all previous and subsequent history could be judged and the present would become subservient to the past, to 'emphasize certain principles of progress in the past and to produce a story which is the ratification if not the glorification of the present' (Butterfield, 1931, p. 2). Those that facilitated this leap forward in human affairs were heroes; those that opposed it political villains. All history, therefore, was a struggle between Absolutist (usually Royalist or Catholic) power and that of the popular will, most often expressed in Parliament and Protestantism. For Butterfield, this led historians to make false connections across periods and epochs – to 'abridgement' – picking out an event they supported or opposed depending on whether it fitted a narrative of unfolding political freedom. Most seriously it suggested that the unfolding constitution was as perfect as any in human history and was the main prompt or context for understanding and writing of English history.

From this perspective, all history worth retrieving was connected to the history of progress. The whig interpretation of history skewed the selection of evidence that was important to this narrative and implied a causation between events that may only have existed in the mind of the historian. Butterfield argued instead that historians should reject links in history that lend history a progressive trajectory, instead they should look for what is unique in any epoch and not for continuities that confirm history as developmental.

These 'fallacies', he proceeded, to 'which all history is liable' include the identification of crucial events or turning points on the road to Protestant constitutional freedoms that we (it was argued) enjoy today. There was then a list of historians that the contemporary historian J. W. Barrow thought belonged to what he described as part of a 'Liberal Descent' or liberal tradition which focused, like William Stubbs' *Constitutional History of England* (1873–8), on constitutional progress or the preservation of the ancient constitution. Probably the first history in this tradition, however, was the *Constitutional History of England from the Accession of Henry VII to the Death of George II* (2 volumes, 1827) by Henry Hallam (1777–1859). He defended the constitution by arguing for Catholic emancipation – publishing on the cusp of some major constitutional reforms – he similarly deplored the persecution of Protestant dissidents under the Stuarts and Tudors. William Lecky (1838–1903) wrote a history of England in the 1870s on the greatest division within English history, namely, that between the Civil War and the peaceful constitutional settlement of the Glorious Revolution of 1688. Whig historians regarded it as axiomatic that these events were stepping stones to the present. So much so that in 1892 Lecky said revealingly that 'we are Cavaliers or Roundheads before we are Conservatives or Liberals' (Collini, 1999, p. 14) thus showing exactly what it was that Sellar and Yeatman were lampooning in the opening part of this section.

Peter Ghosh in a succinct commentary on the whig interpretation of history inevitably went back to Butterfield's critique of the genre that Butterfield insisted was invented by sixteenth and seventeenth century lawyers (Ghosh, p. 1293–4). Yet in the later *The Englishman and his History* (1944), we find Butterfield arguing that while history was based on the notion of unfolding liberty, it was at the very least fortuitous and the result of the English – note 'English' – character. In this respect Butterfield never really escaped from the clutches of the whig approach himself nor, according to Ghosh, could he accept (as a Christian) a non-Christian or secular teleology.

Butterfield's analysis of whig history drew upon a longer current of criticism. Historians such as J. R. Green (1837–83) in his *Short History of the English People* (London, 1878) and Eben William Robertson (1815–74) in his *Historical Essays in Connection with the Land and Church etc* (1872, republished 2010) had said much the same:

> **To look upon the past with the eyes of the present, to judge of its events and of its characters by a similar standard, awarding praise or blame to the men who felt and thought and acted in bygone days, as if their conduct had been shaped in accordance with the ideas influencing their remote descendants, – such has, and is, and ever will be the habit of the majority of living men. . . . The present age simply repeats the habit of the past.**
>
> (Robertson, 2010, pp. vii, viii)

Perhaps the greatest touchstone of whiggish history, however, is the Protestant ascendency of the fifteenth and sixteenth centuries, and the changes in religious practice between about 1530 and 1580. 'Popular' and lay religion was thought by Whig historians to be infused with heresy, witchcraft, superstition, Paganism and magic, while the 'elite', Catholic religion was seen to be a separate force, manipulative and controlling the masses. Protestantism, on the other hand, had greater rationality as folk beliefs gave way to the Reformation and a more diverse Protestant orthodoxy stood against Catholic absolutism and a decadent religious tradition that had run out of steam.

This narrative is challenged in Eamon Duffy's magisterial and ground-breaking book *The Stripping of the Altars: Traditional Religion in England c.1400–c.1580* (1992), in which he argued against generations of school essays and undergraduate theses that assumed the underlying truth of the whig viewpoint that Protestantism was an inevitable part of constitutional progress. Unlike whig convention that has Protestantism carrying the torch of progress, almost destined to usher in the constitution that emerged from the 'stripping of the altars' leading to the Civil War and the Glorious Revolution when Protestantism ran riot into Puritanism, Duffy sees the Protestant influence as exaggerated. Put simply, '. . . late Medieval Catholicism exerted an enormously strong, diverse and vigorous hold over the imagination and the loyalty of the people up to the very moment of Reformation' (Duffy, 2005, p. 4). Instead of 'popular' and 'elite' religious structures, Duffy argues for the notion of 'traditional' religion, which as a Catholic himself (the book is dedicated to the Latin Mass) he takes to be, as one reviewer recalled, 'vibrant, popular, unified and flourishing', a vitality he demonstrated by the use of liturgical books, painted images, saint's lives, devotional treatises, churchwardens' accounts, ecclesiastical court records, personal commonplace books and wills (Ryrie, 2009). Under these circumstances, if Protestantism was to supersede Catholicism, its rise was far from inevitable. Duffy thus, unwittingly perhaps, confronts whiggish assumptions that Protestantism was an irresistible force and Catholicism a moveable object to be brushed aside by the progress of the Reformation and then by the late-seventeenth-century settlement of the Glorious Revolution.

So what has happened to whig history? The 1890s was the critical decade when whig history was weakened by calls for English history to be as scientific as French or German historiography, and by the professional growth of the discipline within the academy (Blaas, 1978). And the critiques of people like Butterfield have been telling. Ghosh goes as far to argue that there is a limited timeline for whiggish history. As empire, economic prowess and independence from supranational bodies such as the United Nations or various European bodies do not survive 1940, nor does the whig approach, save for histories published by that old Whig Winston Churchill in the 1950s. Yet in a reinvented form whig history has survived to the present day in the work of a corpus of prominent historians. Trevelyan's studies not only represented all the attributes, qualities and weaknesses of the whig historical approach, but he also provided a link to the next generation of English historians. Now the emphasis was democratic, popular, multi-national and multi-cultural. It may be no accident that Trevelyan's Festschrift, *Studies in Social History* (1955), was edited by his first doctoral student and the subject of our next section, the historian J. H. Plumb (1911–2001), who created a fresh school of whiggish history and a new approach to writing national history and the consideration of national identity.

Section 3

The 'new Whigs': the school of J. H. Plumb

Sir David Wilkie (1784–1841) was Principal Painter to the Queen. He was a Scot and son of a Reverend from Fife. A friend of the historical novelist Walter Scott and a notable artist in his own right, Wilkie was best known for a history painting begun in 1820 called *Chelsea Pensioners Reading the Gazette of the Battle of Waterloo, 1822*. It was first exhibited at the Royal Academy in that year when its popular appeal demanded the erection of rails to keep the crowds back in an exhibition that would take record receipts. Dating precisely from Thursday 2 June 1815, and the first official confirmation of the British victory over the French, it showed for the historian Linda Colley in her major history *Britons* (2005) a perspective on the 'present crisis' of Britishness, a multi-cultural present that raised questions of what it meant to be British in a post-colonial age, and brought to mind nationalist politics in Scotland that envisaged the undoing of the Act of Union of 1707. These are important considerations and take us back to questions that had once been the chief concern of whig historians. These concerns also explain why Colley and her generation of Cambridge historians that studied under Jack Plumb or are influenced by him are so important to our understanding of post-war English historical writing and suggest continuities with earlier forms.

Plumb was a working-class boy who longed for a Cambridge education. His impact on reformulating eighteenth-century politics and his influence on historiography with his book *The Death of the Past* (1969) has been immense. To those that were taught by him or counted him as a mentor he was to become very important to their professional development. He refashioned his Leicester youth as a son of a 'shoe clicker in the boot and shoe industry' (*Oxford DNB*) to become a 'courtier and connoisseur', eventually embracing Thatcherism with (as he apparently put it himself) all the zeal of a convert. His students remember his collection of fine porcelain in his rooms and the fine wine after seminars. He came to wider public attention in 1977 with a BBC television series called *Royal Heritage* that told the story of the builders and art collectors of the British Royal family and was accompanied by a best-selling illustrated book. He was, as we are also told in an introduction of *The Death of the Past* by Niall Ferguson in 2004, a 'meticulous portraitist' and certainly his life of Walpole and his work on eighteenth-century politics endure.

Unlike Macaulay or the nineteenth-century whigs, Plumb approved of traditional archive research and applied scientific-type methods to questions of the English constitution (Ferguson, 2004, p. xxvii). While he was no crude positivist, he did believe that history was much closer to a science in that truth could be identified through research and that in some degree we could learn what to do in the future by learning from the past – a belief shared with Geoffrey Elton (Chapter 1). Ironic then that Elton's bright young boy was David Starkey and Plumb's (or at least one of them) was Simon Schama, and that years later Starkey and Schama would be themselves rivals as stars of the small screen, presenting history as an edge-of-the-seat drama in which cliffhanging episodes unfolded on a weekly basis. Yet, like Trevelyan, Plumb advocated social history approaches and was, at least in his early days, progressive in both his politics and in his approach to history.

Plumb had immense influence on such diverse historians as Roy Porter, Niall Ferguson, David Cannadine, Neil MacKendrick, Simon Schama and John Vincent, as well as Colley, adding up to what this section will suggest is a school of historical thought and practice – a 'new whig' approach. In so far as we can find a thread running between these diverse historians and the diverse whig historians that preceded them, it is an emphasis on certain defining features (Table 8.1). Emphatically, this is not to suggest that the 'new whigs' believe in a vulgar tautological approach to history, where evidence is read back from the present as a justification for the current constitutional arrangement. Nor do they reflect Plumb's notion of history as science; indeed, any confident notion that history had the ability to inform the future categorically does not run from Trevelyan to Plumb's generation onto the 'new whigs'. Nor further should it suggest a slavish agreement with either his approach or his conclusions. Colley has argued against many of his views regarding the eighteenth century and Plumb himself seems to have encouraged her in this. There are, however, continuities at work.

Table 8.1 Elements of old whiggism in the new

'Old' whig history	*'New' whig history*
Non-scientific; social; political	Non-scientific; cultural; political
Concern with liberty; progress; civilisation	Concern with liberty; progress; civilisation
Constitution; parliament	Constitution; state
English 'exceptionalism'	English 'exceptionalism' within context of national decline
History has a social function	History has a social function
Popular and accessible	Popular and accessible; with emphasis on accessible visual evidence
Emphasis on well-written prose	Emphasis on well-written prose
Biographical approach	Biographical approach
Empire	Post-empire
Narrative driven	Narrative driven

That these diverse historians may indeed be considered as a coherent school of historical thought and writing, let alone that they have synergy enough to be called 'new whigs', is not necessarily a view that is widely held by historians. In order to explore this contention further, therefore, we shall concentrate on Colley's *Britons* in an effort to tease out the elements of what might be meant by a 'new whiggish' approach but then go on to touch on other historians associated with Plumb, in particular Simon Schama.

The first and most obvious feature of Colley's work is that it is present-minded; second, it is popular and public-orientated using the 'poetry and philosophy' of a well-written, well-crafted style; and lastly it tends to be English focused (although Britain is invariably heavily featured). Like many others of the Plumb school of 'new whigs,' Colley is an adherent of biography (she authored a very good biography of one of Plumb's bitter rivals, the historian Lewis Namier). Others who were not students of Plumb such as David Cannadine or perhaps even Peter Mandler, who has no formal or informal connection with Plumb, nevertheless tell a story of the nation and in the case of Mandler support the popular telling of history in books such as *The English National Character* (2006) and *History and National Life* (2002).

Colley's discussion of Wilkie's *Chelsea Pensioners Reading the Gazette after the Battle of Waterloo* (Plate 3) revealed much about her approach to historical writing. The home for military 'pensioners' or a veteran of Britain's former wars was the Royal Hospital Chelsea, a retreat for old and disabled soldiers from 1692. Just nearby in the old Jew's Row in Chelsea, the soldiers are shown getting news of Wellington's victory at Waterloo on that never-to-be-forgotten June day in 1815. They are mostly shown in their uniforms, representing a number of different regiments and ranks.

Many black men fought in the Napoleonic Wars, and one of the retired soldiers shown here is black. He is wearing an elaborate uniform coat and has a ring in his ear. Sweeping leftwards across the canvas we find that the horseman is from a Welsh regiment; while the gathered soldiers are identified as Scots, Irish and English by their clothes and other symbols. They surround the black soldier whose presence not only reminds us of his contribution in war but that he may also be there, it could be further speculated, to state that (even in 1822) no man is a slave when in England (or Britain?). There are signs and symbols of past victories besides the Chelsea Pensioner reading aloud, a veteran from the battle of Quebec in 1759 who stands at the conceptual middle of the painting. Off-centre we can see that the inn sign is 'The Duke of York', a reminder of a battle with revolutionary France while the other public houses bear the mark of the 'The Snowshoes', a 1758 battle from the American War of Independence, and the Marquess of Granby who is a hero both of the Battle of Culloden in 1746 and of the Seven Years' War:

> **Explicit in this strictly imaginary scene is the existence of a mass British patriotism transcending the boundaries of class, ethnicity, occupation, sex and age . . . and it is 'one man's very perceptive interpretation of both the variety and the roots of Britishness.**
>
> (Colley, 2005, p. 365)

It is war (and empire) that brought the diverse nations of Britain together while it was Protestantism that 'first allowed the English, the Welsh and the Scots to become fused together, and to remain so, despite their many cultural divergences' (Colley, 2005, pp. 367–8). To be British was to be against the French; to be Protestant was to be against Catholicism. To be both was to identify with a distinct and 'Chosen People', a providential destiny and with God who had entrusted them with empire, a testimony to their status as the 'Protestant Israel'. Colley again:

> **Well into the twentieth century, contact with and domination over manifestly alien peoples nourished Britons' sense of superior difference. They could contrast their law, their treatment of women, their wealth, power, political stability and religion with societies they only imperfectly understood, but usually perceived as inferior.** (Colley, 2005, pp. 368–9)

Telling the story of 'Britain' as opposed to England has long been the cause of tension among historians. 'British history' has long been seen as problematic in the sense that whig history was concerned more with England. The remaining countries of the 'four nations' or 'three kingdoms' – Scotland, Wales and Ireland – tended to be organised around separate historical accounts of their component national identities while the histories of Irish nationalism and Unionism were given priority. Even Roy Porter who wrote a splendid history of Britain and the Enlightenment did so without much reference to examples outside England. Unfortunately, he never completed a two-volume *Social History of Britain* that was intended by Penguin to replace the classic *English Social History: A Survey of Six Centuries from Chaucer to Queen Victoria* (1944) by G. M. Trevelyan.

In emphasising Britain, however, Colley found a new point of origin for the nation. Against the old whig histories, the founding date is no longer 1215 (the Magna Carta) or 1688 (the Glorious Revolution) or 1832 (the Great Reform Act), but 1707 and 1800 as the acts of Union with Scotland and Ireland. She also wanted to listen to loyalist and patriotic voices, not unreasonably given her subject matter, but at the expense of E. P. Thompson's workers and radicals and the expressions of working class agitation or disquiet. Discussing the Bristol riots of 1831, for example, where there were protests against delays in political reform, Colley insisted that:

> **The growing involvement in politics of men and women from the middling and working classes that characterised British society at this time was expressed as much if not more in support of the nation state, as it was in opposition to the men who governed it.**
>
> (Colley, 2005, p. 371)

Historians have accused her of repositioning the working class as nationalistic and conservative. Even when considering the substantive points of her case, it is difficult to see how differences of class within the nations that made up Britain were suppressed to the degree suggested by Colley and, if they were, how fault lines within the component nations of Britain such as nationalisms and localities, language, religion, and urban and rural divides could be as equally suppressed as the class allegiances that she underplays. Indeed, after her end date of 1837, we know that they are not.

It does appear, however, that there is indeed a present-minded quality to these 'new whig' histories and even a desire to appeal to current policymakers in exactly the way envisaged by the 'old whigs' such as Macaulay. In Colley's more recent book, *Captives: Britain, Empire and the World* (2003), for example, the chapter on Afghanistan compared captives taken in the nineteenth century with the American hostage crisis in Iran in 1979–81 where a weak country could apparently hold captive the citizens of a strong country with impunity, asking historical questions about the limits to the reach of empire and the consequences for foreign policy in the here and now. In a country where Afghans (or at least Muslims) may live cheek by jowl with the 'indigenous' Britons but may not consider themselves to be primarily British, then what is to be done in an environment where terrorism and the threat of terrorism is a real issue. In a 2006 newspaper article, Colley had a solution:

> **[A] chronological history of Britain should become part of the national curriculum. This history need not be built around the reigns of monarchs. It need not obscure the cultural and political differences between Wales, Scotland, England and Ireland, although it should draw attention to the persistent and powerful connections that have always existed between them. And it certainly does not need to be insular, or remotely reactionary. . . . But most of all, schoolchildren need to learn. For how can they grow up to be British citizens if they haven't a clue how Britain came to be what it is?** (Colley, *The Guardian*, 18 May 2006)

Above all, it was the constitution that will make good Britons:

> **Britain possessed many such iconic constitutional and legal documents in the past. American revolutionaries, for instance, borrowed their bill of rights from the document of the same name that was passed at Westminster in 1689 . . . people here often assumed that Britain has no significant constitutional documents. This is dangerous. The Magna Carta, the Petition of Rights, the Treaty of Union, the Catholic and Jewish emancipation acts of 1829 and 1858, the Parliament Act of 1911, the Scotland and Government of Wales Acts of 1998, and more, should all be put on show together somewhere. Copies, and explanations of their significance, should be made available online to every school. Not for the purpose of crude patriotic drum-banging, but in order to encourage people, especially young people, to think hard about what the struggle for citizenship has involved, and what it has meant.**
> (Colley, *The Guardian*, 18 May 2006)

Given this list of British constitutional achievement, it would be surprising if there were not a small roll on the drum and a modest blow on the trumpet, or that her proposal for national exhibitions could do anything else but place the unfolding of constitutional progress at the centre of history. Like the call for a return to chronological history, it did not quite take us back to the whiggish history that Seller and Yeatman by the 1930s perceived to be on the lips of every schoolchild in Britain, every bit as alive as the children's empire literature in the Edwardian period or as vivid as a globe of the time coloured red by British (or is it English?) conquest, but it did give pause for comparison with some of the features of the new whig history.

This section suggests that whiggish history has survived, predominately through the whig approach of Plumb and his School. It seems that above all else whiggism saw constitutionalism as worthy of comment and the 'identities' of the British as the subject of extensive histories. After all, what else is Simon Schama's *Citizens* (1989), a history of the French Revolution, but a sneer at French millenarianism and an attack on hapless French attempts at statebuilding, argued alongside a softly softly defence of the British constitutional arrangement. Likewise, his *History of Britain* (2000), written for consumption on television, was popular, narrative-driven and had a Plumb-like social purpose to tell the story of a nation still in the making with more than a hint of celebration. Because of this, perhaps, Schama is as likely to be called in to the television studio as a voiceover to a Royal Wedding or to pontificate as the votes in an American Presidential election are counted.

Schama's work in many ways epitomises the new whig position. Read alongside Colley's *Britons*, there is no doubt the value placed on constitutional stability. One volume of Schama's *History of Britain* recalled his Jewish father and what it meant to be a 'foreigner' in England and how that belonging played itself out in the midst of economic decline, end of empire and the rise of the European dream:

> **Born and bred in him (for he himself was born in Whitechapel not Botosany) was the sense that being British meant being a European, but also being something else too. Whether that something else extended our sense of place out west into the Atlantic or much further across the world, it was not something, even with the vanishing act of empire, to feel defensive about. Nor should we now. It is true that I argue this as a transatlantic Briton myself, but the increasing compulsion to make the choice which General de Gaulle imposed on us between our European and our extra-European identity, seems to order an impoverishment of our culture. It's precisely the roving, unstable, complicated, pock-marked migratory character of our history which ought to be seen as a gift for Europe. Since it is a past which uniquely in European history combined a passion for social justice with an incorrigible attachment to bloody minded liberty, it is a past designed to subvert, not reinforce the streamlined authority of global bureaucracies and corporations. Our place at the European table ought to make room for our peculiarity or we should not bother showing up for dinner.**
>
> (Schama, 2002, pp. 553–4)

Thus in Schama's work also – extraordinary as so much of it is – we have all the elements of the new whig approach. Its concerns are political and its evidence base is cultural with the visual (such as works like *Rembrandt's Eyes* (1999) or *Landscape and Memory* (1995)) ever present and, like Colley, brilliantly accessible in their descriptions. It focuses on liberty and the growth of civilisation where it charts state action and reaction and his concern is both with empire and its disappearance. Plumb valued good historical writing and Schama, like many others of the Plumb School such as Sir David Cannadine and Linda Colley, now an MBE, is a fine exponent of the art.

In practice

The tradition of history writing discussed in this chapter has been, and continues to be, important and influential. With its origins in the early modern period, the rise of what we refer to as whig interpretations of the past reflected a growing confidence in the British nation, and today can in many respects be seen as a celebration of its stability and progress. This in part explains the wide popular appeal of books written by its leading proponents. As history teachers like to remind us, the thing about history is that it is full of good stories; and few contemporary historians can tell a story as well as Simon Schama, David Cannadine, Linda Colley and others inhabiting this tradition. Few can deny that their narratives are often compelling, and we cannot say that of many postmodern studies.

It is, however, the very appeal of whig interpretations which ought to place us on our guard. Far too easily can we be seduced by their engaging narratives, temporarily abandoning our critical faculties, when we should constantly remind ourselves that these accounts are framed by particular teleologies which tend to articulate notions of progress. Thus the history of Britain is seen variously and reassuringly as the forward march of constitutionalism, liberty, democracy, civilisation or Protestantism. This optimistic perspective is not entirely misplaced. The record of the British history over the past three centuries has suggested real advances in individual freedoms, and in political and religious rights. The problem, it might be argued, is that these advances have often been incomplete and won at considerable cost to others. It is the darker side of progress which is underplayed or ignored completely. Thus, for example, whig interpretations of the British empire stress its achievements in spreading education, free trade and the rule of law, at the same time giving scant regard to its brutal realities. If the unacceptable face of empire is occasionally admitted, then it is viewed as a price that was worth paying. Similarly, while we may see the eighteenth century as a time when the British state was happily unified, there is little regard to those people living at the margins who were simultaneously being subjected to harsh legal and imperial disciplinary regimes. The English tradition, therefore, despite its avowed objectivity is somewhat uncritical in its use of sources. Not only are they gathered and employed selectively, but they are rarely interrogated as evidence.

Summary

The three sections of this chapter have said three things:

- There was some sort of radical shift in the way histories of England were written around 1580. We also saw that different types of people began to write histories of the nation. Somewhere between the age of Elizabeth I and the seventeenth-century Civil War, histories of the nation became much less reliant on fantastic accounts of a land of giants based on biblical prophecy and were transformed into histories of rational political and economic government and of constitution. No longer were historians drawn from the church and various civil authorities; now they tended to be antiquarians taken from a rising class of new professionals who, like Clarendon and Camden, rarely strayed from accounts that could be empirically verified, i.e. proved by the use of our senses. The sources that historians used also changed. Further, this transformation could not have happened without the influence of Italian humanism based upon the characteristics of human beings free from any mystical influence.

- The whig interpretation of history concentrated on national histories that celebrated constitutionalism. In particular, this meant a selection of evidence that picked winners from the past who enhanced and supported the perfecting English constitution and condemned those that remained in opposition to it. This constitutional settlement, reckoned to be the most flexible and equitable that had ever been forged by human hand, in the political and religious heat of the seventeenth century, was underwritten by a Protestantism that itself protected the Englishman from the absolutist tyranny of the Church of Rome. The task of the historian was a very public one: to inform decision makers about the dangers of abandoning the constitution and the advantages of sticking to it. The whig interpretation was part of a liberal tradition of historical thought, nonetheless, that produced giants in the field such as Macaulay and Trevelyan. By the time Sir Herbert Butterfield published his book on the whig interpretation of history in 1931, the approach taken by so-called whig historians was already being criticised.

- The need to write histories of the nation have become no less urgent. Looking initially at the influential work of Linda Colley, which has its origins in a concern about national identity in our multi-cultural present, a school of history is identified that gathered, however informally, around the influential figure of Jack Plumb at Christ's College, Cambridge. As Plumb was a doctoral student of Trevelyan, so Colley was a student under Plumb. She was not alone. Simon Schama, Roy Porter, Niall Ferguson and others such as Neil McKendrick and John Vincent were taught by Plumb while others such as Sir David Cannadine (husband to Colley) were profoundly influenced by him. In the wake of Plumb's conversion to Thatcherism before his death in 2001, these 'new whigs' have written popular, present-minded, English-centred histories of Britain for a democratic, popular audience with – like Trevelyan and Plumb – an emphasis on good writing and constitutional politics.

Discussion document

Here follow two extracts reflecting on the character of monarchy. Vergil wrote the first full-length attempt at a universal or national history based in a humanist tradition; an approach that was to become better established in the following century. Here is an historian that readily considers his predecessors, reflects on the sources that he has to hand and the origins of his subject – in this case the history of England. Any religious connotation or analogy is absent and as such represents a departure from the Chronicle histories that hitherto had been the dominant style. Clarendon, by contrast, is a humanist history of the English Civil War, written while the embers of the conflict still smouldered.

From the beginning of human affairs, great King Henry, all men have striven to perpetuate the memory of virtue and achievements. Hence, surely, cities have been built and named after their founders, hence statues have been invented, hence the great masses of the pyramids and many magnificent works of that kind; hence, too, there have been men who have not hesitated to seek premature death in order to preserve their nation. But since all these things have partly been erased by the passage of time and partly cast into oblivion by forgetfulness, men next started to celebrate these works and deeds in literature, which confer immortality on them all so that in after time men could observe what good deeds were to be imitated, and what bad ones were to be avoided. For just as history speaks of and proclaims men's praises, so it does not keep silent about their disgraces, nor does it conceal them, and so it passes its judgments about what things are of the greatest use for the conduct of our lives, stimulating some to achieve immortal glory and virtue, and deterring others from vice by fear of infamy. And this is the single thing which seems to be lacking from the supreme glory of your realm of English, that, although it is most blessed in all things, its greatness is unknown to a large number of nations since no history exists from which it would be possible to learn the nature of Britain (which is now England), the origin of this nation, the manners of its kings, the life of its people, and the arts whereby its government, as it was founded in the beginning and as it grew, attained to its greatness. It is that true that in a very short work Bede, an Englishman, sketched the history of England from the arrival into this island of Caius Julius Caesar down to his own times (and he lived about 700 A.D.), and before him Gildas cast some light on the antiquity of the British. But after them other men produced works which are so bound in shadows that they cannot shine forth. And latterly some men undertook to write almost day-by-day accounts. But they compiled annals in which both the arrangement and the style was so threadbare that they justly strike us, as they say, as food without seasoning. And yet they were such that, when read alongside the histories of other nations who have had dealings with the English, they can supply matter for the creation of a new work. Having perceived this, I, who had already dedicated myself to investigating old things, began to read, study, imbibe, and copy out these annals of the English and other nations more carefully, and for this reason I elected to gather my material, no matter how raw and unadorned, from all manner of sources, which I might learnedly polish and adorn when considerations of time did not prevent me. Thus I had to begin all over again *ab ovo* [from the origin], as they say, in composing this history I have created with no small effort, and I have entitled it English because such today is the name of the island's greater part, and by far the greatest part of its government. But just as a history is not completed in a small amount of time, so, after being completed and published, it does not acquire credibility, popularity, and authority overnight, particularly among a people whose accomplishments have long remained hidden. For it is the case that in the meanwhile grandsons have heard much from their grandfathers, and the things these grandsons have spread about are believed, although they are only old men's dreams. As a result, if somebody omits these things in his writing, good God, what a drubbing he gets in common conversation! But if afterwards somebody will read this (and every man will read it who delights in the glory and honour of his nation), and shall have come to learn the causes of things, the chronology, and the deeds and sayings of his ancestors, then he will be led, willy-nilly, to approve this new history, to laud it, to praise it to the skies. I have no doubt that this will have some such utility. And perhaps the English reader (and likewise the Scotsman and the Frenchman) will be surprised to find no little in it that is contrary to what is commonly said, and other things which their writers either have not touched upon or have recounted differently. But when they have digested these things, they will undoubtedly understand that old wives' tales do not agree with the truth, and that patriotism has sometimes robbed their writers of their judgment, deprived them of their intelligence, and stripped them of their senses, none of which things have been able to befall me, since I have not written so as to flatter any man's ears, and in the end, the truth being grasped, they cannot help but approve of a history written honourably and sincerely. And you particularly among your Englishmen, most puissant king, if in your grace, gravity and wisdom you will not disdain (as I am confident you will not) to do this openmindedly, then I shall deem myself to have reaped the richest reward for all the years of effort I have spent in the writing. For which reason I have had no hesitation in submitting this work for censure by you first of all men, particularly since you know how to pass right judgment on things that have been done or need doing, being as you have been born for rule and for justice, are endowed with great prudence, are exceptionally well-read in letters both human and divine, and well understand all the goodly arts. And so for your singular virtue you easily surpass, not just the glory of sovereigns alive today, but also the memory of all antiquity. And in this history there are things that will give you no small delight, since from them you may understand the customs of your subject, which have always been constantly taken into account from the nation's beginning, in matters both private and public. Farewell. London, August 1533.

Polydore Vergil, *To Henry VIII, Invincible King of England, France, and Ireland, Defender of the Faith, the Poem of the English History* (1533). Available at: www.philological.bham.ac.uk/polverg/1e.html#letter.

There were so many miraculous circumstances contributed to his ruin, that men might think that heaven and earth conspired it, and that the stars designed it. Though he was, from the first declension of his power, so much betrayed by his own servants, that there were very few who remained faithful to him, yet that treachery preceded not from any treasonable purpose to do him any harm, but from particular and personal animosities against other men. And afterwards, the terror all men were under of the Parliament, and the to make guilt they were conscious of themselves, made them watch all opportunities to make themselves gracious to those who could do them good; and so they became spies upon their master, and from one piece of knavery were hardered and confirmed to undertake another, till at last they had no hope of preservation but by the destruction of their master. And after all this, when a man might reasonably believe that less than a universal defection of three nations could not have reduced a great King to so ugly a fate, it is most certain that in that very hour when he was thus wickedly murdered in the sight of the sun, he had as great a share in the hearts and affections of his subjects in general, was as much beloved, esteemed, and longed for by the people in general of the three nations, as any of his predecessors had ever been. To conclude: he was the worthiest gentlemen, the best master, the best friend, the best husband, and the best Christian, that the age in which he lived had produced. And if he was not the best King, if he was without some parts and qualities which have made some kings great and happy, no other prince was ever unhappy who was possessed of half his virtues and endowments, and so much without any kind of vice.

Clarendon, *The History of the Rebellion and Civil War in England*, reproduced in J. R. Hale, *The Evolution of British Historiography From Bacon to Namier* (1967), pp. 140–1.

Further reading

* *essential*

* **J. W. Barrow**, *A Liberal Descent: Victorian Historians and the English Past* (1981).
Now a classic text. Its argument for coherent Burkean whig tradition takes in some of the important figures we touched on in this chapter, such as Macaulay and Stubbs, as well as others, such as Froude. The chapter 'Protestant island' is especially useful.

Stefan Collini, *English Pasts: Essays in History and Culture* (1999).
Presented as a series of essays on England and Englishness. His opening chapter on 'Writing the national history: Trevelyan and after', along with the introduction, is especially useful to themes covered in this chapter.

Frank Smith Fussner, *The Historical Revolution: English Historical Writing and Thought, 1580–1640* (2010).
First published in 1962, this is an invaluable volume that deals in comprehensive terms with what the author calls the intellectual revolution that fundamentally changed both writing generally and history writing. The result was different types of history books and different types of historians.

Peter Ghosh, 'Whig interpretation of history', in K. Boyd (ed.), *Encyclopaedia of Historians and History Writing* (1999).
A succinct and forceful statement of the importance and genesis of the whig interpretation. It combines both useful definition and a commentary of the genre. It is particularly strong as an interpretation of Butterfield and how Butterfield has been understood and used by historians.

J. R. Plumb, *The Making of an Historian: The Collected Essays of J. R. Plumb* (1988).
Fascinating for its account of Plumb's life at Cambridge and his encounters with Trevelyan, Butterfield and Namier. The first volume is especially pertinent in this respect and is often very insightful and very sharp in its observations.

J. R. Plumb, *The Death of the Past* (1969, 2004).
A well-known work or commentary on historiography and historical practice that makes the case above all for the social uses of history. The 2004 edition is especially useful as it contains a preface by Simon Schama and an introduction by Niall Ferguson.

D. R. Woolf, *Reading History in Early Modern England* (2000).
An essential read for a thorough coverage of this topic area. As stated in the introduction, it is a history book about history books that seeks to place early modern historiography firmly in its social context. The opening chapter 'Death of the chronicle' is very useful for our purposes.

Part 4

VARIETIES

9 Political, social and cultural history

1 High and low politics: a case study of the British Labour Party
2 Social history and its legacy
3 Cultural history and its expansion

Introduction

Approaches to political history have traditionally been divided. High politics and the history of elites has been the preserve of historians who place emphasis on the importance of decision making in the political process. Its sources have been specifically concerned with the private motivations of historical actors in critical positions of power and influence. Popular or 'low' political history focuses on structures of power such as political parties. The opening section of the chapter, therefore, examines the evolution of the British Labour Party from both perspectives: the high politics of its leaders; the electoral sociology and so on that determined its development as a political movement. The second section explains why social history has been so centrally important to historical method more generally but how too it is now part of an approach to the past which once took in a 'history from below' approach, a social-scientific approach or an approach influenced by the totalising history of the Annales School. It draws on a range of disciplines, and now seems as preoccupied with culture and representations as once it was driven by an ambition to retrieve histories of the marginal or powerless. Culture is a chief concern of the third section as we look at how cultural history has emerged as an approach in its own right. Cultural historians have overcome the difficulties in defining 'culture' to create some of the most imaginative histories of popular leisure pursuits, seen not as trivial pastimes but occupying a vital place in the life and identity of people in the past. We look also, therefore, at how culture has been considered by different historians over different periods.

Section 1

High and low politics: a case study of the British Labour Party

The British monarchy has an official website which features '40 facts about Buckingham Palace'. One of these facts concerns the dress codes when visiting the monarch. When the prime minister goes to the Palace after an election supposedly to kiss hands with the head of state, the requirement after every election until the Second World War was to wear formal court evening dress. Except once: after the election of a Labour government in 1924. Then James Ramsay MacDonald (1866–1937) became prime minister of a minority administration. A photograph shows Labour's first prime minister leaving the Palace in a suit with a top hat that was almost certainly borrowed.

MacDonald was to lead the 1931 Labour government and was also to be expelled from the party he had been so instrumental in bringing to power. MacDonald was a Scot from an impoverished background who, before meeting his wife of independent means, once almost died for lack of food. He was the first of his kind and almost the last to date: a working class leader of a governing party of the state; in this case, of the Labour Party. There would not be another working class leader of any party until Leonard James Callaghan (1912–2005) who became Labour prime minister in 1976. (Edward Heath, the Conservative prime minister who preceded Callaghan in the same decade is said by the *Oxford Dictionary of National Biography* to have been brought up 'on the subtle English borderline between the working and middle classes'.) Like MacDonald, Callaghan was raised by his mother in poverty; like MacDonald he was from a non-conformist Christian background; like MacDonald he served both as foreign secretary as well as first lord of the treasury; and like his predecessor, Callaghan found it difficult to manage power in the face of opposition within his own party.

This is not the only approach to politics, an approach preoccupied with leaders, although we shall return to so-called 'high' politics in due course. Politics is about power and political history is about the history of power (Hoffman and Graham, p. 3). Or it is concerned with the history of theories about power, focusing, for example, upon issues connected to the central state or local government, or histories of democracy or citizenship. Histories of 'high' politics have become rarer in recent years, as historians have instead turned to popular politics or 'politics from below', which emphasise electoral sociology, trade unions, the role of pressure groups and the like. So while the machinations of say MacDonald or Callaghan in parliament and in the corridors of power have not been discounted by historians, there is a greater tendency to study the pressures they faced from outside parliament; the impact of the welfare state on social mobility and voting patterns or the demands for political enfranchisement made, for instance, by women.

One way of illustrating how popular politics has made a real impact in historical practice in recent years is to sketch one of the central concerns of twentieth-century British politics, the replacement of the Liberal Party as the main party of progress with the Labour Party. The methods we now associate with popular politics have assisted historians to understand a political rupture that is even today playing itself out. Comparing these methods with a high politics approach by historians such as Maurice Cowling (1926–2005) allows us to see how the British Labour Party has been studied from a variety of angles using tools developed within the sub-discipline of political history.

In tackling this question of how and why the British Labour Party grew and transformed into a party of government (albeit one spectacularly unsuccessful in winning elections until Tony Blair in 1997) political historians conform to trends that can be found in other sub-disciplines of history. Where once there may have been a concentration on class and, say, the sociological make-up of the Labour vote, now there is an emphasis placed on textual approaches and the importance of language used in political debate or the development of policy. There is also now a 'four nations' approach where regional or local variation in the United Kingdom is recognised as contributing to the political processes of the whole. When historians first examined how the Labour Party became the main party of progress in place of the Liberal Party, they looked at sociological factors such as the expansion of the franchise which allowed the working classes to vote in greater number. Now they are more concerned to move away from any form of class-based determinism.

As well as studies of region and nation, popular political history has also been concerned with constitution. This has been especially true of the devolution of power from the political centre to the peripheries. Interventions in this area are overloaded with details of how the constitution works with electoral statistics and a labyrinthine civil service placed in context. Party has also been a concern with both the Labour Party and the Conservative Party surveyed over long periods, and as parties of state their conduct in and out of power is related to economic, social, cultural and constitutional development more generally.

Challenges to the constitution remained very much part of the historical story of the decline of the Liberal Party. In a book that has become a classic, George Dangerfield in his wonderfully written *The Strange Death of Liberal England*, first published in 1935, argued for the significance of the 'hiatus' of the period 1910–14 when the House of Lords threatened to rebel and was thwarted by the Parliament Act of 1911, when Ireland revolted, when suffragette and suffragist protest was at a fairly violent peak, and when trade union activity threatened levels of militancy not seen often in Britain. While it must be true to say that Liberalism did not die because of these constitutional threats, we know that after 1922 the Liberal Party would never govern again unless we count its resurrection via the Liberal Democratic Party who became the junior partner to the Conservatives in the 2010 Coalition.

This brings us to another central concern of popular political history in this period: the *timing* of Labour ascendency, which Dangerfield placed in the period before the First World War (1914–18). The 1918 extension to the franchise and the socialist and trade union militancy that characterises the post-war world are well known but Dangerfield insisted that:

> **the extravagant behaviour of the post-war decade, which most of us thought to be the effect of war, had really begun before the War. The War hastened everything – in politics, economics, in behaviour – but it started nothing.** (Dangerfield, 1997, p. 14)

Historians of popular politics dispute this chronology but they do so from the perspective of understanding the class and sociological make up of the period. Peter Clarke's *Lancashire and the New Liberalism* (1971), brilliantly used a local case study to argue that New Liberalism as an ideology was committed to collectivist solutions that appealed to a segment of the respectable working class. This enabled the Liberal Party to hold at bay the emergent Labour Party until 1914. Then the war introduced new elements in the way that work and the state were organised – such as compulsory conscription and the constitutional claims of women, which divided the party at parliamentary level.

The picture at the local level, in local government in fact, made national politics look different again. Duncan Tanner argued in his *Political Change and the Labour Party* (1990) that the Clarke position was overstated, for although he was right to emphasise the relative Liberal strength until 1914, it was vital to consider the 'politics of place', which offered a different perspective from that of ideology or national political strategies. Others fix on 1918 and the expansion of the franchise to suggest that Labour's rise after the war depended on the emergence of a working class constituency, which from a sociological perspective makes perfect sense but leaves little room for explanations of change focused on power, leadership and personalities.

In some contrast to these wider perspectives, Maurice Cowling, the foremost historian of the 'high politics' approach to political history, took the view that a study of decision making and the wielding of power was the only way to get either a complete historical or satisfactory sociological picture on the rise of the Labour Party. In so doing he was concerned more with social scientific models of power rather than a self-conscious and deliberate attempt to follow in the footsteps of the influential historian Lewis Namier (1888–1960). Namier had made his name by reconstructing power structures in the eighteenth-century parliaments by painstakingly piecing together the career histories of politicians. Cowling claimed that he belonged to a different historiographical tradition from that of Namier; parliament and party was his main concern but he also thought that the interaction between political leaders and their followers was important. In his introduction to the *Impact of Labour* (1971), Cowling said emphatically that:

- it was the high politics of parliamentary politicians that 'mattered';
- politicians and political party ties may have had beliefs but their calculations and strategies were not based on these beliefs;
- parliament was affected by outside pressures from, for example, the media and electorate, but party strategy was decided at the top and this is where the historian should seek evidence.

Politicians from every party had to make strategic decisions in response to the rise of the Labour Party, and that they had a clear responsibility to educate the electorate to act moderately. Accordingly, said Cowling, the Conservatives between 1920 and 1924 'made three long term decisions':

1. To remove Lloyd George, the prime minister of the Coalition government.
2. To take up a role as 'defender of the social order'.
3. To consider the Labour Party as the chief party of opposition and to school the Labour Party to be loyal and responsible in that important constitutional position.

These decisions were not easily made, and they were strongly contested among the leadership, but the Conservatives needed to contain the political upheaval announced by the arrival of the Labour Party on the political scene and at the same time to seek electoral advantage. The consequences were wide ranging for in the next phase of political struggle leading up to the general election of 1924, and subsequently, the new Tory leader, Stanley Baldwin, would now take up the challenge of opposing 'socialism' as a creed that was essentially un-English. Cowling then had a different viewpoint on the rise of the Labour Party and the effect on British politics of the First World War than the historians of popular politics discussed so far.

In his astonishing scholarship and attention to method, Cowling revealed a complex and thoughtful approach to the past and the present but from 'above'. Many have criticised him for ignoring constituency politics and extra-parliamentary activity in say trade unions or the formation of public opinion more generally. He certainly recognised that power from outside parliament permeated into its chambers and, equally, saw the importance of rhetoric as it related to public opinion. He was interested, however, in political language; the motivations for speaking – where and to whom, why and at what moment – more than the actual words themselves. This is why he preferred private letters and diaries over public documents because the former were bound to reveal more than the latter. Finally, he utterly rejected notions of history as science. Historical actions were, he thought, without cause and effect to the extent that the same could be said for phenomena in the natural world. In this sense, his influences could not be Namierite but were rather closer to the approaches of R. W. Collingwood and the Conservative, Michael Oakeshott (1901–90), who also rejected notions of the historian as objective fact gatherer. In short, context was all-important and 'the historian himself was part of the context he investigated' (Craig, p. 468).

Until recently, this overall approach was thought to be part of a so-called Peterhouse School or Cambridge School of Politics and History which narrowly restricted politics and political endeavour to that which took place within the parliamentary sphere, but the able defenders of Cowling such as Philip Williamson and David Craig have argued that he was also interested in a much wider frame of reference, connecting party politicians who wielded individual power to movements in the political landscape of the nation. Thus elite politics was not the only politics that 'mattered', and his use of private sources allowed an understanding of the real motives of political elites. Cowling adopted a high politics approach only because he wanted to get beyond the narrow limits of political sociology that he found ultimately inadequate.

Drawing upon electoral statistics, political thought, biography and memoir, as well as official sources, political historians have thus approached the history of the Labour Party in contrasting ways. The narrative outlined here has drawn largely upon the popular political histories because it has sought to represent the bulk of histories written in this way over recent years and not because Cowling's approach appears to hardly stray beyond the specific cultures of the political elite. We should take notice of David Craig, however, when he says that there is now a narrower gap between political histories of elites and histories of popular politics, or Susan Pedersen's equally wise suggestion that 'high' politics and 'low' politics may have converged with a common focus on political language or rhetoric, making up what is now called the 'new political history'.

'New political history' would cast so-called Labour culture in a somewhat different light. These new histories argue that political parties construct their political constituencies through discourse and vocabulary. Politics from this viewpoint was not built within national party organisations, working within newly equalised constituencies after the mid-1880s, nor can political preference be simply expressed through the sociological make-up of neighbourhoods. Rather it is the sum of the language used to describe or articulate the centrality of say, empire or masculinities and the wider culture. E. H. H. Green (ed.), *An Age of Transition: British Politics, 1880–1914* (1997); Jon Lawrence and Miles Taylor, *Party, State and Society: Electoral Behaviour in Britain Since 1820* (1997); Jon Lawrence, *Speaking for the People: Party, Language and Popular Politics in England, 1867–1914* (1997); all were concerned to suggest that the older electoral sociology is outmoded and deterministic and that more attention should be paid to political rhetoric.

We now also know from the work of Alex Windscheffel in his *Popular Conservatism in Imperial London* (2007), for example, that Conservative Party success at the end of the nineteenth century – a moment when Conservatism in London swept Progressive politics aside – was not simply the result of a politics that held a mirror up to the new suburbs. 'Villa Toryism' was not a newly found class identity that somehow found a natural home in Conservative politics and in which the Conservative Party was but a perfect reflection, but rather the Conservative Party invented a new metropolitan politics. By celebrating empire, the new denizens of the 'Little Palaces' in the suburbs could now see London as an imperial metropolis and saw the Conservative Party successfully *describing* their place in the capital. There is now no longer any reason to suppose that simply by virtue of their class or occupation that the dwellers of the suburbs automatically fashioned Conservatives anymore than the slums of London robotically manufactured Socialists with flat caps that raced pigeons, attended football matches, drank light ale and who were therefore, sociologically speaking, impelled to vote Labour.

Section 2

Social history and its legacy

Since the work of the social historian tends to overlap with that of cultural, political and economic historians, there is no precise definition of the aims of social history, but Adrian Wilson in *Rethinking Social History: English Society 1570–1920 and its Interpretation* (1993) has usefully provided a sense of its scope:

> **The term 'social history', as used in English historiography, covers three different yet overlapping approaches: first, the history of the people; second, what I call the 'social history paradigm', consisting in the historical application of concepts derived from the social sciences; and third, the aspiration to a totalising or integrating history, which has been called 'total history' or the 'history of society'.**
> (Wilson, 1993, p. 9)

These approaches tend to reflect the origins of social history in the nineteenth century when historians turned to the history of the people without the encumbrance of any need to refer to politics. At the time, historians had no analytical tools with which to undertake the task, and so borrowed promiscuously from the social sciences. Perhaps unsurprisingly, the most useful of the concepts employed has been the notion of class, and here the influence of the work of Marx was paramount. Social historians have not been Marxist to a man or woman, but this did not prevent them from approaching the study of societies, communities, even families using the framework of antagonistic class relationships laid down by Marx. As Geoff Eley put it in his autobiographical *A Crooked Line: From Cultural History to the History of Society* (2005), social history saw itself as situated 'within a self-confident materialist paradigm of social totality, grounded in the primacy of class' (p. 89). In more recent years as the influence of Marx has waned, the 'totality' of class has been displaced, or at least complicated somewhat by notions of gender, race and sexuality – all areas developed since the 1960s and discussed elsewhere in this book.

The work done by social historians from the 1960s constitutes a role call of some of the most pioneering work: from urban histories, to histories of public health and histories that explore the lives of working people as radicals or as workers. To take a few examples, almost at random: Benedict Anderson, *Imagined Communities* (1983), is a history of how ideas of nationhood have been used in imperial projects; Leonore Davidoff and Catherine Hall, *Family Fortunes* (1987), is a study of the English middle class family from the late eighteenth to mid-nineteenth centuries; Jack Goody, *The Development of the Family and Marriage in Europe* (1983), is a wider historical study on similar themes; Peter Laslett (ed.), *Household and Family in Past Time* (1972), is a collection edited by one of the most skilled users of social historical data; and the works of Harold Perkin, including *The Rise of Professional Society* (1989) and *The Structured Crowd* (1981), which have done as much as any to establish the worth of social history.

Rather than survey this extensive literature as a means of exploring the concerns of social history, we wish instead to focus on a number of studies that have illuminated the rise of the City of London and a global financial centre. We look in Chapter 15 at how cultural geographers and by extension cultural historians have dealt with the special aspects of the City, now we shall examine the myriad ways in which the development of the City has been treated by historians from different perspectives and, in particular, by social historians.

Most books and articles about the City have concentrated on big finance and grand financiers, the cultural geography and architecture of the City, its local politics, or its role either in national prosperity or national decline. There has also been a popular antiquarian strand of City historiography which has lovingly recreated its vivid associational life through the Livery Companies, or has latterly attempted – prompted perhaps by the genealogist craze – to rescue from oblivion the lives and rituals of the City of London Corporation from humble common councilmen, to members of the Court of Aldermen to those who held the office of Lord Mayor. More recent work, however, has provided fresh and original insights by using social history methodology to retrieve the lives of people not necessary connected to power (as in high political history) or, in the case of the City, primarily concerned with the economy. It is to the social networks that operated in the City that we shall turn as a way of discussing the benefits to be gained for historians of the City who take a social history approach.

The City more generally benefited hugely from slavery. The slave trade was made illegal from 1807 partly because of a belief among legislators that slave owners would thereafter do more to facilitate pronatalism among slaves (the promotion of the bearing of children) and thus render the movement of slaves across the Atlantic unnecessary.

Before 1807, however, and from about 1733, the thirteen colonies situated between French Canada and Spanish Florida provided a 'triangular trade' between West Africa, the West Indies and North America. Here is how it worked: British ships took finished goods to the coast of West Africa in exchange for slaves who were then taken to the West Indies and North America in order to harvest sugar and tobacco or cotton crops in conditions that are almost unimaginable to modern sensibilities. Life on board the slave ships was horrific with slaves often treated dramatically less well than even chattels or goods. Once put to work, 16-hour days were routine for a slave working in sweltering heat with only a 4-hour period allowed for sleeping. To give some idea how bad conditions were in the sugar plantations of the Caribbean, fertility among female slaves was all but non-existent, that is, they stopped reproducing (the southern states of the United States fared somewhat better). These ships then made passage back to Britain loaded down with cotton, rum, rice, tobacco and sugar for the domestic market. It was a trade that made Britain's empire extraordinarily profitable. As London-based merchants were not particularly visible using official sources generated by the state – in the first section we identified as favoured by historians of high politics – it became necessary to expose their contribution by adopting an approach that we cannot fail but recognise as belonging to social history.

When historians have thought of British connections to the slave trade, cities such as Bristol and Liverpool have come to mind for it was from these important ports that many of the slave ships sailed. Less attention has been devoted to London. But the situation is now changing as to the centrality of London; in particular, the City has come increasingly to be recognised in the wider economy and society. David Hancock's book, *Citizens of the World: London Merchants and the Integration of the British Atlantic Community, 1735–1785* (1995), for example, was a wonderfully detailed study of the integrated connections of 'people, material and capital across market sectors' that made the slave trade possible. His argument was that in the eighteenth century a relatively small but tightly integrated network of four London merchants and nineteen of their associates built the Atlantic system, and he set out to reveal the precise nature of the social interconnections which made the whole possible. What were the social logistics which underpinned this network? What was the coordination needed between the counting house situated in the square mile of the City of London, the slave depot that deposited and then distributed the slaves in the West Indies, and the American plantation house? The starting point to answering these questions was an exploration of the relationship between metropolitan centre and imperial periphery using methods and sources associated with social rather than economic history.

Hancock argued that the slave trade of the eighteenth century has conventionally been studied using statistical analysis or biographical narrative. The former has used aggregate data to construct arguments about the commercial and economic forces which created and sustained the trade. In so doing, it has dealt with the movement of markets almost completely removed from the actions and thoughts of the men and women who controlled them. Biographical accounts, on the other hand, focus on the lives of the individuals and families involved in the trade, and have provided genuine insights. Most, however, have been written as if these people operated in a commercial vacuum, and so there is little sense of how these families actually connected with the larger economic forces and apparatuses of the slave trade, which is precisely why the first definition of social history with which we began – social history of the people – can be coupled with the second which allows us to understand the network of merchants operating in the City by using the historical application of sociological factors such as gender, education and sociability or associational life; discovering how they could cohere into a group that historians can study. The third part of the definition of social history was, as it was put, to build a totalising or integrated history which builds to become a 'history of society'.

As an alternative inspired by *Annales* – the determination to comprehend human behaviour beyond the narrow confines of the political by drawing upon other disciplines – Hancock's solution was to combine the statistical and biographical. He thus set out to recreate the complex world of a London merchant community by identifying the 'circles and associates' of those men who built the Atlantic trade and who became, because of the reach of their power and influence, 'Citizens of the World'. Evidence for their integration as a body that worked closely together was revealed by new archives that came to light in the course of his investigation; chief among them, diaries, memoirs and letters. In order to make clear the web of interests at work, Hancock analysed conventional written sources, paid close attention to human behaviour in the past and drew upon other disciplines in order to understand 'impersonal forces', 'reciprocal relationships' and human reactions to events that were located outside or 'below' high politics – in fact an approach that is the very stuff of social history.

Other work has further illuminated the operation of the City beyond the narrowly political or economic. Studying a later period, Ranald Michie, in *The City of London: Continuity and Change 1850–1990* (1992), attempted a fuller understanding of the financial City by breaking up its constituent elements into distinct, functional categories. The Commercial City, for instance, was in decline from 1850. The growth of an integrated railway system, and improvements in communications meant that the City was largely bypassed in the distribution of goods. The City did, however, retain a direct involvement in international commerce in three ways. The first was, more conventionally, through its physical trade passing via City warehouses. The second could be found in its office trade, which handled imports and exports external to Britain. The last was in 'futures', which dealt with traded commodities ahead of actual production or demand. In addition, Michie continued, the Credit City, like the Capital City, sought to furnish loans through the money markets.

In the eighteenth and nineteenth centuries this involved an increasing stream of capital that ran from the country banks to the London private bankers and onto the money markets in the City. Between the 1860s and 1880s this process had been formalised to the extent whereby national banking structures had been set up. For example, both Barclays and the National Provincial had established a national network of branches, while provincial banks such as the ostensibly Birmingham-based Lloyds in 1884 and the Midland bank in 1891 moved their operations to the City. Similarly, older London merchant banks such as Barings and Rothschilds were joined by newer firms such as Morgans and Kleinworts. By the 1860s there were a growing number of City-based imperial and international banks, financing trade between Britain and other parts of the world.

Now this City of banks and insurance offices might, on first glance, offer little of interest to the social historian looking for history generated from below. If the social historian does examine the Stock Exchange or the great insurance companies such as Lloyds, for example, they are as likely to be considered alongside the petty bourgeois businessmen of the City of London Corporation (the ancient local government of the City) who were themselves important traders or manufacturers, shipbuilders, suppliers to the empire, members of parliament and financiers. Their associational life, their clubs, churches, membership of the ancient guilds engendered a rich sense of belonging to the square mile at a time when the City's physical spaces changed rapidly, providing rich pickings for social history approaches. These connections between City representatives and evidence of their 'integration' with recognised City figures is similar to those identified by Hancock among his London merchants who knew the City in the previous century.

By concentrating on the powerless and with its ambition to construct a 'whole' historical picture, social history can also chronicle the informal economy of the City in some detail and link its various parts. The approach taken by social history is distinctive for a number of reasons, not least because it suggests that the peripheral City figures and ideas of what the City symbolised were connected to those powerful figures at its centre in the same way that Hancock could connect the eighteenth-century counting house in the City with the plantation house in America. The Jews, for example, transacted business in St James's Tavern, Duke Street at the edge of the City and held a market there to exchange new and second-hand jewellery. Here honest and straight dealing were watchwords. Trust stood as a *leitmotif* of the City within its institution, while the origins of this culture of trust were located in the informal economy. One foreign visitor to the City in the nineteenth century expressed astonishment at the open doors and free access to banks and offices, the low tables in the counting houses without grating or metal trellises, and the use of small shovels to weigh gold as if it were salt or cloves. Collectively thought of as honest, therefore, the City's institutions enjoyed direct benefits: the motto of the Stock Exchange was *dictum imium pactum* (my word is my bond); at Lloyds, it was *a fidentia* (with the utmost good faith) and at the Baltic Exchange, 'our word is our bond'. That trust, it might be argued by social historians, was as much part of the City, as much located from below as discerned at the top.

The social historian working in traditional mode is likely to take an holistic approach to the City and challenge the dominant image of the City taken by economic historians or historians of high politics. Rarely considered from this angle but who were, nonetheless, part of what we think of as the City are those who serviced its streets and cleaned its offices. If the informal economy of the City is brushed aside in standard economic-driven accounts of the City, so then are City vagrants, the disabled poor such as the legless Irish beggars who travelled on low wooden-wheeled platforms, match-girls, impoverished Jewish immigrants, 'Creoles' or black flower girls, and City 'characters' like 'Poor Jenny' who sold flowers in Newgate Street. What too, of the man who offered muffins and crumpets at Hanway Yard, the Jewish women selling puddings in Old Change, or the 'country wenches', 'dapper clerks,' 'unclassed men', widowers, ex-schoolmasters, and others of former 'superior station' that hovered at the gates of the great City institutions but also at the doors of the workhouse. The social historian then will tend to attempt a recreation of the whole spectrum of the Victorian City but not in order simply, in E. P. Thompson's withering phrase, to rescue the poor and marginal from the 'condescension of posterity' but to argue instead that the bourgeois associations of the City and the penny capitalism of its streets were vital factors in the success of the City. Social history, therefore, allows us to understand how and why the City's associational life and its informal economy – its living and breathing community – were vital to the evolution of modern financial capitalism.

Section 3

Cultural history and its expansion

Writing in 2008, Peter Burke in his book *What is Cultural History?* admitted that it was best to say simply what cultural history did rather than what it is. He had a point. For the approach of historians to the study of culture has been fraught with difficulty and imprecision. A large part of the problem lies in the notion of culture itself. Raymond Williams famously claimed that culture was one of the 'two or three most complicated words in the English language' (Williams, 2010, p. 87), with a complex history of shifting meanings, but then proceeded steadfastly to identify its three main uses:

1. The general process of intellectual, spiritual and aesthetic development from the eighteenth century. What this refers to are the ways in which societies have expressed concerns and aspirations as they entered into the modern world, that is, how artistic traditions, political and religious movements, and philosophical developments have emerged and have come to define and distinguish particular societies, most notably, the 'West' from the 'East'.
2. A particular way of life of a people, period or group, or humanity writ large. Culture here refers to the whole way of life of a people, how it is organised, reproduces and expresses itself.
3. The works and practices of intellectual and artistic activity. This is a variation on (1), but with a rather clearer focus on the specific works of art, literature, scholarship, music, theatre and film.

Now it is not immediately clear which of these areas are of legitimate interest to historians. The study of culture as a whole way of life has been claimed almost exclusively by anthropologists, sociologists and archaeologists, perhaps with good reason. It may well be feasible to grasp the whole way of life of a 'tribal society', a relatively small group such as teenage gang, or an ancient society which has left few remnants as evidence, but a large and complex modern society? And surely works of art are best left to scholars of literature, art, film and so on, who can bring to bear their own specialist knowledge to an understanding of these expressive forms?

The other problem confronting historians was to audit precisely what role culture played in historical change. It is clear for many that, say, music or art, let alone popular recreations such as dancing were mere fripperies when compared to elemental forces such as economic change, political machination and war. And yet there were notable exceptions. In 1870 Jacob Burckhardt, who we first met in Chapter 7, published *Civilization of the Renaissance in Italy*, a study charting the extraordinary flowering of culture at the time. It may have done this by linking Renaissance culture to the classical world rather than contemporary developments, but the fact that it was viewed as the first study of the history of art said something about the acceptance among historians of the legitimacy of inquiries into great cultural movements as indicators of fundamental shifts in human thought and imagination. It is unlikely that a study, say, of the popular festivities of French peasants would have been accorded the same status in the late nineteenth century, although, as we shall see, this is very much the fare of more recent work.

Burckhardt was at the same time a celebration of the rise of bourgeois individualism for this was the trait which underpinned the lives and works of the artists of the time. Implicitly, therefore, he accepted that the social and economic conditions of fifteenth-century Italian society gave rise to particular aspirations among the bourgeois elite which expressed themselves in art. This approach was one that necessarily appealed to twentieth-century historians of Marxist persuasion who were largely responsible for taking on the mantle of cultural history. According to them, art, music, literature and so forth were part of the superstructure of society, and as such reflected or expressed changes in the socio-economic base. Thus Arnold Hauser's *Social History of Art* (1951), to take one influential example, argued like Burckhardt that the art of late fifteenth-century Florence was an expression of bourgeois naturalism which was evident in the deliberate flaunting of artistic skill such as perspective, and which was a direct response to nationalist sentiment boosted by momentous contemporary historical developments, including the discovery of America and the invasion of Italy by France in the 1490s.

In recent years, this approach has been undermined by two connected developments (Burke, 2008, pp. 118–20). First, historians have moved away from an exclusive interest in elite cultural forms to embrace popular culture. Second, culture is no longer seen as a passive response to the socio-economic, but is now viewed as an active force in its own right. Let us consider some examples. As a nice counterpoint to studies of elite Renaissance culture, Peter Burke, one of our most gifted cultural historians, published in 1978 his *Popular Culture in Early Modern Europe*, a study of cultural forms which spanned Europe from the late medieval period (1500) to the beginnings of the industrial revolution (1800). From the outset, Burke spelt out what was distinctive about his approach. Borrowing promiscuously from various meanings of the term, he claimed that culture is a system of shared meanings, values, and attitudes, and the forms (literature, plays, and so on) which are used to express them. In this sense, culture is in part a whole way of life, but not identical with it. Popular culture relates to the subordinate classes, most craftsmen, peasants and their families; to understand it, he claimed, we have to adapt the approach of Burckhardt by borrowing concepts and methods from other disciplines, in particular, literature, folklore and social anthropology. The result was a wonderfully evocative and insightful account of the origins and structures of popular cultural forms, and the extent to which they revealed the nature of the wider societies. The most significant and lasting of these forms was the carnival which took place early each year throughout Europe, but particularly in the temperate south, and represented a celebration of popular sentiment before the austerities and lean times imposed by Lent. It was therefore a brief time of excessive consumption of food, alcohol and sex, when through transgressive acts of social inversion the 'world was turned upside down'. During carnival symbols of this challenge to the dominant social order were pervasive – the king became the fool, the fool became the king, animals rode on humans, fish flew.

Burke was not alone at the time in seeking to approach history from below. The 1970s witnessed a rich flowering of studies of peasant and plebeian cultures from the pens and typewriters of outstanding radical historians. In France, Emmanuel Le Roy Ladurie, a leading member of the *Annales* School, published *Montaillou: Cathars and Catholics in a French*

Village 1294–1324 (1975), a vivid and detailed reconstruction of the life of a small medieval village in the early fourteenth century, which he followed shortly after with *Carnival in Romans: Mayhem and Massacre in a French City* (1979), a dazzling account of when celebrations at Romans in south-west France turned into a people's uprising against repressive authority. In Italy, as we will meet in a slightly different context in Chapter 14, Carlo Ginzburg wrote *The Cheese and the Worms*, which used records around the trial of a sixteenth-century miller to shed brilliant light on the Italian peasant culture. In Britain, Edward Thompson (see Section 1) wrote a series of pieces on plebeian village culture collected together in *Customs in Common*, while Christopher Hill in *The World Turned Upside Down* (1972) and his student David Underdown (1925–2009) in *Pride's Purge: Politics in the Puritan Revolution* (1971), and then more particularly in *Revel, Riot and Rebellion* (1985), effectively rewrote the history of the English Civil War by demonstrating the extent to which the conflict was not merely political and religious, but at every turn cultural. In their eyes, struggles over the status and survival of popular recreations such as sport and theatre, exerted a decisive influence on the course of events. This body of historical work stands comparison with any. It has stood the test of time, and is largely responsible for the richness of cultural history today.

The second challenge to historical studies of elite culture has come from theorists who are seen collectively to inhabit approaches based on structuralism. Structuralists (as opposed to the culturalists against whom they are pitted) seek to invert the relationship between society and its cultural forms. Whereas previously, cultural historians began with economic and social structures as a means of explaining modes of cultural expression such as religion, language and art, structuralists argue that these forms of expression are actually decisive since they – and not, say, the class structure – create the mindsets through which people interpret their experience. A member of the bourgeoisie, for example, does not think and behave in ways defined by his or her position in society, but according to the ideologies they inhabit. Thus, for example, they come to believe that they have a natural right and ability to rule. To state the opposition pithily, but hopefully in a helpful manner: for culturalists, experience tends to structure expression, while for structuralists, expression tends to structure experience. Take, for example, literature. Culturalists have argued that literature is the embodiment or expression of societies, classes and communities because it represents their lived realities, while structuralists argue that literature expresses nothing, rather it shapes the way people view these lived realities. The use of the term 'structures' rather than, say, 'determines' is important, for the vast majority of historians within these camps have no wish to work with crude Marxist visions of base and superstructure, as outlined in Chapter 4. Instead, in their various ways, they see culture as part of the whole fabric of social practices which comprise human activity; the trick is to understand the changing dialogue between cultural forms and social behaviour at particular times.

The origins of structuralism can be traced back to early twentieth-century work on language undertaken by Ferdinand de Saussure (1857–1913) and Roman Jakobson (1896–1982). They perceived that languages operate to create meaning not through vocabularies, which are purely arbitrary, but by systems of rules of which for the most part we are simply not aware. Thus, for example, there is nothing in the word 'table' which signifies the object being described; it is only when we realise that 'table' does not mean chair, or floor, and so on, that it comes to take on meaning. After the Second World War, anthropologists, political theorists and sociologists began to understand that this approach to language had a much wider relevance. In the appropriately titled *Structural Anthropology* (1958), the French anthropologist Claude Lévi-Strauss (1909–2009) claimed that cultures were in effect languages, and operated according to the same system of rules. Myths, kinship systems and rituals were ordered in specific ways; once we understood the underlying structure through application of the tools of linguistic analysis, we could then reveal how they operate to create meaning and hence patterns of behaviour. An example of such a ritual was the meal, which is highly structured like a language, and even if we are not aware of how the structure operates we act accordingly. The courses are rigidly organised (just think of the confusion if treacle sponge and custard was offered before roast beef and vegetables, finishing with pea soup), and tight protocols of eating them are followed. Levi Strauss hoped, therefore, to identify universal structures which underpin all cultural systems; the increasing awareness of the common features of myths suggests he was along the right lines.

What has this concern with structures meant for historians? When Fernand Braudel wrote his magisterial *The Mediterranean and the Mediterranean World in the Age of Philip II* in a prisoner of war camp, he was probably not aware of the latest work in linguistic theory, and yet it is clear he was thinking along similar and parallel lines. He was concerned above all to downgrade narratives of the individual and event that tended to prevail in previous historical writing by instead focusing on the deep historical structures which produce change. This demanded a total history involving society, culture and the physical environment, and not the narrow diplomatic and political histories that had tended to prevail. Fundamental in this approach was his use of time, which can also be understood as language. For Braudel, time was an organising principle in human societies. In the period and place of his study, it operated at different levels. Fundamental was the *longue durée*, a history of recurring cycles which span centuries, but this was mediated by the medium *durée*, a history of trade cycles and demographic change over decades, and finally *histoire événementielle* which charts day to day course of historical change. Thus lives of individuals and events, the normal fare of historical writing, are in fact merely surface manifestations of deeper and more fundamental temporal structures of which we are for the most part ignorant (Gunn, 2006, pp. 14–15).

It is generally the case, however, that this approach to history has been less fertile than that of culturalism. Historians have remained suspicious of what they see as the influence of continental philosophers, although there are some notable exceptions whose work deserves mention. Michel Foucault is discussed more fully in Chapter 5, but suffice it to say here that his studies of madness, incarceration and power all start with the premise that histories which present unified and linear chronicles of events sustaining a sense of stability are not to be trusted. Rather we have to look at how knowledge is produced and operates, for it is on the basis of such sources of meaning and identity (or discourses in Foucault's terminology), that people act as historical agents. Thus people inhabit ordered structured discourses of, say, commerce, economics or bourgeois individualism which impact directly upon how they see themselves and the world around.

There are few historical studies of culture which could be described as purely structural; any such study would probably be quite dull. We have seen in important recent work, however, the incipient influence of structuralism. Simon Schama would resist any tendency to rank him among the structuralists, and yet his *The Embarrassment of Riches* (1987), subtitled *An Interpretation of Dutch Culture in the Golden Age*, clearly owes something to their work. The book is a detailed account of how the burgher world of the Dutch in the seventeenth century constructed a collective sense of identity. The ideology they inhabited determined how they conducted themselves in civic affairs, how they dressed, how they viewed others outside their universe, how they lived within the family, and so on. In *Landscape and Memory* (1995) Schama turned his attention to the ways in which representations of the landscape have entered into the fabric of western culture. He wished to understand the richness, antiquity and complexity of the landscape tradition not by gazing at its obvious appearance but by excavating below to reveal the 'veins of myth and memory that lie beneath the surface' (Schama, 1995, p. 14).

Questions of myth and memory have featured prominently in recent cultural history. Myth, like culture, is a complex term. Commonsensically, myth refers to an untruth, usually one that has grown organically over time to be accepted by many; belief in the ancient continuity of the British royal line, serves as an example. And there are, as we have already mentioned, myths of a universal nature involving human struggle against imposing odds. Historians, by contrast, use the term to refer to an interpretation of events which has distilled the essence of what is a complex picture to convey one which appears cogent, simple and, above all, natural. Myths are profoundly important to the creation of collective identity – just pause to think for a moment of how our senses of Britishness are mythological. By unravelling the ways in which such myths are put together, what particular rhetoric and narrative devices they employ, how, in other words, they are structured, we can better understand their latent power. As examples of recent work we can do no better than refer to the studies of Alessandro Portelli, an Italian scholar of American literature and culture who we meet briefly in Chapter 20 on the subject of oral history and Luisa Passerini, also an Italian, who we introduce in the same chapter as an expert on memory and fascism. Portelli's *The Death of Luigi Trastulli and Other Stories* (1991), for example, shows how the death of an Italian worker on a demonstration in 1949 was selectively remembered by subsequent generations. Such remembrances were not, he claimed, the result of wayward memories but emerged from an effort to make sense of what happened. Similarly, Passerini's *Fascism in Popular Memory* (1987) investigates how the experience of fascism in Italy was subsequently appropriated in popular memory, not as a reliable record but as a means retrospectively of incorporating the experience into narratives that were seemingly rational. We investigate the use of myth in history more fully in Chapter 14.

Memory has for long been of interest to historians. Most argued that memory was the fickle product of the subterranean mind, thereby relegating it to the instinctive and intuitional. This helps to explain the hostility of conventional historians to oral testimony, and yet few appreciated that all documentary evidence was in part built on memory simply because the documents were created in part from memory of the events they described. In recent years, there has been a growing recognition in the work of people like Portelli that memory is not a passive store of images from the past, but an active and dynamic force in the creation of historical thought; one where the silences and gaps are as important as the presences. We all interpret and act from personal and collective memories of past events, most often in the belief that these memories are reliable and secure. Often the indefensible, irrational and horrific in collective memories are deliberately erased or reworked. Memories are thus not stable and inviolable; they are historically conditioned, altering from generation to generation, from place to place.

In *Theatres of Memory* (1994), Raphael Samuel took up these arguments by showing how popular memory of the past is not fixed but actively created, most notably by television, which has become the principal source of unofficial knowledge. Drama documentaries, series such as *Timewatch*, *Who do you think you are?* and *Time Team*, fictional dramas of the past such as *Band of Brothers* and *Madmen*, biographies, anniversaries of events, and even the replaying of old films, may help satiate our appetite for all things past but at the same time they construct popular memories of that past even when the images they present conflict with memories based on personal experience. In Britain, this tension was amusingly exploited in *'Allo, 'Allo*, which parodied the ways in which the French resistance to Nazi occupation had been represented in television drama. Under such circumstances it is the role of the historian to provide correctives where necessary, to reveal how historical memory operates, and develop strategies for a more critical popular historical imagination.

In practice

Recent approaches to social, political and cultural history have opened up a number of important questions for us all to consider. First is the question of theory. Conventionally, historians have not been that much concerned with theory. Working assiduously with the evidence, they tended to see their role as objective chroniclers of historical episodes, leaving the partialities of theoretical abstraction to scholars in the social sciences. That has changed. Historians increasingly recognise that theory has always informed their accounts, and that there is much to be learnt from work in such disciplines as sociology, anthropology and geography. The widespread adoption of notions such as class, structure, consciousness, discourse, identity and ideology has resulted from a welcome dismantling of the rather artificial boundaries that historians have erected around themselves.

Second, we approach differently the role of the individual and the event. Previously, they were sovereign. The task of the historian working in, say, political or diplomatic history was to chart the actions and decisions of individuals who made a difference, and how these were related to the unfolding of events on the national and international stage. This role is for many no longer centre stage. Historical change is brought about not merely through the action of a few, but more importantly through the many. A leader, for example, emerges because he or she is able to articulate and express the fears and aspirations of large sections of the population.

The third question extends the above point by considering the relationship between historical agents and the structures they inhabit. To say that we need to take better account of the popular in our approach to history is not entirely sufficient, for the course of people's lives are shaped by latent structures of which few are conscious. Whether it is the eating of a meal, a parliamentary election, a workplace environment, or deeper and more fundamental processes like geography and climate, we inhabit and are profoundly influenced by structures. To understand precisely how these operate, we have again to turn to the insights of other disciplines.

Summary

The three sections of this chapter have said three things:

- Political history is concerned with politics and politics is about power relations in society, and so its potential brief is extremely wide. In practice, however, political historians have devoted themselves to the study of political organisations which have impacted upon the formal, parliamentary arena. Using a case study of the rise of the Labour Party, we have shown that the study of politics – narrowly defined – can be approached in different ways. An older tradition focused on the role of influential figures and their hold over strategic decision making almost exclusively in the field of formal party politics. Underlying this was the premise that to an extent these individuals lived in rarefied atmospheres, taking key decisions not on the basis of any preconceived ideas or rooted in particular ideologies, but often because they were impelled by peculiar circumstances of the moment, or because of distinctive personal traits. In part as a response to this, there has emerged more recently an approach which is rather more interested in the extent to which the arena of formal politics reflected wider social movements, in the case of the Labour Party, its relationship to working-class culture and behaviour. This approach to politics has also been more concerned to move beyond the boundaries of formal politics to consider political events and movements of all shades of opinion in the extra-parliamentary sphere.
- There is no hard and fast distinction between social and cultural history. A case could well be made for confining the social to the component features of society, for example, class, kinship systems, work and crime, while culture refers to the more closely focused areas of leisure and imagination, such as cinema going, religion, language, manners and music. But the boundaries do not stand up to scrutiny – are peasant rituals, shopping, pubs or racism, for example, legitimate areas of inquiry for the social or the cultural historian? In considering social history, we have simultaneously considered histories of the powerless as well as the powerful. Using the City of London of the eighteenth and nineteenth centuries as an extended case study, we have explored how social historians have been able to reveal how complex social networks and class structures underpinned the rise of the Atlantic system and the City as a financial powerhouse, thus providing a history that has gone beyond the narrow remit of a concern with financial apparatuses controlled by powerful men.
- By exploring cultural history by charting the move from elites in the Italian Renaissance, and the medieval carnival, to history on television we have detected, as in other fields of history, a shift toward the popular in recent years. Cultural historians are now interested in revealing the nature and significance of popular cultural forms which had previously been thought of as trivial and of little worth. Thus the minutiae of daily life – eating, washing, smoking, courting and so on – attract the attention they deserve. The other challenge has come from what we referred to as structuralism, that is, the notion that cultural forms resemble a language and are therefore open to methods developed in linguistics. The task here is to excavate beneath surface appearance to uncover the deep structures that have a profound influence on the course of people's lives. Cultural historians have created a rich and varied body of work in the past 20 years or so which has greatly extended our understanding of the importance of culture in the lives of people, and hence in explaining the nature of historical change.

Discussion document

The extent to which Schama is first describing social history approaches (borrowing from other disciplines as a form of 'shameless eclecticism') and then abandoning this for a pure discussion of culture in historical study is articulated via a discussion of Dutch art. Look out for references to Mary Douglas, Emile Durkheim and Proust as they lend weight to notions of culture as promiscuous and open ended.

In wandering about the Dutch city, bumping into its cultural furniture, I have strayed a good deal from the straight and narrow of the historical method. Shameless eclecticism has been my only methodological guide. The thieving magpie approach to other disciplines may seem, superficially, to be newfangled but it is very old-fashioned. It follows on from the precedent of those venerable nineteenth-century compendia of manners and mores . . . that were part folklore, part antiquarian anthropology and which for all their methodological innocence remain a rich treasure house of arcane and intricate knowledge. . . .

So there is nothing especially daring about a working definition of culture drawn from social anthropology. In this well-established tradition I follow the kind of characterization offered by Mary Douglas of cultural bias as 'an array of beliefs locked together into relational patterns'. In the same essay, however, she cautions that for those beliefs to be considered the matrix of a culture, they should 'be treated as part of the [social] action and not separated from it'. . . . Acting upon one another, belief systems and customs together form what Emile Durkheim called 'a determinate system that has its own life: . . . the *collective or common conscience* . . . is by definition diffuse in every reach of society. Nevertheless it has specific conditions that make it a distinct reality'.

To see this elusive quarry – the *conscience collectif* – in its proper habitat and in action, rather than prone and eviscerated on the sociologist's dissecting table, I have used visual as well as textual evidence. . . . To exploit the bottomless riches of Dutch art – not merely panels and canvases, but architecture, sculpture, and the cornucopia of the decorative arts on glass, ceramic, tapestry – seems so natural and so obvious that is difficult to conceive of any kind of cultural history, even an anthropologically bent one that leaves them out. . . .

Dutch art invites the cultural historian to probe below the surface of appearances. By illuminating an interior world as much as illustrating an exterior one, it moves back and forth between morals and matter, between the durable and the ephemeral, the concrete and the imaginary, in a way that was peculiarly Netherlandish. And the paradoxes crowd in so thickly that the culture seems almost designed as a contrapuntal arrangement. . . . It is a sobering reminder to the cultural historian that the collective image he may try to recover might at best be fugitive and ghostly, like the outline of houses that Proust saw reflected in the Maas at Dordrecht, which trembled into incoherence with every ripple of the evening tide.

Simon Schama, *The Embarrassment of Riches: An Interpretation of Dutch Culture in the Golden Age* (1991), pp. 8–11.

Further reading

* *essential*

Philip Williamson, 'Maurice Cowling and modern British political history' in Robert Crowcroft (ed.), *The Philosophy, Politics and Religion of British Democracy: Maurice Cowling and Conservatism* (2010).
A convincing and very well-informed account of high political history from a major practitioner and former student of Maurice Cowling. It is strongly argued but also covers all relevant historiography on the subject.

Adrian Wilson, *Rethinking Social History: English Society 1570–1920 and its Interpretation* (1993).
An accessible take on social history as an important sub-discipline, covering the developments of social history over a very long period.

* **Peter Burke**, *What is Cultural History?* (2008).
A valuable guide to historical approaches from a widely published historian in an area in which he is well qualified to comment.

Peter Burke, *Varieties of Cultural History* (1997).
A lively account of the origins of cultural history that is accompanied by some equally valuable essays on memory, mentalities and gesture.

Lynn Hunt (ed.) *The New Cultural History* (1989).
A critical intervention in the subject, it should be read both for its important introduction and for some notable essays, particularly Roger Chartier's.

Paul Readman, 'The state of twentieth-century British political history', *Journal of Public Policy*, vol. 21, no. 3, 2009, pp. 219–38.
Underlines and gives an overview of many of the debates in political history that have been sketched in this chapter.

10 Feminism, gender and women's history

1 History and feminism
2 Women: hidden from history
3 Gender and identity

Introduction

This chapter describes how history has been transformed by gender: both in ways that the subject is now researched and written; but also how historians have read evidence to include both women and then gender issues more generally. The opening section tackles the problem of gender versus class, and investigates more generally how female experiences in the past have prompted a massive historiography among different strands of feminist thought. It is chiefly concerned with various forms of feminism, from conservative feminism that traditionally saw women as natural beings, who as wives as mothers have attributes best suited to the domestic sphere, or Marxist feminism, which tended to place class as its main concern. These approaches to the history of women have transformed male-dominated histories. Now histories are sensitive to gender, a transformation that is charted in Section 2. The roles of women in history and an attempt to write women back into history during the 1960s and 1970 is considered, as is the rise of a political feminism during that period. In Section 3, we explore questions around femininity and masculinity, and in this context outline the significance of recent work on witchcraft with due consideration paid to approaches to the past which borrow from psychoanalytic and linguistic techniques of understanding human behaviour from a gendered point of view.

Section 1

History and feminism

Betty Wardle, a housewife of Outwood, near Lever in Lancashire, England, recalled her working life in a coalmine in an interview with the Royal Commissioners in 1842. Having worked since the age of six wearing a belt and chain (not uncommon for mineworkers in her day) she had given birth twice underground, bringing the last baby to the surface in her skirts. The reason why she could recollect this, she told her incredulous interviewers, was that the infant had been born the day after her marriage. These were clearly desperate circumstances and as these interviews are all too rare testimonies from female industrial workers during the early-Victorian period, they reveal for the historian a harrowing account of how women balanced work with an almost unimaginable burden of maintaining a family. 'Independent' is a word used frequently by Commissioners sent by an anxious Parliament to describe these women workers. They found girls in Bilston, Staffordshire whose language and conduct they described as unfeminine: riding astride horses, drinking, swearing, fighting, smoking and singing. Yet, like the children who worked in factories and mills, the 'little elves' described by the Scots manufacturer Andrew Ure (1778–1857), these women were also described as happy with their lot and should, it was concluded by the Commissioners, be 'no objects of pity'. In Darlaston, near Walsall in the West Midlands it was found, for example, that women went into public houses, ordered beer and smoked pipes: all category errors for a Victorian society that in its most evangelical Christian phase in the years before the 1840s saw women as 'helpmeets' or 'angels of the hearth'; the very bedrock of domestic stability. They were, it was thought, the 'chief sufferers' of the industrial process, victims of capitalism which raw in tooth and claw extracted an unacceptable toll from the weakest in society. When Parliament heard the verdict of the Royal Commission, it lost little time in banning women from working underground, but not because they were victims of the industrial process. It was because to do otherwise would have upset the established order of relationships between the sexes.

This story about the struggles of women as mothers, daughters and sisters in a harrowing and brutal moment of Britain's industrialisation touches on issues of vital importance to feminist history. Some might argue that the history of these women fills a significant gap in our reading of the industrial revolution. For most feminist historians, however, it is not merely or principally a matter of providing a more complete picture by the inclusion of women; it is more a question of approaching the past with due regard to the complex and dynamic relationships between men and women.

What sorts of questions would a feminist historian therefore ask of the experience of these women? That they were forced to work under such conditions was clearly a matter of their class and the logic of capitalist exploitation which underpinned the industrial revolution, but did it also have something to do with their gender? There is a tension between approaches which see class and gender as the most important aspect of the historical experience, and feminist historians have attempted to weigh the balance between them with greater accuracy. Given that women had on average less physical strength than men, why were women chosen? Was it because employers could pay them less? If so, why was it that the majority of people accepted the fact that women should be paid less than men, even if the work they were doing was identical? And why was the Commissioners' report so anxious about the state of these women? Were they troubled that employers, by subjecting these women to such toil, endangered their health and general well-being? Or was it rather that the existence of these seemingly strong and independent women actively challenged male-dominated, patriarchal perspectives that women should be confined to the domestic sphere in subordinate and supporting roles to the male head?

All brands of feminist historiography have taken into account the female historical experience. Yet this otherwise anodyne observation does not begin to reflect the multifarious political ideologies and traditions that are 'feminist'. Three main strands within feminism – Conservative, Liberal and Marxist – have emerged out of feminist politics in the modern period and have affected the writing of history.

Victorian women such as Mrs C. M. Yonge (1823–1901), Mrs Humphrey Ward (1851–1920) and Octavia Hill (1838–1912) articulated the principles of conservative feminism in the so-called first wave of feminism at the end of the nineteenth century. As prominent campaigners, authors and charity workers, they saw women's true natures as best developed in the home on behalf of the family. These conservative women opposed female political activity (like paid employment) because it took place in the public sphere that they assumed to be competitive and therefore unfeminine. By the end of the nineteenth century, however, philanthropy and a religious duty to do good works, allowed conservative women alarmed by the social dislocation of the new urban centres to go into the slums and courtyards of the poor. Philanthropy was seen as an extension of the domestic sphere and therefore was an activity permitted to women; a world away from the corrupting influences of public discourse, Parliament, courts of law and so on. Many of those that occupied private as opposed to public spaces did so in the context of a dominant religious sensibility and clearly thought of themselves as leading moral lives. Despite differences in religious affiliation, wealth and politics, these conservative women wanted to maintain separate roles for men and women in a moment of rapid and destabilising change. These separate spheres articulated the different meanings of masculinity and femininity at the time. To be a man was to be serious, upright, respectable and honourable. If women were retiring and emotionally vulnerable, men should be brave, honest, self-disciplined and hard working whilst also displaying tenderness and care for others. A true gentleman was masculine in every sense.

Liberals had no such reservation about the public role of women. John Stuart Mill in the nineteenth century outlined a humanist case for feminism, that is, he saw human beings as sharing characteristics such as altruism and a desire for social justice regardless of gender or social differences. Mill believed that the unequal treatment of men and women was wrong; that these inequalities offended against reason and conscience, and that social or environmental reform could overcome biological differences like motherhood. The emphasis here on overcoming biological differences was important because it suggested that women could not be defined by their natural attributes such as an ability to give birth. Accordingly, liberal feminists such as Mill argued for state intervention in areas such as child welfare that had previously been part of women's domestic preserve and called for the related need of women to enjoy equal participation in the workplace. Women were different but they could be equal.

Both conservative and liberal feminist ideologies have fed into the writing of histories, but Marxist-inspired feminism has probably enjoyed the most influence. Marxists met gendered histories initially with derision, fearing that writing women back into the historical record threatened the primacy of class as a mode of analysis. That fear has been well founded. There was a time when historians told big stories about class. These grand narratives are still around, of course, but they no longer for the most part connect to a political project such as Marxism. This is largely because histories sensitive to gender and race have usurped grand narratives about class, using a range of sources which describe the past from the point of view of belongings and identities constructed outside or alongside those of class. That these gendered histories could have been written since the signal year of 1970 (as we shall argue in the next section) is overwhelmingly because we no longer see ourselves as simply members of a social class but feel our identities to be more fluid; accordingly writing sexuality, ethnicity and religious backgrounds, as well as gender, back into history.

For Marxist historians, history is the nature of the sexual division of labour within capitalism. Women in most historical accounts form a largely unskilled, disorganised 'industrial reserve army'. In times of labour shortage they could be utilised or 'called-up' to maintain employment, job insecurity and low wages. Thus, the economy mirrored social divisions between public and private spheres: the latter located in the home, a domestic economy that supported capitalism through the reproduction of workers. From a Marxist perspective, 'gendered' approaches to the past could add little as all history was the history of class struggle: gender blind, and race neutral.

Some feminist historians who had shared this Marxist perspective soon argued for a 'patriarchy first' model of history. This acknowledged that the capitalist system worked in favour of the propertied but, more significantly, that it worked also to the advantage of men with men wielding power as men, not as capitalists or workers. This more gendered approach to historical research, as we shall see in more detail in Section 2, won considerable support in the 1970s and beyond. More recently, however, an influential study of the lives of working class women in Burrow, Preston and Lancaster between 1890 and 1940 by Elizabeth Roberts (1996), resisted the 'patriarchy first' approach by arguing that the lot of women in the industrial working class was a result, not of patriarchy, but of poverty. Gender is given no more priority than 'work' or 'production' as a prime focus of research although the subject matter remains focused on women.

The notion of 'separate spheres' prompted some feminist historians to understand the history of women through a 'domestic ideology', that is, the view that women's rightful place in society was within the home as wives and mothers. Discussion has often focused on the role and place of middle class women within the political and economic milieu of the nineteenth century. *Family Fortunes: Men and Women of the English Middle Class, 1780–1850* (1997) by Leonore Davidoff and Catherine Hall is a prominent example. Davidoff and Hall compared industrial Birmingham with rural Essex and Suffolk, looking at the private and public lives of banking, trading and farming families to conclude that a new sexual division of labour emerged by the mid-nineteenth century based on economic success, domestic happiness and at least some cooperation between the sexes. The home fulfilled the evangelical idea of a 'cottage religion' where women were considered theologically as the helpmeet of men – spiritually equal, if socially and politically unequal. If mid-century women were modelled on the biblical Eve, a mixture of mother and temptress, by the end of the century they began tentatively to enter the public sphere when philanthropic work was thought to match the inherent female qualities of purity, sympathy, gentleness and obedience.

The debate between the importance of capitalist economic relations to the lives of women and the power wielded by individual men has been informed by a gendered reading of primary sources. In this, feminist approaches have transformed our understanding and writing of history. Take, for example, the historiography of industrialisation. The Marxist historian Eric Hobsbawm assumed that few married women were in paid employment during certain phases of industrialisation and therefore should not be considered to have been part of the industrial proletariat. Maxine Berg, in contrast, concentrated on the presence of female labour in the workforce at a time of rapidly changing technologies. She especially highlighted the significance of family labour and the family wage, that is, the combined income of men, women and even children, although their precise role has been open to debate. Some Marxist historians see the family wage as a side-effect of the casualisation of the workplace inherent in capitalist production which deskilled work allowing women to take over tasks previously done by men, while 'patriarchy first' historians dismiss the family wage as a concession to male breadwinners, while others argue that it was a necessary negotiation between men and women in a family setting. Jane Humphries, for example, suggested that the family wage was not 'a sexist device adopted by nineteenth-century working class men'. Rather it was 'a strategy adapted by both men and women against exploitation by the capitalist system' (quoted in Roberts, 1995, p. 15).

The 1842 Mines Regulation Act, the topic with which this section began, was perhaps the first discriminating labour legislation aimed at women and an early example of the state regulation of women's work. It has been used by historians to argue for the importance of gender to narratives of industrialisation. The intervention of feminist thinking to the process of historical thinking and writing has been transformative and if applied to the evidence gathered by the Royal Commission can reveal levels of meaning that without gendered approaches to history would remain obscure. Much of this new sensitivity to women in the writing and reading of history was due to the contribution of those socialists and feminists who in 1970 gathered at a conference to argue that women be written back into history. We shall now make a beeline to this Oxford conference.

Section 2

Women: hidden from history

Much of the history of industrialisation has been centred on the male experience. Before 1970, labour history and conventional political histories that dealt with, say, high politics or the politics of government, tended to tell the story of male power. Unsurprisingly then some of the more traditional right-wing historians were in the feminist firing line but so also were historians such as E. P. Thompson – in fact, E. P. Thompson in particular. His classic *The Making of the English Working Class* (1963) was essentially a study of the formation of a male culture; women were present only at the margins. Thus his various accounts of radical movements in pre-industrial society argued that a largely homogeneous (and seemingly male) proletariat had gone underground during the state oppression associated with the French wars only to remerge during the 1820s as a major political force in the land. The essay that really riled feminists, however, was that on wife sales republished in *Cultures in Common* (1991). This explained how a largely male plebeian class had used unofficial forms of divorce to assert their independence from the patrician ruling class and in so doing demonstrated their independence as a class. As a thesis it attracted venom from feminists precisely because it tended to focus on men in the history of class struggle at the expense of women's experiences, suggesting that women had not resisted either capitalist or patriarchal power. Thompson protested that he was simply following evidence presented to him in the archive, but from the 1970s onwards feminist historians would re-read the primary sources, and in so doing bring some balance to what they believed to be a skewed historical record in favour, as the joke went at the time, of 'his – story.'

Eric Hobsbawm, to take another notable example, put together a collection of his writings entitled *Labouring Men* which foregrounded the conditions of the male working class in different industries and their struggles for improvement. Thirty years ago Thompson and Hobsbawm, even though part of a radical historical tradition, represented more conventional histories of manual labour and trade union struggles which for the most part had been dominated by men; but then a wave of feminist scholarship began to revisit these histories.

In 1970, a National Women's Liberation Conference was held at Ruskin College. Convened by leading feminists including Sheila Rowbotham, Sally Alexander and Anna Davin, the conference marked the beginning of a new wave of feminist scholarship. Initially, conventional historians viewed these developments with suspicion, even ridicule. Some saw an interest in gender as a passing fashion, others were unwilling to accept that gender was as important a determinant of the human experience as class or race. In the years that followed, however, many of those who attended became prominent feminists and their ideas of gendering history were (almost) totally accepted into the mainstream of historical writing. The feminists of 1970 also made a significant breakthrough in institutional terms, breaking through into the upper echelons of the academy, influencing many academic disciplines and creating the sub-discipline of 'Women's Studies' that saw women as exclusive historical subjects in their own right. From this movement came a host of journals in the 1970s, founded within a few years of each other, such as *Feminist Review* and *History Workshop Journal*, the latter subtitled at its inception as 'a journal for socialist and feminist historians'.

A fresh subjectivity was also introduced into the writing of history in 1970 with the personal experiences of women writers finding an outlet in their writing. It was probably the radical American feminist, Carol Hanisch, who coined the phrase in 1969 that the 'political is personal'. Its enduring meaning was that for women their personal problems had become political problems and for them barriers between the private and public spheres had largely broken down. For a number of reasons then, 1970 proved to be a breakthrough in a consciousness that women and women historians had something important to say. Although this generation of women influenced the way many historians today read, research and write history, it is important to note that they were not the first to attempt histories from a female perspective. Historians such as Ivy Pinchbeck (1898–1982), Eileen Power (1889–1940) and the great M. Dorothy George (1878–1971) had all researched and taught history in a man's world. Their books have continued to have an enduring appeal. Similarly, Mary Beard's *Women as a Force in History* (1946) enjoyed an afterlife in the 1960s, perhaps because it argued across a long period (from prehistoric to modern times) and because its polemic against the 'myth' of female subjection in history appealed to the new feminist historians who by now enjoyed a large and popular audience associated with women's liberation.

In order to 'liberate' women or even to celebrate women's role in history, however, first they had to be 'found'. *Hidden from History* was the title of a book by Rowbotham (1973). Its subtitle, *300 Years of Women's Oppression and the Fight Against It,* said much about the stance of women fighting against sexism and injustice both in the workplace and the home at this time of radical change. Like Beard, Rowbotham attempted to write women back into national historical narratives over a long timeframe, starting with 'early capitalism' in the seventeenth century and ending around the First World War. Also a product of feminist politics of the 1970s it crystallised discussions among politically aware women. Published by Virago, the first major publisher dedicated to literature produced by women, it bore witness to an approach that was to transform the writing of history.

By the time Joan Kelly published her brilliant study 'Did Women have a Renaissance?' (Kelly, 1984), questioning whether the Italian Renaissance was a time of great cultural change for women, gender-sensitive histories were routine. Kelly's book, however, did mark a significant landmark in writing women back into history. Like so many feminist commentators in the 1960s and 1970s, Kelly argued that woman is a cultural being, who could never be defined solely by her physicality or body. This notion established that women could transcend their roles as mothers or wives, with Kelly adding that 'the relations between the sexes is a social and not a natural one' but also that gender relations were not biologically given but historically created (Kelly, p. 1). Within this framework, Kelly's reinterpretation of the Renaissance (defined traditionally by the consolidation of states in Italy from 1350 to 1430, the development of a mercantile and manufacturing economy that could support these states, and a set of social and cultural relations that emerged from these new relations) was important. She took issue with the periodisation of the Renaissance, implying that if the Renaissance as a moment of cultural renewal happened for women, it did not occur between the terminal dates chosen by male historians. To measure how the Renaissance affected women, Kelly identified four major areas of social and cultural life. The first was the regulation of female sexuality when compared to men. The second was in the economic and political roles for women compared to men and their relative access to property, politics, power and education. Third, the roles women played in shaping their society. The fourth was the emergence during the Renaissance of an ideology about women that represented their 'sex-role' in the cultural production of art, literature and philosophy. This role, Kelly further noted, was performed within the constraints of 'courtly love'; noble and chivalrous love that demanded that women of high social standing marry well and obey the rules of chastity, etc. and which as a result acted as a brake to women's freedoms. In essence, according to Kelly, personal and public life separated the sexes in Renaissance society. From this a gender division emerged which Kelly argued marks the origin of the modern relation of sexes; that is, separate spheres where men exist and thrive in public spaces and women are constrained within the domestic or private sphere. If a Renaissance happened for men, it happened very differently for women, something we could only know by retrieving the hidden lives of women.

By the 1980s, the wheels had started to come off the Marxist bus. In that decade, Sally Alexander observed in an article in the *History Workshop Journal* that Marxist ideas about the 'determining social relationship between wage labour and capital, exploiter and exploited, proletarian and capitalist' were unsustainable (p. 00). Women's history and feminism had together proved that 'subjective identity is also constructed as masculine or feminine, placing the individual as husband or wife, mother or father, son or daughter, and so on' (p. 132). These identities may be conveyed in political language and may occasionally turn into political action but were not necessarily expressed in the form of class interests. Nor could we understand the female historical experience through a simple analysis of their roles which were largely determined physiologically.

Anne Clark's *The Struggle for the Breeches: Gender and the Making of the British Working Class* (1995) was a conscious attempt to challenge these narratives not simply by replacing a history of male labourers with a history of female members of the working class, but instead by integrating considerations of gender into the analysis of class. By comparing the experiences of male artisans with female textile workers, she demonstrated that the story of the industrial revolution was not merely about productive relations at work, but also featured histories of families and communities, and here women played a vital role. Indeed, the industrial revolution could be recast as a struggle over gendered divisions of labour.

That women and men experienced industrialisation and working class culture in very different ways was also explored by Catherine Hall. Her 1990 article 'The tale of Samuel and Jemima: gender and working class culture in nineteenth century England' put yet another nail in the coffin of the triumphal narrative of (largely male) labourers and artisans and revealed women in history where once they had been 'hidden'. Taking the account of the radical Samuel Bamford's experiences at the Peterloo Massacre in August 1819, she contrasted it with the story told by his wife Jemima Bamford around the same event. Each account conformed to gender stereotypes: he marched and organised the protesters; she acted as mother and support to the men. These testimonies were not new; they had been available to historians for some time, but Hall, like Clark, showed that accounts of the working class in the workshop or factory where skills fell inevitably to men tell only part of a more complicated story. This new reading of sources did two things: it placed women and gender at the heart of labour narratives; but also, as Clark put it, 'ultimately muted the radicalism of the British working class' for within radical culture women were defined principally as wives and mothers (Clark, 1995, p. 271).

One prominent example of the rereading of what had been thought of as the conventional sources of social history was undertaken very effectively by a former student at Ruskin College during these tumultuous times. Sally Alexander was a key figure in these new radical circles fusing, like so many of her contemporaries, the writing of history with political activity. Her long essay on 'Women's work in nineteenth-century London: a study of the years 1820–50', was a passionate example of how women's history could interrogate previously well-worked historical sources to reveal the roles of women in the past. The 1851 Census in the hands of male historians had been curiously silent on women's work, but with a close and creative reading by Alexander, women's roles were revealed not only in the domestic sphere but also in a host of occupations, even if most of them were low status and poorly paid. She thus located a division of labour based on gender, income and skill, thereby demonstrating how patriarchy and capitalism worked hand in glove to ensure 'the economic dependence of women upon their husbands or fathers for a substantial part of their lives' (Alexander, 1976, p. 77).

One of the most eminent of feminist theorists in the United States, Joan Wallach Scott, made a telling intervention in 1986 with an essay entitled 'Gender: a useful category of historical analysis'. Scott had long rejected women's history *per se*, that is, an historical approach that simply retrieves women from historical oblivion, and was critical of any analysis that involved men and women in relationship to one another because it limited gender histories to histories of power struggles between them. Scott followed this with her important book *Gender and the Politics of History* (1988), in which she retained an interest in power and politics, although not through the lens of class or gender, but the production of knowledge about sexual difference or class. The chapters of her book reflected a lifetime seeking to understand gender inequalities and the importance of gender differences in history. Accordingly, she devoted separate essays to the relationship between gender and class, especially in labour histories of the previous 30 years, the affect of feminist history, the role of discursive histories and the uses historians make of representations that construct meanings about class and gender, offering insights to her own field of French labour history. Gender was thus an historical category that, created through discourse, could be analysed.

Reflecting on the state of knowledge about women in early modern Europe, Merry Wiesner (1993) summed up the major advances which had taken place. Feminist history began with studies of 'women worthies' as a means of revealing figures who had previously been hidden. What was the contribution of women as individuals and groups to the great artistic, scientific and intellectual movements of the time? This question has continued to inform research, but it has been augmented by different questions as historians have come to appreciate the limitations of analyses which simply attempt to place women on the historical agenda. More interest followed in excavating the distinct female experience in the private and domestic spheres. Here biological experiences around menstruation, pregnancy and motherhood have yielded fine studies, as have friendship networks, devotional practices and patterns of consumption and taste, particularly so given that many of the topics were scantily documented in public archives. Finally, the creation in the early modern period of a gendered division between public and domestic spheres has been subject to scrutiny, and related to this, questions around the emergence of distinct identities of femininity and masculinity investigated. In certain respects, this trajectory has also been evident in recent feminist histories of other periods and across different parts of the world.

Section 3

Gender and identity

Monks with lactating breasts, boy children turning into girls, animals turning into human beings and vice versa, are all medieval and early-modern representations where sex, sexuality, identity and gender are very much more ambiguous than images of women and men were to become after the eighteenth century. In Renaissance and medieval paintings, Jesus is depicted with breasts flowing with maternal milk for the soul, or his wound from the Crucifixion is open (it has been argued) like a vagina, symbolic of the largely feminine compassion of God's only begotten son. His heat, moisture and bodily fluids had the power to purify through the sacred juices of his blood, semen and milk – themselves all signs that Christ was independent of sex or gender or else was feminine. God made flesh with female attributes inverted or neutralised ideas of Jesus as a man, making a huge impact on Cistercian and other traditions within the Catholic Church.

Caroline Walker Bynum has explained this gender ambiguity in her books *Jesus as Mother: Studies in the Spirituality of the Middle Ages* (1984) and *Holy Feast and Holy Fast: The Religious Significance of Food to Medieval Women* (1987). Fasting was a means of female self-control, erotic expression and a way of controlling their space in the context of a male-dominated church. In defiance of their husbands and families, religious women, according to the sources, would drink pus from the sick while abstaining from ordinary food. Or else they would give food away to the poor or live for years on the bread of the Eucharist alone until the normal functions of the body such as menstruation or excretion ceased. As Christ was in the Eucharist broken and sacrificed for humanity, hunger through fasting became a sign of female vulnerability and women's inherent understanding of the suffering of Jesus on the cross. When women consumed the blood and body of Christ they became his flesh, thereby fusing their own female identities to the extent that it made it impossible to base those identities purely on their sex.

Bynum's work is an example of how to move women's history on from its initial project of simply writing women back into history in ways that we saw in the last section, to a history that addresses issues around the relations between genders and gender identities. Bynum's approach to medieval aesthetics and food concentrates on the experiences of women themselves but also, critically, on feminine and masculine attributes that she finds in ritual, symbolic practices, cultural artefacts and so on. From Bynum's analysis, therefore, men and women in her medieval world are 'fragile constructs', and the usual way of constructing women around what they do in the family, or by the functions of their genitalia, underplays what it was to be feminine in medieval culture.

Such new approaches drew in part upon psychoanalytic techniques which have been especially useful to historians concerned with the irrational and with human experiences where *social* anxieties bring out *individual* psychic behaviour: instinct, emotion and bodily drives that were suppressed and where by the eighteenth century both private and public conduct was mannered, restrained and disciplined. Histories using these techniques have been concerned with how these changes in society influenced individual psyches. The problem is to understand a subjectivity or, to put it another way, personal responses from women that involve fantasy, memory, sexuality, the unconscious and gender ambiguity (as we saw with the example that opened the section).

So how has the important question of gender identity been approached in recent years? Feminist thinking about identity has drawn problematically upon the work of Freud, in particular his notion that children develop senses of identity through identification with their father, a process that leads to a sense of estrangement for girls. To deal with this problem, feminists such as Julia Kristeva have sought to define a distinct feminine identity by looking at the ways it is constructed not through biology but through language, that is, how images and the written and spoken word in, say, art and literature, come to define sexual difference.

Such ideas suggest that identity is never fixed or stable, but dynamic and subject to change over time brought about by the particular rhetoric of difference employed in society.

No work has had more influence on thinking around femininity than Simone De Beauvoir's *The Second Sex* (1949). The title itself referred to the notion that the terms masculine and feminine are asymmetrical, for the male is considered as the norm in society, against which the female is the other. Using a synthesis of biological, psychological and Marxist theories, De Beauvoir then explored how the creation of this female other can be traced to prehistory. In virtually all societies women's relegation to their unique capacity for reproduction underpinned the sexual division of labour and may have led to their subordination. It is not merely or primarily a matter of biology, however, for this ordering is not given, a product of biology, but is created:

> **One is not born, but rather becomes, a woman. No biological, psychological, or economic fate determines the figure that the human female presents in society; it is civilization as a whole that produces this creature, intermediate between male and eunuch, which is described as feminine. Only the intervention of someone else can establish an individual as an *Other*.**
>
> (De Beauvoir, 1997, p. 295)

Feminist historians working within this paradigm have understandably been interested in masculinity as well as femininity. One of the more important studies has been Graham Dawson's *Soldier Heroes: British Adventure, Empire and the Imaginings of Masculinities* (1994), in which he explored how masculinities are fashioned in the national imagination. The soldier hero, he argued, has been a remarkably enduring figure in the western tradition, in part because it was bound up with the emergence of the modern nation state. Henry V, Drake, Nelson and a host of others were constructed and remain potent symbols of British national identity. What such figures represented were 'true Englishmen', the status of whom was complemented and completed by visions of domestic femininity at home, vulnerable and requiring protection.

Processes of representation and identification have shaped the cultural production and circulation of images of the soldier hero. War adventures, comics, television series, novels, tourist sites and now computer games helped to sustain an intense fascination with the military side of conflict in contemporary society, but the processes have long been evident. In detailed studies of Sir Henry Havelock, hero of the Indian uprising in 1857, and T. E. Lawrence (of Arabia), Dawson showed how the psychic and the social intermeshed in the production of powerful public narratives which furnished idealised forms of masculinity to allay anxieties generated in a world deeply divided by nation and ethnicity, class and gender. In other words, such heroes offered (and continue to do so), psychic reassurance of the eventual triumph of 'good' over the threatening sources.

In a similar fashion, Mrinalini Sinha's *Colonial Masculinity: The 'Manly Englishman' and the 'Effeminate Bengali' in the Late Nineteenth Century* (1995) demonstrated how important notions of masculinity were for the British imperial enterprise. She started from the premise that the identities of coloniser and colonised were never fixed or self-evident, but had to be constantly defined and redefined in the context of the imperial social formation. As a result of this, their interrelationship was rearticulated according to the changing imperatives of British rule. As one aspect of this, the figure of the 'manly Englishman' was counterposed to the 'effeminate Bengali' in a descending scale as a means of asserting and maintaining authority. Senior officials within the administrative and military apparatus of rule were constructed as 'manly', while the corpus of politically self-conscious Indian intellectuals, dominated by middle-class Bengalis, who were recruited into the colonial service were seen as 'effeminate'. This representation of Bengalis in colonial discourse as an unnatural or perverted form of masculinity coincided precisely with their rising demands for a share in the economic and political privileges enjoyed by the British. This was not a blatant imposition, but more subtly and powerfully, this categorisation came to be adopted by the Bengalis themselves.

It would be remiss of us to close this chapter without mentioning a topic which has attracted considerable interest amongst feminist historians. In the West of the sixteenth and seventeenth centuries between 50,000 and 100,000 people were tried and executed as witches, the vast majority of them were women, and most of these were old and poor. Within the vast literature devoted to the topic a variety of social, cultural, economic and psychoanalytical explanations has been offered. Christina Larner (1981), for example, has argued that the Reformation saw an intensification of religious commitment, proof of which was sought by male rulers in fighting religious wars or suppressing heretics within their kingdoms. Social and economic approaches have pointed to the felt need for communities to find explanations for the periodic famines created by bad harvests, and the attendant increase in vagrant populations. Such thinking has informed specifically feminist perspectives. Mary Daly (1979), for example, has argued that at this time of profound uncertainty many women were seen to challenge normative views about their position in society, even by confronting male supremacy, and witch hunts were one means of suppressing and eliminating the perceived threat posed by independent women who inhabited spaces beyond conventional social norms. In this context the figure of the witch was literally demonised through association with the Devil, and was seen to possess those attributes of aggression, independence and sexuality which set her apart from the acceptable woman of chastity, obedience and domesticity.

Starting with *Oedipus and the Devil* (1994), the work of Lyndal Roper has signalled a more determinedly psychoanalytical approach to an understanding of witchcraft. The work was prompted by an unease about the relationship between culture and individual subjectivity, in particular about what she considered to be the excessive emphasis on the cultural and linguistic creation of identity. Witchcraft and the figure of the witch cannot be understood fully without reference also to psychic dimensions, that is, the extent to which fantasy, memory, subliminal desire, and the unconscious intervened. The irrational and unconscious were vital dimensions of the witch craze and associated beliefs in such rituals as sex with the Devil, diabolic Sabbaths and cannibalism, and our task is to reveal how they informed the nature of masculinity and femininity, the cultural impact of the Reformation and Counter-Reformation, and the vital role of witchcraft and magic at the time. Such a perspective has broader implications for it invites us to reconsider the Reformation, not as heralding the birth of the rational, ascetic individual who paves the way for the modern world, but as a time of renewed interest in magic and the irrational.

In practice

Historiography has tended to be a male preserve. Not only have a large majority of studies been undertaken by men, but they have featured men as the movers and shakers of history. History is often said to be written by the victors, that is, historians who have recorded the triumphs of nations and empires. But this can apply also to gender, for men who have dominated the recording of history have chosen to write about the exploits of other men who have dominated nations and empires.

There were notable exceptions. Talented women historians have documented the lives of women, thereby revealing the contribution made by prominent and lowly alike to the functioning of past societies. This may have been a conscious attempt to place women onto the historical agenda, but it had its limitations, for histories which attempt fully to integrate the female experience require more than the inclusion of women in order to fill the gaps – they require a fundamental realignment of historical thinking around the fault lines of past societies. To class divisions we must add those based on gender and race, understood as a dynamic and integrated whole.

These have been the concerns at the centre of the wave of feminist historiography which emerged during the 1970s. Dismissing conventional historical accounts and those inspired by Marxism as sexist, that is, dominated by a tendency to record the male historical experience, feminists set about rewriting history. There were different currents, and different political projects, but shared was a desire to integrate more fully the female experience into history. Here the most satisfying attempts were not those which concentrated exclusively upon women, but considered history as driven by women and men in relation to one another. It was impossible to approach matters of class formation, the industrial revolution, family, community, nation state or empire, they argued, with a blindness to gender relations.

In recent years questions of gender subjectivity and identity have attracted attention. We now have a much better understanding of the importance of notions of femininity and masculinity to the organisation of society into separate spheres, political and industrial struggles, conflict and the imperial project. Here again, approaches differ depending upon the roles attributed to physiology, culture and language in creating gender identities. Most recently, psychoanalytical approaches have instead argued for the crucial role of the unconscious and fantasy. In no area has this been more important or revealing than with regard to witchcraft.

All historians are under an obligation to remember that approximately half of all societies comprised women, and any account which marginalises the female experience is impoverished not only because it takes undue account of women but equally because it provides a one-dimensional interpretation of the male experience.

Summary

The three sections of this chapter have said three things:

- That feminism is not simply defined by equal rights but is construed differently from within different ideological positions. Conservative feminism believed that women had natural attributes such as motherhood which were best expressed in a domestic setting. In contrast the public sphere was competitive and the opposite of genteel: the very antithesis of what it meant to be a woman. Liberal feminists recognised these feminine attributes and qualities but argued that the disadvantages of biology, such as child-rearing, could be mitigated by public policy. Marxists originally downplayed gender differences, preferring instead to concentrate on class. The emphasis on gender-led history among female Marxist historians, however, led to dissatisfaction with the Marxist attempt to retain class as the primary means of analysing inequality in a capitalist society over time. Histories where class was the primary object of analysis were challenged by feminist historians who now insisted that the most important tool for historians was not class analysis but a 'patriarchy first' analysis where class exploited class but men, more importantly, exploited women. While this approach proved fatal for Marxism, histories of patriarchy also became questionable. Nor did the 'domestic ideology debate' (whereupon men and women occupied public and private spheres respectively) prove satisfactory as an explanation for the role of women in history with liberal, radical and Marxist feminist stances outlasting their conceptual usefulness.
- Women-centred histories in the early days of feminist agitation, especially since 1970, have successfully reintegrated women back into the historical record. By foregrounding women as an object of study, innovative new histories were researched and written by an extraordinary generation of women activists and historians. These women, however, could not go beyond the early and necessary task of reappraising the standard tests used by (male) historians and create histories where men and women were treated together or where the story of women was constructed in the shadow of men. This meant that there were an increasing number of histories of women that concentrated on their exclusion from public life. Women's bodies and sexuality were stressed as well as their relationship in one way or another to men. These gendered histories, however, became very influential indeed and it is now quite impossible to imagine histories without a sensitivity to gender issues.
- An interest in identity has led to some innovative histories that consider subjective issues such as emotion, fantasy or the unconscious as legitimate areas of historical study. Questions of femininity and masculinity have opened up interesting avenues of inquiry into national and imperial cultures. In the meantime, witchcraft continues to attract enormous interest, and remains useful as a vehicle with which to explore issues around gender, identity, culture and the body that go the very heart of feminist history.

Discussion document 1

These testimonies give us a rare glimpse of female voices speaking in a reasonably unalloyed way. Certainly we cannot take these testimonies to have been conveyed without some 'polishing' and 'shining' by those that asked the questions and collected the answers. However, these are the legitimate voices of women and are immensely useful to historians, not least to historians interested in issues of sex and gender. By using evidence from this document, look at different ways of reading evidence from class, patriarchal and psychoanalytic perspectives.

My mother's ignorance of household duties; my father's consequent irritability and intemperance; the frightful poverty; the constant quarrelling; the pernicious example to by brothers and sisters; the bad effect upon the future conduct of my brothers and sisters; one and all of us forced out to work, so young, that our feeble earnings would produce only 1s a week; cold and hunger, and the innumerable sufferings of my childhood, crowd upon my mind and overpower me.

Parliamentary Papers 1842, vol. XIX, p. f 131.

Betty Wardle, housewife, Outwood, near Lever, was asked: Have you worked in a coal-pit? – Ay, I have worked in a pit since I was six years old.

Have you any children? – Yes. I have had four children; two of them were born while I worked in the pits.

Did you work in the pits while you were in the family way? – Ay, to be sure. I had a child born in the pits, and I brought it up the pit-shaft in my skirt.

Are you sure that you are telling the truth? – Ay, that I am; it was born the day after I were married, that makes me to know.

Did you wear the belt and chain? – Yes, sure I did.

Parliamentary Papers 1842, vol. XVII, p. 163.

Where women are encouraged to work below they get husbands very early, and have large families, and the children are much neglected, as they have been themselves. There are a vast [number] of women work in the pits, and the employment very much unfits them for the performance of mother's duties; and they frequently cause men to leave their homes, if homes they may be called, and drink hard; the poor bairns are neglected; for in time the women follow the men and drink hard also . . .

Joseph Fraser, age 37, coal hewer; Parliamentary Papers 1842, vol. XVI, p. 442.

It is now four years since the practice of employing females and very young children ceased in these mines, and I have evidenced the advantage of the change religiously, morally, and socially.

In these works, since the discharge of women, marriages have been formed with greater care, and more appropriately: few now marry till 23 or 24, and we have not had a bastard child since the disemployment of females. On the old system men married from the advantage, their physical strength might procure them, than any degree of affection. Men labour here regularly and average eleven or twelve days in the fortnight, whereas, when they depended on their wives and children, they rarely wrought nine days in the same period. Colliers are now stationary, with very few exceptions; the women themselves are opposed to moving since they have left the benefit of homes.

John Wright, manager of coal-mines in Lasswade, east of Scotland; Parliamentary Papers 1842, vol. XVI, p. 451.

While working in the pit I was worth to my husband 7s a week, out of which we had to pay 2s 6d to a woman for looking after the younger bairns. I used to take them to her house at 4 o'clock in the morning, out of their own beds, to put them into hers. Then there was 1s a week for washing; besides, there was mending to pay for, and other things. The house was not guided. The other children broke things; they did not go to school when they were sent; they would be playing about, and get ill-used by other children, and their clothes torn. Then when I came home in the evening, everything was to do after the day's labour, and I was so tired I had no heart for it; no fire lit, nothing cooked, no water fetched, the house dirty, and nothing comfortable for my husband. It is all far better now, and I wouldna gang down again.

A mother of four children, formerly working in Pencaitland colliery; *Mining Commissioner's Report*, Parliamentary Papers 1844, vol. XVI, p. 4.

The girls who work on the pit-banks are well grown, healthy, and strong; but thin, sinewy, bony, and very unfeminine. . . . They are in most instances as gross and immoral in their language and conduct as the men who first made them so.

From their constant association with men, and from the nature of their work, one of these girls, in her coarse great coat, with her hands in her side-pockets, presents a picture of rude jovial independence of life, and recklessness of all refinements and delicacies of sex, which often makes an observer forget the objectionable characteristics of the individual in his sense of the uncivilized circumstances by which she has become so unlike the rest of her countrywomen.

They drive coal-carts, ride astride upon horses – sometimes two or three upon a large long-backed horse – drink, swear, fight, smoke, and sing, and care for nobody. Being very happy, they are certainly no objects for pity, but surely their circumstances are of a kind in which girls should never be placed.

Report on the town of Bilston, Staffs; Parliamentary Papers 1843, vol. XV, Q. 65.

There are a great number of illegitimate children born here (Darlaston); many of the girls have from three to four children each; and they work for and support their children and themselves without a murmur. The effects of early work, particularly in forges and on the pit-bank, render these girls perfectly independent. They often enter the beer shops, call for their pints, and smoke their pipes, like men; indeed, there seems little difference in their circumstance from those of the men, except they are the chief sufferers.

Parliamentary Papers 1843, vol. XV, Q. 62.

E. Royston Pike, *Human Documents of the Industrial Revolution in Britain* (1966).

Discussion document 2

If political and gender theory has proved important in recent decades to the development of historiography, then these extracts may allow us to discern the role and importance of ideology. Here then we have viewpoints from conservative, liberal and radical perspectives. Each extract reveals the essential elements of the ideas that have had a formative influence in the writing of histories. The third extract makes clear the distinction between separatist radical viewpoints and the more usual class-based Marxist position.

> I have no hesitation in declaring my full belief in the inferiority of women, nor that she brought it upon herself. I believe – as entirely as any other truth which has been from the beginning – that woman was created as a help-meet to man. How far she was then on an equality with him, no one can pretend to guess; but when the test came, whether the two human beings would pay allegiance to God or to the Tempter, it was the woman who was the first to fall, and to draw her husband into the same transgression. Thence her punishment of physical weakness and subordination mitigated by the promise that she would be the means of bringing to renovate the world, and break the domination of Satan . . . The Blessing conferred upon the holy Mother of our Lord became the antidote to the punishment of Eve's transgression; and in proportion to the full reception of the spirit of Christianity has woman thenceforth been elevated to her rightful position as the help-meet.

C. M. Yonge, *On Woman and the Church* (1876) quoted in James R. Moore (ed.), *Religion in Victorian Britain*, vol. III, pp. 95–7.

> In the preceding argument for universal, but graduated suffrage, I have taken no account of difference of sex. I consider it to be as entirely irrelevant to political rights as difference in height or in the colour of hair. All human beings have the same interest in good government; the welfare of all is alike affected by it, and they have equal need of a voice in it to secure their share of its benefits. If there be any difference, women require it more then men, since, being physically weaker, they are more dependent on law and society for protection. Mankind have long since abandoned the only premises which will support the conclusion that women ought not to have votes. No one now holds that women should be in personal servitude; that they should have no thought, wish, or occupation, but to be the domestic drudges of husbands, fathers or brothers. It is allowed to unmarried, and wants but little of being conceded to married women, to hold property, and have pecuniary and business interests, in the same manner as men. It is considered suitable and proper that women should think, and write, and be teachers. As soon as these things are admitted, the political disqualification has no principle to rest on. The whole mode of thought of the modern world is with increasing emphasis pronouncing against the claim of society to decide for individuals what they are and are not fit for, and what they shall and shall not be allowed to attempt. If the principles of modern politics and political economy are good for anything, it is for proving that these points can only be judged of by the individuals themselves: and that, under complete freedom of choice, wherever there are real diversities of attitudes, the great number will apply themselves to the things for which they are on the average fittest, and the exceptional course will

only be taken by the exceptions. Either the whole tendency of modern social improvements has been wrong, or it ought to be carried out to the total abolition of all exclusions and disabilities which close honest employment to a human being.

J. S. Mill, *Representative Government* (1861, 2009, pp. 143–4).

In the fall of 1967 small groups of radical women began meeting in the United States to discuss the problem of male supremacy. At that time the majority were committed to organizing a women's liberation movement with the larger radical Movement. Indeed, most early women's liberation groups were dominated by 'politicos' who attributed women's oppression to capitalism, whose primary loyalty was to the left, and who longed for the imprimatur of the 'invisible audience' of male leftists. 'Feminists,' or radical feminists, who opposed the subordination of women's liberation to the left and for whom male supremacy was not a mere epiphenomenon of capitalism [a Marxist term meaning a phenomenon such as ideas, gender relations etc, secondary to the economic or material base, as covered in Chapter 4], were an embattled minority in the movement's infancy.

However, within two years radical feminism has established itself as the most vital and imaginative force within the women's liberation movement. Radical feminism rejected both the politico position that socialist revolution would bring about women's liberation and the liberal feminist solution of integrating women into the public sphere. Radical feminists argued that women constituted a sex-class, that relations between women and men needed to be recast in political terms, and that gender rather than class was the primary contradiction. They criticized liberal feminists for pursuing 'formal equality within a racist, class-stratified system,' and for refusing to acknowledge that women's inequality in the public domain was related to their subordination in the family. Radical feminists articulated the earliest and most provocative critiques of the family, marriage, love, normative heterosexuality, and rape. They fought for safe, effective, accessible contraception; the repeal of all abortion laws; the creation of high-quality, community-controlled child-care centers [sic]; and an end to the media's objectification of women. They also developed consciousness raising – the movement's most effective organizing tool. And in defying the cultural injunction against female self-assertion and subjectivity, radical feminists 'dared to be bad.' By 1970, there was such enormous interest in radical feminists that some even have argued it was on the verge of becoming a mass movement.

Alice Echols, *Daring to Be Bad: Radical Feminism in America 1967–1975* (1989), pp. 3–4.

Further reading

* *essential*

Sally Alexander, *Becoming a Woman: And Other Essays in Nineteenth and Twentieth Century Feminist History* (1984).
Alexander has been an important figure in women's history and feminist studies since she was a student at Ruskin College. These essays represent the intellectual and theoretical development of her work.

Sheila Rowbotham, *Hidden from History: 300 Years of Women's Oppression and the Fight Against It* (1973).
Rarely does a history book so perfectly reflect the times in which it was written. Almost a pamphlet for the liberation struggle it nonetheless is a scholarly attempt to write women back into the historical record.

Joan Kelly, *Women, History and Theory: The Essays of Joan Kelly* (1984).
Contains all her key essays, including 'Did women have a Renaissance'? and deals with periodisation, social analysis and theories of social change from a gendered and feminist standpoint.

Joan W. Scott, *Gender and the Politics of History* (1999).
This is not a simple read but nonetheless as a collection of essays that span a long and important career in gender history and theory, an important one. The sections mentioned explicitly in the text above should especially be consulted.

John Tosh, *Manliness and Masculinities in Nineteenth Century Britain* (2005).
An innovative collection of essays that open up a genuine new area of study. His emphasis on both the family and empire effectively explores the interaction between theory, masculinity and patriarchy in history.

Judith M. Bennett, *History Matters: Patriarchy and the Challenge of Feminism* (2006) and Judith M. Bennett, 'Forgetting the past', *Gender and History*, vol. 20, November 2008, pp. 669–77.
Bennett very ably makes the case for history in the wider field of gender studies. In the 1970s, she argues, feminism and history were closely linked. Now feminists embrace political and theoretical positions that seemingly don't need an historical perspective, although patriarchy remains alive and well.

* ***American Historical Review***, vol. 113, no. 5, December 2008.
Revisits the work of Joan Scott from a variety of angles; particularly interesting is the essay by Joanne Meyerowitz, 'A history of "gender" ' and 'Unanswered questions' by Scott herself.

11 Public history

1 What is public history?
2 The consumption of public history
3 Producing public history
4 Public history as contested knowledge

Introduction

This chapter will examine public history and its chief elements: present-mindedness, promiscuous in its choice of what constitutes historical evidence, multi-disciplinary and anti-expert. It reaches out to historical constituencies such as family historians or popular collectors who are quite untouched by university style history, what is called here the 'academy'. These are not necessarily readers of popular histories that fill the shelves of booksellers but local and community 'historians' who are themselves potentially well placed to tell their own stories without acting as passive participants in histories written by professional historians. However, if these are the claims of its advocates, public and popular forms of history have a soft underbelly. At its worst, academic historians perceive public history as untheorised and uncritical. History becomes heritage, nostalgic and conservative, packaged in such a way that celebrates the past by dressing it up to encourage social consensus, an antiquarian ruse to make us believe that consent and conformity is a natural feature of the present. By collecting evidence of past societies, public historians have allowed those scholars working in the academy to rewrite histories in ways that would have remained quite impossible without their intervention. In so doing, the basis of historical knowledge is challenged. In order to explore these issues, the first section uses the Battle of Cable Street in 1936 as a way of discussing the range and scope of sources used by the public historian, the definition of public history, how it differs from the publishing phenomenon of popular history and is perceived differently across the world. Section 2 explores differing views about heritage and the 'heritage industry' and the ways that the past is conceptualised, and ways too that public history is 'consumed' by the general public. While public history seems to be a different enterprise from university history, it nevertheless produces evidence that professional historians and students can utilise. This is the subject of the third section while the last section explores the tensions created between public history and the academy in what precisely constitutes historical knowledge.

Section 1

What is public history?

According to local folklore, in October 1936, Catholics, Jews and Communists fought a pitched battle on the streets of East London against the so-called 'Blackshirts', or British Union of Fascists, led by English aristocrat Oswald Mosley (1896–1980). The Battle of Cable Street has passed into mythology, especially among those on the left of British politics who still regard it as the opening salvo in a longer battle for multicultural and multiethnic solidarity. Reputedly, priests took up arms alongside rabbis to oppose a brand of fascism largely modelled on Mussolini's fascists in Italy and which along with German Nazism now choked mainland Europe like a miasma. Waves of protesters dispersed Mosley's Blackshirts with no help from London's police force who had allowed the march to thread its way through areas heavily populated by Irish and Jewish immigrants. 'They shall not pass' was the rallying cry of the anti-fascists that day, a slogan borrowed from the Spanish Civil War. As a cause célèbre of Popular Front politics from the period, it is immensely important as a moment when otherwise divided and disparate groups came together under a unified banner, while the defeat of the Blackshirts cleared the political air by removing any lingering odour of anti-democratic politics in Britain.

Conventional historical approaches can help to understand the main facets of this event. Political historians would be keen to tease out the power relations at work that day: the machinations of Communist, trade union and leftist politics, the internal dynamics of Jewish groups (pro- and anti-Zionist, socialist and reformist, religious and secular), the tactics of the London Metropolitan Police, the divisions within Fascist ranks and so on. Similarly, social historians may be less interested to divine power relations, feeling themselves better placed to consider gender relations at work on that day, the role of children and young people, religious influences and the like. Methodologically the social historian may well be more sensitive to oral history approaches (as we will see in Chapter 20), exploring the living testimonies of those that actually experienced these momentous events, comparing these witness testimonies with newspaper records, contemporary diaries and so on. Cultural historians, perhaps influenced by related subjects such as social or cultural anthropology, psychology, sociology, geography, may be more inclined to look closely at the expressive aspects associated with the day such as posters and banners, language, the role of leadership cults, the socio-economic make-up of the participants, the use made of public space and so forth. Public historians, on the other hand, may well employ a synthesis of these approaches but will focus instead on surviving public nomenclature such as street names and buildings – in particular, how the event resounds in the present.

What precisely then is public history? There is no ready and encompassing definition, but with the words from Robert Kelley, a practitioner of public history, we may have a start:

> **In its simplest meaning, Public History refers to the employment of historians and the historical method outside of academia: in government, private corporations, the media, historical**

> **societies and museums, even in private practice. Public Historians are at work whenever, in their professional capacity, they are part of the public process. An issue needs to be resolved, a policy must be formed, the use of a resource or the directions of an activity must be more effectively planned and a historian is called upon to bring the dimensions of time: this is Public History.** (Kelley, 1992, p. 111)

He tells us that public history and public historians are anything but creatures of the academy, or a trained professional vanguard, but as museum curators, tour guides, genealogists, they take the historical record beyond the fetishised scholarly footnote and cloistered academic seminar into a less rarefied public consciousness.

Shifts in contemporary preoccupations of the historian change over time and necessarily alter the subject position of history, revealing new vistas, sources and perspectives; the same might be said of the altering professional, geographical and social position of the historian. Public history has been particularly adept at meeting these changes, especially given its promiscuous approach to historical evidence. Raphael Samuel, for instance, an enthusiast if not a pioneer of public history approaches, made much of incorporating unofficial sources into the canon of history, and giving due regard to scholarship generated outside of professional history and the academy as the product of what is essentially a social form of knowledge. Therefore, the genealogists, canal enthusiasts, railway buffs and amateurs that people his *Theatres of Memory* (1994) enjoy equally the status of historians alongside the professoriate of the old universities as both consumers *and* producers of history. Emma Wilner sees public history not simply as history practised outside the university, however, but as the dissemination of history through a broad medium of methods and approaches:

> **Public history is history, practically applied. It is based on the understanding that history is not taught solely in the classroom, but is learned in a variety of places, and in a variety of ways. Public historians disseminate historical information to a wide audience through institutions such as archives, historical houses or societies, museums, consulting firms, history libraries, and Web sites. They are providers of primary and secondary source materials, and they often present information to patrons so that the patrons can form their own ideas of history and historical events through exhibits and research. My particular experiences with public history are diverse, and they have helped inform my definition of public history. In providing historical information to visitors, public historians give these visitors a chance to form their own opinions and ideas about history and to create books, essays, dissertations, works of art, and other products that in turn shape other people's ideas about history. Practical and entertaining, applications of history are what set public history apart from classroom history, and both have their place in the overall process of teaching history.** (Wilmer, 2000)

It is historians working outside the academy that have been responsible, it should be emphasised, for actually producing historical evidence, adding to the sum of our historical knowledge, say by collecting political badges generated after the Battle of Cable Street or creating forms of public art (as will shall see below). Moreover, the popular disseminators of history have encouraged the consumption of history by and to a wider public. Public history and public historians have done both these things: produced historical evidence as collectors of evidence that historians working in the academy can readily use, consumed popular forms of history, and have sometimes done both of these things simultaneously. Public history, then, is concerned to study the events of history but also its traces (see Plate 4).

The bottom frame of Plate 4 is a photograph of the battle taken on the day that it took place, shop signs hanging from the Jewish-owned shops, burning barricades, paving stones ripped from the pavement. The top frame is a detail of the massive mural that today takes up a side of a building on Cable Street. The photograph constitutes the primary remains of the battle, perhaps taken by a participant and rescued as historical evidence only later. The mural emerges later as a public memoriam to the event, although as a representation of officially sponsored street art, it has its origins in semi, if not wholly, illegal gable-end graffiti. The historical moment that gave rise to the Battle of Cable Street has passed – as have the making of films about the battle, or the historical circumstances that gave rise to the mural and even films about the making of the mural, they too have all passed. Yet the event itself, and subsequent public expressions of the event, all have histories that exist in public narratives or stories about the battle. This interface between historical evidence in its primary form influences history in its secondary form and vice versa; whether it is a mural, a school play or even in a more nebulous form, as local legend, they all survive and evolve, and eventually transform, taking on lives of their own.

To the public historian, representations of the event enjoy equal resonance with the event itself, building and layering to become part of the received account of what went on during that October day in 1936. Whether via a photograph as primary source or mural as secondary source, these historical echoes exist in a more durable half-life of the battle and its responses, in public spaces such as the Internet, opening up discussions about 1930s fascism in Europe more generally as well as informing current debates about multiculturalism, citizenship and national identity. This is how public history operates in the historical present.

Indeed, using a wide variety of media, collecting oral histories or making a film, aid accessibility to history as a genre and produce yet more knowledge about the public aspects of an historical event such as this. In addition, the advent of digital cameras means that films made on very small and very sophisticated movie cameras facilitate both the production of more narratives about the battle but also determine how stories about it are consumed. Online technologies such as blogs and wikis or moderated online discussions have precisely this dual function as producers and disseminators of yet more knowledge about the battle. The use of technologies that help to develop a more critical understanding of how to analyse history produced and consumed in a public forum has become one of the defining aspects of the public history approach.

Public history, however, is not simply the type of popular history that is now ubiquitous on cable television channels and in the best-selling lists of paperback history, some of them excellent. Simon Schama and his BBC *History of Britain* programmes and accompanying volumes and books, Richard Hamlyn's award-winning *The Invention of Clouds* (2001), Dava Sobel's *Longitude* (1998), or Adam Hochschild's *Bury the Chains: Prophets and Rebels in the Fight to Free an Empire's Slaves* (2005) are not, to use a term from the nineteenth century, 'curious histories', but have made a real contribution to historiography. These popularly consumed histories illustrate popular sentiments about what at any one moment is important in history whether or not these histories finally migrate to television or radio. Schama's volumes are constructed wholly from the point of view of a professional historian; with Hamlyn, Sobel and Hochschild, although their perspective originates outside professional history, they too kick over the traces of a given historical phenomena while attempting to engage with a mass audience.

What then is the extent of public history's concerns? It champions the democratisation of the archive and of accessible history but it is perplexingly difficult to fathom the depths of its interests: treating the public histories of the ancient stones of Avebury at one turn (as a study of history and heritage) and the historical plight of red squirrels at the next (as a study of history and nationalism) (Kean *et al.*, 2000). The definition of what public history actually *is*, therefore, must be tempered by what it is *not*, that is, how it differs from political, social or cultural history or from popular histories.

Public history also differs in its practice across the world. It began life in Australia and the United States and accordingly is seen in those places in a somewhat different light than it is in Europe. In Australia, the term has inspired histories based on the indigenous Aboriginal population; in the United States, it serves a more consensual vision of the past, dealing with almost endless lists of individuals and organisations whose interests range from genealogy to the corporate past. Britain, however, hosts a weaker strand of public history. In so far that it has bothered to be reflective about its own existence, public history British-style imagines itself concerned with bottom-up history, a sub-genre of the new social history of the 1960s that, as we saw in Chapter 9, is couched in class conflict or else is a celebration of heritage. Therefore, a single definition that crosses geographical boundaries is elusive.

If Australian, American and British approaches to public history differ, they are all concerned to widen the public audience for history while employing diverse ways of disseminating history using museums and other forms of popular culture. In this way local and family experiences are brought alive through plays and art works, community histories, or through old newspapers, poor law records, diaries and memoirs and travel writing, giving renewed vigour and life to present-day issues such as family breakdown, gender equality, child cruelty, moral sexual dilemmas, 'anti-social' behaviour, and developing ideas of masculinity or citizenship. This approach has profound implications for the role of the historian in a modern society in the here and now but it also asks searching questions about the public function of academic history.

Philip Scarpino, writing in the dedicated journal *The Public Historian*, argued that if public history is concerned with unusual sources and with unusual approaches to sources, with opening up the archive to a wider historical public and with addressing a wider historical public, it is only because the academic world continues to confine itself to a relatively limited audience:

> **As public history has evolved from a quest for 'alternative careers' to a way of understanding and practicing the craft of history, it has on the campuses run headlong into the sacred trinity of research, teaching, and service – with the greatest of these being research embodied in refereed publications. . . . Despite the peer review and many other strengths, the present reward system has contributed to an unproductive 'academic vs. public' debate; encouraged a trend towards co-opting public history by defining it as another specialized subfield and obscured the common ground shared by the community of professionals who practice the historian's craft. As historians, we all do research, we all analyze and interpret our findings, and we all communicate the results. The primary difference between public and academic history is in the area of communication – in the audiences that we attempt to reach and in the products that we use to convey our scholarship to those audiences.** (Scarpino, 1993, pp. 55–61)

Professional historians working in universities have begun to argue, however, that we need to take popular forms of knowledge about history as seriously as knowledge generated in the academy. Some of these sentiments may have been encouraged, in Britain at least, by the 'quest for alternative careers' among those academics tenuously employed within the academy. In other words, addressing a wider historical public in the way attempted by public history has become the side effect of changes introduced into higher education. These include an increased student population, an attempt to increase skills levels and to introduce greater cooperation between universities and the private sector, linking funding for research to knowledge transfer initiatives. Because of structural changes within universities, especially the 'new' universities who now work in a wholly different climate from the ancient universities (now operating in a global marketplace) or the Russell Group or the 'red-bricks', there is an increasing division between institutions that predominately teach and institutions that maintain the traditional mix of teaching and research with funding distributed accordingly. Public history, therefore, has a very practical use for a stratum of professional historians who cling onto the profession by their fingertips, as well as others whose business is the past more generally, who did not teach or research history in a university setting, but who potentially challenge the status of the professional historian as expert.

Definitions of public history are elastic enough to stretch across geographical borders and to allow the Australian, American and British experiences of public history to mean something different in each context. The focus of public history is the non-expert, and since the sources associated with public history are various, historical knowledge among 'untrained' historians working outside universities tends to be knowledge which is socially constructed. If this distinguishes public history from mainstream, university-based history, then it is because public history engages with forms of history inevitably connected to a wider public. This in itself creates problems. To engage with the public, to really be the public face of what history is and to do this successfully, public history must be accessible and interesting but must also develop as a recognisable genre of history. It is because history in its popular and public forms is so very familiar that it is sometimes difficult to argue that it has the same scholarly weight as conventional history. In effect it is a struggle to ensure that it is taken seriously at all, especially since one of its strengths is that it is indeed accessible and to some degree anti-authoritarian.

Hilda Kean is a pioneer in diverse forms of public history in Britain and she insists this new approach to evidence 'exists inside – and outside – the archives, in the local streets of the present, in graveyards and cemeteries, souvenirs and trinkets, photos [sic] and maps, memories and stories' (Kean, 2000, p. 00). In doing family history as one important aspect of 'non-expert' led public history, the 'archaeology of lives' as Kean put it, we are as likely to use the 'unofficial' sources of family photographs, diaries, and so on as the 'official' sources of the state such as census returns, probate, ecclesiastical records, and court case files. According to Kean, public history is not only about the 'historical self' in the historical present or challenging the historian as expert, it is also about collaboration across fields and a commitment to what she calls 'praxis'; that is, history as it affects people and communities:

> **Public History acts as an umbrella, under which the historical mind can be brought to bear on areas of research and thought which are too often seen as mutually exclusive. It draws upon the magazine racks of W. H. Smith for source material as much as it draws on academic texts. It looks as much to images and textual conceptions on commercial packaging and television advertising as it does to the art gallery and museum. It seeks oral opinion conveyed**

through the domestic images recorded by camcorder, constructed images and visual texts on television, and the holistic nature of the idea of knowledge expressed by the Internet. Public History relies on a collective and collaborative effort of people often working in different fields. This very process, of itself, helps to avoid academic navel gazing. In examining the 'historical self' in the concept of our perception of time and sense of place, for instance, then necessity for the enlargement of our terms of reference becomes apparent.

(Kean *et al.*, 2000, pp. 13–14)

There is one very real sense, therefore, in which public history has served to widen our horizons as historians and if we use family history as but one example of the practice of public history, we will find that millions practice it. History from this perspective has never been more popular.

Public history as a popular form of history acting as an 'umbrella' for different approaches to history has indeed drawn upon a range of both familiar and unfamiliar sources, and this, if nothing else, will be its legacy. Nevertheless, one distinguishing feature of public history is the way it is consumed by a television watching, 'big house' visiting public, which now in many ways seems quite smitten with all things past. This consumption of the past, very much associated with history outside of the academy and the ways in which it connects in a controversial way to the 'heritage industry', will be the subject of the next section.

Section 2

The consumption of public history

Sir Edwin Landseer (1802–73), Victorian court artist par excellence and a great favourite of the Queen, did not exaggerate the ancient splendour of the scene when he painted Victoria and Albert as royals from the fourteenth century, Edward III and Philippa of Hainault. The occasion was a sumptuous and extravagant Plantagenet Ball in May 1842. The young Queen and her Prince wore medieval garb amid a hall decked in medieval decor designed at huge cost (Schama, 2009). The antiquarian James Planche recalled how Victoria and Albert dressed up this way, self-consciously re-enacting the story of a Queen in the Middle Ages who made a successful plea to her 'warrior husband' to spare the burghers of Calais. Schama was keen to emphasise not only the enormous cost of the ball staged at a time of particular economic distress in the industrial areas, but that the proceeds of the ball were donated to the unemployed weavers of Spitalfields.

For Schama, therefore, the acting out of a medieval story of clemency by the appeal of a Queen to her 'King' was no longer simply a fable about the saving of Calais burghers as an example of medieval royal compassion but instead 'is given a modern gloss as a philanthropic melodrama of the nineteenth century' (p. 127). This worked well enough as a reading of early-Victorian class relations at the time. However, our concern is to explain how heritage is employed as an historical narrative, and its relation to public history.

The historian Peter Mandler in *The Fall and Rise of the Stately Home* (1997) dedicated the opening chapter of his book to the 'Victorian idea of heritage':

> **Whatever the truth of this, it is clearly not necessary to explain the Victorian turn to history – as British historians, less comfortable with cultural nationalism than their French or German counterparts, tend to do – by reference to ruling-class anxieties about the pace of social change and the fear of political upheaval. The use of history is not necessarily prescriptive or conservative, and is often very far from being a device of social control. On the contrary, elite culture's longstanding disregard of national history in favour of classicism and cosmopolitanism gave the past an intrinsically democratic appearance. Long before the early Victorian period of cultural democratization, political radicals had made arguments for constitutional change based on the idea of a lost 'ancient constitution', more popular and national, which had been subverted in the recent past but which could still be reconstructed. It was a natural instinct for advocates (*not* opponents) of change in a highly stable and hierarchical society to seek a pedigree, a tradition for their programme. In much the same way, the Victorian culture industry called into existence an old world to redress the new.**
>
> (Mandler, 1997, pp. 28–9)

Here we find the Victorian discovery of the 'olden times' which served to confront anxieties about rapid change or acted as a side-effect of what Mandler calls 'cultural nationalism' – the building of the nation through the use of history. Heritage became a foil to all things modern and this explains the clothes worn by Queen Victoria and the Prince Consort on that May evening in 1842 and again in June 1845 and June 1851 when they became Georgians for the evening or mimicked the style of the Restoration. Yet we need to dig deeper still if we are to understand the power of heritage in the public understanding of history, especially in contrast to the type of history conventionally practised in university departments today.

Significantly, Mandler was rightly reluctant to dismiss heritage in the nineteenth century or in the present-day as a symptom of ruling-class anxieties about the pace of change and the fear of political upheaval. Before the reforms of the 1830s, the aristocracy quite often looked less to national history as a way of defining the nation, preferring instead to view the past by concentrating on the classical civilisations of Rome and Greece. With the gradual displacement of the aristocracy as a governing class, the past became for the newly enfranchised classes 'intrinsically democratic' and progressive. Heritage became a way of remaking the nation in the image of the new governing classes. After all, as Mandler said, it was radical opinion that lamented the disappearance of the 'ancient constitution', an indigenous and localised constitution displaced by the centralising tendencies of the so-called 'Norman Yoke' after the invasion of 1066. Radicals looked back (not forward) to what they believed was a perfect Anglo-Saxon constitution that had been swept away by the Norman regime.

Changes in the constitution during the nineteenth century, however, and the inclusion of new classes within the pale of the constitution inspired what Mandler further called the 'culture industry'. This culture industry, probably for the first time, facilitated the consumption of history among the masses, remaking the present through Victorian architecture and the 'improved' built environment; taking the nation back to its medieval foundations. This process of historicising the nation meant that when Victoria and Albert donned medieval clothes at the Plantagenet Ball of May 1842 and gave the proceeds of this exquisitely grand event to the unemployed it could be coherently argued by contemporaries that, as Mandler put it, heritage 'called into existence an old world to redress the new' (Mandler, 1997, pp. 28–9). From this vantage point, heritage 'is not necessarily prescriptive or conservative, and is very far from being a device of social control'.

This is important to note when we consider the role of heritage in public history; to understand heritage is to understand how a past is created and consumed, and to judge to what extent public history is useful within the canon of history as a discipline. Patrick Wright wrote his provocative and wide-ranging *On Living in an Old Country: The National Past in Contemporary Britain* (1998) upon returning from a spell abroad when he found Britain tottering on the brink of a Conservative-led Thatcher government and its population enthralled with what Wright contended was essentially backward-looking tradition. The 'heritage industry', according to Wright, confirmed a cultural conservatism in the country by restructuring a monolithic national identity through an appeal to jingoism and imperial values, and the way that 'heritage' was consumed merely confirmed to Wright a populace stupefied by images and narratives of an apparently consensual past. By trooping around the big houses and castles of rural Britain, people were living the imaginative life of the gentry while being encouraged to forget the vicious class distinctions manifested in life below stairs. Nowhere was this truer than in properties owned by the National Trust, the same organisation whose founders, so we have learnt from Stephen Fry at the very opening of this book, were anything but conservative or prescriptive.

The National Trust is not an organisation where history is passively consumed but where activity and popular participation are in evidence. The 'One Day in History' event in October 2006, for example, was an event organised by the National Trust precisely to encourage public participation in matters concerned with the past and to produce a level of popular interest that most historians working in the academy could only dream about and one relevant to the lives of many millions of people. Heritage has been a major concern of public history in Britain where monuments and the packaging of the past – National Trust tea towels and cream teas – have been seen as an object of legitimate study. For Wright this packaging has prevented an historical public from realising the harsh realities of history. Yet this 2006 event held by the National Trust saw a million badges sold, 10,000 postcards completed, 20,000 declarations of support for the National Trust, 46,000 blogs registered online and 1 million people accessing a virtual heritage site. History from this perspective appears designed less as a trick to manufacture consent and more as a way that a mass audience for history could be galvanised into action; after all the encouragement of mass participation is an aim of public history. To its detractors, however, the consumption of history succeeded only in 'prettifying' the past, dressing it up in order to support political consensus and suppress political divisions in the present.

On a slightly different trajectory from that of Wright, David Lowenthal has identified nostalgia as a feature of our everyday lives, above all how we deal with the boundaries that he argues separate history from heritage. *The Heritage Crusade and the Spoils of History* (Lowenthal, 1998) saw heritage and the adherence of a vast public to an uncritical past as essentially situated against progress. Both Wright and Lowenthal, despite their erudite and theoretically sophisticated take on what after all to the discipline of history is an important question – that of history's relation to the past – saw the consumption of history by a non-professional public as regressive. In so doing, it might be argued, they ignored the myriad ways in which amateurs and enthusiasts add to the sum of historical knowledge and how the 'heritage industry' throws up legitimate historical evidence that can be used by historians working in the academy.

Used, that is, by historians like Raphael Samuel who revived the argument suggested in Section 1 of this chapter: that studying the consumption of the past should be part of what public history does. In precisely this spirit, Samuel undertook research in his local supermarkets. What he found were products literally wrapped in traditional images from the past and drew conclusions from this evidence into how the past reacts with the present in contemporary culture. To Samuel, history could be done in the supermarket:

> **The shelves of the supermarkets are full of newly-minted traditional goods – ploughman's pickles, 'country ales', 'Wiltshire' mustard, 'Norfolk' turkeys, and an astonishing range of technicoloured English Cheeses in which county is distinguished from county by its speckles. Sainsbury's offer 'harvest slims' crispbread and 'all-fruit preserves'. Tesco market their own farmhouse brunch. Heinz have turned from the vivid oranges and browns of their 1960s tins to the yellowy-greenery of their 'ploughman's' pickles.** (Samuel, 1995, pp. 106–7)

Our apparent care for the environment was revealed in 'dolphin-friendly' tuna; county-based 'technicoloured cheeses' emphasised local belongings and wrappings with bucolic images of England suggested our country longings. Furthermore, 'newly-minted traditional goods', a contradiction between the needs of now and a longing for then – products once synthetic and flush full of chemical additives, now revealed our ecological soundness. Samuel was undoubtedly right about the importance of consumer packaging as a sign of present-day obsessions about the past – his examples reflect the place given to tradition and are true to the time he researched and wrote his book. Now we are more likely to see products wrapped in ways that represent our aspirations for a world village or take into account our concerns for ethical or 'fair trade' products. These preoccupations will undoubtedly change again and given that we have established that public history is concerned about uses of the past in the present, that it attempts to reach a mass audience, challenge the practices of the professional historian as expert and reconceptualise what constitutes the archive, the public historian ought to monitor the changes in the consumption of heritage. Indeed, the type of evidence suggested by Samuel makes up the very stuff of public history.

Yet a view of public history that concentrates only on heritage and the public consumption of history will fail to take account of public historians as producers of historical knowledge, non-professional historians who by the simple act of collecting artefacts or ephemera of the past have added to history as a social form of knowledge. It is to these producers of public history archives that we now turn.

Section 3

Producing public history

One way of illustrating the importance of such producers is to look at the collections of George Thomason, a seventeenth-century London bookseller and collector of political tracts from St Paul's Churchyard in London, and Robert Opie, who has collected the most

Plate 1 *View from Mount Holyoke, Northampton, Massachusetts, after a Thunderstorm – The Oxbow* by Thomas Cole, 1836

Source: Bridgeman Art Library Ltd: Metropolitan Museum of Art, New York, USA / Photo © Boltin Picture Library

Plate 2 World map of Hecataeus

Plate 3 *Chelsea Pensioners reading the Gazette of the Battle of Waterloo* by Sir David Wilkie, 1822

Source: English Heritage Photo Library

Plate 4 Mural of the Battle of Cable Street in 1936 now located in Cable Street itself (above) and a contemporary photograph taken at the time of the battle (below)

Source: Alamy Images: Mary Evans Picture Library (above), David Hoffman (below)

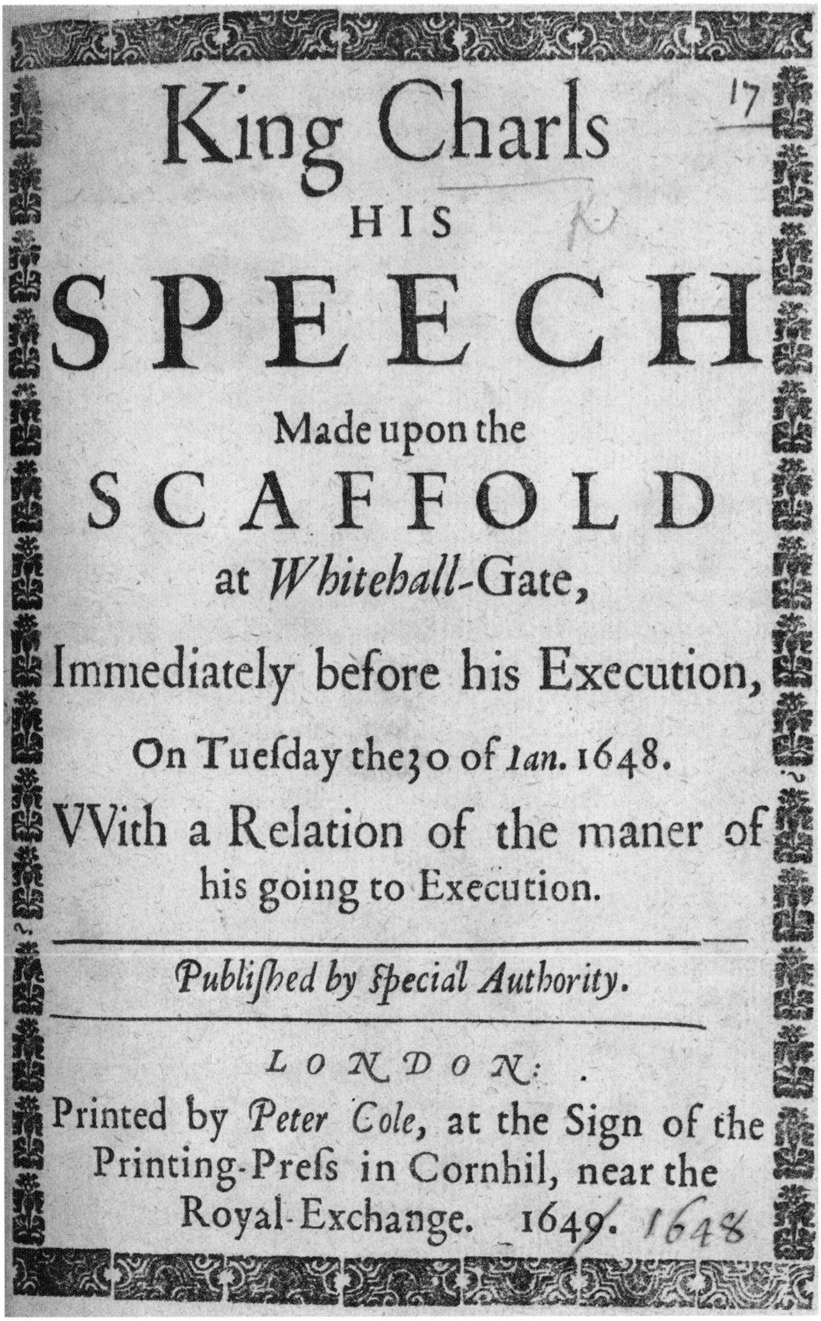

King Charls
HIS
SPEECH
Made upon the
SCAFFOLD
at *Whitehall*-Gate,
Immediately before his Execution,
On Tuesday the 30 of *Ian.* 1648.
VVith a Relation of the maner of
his going to Execution.

Published by Special Authority.

LONDON:
Printed by *Peter Cole*, at the Sign of the
Printing-Press in Cornhil, near the
Royal-Exchange. 1649.

Plate 5 Title page from the final speech of King Charles I, which contains a transcript of what the King said before his execution in January 1648

Source: © The British Library Board

Plate 6 *The Heart of the Empire* by Niels Moeller Lund, 1904

Source: Guildhall Art Gallery

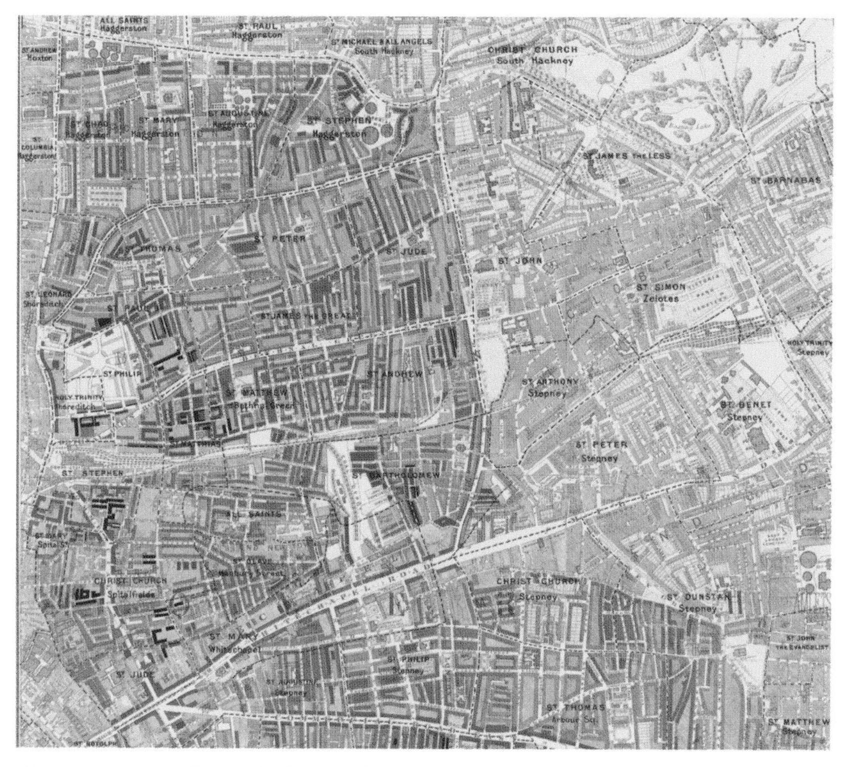

Plate 7 A section from Charles Booth's poverty map of London, 1898–9

Source: The Library of the London School of Economics and Political Science

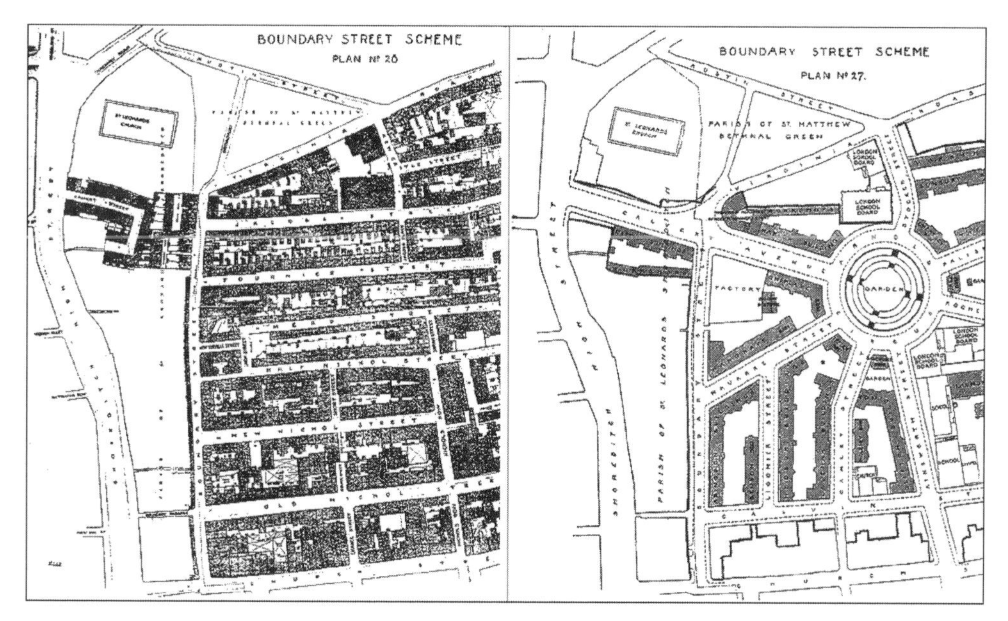

Plate 8 Booth and LCC 'before' (left) and 'after' (right) maps of the Boundary Street development from the 1890s

Source: The Open University

Plate 9 The unemployed in the East End of London: applicants for the relief fund, *Illustrated London News*, 27 March, 1886

Source: © Illustrated London News Ltd/Mary Evans Picture Library

astonishing archive of junk leftovers from our own consumer society. It is almost impossible to imagine a reading of the seventeenth century that does not acknowledge the importance and worth of the Thomason Collection of Tracts held at the British Library. Now bound into about 2,000 volumes these 22,000 pamphlets, tracts and early newspapers (Plate 5 shows one example) together give a unique account of the political and religious controversies at a moment of fundamental change in England. Thomason acted as an unofficial commentator on the unfolding drama that he himself was a witness to. He collected a remarkably diverse literature that would never have survived if he had not deferred to his own historical sensibilities, possessing the presence of mind to realise that he lived in momentous times. Nor was this collection put together without considerable financial cost to himself and with his own safety on occasions being compromised – he went to prison briefly in 1651. Faced with danger to the collection and himself, he even moved it from location to location to ensure its safety. As he collected the documents of Civil War, the rise of the Commonwealth under Cromwell, the Interregnum and finally the Restoration of the monarchy, he also annotated these printed materials. Here was a public historian providing us with documents, priceless sources which would become the basis of future histories.

In less personal danger but no less heroically, Robert Opie brought together a fantastic collection of packaging and advertising memorabilia, which, but for his determination to record the fleeting imagery of what we might consider to be everyday and mundane, might also have disappeared into the ether. His attention to the flotsam and jetsam of a consumer society and his willingness to repackage the collection as nostalgia is not, it might be argued, comparable to Thomason's efforts in the seventeenth century. Yet, his collection of drink cans, old radios, pedal cars and 'traditional' lawnmowers only hints at his contribution to the documentation of our own age and will one day prove its worth as an astonishing archive. If this collection will be a boon for historians in the future, then we have its conceptual moment articulated by Opie himself when he describes the founding of the collection on a Sunday afternoon in Aberdeen:

> **It was impossible to get anything to eat on a Sunday, at least in those days in Scotland. I found a vending machine and purchased a packet of Mackintosh's Munchies and a packet of McVitie's and Price Ginger Nuts. These machines made a good sound in those days – a real 'crunch' when they came down. I got back to my room at the hotel and I was consuming the Munchies, I suddenly looked at the pack and thought, 'If I throw this away I will never, ever, see it again, and yet here is a whole wealth of history!' It was something along those lines. But you see, I was looking at the packet as if it were a stamp, something that I had been saving for thirteen or fourteen years up to this point. So I had had my 'apprenticeship' and I had come to this pivotal moment. I can virtually remember the room I was in. The sudden realization came to me that this was something I should be saving, and I thought what an enormous part of social history I was about to throw away. That packet was going to change and develop into other things. It was no longer going to be priced at seven pence, it would soon be priced at eight pence, or whatever it was. Yet I was about to throw it away, damage it. I knew I should be saving these things. The next packet was the McVitie's one. I still have these things, and they have a date on them. It still says 'wrapped in Sellophane' on them. Spelt with an 'S'! I had my training – as with Matchboxes [an earlier obsession]. I would write the prices in and the date and everything else. When I went up to my friends in Scotland, I was already saying, 'Can I have those packets?' When I got home, my mother was told about the momentous event and from that time in, I have saved every packet that I've consumed the contents of.** (Elsner and Cardinal, 1994, pp. 32–3)

Clearly this is seriously obsessive behaviour, a point illustrated when he talks elsewhere in the interview about the thrill or 'the play' between 'what's useful to save and what's boring to save', emphasising that the subject matter is not the overriding stimuli but rather the act of collecting itself. These are not the instincts of an historian, nor even, as we shall find out in Chapter 19, of an archivist. The result, however, is most certainly useful for historians yet to be born who will be able to enjoy a vast archive based on the cultures of twentieth-century consumption. Public history, at least in this guise, provides a useful mode of historical production, concerned as it often is with consumption patterns of the everyday, with contemporary politics and family relations. This in itself affords angles of interpretation of sources not considered as such in the circles of traditional history.

Perhaps the most straightforward way of approaching public history is as a method to reconfigure the archive in ways done by public historians like Thomason and Opie, producing collections useful to scholars. Let us examine this point more fully by considering war games, war gamers and uses made of the past by children's board games made during the Second World War. The work of the public historian is as likely to be found in the magazines of war gamers as in the journals of the military specialist at Sandhurst, for gamers display an impressive ability to engage in complex arguments about the accuracy of the historical record and in present-day historical debate. In an edition of *Miniature Wargames* from 1980, one public historian asked whether Constantine III was 'just another usurper?' This is a question to grace any university examination paper. In another, we find history told as a narrative of flashing swords and booming guns with the rhetorical flourish at the end – 'Bloody, isn't it?' Being both informed about the conventions of an historical approach and able to make history engage and excite is one of the interesting features of public history practised in this way. It takes precisely the approach no longer taken by school or university history departments, which may, of course, account for its popularity among a large group of people who nevertheless imbibe history in a variety of ways and work tirelessly with the stuff of the past. If nothing else, it appeals to boys:

> **Personally, I am drawn to the Pechenegs (800 AD to 1050 AD). Admittedly as a nation they did inspire the proverb 'As stupid as Pecheneg', but on the other hand they did decline the orders of a Byzantine emperor to attack the Turks with the polite response that they did not wish to comply as the Turks were fierce and more numerous, and they sincerely hoped that the Emperor would be tactful enough not to mention the matter again. A glance at the Army List shows, however, that it is possible to upgrade the Pechenegs from the 'cowardly' to the 'pragmatic'.**
> (Anon, 1989, p. 13)

And:

> **If you wish to hijack the mob first both players state exactly where they want the mob to go and what they want to attack. Both then roll a dice and the winner has control of the mob which now must move to its new destination. If the loser has lost by more than 7 he is rendered limb from limb. Bloody, isn't it?**
> (Webster, 1989, p. v)

These sources give us a strong indication of how at any particular moment in history the past in a dialectic relationship with the present actually plays out in areas of everyday life that would otherwise go unnoticed. Board games manufactured and played during the years 1939–45 are sources open to interrogation from a number of angles. They may even take us back to our opening concern, the public manifestation of attitudes to fascism and anti-fascism in Britain that we saw writ large at the Battle of Cable Street and on the mural created in its memory. Played in the air raid shelters of the Blitz, games like 'Decorate Goering – A Party Game', 'The Allies Dart Game' and 'Chase Your Enemy' showed the German Foreign Minister Ribbentrop with a snake's body and a cave-man club or Goering as a victim of a patriotic version of 'Pin the Tail on the Donkey'. Similarly, in the *Dandy* comic Goering became Hermy in 'Addy and Hermy – The Nasty Nazis', Desperate Dan punches Hitler, and anti-Italian racism (that certainly survived into our childhoods) is manifest with Mussolini portrayed as 'Musso the Wop' ('the bigger der flop'). Once again, as in the study of the Battle of Cable Street and the mural that came from the battle, the concern from a public history angle is with the event itself but also with the traces of the event in the present.

These board games work as part of a study of propaganda, of attitudes to warfare as derring-do adventure, as a study of childhood during this critical period or even, if we examine the raw materials from which they are made, an indication of the level of shortages during the conflict when the Norway campaign in 1940 cut off supplies of cardboard. They also demonstrate that the evidence for public history is (a point made by Hilda Kean in Section 2) as likely to be fished out of the attic as dug up in the more conventionally defined archive. The question that Section 4 will seek to answer is whether public history really constitutes a serious alternative to conventional historical approaches.

Section 4

Public history as contested knowledge

David and Andrew Whelan from Leeds took out their tools for 'doing' history and made their steady way to a field somewhere near Harrogate in England. This father and son metal-detecting team from Yorkshire had already secured permission from a local farmer to scour his land for 'treasure', the sort of 'treasure' that classicists and historians working in universities prefer to call 'evidence'. On their hands and knees they managed eventually to unearth 617 silver coins, some gold rings and silver bars, all stuffed hard into a silver vessel decorated with depictions of animals and vine-scrolls. Some coins related to Islam and came from areas that stretched from Russia and Afghanistan to Scandinavia, Ireland and the far reaches of Continental Europe. In so doing, these amateur archaeologists (as we might now think of them) added to the sum of expert knowledge, emphasising the multicultural nature of Britain's ancient history:

> **Jonathan Williams, the British Museum's keeper of prehistory and Europe, said that the 'remarkable' find shed new light on a period overshadowed by bloodshed and brutality. 'This was a crucial moment in the country we now live in,' he said. 'The treasure may have been buried for safekeeping by a wealthy Viking during the conquest of the Viking kingdom of Northumbria in AD 927 by the Anglo-Saxon King, Athelstan. He could have been killed – or even forgotten exactly where he buried it.'** (*The Times*, 20 July 2007, p. 25)

From this perspective, history is as much an activity as a profession. It takes its evidence from all around, never privileging the 'official' written document over the 'unofficial knowledge' that decorate our public spaces. Public history, therefore, is practised in the spaces that we do not recognise as relating to history at all. Could metal detecting, for instance, be credibly seen as the binary opposite of the established methods of archaeology? Could elite biographies as a way of retelling power relations be in reality regarded as less important than family history? Professional historians view family history with scepticism for two chief reasons: first, it lacks a real overarching purpose and a necessary sense of detachment; second, it can collapse quickly into nostalgia, symptomatic of felt absences in the present. 'Top people's' biography is not treated with anything like that routine scepticism. Yet, as we know from accounts of the Labour governments in the 1960s, written in diary form or in the form of memoirs by Tony Benn, Barbara Castle and Richard Crossman, we know that while all these people were in the same Cabinet, attending the same meetings, they give radically different versions of events and, unaccountably, place themselves centre stage.

Nor can we confidently know what is omitted in elite biography. The former Conservative Prime Minister John Major wrote his voluminous memoirs without ever mentioning his extra-marital affair with Edwina Currie. Much of the 'contested knowledge' that Paul Martin, historian, theorist of collecting and part of the new wave in museum studies describes in Table 11.1, is what he calls 'rarefied' approaches to the past which have been transformed by a 'popular' counterpart. Learned academic journals from a public history angle are less important to the historical public then the potted histories of a holiday destination featured by an in-flight magazine. Similarly, television programmes that invite an audience to bring along their family heirlooms or antiques for scrutiny have, at least in Britain, attracted stunning audience figures while emptying the lofts or attics of the nation. If it is true to say, therefore, that history is now popularly understood through television and film, then in this respect at least, probably the most watched 'historian' in the field today is the actor and director Mel Gibson, with his wildly inaccurate historical dramas that seek to take the lid off Jewish or Anglo-Saxon plots to domicile subject peoples.

The spin-off to all this is a welcome interest in history more generally, rather in the same way that the brass-rubbing craze of the 1960s and 1970s made the past genuinely popular. The practice involved tracing the outside of tombs and monuments in order to gain a likeness, stoking a renewed public interest in heraldry and medievalism more generally. Remarkably, this practice became so popular that, in some churches and cathedrals, facsimiles replaced the originals, raising questions about how we understand the place of the 'original', thus

Table 11.1 Contesting knowledge – a table of binary opposites

Rarefied domain	*Popular domain*
Archaeology	Metal detecting
Elite biography	Family history
Classical music	Popular music
Academic journals	Popular magazines
Classical literature	Pulp fiction
Antique appreciation	Popular collecting

Source: Taken from Martin (1999).

promoting another craze of later decades: conservation and yet another area in which public history works. In the same way, public history has undoubtedly brought a new perspective to conventional historical study. It has questioned the definition of who a historian is and what history does. In this respect, it has enfranchised whole classes of enthusiasts hitherto too often summarily dismissed by professional historians.

Social sciences have been rather quicker off the mark than the arts or humanities regarding questions of cross-disciplinarily activity and the use of knowledge gleaned from outside the academy. Sociologists of medicine, religion and environmental politics have all confronted the problems associated with maintaining the status of the expert: the doctor, the cleric, the scientist. Natural scientists are arguably even quicker to break down barriers between the amateur and the professional expert, a legacy, perhaps, of the gentlemen scientists of the eighteenth and nineteenth centuries. In the United States, amateur astronomers complement the academy by identifying comets, variable stars and stellar occultations; field biologists help collect data for bird counts and enumerate flora and fauna, and geologists do likewise for the study of rock formations to the extent that together there is now a Society for Amateur Scientists actively engaging with professional science. In Britain, the Zoological Society of London (ZSL) regularly appeals for amateurs to join the search for dolphins, porpoises and seals in the Thames Estuary. Meteorologists rely on public feedback on weather conditions, while archaeologists have long appreciated volunteer diggers and even, as we have seen in the opening example of this section, appreciate amateurs with metal detectors as unpaid scouts for future sites.

In practice

We have attempted in this chapter to suggest that contemporary historical practices take different forms. Usually thought of as a discipline confined to the rarefied atmosphere and structure of the academy to be pursued by appropriately qualified historians, what is often overlooked is the fact that history features powerfully in the public imagination, and there are many other 'lay' practitioners who undertake research that could be considered to be history. Indeed, before the emergence of history as a profession in the nineteenth century, the vast majority of historians of repute were amateurs. Today, people who delve into their family history, community activists who attempt to reconstruct aspects of an historical event such as the Cable Street riots, writers of broadcast history programmes, local historians who explore the historical significance of particular lives or buildings, and heritage workers who conduct guided tours of buildings or streets all enthusiastically practise and disseminate forms of history despite the fact that many have not been through the rigours of formal historical training.

The existence of this popular, public history has posed many challenges to history as a profession, and this has created real divisions. Some historians have welcomed the emergence of public history. For them, it has served to democratise the practice of history and to change for the better the social production of historical knowledge. There is no obvious reason, they argue, why history should be confined to the academy, or for the academy to define what constitutes legitimate historical knowledge. Too much history is inaccessible since it is written for a small audience of like-minded individuals. In contrast, others argue that public history is not progressive for it produces knowledge for a popular audience which rarely goes beyond commonsensical understanding. The heritage industry, for example, manufactures representations of the past for mass consumption which, in pandering to populist nostalgia, remains conservative and incapable of addressing critically sources of conflict and dissent.

All this suggest that history matters. The huge interest in various forms of history indicates that people are attracted to stories about the past, and these are part of an endeavour to make sense of who and where they are in the present. Perhaps under these circumstances, history is too important to be left to the historians. If that is the case, we as historians have a responsibility to widen and hence democratise the production and dissemination of critical forms of historical knowledge.

Summary

The four sections of this chapter have said four things:

- Public history is defined by its approach to evidence, its appeal to a popular audience, its interest in the way the past is represented in the present and its scepticism towards history as a profession. These elements were explored by looking closely at the Battle of Cable Street in 1936, which was a street riot and proved to be an earthquake for modern multiculturalism, perhaps, but the aftershocks that followed it are the concerns of public history. It should be emphasised, as it is in the first section, that public history has taken on different guises in different countries: notably, in the cases of Australia, the United States and Britain.
- Heritage is the prominent way that the past is consumed by a mass public. The debate about whether heritage and the 'heritage industry' (say through its presentation in the work and activities of the National Trust) was seen by historians such as Patrick Wright or Raphael Samuel as either conservative or progressive depended on its context. Because of these divisions in understanding the role of heritage as a suppressor of present day dissent or a device that passively consumes the past – it remains an approach to research that has much promise.
- Although public history is primarily concerned with the consumption of past narratives through a language of heritage public historians have also been prominent in the production of historical knowledge, say through collecting objects from everyday life. How so doing, definitions of history and who can claim the title of historian is brought into relief while the archive is redefined to be more promiscuous than in other genres of history.
- Public history approaches may challenge the very basis of what is conventionally regarded as the limits of historical knowledge. This section sought to demonstrate how conventional notions of, say, archaeology, biography or classical literature is overshadowed by, say, metal detecting, in-flight magazines or pulp fiction.

Discussion document

As a review of a book on uses of photography and landscape, Patrick Wright gives a multi-layered and rich account of the possibilities of using the techniques of aerial photography to understand landscape and architecture by constructing a public history-driven narrative of changes in these areas. This may also raise questions about the veracity and use of historical knowledge gained through these methods.

A former member of the Royal Flying Corps, he was also a pioneer of aerial archaeology, finding new use for a photographic technique that had been developed for reconnaissance purposes during the First World War. Aerial archaeology approached the landscape as a witness that might be coaxed into disclosing evidence of everything that had ever happened to it. Its findings, however, were not just romantic. 'Woodhenge' was first detected by these means in 1925. Having enlisted the help of the RAF in his searches, Crawford also found the site outside London that Stukeley in the 1770s had (wrongly) claimed as one of Caesar's camps, and which was now shown to be threatened by 'the rising tide of villadom'.

Aerial photography was shaped by a Modernist imagination. Dynamic, abstract and defamiliarising, it could also counter the 'grim narrative of irreversible obliteration' by insisting on the 'ineradicable remains of the distant past' – as if the ribbon development was the transient and temporary thing, and the advancing junk landscape that John Betjeman and others at the *Architectural Review* would deride as 'subtopia' was the thing that would fail to last.

The Second World War saw this 'archaeological imagination' pulled in new directions. The artists despatched around the country for the Pilgrim Trusts 'Recording Britain' scheme produced images of buildings and landscapes judged threatened by the Council for the Preservation of Rural England, and the threat was not necessarily provided by Hitler or the new war effort. Yet, as Hauser indicates, pre-war anxieties about the 'tide of modernization' threatening the British landscape were 'largely eclipsed' as propaganda demanded a new 'catalogue of hallowed sites and social practices marked by time'. Places were rehallowed with lines from the great national poets, as in Humphrey Jennings's film 'Words for Battle'. Michael Powell and Emeric Pressburger began making 'A Canterbury Tale' in 1943, not long after Canterbury had been bombed. Their film reaffirms the links between history and place, while also, as Hauser argues in a captivating digression, offering its own variation on the story of Hollywood's 'The Wizard of Oz' (1939). Among the institutions that carried the 'archaeological imagination' into the nineteen fifties, was the National Buildings Record, founded in 1940, a year of grievous destruction and loss. The desire to record historical buildings was soon enough accompanied by an interest in the imaginative potentiality of 'Damaged Britain'. Destroyed churches would be preserved as war memorials, but bomb-sites became places of discovery too – like one near London's Cannon Street Station, where a Mithraic temple was discovered in 1954. By that time W. G. Hoskins, pioneer of 'history on the ground', was ready to take on the cause with his influential *The Making of the English Landscape*, first published in 1955, and written in the conviction, presumably shared by the author of this original and highly suggestive study, that 'the English landscape itself, to those who know how to read it aright, is the richest historical record we possess'.

Review by Patrick Wright of Kitty Hauser, *Shadow Sites: Photography, Archaeology and the British Landscape 1927–1955* (2007), in *Twentieth Century British History*, vol. 19, no. 2, 2008, pp. 239–42.

Further reading

* *essential*

Hilda Kean *et al.* (eds.), *Seeing History: Public History Now in Britain* (2000).
A collection of essays that outline the plethora of ways in which public history approaches to the past have influenced historical approaches. Essays include Bruce Wheeler, in 'Language and landscape: the construction of place in an East London borough'; Paul Long, 'But it's not all nostalgia: public history and local identity in Birmingham'; and Peter Claus, 'Managing boundaries: history and community at the Bishopsgate Institute'.

John Elsner and Roger Cardinal, *The Cultures of Collecting* (1994).
Covers to some extent the trends of public history which are apparent in the world of professional museum studies but also in popular forms of collecting.

* **Raphael Samuel**, *Theatres of Memory: The Past and Present in Contemporary Culture* (1995).
Sometimes repetitive and overloaded with examples, this is nevertheless a remarkable manifesto for a democratic approach to history, taking into the ranks of 'historian' all manner of amateur practitioners of public history.

Ludmilla Jordanova, *History in Practice* (2006).
Chapter 6, 'Public history', covers American and Australian models of public history and arrives at different conclusions.

12 Global histories

1 The challenge of global history
2 The origins of global history
3 Enter 'new world history'

Introduction

This chapter focuses on the genre of world or global history. Section 1 discusses contemporary interest in globalisation, and investigates whether processes which operate at a global level are a modern phenomenon or have their lineages in the distant past. It shows that many of the features which are now considered to be part of globalisation can be traced back to earlier periods, although recent years have experienced an acceleration of globalisation. It is possible, for example, to devise a periodisation of global history based on such features. Section 2 develops this theme by looking at the extent to which writers of the premodern period shared a concern to think beyond their immediate environments, whether local or national. Here we examine the accounts of some of the great travellers who were responsible more than any others for bringing an awareness of other regions of the world to popular attention, and helped to lift Europe from what might be thought of, in modern terms, as medieval ignorance. Such accounts were marginalised when history emerged as a discipline in its own right during the nineteenth century and turned its interest to nationalist narratives based on notions of the nation state that are associated with the period after the French Revolution. Finally, the chapter considers the promise of fresh approaches to world history which have appeared in the last 30 years, not only in how these accounts reveal a multiplicity of global interconnections, but also in challenging views of historical change that have placed the West at centre stage.

Section 1

The challenge of global history

It is said that on the occasion of a visit to Europe in the 1960s, Chou En Lai, one of the leaders of the Chinese revolution, was asked what he thought about the impact of the French Revolution. 'It is too early to say,' he replied. It was a mischievous but astute observation. The Revolution was of such momentous significance that its reverberations are still being felt, and these, like ripples on a pond, have extended further and further until they have reached every corner of the globe. He appreciated that it was merely part of a crisis which affected and was manifest in popular uprisings in many global theatres. Equally, this crisis gave birth to a host of ideas about human rights, citizenship, and democracy which inform the lives of so many of us today, and yet are still being contested. Chou En Lai thus revealed a sensitivity to how such events operated on a world stage, and to the notion that they can only be understood in global terms.

If history has operated on the global stage ever since human societies had the potential to trade over long distances, it is only in recent years that the historiography of world history has revealed something of its potential for understanding more fully critical moments in the human story. It has done this by demonstrating that such moments were not bounded by distinct regional or national movements, but emerged from complex interconnections which reached across land masses and oceans. This, therefore, is the task of global history. World or global history is not necessarily a history of the world (although, there are fine examples of this), but can be importantly a history of a country region or episode that recognises and takes account of the contact and connections, linkages and interrelationships that have characterised human contact over centuries and which ought to be reflected in our histories. This is critical to note if we are to understand what it is that this chapter is seeking to convey.

The chapter then explores the significance of a global imagination to the study and writing of history. Its argument is that by overcoming regional boundaries which have defined much of the historiography, world history promises fruitful and challenging perspectives on the nature of historical change. A good point to start is Eric Wolf's *Europe and a People without History*, which opens with the following: 'The central assumption of this book is that the world of humankind constitutes a manifold, a totality of interconnected processes, and inquiries what disassemble this totality into bits and then fail to reassemble it falsifies reality' (Wolf, 2010, p. 3). First published in 1982 and again in 1997 and 2010, it is an eloquent statement of what he saw as one of the crucial problems besetting intellectual inquiry, and serves nicely as an introduction to some of the concerns of this chapter. From some of the earliest records of human existence it is apparent that people have travelled across land masses, seas and oceans to make contact, and enter into economic and cultural exchange with others. These patterns of intercourse deny that human societies were enclosed and sealed off, but readily fused with others. The implications of this insight are profound. First, apart from a few isolated communities, societies have existed, indeed have been actively formed in relation to others. Second, under these circumstances, if historians try to separate societies by considering them as impervious to outside influences, then we run the risk of providing a distorted account of their identities, histories and cultures.

Eric R. Wolf (1923–99) proceeds with examples of these 'interconnected processes'. Ecologically, New York is hit by the Hong Kong flu; European grapevines are devastated by American plant lice. Economically, when oil wells in the Persian Gulf cease production, generating plants in Ohio are forced to shut down; when the United States suffers an unfavourable balance of payments, American dollars drain into the bank accounts of Frankfurt and Yokahama; Italians manufacture Fiat cars in the Russian Federation. Politically, European wars reverberate around the world; American troops are stationed on the rim of Asia, and Finns guard the border between Israel and Egypt. Wolf chose these examples in the early 1980s; think of what has happened since then, and how the unfolding of world history around such incidents as the destruction of the twin towers in New York on 9/11, 2001, the invasion of Iraq in 2003 and the banking crisis of 2007/8 has given his message even greater weight.

What may be true of the present is equally so of the past. Diseases brought by the Spanish to South America in the sixteenth century decimated the native populations; from that time, American plants such as the potato, maize and manioc spread through the Old World. Beginning with Portuguese incursion into Africa during the fifteenth century, but reaching a peak in the eighteenth, enslaved Africans were forcibly transported to the New World. With the abolition of the British slave trade early in the nineteenth century, indentured labourers from China and India were shipped to South East Asia and the Caribbean. As a result of early contact with Asia in the sixteenth century, Europeans learnt from skilled Indians the techniques of producing fine cotton textiles and, from the Chinese, the art of making porcelain. From that time also Arabic numerals were widely adopted, and Europeans entered into a long – and deadly – relationship with native American tobacco.

Such examples, concludes Wolf, demonstrate 'contact and connections, linkages and interrelationships'. Yet scholars who seek to understand the past choose largely to ignore them. Instead, historians, economists and political scientists take nations, separated by historical and cultural boundaries, as their paradigm. We might then well ask why an anthropologist like Wolf had such a keen sense of the importance of world histories. The argument in this chapter is that all disciplines which seek further understanding of the development of human societies, looking beyond the artificial barriers imposed by national boundaries, need to have an historical imagination, that is, a sense of historical change and how the past continues to live in the present. And it is not merely a question of taking a broader view; there is an imperative to recognise and appreciate the contribution of those who have been written out of the historical record. What does the title of his book reveal about Wolf's approach? Does it seriously suggest that peoples outside Europe have no history? On the contrary, it soon becomes clear that it is precisely the histories of those peoples which have been grievously ignored by writers of European history, and now as a matter of urgency need to be placed onto the agenda.

Since the publication of Wolfs' book, there has been a phenomenal growth of interest in globalisation. It is difficult these days to switch on the radio or television without hearing an economist, politician, sociologist or even historian talk of globalisation as if it was part and parcel of conventional wisdom. More importantly, globalisation has emerged as a political issue of some magnitude. When linked to war, hunger, corporate greed or ecological catastrophes, globalisation has the ability to mobilise increasing numbers of activists onto the streets to campaign against what they see as the damage caused by global processes to those who live and work at the margins.

Sadly, our understanding of globalisation does not quite match our enthusiasm for or against its role in the contemporary world. So what are its defining features and how does it link to the writing and understanding of history? The following have all been proposed by writers in the past 30 years, and summarised by the political theorist David Held and his co-authors in *Global Transformations* (Held *et al.*, 1999):

1. An intensification of connections among nation states, leading to a diminution of state policy, and a decline in the importance of the nation state.
2. The emergence of political, economic and cultural bureaucracies which operate on a global scale, including multinational firms, banks, the International Monetary Fund, and the United Nations.
3. The creation of global cities that act as hubs of global interaction such as London, New York and Tokyo.
4. A dramatic increase in the flows of commodities, peoples, information and cultural products. Millions of people now move around the world in search of better jobs and opportunities, or in order to find refuge from persecution. Consumer and perishable goods now reach our shelves in the West from virtually every corner of the globe. The World Wide Web has transformed the speed and passage of information.
5. The worldwide spread of western-style consumerism. Western brands such as Coca-Cola, MacDonald's and Apple, rituals of consumption, and shopping malls identical to those found in London or Chicago are to be found from Delhi and Beijing, to Abu Dhabi and Rio de Janeiro.

On reflection, there are probably few who would disagree violently with such a list. Under these circumstances it would be tempting to consider, as many do, that globalisation is a process brought about by the ways in which corporations, banks, communications and the movement of people have increasingly transcended national boundaries in the post Second World War period. The problem is, however, that if we scrutinise the historical record it is apparent that these processes have been in place for a very long time.

This is where some of the difficult problems arise. For while there may be a degree of consensus on what globalisation is, there is little on when it actually began. Many of the features of globalisation can be traced back centuries. The following periodisation usefully lays out how global processes have originated and changed over time (Held *et al.*, 1999):

Phase 1 Premodern (before 1500)

- Early imperial systems.
- World religions.
- Nomadic empires and agrarian expansion.
- Plagues and pandemics.
- Long-distance trade.

Phase 2 Early modern (1500–1800)

- Political and military expansion.
- Europe and the new world: demographic, environmental, epidemiological flows.
- Development of European empires.
- New transatlantic exchanges.

Phase 3 Modern (1850–1945)

- European global empires: military, political, economic, cultural flows.
- Global circulation of western secular discourses and ideologies.
- Transatlantic migrations.
- Asian diasporas.
- Development of a world economy.

Phase 4 Contemporary (1945–present)

- Cold war and post cold war global military relationships.
- Systems of global governance and international law.
- Economic globalisation: trade, financial markets, multinational production and investment, technology transfer.
- Global environmental threats.
- New patterns of global migration.
- Global spread of media multinationals, western popular culture and thought.
- New global networks of communication and transport.

We could write many histories of human interaction across many areas and themes but let us take, for example, the case of industrialisation. Here is a story familiar to many and one that we will discuss further in Chapter 17. Sometime in the late eighteenth century, Britain led the industrial revolution. A combination of advantageous natural resources and native genius created a system of factory production which guaranteed for the first time in human history self-sustained economic growth. The revolution was initially based on the manufacture of cotton goods in the large mills of the north, but later, through the production of iron and steel, reached into every corner of the economy, transforming the working lives and living conditions of the people for ever. The problem with this narrative is its insularity. Simply stated, we cannot understand the industrial revolution exclusively as a British experience. In a remarkable passage from his massive study of capitalism penned about 150 years ago, Karl Marx provided an alternative interpretation:

> **The discovery of gold and silver in America, the extirpation, enslavement, and entombment in the mines of the aboriginal population, the beginning of the conquest and looting of the East Indies, the turning of Africa into a warren for hunting black skins, signalised the rosy dawn of capitalist production. These idyllic proceedings are the chief memento of primitive accumulation. On their heels treads the commercial war of the European nations, with the globe for a theatre.** (Marx, 1974, p. 345)

Marx thus locates the origins of industrial capitalism in the nascent colonial system rather than in the textile factories of England. The flow of plunder from the Spanish colonisation of South America and later the British annexation of India, the wealth created by the slave trade, and the establishment of a world market enabling manufactured goods to be sold, all helped to create the conditions which underpinned the industrial revolution and the ascent of capitalism. The origins of capitalist production, therefore, are not necessarily to be found among English textile weavers alone, but have to be sought also among the cotton producers of India, America and Egypt, and the sugar workers in the slave plantations of the Caribbean, for here too can we find the skills, technology and forms of labour organisation which have come to be seen as typically capitalist (Williams, 1966). Historians have for the most part been reticent to grasp the potential of global history. After all, the challenge is a formidable one. Historians trained in western academies tend to be conservative creatures, resistant to new ways of looking at the world. History is written by the victors, and so they have been taught that the West is a society that has developed independently of other societies and civilisations, according to distinct stages from ancient Greece to Rome, Christendom, the Renaissance, the Enlightenment, ending up with the advanced capitalism of North America, the zenith of human civilisation (Wolf, 1997, p. 5). This teleology marks and celebrates the historical unfolding of a self-contained and self-fulfilling prophecy: why do we need to take account of peoples outside its orbit? Historians are also encouraged to become increasingly specialist, especially in research which is more tightly bounded by period and location. Under such circumstances, it requires something of a bold imaginative leap to think across narrowly defined contours and embrace different historical experiences, and to overcome a profound historical amnesia by thinking sympathetically about 'the people without history', that is, those who have rarely featured in conventional historical accounts. This is nothing less than a confrontation with all they have been taught, and yet some have started to pave the way.

Section 2

The origins of global history

Histories in the form of genealogy, myth, biography, dynastic chronicle and military conquest have existed ever since people developed a sense of the passing of time. Most of these were culturally and geographically limited, and were meant to establish and help maintain the authority of particular peoples, groups and families. There were also, however, a relatively small number with inquiring minds who were interested in exploring beyond the boundaries of knowledge in which they had been raised, to nurture a sense of world history. They tended to come from the intellectual powerhouses of the time. In China of the first century BCE, for example, Sima Qian, the official historian of the Han Dynasty, gathered and synthesised evidence from early times and from far distant lands to provide a narrative reaching beyond its formal boundaries (Manning, 2003, p. 33). Some were travellers who undertook remarkable journeys across the known world, later to record their observations on the nature of the civilisations and peoples they had encountered.

A few examples must suffice. Marco Polo (1254–1324), the son of a Venetian merchant, set out in 1271 on a journey along the silk route to Xanadu (Shangdu), capital of the Mongol empire, where he was reputed to have stayed for over 20 years. He was not the first European to visit China, but he travelled much more extensively than his predecessors. On returning to Venice in 1295, he published an account of his travels which was a huge bestseller even though much of the book was regarded as fiction by contemporary readers. Whatever its authenticity, the travelogue opened European eyes to East Asia for the first time, and retrospectively established his reputation as one of the great European travellers. Thirty years after Polo's return, the lesser-known but much more widely travelled Moroccan scholar Ibn Battuta (1304–68/9) embarked on a 75,000 mile journey traversing the Islamic world from Africa, across the interior of Asia, and then onto China. Returning finally to Morocco in 1354, he dictated an account of his travels which was then forgotten, even in the Islamic world, until recently when its rediscovery and translation into English belatedly sealed his reputation as the greatest of medieval travellers and the most reliable chronicler.

This important tradition of writing continued. In the sixteenth century, al-Hasan al-Wazzan (1488–1548), born in Granada, raised in Morocco, also travelled around the Islamic world. As Leo Africanus, he published *The Description of Africa*, which revealed the complex ways in which the histories and cultures of the African, Muslim, Christian and Jewish worlds were interlinked (Zemon Davis, 2007). Take, for example, the vital question at the time of the spread of disease. Syphilis, he claimed, was introduced into North Africa and subsequently spread by Jewish women, many of whom as prostitutes had transmitted the condition to Muslim men:

> **Don Fernando, King of Spain, chased the Jews from Spain. Many of the Jews who came to Barbary . . . carried the disease from Spain. Some unhappy Moors mixed with the Jewish women, and so little by little, within ten years, one could not find a family untouched by the disease. At first the disease was judged to be leprosy, and those infected were chased [from their houses] and forced to live with the lepers. Then, as the number of those infected increased every day, it was discovered that many people in Spain had the ailment. So the people who had been chased from their houses returned to them.**
>
> (Cited in Zemon Davis, 2007, p. 137)

Once the disease spread in North Africa, al-Wazzan continued, it inflicted great damage on the cities of Tunisia and Egypt. By contrast, nomadic Arabs and people in the 'Land of the Blacks' (Numibia) were unaffected. It was therefore believed that in order to be cured it was sufficient to breathe the air of the countryside. More recent studies have challenged the account by demonstrating that the syphilis was in fact brought from the Iberian peninsula by both refugee Muslims and refugee Jews; if that is the case then al-Wazzan's interpretation of events was misleading, probably because it was shaped by a number of anxieties about sexual relations between Muslims and Jews, and the 'civilised' values of Arabic cities when compared with nomads and blacks.

Travel accounts like these played a crucial role in helping to lift Europe out of the superstition and religious dogma of the medieval period. By opening up the minds of Europeans to an appreciation of lands and peoples previously seen as fabled, even monstrous, thereby uncovering remarkable sources of knowledge from which Europe had been excluded since ancient times, they helped pave the way for the intellectual revolution of the Renaissance and laid the foundations too for the eighteenth-century Enlightenment. These intellectual transformations in turn provided fertile ground for the planting of novel ideas about world history. The Renaissance witnessed the first flowering, even though its thought remained highly contradictory. The supreme political theorist of the time, Machiavelli, embraced the idea of western civilisation, but linked the cultural flowering witnessed in Italy directly and linearly to the Old World, notably the classical era. He therefore had no need to engage with the world outside Europe. Others were more mindful of the existence of other peoples, most especially after the 'discovery' of the Americas at the end of the fifteenth century. For the historian Francesco Guicciardini (1483–1540), the existence of native Americans raised a host of vital questions about the human condition. How was it, he asked, that such people, many of whom lived in highly organised and successful societies, had been able to progress without knowledge of the Bible or European thought? The opening up of the Americas therefore invited reconsideration of the whole of the past, and offered possibilities for future progress.

The Renaissance laid the foundations for the ascent of the West in part by mapping, however patchily, the non-European world. It was not until the Enlightenment, however, that these other cultures were studied seriously, and the lessons learnt applied to an analysis of contemporary western society. Chapter 3 was devoted to the impact of the Enlightenment on the writing of history, and we have no wish to repeat the arguments here, but it would be worth saying a little about how Enlightenment figures furthered the study of world history. Combined with a commitment to rational inquiry based on the laws of natural sciences, many writers were fascinated by societies beyond Europe and determined not only to learn more about their distinct cultures but also to think of ways they could be brought together imaginatively into a grand evolutionary scheme. Thus one of the leading Enlightenment figures, Denis Diderot (1713–84), began to compile the *Encyclopédie des Sciences, des Arts et des Métiers* in 1751 with the aim of collecting all the knowledge scattered over the face of the earth. By the time the 28th volume had been published 14 years later, an enthusiastic reading public could learn from the entries of nearly 200 leading writers about, say, the vital contributions made by Islamic intellectuals to the modern world, and the important advances in science and philosophy made by ancient Indian and Chinese civilisations.

Simultaneously, many Enlightenment thinkers were busily applying themselves to the task of locating different civilisations in an evolutionary hierarchy. Some of the foundations for this reasoning had been laid earlier. Jean Bodin (1530–96), a French professor of law, wrote *Methodus ad Facilem Historiarum Cognitionem* (1566) in which he reinterpreted the course of world history by identifying three crucial geopolitical regions. The first two millennia had been dominated by the Orientals including Babylonians, Persians and Egyptians because of their knowledge of philosophy and mathematics. They were displaced by Mediterranean peoples (Greeks and Romans), who through politics and practical knowledge controlled the next two millennia. Finally, Northern peoples, that is, Europeans, ascended to power through their skills in warfare and mechanical inventions, and their ability to utilise the scientific and philosophical work of ancient Greece and Rome. The English philosopher John Locke (1632–1704), now widely recognised as one of the founding figures of the Enlightenment, published in 1690 *Two Treatises of Government*, which opened the path for what later became known as the stages theory of development which we have already discussed in Chapter 2. Challenging scriptural and ancient accounts which suggested a universal scheme of societal evolution, Locke argued that primitive modes of human subsistence, such as found in hunter-gatherer and early pastoral societies, existed at different times in the development of Asia and Europe, thereby suggesting that their civilisations had progressed at different rates.

How, Enlightenment thinkers asked, were different civilisations to be ranked according to their state of advance? Just as the discovery of 'civilised' native American societies had posed awkward questions about the status and relevance of Christian knowledge, so astonishing revelations in the *Encyclopédie* about the achievements and longevity of Indian and Chinese civilisations prompted demands to know precisely how these were to be located in the grand order of things: if not at the apex of European civilisation, or at the level of Africa, which was dismissed as pagan and primitive, then where? In the eighteenth century, particularly with the writings of Adam Smith, Jacques Turgot and Quesnay, the stages theory of development reached maturity. Using overarching and teleological schemes which identified different societies on the basis of their division of labour, commodity exchange and accumulation of capital, they identified various stages through which these societies had passed, from the primitive nomadic ones found in the South Pacific to the advanced commercial nations of Europe. What distinguished these studies was their use of abstraction. None was intended to be a detailed account of historical change, rather the historical record was selectively called upon to support grand, overarching theories about the nature and development of human societies. Influential writers such as J. G. von Herder and G. W. F. Hegel continued something of this tradition into the nineteenth century, as we witnessed in Chapter 4. Thus Herder's *Ideas for the Philosophy of History of Humanity* (1784–91) emphasised the unity of humankind, but argued that divisions appeared on the basis of ethnicity, and it was the 'national genius' possessed by particular ethnic groups that drove historical change. And Hegel's *Lectures on the Philosophy of History* (1837) saw human desire for freedom as the moving force of change toward an ultimate universal spirit. Both drew upon historical examples from around the world, but the focus was on national progress, and the nation was invariably European. Despite his sensitivity to the importance of the world outside Europe, even Karl Marx in his emphasis on the advanced stage of (European) capitalism can be viewed in the same light.

Evident in these writings was the germination of the idea of the nation, and it was this which was to determine the course of historical writing over the next two centuries. It was no accident that the rise of the nation state during the nineteenth century coincided with what has been seen as the coming of age of history as a scientific discipline in its own right, for the foundations of historiography were laid by historians who pioneered studies of the nation. We encountered Leopold von Ranke in Chapter 4 and know something of his approach to evidence, but he can be located also within the changing paradigms of global history. Influenced by Hegel, von Ranke worked within a tradition of philosophical idealism, that is, a system of historical thought based on the application of more abstract rational principles such as the progress of civilisations rather than factual evidence, which he never really abandoned; indeed, he left unfinished at the time of this death an ambitious history of the world. And yet, unlike Herder and Hegel, this idealism was tempered by an attempt to recover the past 'as it really happened' through a meticulous and painstaking examination of documentary sources.

For those fledgling historians seeking to establish themselves, their discipline and their nation, this was an exciting prospect, and so was launched a vast project to record and disseminate the histories of nation states to patriotic audiences. Jules Michelet's *History of the French Revolution* (1847–53), Lord Macaulay's *History of England from the Accession of James II* (1849–61), George Bancroft's *History of the Unites States of America from the Discovery of the Continent* (1873–74), and a host of other sizable nationalist narratives both illuminated the past and provided lessons for the present. The skills demonstrated in gathering, assessing and interpreting documentary evidence, and the enthusiastic response of a reading public, helped to establish the dominance of national history and the virtually unassailable authority of the professional historian trained in the West (Manning, 2003, p. 28).

This paradigm has survived more or less intact to the present day, the difference being that historians have become so specialised in their interests that they tend to talk to one another rather than reaching out to a broad audience. There have been notable exceptions, in particular studies of world history which engaged with a more popular audience in the aftermath of the horrors of the First and Second World Wars, but somehow they have not successfully entered the canon. A few examples must suffice. In 1918 Oswald Spengler published *Decline of the West*, in which he charted the rise and fall of successive civilisations. It was a profoundly pessimistic vision of a world which he saw as standing on the edge of the abyss. According to Spengler, there was no universal science or spirit of humanity, rather cultures had their own character and way of reasoning which meant that there was little communication among them. Each, however, went through a predetermined path of development. Starting from a heroic age of war and religion, cultures were then subjected to the influence of industrialisation, urbanisation and science, which led to commercialisation and the domination of the masses. Chaos and a loss of creativity were the inevitable result. H. G. Wells' *The Outline of History*, published in 1920, was a skilful synthesis of the work of world historians stitched together by a single vision. Written in the immediate aftermath of the First World War, the book was meant to answer the need expressed by people for an understanding of the unfolding of the events of world history rather than the narrow national histories they had been taught at school. Wells set about what soon appeared as an epic task because he was persuaded there were no 'proper' historians who were 'sufficiently wide and sufficiently shallow to cover the vast field of the project'. The story he told was one of progress, of lives of countless people struggling toward consciousness and understanding until we reach the world of today with its tragic confusions and perplexities and yet so full of promise and opportunity.

Arnold Toynbee's 12-volume *A Study of History* (1933–61) is the most comprehensive attempt to chart the course the rise and fall of world civilisations while paying due regard to those cultures of Asia, South America and Africa that had been systematically ignored by others. Having said that, *Study* is not a narrative history of the world based on original sources, but a comparative and synthetic analysis of all the world's civilisations which relies heavily on the work of previous historians. Thus, like Spengler, he chronicled the changing fortunes of civilisations, using as a template the idea of genesis, growth, breakdown and disintegration, and to an extent shared his pessimism, but he stressed the critical role of human freedom, and posed a universal spiritual renewal as a solution to the world's ills. This suggests that the study of, and respect for, religion was a key to understanding

Toynbee's approach, but at the same time he was at pains also to incorporate the impact of Enlightenment reason, and rejected any religious dogma that conflicted with reasoned argument and evidence.

Finally, Lewis Mumford's trilogy *Technics and Civilization* (1934), *The Culture of Cities* (1938) and *The Condition of Man* (1944) appeared at the same time as Toynbee's magnum opus, and also focused on the changing fortunes of world civilisations. He argued that the twentieth century had witnessed the steady disintegration of western civilisation quite unlike those of the Greek, Roman, Chinese or Indian experiences. The loss of faith in progress and the end of expansion can only be reversed by restoring balance in the community and the human personality through drawing upon human energy, knowledge and wealth without being discouraged.

What is interesting about these authors is that none was a 'proper' historian; indeed, their engagement with history was highly ambiguous. Perhaps this is because no historian was sufficiently ambitious or reckless to take on the task. Spengler had studied philosophy and history as an undergraduate, but was equally interested in science and art. He failed his doctoral dissertation of Heraclitus, and remained outside the academy, choosing instead to teach in a school. He was deeply critical of the evidence-based approach of historians. Wells' mind was seemingly too eclectic and expansive to be confined to history. He had no academic post, making his name as one of the best-known writers of early science fiction. When confronted with the immensity of the world history he had embarked on, Wells decided that a writer of speculative essays and works of fiction was better qualified than an historian. Toynbee studied archaeology in Athens for a time, and although he did have a chair in Modern Greek and Byzantine Studies for five years, he went on to the Royal Institute of International Affairs and later the Research Department at the Foreign Office. And Mumford did not complete his undergraduate degree, had no academic post, and considered himself a writer rather than an historian, urban theorist or literary critic. It is almost as if the discipline of history and the training of historians militated against an imagination of the world required in undertaking such a study.

Section 3

Enter 'new world history'

There emerged in the aftermath of the Second World War another current of world history. Less concerned with broad synthesising narratives covering long historical periods, or with the articulation of overarching themes such as progress, spirituality and reason, its protagonists chose rather to focus on more discrete historical problems within a global context, using as evidence fairly conventional documentary sources. The shift was so dramatic that we might well wonder if we are still talking of the same species of world history. Two remarkable studies from seemingly unexpected and unlikely sources led the way. In 1944, Eric Williams, a Trinidadian who had just completed a doctoral dissertation at Oxford, published *Capitalism and Slavery*. Bestriding the continents of America, Africa, Europe and India, Williams confronted much of the orthodoxy which had beset the study of the institution of slavery, in particular the belief that it was an enclosed system of exploitation, and that its eventual eradication owed most to the determined campaigns of enlightened Britons led by William Wilberforce. Like Marx, he identified the links between the slave trade and the industrial revolution, arguing that profits from slavery provided the necessary finance for the early entrepreneurs. And the whole wretched system was not eventually abolished because of Wilberforce; rather, British capitalists realised that the trade, no longer profitable and increasingly under threat from slave revolts, was a liability. Better by far to do away with it and claim the moral high ground. The book launched a brilliant wave of historical scholarship on world slavery which continues to this day, and although details of Williams' arguments have been subjected to criticism, all historians work with the agenda he first laid down.

While imprisoned by the Nazis during the Second World War, the French historian Fernand Braudel (1902–85) began work on an ambitious project. In 1949 his labours saw fruition with the publication of *The Mediterranean and the Mediterranean World in the Era of Philip II*, one of the truly seminal works of the twentieth century. Before the war Braudel had, significantly, spent nearly a decade teaching in the French colony Algeria, and later became an important member of the *Annales* group, an influential cohort of historians organised around the journal *Annales d'Histoire Économique et Sociale*, which was committed to a larger and more open approach to history. The book, however, sealed his reputation.

Braudel dedicated it to his fellow historian Lucien Febvre, and for good reason. Febvre, along with Marc Bloch, had founded *Annales* in order to promote a new, larger and more human history accessible to audiences beyond the academy. They were highly critical of traditional approaches, and were relentless in their attacks on elite political or diplomatic histories. They wished to downgrade the status conferred on individuals and events, and instead set out to understand and reveal the deep structures that underpinned human behaviour as a means of writing what they called a 'total history'. In so doing, they borrowed freely from the insights of other disciplines, most notably, geography, sociology and anthropology.

Conceiving the Mediterranean during the Renaissance as a part of world history, Braudel's account knew no national or cultural boundaries but embraced the ancient regions of Iraq and Egypt, the Sahara, Europe and Russia. And eschewing the traditional focus of historians on the rich and powerful few, and times of rapid change, he broadened his approach to include details of the lives of ordinary people which changed only slowly and over long periods of time. All of this was informed by a deep knowledge and profound historical imagination.

Interestingly, the book started out in 1923 as a fairly conventional study of Philip II's Mediterranean policy. Braudel claimed that his teachers strongly approved of it for it conformed well to the pattern of diplomatic history which was little concerned with the broader economic and social movements that affected the lives of the mass of people. Thus he began to write about the roles played by the Spanish king and his counsellors through changing circumstances, thereby reconstructing a model of Spanish foreign policy of which the Mediterranean was one small part. While thus engaged, Braudel came to recognise that beyond the intervention of Spain, the Mediterranean had a history and destiny of its own, a 'powerful vitality' which suggested that it deserved to be treated better than a 'picturesque background' to the actions of the Spanish court. He therefore embarked on a history of the Mediterranean in its complex totality. Thus, beginning with an account of the relationship between humans and the environment, the passage of which is almost imperceptible, he proceeded to inquire into how economic systems, states, societies and civilisations worked, and finally described how these profound underlying currents shaped the lives, decisions and behaviour of individual men (and, yes, it was mostly men).

Critics may at this juncture inquire whether a study of modern slavery or of the Mediterranean, no matter how broadly conceived, can be legitimately considered as a world history. It is a good point, but one based on a rather pedantic approach to the topic. Of course, neither Williams nor Braudel set out to write a history of the world; Williams did not even write a world history of slavery, saying nothing about its ancient forms, and Braudel's historical sweep was fairly narrowly defined. What Williams showed with great skill was how modern slavery was built not merely upon the Atlantic system that united America with Europe, but interconnected also Africa and Asia, and it is this which qualifies it as a world history. And what Braudel did similarly was to show how the destiny of the Mediterranean was intimately linked to all the civilisations that comprised Europe at the time, as well as some in Africa and the Middle East. World history does not require that every corner of the globe be covered in a grand work of synthesis; rather, what is important is that we reveal Wolf's 'totality of interconnected processes' in ways that transcend conventional national, cultural, and even regional boundaries, so shedding a powerful new light on older historical problems. This explains the enduring influence and appeal of Williams and Braudel.

But if the critics are insistent that world really does mean world, then the foundational text for the new world history was William McNeill's *The Rise of the West*, first published in 1963. As the title suggests (note the inversion of Spengler), this was a study of how the West ascended to world dominance, seen not as part of a linear and triumphant trajectory from the ancients, or as part of what some have seen as European exceptionalism, but as the unfolding of awkward and complex interrelationships with other world powers such as the Ottomans in which knowledge was diffused freely across cultural boundaries. This was history writ large, perhaps not surprising since McNeill worked with Toynbee in preparing the last volumes of his monumental series. Unlike Toynbee, however, he avoided the identification of particular patterns in the historical record, which for him derived not from the evidence directly but from the imposition of abstract themes such as secularisation, and addressed the evidence directly to create chronologies which offered a range of novel perspectives not only on the West but on world history. Given the focus on the ascent of the West, there was a certain inevitability about the criticism that the book overstated its power, and thereby understated the contribution of China, Africa and the Islamic world, but it did give a considerable boost to the study of interactions, and eventually a less skewed picture of the relationship between the West and the rest, to use a phrase adopted by Niall Ferguson in a book called *Civilization: The West and the Rest* (2011), but which argues in the opposite direction.

Since these pioneering studies we have seen a great flowering of a new world history. Some of our leading historians have been emboldened to take on afresh the task of writing grand syntheses. Hugh Thomas's *An Unfinished History of the World* (1979), Felipe Fernández-Armesto's *Millennium* (1995) and Christopher Bayly's *The Birth of the Modern World, 178–1914* (2004) all demonstrate wide erudition, and have opened up new avenues of inquiry into the ascent of the West, the role of industrialisation and conflict, and the contributions of empires. And many undergraduates have benefited from books such as Wolf's *Europe and the People without History* (1982) and the more recent textbook *Worlds Together, Worlds Apart* (2008) put together by Robert Tignor and his colleagues at Princeton University. Equally, world history has immeasurably enhanced our understanding of topics such as slavery, modern empires, the epidemiology of diseases, diasporic movements, the transfer of technologies, ecological change, commerce and trade, and the transmission of culture.

There is a now a considerable body of work to feast upon, the pick of which is as rich and satisfying as any history published in the last hundred years. Take, for example, Marshall Hodgson's *Venture of Islam.* A colleague of McNeill at Chicago before his untimely death in 1968 at the age of 47, Hodgson published posthumously a three-volume magisterial survey of Islamic civilisation from before the birth of Muhammad to the mid-twentieth century. *The Venture of Islam* (2011) succeeded spectacularly in countering what Hodgson saw as the western bias in world histories by locating Islamic civilisation within the extraordinary mix of other cultures with which it came into contact.

It is difficult to choose from among the works comprising the historiography of slavery, but David Brion Davis' *The Problem of Slavery in Western Culture* (1966) is a quite wonderful comparative survey of how slavery was viewed from antiquity to the 1770s. The field of the history of empire has also benefited greatly. Some time before his history of the modern world, Bayly published an account of the reconstitution of the British empire following the loss of the American colonies. Brief and speculative, *Imperial Meridian* (1989) is bursting with ideas about how this episode can only be understood in the context of a world crisis during 1780–1820, and repays careful scrutiny.

So what does this new genre offer? One of the most powerful features of world history is the challenge it poses to ways in which the West has been foregrounded in dominant historical narratives. By locating the West in the context of Afro-Eurasia as a whole, we begin to understand more fully its complex trajectory, and simultaneously accord space to other world powers and peoples. As we have seen, Wolf's *Europe and a People without History* was a sustained critique of western centrism, but the most powerful assault was launched by Marshall Hodgson, who had not only published the *Venture of Islam* but pioneered world history. Using examples from cartography and the status of Greenwich Mean Time, he argued that the West has dominated notions of geographical space and time (Hodgson 1993). How did this come about? Of course, the West actually did ascend to world dominance, but equally important was the story it told of its own rise to power. According to this narrative, the history of civilisations began in Egypt and Mesopotamia, that is, the East, but then passed successively to ancient Greece and Rome, and Christendom of northwestern Europe where medieval and later modern life developed. During this time, the torch of science was temporarily held by Islamic civilisation until it was rightfully assumed by Europeans. It is true that China, India and Japan also had important civilisations, but they were on the margins of world history and contributed even less than Islam to the modernising impulses of Europe. Africa is not even mentioned.

We must locate the history of these civilisations with greater precision. Until 200 years ago the vast majority of the world's population lived in the Afro-Eurasian landmass. Conventionally this is seen to comprise Europe, the Middle East, India and the Far East, each of which developed autonomously, but in fact they were secondary groupings fused together in a single complex of economic and cultural development promoted principally by trade and diasporic movements. Well into the Middle Ages, Europe, which appeared as little more than a north-westerly outpost to Eurasia, played a peripheral and backward role, evident in the fact that the flow of learning was overwhelmingly from the 'East', something we saw in Chapter 7 when comparing the relatively puny library belonging to Bede in the sixth century with contemporaries from the Islamic world. But Europe was on an upward march, in part through the use of weapons technology, navigation and ships which had originated in China and the Islamic world. At the cusp of the modern era – roughly the long eighteenth century – power was distributed among these three powers. There was no inevitability to the eventual rise of the West to dominance; it was a process dependent on the common conditions which had underpinned Eurasian culture, and which were now beginning to break down.

We must therefore distinguish the history of the West from word history. 'Just as an understanding of the history of Europe cannot be reduced to the history of England because industrialisation first developed there, so the history of the world cannot be reduced to the history of the West, because industrialism first spread there' (Wolf, 1997, p. 2010). The West was one region among others and in premodern ages was distinctly peripheral to the main contours of historical development. Even now it does not define the modern world. Instead of posing the dichotomy of 'East' and 'West', therefore, historians should find ways of thinking about interregional exchanges and mutualities. This is not merely a matter of geography, for such a project also requires that they address anew the question of periodisation which has been largely defined by the western experience. When, in other words, was the medieval, the premodern, or even the modern?

These are some of the important questions addressed by Dipesh Chakrabarty in *Provincializing Europe* (2000). His argument is that the so-called European age yielded to other global powers sometime toward the middle of the twentieth century, and the idea that the European experience can somehow stand for a universal human history no longer obtains. Important though Europe was to the development of the modern world and concepts such as citizenship, the state and human rights, Europe cannot be seen as a unity, nor in isolation from the non-European world. We need, therefore, to talk of different Europes with different historical trajectories, each of which had a distinct relationship to the colonised world. The imperial experience was integral to the genesis of the modern world, and therefore it is necessary to trace carefully the genealogies of those ideas which have framed modern societies. This does not mean a rejection of all things European, such as modernity, liberalism, science and reason, but rather a recognition of the necessity to 'provincialise Europe'. Without an understanding of its elements and their relationship to regions of the non-European world no longer seen as subordinate, our grasp of the complex totality of world history will remain skewed and unreliable.

In practice

Whatever sort of global history is being written, the task is not a simple one, nor one for the faint hearted. Traditionally, an historian is trained to be a specialist, or soon becomes one as a means of carving out a niche in what is a competitive market. Global or world history confronts this tradition in a direct way, for it requires the historian to transcend such limitations by thinking on a much wider canvas. It is possible to write a history of Britain, for example, without venturing beyond its shores. But this would be an insular and impoverished history. 'What do they know of Britain', inquired Rudyard Kipling, 'who only Britain know?' Given that the rise of Britain to world power happened because it was able to dominate other countries and at the same time defeat its imperial rivals, means that any self-respecting history needs to take account of those relationships, and that in turn requires detailed study of the histories of other countries.

Quite apart from the sheer scale of such a venture, certain problems arise which can only be alluded to briefly here. To write an account of the relationship to another culture, it is necessary to understand how the culture works not from the perspective of an outsider, but from the inside. This in turn requires some knowledge of other languages, thus providing access to archival sources. To illustrate the point, consider Britain's colonisation of India. It would be possible to write a top-down history of how Britain imposed its rule, but it would be highly skewed. Britain was never able to exercise complete authority; it had therefore to enter into dialogue with individuals and sections of Indian society. How that dialogue worked depended in part upon how Indians themselves viewed the occupation of their country by a foreign power, how they viewed attempts to interfere with their own ancient customs, rituals and beliefs. Some of these responses may have appeared in English, but even here without an appreciation of the codes, philosophies and histories that shaped them, our understanding is impoverished.

The promise of world history, however, is considerable, so that if we are prepared to put in the work and have the imagination, then the discipline of history may at last be able to shed the legacies of its founding impulses.

Summary

The three sections of this chapter have said three things:

- There is real promise in the study of global or world history. In many respects we live in an age of globalisation, for rarely has a single topic entered so pervasively into media commentary, or been able to mobilise so many people onto the streets around the world. It is hardly surprising under these circumstances that some historians have turned to the global as a means of better understanding the past and therefore the contemporary world. And yet ever since the past was chronicled there have been writers who have demonstrated a desire to move beyond their geographical and cultural boundaries to think more expansively about other, far removed cultures, and the interrelationships which propelled historical change. We saw that, in premodern periods, many of these were travellers who wrote detailed accounts of their experiences. Many of these were hugely popular and brought an awareness of other countries, civilisations and cultures to an eager public.

- The western nation state in the nineteenth century rose when history emerged as a discipline in its own right. Narratives charting the development of individual nations came to be accepted as part of orthodoxy, a marker of what proper research and writing was all about. And yet there remained historians wedded to global perspectives: Hegel, Herder, and to an extent Marx, were all acutely sensitive to the importance of a global imagination. What distinguished their work, however, was a use of evidence to illustrate the role of abstract categories as the driving forces of change. Freedom, progress and class struggle were erected as grand themes to help chart the unfolding of history over time.
- The cataclysmic events of the twentieth century compelled some writers to return once more to the matter of grand, overarching themes as a means of shedding light on human frailties. In their different ways, Spengler, Toynbee and Mumford addressed themselves to this problem by taking up the mantle of their nineteenth-century predecessors. In the aftermath of the Second World War, a number of path-breaking studies heralded an approach which eschewed grand narratives, instead placing stress on revealing the complex interrelationships that existed among different regions of the world as a more satisfying way of explaining change, whether of civilisations or of events which have had a profound impact on human affairs. In so doing, such accounts have displaced the centrality of the West evident in nationalist narratives, and forced onto the agenda previously marginalised world cultures.

Discussion document 1

The following is a brief extract from the writings of the great fourteenth-century Muslim traveller Ibn Battuta. It has an approach and a style which is surprisingly modern – it probably would not be out of place among travel accounts published today. Few, however, would consider it a work of history. Having said that, although it is not a narrative of the past, it is informed by a deep sense of the histories of civilisations, by religions and places; much of which is enriched by a comparative perspective.

The great river Nile

The Egyptian Nile surpasses all rivers of the earth in sweetness of taste, length of course, and utility. No other river in the world can show such a continuous series of towns and villages along its banks, or a basin so intensely cultivated. Its course is from South to North, contrary to all the other great rivers. One extraordinary thing about it is that it begins to rise in the extreme hot weather at the time when rivers generally diminish and dry up, and begins to subside just when rivers begin to increase and overflow. The river Indus resembles it in this feature. The Nile is one of the five great rivers of the world, which are the Nile, Euphrates, Tigris, Syr Darya and Amu Darya; five other rivers resemble these, the Indus, which is called Panj Ab [i.e. Five Rivers], the river of India which is called Gang [Ganges] – it is to it that the Hindus go on pilgrimage, and when they burn their dead they throw the ashes into it, and they say that it comes from Paradise – the river Jun [Jumna or perhaps Brahmaputra] in India, the river Itil [Volga] in the Qipchaq steppes, on the banks of which is the city of Sara, and the river Saru [Hoang-Ho] in the land of Cathay. All these will be mentioned in their proper places, if God will. Some distance below Cairo the Nile divides into three streams, none of which can be crossed except by boat, winter or summer. The inhabitants of every township have canals led off the Nile; these are filled when the river is in flood and carry the water over the fields.

Upriver

From Cairo I travelled into Upper Egypt, with the intention of crossing to the Hijaz. On the first night I stayed at the monastery of Dayr at-Tin, which was built to house certain illustrious relics – a fragment of the Prophet's wooden basin and the pencil with which he used to apply kohl, the awl he used for sewing his sandals, and the Koran belonging to the Caliph Ali written in his own hand. These were bought, it is said, for a hundred thousand dirhams by the builder of the monastery, who also established funds to supply food to all comers and to maintain the guardians of the sacred relics.

Thence my way lay through a number of towns and villages to Munyat Ibn Khasib [Minia], a large town which is built on the bank of the Nile, and most emphatically excels all the other towns of Upper Egypt. I went on through Manfalut, Asyut, Ikhmim, where there is a berba with sculptures and inscriptions which no one can now read – another of these berbas there was pulled down and its stones used to build a madrasa – Qina, Qus, where the governor of Upper Egypt resides, Luxor, a pretty little town containing the tomb of the pious ascetic Abu'l-Hajjaj, Esna, and thence a day and a night's journey through desert country to Edfu.

Ibn Battuta, *Travels in Asia and Africa 1325–1354*, translated and edited by H. A. R. Gibb (1929). Available at: www.fordham.edu/hallsall/source/1354-ibnbattuta.

Discussion document 2

This is a brief extract from C. A. Bayly's *Imperial Meridian*. The book is a study of the period 1780–1820, so it hardly qualifies as the sort of history of the world written by Toynbee. But it is a world history because it demonstrates the global nature of the crisis that beset these decades. Specifically, it focuses on the problems faced by Britain following loss of the American colonies, and the solution it found in the turn to India and the establishment of imperial rule there. But, he argues, these were revolutionary decades, and so the crisis experienced by Britain has to be placed in the context of global turmoil. The extract charts the extraordinarily wide ranging and unexpected course of events which followed the state's attempt to solve the financial deficits of the East India Company, which simply could not be allowed to fail given its importance to the economy as a whole. It serves well to illustrate in action the global interconnections and linkages which world historians are determined to reveal.

All the same, the interlocking effects of the imperial crisis did tie some parts of Britain's overseas enterprise together in new ways. The lines for advance during the next round of international war and conflict were laid. In a global historical perspective, the development of the China trade after 1783 was scarcely less important than the independence of the United States. Government needed to repair its battered finances by plugging gaps in excise revenue caused by smuggling and evasion. It also needed to bail the East India Company out, now that its growing United States market was forfeit to the New England merchants. The result was the 1784 Commutation Act which had momentous consequences throughout Asia. By reducing the duties on China teas from 120 per cent to 12.5 per cent, the British government strengthened its own tax base and bailed out the Company by stimulating a vast rise in tea imports. Increased tea imports to the UK and Ireland, in turn, gave a further boost to sugar sales (and incidentally to the slave trade). It also forced India to produce and sell much more raw cotton to China and laid the foundations for the opium trade. For the Chinese would not yet take significant quantities of British manufactured goods (as Macartney's 1792 Embassy to Peking was dismally to show).

Further consequences followed. Bombay grew rapidly and the possibility of war for trade with the Marathas who controlled the cotton-growing areas of Gujarat increased. It also became profitable for the first time to bring central Indian raw cotton down the Ganges to Calcutta for export to China. So a whole range of peasant producers and small towns between inland India and Bengal was galvanised into production and the economic foundations of British rule in central and upper India were laid. Finally, the need for an entrepôt on its China trade route encouraged the East India Company to bid for Penang on the Malay coast. This was to be the harbinger of Britain's growing stake in the Indonesian Archipelago and the China coast.

A simple accounting of the destination of British exports and the origin of imports before and after the 1783 watershed will not illuminate these important developments in the history of empire and international capital. For the foundations of Penang was an event in the history of Chinese overseas enterprise as much as British. If there was continuity over the boundary of 1783, however, it was in the onward roll of international conflict. For the Eurasian wars to redivide the world's resources intensified once again after 1793. Not only did plague, poor harvest and the abrupt redirection of trade routes intensify the conflicts between states, but the cumulative effect of the crisis on townsmen and peasants over much of Eurasia brought about a remarkable convergence of movements of resistance, millenarian revolt and liberation. The Gallic Great Fear spread across Eurasia and America to merge with the moral panic of Asians convinced that religion and identity was in danger. It was against this background – the background of the first true world crisis since the Mongol invasion – that the British discovered the ideological and political will for a more vigorous world empire. It was then that those creole elites – in Ireland, Canada, Caribbean or India – which, as late as 1783 might have hoped for a future of profiteering outside the ambit of colonial governors and their taxation, moved more smartly into line.

C. A. Bayly, *Imperial Meridian. The British Empire and the World, 1780–1830* (1989), pp. 98–9.

Further reading

* *essential*

Marshall G. S. Hodgson, *Rethinking World History: Essays on Europe, Islam and World History* (1993).
A posthumous collection of essays by one of the pioneers of world history in which he argues lucidly and persuasively for the importance of a global history to an understanding of the West.

* **Georg G. Iggers and Q. Edward Wang**, *A Global History of Modern Historiography* (2008).
An ambitious book that examines historical thinking and writing from around the world since the late eighteenth century. Accessible and learned, but even at 400 pages plus, the coverage is spread a little thin.

Patrick Manning, *Navigating World History: Historians Create a Global Past* (2003).
This is not only a well-informed survey of the terrain of world historiography, but provides useful nuts and bolts guidance on how this complex field can be approached. To be consulted rather than read from cover to cover.

Michel-Rolph Trouillot, *Silencing the Past: Power and the Production of History* (1995).
A brief but brilliant study of world history, not in the form of a survey or critical reflection, but one that uses a concrete episode – the Haitian slave revolt – to demonstrate how Western historiographical power has operated to distort the record.

* ***Journal of World History***.
Edited by Jerry Bentley at the University of Hawaii, this is the official journal of the World Historical Association. Patchy at times, but essential reading for those who wish to keep abreast of the changing paradigm of world history.

Part 5

APPROACHES & DISCIPLINES

13 Visual and literary cultures

1 Ways of seeing: paintings, photographs and architecture
2 Film history and its conventions
3 Literature and its uses

Introduction

Visual cultures provide sources of historical evidence that can greatly enrich understandings of the past and as such are open to the methods that historians bring to evidence of all kinds: whether it be evidence that can be seen or evidence that is read. In the opening section we consider from these perspectives the roles of architecture, paintings and photographs in the making of historical narratives. Using the example of ecclesiastical history in the Victorian period we look at religious painting, the religiously inspired gothic revival that re-introduced Catholic forms of liturgical worship to churches in England and Wales, and the architecture that reflected these currents. Photography has provided us with other 'ways of seeing' historical evidence and we use the first and last media war – Vietnam – as an example of this. We see here how photography has an ability to mislead and dramatise. The second section discusses how film reflects society and culture but also how it intervenes in society and even changes it. In order to examine the tension between film reflecting history and changing it, we look at popular film, documentary and propaganda as legitimate subjects for the historian to interrogate. The final section takes as its focus the novel and how it too can hold up a mirror to society and as such may be worthy of examination, telling us something about our contemporary preoccupations with the past. By discussing the novel in this way we see how the boundaries of historical and purely fictional narrative have been blurred in ways that also provide both challenges and opportunities for the historian.

Section 1

Ways of seeing: paintings, photographs and architecture

As historians we should read visual sources as if they were written texts: as words or signs to be deciphered, understood and interpreted. Visual sources include paintings, photographs and architecture and are legitimate sources for historians to use on their own or as supplements to other more conventional sources. Places of worship, for example, are expressive ways of reading the past; that is, their stones or stained glass windows can be read in ways that chart change. One example is the *Sagrada Familia* (Church of the Holy Family) in Barcelona, which is an elaborate testimony to the uniqueness of its architect, Antoni Gaudi, and although uncompleted in 1926 when he was killed by a tramcar, it can be read as a Catalonian monument against the order and conventions of Spanish fascism and authoritarianism during the Civil War of the 1930s. Similarly, the architectural relics of the so-called 'Golden Age' in Spain, when Jews, Christians and Muslims lived all too briefly in harmony during the Middle Ages (eighth to eleventh centuries), tell a story in the very stones and bricks of Spain; the stylistic and cultural hybridity evident in the wondrous Cordoba mosque or the magnificent Santiago de Compostela cathedral in Galicia provide abundant testimony to the period.

Occasionally historians can derive as much from absent or hidden visual evidence as from those buildings that remain standing; structures that no longer exist or are dilapidated, or those that have been transformed beyond recognition, such as the synagogues in Cordoba or Teledo which were either turned into churches (like the Cordoba mosque) or usurped for other purposes. By noting where the synagogues of medieval Spain were sited, we soon learn that they are quite unlike the soaring majesty of the cathedrals or the mosques whose spires or golden domes express nothing if not confidence. The synagogues, in contrast, are located in twisted back alleys and only ask to be left alone. This visual evidence surely tells us as much as any fading written parchment or document.

If the Spanish 'Golden Age' of religious tolerance began with the Muslim invasion in 711 and ended with the expulsion of the Jews in 1472, then the Golden Age of culture in Spain was yet to begin. The Golden Age of literature, poetry, painting and print, however, is said to commence with the undisputed monarchy of Isabella and Ferdinand over a united Spain in 1479 (or else when Columbus 'discovered' the New World in 1492) and to end in 1700 with the demise of Charles II, the last of the Hapsburg monarchs. By that time, plunder from the New World had taken Spain to the top of the European pecking order until decline set in with the Treaty of the Pyrenees in 1659 and the end of the Franco-Spanish War. Castile, Aragon, the Muslim Kingdom of Grenada, and Portugal on the Iberian Peninsula together contributed to what most historians would agree to be a cultural rebirth. Here there are rich pickings for the historian. Writers such as Cervantes (d.1616) and Gongora (d.1627) also coincided with a boom in sculpture, classical architecture and painting. Added to the writings of Cervantes is the 'exuberance of the Baroque, the paintings of the Zurbarin,

Murillo, and El Greco, and culminating in a blaze of glory with the paintings of Diego Valazquez' (Sureda, 2008). According to Jonathan Brown in his *Painting in Spain 1500–1700* (1998), however, there is a contradiction in this explosion of culture. Spain had an enormous influence on Italy and the Netherlands (even after the formation of the Dutch Republic in the late sixteenth century), and it continued to keep a diplomatic presence in European courts. Yet, the political dominance of much of Europe did not extend to the dominance of European culture. Rather the opposite; as Jean Sureda has argued, the existence of Spanish culture during this time was hardly acknowledged until the period was very nearly over. This raises a question that we shall return to throughout: what precisely is the link between visual culture and literature and the historical context that can be said to have given it life?

How then can we use visual (and in Section 3, literary) sources such as these examples from Spain? How can we take account of the presence, indeed the sometimes loud and obvious presence, of the spire and the golden dome, yet at the same time take stock of the absence of this type of evidence – the synagogue built below the skyline, often sunk beneath ground level and away from the main thoroughfare, constructed almost surreptitiously and now all but erased from history? This chapter will be concerned with just these types of questions in the areas of architecture and paintings but also photographs (maps remain part of the subject matter of Chapter 15). Clearly we face a choice about how we deploy visual sources: either as a 'snapshot' or 'mirror' held up to reality *or* as visual evidence that is, in the words of the historian Peter Burke, 'a system of signs or conventions' (Burke, 2007, p. 184) which the historian must unpick. Each approach, however, presents us with a different problem. Too often, it has been argued, historians have been content to settle on the former, to see visual evidence as simply evidence that reflects or illustrates reality. Here visual sources are minimised in importance, appended to the narrative as a way of giving life and colour to the more serious matter of the written text, but not used as evidence in their own right. Little attention is paid to critical analysis of how a source adds to our historical knowledge. There are, of course, exceptions to this rule. From historians working on the 'deep time' of pre-history, evidence such as the interpretation of cave paintings has been the only way to piece together a narrative, while objects such as the Bayeux Tapestry appear to tell the complete story of the Battle of Hastings in 1066, presenting an opportunity to place into context other complementary or conflicting evidence.

More profitably, visual evidence can be read as a series of signs: the portraits of a king or the photograph of an American Civil War battlefield are raked over for telltale symbols of everyday life and mores. The dress and deportment of a leader – from the posture of Elizabeth I to Mussolini, the Italian fascist leader, jogging bare-chested – tell us everything we needed to know, it would seem, about femininity and masculinity in their clothes, posture or deportment at these very different historical moments. Or about class: the aristocracy in photographic portraits tended to steer their gaze away from the camera while the working class or the poor look straight down the lens. There is then more to visual sources than the opportunity to bolster an historical narrative researched in conventional ways. Historians need to peel away the layers to reveal a story to be told.

If visual sources were indeed enough to make a history, then we could tell the story of twentieth-century totalitarianism by simply looking at or examining its built environment. From the plans of Albert Speer for a new Berlin – Germania – that would in all its classical glory have at its centre a great hall which could accommodate 180,000, and the return of Italian fascism to imperial Rome for its own architectural inspiration, or the Soviet Union's expression of modernity in the planned monument to Lenin and an underground system of trains that ascetically rivalled the interior of any western opera house we can learn much about the mindset of the various authoritarian regimes.

Visual images

As an introduction to some of the ways in which images have been used to shed light on historical episodes, consider Marcus Wood's *Blind Memory* (2000), which explored the visual representation of slavery in Britain and the United States over 1780–1865 (when the slave trade was finally abolished in America). Wood argued that despite the fact that much of the vast historiography of slavery uses images, these are rarely subject to the close critical reading employed on written sources. Maybe, he reasoned, this is because there abides a questionable belief that pictures speak for themselves, or that only a tiny proportion of this imagery can be thought of as high art. To overcome this neglect, he embarked on an analysis of oil paintings, rough wood cuts, graphic satire, photographs, book illustrations and advertisements, all of which helped to represent the slave trade, the enslaved and the enslavers. From the outset, however, he faced a dilemma: can art which attempts to describe horrors such as slavery be understood using aesthetic criteria? His answer is yes, but there are limits, for the actual experience of those enslaved stays beyond our comprehension for ultimately the imagery was created by whites.

Harriet Beecher Stowe's *Uncle Tom's Cabin* is included in the case studies. The book appeared in 1852, and has been regarded as one of the most significant and popular statements on slavery. Wood is interested in how the power of the novel was 'drowned in a visual rhetoric of colossal vulgarity' (p. 143), that is, how the illustrations helped to convey representations of black slaves in ways which were more telling than the written text itself. Indeed, the imagery transformed the book, and in so doing provided genuine insight into how English and American audiences wished to remember slavery, and how it shifted the language of racism in the mid-nineteenth century.

These stories cannot simply be told with visual images and must instead take account of other evidence and more generally evoke a wider historical context. This does not mean, however, that we forsake visual evidence as we shall find out now when we look at the uses church historians have made of architecture or the built environment.

Architecture

But first we need context. The Church of England faced four important challenges between the conclusion of the French wars in 1815 and the First Reform Act of 1832: their churches were located for the most part in rural areas while the population increasingly lived in cities; dioceses were often large and unmanageable and their finances were poorly balanced. Lastly, the governance of the state church lacked adequate representation by Anglicans because the liberalising Whig reforms of the 1820s had eased restrictions on those non-conforming Protestants such as Methodists who were not members of the Church of England, the 1829 Catholic Emancipation Act had brought Catholics within the pale of the constitution, and the great reform of 1832 boosted middle-class representation. Together these constitutional reforms widened the class and religious composition of Parliament so that the legislature was no longer the exclusive domain of Anglicans. How then could the Church of England remain as an established church, a church of the state, when some of its lawmakers belonged to rival religious traditions? The answer was to rest the authority of the church, not on the state as had been the case since the Reformation, but instead on apostolic descent. This authority derived from the early church, that is, from Christ's Apostles, and the continuity of their ministry through deacon, priest and bishop. This necessitated in some measure a belief in the Catholic roots of the Church of England. If the reforms of the 1820s and 1830s were a response in part to the problem of an increasingly urbanised working class which was denied a voice and refused to attend church regularly, their unintended consequence was to remake an established church whose authority and popularity among the working class had long been undermined.

The reaction to these trends was reflected in the 'overlapping circles', as Paul Avis put it in his *Anglicanism and the Christian Church: Theological Resources in Historical Perspective* (2002), of the 'High' and 'Low' parts of the church which came to terms with initial objections to non-Anglican representatives sitting in Parliament and to a non-Anglican franchise that would increasingly elect its representatives on a non-sectarian and non-confessional basis. Before going any further, we should probably define what is meant by 'High' and 'Low' parts of the Anglican Church of England:

> ***High*: respect for the priesthood and the venerable nature of the church; emphasis placed on the apostolic succession; use of more Catholic forms of worship known as 'Ritualism'; maintenance of the founding 39 Articles or Tracts of the Church of England dating from 1562 that mark off Anglicanism from Catholicism but also have continuities with the pre-Reformation Roman Catholic church, known as Tractarianism; Marion devotion or worship of Mary as mother of Jesus.**
>
> ***Low* (or Evangelical): emphasis on the Word, the authority of the Scriptures and less on the priesthood and episcopacy or church hierarchy; preaching; personal piety and conduct; plain and more Protestant forms of worship with hymns and music favoured over ritual; conversion and the need to 'spread the Word'; Hell and eternal salvation; substitutionary atonement through the crucifixion of Christ; stern and serious belief organised around the principles set out by the Evangelical Alliance in 1846.**

In 1833 the reformed parliament attempted to pass the Irish Temporalities Act. This would reorganise the church in Ireland and support the training of Catholic priests at the Maynooth seminary in Ireland which at the time (from 1800) was part of the established Anglican Church. One result of this development was the formation of the Oxford Movement (also known as the Tractarians) in the 1830s which led directly, via the Cambridge Camden Society and the Church Union in the 1860s, to:

1. a long-running protest against an Erastian parliament; that is, a Parliament made up of non-members of the Church of England who could influence the governance of the established church; and
2. a Ritualist movement that wanted to return to more Catholic, pre-Reformation styles of worship.

These developments can be traced through ecclesiastical and secular architecture in particular the marked contrast between late-Georgian functionality reflecting practical use in an age when these religious disputes were largely absent, and Victorian aestheticism which was suffused with ideas and meaning related to internal turmoil within the church and which found expression in the architecture of chapels, churches and cathedrals.

The 'quest for reverence' by the established church promoted the building of new churches and the restoration of others which in their architecture and use of internal space represented a return to High Church traditions notable in the use of altar frontals, the lighting of candlesticks, wearing of surplices, and the separation of pews and benches. Thus Ritualism as a return to Catholicism placed importance on the role of liturgy, sacraments and priesthood, consistent with the High elements of the church.

Then in the nineteenth century came the revival of the gothic, which recalled a more spiritual, pre-industrial age and was thus regarded as the only proper form of architecture for a pious Christianity. Unlike the classical styles of the previous century, which reflected the pagan-inspired styles of Greek or Rome, the gothic was considered fitting for what was to be a period of church reconstruction.

The trend towards Ritualism, according to architectural historian Nicholas Pevsner (1903–1983), meant that 'medieval churches were naturally re-medievalized in the approved manner' in mid-nineteenth-century London and elsewhere; while classical churches were 'treated with remarkable respect' (Pevsner, 1998, pp. 40, 41). Classical architecture was characterised by horizontal order emphasised by the use of different columns – Doric, Ionic, Corinthian – and rounded arches. Domes were another feature and these were built to mathematical precision. Buildings in this style included St Paul's Cathedral in London, St Peter's in Rome and the White House in the United States. Gothic architecture, on the other hand, often emphasised the vertical and might include pointed arches, flying buttresses and lofty spires, and had been most evident in Northern France in the 1100s from where it spread across Europe. Unlike classical architecture, gothic buildings tended to strive for height and vertical emphasis and not for the symmetry and order of classical architecture. Furthermore, the surfaces of gothic buildings were often covered with an abundance of carvings, sculpture and detail. In earlier incarnations of the gothic such features as the 'triple lancet' windows were typical (three narrow, pointed arched windows in a cluster together), but in later gothic buildings, wide windows and stained glass were the norm. Most English cathedrals had extensive gothic sections, but typical buildings in this style included Chartres Cathedral in France and both Westminster Abbey and the Houses of Parliament in England, although the latter had a compromised English perpendicular.

Painting

Paintings are also cultural texts and therefore potentially important sources of historical evidence. They may be imaginative, but paintings possessed a language, sense of narrative and symbolism which reflected or challenged broader societal values. The task of the historian is to read paintings as a means of revealing precisely how they operated to create meaning for the audience. To pursue these ideas, consider the important body of work which was produced at the time of the industrial revolution. What kind of records were these paintings? Were they reliable records of the experience, or did they attempt to express either the sense of wonder or horror which greeted the industrial revolution? Did, for example, the landscape of industrialisation with its fearsome and noisome machinery pumping out black, fetid pollution evoke feelings of awe and terror in the same way that human beings would once have responded to the power and might of nature? And how far can we go in suggesting that the idea of an industrial revolution was actually constructed through its representations? In other words, have we understood the industrial revolution, not through the data collected by economic historians (as we will see in Chapter 17), but through the more evocative images (and text-based reportage for that matter) that accompanied it?

The imagery of industrialisation was explained in magisterial detail by the art historian Francis Klingender (1907–55) who in his *Art and the Industrial Revolution* (1972) com—prehensively recorded the rise of industry in its expressive aspects. From John Constable and his painting of the *Chichester Canal* in 1828, to J. M. W. Turner's painting *Rain, Steam and Speed* (1844), which terrifyingly portrayed a new-fangled steam train at full throttle (perhaps at 30 miles per hour), or the science-based paintings of a prominent member of the Birmingham-based Lunar Society of scientists and industrialists, Joseph Wright of Derby, to the nightmarish visions of 'Mad' John Martin who sketched industry on a biblical scale as a vision of Hell, it is clear that artists responded in very different ways to the new age of industry and science, and from these responses we can gain insight into some of the hopes and anxieties of the nation as a whole.

Less obvious as a portrayal of the impact of the smoke stacked and 'dark satanic' image of the industrial revolution was the work of the late-Victorian Pre-Raphaelites. Founded in 1848, the Pre-Raphaelite Brotherhood painted in vivid colour and detail, seeking a return to the simple styles of the Italianate painters of the early fifteenth century, that is, before the painter Raphael. They often chose historical subjects and as such might be useful as a reflection of the manners and concerns of their day. Take, for example, *Convent Thoughts* by Charles Allston Collins, which was painted in 1851 (reproduced as Discussion Document 2). Collins was not strictly speaking a member of the Brotherhood but he was close enough to a prominent Pre-Raphaelite, Sir John Everett Millais, for this painting to be considered a solid example of the more gothic phase of the Pre-Raphaelites – part of the same gothic revival that we discussed in the section on architecture. The initial task is to ask what the source is about. It shows a Nun holding a passion flower which symbolised the crucifixion of Christ. One hand holds a book (the *Annunciation*) that also reveals other religious images, her finger notably keeping open a page of the illuminated manuscript at the *Annunciation*, when an angel visits the Virgin Mary. The garden is walled or enclosed and lilies float on the clear water – another symbol of Marion devotion. Its frame also has semiotic value which can be decoded to reveal more about the symbolism of the whole. Ornately decorated, it carries the Latin inscription 'As the lily among the thorns', taken from the Song of Solomon, and this provides us with some sense of the biblical roots of the painting's conception.

We would need to know more about the genesis and development of the painting itself, to understand its context. It was begun in 1850 outside Oxford at Botley and the flowers were painted in the garden of Thomas Combe in Walton Street. Combe was a notable supporter of the Brotherhood. We also know about the model, the costume worn by the model and the anxiety of the painter to emphasise the open book. How then could we possibly conclude that the painting's real object was industrialisation and a protest against industrialisation? The Pre-Raphaelites had a similar sense of retrospect, bemoaning a society that was now in every aspect mechanical. In this sense, while the painting features no direct evidence of a concern with the industrial revolution – there is not a factory in sight – it is concerned with what Thomas Carlyle knew to be the mechanisation of head and heart and what the Brotherhood believed to be the mechanisation of art, and as such cannot be divorced from the industrial revolution and reactions to industrialisation that were going on all around them. Paintings then can be sources for historians to use as much as the reading of buildings.

Photography

Although Pre-Raphaelite paintings appear to have been rediscovered in the mid-1960s, Raphael Samuel reflected in *Theatres of Memory* (1994) on the extent to which social historians of his generation neglected visual evidence, particularly photographs. Social historians were thus more inclined to ignore photography as adornments to other, more conventional sources. Only with the trend towards 'history from below' did photographs become anything other than adornments to text-based commentaries. In a landmark article by Alex Potts in the *History Workshop Journal* (1988), the disjunction between the 'visual language' used to describe Victorian London and the way it was reported in newspapers and the like was explained. Now historians such as Lynda Nead in her *Victorian Babylon: People, Streets and Images in Nineteenth Century London* (2000) routinely use visual culture as part of their work, including photographs with advertisements, for example, treated as primary sources.

Historians need to be aware of the different uses to which photography has been put. Many photographs of 'ragged', 'shivering' children on the streets of Victorian London, for example, were faked. Used by charitable organisations as a means of raising money, they were actually the result of children hauled into a photographers' studio to pose as 'Street Arabs'. Contrast these with the photographs of a British soldier who in 1945 captured for a generation the horror of Bergen Belsen concentration camp.

Photography then is not the simple recording of a factual subject. It is just as open to manipulation as any work of art and its provenance is every bit as significant. The art critic John Berger wrote *Ways of Seeing* (1990) in the wake of a 1970s television programme and was heralded as a path-breaking responder to Lord Clark's magisterial but more traditionally minded television series *Civilization: A Personal View* (2005). Berger made it clear that how we see things is critically influenced by what we already know and what we already believe. For Berger, photography in particular had irrevocably changed our perspective. Unlike say a portrait that stands staring at us and us at it, there was now a facility for the camera to subvert previous constraints of time and space by constantly changing angle. There was no longer a static centre to our gaze but a centre that moved.

Now, it is true that styles of painting such as Impressionism and Cubism sought to confront the relative lack of mobility of paintings but with photography came the ability for paintings to be photographed and looked at in close detail, or one part of a painting to be juxtaposed with an other, or even another image introduced altogether. This ability to reproduce photography challenged the mystique of art based on its originality or uniqueness. All this posed questions for the historian of photography or for historians who wanted to use photography as evidence – historians such as Susan Sontag (1933–2004).

Take, for instance, the astonishing photography of the Vietnam War. It has been estimated that around 58,000 Americans were killed in the decade from 1963 and close to

2 million Vietnamese. The conflict was played out on a domestic front with American culture producing approximately 750 novels, 250 feature films, 100 shorts and nearly 1500 personal recollections of one sort or another. The war, or at least a popular notion of the war, was thus created in many senses through its representations, which included photography.

Photographers did not simply record the horror of Vietnam but in many ways also were combatants; certainly in how it was being fought at home but also in the price they paid for their proximity to the fighting. Reporters were given free access to the conflict in a way that is now unthinkable, and in the process many of them lost their lives including Britain's Larry Barrows and America's Robert Capa. One war photographer who survived and whose extraordinary work remains for the scrutiny of the historian is Don McCullin, whose book *Sleeping With Ghosts* (1996) reveals the power but also the limitations of a history of war using photographs. A review of the book probably summarises the shortcomings of this recollection of a career in conflict photography:

> **McCullin doesn't shoot propaganda photos; in fact, his purpose is to show the horror of the conflict. But the nature of the job determines the side he shoots from. He is there for the duration of the assignment, and then goes onto the next one. He photographs some of the most political moments in history, but the nature of the job requires disconnecting the politics, and the images of them, from the politics which produce them.** (Bacon, 2006)

So, like our discussion about architecture and paintings as evidence, it seems, not unsurprisingly perhaps, that photography as a source also needs context. In this instance, we can discern that there are questions to be asked about the composition of the photographs and in fact there are accusations that the photographs appear to be 'over composed' (Bacon, 2006). There is also concern expressed in the case of McCullin that he got too close to the American soldiers and that the camera's perspective is from the side of the Americans. Conversely, there might be an argument that he is too detached, with war treated merely as a landscape, like his beloved Somerset in England's West Country, where he retired, or the urban landscapes of his impoverished London youth. In either case we need to know context and, as with a painter, something of the life and background of the photographer.

Section 2

Film history and its conventions

It might be argued that we can tell the story of the West through film. *Shane* in 1953, for example, drew on a real historical incident, the Wyoming's Johnson County War, and its director George Stevens witnessed real death and destruction in the Second World War when he made a documentary of the D-Day landings. Or Anthony Mann's 'psychological' Westerns of the same period which are full of post-war angst and damaged heroes, through to the more realist accounts of Clint Eastwood's *Unforgiven* in the 1990s or the first 20 minutes or so of *Saving Private Ryan*, which once again takes us back to the grim triumph of the Normandy beaches.

Film history as a sub-genre has displayed increased sophistication in dealing with film as historical evidence. Studies such as the 1969 collection *Film and the Historian*, John Grenville's *Film as History: the Nature of Film Evidence* (1971), Raymond Durgnat's *A Mirror For England: British Movies from Austerity to Affluence* (1970) and Jeffrey Richard's *Visions of Yesterday* (1973) have been particularly significant. How, therefore, can film be read in this way? Take, for example, *Dances with Wolves*, a feature film directed by and starring the well-known Hollywood actor Kevin Costner in 1990. This is a story about a Union Army Officer, Lieutenant John J. Dunbar, who, injured in a US Civil War battle, finds himself posted to the western frontier. Here he encounters and befriends his Sioux neighbours. In some ways the film recalls *Little Big Man* starring Dustin Hoffman made some 20 years earlier. *Little Big Man* recounts the story of Jack Crabb who at well over 100 years old is interviewed by an oral historian about his life among the indians, his encounters with General George Armstrong Custer and his role as a scout at Little Big Horn. Both films discuss and stress the humanity of a people transformed – annihilated on occasion – by the invasion of another (European) civilisation and how this common humanity is unrecognised by the conquering power. *Dances with Wolves* therefore testifies to a post-Vietnam, post-Cold War sensitivity in late-1980s America to the role and place of minorities when faced with overwhelming power. This is symbolised by the stark warning given by Dunbar to the tribal elder, Kicking Bird, when he warns that the white man will invade the land in 'numbers like stars'. In *Little Big Man* the tribe are not Pawnee or Sioux but are called simply 'human-beings'; one member is openly homosexual and all, even the elders, are sexually active, demonstrating their basic humanity and 'sameness' to us, although 'we' do not always live up to the label 'civilised'.

Each film was a product of its time. No matter how realistic the buffalo hunt was in *Dances* or the encounter that Hoffman's character, Crabb, has with the almost mythical figure of Custer in *Little Big Man*, neither film can tell us about the American West. As such they are not historical sources. They might, however, say something about American attitudes to imperialism and liberal multiculturalism in the post-war period, and the folk memories of the West that survived in American society and culture.

In a similar way, David Lean's adaptation of the Charles Dickens classic *Oliver Twist*, made by a politically conservative director at the height of the Labour Party's power in 1948 when the modern welfare state was coming of age, says something about contemporary attitudes in post-war Britain. 'Please, Sir, I want some more', a plea from Oliver for a second helping of food, had a particular resonance when shown in the austerity of the period. It is a source, therefore, that can only reproduce an almost mythic idea of Victorian England but in so doing may say something about attitudes to Victorianism in the post-war period.

Documentaries and news coverage have, on the face of it, no such problems of interpretation and analysis. Surely we are simply watching events unfolding, unadulterated and straightforwardly. Of course, this is rarely the case. Pathé News was a prominent voice in a range of media. After expanding to London in 1902 it continued to appear in cinemas until 1970, accumulating 3500 hours of filmed history amounting to over 90,000 individual items, all of which is now available online and provides a wonderful resource for analysis of the genre (www.britishpathe.com). While the newsreel is, of course, invaluable as a primary source we as historians have to decide its purpose, its audience and, in its selection of material, what it wished to convey. Most of all we have to determine, in both documentaries and newsreels, when 'fact' becomes the manipulation of fact; in short, when it becomes propaganda.

Leni Riefenstahl's *Triumph of the Will* is probably the most notorious of propaganda films. It was an account of the Nazi Party congress in 1934, and clearly sets out to celebrate German power and the role of Hitler as its great leader and saviour. It begins in the clouds as Hitler's plane begins its descent to the ground accompanied by the strains of Wagner. Above all, its use of aerial photography, telephoto lenses and the clever movement of cameras, reminds us of the importance of symbols and images. As Riefenstahl intercuts the main players such as Hitler and Hess, the use of angles and close-ups make it a classic of the genre and above all technically and artistically advanced. We should, therefore, be routinely sceptical about documentary film as an historical source, treating it as we would any other text.

The documentary film has probably been most utilised by historians concerned with the Second World War, and has been studied by Anthony Aldgate in *Britain Can Take It* (2007). The title comes from a short propaganda film, *London Can Take It* (1940), which was made under the inspired direction of Humphrey Jennings, a documentary filmmaker and a founder of Mass Observation, using much newsreel footage of the Blitz. The film, which was intended principally for an American audience as a means of persuading them to join the war, depicted a determined people stoically facing down a cruel enemy. This should be considered against the Mass Observation archive at www.massobs.org.uk/index.htm, which suggests evidence of mass hysteria among the population, and the presence of criminality, greed and selfishness – a very different picture from the received idea of wartime Britain as a plucky, united and determined nation.

Perhaps the most notable film dealing with Britishness during this period is Michael Powell and Emeric Pressburger's *The Life and Death of Colonel Blimp* (1943). Funded by the government, it polemically warns against the complacency generated by victory in the First World War, evident in the traditions of the military and Allied procrastination at a moment of total war when the British faced a vicious enemy. The film opens with a war game staged between two sides made up of British soldiers. When one side cheats the eponymous hero of the film, Mayor General Clive Wynne-Candy, is outraged. His reaction makes clear that veterans of 1914–18, and battles before that, have not realised that the arrival of the Nazis in modern European conflict means that the 'rules of the game no longer apply'. Subliminally, perhaps, the message was also conveyed that the 'rules of the game' would also apply to domestic politics in the post-war world. In a flashback, our hero is seen as a young military man, a career soldier, on leave from the South African war, being sent to pre-war Berlin to refute German 'lies' or propaganda regarding alleged British atrocities in South Africa. Here amid the nationalist fervour of a beer hall, he fights a dual with the Prussian Theo Kretschmar-Schuldorff, played by the actor Anton Walbrook, using all the ritual associated with Prussian military prowess. Both men are wounded but become friends, giving us a sense of a shared European civilisation which is not broken (at least by the British) after the devastation of the First World War. Post-war his friend becomes estranged, however, threatening as a disenchanted German to drift towards the Nazi party before finally returning to Britain seeking sanctuary (he had been imprisoned there during the previous war) determined as a good German to oppose the Nazi onslaught on his country. This storyline is instructive in that it attempts to describe the British to themselves and also to emphasise that the enemy they now face is different, infinitely more brutal and ruthless than anything Europe had hitherto faced. It also prepared the ground for the post Second World War message that although every Nazi was a German, not every German was a Nazi.

Film – documentary or feature – gives us a sense of context, a way in which historians can better understand a period or historical moment. A case study that will make this point well is the way in which film, at least some film, made during 'the sixties', is an example of counter-culture during this distinctive time of fundamental change (Chapter 2). Part of this new approach to art, of course, was film. In this sense film could both reflect the period under review and influence its development. We will look briefly then at two major films: *Saturday Night and Sunday Morning* (1960) and *Dr Strangelove or How I Learned to Stop Worrying and Love the Bomb* (1964).

Saturday Night and Sunday Morning was premiered in 1960 and immediately fell foul of both national and local censors (the English county of Warwickshire banned it because the main character appeared to enjoy the illicit sex portrayed). Directed by a central European Jew, Karel Reisz, and produced by the future producer of the Bond franchise, Harry Saltzman, it centred upon the life and times of a working-class character played by a youthful and then largely unknown but classically trained actor, Albert Finney, who played Arthur Seaton. Its screenplay was by an equally little known Alan Sillitoe, himself a working-class lad from Nottingham where the film was set. Seaton, a semi-skilled factory hand, looked with distain at the older men on the production line as defeated and cowered by the depression of the 1930s, and was motivated only by hedonism: 'everything else is propaganda'. *Saturday Night* in that sense was a faithful attempt at social realism (Sillitoe used his mother's house in Nottingham for some of the key scenes), and documented accurately the changing shape of working-class communities as a greater affluence began to take hold in the post-war period.

With a co-starring role for the glamorous Rachel Roberts, *Saturday Night* also proved to be an early source for the period in that its sexuality was both overt and dismissive of conventional family structures. The last scene proved especially provocative, with Seaton and Robert's characters lying on a grass plain on the edge of the city, planning an imminent marriage. With the building of a new housing estate in the background, symbolic perhaps of the coming of a new consumer age, Arthur throws a stone in its direction and off screen we can hear the sound of breaking glass. Finney reflected in an interview in 1972 that this was the first stone thrown in a future protest against consumerism and a materialist society. Reisz, on the other hand, saw it for what it was: surrender to domestication and the last gesture of a defeated rebel; particular and peculiar to this character in this film. Yet, the film can serve as a point of historical argument about the character or the meaning of 'the sixties' as a discrete period and as such should be noted as a clearly useful primary source that helps us to understand the 1960s *as* a period.

Dr Strangelove or How I Learned to Stop Worrying and Love the Bomb, released in 1963, is political in another sense and also frames much of what historians argue make up the counterculture of 'the sixties' as an epoch. Directed by Stanley Kubrick, it was described by him as a 'nightmare comedy'. Its anti-war message is conveyed by the multiple roles played by Peter Sellers as the dense RAF officer, as the mad scientist and Nazi refugee, and as the hapless President of the United States. Like *Saturday Night*, Kubrick's film has been presented as a leitmotif of the sixties. It resonates with the paranoia of a Communist plot to topple the free world, its Cold War rhetoric, its hope and despair surrounding the life (and then death) of a young President like Kennedy and, most of all perhaps, the realisation after the Cuban Missile Crisis that the plot, which ends with country music star Slim Pickins riding a nuclear warhead into oblivion, was not so far-fetched. Historians can treat this as a legitimate source because it reflects the machinations of the Cold War itself, both its advocates and detractors, even if they are portrayed as absurd. Indeed this very fact will give some sense to future historians how humour became a weapon of mass destruction for political or military figures who would have the general populace believe every last detail of Cold War propaganda.

The historian then must ask questions of film in the same way that questions must be asked of architecture, paintings and photographs. How, for instance, did film reflect processes of social and cultural change in Britain circa 1960? To what extent did film present an authentic picture of working-class life or international relations? What are the stylistic characteristics of sixties film that make them 'realistic'?

Since the 1970s film history has tended to converge with social history and therefore opened up new areas of inquiry (see Chapter 9). Thus writers have examined the process of filmmaking, the role of the studios, censorship and the state, and cinema exhibition. A good example of this new body of work is Sue Harper and Vincent Porter's *The Decline of Deference: British Cinema of the 1950s* (2003) which examined production and distribution of film, finance, the use of language and reception theory (what the audiences thought about these historical 'texts'). Some of these observations can be made of the historical novel.

Section 3

Literature and its uses

We wish to turn finally to the historical novel, which has formed an important element in how a wider public has imagined the past. When Watson and Holmes inadvertently meet in a City opium den called the Bar of Gold in Upper Swadham Lane, 'a vile alley lurking behind the high wharves which line the north side of the river to the east of London Bridge', we not only travel into London's back streets ('Between a slop-shop and a gin-shop') but journey downwards into its darker places, via a 'steep flight of steps leading down to a black gap like the mouth of a cave'. A respectable City man, Neville St Clair, has disappeared near this unsavoury house run by a 'rascally lascar', a 'man of the vilest antecedents'. Like the gothic-inspired *Mysteries of London* genre associated with the 1840s we are sucked into a place of darkness and danger and, like Tom Alone in Charles Dickens' *Bleak House*, the reader is reminded about how bad blood corrupts: 'There is a trap-door at the back of that building, near the corner of Paul's Wharf, which could tell some strange tales of what has passed through it upon the moonless nights' (Conan Doyle, 1891). The appearance of a trap door is, of course, familiar. It takes us back to mid-century melodrama, 'penny dreadfuls' that told, for example, of that Demon Barber Sweeny Todd who made his way between his shop in Fleet Street to his pie-making accomplice, Mrs Lovett, in nearby Bell Yard via an underground passage.

What then as historians are we to make of Sir Arthur Conan Doyle's story, *The Man with the Twisted Lip*, serialised in *The Strand Magazine* from July to December 1891? One reading would take note of this alternative layer of the City's economic life. Indeed, we know that many figures in the City lived a precarious existence – moving freely up and down the social scale. Many 'City men' straddled many types of existences and so this fictional story could tell us something about notions of identity in the period. Let us look in detail at the story as an example of how an historian might read such a text.

The hero of the short story, St Clair, moved to Lee in Kent as a gentleman who 'appeared to have plenty of money'. He bought a large villa and eventually married the daughter of a local brewer. And as a 'gentleman' he had no occupation. However, St Clair was said to be 'interested in several companies' and travelled into the City by train in the morning and returned by the 5:14 from Cannon Street every night. A man, it would seem, without any side and absolutely without problems. His wife makes an unplanned trip to the City on an errand and to do a little shopping (risqué behaviour unaccompanied by a man) until, like the stories that we associate with the *Mysteries of London* genre, she finds herself in a lesser-known part of the City. Glancing up at a window (of an opium den as it turns out) she glimpses her husband, who quickly jerks out of view. The police are called and so eventually is Holmes; one man that can make sense of the confusion and dangers of modern London. Save for clothing and a trickle of spilt blood leading down steps towards the perilous tides of the Thames, there is no sign of St Clair. Finally we learn that St Clair has taken 'employment' in the lucrative business of professional beggary, although in order to avoid the police regulations he pretends to a small trade in wax vestas (matches). Here, after changing clothes at his den in Great Swadham Street, he proceeds to Threadneedle Street: 'upon the left-hand side, there is, as you may have remarked, a small angle in the wall. Here it is that this creature takes his daily seat, cross-legged with his tiny stock of matches on his lap, and as he is a piteous spectacle a small rain of charity descends into the greasy leather cap which lies upon the pavement beside him' (Doyle, 1891). That the fictional St Clair 'could every morning emerge as a squalid beggar and in the evenings transform [himself] into a well-dressed man about town' stretches reality but by reading a fictional account about the 1890s that was written in the 1890s, we may identify a real, not fictional, anxiety about the nature of identity in this decade. As has been a constant refrain during the whole of this chapter, more context is needed to finally prove the point.

We have noted that this is far from a true account and is not intended to be true in any conventional sense. By looking briefly at the context provided by Ed Glinert in *A Literary Guide to London* (2000), it appears, not for the first time, that Doyle mistakes his London topography. Conan Doyle describes the streets and byways of London, but by following the movements of his characters we can deduce the true setting of the story. The true setting was apparently west of the bridge (not the east) around the recently demolished Paul's Wharf which was situated immediately south of St Benet's Church and St Paul's Cathedral.

It is a useful example for us to use as it makes us as historians ask questions about the boundary between history and literature.

The boundary is not rigid or well defined. Indeed, until the emergence of what we would consider historical writing in the nineteenth century, it was difficult to detect. Historical accounts were suffused with fictional elements such as narratives and conversations which were clearly the invention of the authors. With the emergence of historical writing and literature as genres, boundaries began to be drawn between them. This segregation was encouraged by the new disciplines of historiography and literary studies, both of which attempted to carve out particular niches for themselves. Not that this was entirely successful. While it may be said that in general historians used literary sources as a means of illuminating context, and literary scholars used historical context as a means of illuminating literary forms, there were those who clearly felt comfortable in both camps. Thus, fine studies such as Michael McKeon's *The Origins of the English Novel* (1987) and James Chandler's *England in 1819: The Politics of Literary Culture and the Case of Romantic Historicism* (1999) cannot readily be defined exclusively as history or literature.

Morag Shiach's *Modernism, Labour and Selfhood in British Literature and Culture, 1890–1930* (2004) provides us with the opportunity of exploring this further. Shiach's background is in literature rather than history, but she drew upon both. She was concerned to explore the nature of modern forms of labour, specifically with the ways it was experienced and represented in the period. The years 1890–1930 were chosen deliberately, for the period was coterminous with the moment of modernism when distinct forms of labour and notions of the self emerged. These issues may seem to be the provenance of the historian, and yet Schiach chose to chart the shifts which occurred by using primarily literary sources. What particular technologies, she asked, reshaped our understanding of labour and the self? How did writers and artists seek to capture and at the same time create such understanding? With these questions in mind, Shiach explored the writings of D. H. Lawrence, Sylvia Pankhurst and others to show that work came to define human individuality at the same time as more efficient work routines, new technologies and intense divisions of labour, most notable among women employed in the sweated trades, reduced the number of hours worked.

Something of this relationship between literature and history (at least apparent in its literary style and lavishness) can also be found in Orlando Figes' book on the Russian Revolution. It does not deny that historical truth is important or possible nor is its research based on the simple collection of facts despite what Michael Bentley has called its 'persuasive authenticity' (Bently, 2005, p. 160). Rather it told a good story and retained what Martin Weiner (1998) called 'literary characteristics', even if the story was based on sound knowledge of what happened in the past:

> **On a wet and windy morning in February 1913 St. Petersburg celebrated three hundred years of Romanov rule over Russia . . . The city bustled with sightseers from the provinces, and the usual well-dressed promenaders around the Winter Palace now found themselves outnumbered by the unwashed masses – peasants and workers in their tunics and caps, rag bundled women with kerchiefs on their heads. Nevsky Prospekt experienced the worst traffic jams in its history as trams and horse drawn carriages, cars and sleighs, converged on it. The main streets were decked out in the imperial colours of white, blue and red; statues were dressed in garlands and ribbons; and portraits of the tsars . . . hung on the facades of banks and stores.**

> **Above the tram lines were strung chains of coloured lights, which lit up at night with the words 'God Save the Tsar' or a Romanov double-headed eagle and the dates 1613–1913. Out-of-towners, many of whom had never seen electric light, stared up and scratched their heads in wonderment. There were columns, arcs and obelisks of light.** (Figes, 1997, p. 3)

It was a story told using literary devices: we are told about the weather, traffic jams, the street bunting and the decoration of the trams as people 'stared up and scratched their heads in wonderment', yet it is unmistakably a history and not fiction.

We can reveal more about the complex relationship between fiction and historical truth through a discussion of Simon Schama's *Dead Certainties* (1991), as it provides answers to questions that cannot be answered by conventional historical method and reflects on the process of how narratives are created. Like Figes, Simon Schama used literary devices. Let us first establish the 'plot' or rather the historical narratives as presented by Schama. He adopted two main storylines. The main narrative was the fate of General James Wolfe, killed in 1759 by the French in Quebec. Within this narrative there were sub-narratives that speculate on his demise, what Schama called 'the many deaths of General Wolfe'. Most notable, perhaps, one by these 'deaths' was recounted by a soldier using fictionalised dialogue. The second main narrative was an account of the murder by Wolfe's biographer, Francis Parkman, whose book published in 1884, *Montcalm and Wolfe*, ensued that Wolfe would be remembered as a national hero. Schama explained his approach:

> **Both the stories offered here play with the teasing gap separating a lived event and its subsequent narration. Although both follow the documented record with some closeness, they are works of the imagination, not scholarship. Both dissolve the certainties of events into the multiple possibilities of alternative narrations . . . These are stories then, of broken bodies, uncertain ends, indeterminate consequences. And in keeping with the self-disrupting nature of the narratives, I have deliberately dislocated the conventions by which histories establish coherence and persuasiveness. Avoiding the framing of time sequences supplied by historical chronologies, the stories begin with abrupt interventions – like windows opening suddenly – and end with many things unconcluded.** (Schama, 1991, pp. 320–1)

A third, minor, narrative concerned the representation of Wolfe's death in the famous painting in 1771 by the Anglo-American Benjamin West. All these stories, however, explored a 'border country' between fiction (what is made up) and history (what is constructed from evidence). This was very much in keeping with the close relationship between literature and history. In this sense *Dead Certainties* was of a piece with the new cultural history, discussed in Chapter 9, which was at a high point when the book was researched and written.

Dead Certainties offered multiple endings. This alone, perhaps, gives historians a boundary across which we dare not pass. We can, however, identify the detective elements that may characterise some forms of historical research and which link Sherlock Holmes' *The Man with the Twisted Lip* and *Dead Certainties*, suggesting very clearly how truth can be located in a number of different guises, even if the gathering of truth for an historian must be governed by agreed rules and approaches.

Bearing this in mind, historical novels, such as those by best-selling novelist Philippa Gregory, add context and spice to the study of history. Historical novelists weave their fictional storylines around historical events, thereby bringing them to life. In doing this they face accusations of inaccuracies or of being downright misleading. They can certainly be accused of undue simplification. Whereas it may be difficult to memorise a set of dates, and to work out the complicated relationships that existed in royal courts of old, it is easier to follow and remember a developing scandal, complete with the satisfying gossip that surrounds it, and to grasp the possible implications of such allegations or discoveries on an individual level, in a living, social context. This provides the readers of historical fiction with a basic scaffold on which to hang what they subsequently learn, as new knowledge which will fit into the time frame of the novel, or relate to its characters. Artefacts such as historical costumes, whether described by the novelist or recreated in a television or film adaptation, may also add something that is nevertheless basically factual. To take a very simple example, it may be difficult to remember the order and fate of Henry VIIIs' wives; it is much easier to remember how Anne Boleyn laboriously immersed herself into the king's life, how her teasing drove him to divorce or, more accurately, to repudiate the unfortunate but very dignified Catherine of Aragon. It is similarly simple to remember that Jane Seymour was seen as the quiet, gentle, modest antidote to Anne Boleyn's tempestuous legacy (however erroneous this view may have been). And so on with the rest of the wives.

Furthermore, in a historical novel, information is organised differently to most history narratives. Whereas history tends to focus more on 'themes', such as foreign policy, religion or the economy, a historical novel has the freedom not to be analytical, or to search for cause and effect over time, or anything else that historians may be looking for such as replying to the work of another historian. Rather, a novel can take pains to describe an everyday life where foreign policy, religion and the economy all mesh together, much as they do in reality. Or, indeed, where public discourse takes on the peripheral role which it does in most ordinary lives. In the genre of literature, a Tudor can shed history itself and stand in the present as a human being that once laughed and loved just like us.

Another quality of historical novels is that they give a voice to minor-league historical players. For example, *The Other Boleyn Girl* (one of Philippa Gregory's novels since made into a successful film) gave a voice to Anne Boleyn's sister. In so doing, Gregory was able to explore different relations in the Tudor court – those between two sisters vying for success and attention or those between Henry VIII and his mistresses (not only Mary Boleyn but also Bessy Blount, who bore Henry a son, among others), not to mention the power struggles of the country's leading families who were all trying desperately to thrust their young women into the king's bed (whether or not they were already married to other men, as was Mary Boleyn). So this is an engaging story that can reinforce the reader's suspicion that not everyone in the Tudor court was a Cranmer or a Wolsey, but that other, lesser-known figures played major roles in the formation of our history. These relationships also allow the author to explore some of the traditions and 'rules' of the Tudor court – for instance, a mistress of Henry VIII had to separate from her husband so that the king could be sure that the offspring – however illegitimate – was his.

It is important to bear in mind that historical novelists tend to take artistic licence with the facts, often by insinuating characters (fictional or factual) where they did not necessarily belong. Sometimes they point this out in a disclaimer, sometimes not. Gregory who is an escapee from academia has taken flack from this direction. Although historical novels can be invaluable in helping bring history to life, they must be weighed against more methodologically sound historical research – their purpose is, after all, to entertain more than to educate. Perhaps the greatest strength of the historical novel, however, is an ability to set alight the imagination, to prompt an independent search for more information about a specific event, personage or detail that especially captures the interest. As Gregory herself has said, 'The historian uses speculation to bridge between one known fact and another, the novelist uses the imagination to create a story which links all the facts' (www.philippagregory.com/category/debates). This is a controversial and dangerous contention for the historian but it is certainly one worth thinking about as we read, research and write. It is interesting to note, however, that historical novelists now make a point of researching the period in which they immerse their reader and as often as not provide their readers with a bibliography of historical sources.

We also have to understand that history and all the forms of visual and text-based evidence considered here – architecture, paintings, photographs and literature – are not in all times and all places easily differentiated. B. W. Ife, in *Reading and Fiction in Golden-Age Spain: A Platonist Critique and Some Picaresque Replies* (1985), looked at sixteenth-century vernacular poetry with its emphasis on romance, sentimentality and chivalry and found they were neither fictive nor entirely truthful; they were more like hybrid accounts that swept aside conventional boundaries of history and poetry. As such, it may be less controversial to say that the historical novel, like the verse-based epic that came out of Spain where we began the chapter, is capable of speaking its own truth.

In practice

As a discipline which emerged in the nineteenth century under the guidance of von Ranke, history has tended to rely almost exclusively on documentary evidence for its sources. For most historians, written documents are the most reliable to hand and thus provide the best access to the period under study. Belatedly, other sources broadly considered as visual are now treated with seriousness. Paintings, photographs, films and architecture are thus increasingly employed as legitimate sources of evidence. In certain respects this is surprising given that they are works of the imagination, and therefore not 'reliable' sources. And it is true that our techniques for reading them are little developed in comparison with those which are brought to bear on documentary evidence, and yet when used skilfully images have been able to shed important new light on historical episodes.

Take, for example, the architecture of churches, which arguably can reveal as much about religious power and struggle as tomes of doctrinal debate. In the premodern period when popular culture was overwhelmingly visual and oral, churches were extraordinarily powerful statements of authority. How was this authority expressed? Their size and height alone dominated the landscape for miles around, and thus churches remained as visual reminders of the presence of religious authority. But a more detailed reading of, say, the internal space of the church can reveal a great deal besides about how ecclesiastical power was exercised over the congregation gathered there. The nature of the profound religious tensions between Catholicism, Anglicanism and the various strands of Anglican non-conformity in Britain can also be beautifully elaborated by the style of their churches, and the ordering of space.

▶

In a similar way, paintings, fiction and films are works of the imagination which both reflect historical reality and create it. To be used as evidence, some tricky questions need to be asked of them which do not normally spring to the minds of historians. Who created them, and for what reason? What purpose did they serve? How did they work to create meaning? How were they read by the audiences? What, therefore, do they reveal about particular historical moments? A film such as *London Can Take It* may at first glance appear to be an accurate portrayal of how Londoners responded to the Blitz. It uses, for example, original documentary footage of the destruction. And yet it is clear that some of the scenes are highly staged, that the events are structured to tell a particular story which is emphasised by a narrator who happens to be American. Research reveals that the film was intended for an American audience, as a means of encouraging them to enter the war (it is said that in this respect the film was entirely successful, bringing forward US involvement by six months).

Such sources can greatly enhance historical understanding and imagination just so long as the appropriate skills of analysis are employed, and – importantly – they are always located firmly within particular historical contexts.

Summary

The three sections of this chapter have said three things:

- Architecture, painting and photography can be used by the historian in a number of ways. Visual culture can serve to underline a point already established by looking at more conventional historical sources or can be viewed as evidence that is open to historical analysis. Above all, provenance and context need to be established beyond reasonable doubt. In both architecture and art, the example of Victorian religion is used as an illustration of how context matters. The photography section is, perhaps, a little more sceptical about its uses for the historian and takes the example of photography of the Vietnam War to ask questions about how images were used during the conflict.

- Film – feature film, propaganda, home movie making and so on – can serve the historian but needs to be treated with caution. It focuses on social realism and the urge to depict reality as a way of tracing how different types of film work for the historian. By looking closely at *Saturday Night and Sunday Morning* (1960) and *Dr Strangelove or How I Learned to Stop Worrying and Love the Bomb* (1963) we made some headway in understanding how these films came to characterise 'the sixties' as a period of 'counter-culture'. Yet, we also found that this period was more than the sum of these otherwise excellent films and so once again were left wondering about the limits of sources. We certainly needed to understand a broad range of contextual knowledge about how these particular films came into being and whether they reflected society or, as is more likely, shaped it. The same rule would apply to the use of propaganda in history and its use to historians as evidence.

- Historical fiction exists on a different register to either of the previous topics in this chapter. Preoccupation with culture in literature and history has tended to make fiction writers more historically minded and historians more sensitive to the multiplicity of endings and narrative trails that fiction might open up. Thus we look at a work of fiction by Sir Arthur Conan Doyle and compare it with a history by Simon Schama, looking for ways that historical truths and historical inaccuracies can both be found in historical fiction and history itself. It also becomes apparent how each of these stories can be situated in a dominant narrative and that both the text and context of the source remains important to what historians do.

Discussion document 1

These extracts may give some indication of the social fears that were unleashed by the language employed by the gothic in fiction but which may well transfer to commentary that we would be pleased to regard as historical evidence. The first uses light and darkness as moral indicators while the second reveals a popular device at the time: the notion of the ancestral curse which itself, you may decide, is a commentary on contemporary society.

> Ye are fallen, said I, ye dark and gloomy mansions of mistaken zeal, where the proud priest and lazy monk fattened upon the riches of the land, and crept like vermin from their cells to spread their poisonous doctrines through the nation. . . . See how the pure light of heaven is clouded by the dim glass of the arched window, stained with the gaudy colours of monkish tales and legendary fiction; fit emblem how reluctantly they admitted the fairer light of truth amidst these dark recesses, and how they were debased in genuine lustre! The low cells, the long and narrow aisles, the gloomy arches, the damp and secret caverns which wind beneath the hollow ground . . . seem only fit for those dark places of the earth in which the habitations of cruelty. . . . Farewel, ye once venerated seats! Enough of you remains, and may it always remain, to remind us from what we have escaped and made posterity for ever thankful for the fairer age of liberty and light.

Anna Laetitia Barbauld, 'On monastic institutions' in *The Works*, 2 vols. (1825), ii. 195–6. Quoted in Robert Mighall, *A Geography of Victorian Gothic Fiction: Mapping History's Nightmares* (1999), p. 1.

> But he has his revenge. Even the winds are his messengers, and they serve him in these hours of darkness. There is not a drop of Tom's corrupted blood but propagates infection and contagion somewhere. It shall pollute, this very night, the choice stream . . . of a Norman house, and his Grace will not be able to say Nay to the infamous alliance. There is not an atom of Tom's slime, not a cubic inch of any pestilential gas in which he lives, not one obscenity or degradation about him, not an ignorance, not a wickedness, not a brutality of his committing, but shall work its retribution, through every order of society, up to the proudest of the proud, and to the highest of the high.

Charles Dickens, *Bleak House* (1853–4). Quoted in Robert Mighall, *A Geography of Victorian Gothic Fiction: Mapping History's Nightmares* (1999), p. 75.

Discussion document 2

Convent Thoughts, was painted in 1851 by Charles Allston Collins, a painter close to the Pre-Raphaelite movement. Treated as a document, it raises questions of Victorian social attitudes to religion and modernity and as such may be discussed from the point of view of the methodology needed to understand visual sources.

Source: Bridgeman Art Library Ltd: Ashmolean Museum, University of Oxford.

Further reading

* *essential*

John Berger, *Ways of Seeing* (1973).
A path-breaking response to Lord Clark's magisterial but more traditionally minded television series *Civilization* (1969). Influenced by the Marxism of Walter Benjamin, it looked at the importance and significance of the copy in modern representational imagery from the portrait to the advertisement. It is an argument and approach that historians would do well to understand.

* **Peter Burke**, *Eyewitnessing: The Uses of Images as Historical Evidence* (2001).
A book that does exactly what it promises; dealing with the problems and opportunities that visual culture as evidence presents to the historian. In this respect, it is invaluable.

Sue Harper and Vincent Porter, *The Decline of Deference: British Cinema of the 1950s* (2003).
Represents a significant breakthrough in the histories written about the influence of film on history as a discipline. This is because it focuses on the production and distribution of films, finance, the use of language and reception theory (i.e. what the audiences thought about these historical 'texts').

Francis Haskell, *History and its Images: Art and the Interpretation of the Past* (1993).
An authoritative if fairly conventional approach to art and its interpretation by historians.

14 Anthropology

1 Pens and pith helmets: the influence of anthropology on history
2 Functionalism and structuralism: understanding the Lord Mayor's Show
3 Myths and history: Jewish conspiracies and the 'blood libel'
4 The 'dying god': Captain Cook and ethnohistory
5 Microhistories: cheese, worms, night battles and ecstasies

Introduction

This chapter will begin by outlining the differences between anthropology and history before going on to explore the considerable areas of common ground between the two disciplines. The use of ritual in historical studies influenced a whole generation of historiography, especially apparent since the 1960s. In the course of the discussion in Section 2 we will look at how theories like functionalism and structuralism, so influential in anthropology, were understood by major historians such as Alan Macfarlane, Keith Thomas and Natalie Zemon Davis. The third section will examine the rich and fascinating universe of history and mythology within the framework of anthropology. The case study used here is the so-called 'blood libel' which across centuries and different cultures has maintained a myth that Jews require blood for their religious rituals. Anthropological approaches used by historians have gone some way in obtaining more sophisticated historical explanations for why this myth has enjoyed such extraordinary longevity. The common ground between anthropology and history includes the use of historical methods by anthropologists interested in ethnography that in turn has significant impact on how historians approach social and cultural history – a relationship that we find entwined in Section 4. Without sensitivity towards pre-literate societies such as those encountered in the anthropological writings about Captain Cook we would never have understood the full circumstances of his death. Finally, we will look at how microhistories, influenced by approaches associated with social anthropology seek 'to detect the large in the small'. Here the work of Carlo Ginzburg is recognised as especially significant.

Section 1

Pens and pith helmets: the influence of anthropology on history

Emma Crewe's *Lords of Parliament: Manners, Rituals and Politics* (2005) studied the cultural practices of peers in the British House of Lords: 'Most were mystified by why I was there, and some seemed displeased that I had done research in East Africa and South Asia, as though ceremonial robes of ermine (the winter coat of the stoat) [worn by peers on ceremonial occasions] should not be considered in the same light as those of fish skins, or feathers, or cowry shells and they were puzzled when I lingered on aspects that appeared to them to have little to do with politics' (p. ix). In the same way that anthropologists have understood their own societies by using insights gathered while investigating the lives, rituals and narratives of societies very different to their own, historians have applied the methods of anthropology in order to study another 'foreign country' – the past.

What is anthropology? With Greek roots – *anthropos* and *logos* – anthropology is concerned with 'the study of man', and yet there are a number of branches to anthropology; in this chapter we will deal with social or cultural anthropology. Social and cultural anthropology are often used interchangeably, while 'cultural anthropology' tends to be associated with American anthropology; both social and cultural anthropology studies non-western societies and peoples.

Put at its simplest, social or cultural anthropology is the study of societies that are considered to be either 'primitive' or 'complex'. (Quotation marks are used here because the terms 'complex' and 'primitive' are value-laden – 'complex' being somehow better than 'primitive'.) 'Primitive' may mean 'exotic' or can be used as a byword for pre-industrial societies and 'complex' may mean the study of behaviours or mythologies of a distinct group within industrial or 'advanced' societies. Occasionally we find anthropologists seeking to understand more about 'complex' societies by applying methods usually associated with the study of 'primitive' societies. Biological anthropology, on the other hand, is the comparative study of both humans and primates, and asks questions about evolution, genetics, physical growth and ecology.

While there is no succinct definition of what anthropology *is*, it does have methodologies which serve to distinguish it from related disciplines such as sociology and history. The methodologies of anthropology are diverse but usually involve participation and observation – ethnographical research in which the anthropologist as observer goes amongst those who are to be observed. The methods of anthropology help historians to read language, images, gestures, sounds and objects and a system of signs that are to be found in spoken, written and visual documents.

What then is special about anthropology and how might historians learn from its approaches? Anthropology as a discipline developed both intellectually and institutionally through the eighteenth and nineteenth centuries. It had its origins in the experience of

European imperial expansion. Explorers, colonial officials, traders or missionaries of church or chapel would be dispatched to locate, govern, plunder and convert unfamiliar non-European societies; the success of this venture depended in part upon learning about the nature of the peoples they encountered. Yet this process does not begin to explain the changing institutional or theoretical framework in which anthropology as a discipline developed, operated and continues to operate. Early anthropological endeavour crystallised into a more familiar modern shape with the creation of the Royal Anthropological Institute of Great Britain and Ireland (RAI) in 1871. The RAI was an amalgamation of the Ethnological Society of London founded in 1843 and the Anthropological Society of London which had emerged in the 1860s. Unlike its amateur forbears (the word 'anthropology' first appeared in the *Edinburgh Review* in the early-1800s), or the Paris-based *Société des Obervateurs de l'Homme*, founded as early as 1799, the RAI was a learned institution which expressed its professional aspirations through discussion and debate, meetings and conferences, the promotion and dissemination of research findings, the maintenance of standards and employment opportunities and the provision of bibliographic services.

By the late-nineteenth century when anthropology had pushed its way into the halls of the universities, it was an institution that was already seen as halfway respectable. The American Anthropological Association was founded in 1902 and, most recently, these professional institutions have been joined by the Association of Social Anthropologists of the Commonwealth (1946), the European Association of Social Anthropologists (1989) and the World Council of Anthropological Associations, founded in Brazil in 2004.

The establishment of the RAI in the nineteenth century announced a breakthrough in ideas and approaches to anthropology which was to have a profound effect on the usefulness of anthropology for historians and the attraction of history to anthropologists. Between the 1840s and the 1870s a theoretical storm in the discipline was brewing, and we can date the rather awkward relationship between social or cultural anthropology and history from this moment. Anthropology as a discipline was quite often couched in Darwinist or evolutionist terms and at first anthropology regarded itself as a behavioural science – using scientific method to study the behaviour of living creatures. A recognition that the past could bring context to studies of 'primitive' societies and peoples led to accusations that history as a discipline was less rigorous than anthropology. By the 1920s, anthropologists working in the field had dismissed any attempt to construct a history of the tribe as simply 'guesswork'. Historians were themselves regarded as theoretically primitive or backward while history as a discipline was thought to be conservative and traditional in outlook, producing research that often failed to consider exotic societies. Fixated on documentary or written archives, correspondence, diaries, and so on, blind to non-literary societies, history was thought ill-equipped to investigate anyone besides those that had produced the archive – the colonisers, not the colonised. There seemed then to be little alternative to imperial histories which recounted the experiences of explorers, traders, colonial officials, missionaries – all set within a perspective of imperial expansion, free-trade and evangelical Christianity.

In the twentieth century, the relationship between history and anthropology fluctuated and was dependent on developments in each discipline. E. E. Evans-Pritchard (1902–73), for example, trained as a historian before turning to anthropology as a postgraduate. He saw history as central to the approach that anthropology should take in its encounters with

E. E. Evans-Pritchard

Source: Pitt Rivers Museum, University of Oxford.

people from other cultures. His book on witchcraft, oracles and magic among the Sudanese Azande (a people located in Central Africa between the Nile and the Congo) was significantly entitled *The Azande: History and Political Institutions* (1971). The photograph above may seem to suggest that Evans-Pritchard compares very well with the image of the pith-helmeted anthropologist–explorer but he remained firmly wedded to historical method, and was emphatic about understanding the history, culture and social system of his subjects. This was a point made in a pamphlet published in 1961, but originally given as a lecture at the University of Manchester in 1950, entitled *Anthropology and History*. This pamphlet had a colossal influence on a young generation of historians starting to engage with a new kind of social history.

In 1970, Alan Macfarlanes' *The Family Life of Ralph Josselin; A Seventeenth-Century Clergyman: An Essay in Historical Anthropology* and his later studies of witchcraft in Tudor and Stuart Essex, pioneered work produced within functionalist anthropology in a historical context. This started a trend that would help to redirect the way in which whole areas of historical research and writing were undertaken. Historians like Keith Thomas, soon to be famous for his magisterial *Religion and the Decline of Magic* (1971) but then working in the relatively untrodden field of women's history, acknowledged this debt.

By the 1970s, therefore, 'context' was reintroduced to anthropological study. With both disciplines in a reforming mood, the result was a rapprochement of anthropology towards history and vice versa. On the one hand, anthropologists rediscovered older bodies of ethnographical writing, and so developed a renewed interest in the provenance and progeny of their discipline. On the other hand, approaches used by historians were finding currency among anthropologists. By the 1960s, both Victor Turner (1920–82) and Clifford Geertz (1926–2006) were making imaginative use of available historical evidence, developing an anthropological and historical interest in culture, ritual, performance and symbolism. Turner in particular argued that anthropologists should turn their attention to medieval religious politics as a well-documented period open to the methods of anthropology. The emphasis on ritual in particular was to have a profound influence on historical research and writing in precisely this period.

Bernard Cohn (1928–2003), whose interest in the Indian caste system was already well known, wrote an article entitled 'History and anthropology: the state of play' (Cohn, 1980; see also Cohn, 1987). The central idea was that 'history can become more historical in becoming more anthropological' and that 'anthropology can become more anthropological in becoming more historical'. In recommending a growing conjunction between anthropology and history, Cohn set in train a coming together of the two disciplines. Culture and how culture is constituted and represented, particularly in the historic 'otherness' of non-western peoples, formed the basis of this new hybrid of historical anthropology.

Others took up the cause. John Adams recommended that historians take up anthropology's interest in the everyday, the meanings of the mundane and commonplace, and also be more self-aware of historical method and theory than they had heretofore been inclined to be. Historians, he contended, had become too preoccupied with what they took to be anthropology's fascination with the exotic and that cultural history was setting off hurriedly in pursuit of the unusual rather than the typical. From the historians' camp, Natalie Zemon Davis argued something similar. Anthropology, she suggests, can help historians to free themselves from the need to order events in terms of relative importance and so constructing narratives that hide the detailed fabric of life behind the great tapestry of the story. Anthropology can lend itself in practical ways by leading the eye of the historian towards 'the living processes of social interaction', providing ways of 'interpreting symbolic behaviour' (behaviour in history, such as faith, that can be seen as a symbol or sign of some historical phenomenon or experience) and understanding 'material cultures' or the understanding of non-literary cultures (Adams, 1981, pp. 253–65).

Peter Burke, a historian who has made a very specific engagement with historical anthropology, has summed up the influence and utility of anthropological approaches to history by emphasising a number of areas of impact:

1. There is an emphasis on qualitative over quantitative evidence. Historical anthropology tends to emphasise the use of imagery, symbolic meanings, social and cultural processes and so on over the statistical and the numerical. In fairness, the quantitative approach (related to the measurable quantity of something) has always had a place in the discipline of history, but the relative emphasis definitely falls on the qualitative (the quality of observation or evidence and its utility for historians).
2. The use of microhistory as highly intensive local studies of the type written by Emmanuel Le Roy Ladurie and Carlo Ginzburg are entirely characteristic of social anthropology and now of history. Understanding societies by examining communities at smaller levels of social aggregation is analogous with the practices of social anthropology.

3 The third area where historical anthropology helps to augment the work of the historian borrows specifically from the anthropologist Clifford Geertz who is concerned about the interpretation of culture (Geertz, 1973). Culture for Geertz, following the German social theorist Max Weber (1864–1920), is a 'web of significance' of our own making, and the job of the anthropologist (and the historian) is to find its meanings. Historians often analyse events and processes in the past in terms that would not have been intelligible to the contemporaries who acted out those events and processes. Geertz, on the other hand, used the term 'thick description' in his famous account of the 'deep play' of the Balinese cock fight which provided a layering of detailed description of the event, and built a picture and an explanation that would be intelligible to the people of that time and place. The cock fights in Bali, therefore, were seen as symbolic enactments of local status conflicts.
4 Historical anthropology imports into history a concern with the role of symbolism in everyday life and this applies to cultural life in the form of art, work, clothes, food, gesture (such as the wink that can be either flirtatious or conspiratorial) and so forth. The desire to unpack symbols is nicely described in Robert Darnton's *The Great Cat Massacre: And Other Episodes of French Cultural History* (1984), which asked why the ritual slaughter of cats was found funny by Parisian journeyman printers in 1730. Briefly, the torture of cats was something important in the 'rough music' of the religious-based charivaris in parts of early-modern France and in rituals associated with witchcraft. It was deemed hilarious by the workers to subvert these rituals by killing the cats of their masters' wives and in so doing they turned tradition against the bourgeoisie. This, according to Darnton, anticipated the revolutionary events of the 1780s and 1790s.

Anthropologists who study communities and social groups once traditionally concentrate their energies on the study of peoples living in parts of the world remote in space and in culture from that of the western industrial societies to which they themselves belong. This makes the appearance of difference an inescapable, even blinding fact. More often, especially for functionalist or structuralist anthropologists, who we shall define and examine in closer detail in the next section, their business involves trying to spot recurrent patterns contained within the ritual and symbolic practices in the systems they are trying to read. Now anthropologists are just as likely to study rural communities or discrete urban groups within modern industrial societies and they are often acutely sensitive to particularities and difference within what historians might too easily see as homogenised mass culture. Many historians have learned another habit of mind from anthropology, and one that many more historians could do with learning, that is, to read against the grain of generalisation: to work against our instincts and to hunt down the particular, the peculiar and the odd and understand what it meant to people in the past. Approaching historical subjects from the point of view of an anthropologist, seeing them 'as a race apart', makes for better historians who have fully absorbed lessons learnt from the 'pens and pith helmets' of the pioneering historians and anthropologists that we will review in this chapter. Above all, it is the ability to 'decode' behaviours and cultures, skills borrowed from anthropology, which retains ultimate value for historians. It is to the theories that underline these approaches that we shall now turn.

Section 2

Functionalism and structuralism: understanding the Lord Mayor's Show

Sometimes peaceful, sometimes not, the Lord Mayor's Show before the mid-nineteenth century travelled by water up the Thames from London Bridge to Westminster and was held each year on the 'Glorious Ninth' of November. Later it progressed through the streets of the City of London and by the 1870s it had become 'a holiday show' with the Committee of the Stock Exchange authorising a day off for its members since little business was done in the City anyway. In 1880, the *Daily Telegraph* spoke of the City as the 'finest site in Europe', and it's Show as being 'alive with holiday makers'. By then the Show had reallocated to the first Saturday in November when thousands turned up, not just from the London suburbs and the Home Counties, but from across England. This was a ritual known and revered across the empire.

One of the features of the Show by the 1880s was an overwhelming concentration on historical images, great men and glorious events, drawing on symbols well known to a wider historical culture. Yet, the late-Victorian City of London was truly modern; but to be truly modern was also to be in touch with antiquity and tradition. The Lord Mayor's Show celebrated a local office that dated back a thousand years and recounted the national story in an imperial age.

What are we to make of the changing contours of this ritual that had been played out annually on the streets of the City of London for centuries? Clearly ritual of any kind depends somewhat on context and meaning and that meaning can be often masked or layered. Anthropologically then there are perhaps several questions that can be asked about a ritual such as the Lord Mayor's Show. Any explanation of the place of the pre-modern office of Lord Mayor operating in the modern world must successfully explain the relationship that the City had as a modern centre of finance with tradition or historical memory. It must also answer other questions thrown up by anthropological method. What was the function of the Show, did it support existing social structures by simply representing them, did it legitimise social authority by concealing that authority in 'harmless' ritual and how much can this ritual tell us about City society – about dissent and rebellion, as well as change? To what extent was the Show malleable, not so much a receptacle for uncontested narratives about the national past, of tradition and continuities, but open to different groups and contested views of that past?

Answers to the apparent paradox of the Show, which apparently represented simultaneously the modern and the archaic, is found in anthropological explanations from both functionalist and structuralist viewpoints.

Functionalism developed during a period when anthropologists did not much value history. During the 1920s and 1930s the pioneering Polish anthropologist Bronislaw Malinowski (1884–1942), for example, took little account of the history of people and societies that he described in *Sexual Life of Savages* (1932). His interest was in societies regarded as static and 'backward', evidenced by their primitive reproductive practices, their apparent ignorance about the process of procreation and their indiscretion in publicly describing their own sexual lives:

> **An interesting personal account was given to me by Monakewo . . . It was hardly discreet of him to speak of his mistress by name; but the ethnographer's love for the concrete instance may excuse my not emending it.**
>
> **'When I sleep with Dabugera I embrace her, I hug her with my whole body, I rub noses with her. We suck each other's lower lip, so that we are stirred to passion. We suck each other's tongues, we bite each other's noses, we bite each other's chins, we bite cheeks and caress the armpit and the groin. The she will say 'O my lover, it itches very much . . . push on again, my whole body melts with pleasure . . . do it vigorously, be quick, so that the fluids may discharge . . . tread on again, my body feels so pleasant'.**
>
> (Malinowski, 1932, pp. 286–7)

Malinowski was concerned to understand the varying needs of the human organism and how those needs related to the social system to which the individual belonged. Central to his view is the idea that society is a system in which social processes like courtship and marriage and artefacts such as shrines and other objects of religious veneration are to be understood through the *function* that they fulfil within that system. The object of studying a society, therefore, is to appreciate how it works as a system at any given time rather than how it had historically developed.

Malinowski is known as the founder of functionalist anthropology because of this emphasis on understanding objects, rituals, symbols and practices through their social functions. In this he inherited much from the French sociologist Emile Durkheim (1858–1917), who stands at the head of this tradition of sociology and anthropology. The legacy of Malinowski is clearest in the work of English anthropologist A. R. Radcliffe-Brown (1881–1955) who argued that the function of cultural phenomena like social ceremonies and the structures of kinship was social maintenance, or the conservation of society in its current arrangements.

We introduced the anthropologist Alan Macfarlane in the last section. Like Evans-Pritchard, Macfarlane trained as a historian, and went on to produce works of historical erudition and value within both disciplines. In a review of the developing relationship between history and anthropology, published in the *Times Literary Supplement* in January 1973, Macfarlane explained the benefits that a functionalist anthropology can bring to the study of history:

> **[A]nthropology is based on a timeless but satisfying explanatory system which has been termed 'functionalism'. Rather than seeing the roots of actions and thoughts in random past events, it was argued that both actions and ideas could be explained by their present 'functions'. This was especially important since it helped to de-mystify much of what had earlier been dismissed as 'irrational' or 'superstitious'. For example, witchcraft beliefs serve a 'function' in many societies, both to explain misfortune and as a form of social control. . . . Functionally a witch doctor is only a psychiatrist writ large.**
>
> (Macfarlane, 1973)

In 1981, Macfarlane, who by then was aware of the limits of functionalism, reviewed Thomas' book in *History Today* and reflected on its ground-breaking qualities. He argued that *Religion and the Decline* had introduced fresh ways of looking at previously obscure sources such as the records of the ecclesiastical courts or astrologers' notebooks, making respectable research on fairy beliefs, popular prophecies, village healers and popular religion. Besides anything else, it remains a really fabulous read. Thomas was well aware of how functionalism, derived from anthropology, could be applied to an historical subject. Take, for example, the disputes which emerged in the guise of accusations of witchcraft practice, which in reality were apparent only because of structural weaknesses in that system caused by 'the position of the poor and dependent members of the community':

> **Witch-beliefs are therefore of interest to the social historian for the light they throw upon the weak points in the social structure of the time. Essentially the witch and her victim were two persons who ought to have been friendly towards each other, but were not. They existed in a state of concealed hostility for which society provided no legitimate outlet. They could not take each other to law; neither could they have recourse to open violence. In Africa accusations of witchcraft frequently spring from conflicts within the family, for example, between the co-wives of a polygamous husband. But in England the witch and her accuser were very seldom related. The tensions which such accusations usually reflected arose from the position of the poor and dependent members of the community. The charges of witchcraft were a means of expressing deep-felt animosities in acceptable guise.**
>
> (Thomas, 1973, p. 669)

Using the tools of anthropology then, historians can know why witches were found on the boundaries of the village and on the margins of society. Interestingly, again according to Macfarlane, it was a book researched and written precisely at a moment when functionalism was subject to a devastating attack by an alternative theoretical tradition, that is, structuralism.

Claude Lévi-Strauss (1909–2009) is generally regarded as the most influential anthropologist of the second half of the twentieth century and is considered as the modern founder of structuralism (see Chapter 10). Simultaneous to the development of structuralism and perhaps of greater moment to the historian was the birth of semiotics, which Lévi-Strauss regarded as a limb of anthropology. Semiotics, put at its crudest, is the study of signs. For Ferdinand de Saussure (1857–1913), Swiss linguist and originator of structural linguistics, it was 'the study of the role of signs as part of social life'. Applied to the archive, especially to visual sources, semiotics has attractions for the historian; it seeks to get beneath the 'surface features' of phenomena, and reveal how the organisation of signs and systems as a form of language create meaning. In this way, the definition of 'language' may be widened to include 'images', 'gestures', 'sounds' and 'objects', all of which have systems of signs and symbols.

One example of the usefulness to historians of 'reading the signs' can be examined through something common to us all: death. Rituals of death are culturally constructed and change over time. In most societies and in most times, after death we find a ritual or process of mourning and a sign of mourning is that we might wear clothes that are different to our everyday clothes. In the West the symbol of mourning has been traditionally black; in India it has been white. Only particular knowledge of the context can allow us to know what a particular sign or symbol means and what it means in any one historical period or place.

Section 3

Myths and history: Jewish conspiracies and the 'blood libel'

Anthropologists are also deeply interested in myth and mythology; in many respects the interpretation of myth as a cultural artefact is fundamentally what anthropology is about. History, on the other hand, has always had a more troubled relationship with the mythic and mythological. We shall examine these relationships by looking more closely at a myth that survived across centuries and across cultures and many different types of societies and still exists despite being verifiably untrue. This is the myth that Jews require blood for their religious rituals and practices.

Martin Luther (1483–1546) who was a priest in a critical moment of Christian reform was once a friend to the Jews, calling them the 'blood-relations of our Lord'. He even announced to the Catholic Church that 'if you become tired of abusing me as a heretic, that you begin to revile me as a Jew'. It was the bit about blood that stuck, however, especially after 1543 when he wrote his now infamous *The Jews and Their Lies*. No longer did he defend the Jews as kith and kin ('as blood-relations' to Jesus the Jew), now he stirred mythologies about Jews and Judaism that only confirmed Christian prejudices of a people who had, they thought, conspired to kill Christ by initiating and prolonging the 'Passion' or crucifixion. From early medieval times, the Jews stood accused as consumers of blood for the ritual purposes of making *matzah* (the unleavened bread Jews eat at Passover). This blood was extracted from Christian children. 'William' in Norwich in 1144 and 'Hugh' in Lincoln in 1255 were both said in various ways to have been crucified by Jews and drained of blood for these ritual purposes. There were similar reports of incidents in England after this period which were transported in subsequent centuries to mainland Europe, to Germany and France in particular, with truly terrifying consequences. It was blood that Jews needed to dab on the eyes of their young, as everyone knew in medieval Europe that Jews were born blind and needed the blood of a Christian child in order to see. They needed Christian blood in order to heal their circumcision – a stubborn reminder of their adherence to the old covenant and denial of the new. Everyone knew too that Jewish men menstruated. The mythology then of Jewish culpability in the death of Jesus and Jews as a 'cursed people', the 'children of the Devil', laid the groundwork for what has become known as the 'blood libel'.

How this mythology has transliterated across cultures and religious traditions, retaining a remarkable coherence, keeping its basic shape, is a deep-seated historical problem that is not confined to Europe. Indeed, the most infamous incident of the myth of Jewish cannibalism emerged dramatically in Syria in 1840 with the so-called Damascus Affair (Green, 2010, pp. 133–41).

An arresting example of this myth travelling over time, distance and culture, however, is when it reached the United States. The conversation related below happened in the immediate aftermath of the disappearance of a four-year-old girl in September 1928 from a small town in up-state New York. The child was found safe – she had apparently fallen asleep in the woods – but crowds continued to congregate near the local synagogue with accusations that Jews had been responsible for her kidnap. The 'foreigner' in question was a recent immigrant from Salonika in Greece and provides the direct link back to European mythologies about Jews.

> ***Mickey McCann*: 'Can you give any information as to whether your people in the Old Country offer human sacrifices?'**
>
> ***Rabbi Brennglass* (indignant): 'I am surprised that an officer of the United States, which is the most enlightened country in the world, should dare to ask such a foolish and ridiculous question'.**
>
> ***McCann*: 'Was there ever a time when the Jewish people used human blood?'**
>
> ***Rabbi Brennglass*: 'No never, that is a slander against the entire Jewish people'.**
>
> ***McCann*: 'Please don't think that the idea originated with me; somebody else, a foreigner, impressed me with it'.**
>
> (Perry and Schweitzer, 2002, pp. 43–4)

All societies have myths. They provide a sense of who we are, where we come from and why we are here but they do not necessarily relate to real or even plausible accounts of the past. While we have comprehensibly established that there are myths that existed and exist about Jews, we might have chosen to focus on myths that Jews may have about themselves or about others. We could have raised the more general question of conspiracy and myth in history, or focused on other groups that have historically featured in myth-making over the years.

In one view, myths are a fanciful collection of stories created for important reasons but they do not amount to accurate descriptions of the past as it is understood by historians. The functions of myths are acknowledged but they are the proper concern of other disciplines such as folklore or anthropology. This does not mean that the historian is not interested in myth; as we have seen, it is simply too important to be ignored. Even if we think that the myths of the ancient Greeks, for example, do not describe accurately the development of Athens or Sparta, the history (including politics, sociology, culture and economy) of those societies cannot be understood without appreciating the great importance of their myths to *them*, for the thoughts and deeds of people in the past are guided by what they believe to be true as much or more than by any objective reality that can be dug up in the archives.

Historians have adopted a number of different positions regarding the relationship between myth and history. Some, like Eric Hobsbawm, have seen myth and history locked in a competitive struggle to explain reality. *The Invention of Tradition*, edited with the anthropologist Terence Ranger, caused quite a stir when it was published in 1983. According to the contributors, myth acts as a sort of illegitimate history, explaining past events in a way entirely subservient to the prevailing interests of dominant groups within society. The Aryan myth, the myth that some North European peoples share a common and racially pure origin, so central to Nazi ideology, is one example. Another might be what the historian Angus Calder has called the *Myth of the Blitz* (1991), which finds a population under German attack in London during the Second World War but who are themselves locked in a competitive struggle for survival, not unified on a common front but 'all in it together', a myth that has been handed down to Britons as victors of the war.

Such myths are seen by Hobsbawm and others as being essentially untrue, harmful and must be combated. The main means of fighting against pernicious myth is history. History, as a discipline, with its methods, formal procedures and insistence on the use of evidence, is said to provide an alternative account of the past that challenges the political manipulation of myth. Thus, one job of the historian is to debunk myth, whether it is the myth of the grasping, manipulative, conspiratorial and blood-thirsty Jew or the western myth, according to Edward Said's *Orientalism* (1979), of the so-called destructiveness of the 'Arab mind'. It is all the better then, when refuting these migrating, transforming, durable mythologies, that we have the tools of anthropology at our disposal.

Section 4

The 'dying god': Captain Cook and ethnohistory

In popular perceptions of their roles, anthropologists and historians cut very different figures. The anthropologist wears a bush hat or pith helmet and tirelessly trudges up mountains or hacks through jungle in search of lost tribes and ancient, unchanging, folklore. He or she is a cross between Indiana Jones and a colonial official associated with the imperial literature or poetry of Rudyard Kipling (1865–1936). The historian heads resolutely in the opposite direction, plunging ever deeper into the mysterious and dusty world of the archive, meticulously piecing together our collective past. A dishevelled figure that stands guardian as a remembrancer of how we became who we think we are. Despite their comic pastiches, the traditional images of the adventurous anthropologist and the book-bound historian do nonetheless reflect persistent differences in subject matter and approach. Anthropologists do sometimes study people who live in remote places and historians do spend a lot of their time in archives. However, neither of these images will do for the present day. Anthropology is now a highly theoretical discipline and is as much a creature of the library as of the field trip. Historians have long woken up to the fact that they have a claim on the whole of human experience and are no longer confined to the archives alone.

Ethnohistory looks at the variety of human existence from an historical point of view but quite often using evidence gleaned from indigenous sources. Now absorbed within cultural anthropology in keeping with its American roots, it is one area where history and anthropology more generally have come closest to shading one into the other. Ethnohistory began in the United States in the early and mid-twentieth century as an attempt to understand the culture and history of native-American peoples from the inside. Edward S. Curtis (1868–1952), for instance, between 1907 and 1930, captured the popular culture of the native Indian by photographing 'the old time Indian, his dress, his ceremonies, his life and manners' which has provided an archive for both the anthropologist and historian alike (Library of Congress, 2009).

From the anthropologists concerned with the history of societies that were pre-literate and often small in scale, ethnohistory became open to linguistics and archaeology while vocabulary and the structure of language became the primary materials of historical inquiry. This type of cultural anthropology tries to free itself from the historian's traditional dependence on documents, focusing instead on oral traditions, storytelling or the artefacts of material culture such as pottery, earthenware and similar objects, visual images and artwork. The emphasis on orality, objects and the visual allows histories of non-literate societies to be written. There are then moments when not only does anthropology throw light on an historical question but that history has complemented the work of anthropologists.

By looking closely at the murder of Captain Cook, it can be seen how successful enthohistory or cultural anthropology has been in suggesting plausible explanations. The more standard account of Cook's life and death has become a part of the narrative of the expansion of Europe into the non-European world: of heroic discovery and sacrifice, of a civilising force and *noblesse oblige*, of a Christian mission to savage peoples and to bring further glory and riches to the mother country. The job of the historian is to interrogate this narrative, not simply to debunk it, but to understand it in the context of the history of the British empire and also, and this is critical for any consideration of Marshall Sahlins' important approach to cultural anthropology, in relation to the rituals of the Hawaiians themselves, for more than anyone else, Sahlins has led the way in interpreting the mutual discovery of James Cook and the Hawaiians in a way that makes sense in relation to Hawaiian culture as well as British imperial history.

In his book *Islands of History* (1987), as well in longer treatments of the subject in academic journals and elsewhere, Sahlins' starting point was to ask what the Hawaiians themselves understood to be happening when Cook anchored off their shores and to insist that societies such as these have their own histories and cultures, although they have been influenced by Europe and the West. Princeton anthropologist, Gananath Obeyesekere, takes up this theme in his book *The Apotheosis of Captain Cook: European Mythmaking in the Pacific* (1997), arguing that the deification of Cook was a European invention which presented the 'natives' as dupes, a representation of 'primitive' peoples that lives on in western popular imagination.

On 17 January 1779, the ships *Resolution* and *Discovery* sat at anchor in Kealakekua Bay on the black-sanded shore of the island of Hawaii. The British seamen, confined for month after month on the long sea journey across the Atlantic, through the treacherous waters off Cape Horn and the endless watery wastes of the Pacific, thought they had landed in paradise. In the memories of generations of British schoolchildren, their commander Captain James Cook (1728–79) has been credited with discovering the island. Hawaii was of course already known to its own native inhabitants, even if they had a very different understanding of how their home related to the rest of the universe from that of their putative discoverers. Cook and his crew remained among the Hawaiians enjoying lavish hospitality, the sexual favours of the women and the sumptuous bounty of the verdant green island. As is famous from the crews' own accounts as well as that of historians subsequent to the event, they were treated as if they were gods in a land of natural splendour and plenty.

Cook's discovery, the way that he arrived, and the timing of his presence led to his deification by the islanders – he was thought to be *Lono*, the god of natural growth and reproduction. This god lived among them for a time. When Cook returned to his ship, the islanders thought they had been abandoned by their god, and their child-like generosity turned suddenly to fury as their savagery won out over their natural nobility – or so it appeared from a European perspective. When, on 14 February, Cook returned from the ship with some marines to take the Hawaiian king, Kaniopu'u, as a hostage against goods stolen the previous evening from the *Discovery*, the islanders brutally murdered their fallen idol. The encounter, once peaceful and friendly, had turned to bloody confrontation: 'the structural crisis, when all the social relations began to change their signs' (Sahlins, 1987, p. 107).

Sahlins' explanation involves seeing the incident from the point of view of the Hawaiians, taking note of the local ritual cycles of the year. Cook's appearances and reappearances happened to coincide with the expectations of local lore and custom in relation to the movements of *Lono*, of sexual overtures made by the Hawaiian women who in keeping with their own knowledge of the rituals and narratives of their role in this performative cycle were 'looking for a lord' among their visitors whose very presence, in turn, was part of the prophecy of local religious belief. In this sense, quite apart from the conduct of Cook and his men, or the 'savagery' of the 'child-like' indigenous peoples, the encounter between 'native' and 'European' ended in the way (for the islanders) it was expected and deigned to have ended: a face-off between king (Kaniopu'u) and god (Cook) in which the king was destined to prevail. Cook, as the 'dying god' *Lono*, unwittingly played out the death rituals of local religious custom and, therefore, that of his own death.

Sahlins here posed a challenge to structuralism. According to Sahlins, Cook's death was certainly the result of a 'structural crisis' but that it was predicated on a remarkable set of 'ritual coincidences'. These could only be explained through an understanding of the particular indigenous culture of Hawaii. While not entirely rejecting Lévi-Strauss's linguistic frame of reference, his is a synthesis of a structuralist approach but with a heavy emphasis both on history and the importance of local custom or culture. This approach yields a plausible account of what went on that St Valentine's Day in 1779 in ways that we might never have considered possible. Only by recognising the structures of this society, its symbols and signs, and using the tools of anthropology, could historians challenge existing explanations of the circumstances of Cook's death.

This interest in the impact of the West and particularly the impact of states expanding outside of their territorial boundaries amounts to common interests for the anthropologist and historian. The recent contribution of Sahlins is particularly suggestive here. Assumptions are often made about the impact that contacts with developed western societies have had on the others that they encountered in the course of their economic and political expansion. Key to these assumptions is the idea that the local, the culturally particular, the distinctive folk-ways and ways of life of native peoples, was disrupted fundamentally by imperial contacts. More recently, the globalisation of the world economy and the expansion of western-based multinationals such as Macdonald's and Coca-Cola have had a homogenising effect on local cultures – making all cultures look the same, simplifying them into the workings of a basic machine, as the anthropologist Edmund Leach (1910–89) argued. When we arrive at our 'exotic' holiday destination it also has already been 'spoiled', reduced to a bland similarity in the face of a dominant western culture as regional and local cultural forms are obliterated. Sahlins makes a strong case for recognising the resistance of these cultures. Not that they remain unaffected either by imperialism or modern capitalism but that they are capable of engaging with and absorbing cultural influence on their terms as well as on the terms of the greater economic powers. They exist as genuine hybrids of the general and the local and this may mean that local cultures are more resilient than we give them credit for.

The problem is that historians remained for a very long time well equipped to research and write the history of the British venturers and imperialists from the manifold sources available but less able to research the history of the Hawaiians. Not so anthropologists. They are, after all, expert in the interpretation of non-literate cultures and cultures at the point of first contact with Europeans. If we do not understand the part that Hawaiian history played in these events and the part that these events and subsequent relations with Europeans played in later Hawaiian history, we will never fully understand the imperial past and the events that take place after the 'age of empire'. In the case of the death of Cook this might have always meant a search for explanations from one (European) side of the equation but by considering the local and the discrete we now know better. It is to the local and the discrete, or the 'micro' that we now turn.

Section 5

Microhistories: cheese, worms, night battles and ecstasies

Foregrounding aspects of the cultural life of two communities in the remote Friuli region of north-east Italy, the intellectual development and ideas of a poor sixteenth-century miller known as Mennochio are traced through their many intricacies. Mennochio was strikingly literate for someone from such lowly origins, although Friuli had surprisingly high levels of popular literacy. From his reading of learned texts, from the folk-culture of his region and from the fertility of his own imagination, Mennochio conjured up his own cosmology. Creation, he argued to his neighbours, consisted of ripe cheese and life was made up of maggots and worms living upon its substance. His view of the universe, that it had anarchic beginnings, questioned the Christian understanding of a God, of design. He even questioned the divinity of Jesus. His querulous and incautiously talkative nature soon attracted the attention of religious and civil authorities. Interrogation, prosecution and ultimately conviction followed and, although found guilty of being a *heresyarch*, someone who not only repeated heresies but actually created them, Mennochio was sentenced only to prison. His confinement lasted until the authorities were persuaded that he was truly repentant, whereupon he was released but warned under the direst penalties never to lapse into his old heretical ways. For a number of years he was silent but gradually his need to express his views and propound his own theology fought its way to the surface; he began to once more harangue his neighbours. This time the courts acted with swift severity and, on being found guilty for a second time, Mennochio was executed.

Carlo Ginzburg is the author of *The Cheese and The Worms: The Cosmos of a Sixteenth Century Miller* (1982), a fine example of a microhistory, a small-scale and highly localised attempt to reconstruct cultural processes and social relations in great detail. Heavily influenced by historical anthropology, this approach made the local and the particular its starting point. By the 1980s, following the pioneering lead of historians like Keith Thomas during the 1960s and 1970s and the impact of 'history from below', a number of historians developed new areas of the history of culture: turning their gaze not to the world of the high culture of social elites but, like the historical anthropologist who studied the lowly tribesman, to the world of the common people: the peasant, the villager and the urban poor.

Ginzburg scouted out historical detail in symbols and signs, squeezing these signs from the smallest and the most insignificant historical trifle and then describing and connecting that evidence on macro social structures. We will look now at two of his major works in order to fathom how he managed to tease out the larger trends and concerns of history in the tiny and seemingly insignificant. His particular skill was in reading signs and in those signs detecting a rich context for the more important structures to be found in society. In doing this, in concentrating on the discrete, he draws upon an approach of Italian (and to some extent, French) historiography this has, as its starting point, the local.

In the second of his noted works, *The Night Battles* (1983), Ginzburg analyses what appeared to be the incidence of a secret cult known to themselves as the Benandanti, again in a remote Friulian community. Extensive records created by Dominican inquisitors sent by the Catholic Church to investigate them, suggest that these people believed that in a nocturnal dream world battles were fought out between the Benandanti and forces of darkness trying to invade their world while they slept. The Inquisitors wanted to know if these stories of 'nightbattles' were related to witchcraft and, in particular, if they contained any evidence of demonic activity: did the devil have a hand in the these dream world events of the night? In different ways through the intensive description of the life of Mennochio and the nocturnal world of the Benandanti, Ginzburg is interested to retrieve aspects of popular culture at the most humble levels of society and in its more remote geographical reaches: a long way from the concerns of high politics and court society. In this he represented, like Sahlins, a venture into the field of historical anthropology. As Ginzburg himself would acknowledge, however, there were issues of methodology to be attended to here. Popular culture cannot really be understood outside of its interactions with elite, literate culture. For Mennochio, it was his literacy, his reading of learned texts, that was one source of his own private cosmology that finally led to his destruction. In the case of the Benandanti, what we know of their beliefs we recover from records produced by their inquisitors who not only recorded what they were told of the views of the poor villagers but also framed and wrote the questions they were asked. We also have to recognise that the inquisitors conducted their inquiries over such a long period that the responses of the Benandanti might well have come to take on the meanings and shapes implicit in the kinds of questions they were being asked.

The poor peasants may have been providing the answers they thought were expected of them; popular culture may have learned to mould itself around the preconceptions of the inquisitors themselves.

In his third and by far most ambitious work, Ginzburg's new edition of *Ecstasies: Deciphering the Witches' Sabbath* (2004), investigated why ideas of a conspiracy against Christianity spread in the early part of the fourteenth century. Why accusations of conspiracy were first aimed at discrete social and ethnic groups – lepers, Jews, Muslims or conspiring combinations of these groups – and then ended up with witches as the arch-conspirators, their numbers drawn from the general population. It was only then that Christian society could imagine that it faced a single external enemy: the devil, and it was this idea of a conspiracy of the devil that came to dominate Europe over the next two centuries:

> **From a relatively restricted social group (the lepers) one passes to a larger, but ethnically and religiously delimited group (the Jews), finally reaching a potentially boundless sect (male and female witches). Like the lepers and Jews, male and female witches are located at the margins of the community; their conspiracy is once again inspired by an external enemy – the enemy par excellence, the devil.** (Ginzburg, 1992, p. 72)

Ginzburg wanted to establish where this phenomenon began and his use here of historical anthropology is unmistakable. His starting point is the internment of lepers and the prohibition on their having children, and then the mass murder of French Jews in the spring of 1321. Burning at the stake, the confiscation of property and the exclusion from trades and commerce was followed by accusations that Jews were behind the Black Death, more burnings, and eventually to expulsion from France under royal edict. He works back to these events by investigating the provenance of the Witches' Sabbath which comprised homage to the devil, rejection of Christ and the Christian faith, magical ointment, sacrifice of children, animal metamorphoses, magical flying, nocturnal gatherings, feasting and sexual orgies. In doing this, focusing on a particular time and place (fourteenth- and fifteenth-century France) he hoped to chart how conspiracy, or the idea of conspiracy, worked and from whence it came. Moreover, he also wished to determine how the microhistory of a small community, a discrete group, a lone individual, could impact on the mighty structures of church and state.

For all of Ginsburg's erudition, he did what all good historians should do: he connects evidence; he drew conclusions from the particular and applied those conclusions to the general. Above all, he treated chronology with tremendous respect: poring over evidence year by year, day by day and hour by hour. His influences were anthropological and he has an astonishing ability to read signs and tear symbolic fragments of evidence from one context and apply them imaginatively to what was previously thought to be an entirely unconnected context. His inspiration, however, was surely that of an historian seeking to understand human change.

In practice

At first sight there appears to be little in common between history and anthropology. History, after all, is concerned with the study of past societies, while anthropology explores societies in the present. The work of the founding anthropologists in the early nineteenth century was very much part of an imperial project for it arose from a need to understand more about the societies which the imperial powers – most particularly the British in India and Polynesia – encountered. Thus the aim was to understand as a means of better controlling the ways in which these 'primitive' societies operated, and although there may have been passing reference to the histories of these societies, the overriding concern was to reveal the significance of their ritual beliefs and activities, and the role of myth and custom.

In the course of the twentieth century, the relationship between history and anthropology altered. Anthropologists increasingly recognised the importance of providing historical context, but more important was the acceptance among historians of the value of anthropological approaches. Their interests remained in past societies, but many began to appreciate that the ways in which anthropologists had approached an understanding of, say, ritual and symbolism, could be applied to the past. Thus in the postwar period, we have witnessed the creation of a body of work about past societies by scholars who to great effect have straddled the worlds of history and anthropology. To take one outstanding example, Keith Thomas' *Religion and the Decline of Magic* was a path-breaking attempt to understand an important moment in European history, and he did so by viewing with the eyes of an anthropologist how and why societies at the time responded to the rise of religion, and the impact it had upon ancient folk beliefs and rituals.

Anthropology has also encouraged a certain theoretical awareness amongst historians. Although functionalism and structuralism were not the exclusive preserve of anthropology but were developed also in disciplines such as sociology and literary studies, historians learnt most about their practical application from anthropologists. For historians, functionalism provided a means of explanation of the 'whole way of life' of a society through an understanding of what particular functions were served by customs, rituals or particular patterns of behaviour more generally. An emphasis on the maintenance of social coherence, however, has over time led to a loss of confidence in functionalism. Rather more important has been the influence of structuralism. Here a preoccupation with revealing the hidden structures of social mores, read more or less as a giant language, has led to an influential body of historical inquiry, deeply critical of more traditional approaches.

Finally, anthropology has opened up an interest within history with the whole question of myth. It is no exaggeration to say that we live through myths as taken-for-granted systems of beliefs, and anthropology has played a vital role not only in explaining to historians the importance of myth, but also in providing them with the tools to untangle their inner workings and social consequences.

Summary

The five sections of this chapter have said five things:

- Anthropology and history, where once separated and remote, began to find commonality in method and approach. Much of this commonality was organised around a shared understanding of culture. The first section traces the progeny of social or cultural anthropology and the use historians began to make in the 1960s and 1970s of anthropological approaches to ritual in particular. A hybrid historical anthropology learnt how to decode symbols.
- An understanding of the signs and symbols that make up any study of so-called primitive societies can be utilised to know how the apparently ancient ritual of the Lord Mayor's Show in nineteenth-century London, perhaps held in the most modern place on earth, could be understood through its cultural symbols. As historians became more anthropological and anthropologists became more historical, then areas of study such as religion, magic and witchcraft became open to different methodologies.
- The importance of myth to anthropology is an area of shared concern to the historian. By looking in some detail at the myth of the Jewish blood libel, that is, the accusation that Jews require blood for their religious rituals, we ask how myth travels across time and geography. Clearly myth has a role as being important to those that believe the myth but, because of that, it also becomes important to the historian.
- The approaches of anthropologists to preliterate societies can give an invaluable insight to historians of, say, imperialism. The example given here is the death of Captain Cook. Without knowledge of local customs and religious beliefs, his murder would be seen simply as an irrational act of a 'child-like' 'primitive' people. Instead, we now know that the natives' understanding of religious destiny makes his demise entirely rational – to them.
- The anthropological fixation on social systems, symbols and an emphasis on the interpretation of culture has led historians to look very closely at the microhistory of phenomena that for all intents and purposes appear quite unconnected. The extraordinary work of Carlo Ginzburg is looked at in some detail and, in particular, his painstaking use of what would be otherwise considered to be unconnected fragments of evidence.

Discussion document 1

The use of anthropological method in observing national consciousness and the 'grammar' of belonging is both engaging and seductive. The subject matter here is Englishness but it might be applied to any advanced society. But is it applicable to national belonging in the past? Is there such a thing as national traits among the Tudors that can be determined among the Victorians?

> The rules of English weather-speak tell us quite a lot about Englishness. Already, before we even begin to examine the minutiae of other English conversation codes and rules of behaviour in other aspects of English life, these rules provide a number of hints and clues about the 'grammar' of Englishness.
>
> In the reciprocity and context rules, we see clear signs of reserve and social inhibition, but also the ingenious use of 'facilitators' to overcome these handicaps. The agreement rule and its exceptions provide hints about the importance of politeness and avoidance of conflict (as well as the approval of conflict in specific social contexts) – and the precedence of etiquette over logic. In the variations to the agreement rule, and sub-clauses to the weather-hierarchy rule, we find indications of the acceptance of eccentricity and some hints of stoicism – the latter balanced by a predilection for Eeyorish moaning. The moderation rule reveals a dislike and disapproval of extremes, and the weather-as-family rule exposes a perhaps surprising patriotism, along with a quirky appreciation of understated charm. The Shipping Forecast ritual illustrates a deep-seated need for a sense of safety, security and continuity – and a tendency to become upset when these are threatened – as well as a love of words and a somewhat eccentric devotion to arcane and apparently irrational pastimes and practices. There seems also to be an undercurrent of humour in all this, a reluctance to take things too seriously.
>
> Clearly, further evidence will be required to determine whether these are among the 'defining characteristics of Englishness' that we set out to identify, but at least we can start to see how an understanding of Englishness might emerge from detailed research on our unwritten rules.

Kate Fox, *Watching the English: The Hidden Rules of Englishness* (2004), p. 36.

Discussion document 2

Emmanuel Le Roy Ladurie investigated in great depth the late-medieval history of a small village called Montaillou in the Langedoc region of France. Montaillou was a community of religious dissidents known as Cathars on the eve of prosecution for heresy. The research is based upon the large archive of manuscripts that survive concerning this socially and geographically well-defined community.

Arnaud Gelis himself was reasonably well off and probably owned his owned house (i.128). He was a glutton for work, and liked to sit in the sun (i.550). He was employed as a canon's servant and subsequently as an assistant sacristan. But his chief role, like that of the modern historian, was to act as mouthpiece for the dead.

Sometimes he might even act as intermediary, not between living and dead but between one dead person and another (i.134). Gelis carried out his functions as messenger of souls with professionalism and discretion, keeping his information to himself once he had imparted it to those concerned. For the Inquisition to suppress the messengers of souls was to encourage people to indulge in direct communications with ghosts, and there was then a danger of ghosts appearing in person to everyone everywhere.

The Church itself tried to replace the idea of ghosts with that of souls. According to Christian theology souls, after death, flew like arrows to Paradise, Hell, or Purgatory. This again prevented the living from addressing their departed loved ones directly and there was a danger that, with their well-known love of the supernatural, they would be tempted to try themselves to speak with demons. (In the good old days of Guillaume Fort and Arnaud Gelis, demons might have had contact with the dead, but they were not in direct touch with men of flesh and blood.) The later developments opened the way to witchcraft.

The payments Gelis received for his services were not excessive. When he did not perform his errands satisfactorily among the living, the dead would requite [sic] him with a cudgelling (i.136, 544). The living paid him with cheese or an invitation to a drink or meal, or perhaps a little money (i.137, 538, 543, 544, 547). This was not unreasonable, considering the risks Gelis took vis-a-vis the Inquisition, into whose clutches he finally fell.

But for a long time his relationship with the official clergy was far from disagreeable. He often went to church, and his own utterances were influenced by what he heard from the pulpit and in the sacristy. He stood at the intersection of a certain supply and demand. He established a whole clientele of living women who wanted to have Masses said for their dead husbands or fathers or children, and these he guided towards the priests of his acquaintance who asked nothing better than to recite offices for them, for a consideration. He did encounter a few sceptics among the living. But what he had to tell was so congenial to the mentality both of the masses and of the elite, and what he did was so genuinely useful, both domestically and socially, that he was assured of a good supply of faithful customers, most of them women (i.550).

Emmanuel Le Roy Ladurie, *Montaillou: Cathars and Catholics in a French Village 1294–1324* (2002), pp. 350–1.

Further reading

* *essential*

Clifford Geertz, *The Interpretation of Cultures* (1973).
A brilliant collection of essays which captures so much of the productive sharing between anthropology and history. The essay on Balinese cock fights is perhaps the most important and certainly the most memorable to non-specialists.

Carlo Ginzburg, *Myths, Emblems, Clues* (1990).
Again a collection of essays which serve to support some of the themes developed throughout this chapter and also to provide a sketch of Ginsburg's intellectual development.

Alan Barnard and Jonathan Spencer (eds), *Encyclopaedia of Social and Cultural Anthropology* (2002).
These are complex issues and this volume, while comprehensive, does not go out of its way to simplify the discussion of areas such as 'functionalism' and 'structuralism'.

* **Marvin Perry and Frederick M. Schweitzer**, *Antisemitism: Myth and Hate from Antiquity to the Present* (2002).
A comprehensive account of the mythologies and misunderstandings of Jews and Judaism which have been built up and relayed across centuries and cultures.

Robert Deliege, *Lévi-Strauss Today* (2004).
A very good retrospective of the enormous contribution made by Lévi-Strauss to the social sciences. It combines biographical insights with clear explanations of his theories to a range of disciplines, although not especially to history.

* **Simon Gunn**, *History and Cultural Theory* (2006).
A fine tool for historians wanting to understand the theoretical positions that have impacted on history. For the purposes of social and cultural anthropology and history, Chapter 3 is very useful indeed.

* **Marshall Sahlins**, *Islands of History* (1987).
The central text of Section 4 – follow the references in the text.

* **Marshall Sahlins**, *How 'Natives' Think: About Captain Cook, For Example* (1995).
This serves as a reply to Obeyesekere. Again do follow up references from the text, particularly as Sahlins is a prodigious writer in the academic journals. It also has the advantage of setting out the author's summary of *Islands of History*.

Marshall Sahlins, *Historical Metaphors and Mythical Realities: Structure in the Early History of the Sandwich Islands* (1981).
A short pamphlet but one which outlines the theoretical contours of the argument very well.

Marshall Sahlins, *Apologies to Thucydides: Understanding History and Culture and Vice-Versa* (2004).
Should be read as the authoritative account from this particular author on the relation between anthropology and history.

Emmanuelle Le Roy Ladurie, *Montaillou* (1978).
Entertaining and important, Le Roy Ladurie's research was based upon the large archive of manuscripts that survive concerning Montaillou and the terminal dates he uses are quite precise – 1294 to 1324. The emphasis of the book concerns the 'Cathars and Catholics in a French village' at a time of extreme duress. While by no means the first history of a small community, this was a ground-breaking work in microhistory.

Carlo Ginzburg, *The Cheese and the Worms: The Cosmos of a Sixteenth Century Miller* (1982).

Carlo Ginzburg, *The Night Battles: Witchcraft and Agrarian Cults in the Sixteenth and Seventeenth Centuries* (1983).

* **Carlo Ginzburg**, *Ecstasies: Deciphering the Witches' Sabbath* (2004).
All these books are exemplars of the anthropological approach. The last probably has the most developed introduction to the theoretical contours of microhistory.

15 Geography

Introduction

Geography and its methods have been especially useful to historians in recent years, particularly for those historians working on urban topics and on empire. The first section acknowledges the way place and space have been understood in both urban and imperial studies and charts the development of historical geography as a sub-discipline, closely related to both anthropology, which we dealt with in the last section, and sociology, which is the subject of the next. This section, therefore, will concentrate on the contribution of historical geography and its importance to the historical method in the study of space or place, using examples that illustrate how geographical approaches to history have become critical to historians. By the end of the section we will have a robust idea of why geography counts in historical analysis more generally and why it is important to history. The second section investigates empire geographies: geographies closely aligned with postcolonial criticisms of imperialism, postcolonial discourses and the problem of how power was wielded in imperial spaces, in both the past and the present. The final section concentrates on urban spaces and the mapping used by Charles Booth, the late-nineteenth-century statistician, philanthropist and social investigator. Maps have been a constant if changing focus for historical geography and are useful as a way of illustrating the extent to which geography has moved away from the social sciences and towards the arts or humanities, facilitating the use of maps as historical sources.

Section 1

History, space and place

Space and place orientate historians, allowing us to analyse historical context in a dimension other than time. Historical or cultural geography helps us to understand how spaces or places change. H. G. Well's hero in *The Time Machine* (1895), known only as 'The Time Traveller', shifted forward in time without moving a muscle. His vantage point stayed constant as, sitting in his machine, he slipped further into the future or retreated into the past. At its simplest, historical geography charts change in a single place, looking out for altering power relations in that place or examining cultural, social, political relations in comparison to other places. Historical geographers are interested in places: what it is that they represent over time, yet proceed with the conceptual framework of other historians, rather than the more familiar concerns such as the movement of tectonic plates, river courses, volcanoes or climate fluctuations.

A brief focus on a place can reveal much. An example is Bank junction at the heart of London's financial district. The City was both iconically and in reality the financial and imperial powerhouse of British imperialism; it provided much of the money for expansion and was where a good deal of global business was transacted. This business was not just undertaken in the abstract form of loans or insuring the world's shipping against risk, for instance, but could be seen and experienced in an actual space. As a confluence of roads abutting the Bank of England it is a space that has unsurprisingly attracted a good deal of attention from historians, precisely because in the nineteenth and twentieth centuries it was where modern capitalism existed at its essence and from where it developed overseas. Niels Moeller Lund (1863–1916), a painter born in Denmark, focused on this place in his *Heart of the Empire* (Plate 6), which is a painting that looks down at Bank Junction and the Mansion House from the roofscape of the Bank of England, while gazing further afield to older spaces in the City such as St Paul's Cathedral. Some historians see this as an image of national identity that is uniquely organised around the business zone of an important urban place, the very epicentre of Britain's imperial might.

Taking this painting as a single source historians may be forgiven if they determined that this landscape defines the City as exclusively modern, bereft of a residential population, even if the use of other (written) sources would identify a flourishing associational life. Lund's portrayal of City space picked out cathedrals and churches, the halls of the Livery Companies and with the view of the Lord Mayor's Mansion House, the City Corporation as the ancient local government of the square mile, all nestling between the cracks of the otherwise dominant financial palaces. Just by looking at this painting and other contemporary sources it is possible to conclude that places celebrated for their grandeur and modernity sat cheek by jowl with historic sites and buildings. To put it another way, it is a space that contains the fragments of the past as well as the essence of the present. Yet by using only the conventional tools of history, we would be in danger of associating the City only with modernity – with finance and capital.

One way of amending a received view of the City as being simply about business and power might be to use approaches developed by historical geographers. By fixing our gaze on place we focus down to the level of the street, finding the workers that serviced its business. Then the City of London becomes more than the sum of its economic interests. Rather it is a place that contains pockets of overcrowding, working-class housing and poverty and is alive with social dangers such as criminality and violence. In order to examine this same place in an entirely different light we would need to turn to other sources. Contenting ourselves with visual sources for the moment, we find another painting influenced by Lund's study of the City as the bustling and noisome centre of a great empire. Frederic Marlett Bell-Smith (1846–1923), an émigré to Canada in 1867, in many ways stands in contrast to Lund. Bell-Smith was influenced partially by Lund, but unlike Lund he gave a strong sense of how City spaces were about much more than big business. Painted in 1909, Bell-Smith's *The Heart of Empire* emphasised the workforce of a City that was miles away from the impression of the City as almost unpopulated, jam-packed with imperious buildings. Featured instead in the foreground are ordinary working-class Londoners. Thus we find a newspaper boy, costermongers, soldiers and sailors, drivers, and a motley collection of pedestrians going about their daily business against a backdrop created by the imposing architecture of financial power.

The City of power, modernity and business may be one way (it might be concluded) to understand the City in history but it can be seen that these spaces were populated by the poor and powerless. In either case, the consideration of place has yielded considerable benefits. Thinking about this place as essentially contested is, therefore, an example of how geographical approaches can be useful to historians. While historians have been keen to map the City's boundaries and write copiously about its function within modern capitalism, it is only by using geographical approaches to place can we begin to see the City's history as existing in social and economic layers: from the stockbroker and the clerk to the newspaper boy, carriage driver, chestnut seller and sailor. By looking closely at the City's diverse spaces through the lens of historical geography, we get an alternative view of the City that is not dependent on a simple nexus between modernity (what it means to be modern), business and empire.

From this example, we should have some idea of what historical geographers do and some sense of the range or limits of their concerns. Yet we should pause to recognise that the work of historical geographers is premised on the notion that historians cannot take place as given – a mere backdrop where events are played out. Places, such as the City of business or the City of the casual poor, are cultural places that affect the thoughts and behaviour of those that inhabit that place. To be 'something in the City' can mean several things, but in any case, the place represented by either of our paintings has a significance in its own right. Before we go any further, we ought to establish an uncluttered and straightforward definition of historical geography that can be applied easily to other historical situations.

Historical geography is the study of places in the past. As found in the chapter on anthropology (and will be found with sociology), it is as easy to find what it is that historical geographers do as what historical geography is. But this description of what historical geographers do will only get us so far. Let us therefore take as an example of the actual use of geography in history, the *Annales* school in France. Part of the cross-disciplinary work of *Annales* (also discussed in Chapter 9) spans the twentieth century and became predominant in the use of geography by historians. Fernand Braudel wrote a magisterial work of history that was influenced enormously by geographies of his chosen region – the territory that borders the Mediterranean. His book *The Mediterranean World in the Age of Philip II* was first published in the late 1940s and concentrates on climate, terrain, agriculture, cities and trade, transport and demography – all the raw materials of geography. He used geography (mountains, plateaux, hills, foothills, plains, and so on) before he got to the people, their economy and then the history of the people.

The latest definition of geography and its relationship to history has in more recent years come from the historical geographer, David N. Livingstone. His *The Geographical Tradition: Episodes in the History of a Contested Enterprise* (1992) hit on the idea of geography as a developing discipline, its preoccupations and approaches changing with society. Once, according to Livingstone, the geographer was concerned with the scientific problem of navigation. One thinks immediately of the Royal Geographical Society in this respect. Later involved in Enlightenment-driven science, he goes on, geography became 'an instrument of imperialism', manipulated to serve the interests of racial theory. At another moment geography has helped find geographical patterns of diversity, adapting models of evolutionary theory and the importance of regions and 'zones' which have all fed into urban sociology (see Chapter 16). It has been concerned with environment and resources. It has gone through phases where quantitative methods have been embraced, and phases (such as the City example above) where culture and imagination have been all the rage. It has been against pure fact gathering where human agency or action is suppressed or minimised in favour of what Livingstone calls 'the quantitative tabulation of economic data', the act of working out statistics (Livingstone, 1992, p. 356).

The assumption that cultural-historical geography is focused entirely on place, locality, values and social theories that make sense of modernity would be mistaken; cultural politics, iconography and the reading of landscapes are the main focus in Britain and, as has been seen, can all be read like any other text. Britain in fact has been host to the 'new cultural geography' with Denis Cosgrove, Peter Jackson and Nigel Thrift prominent in this respect. Other geographers such as Doreen Massey and David Harvey have influenced historians but it would seem have not themselves been unduly influenced by any sort of historicism. In the meantime, historical geography in North America has been more concerned with the reconstruction of landscapes and the role of landscape in society.

Different places and spaces have been historically influenced by a nexus of patriarchy and capitalism and have (or had) the ability to control lives depending on sex or gender (Rose and Ogborn, 1988). The separation of men and women in poorhouses or asylums, schools, factories, religious institutions or in the home were given as cases in point. Yet they have received very little attention from historical geographers and, it has been argued, women remain hidden from geography. There have been attempts to redress this omission but most work in America, for example, remains locked within the more traditional cultural geography associated with the important pioneering work of Carl Sauer (1889–1975) with its empirical and non-theoretical flavour (Dennis, 1991, pp. 265–88).

Perhaps the most interesting historiographer and urban activist that takes us forward in understanding the urban from a cultural history point of view was the extraordinary work of Jane Jacobs (1916–2006). Cities to Jacob were the historical powerhouses of advanced civilisation and the economic roots of any complex culture. Her *The Death and Life of Great American Cities* (1961), *The Economy of Cities* (1969), *Cities and the Wealth of Nations: Principles of Economic Life* (1984), *Systems of Survival: A Dialogue on the Moral Foundations of Commerce and Politics* (1994) and *The Nature of Economies* (2000) posit the city as an organic system with all the moral life of an advanced life form. In a sense it might be argued that her optimism about the power of cities to both represent all of humanity and to simultaneously hold up the potential to transform it was the antithesis of Lewis Mumford's work on the city. Mumford, who in *Cultures of City* in 1934 and *City in History* in 1961 was, for all his humanity, largely pessimistic about modernity and the accompanying mechanisation of urban life. Not until the end of her life did Jacobs reveal her own pessimism about the weakening of social responsibility, the cheapening of culture in North America and the general amnesia about history – something that her *Dark Age Ahead* (2004) both articulated and predicted in areas as diverse as education, the family and the affects of technology. In so doing she evoked a diverse range of historical examples, examples that she felt could allow lessons to be learnt and a remedy put in place even at this late hour.

Historical geography has moved now towards postmodernism. This, in brief, has led to a concern not with the accumulation of facts about place but with how place as been represented in what might be called cultural texts. Edward Said, and in particular his book *Orientalism* (1978), has been enormously influential in the area of postcolonial theory (see Chapter 5). Said described how knowledge and culture can work together in the application of power. Through representations of its culture, the 'Orient' could be viewed by the West as backward and exotic, while the West could be seen by comparison as modern and rational. That the British had mapped Egypt in the 1880s meant that they could describe the Middle East and eastern cultures in their own terms: through western texts – mostly paintings and literature gathered through journeying to the East – and thereby, because of this knowledge, they could rule over place and peoples. Another, perhaps more accessible example of the relationship between language, culture, knowledge and power, is *Translations* by the Irish playwright Brian Friel. First performed in 1980, it is a play about the mapping of Ireland by the English-based Ordnance Survey in the 1830s and the forced introduction of English to Irish schools. Names given or imposed on a place affect its cultural identity.

As in the example given by Said, to have knowledge of a place is to have power over it. Maps and mapping, therefore, have become as instrumental to the study, for instance, of imperialism as they were once vital to imperialism itself. This relationship between maps and space, including maps of empire, as will be seen in the following sections, has become equally invaluable to historical geography.

Section 2

Geographies of empire

The Victorian author Charles Dickens wrote a book in 1838 which brought to life one of the most reviled characters created in the English language. Dickens notoriously portrayed Fagin as a Jew who manipulated the children of London's slums into learning the dark arts of robbery and picking pockets. In a famous scene from *Oliver Twist*, Fagin traversed the highways and hidden spaces of the city, criss-crossing through back alleys and underpasses, apparently knowing the city in ways considered wondrous yet sinister by contemporaries. A contrast, perhaps, is Joseph Conrad's *Heart of Darkness*, a novella serialised in 1899 before it was published as a book in 1902. His hero, Marlowe, a seaman and wanderer, did not penetrate the heart of the city like Fagin but went in the opposite direction, taking a psychological journey to the edges of the imperial imagination – going to the borders of what reasonably could be known.

These examples from literature illustrate how important geographies – the understanding of place – are to our efforts as historians to tease out how place influences history. The metaphor of centre and periphery is especially significant to our historical understanding of both urban spaces and empire spaces. That is to say, the urban is imagined at the centre of our understanding of place and the empire at the periphery, by definition on the borders or edge, and occasionally in the way it is described it can, like in *Heart of Darkness*, tip over into the mythical or menacing. We touched on this metaphor in the first section when discussing Lund's painting that focused on the roofscape of the mighty imperial City (in the centre) but then adjusted its gaze out towards the colonies (on the periphery). Geographies of the urban and geographies of empire both in a sense rely on knowledge of, as historical geographer Felix Driver put it, 'cultures of exploration' that existed in both Dickens' London and Conrad's Africa. This section will therefore concentrate on how geographies of empire and geographies of the urban interacted and how historical geographers have treated this interaction.

Driver's chapter on social investigation in the 1890s metropolis in his *Geography Militant: Geography, Exploration and Empire* and Alan Lester's work on *Imperial Networks: Creating Identities in Nineteenth-Century South Africa and Britain*, both published in 2001, connect urban with empire geographies. Driver noted the influence of domestic accounts of London such as that of the Salvationist William Booth and his much-read *In Darkest England* (1890). (William Booth is not to be confused with his namesake Charles who will be discussed later.) This book is in many ways graphic and hard-hitting. Typically for an evangelical tract of the period it was both keen to save souls and dire in its warnings for those that choose the wrong path in life. The Salvation Army under Booth became a feature of the industrial metropolitan landscape and with tambourine and military-style uniform, Booth and his followers explored London at the same time that they rescued its miserable and downtrodden people. It was also a book that in turn was influenced by the publication in the same year of the explorer and journalist Henry Moreton Stanley's *In Darkest Africa*. As Driver put it in his *Geography Militant*, 'The language and politics of exploration abroad were recycled in the context of debates over social policy at home as the frontiers of geographical knowledge were mapped onto the heart of empire' (Driver, 2001, p. 23). There was then a relationship between exploring the 'unknown' city of the poor and destitute and exploring the unknown paths and tributaries of empire.

In some ways, the centre/periphery metaphor is considered somewhat dated. Yet, both Driver and Lester demonstrated a mutual interest in knowing how the exploration of foreign lands abroad linked with a growing knowledge and exploration of the unknown city. The metaphor is still useful then as a way of explaining the extent of historical geography's interests and preoccupations. Lester recounted how each settler colony was a hub for communication between 'certain social and political groups that concerned themselves, even if only periodically and half-heartedly, with events at the margins of empire' (Lester, 2001, p. ix). Exploring London and exploring empire forged both the identities of people that occupied these spaces and informed discourses about these spaces. Historians sensitive to the methods and approaches of historical geography have been keen to stress how describing unknown metropolitan and imperial spaces helped map those places onto the contemporary imagination. John Marriott, for instance, argued in *The Other Empire: Metropolis, India and Progress in the Colonial Imagination* (2003), that imperial centre and colonial periphery, to some extent, constructed each other through what he called a 'unitary field of analysis'. Issues of poverty and race pressed on the 'explorers' of both London and Delhi and are described in London-published evangelical tracts and Indian travelogues in very similar ways, although the extent of this shared way of describing these different spaces may have been somewhat less apparent than Marriott had initially thought. In any case, that influences between centre and periphery are interlocked and are reciprocated is an idea which has proved to be tremendously useful to historical geographers, urban historians and historians of imperialism.

It is the emphasis on power and uses of power in the colonial and postcolonial interest, that is, how imperial powers took over space and used it for their own purposes, that has excited most interest among historical geographers. The expression of this power can be found in the mapping of empire geographies and its importance to the work of historians.

According to Eric Wolf in his enormously influential *Europe and the People Without History* (1983), to understand the world of 1400 we must begin with geography and space – how the world was spatially ordered and how that ordering was transformed by the opening up of the Americas at the end of the fifteenth century. Wolf, first discussed in Chapter 12, was trained initially as an anthropologist and then turned to geography. His emphasis was on topography, the climate, and the extent to which these factors influenced the development of trade routes and the interconnections between people within the overall context of the rise and fall of empires. Many travel accounts, for example, that may have helped understand how space was organised globally remained little known or never saw the light of day; whether these accounts were published and distributed depended upon varieties of social, economic and political factors. Although it is possible that some of these travel accounts were written with a degree of objectivity, and that others contained a substantial amount of imaginative writing, such distinctions would have meant little to the medieval reader. Places like India and China were so beyond the mental horizons of people in the 'known world' that they simply had no way of assessing the validity of travellers' accounts.

This is why maps became a more direct and accessible way of conveying a sense of the spatial ordering of the world and why they remain such invaluable sources for historians. We cannot think of maps as inert records of landscapes or passive reflections of objects – these are above all socially constructed images. They cannot be judged in terms of their veracity or falsehood, but have to be viewed as ways of representing, conceiving, articulating and structuring the human world – and as such they are influenced profoundly by the social relations from which they were created. This was true at the very origins of mapping. Their production was subject to all the factors relating to literature; indeed many of the early maps were drawn from literary accounts, including biblical accounts, such as a map of the Garden of Eden, which before the advent of accurate techniques of surveying, are to our eyes so fantastic.

So what was the state of cartography in 1400 and how from maps can we get a sense of how people *at the time* saw the world? How too does the development of cartography connect to imperial geographies? Maps have been around for many centuries. The earliest-known example is from 5 BCE. Perhaps not surprisingly, it was the Romans who put cartography on the map. There is an important historical lesson here which links to what has already been said in this section. Maps have always been associated powerfully with empire in that they were used actively in the pursuit of colonial objectives. Lands were claimed on paper before they were effectively occupied, and so in a way anticipated and facilitated empire. Surveyors marched alongside soldiers, initially mapping for reconnaissance, and then for general information, and eventually as a tool of pacification, civilisation and exploitation of the colonies. Maps were used to legitimise the reality of conquest and empire.

Strabo (64 BCE–20 CE) was the first great Roman geographer. Ptolemy (90–168 CE), who with some justification can be described as the father of modern geography, followed him. He did not really extend the spatial knowledge of Strabo, but ordered it in a more systematic way. It was Ptolemy who established the convention that places north at the top of a map, using a grid of latitude and longitude, who perceived the earth as a sphere divided into 360 degrees, and who devised a means of projecting the spherical earth into a flat map. He gave his name to this and so maps today are consequently labelled Ptolemaic.

Europe lost its supremacy over cartography in the Middle Ages. Roman Catholic orthodoxy dictated that the special ordering of the world be determined by Christian principles. So emerged what came to be known as 'T-O' maps, as represented in the diagram below.

A 'T' in an 'O' or circle represented everything that was known in the universe: Europe, Asia and Africa (beyond Asia was Paradise). The 'T' represented the large oceans: to the

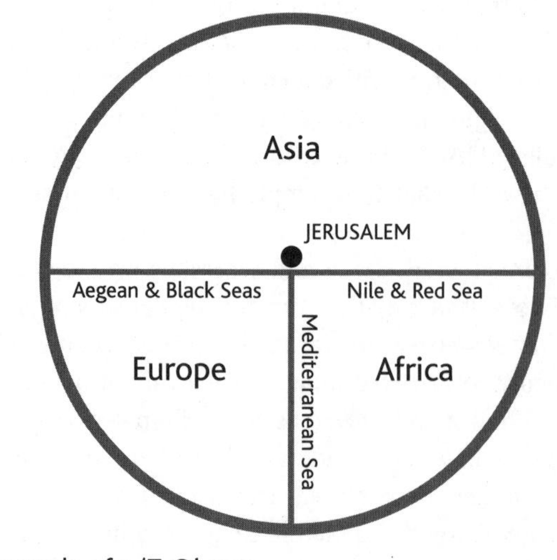

An example of a 'T-O' map

left the Black and Aegean Seas, to the right the Nile and Red Seas and through the middle, the Mediterranean. Jerusalem was at the centre of the world.

Such maps must be among the most expressive and ideological of all cultural objects. They describe not only the perceived world spaces of the Christian period from the Middle Ages to the great age of discovery, but reveal the minds and values of their creators. Their portrayal of space is replete with Christian ethnocentrism and the marginalisation of alien, that is, non-Christian peoples. For on these maps, the peoples of Africa and Asia are divided off from those of Europe. Indeed, the whole map divides the world into Noah's post-flood allotment of the world to his sons: Asia to Japhet, Europe to Shem and Africa to Ham; the first son, being the eldest, receives the largest land mass. Occasionally, a fourth area is depicted, boldly separated from the others. Here resided the people that were most unlike westerners – an antipodal region somehow beyond description.

Cartography was transformed by the so-called age of exploration, attendant upon the ascent of the West in line with the argument that geographical approaches changed in response to the anxieties of the time in which they are situated. This began in the Renaissance in the fifteenth century. Scholars rediscovered the works of ancient geographers such as Strabo and Ptolemy at the same time as they embarked on an unprecedented wave of discovery (see Chapter 7).

Portuguese and Spanish explorers and navigators were the most determined and ambitious. The Portuguese made their way down the coast of West Africa and eventually around the Cape of Good Hope in search of a sea route to India, completing the return journey in 1498. At the same time Columbus set off westwards across the Atlantic in the hope of reaching the rich empires of China and Japan. When he reached the Caribbean, he thought he had found Indians, laying the foundation for the distinction between East and West Indies. Soon after, Pedro Álvares Cabral, Portuguese navigator and explorer, sailed from Lisbon and accidentally discovered Brazil on his way to India.

These discoveries opened up the world to Europe, so transforming its sense of space and its geographical imagination. The entire project of discovery was in one decisive sense a direct refutation of Christian cartography; in another, it altered the use of maps – no longer were they seen as visual commentaries of divine purpose, and as repositories of legends, monsters and marvels, but as instruments to use practically. Cartography became a matter of transcribing and measuring the visible world, rather than a means of speculating on its nature, form and structure as the ancients once thought. Thus the discovery of the Americas was not merely a matter of finding some new land mass, but also of rethinking a world that could contain it. To do this it was necessary to reinvent the world. In the geography of the fifteenth century, there were no Continents and no oceans. The world was seen as an island – something essentially insular, self-enclosed, surrounded by the dark, inhuman and unknowable void of the deep waters. It was not that the ocean was as yet empirically unknown, but rather that it was, in principle, unknowable. The ocean had been a nothingness or void that marked the boundaries of the world – now it was necessary to think of the world as discontinuous, divided by an ocean that became no more significant than a river or a mountain range that divides two land masses.

This process of learning and development focused on space and the imagination of space had a tremendous effect on the modernising process. The need now was to understand and map urban centres.

Section 3

'How to lie with maps': maps, methodology and the metropolis

Shetland is not located in a box, just off the coast of mainland Britain. Yet it is shown as if it is nearer to Scotland than it is to Norway and every evening this falsehood is represented on BBC weather maps and across countless news organisations. London Underground lines do not move in straight lines (like the schematic map designed by Harry Beck in 1931) but in reality travel in crooked and circular motions; topographically (the features on the ground such as a railway) are correct but geographically incorrect. Maps are the stuff of historical geography and maps lie. One commentator, Mark Monmonier, in his book *How to Lie with Maps* (1996) argued that maps in general are a 'selective, incomplete view of reality' that, like speeches or paintings, are authored collections of information subject to distortions arising from ignorance, greed, ideological blindness, or malice' (p. 2). Not all maps, of course, and not always. As the last section witnessed, the way we see maps has changed radically over time. From the perspective of historian Jeremy Black in both his books on this subject, *Maps and History: Constructing Images of the Past* (2000) and *Maps and Politics* (1997), maps are selective in what they show, and convey a sense of art or artifice; that is, they are constructed, or, to a limited extent at least, made up. The argument of this section, therefore, is that cartography is not a science: objective, precise, technically mathematical; it is now a branch of the arts. Cartographers can now make maps with pin-point precision but the choice of what to map, what to include and exclude in a map, what colour legend to use, are all subjective judgements.

Two views of maps as mathematically accurate and faithful to an objective truth (like a photograph) and maps as an interpretation or representation of reality (like a painting) are played out in the methodological problems that historians face in the interpretation of maps and their use in the past. Perhaps one way of illustrating this tension is to look closely at Charles Booth, the nineteenth-century philanthropist and social investigator (see Chapter 17). Booth was an innovator in urban cartography but before discussing his contribution in this area, more needs to be known about the man and his methods.

Charles Booth (1840–1916) was concerned with social statistics and social reform. He was also concerned with morality and with moral character – facets that every individual ought to have as part of a civic ideal. This stance was not uncommon among his Victorian contemporaries. A lack of civic virtue was judged against the notion of 'fitness', recalling perhaps, the social reformer John Bright's appeal for constitutional rights in 1867 to be extended to the 'fit', that is, those that had the rationality and property to grasp the rights and obligations of the franchise and thereby of full citizenship. A lack of the wherewithal to be fit and independent would suggest a failure of moral will and was a sign of defective citizenship; although for Booth this might be explained by defects in the social environment. The Left, therefore, has tended to dismiss Booth, with historians E. P. Thompson and

Eileen Yeo (most notably) regarding him as a middle-class moralist with inferior informants and little direct contact with the working class.

Booth's ability to be detached is important for our consideration of him as urban map-maker because it would inevitably say something about the nature of his maps. The point about Booth in this respect is that his own perceived sense of what constituted a 'fact' was but a short conceptual hop from what we now can see clearly as the fiction of late-Victorian novelists, artists and journalists. Fiction, art and reports filed by sensationalist journalists to the mass-circulation journals and newspapers of the Victorian age is collectively called social reportage. Both Booth and the social reportage of the time drew on official reports for their ideas, although there is no guarantee that either parliamentarians or those that sat on Royal Commissions and the like could declare themselves entirely free from assumptions about the London poor which social reportage expressed in such vivid and vulgar colours. If social reportage is the sum of literature, art and journalism, perhaps its most detailed and lurid exponent was Henry Mayhew, a journalist and social investigator in the 1840s and 1850s. His sensational descriptions of poverty and criminality were part and parcel of social reportage, an influence that if anything intensified between 1889–1902 when Booth wrote the bulk of his reports about London poverty, industry and religious influences. The language used by Charles Booth places grave doubt on his claim of scientific objectivity. The influence of these descriptions that seem to chime so perfectly with what science thought it knew about human evolution (and degeneration), one might argue, is reflected in the way Booth constructed his maps.

Like Booth in his *Life and Labour of the People in London* (1889–1902), historians want to map the unknown, to explore, but also to find the 'underlying' truth of places like London as a 'myriad of subcultures'. Booth's groundbreaking attempt to use statistical material in order to provide a social classification for all London's streets, displayed in the colour coding of his *Descriptive Map of London Poverty* in 1889, was startlingly innovative. These distinctions are given expression in the form of a map, that is, are represented spatially in Plate 7.

Bearing in mind Booth's use of contextual evidence in the construction of his maps, we might want to ask: did Booth's maps describe poverty as he intended or were they a distortion of reality, more a reflection of Victorian moral values? Table 15.1 shows the method Booth used to classify classes: black represents 'the lowest grade', while yellow is the lightest and most transparent of the primary colours and is ascribed to the wealthy.

Table 15.1 Booth's street classification

Colour code	*Social character*	*Class groups*
Black	The lowest grade	A
Dark blue	Very poor	B
Light blue	Standard poverty	C, D
Purple	Mixed with poverty	C, D + E, F
Pink	Working-class comfort	E, F
Red	Well-to-do	
Yellow	Wealthy	

The use Booth made of colour should make historians wary, and an analysis of this may go some way to answering the central question about the accuracy of Booth's maps and the imposition of Victorian moral values on what Booth would have claimed to be the objective claims of science. We need to take into account the contexts raised so far and to interrogate his mapping as we would any other source. Any historian worth his or her salt should ask questions, although answers to these questions now are not our chief concern. Were Booth's choices influenced by the technical limitations of printing at the time? Was he influenced too by contemporary innovations in art such as Pre-Raphaelite art and his friendship with the Pre-Raphaelite artist, Holman Hunt, thus explaining his own innovative use of colour coding? Might his own cultural presuppositions and perceptions of social hierarchy have found expression in darkness as a byword for vice and depravity while light colours suggested civility and virtue? To what extent was Booth open to contemporary assumptions and theories regarding the degenerate nature of the poor (Englander, 1995)?

The language of the reports and notebooks (as the historian Geoffrey Crossick and others have argued), like his maps, was shaped by contemporary concerns that the respectable working class would be infected by an underclass. We know that Booth supported the exclusion of the 'residuum', or those thought by biological predisposition to sully the gene pool of an imperial race, who by necessity had to be banished to labour colonies. In this, Booth only succeeded in holding up a mirror to late-Victorian respectability and social theory. Whether Booth and others presented a true representation of their subject, or rather more simply mapped moral prejudices, have implications for Booth's methodology and for his claims of value-free investigation. It also tells us something about our use of maps as historical sources – whether, indeed, they might be considered to be more like photographs or more like paintings.

Booth, like contemporary sensationalist journalists, writers and social-realist artists, wanted to map the unknown. He also claimed that he wanted to get beneath the more lurid accounts of the urban poor. That is perhaps one reason why the emphasis placed on cartography by Booth was very innovative – he wanted to present his findings as unimpeachable science. When he displayed his map of London at Toynbee Hall and the Oxford House settlement at Bethnal Green in London's East End it measured an enormous 16 ft by 13 ft. Its scale was 25 inches to the mile and he had it specially hand coloured by his staff.

David Reeder (1995) has discussed this innovation in social cartography. The subjectivity of Booth's maps drawn from his poverty survey, suggested Reeder, derived from Booth's initial feeling that the metropolis was essentially so large and so diverse that it was unknowable. He proceeded to explain that Booth was keen to provide a context to his data that could not be strictly quantifiable, that reflected the fluidity and almost mystery of London life, but went much further in portraying more data on his maps than was strictly necessary. This suggested, perhaps, a continuing need to understand, not simply what he *thought* about London, but how he *felt* about London it all its disturbing complexity. This subjectivity was compounded, it could be argued from a reading of Reeder, by the very methodology of the survey itself – its use of School Board Visitors, schoolteachers, policemen, clergymen, social workers and local administrators to collect data which, no matter how widely gathered, could never be free from the inherent bias of those that collected the information. That Booth thought that this bias could be eliminated by the sheer weight of the collected data, suggests a naivety about the nature of social investigation as a credible science.

It owes something to Booth's mistaken assumption, moreover, that information (and by extension the representation of information on his maps) could ever be an unsullied truth; it also tells us a great deal about contemporary assumptions about how space and place affected shifting poverty patterns and the movement of people. Booth's study was informed, for example, by standard assumptions about Jews and the Irish and some dogmatic views about areas that seem somehow inherently of the 'lowest grade'.

One way to consider to what extent Booth may have simply mapped his subjective moral values is to place two of Booth's maps side by side (Plate 8). The map on the left is a representation of an area in East London called the Old Nichol, what Arthur Morrison called in his fiction, the Jago, an area explored forensically by Sarah Wise in her *The Blackest Streets: The Life and Death of a Victorian Slum* (2008). High Street Shoreditch and Hackney Road bound it to the north with Spitalfields to the south. On the right is the same area portrayed after the newly created London County Council (LCC) had built the model Boundary Street Estate by clearing 15 acres of slums, displacing 6,000 slum-dwellers and providing new, modern, housing for 5,500 people. The Jago, or Old Nichol, was characterised by dirt, decay and degeneracy. A local clergyman, the pugnacious Reverend Osbourne Jay, had been resident in the area at Holy Trinity Shoreditch since 1886 and recorded his shocking experiences in his evocative *Life in Darkest London* (1891). Five years later, Morrison's *The Child of the Jago* cast Jay as Father Stuart and Toynbee Hall as the 'East End Elevation Mission' and arrived at similar, pessimistic, conclusions about the area. While the Old Nichol, imagined by social and literary observers as intemperate, violent, crowded and dark, the development promised temperance, order, space, and light. Put simply, as seen by contemporaries, it was an exercise in social cleansing. The two maps, both from Booth's survey, give some sense of the scale and scope of the demographic shift that occurred, and is a dramatic example of how historical geography and maps can record change over time.

Plate 8 takes a close-up of a 'circle with tentacles', featured in Booth's poverty map represented here. Both these representations (before and after) should be treated with care for their combined effect on those in Booth's team charged with representing social reality in his maps. Maps used in isolation rarely give a wholly convincing account; indeed there are three alternative sets of evidence that contradict the generalised negative descriptions of the area represented by Booth on the left-hand map. The ramshackle street on the left in Plate 8, is contrasted with the 'post-development' map on the right, from *Description of the Boundary Street Scheme* published by the LCC in 1896, which underlines a perceived significant improvement in the area: namely the replacement of the original inhabitants by artisans and clerks. Yet the map on the right is a blueprint or prospectus, an account of a space in the throes of becoming a different kind of space. In it we are invited to *imagine* that the factory provides steady work, not casual work, for residents who live nearby. As the School Board building is represented on the map, indeed a plethora of School Board buildings, they fulfil the promise, not the actuality, of public education. The reader of this map is invited to muse, to daydream that, when the day is done, the citizen, maybe the very citizen looking at the map, might stroll to a place of recreation: the centrepiece of the development, the garden or bandstand as it eventually became. Again, students of historical geography and students of the metropolis must ask, considering its topographical accuracy, whether these features were exaggerated in number or size. This is most certainly the case with the bandstand, which in fact is a lot smaller. Does this map really represent space that is scientifically constructed and objective? We would suggest not. Booth was reported in an obituary to have protested otherwise:

> **East London lay hidden behind a curtain on which were painted terrible pictures: starving children, suffering women, overworked men; the horrors of drunkenness and vice; monsters and demons of inhumanity; giants of disease and despair. Did these pictures truly represent what lay behind, or did they bear to the facts a relation similar to that which the pictures outside a booth at some country fair bear to the performance or show within? This curtain we have tried to lift.** (Quoted in Abbott, 1917, pp. 195–200)

Either way, it should be reiterated that Booth's maps were constructed like any other artefact: subjective in their representation of what might be or be regarded as one view, but are only one view of social reality – a reality or knowledge that can be at least partly unlocked using the tools of historical geography.

Maps can present a facet of history that is colourful and evocative. In the nineteenth century, maps were seen in mathematical terms: a form of knowledge final in its conclusions – assuming an Enlightenment notion that the information contained therein was transparent, objective, neutral and 'scientific'; both verifiable and falsifiable. There has been a shift in the perception of what it is that we think maps can do. Maps are not simply mathematical but they evoke the 'remembered, the imagined, the contemplated' (Cosgrove, 1999, p. 2). Maps depict neither the material nor the actual but instead they convey the immaterial or the desired. From this perspective, the map is just another cultural 'sign' that is selective, that omits, that is essentially opaque – we also look now as much for its silences as its obvious pronouncements.

Why is there this shift in our understanding of maps? One factor is our use of information technology. When maps are used online, for example, the spatiality is altered and the data synthesised; spatial coordinates are juxtaposed and manipulated. This is surely a decisive move away from Booth's flap-top table mentioned above – no matter how impressive in size, no matter how vivid its colours, no matter how plural its audience. What emerges from a brief study of the geography of the Victorian metropolis and the use of social cartography, or social mapping, is that maps can be used to investigate, communicate and inform, but as a primary source must be read with immense caution.

In practice

It is something of an aphorism that historians are interested in time, while space is the concern of geographers. Thus history is built around notions of the passing of time considered for the most part as a process of linear progress within a space which is never questioned. In this scenario, space is a given, a constant, a background against which historical events unfold. Now it has been apparent since the work of Einstein that time and space are not constants, but since these distortions are only apparent under extreme conditions at the subatomic level, they hardly have relevance for historical processes. It is therefore only in recent years, largely under the influence of geographers and sociologists, that space has come to be recognised as a dynamic dimension of historical change. Far from being an inert backdrop, physical space and the ways in which it has been represented have contributed massively to the ways in which historical actors have behaved. Thus the work of influential writers including Fernand Braudel and Eric Wolf have shown that geography matters because the physical landscape defined and set limits to the movements of people, and these limits have had a profound bearing upon what was possible.

Equally importantly, we are defined and define others in part by the ways in which space is represented and experienced. This process is ultimately political because there have been constant struggles to define the nature of particular spaces. It is no exaggeration to say that those who have been able to define, order and represent space have tended to be the ones who have prevailed in struggles, either at the micro level of, say, individual households, or at the macro level of the global. Thus European imperial endeavour was built not only upon the appropriation of space, but also its representation in particular ways. To define a space as wild, untamed or a wasteland was often a vital prelude to its subsequent annexation by colonising forces. And we have seen from Chapter 11 that the isolation of domestic space in early modern Europe was crucial to the history and politics of gender relations.

No sphere of activity in this regard was more important than cartography. The making of maps was never an attempt to capture in a neutral and accurate way physical space. Maps were very much part of an endeavour to define and hence ultimately control space, and it was no accident that all the major advances in cartography occurred at times of imperial expansion. Maps also played a vital role in ordering space at a more local level. The metropolitan poverty maps created by Charles Booth, for example, represented in distinctive ways the spatial distribution of the poor but were also deeply inflected by ideological assumptions about who and what the poor were.

We need therefore to keep constantly in mind the spatial dynamics of historical processes. From mountain ranges and oceans to cities and even streets and houses, space has played an import role in determining how people moved, and defined themselves and others.

Summary

The three sections of this chapter have said three things:

- The methods of historical geography are important in understanding place and the changing nature of places. Geography has been particularly important in charting empire and understanding the role of place in urban environments. The main point to grasp from this section, however, is that how we define what historical geography is has been largely dependent on the changing nature of what historical geography does. On occasion, it has embedded itself within the sciences, at other times it has focused on 'softer' evidence such as language or culture. It has gone through a postmodern phase where 'representations' of phenomena have become more important than the phenomena itself. In either case, it can be safely stated that historical geography is set apart from physical geography and its focus on place and the comparison with place in the past has proved to be both useful and innovative to historians.

- Empire geographies have explored in some depth over recent years the relationship between centre and colonial periphery and the way cartography proved to be an aid in the imperialist project. Indeed the focus on the centre/periphery metaphor in understanding both urban and imperial spaces continues to yield some fascinating historical questions. One such question is the nature of the relationship between so-called urban social investigators in the past, anxious to understand and map the 'poor man's country' and the imperial explorers who wanted to chart the boundaries of the known world. By looking closely at the way mapping has evolved since 1400, it was possible in this section to see how mapping the world could assist (for the West) the process of ruling the world. In this sense, geographers quite often have been at the forefront of what it meant to be modern. Without the tools of historical geography, we would have remained quite ignorant of this process.

- Urban geographies have exposed the constructed nature of map-making as, in the case of Charles Booth in the nineteenth century, the result of subjective moralising not objective 'scientific' approaches. By taking Booth as a case study, it became possible to see how mapping social phenomena could appear objective and scientific but in reality owed more to subjectivity and the moralising (if well-meaning) of a late-Victorian gentleman. Indeed it was suggested in this section that Booth was very much influenced by contemporary social reportage; that is, portrayals of the poor and of different ethnic groups (notably Jews and the Irish) by sensationalist journalism, slum literature and paintings that claimed to be socially realistic. Mapping and the historical study of place remain vital as a facet of our overall historical understanding.

Discussion document 1

Braudel's book and his work more generally represents an approach to history which grasps the main relationship with which geography is concerned; that is, the environment and the influence in turn that humans have had on that environment. The medium for this investigation is history. The second extract is an informed commentary on Braudel. The extent to which Braudel provides a workable framework for historical geography is open to discussion.

The first part is devoted to a history whose passage is almost imperceptible, that of man in his relationship to the environment, a history in which all change is slow, a history of constant repetition, ever-recurring cycles. I could not neglect this almost timeless history, the story of man's contact with the inanimate, neither could I be satisfied with the traditional geographical introduction to history that often figures to little purpose at the beginning of so many books, with its descriptions of the mineral deposits, types of agriculture, and typical flora, briefly listed and never mentioned again, as if the flowers did not come back every spring, the flocks of sheep migrate every year, or the ships sail on a real sea that changes with the seasons.

On a different level from the first there can be distinguished another history, this time with slow but perceptible rhythms. If the expression had not been diverted from its full meaning, one could call it 'social history,' the history of groups and groupings. How did these swelling currents affect Mediterranean life in general – this was the question I asked myself in the second part of the book, studying in turn economic systems, states, societies, civilizations, and, finally, in order to convey more clearly my conception of history, attempting to show how all these deep-seated forces were at work in the complex arena of warfare. For war, as we know, is not an arena governed purely by individual responsibilities.

Lastly, the third part gives a hearing to traditional history – history, one might say, on the scale not of man but of individual men . . . that is, the history of events – surface disturbances, crests of foam that the tides of history carry on their strong backs. A history of brief, rapid, nervous fluctuations, by definition ultrasensitive; the least tremor sets all its antennae quivering. But as such, it is the most exciting of all, the richest in human interest, and also the most dangerous. We must learn to distrust this history with its still-burning passions, as it was felt, described, and lived by contemporaries whose lives were as short and as short-sighted as ours.

Fernand Braudel, *The Mediterranean and the Mediterranean World in the Age of Philip II*, Preface to the 1st edition (1949).

The first aspect of this 'world' is geographical: 'man in his relations with the environment that surrounds him' (p. xiii). Here, the significant movement is almost imperceptible and is complicated by the ceaselessly revolving inner cycles of seasons and years. Its 'time' is that of geography (p. xiv). The second aspect is that usually dealt with by social and economic historians: the histories 'of the groups, of the structures, of the collective destinies, in a word, of the group movements' (*des movements d'ensemble*; p. 308). Here, the motion is 'slowly rhythmed' (*lentement-rythmée*), and the time may be called 'social.' In practice, this is a 409-page essay on the social and economic history of the area mainly during the sixteenth century. The third element is that usually dealt with by the traditional historians: the 'short, quick, nervous oscillations' of men of action. It is thus only in the last section of the book (354 pages) that the events of Philip's reign are recounted.

Bernard Bailyn, *Braudel's Geohistory – A Reconsideration* (1951).

Taken from Jacques Revel and Lynn Hunt (eds), *Histories: French Constructions of the Past*, vol. 1 (1995), pp. 87, 351.

Discussion document 2

The City is a landscape that has been raised as a 'symbolic heartland' and an 'historical inner core' – as a meeting point where the claims of the local (the 'archaic' City Corporation) and the demands of global interests (modern capitalism) do battle – and on the other hand, where historical tides carve out the 'City of history', as Jane Jacobs described its post-imperial present. How far the history of a place can provide useful questions and serviceable answers for the historian is a discussion that is surely prompted by the work of Jane Jacobs whose work over nearly half a century has added much to the historical knowledge of cities.

The title *Edge of Empire* does not refer to sites literally on the periphery of an imperial geopolitical regime. The British empire has in all but a few cases officially ended and the nations and peoples once part of its reach are in a state precariously registered as post-colonial. There is in theory no empire, no centre, no edge. Of course this is an official state which is challenged by the present as we know it: there are centres, there are peripheries, there are persistent structures of domination and subordination. The ongoing presence of anti-colonial politics attests to this. But the social and spacial demarcation of such uneven politics is no longer as clear as it once was. The structures of power that gave rise to empire live on in a more disorganised fashion. And any lingering certainty imperialism has is daily challenged by diasporic settlements, new nationalisms, indigenous land rights claims as well as a plethora of other events. That is, British imperialism lives on in the present but it is also always at its 'edge' point. This book describes this politics of the 'edge' in terms of the unstable negotiation of identity and power which occurs in and through the space of the contemporary city. The 'edge' of the title *Edge of Empire* evokes not a literal edge, the periphery, but . . . [the] 'profound edge', the 'unsafe' margin which marks not only a space of openness but also the very negotiation of space itself . . .

The relations of power and difference established through nineteenth century British imperialism linger on and are frequently reactivated in many contemporary First World cities. Yet in these cities there are also various challenges made to imperialism by way of what might be thought of as postcolonial formations. These expressions and negotiations of imperialism do not occur *in* space. This is a politics of identity and power that articulates itself *through* space and is, fundamentally, *about* space. This is plain enough to see in terms of the grand territorialisation of the building of empire, but it is also evident in the politics associated with contemporary processes of urban redevelopment, which is the main focus of my book. Changes to city spaces may occur within a calm consensus but more often than not may result in protracted struggle or in self-conscious gestures of reconciliation. The politics is rarely only about how space is to look and function, about competing architectural aesthetics or urban planning ideologies, although such concerns may well provide the dominant discursive form of these struggles.

These place-based struggles are also arenas in which various coalitions express their sense of self and their desires for the spaces which constitute their 'home' – be it the local neighbourhood or the nation home, an indigenous home or one recently adopted. The politics produced by places in the process of becoming or being made anew is, then, also a politics of identity in which ideas of race, class, community and gender are formed. This politics of identity and place is not simply built around structures of power internal to the city itself or even to globally linked processes of urbanisation, is undeniably a politics that occurs in and is concerned with the city, but for many groups it is also a politics constituted by a broader history and geography of colonial inheritances, imperialist presents and postcolonial possibilities.

Jane M. Jacobs, *Edge of Empire: Postcolonialism and the City* (1996), pp. xi, 2–3.

Further reading

* *essential*

David N. Livingstone, *The Geographical Tradition* (1992).
This has proved to be a seminal work in its comprehensive treatment of the changing meaning of geography and its relationship to the discipline of history.

Felix Driver, *Geography Militant: Geography, Exploration and Empire* (2001).
Driver takes a comprehensive view of the whole panoply of empire geographies, looking closely at the role of explorers and scientists but finishes with an interesting and important chapter on descriptions of empire in the context of late-Victorian London.

Jeremy Black, *Maps in History: Constructing Images of the Past* (1997).
This should be read in conjunction with the author's *Maps in Politics*, published in the same year. Both books are especially strong on warning about the opportunities and pitfalls of using maps as sources.

Eric Wolf, *Europe and the People Without History* (1983).
This is an extraordinarily ambitious world history written not by an historian but by an anthropologist. Not only does it challenge triumphant narratives of the rise of the West, but puts squarely on the agenda the importance of space to an understanding of historical change.

16 Sociology

1 Is sociology of use to historians?
2 History and the problem of the sociological method in understanding class, authority and the city
3 History, sociology and religion

Introduction

Sociology is one of the major disciplines from which historians borrow. The first section charts the development of academic sociology and the length and importance of the relationship that exists between the two disciplines. It concentrates on the development of sociology in the 1950s and 1960s and the reaction of historians to its development in the 1960s and 1970s, especially moves to construct a workable hybrid known as 'historical sociology'. Its chief aim is to access how far sociology is useful to historians by using sociological approaches to understand the phenomena of mutiny in twentieth-century France and Russia. The second section examines both the opportunities and problems presented to historians by conventional sociological methodology in the research and writing of history. It is seen how history uses different sources and methodologies, but also how sociological concepts such as charisma, status and social stratification are tremendously helpful in understanding past societies and the roles of individuals within those societies. The case study of secularisation and religiosity, confronted in the third section, is a problem that is common to sociologists and historians alike. Its study has shifted approaches to religion and irreligion in the past 20 years, revealing the various uses of sociological methodology in this area but also demonstrating how historical research can sharpen sociological theory.

Section 1

Is sociology of use to historians?

Drunkenness led to gambling and insubordination, while the pillage of property disintegrated into rape and murder, according to Anton Denikin (1872–1947), a First World War infantry commander who was later to lead White anti-revolutionary forces against the Red Army. His description of mutiny in July 1917 among the 2nd corps from the Caucasus and the 160th infantry division was both vivid and disturbing as an account of the Bolshevik revolt in the Russian army (Denikin, 1975). How did it compare with the mutiny of 30,000 French soldiers in May 1917? This on the face of it was also a revolutionary act, or at the very least one designed to sabotage the Allied war effort.

For historians, mutiny and war have often gone hand in hand. We intuitively assume that the blood spilled in combat, and the confusion and emotional pain of men wrenched from their families and homes, are together enough to explain the root causes of mutiny, and that our only task, difficult though it may still be, is to locate the *particular* circumstances of a rupture in wartime convention and hierarchy. Yet we could not be more wrong if we were to take this approach or at least we would neglect the insight and conceptual tools lent to us by sociology.

Sociologists are not usually concerned with particular historical circumstances but want instead to explain *general* phenomena such as power relations, the legitimacy of authority, the way bureaucracies and states work, and the mechanisms that make modern societies function. As such, sociology can help historians understand the particular by locating it within wider historical processes which reach across space and time. Sociologists have long recognised that authority (the right to exercise political, social and cultural power) and bureaucracy (an administrative system run along rational and well-defined lines) are both by-products of modern societies. Concepts that seek to understand authority and bureaucracy can perhaps also be used to explain acts of mutiny in surprising and unexpected ways. We know, for instance, that armies in wartime are under stress, that they rely on patterns of authority as much as they rely on the supply lines that bring them food, water and ammunition, and that consequently the political and economic machinery of a state at war demands bureaucratic organisations. With these assumptions in place, Tony Ashworth's *Trench Warfare 1914–1918* (1980) posed broad, sociological questions about the First World War and the nature of combat more generally: Why were some trench fighters more zealous, aggressive and disciplined in their combat roles than others? How were some men more able to endure the harshness and horrors of combat than others? What exactly was this ability to endure? He explained that men fought because of an aggressive military tradition, and that ideas of masculinity (what it meant to be a man, see Chapter 10) and abstract values such as patriotism drove soldiers forward in the most difficult circumstances. Finally, and perhaps the explanation that has most immediate use for historians, men fought because of social relationships among fellow combatants.

There is, however, another side to this question. Ashworth identified what he called 'the live and let live system' which influenced the conduct of battle. Generations of war movies have conditioned us to believe that hostile armies fight it out without restraint; shots ring through the air and explosions resound in the middle of battle with one side pressing ever forward and another pulling back beyond the lines. Orders to go forward or pull back are conveyed from aloof bureaucracies, politicians and generals instructing their armies to advance or retreat. In reality, according to Ashworth, combatants on each side do fulfil their roles but rarely do any more than the bare minimum required of them; indeed, there were tacit agreements on each side to go only through the motions of combat. You shoot, for example, only when shot at. These conclusions were supported by various sociological studies of the Second World War and the Vietnam War, which have revealed how few guns were fired, and among the small minority of soldiers that did fire their weapons, how little ammunition was expended. How do we explain this sociologically and historically?

With the emergence of modern warfare and the increasing influence of a bureaucratic state (the civil service, parliament and the military) came a realisation that each man was but a small part in the war machine. 'Social exchange' or the basic relationship between combatants in these circumstances was, as Ashworth put it, governed by reason, rather than martial values, masculinity, patriotism or the fellowship of other soldiers. Unless fired on, it made sense not to fire back, because this is the most reasonable way to deal with a situation where rank and number meant that a man was but a small cog in a massive and merciless killing machine. The only exception to this doctrine, it appeared, was when a fellow soldier was killed randomly (say by a sniper), engendering a certain rage among his comrades and an active urge for revenge, but even this took the form of a ritualised aggression.

From this reading of what the sociologist Max Weber saw as a natural and inevitable consequence of a modern state, a bureaucracy growing inexorably and an increasing rationality among its citizens, emerged an historical explanation of why soldiers did not lay down their arms as part of a dramatic or sudden mutiny, turning against their officers. Instead, mutiny can now be seen as a relatively small escalation, albeit a critical escalation, of a strategy of avoiding conflict among rank and file soldiers. From a sociological angle, the French mutiny of 1917 was no mutiny at all; these soldiers did not turn tail and run, nor, however, did they allow the Germans to advance. It was simply an extension of the 'live and let live' doctrine; an inertia that was a rational response from the soldiers to their enfeebled position in a bureaucracy that had denied them privileges such as leave to visit home.

The great mystery of this event for historians, however, has always been the question of why the Germans never once rumbled that the French had mutinied. Now that we know that French soldiers always minimised their firepower (save in exceptional circumstances), this phenomenon can be explained adequately – the Germans were already used to infrequent firepower coming from the French side and in all probability were applying the same doctrine themselves. In other words, we know from the application of sociological methodology that the behaviour of the French did not change significantly, at least not to a degree that the Germans would have noticed.

In addition to strategies of inertia and the occasional controlled aggression prompted by specific instances of, say, a sniper round, there were the even more occasional instances of the more formal truce. This may explain the fraternisation between the Berkshire and Saxon regiments during Christmas 1914 when British and German soldiers significantly reduced fire on Christmas Eve, ceased fire on Christmas Day and notoriously put up trees, sang carols and even played a football match or two. (The Germans won 3-2, probably on penalties.) Firing began slowly again on the day after Christmas.

We can also see by using sociological methodology, that the Russian mutiny with which we began this chapter was indeed a mutiny based not on a temporary withdrawal from action, but a conscious attempt to overthrow direct military authority. Officers were attacked for *political* reasons, and here sociological ideas of social stratification and Marxist class analysis may be effective tools of historical understanding along with Weberian notions of bureaucracy and the rational response of individuals within that bureaucracy. Where Weberian explanations for mutiny may look at dysfunction within the ranks caused by an increasingly remote bureaucracy that creates an 'iron cage' for those within it, Marxists would look to class relations within the ranks – say between officers and ordinary soldiers – who are, after all, only proletarians in uniform and who are bound to assert their own interests inimically to the higher ranks. Using the tools of sociology then, we can understand historical phenomena such as mutiny and, more than this, we can distinguish between different types of mutiny. Yet the relationship between the two disciplines has not always been so productive.

The differences between history and sociology can be traced back to their emergence as disciplines during the nineteenth century. The task of historians, it was believed, was to record the past as it actually happened (see Chapter 1). The emphasis was therefore very much on the expert use of historical evidence to put together a persuasive account of an event, person or period. Sociology, in contrast, drawing upon scientific approaches, sought to reveal the general laws which governed society and the individuals who comprised it. The intellectual founders of sociology assumed that, by learning everything about human beings and human society, knowledge could be used to transform human nature itself. Auguste Comte (1798–1857) was a French philosopher who coined the phrase 'sociology'. Comte understood that to understand any society we need a *social* science as an extension of the natural sciences; the latter influenced most profoundly by the seventeenth-century scientist Sir Isaac Newton. Newton's natural laws were reapplied to the study of society by early sociologists. In the same way that Newton could theorise gravity and motion and argue that the universe responded to universal not fragmented laws, so social scientists could feasibly understand society by a thorough investigation of society using similar universal approaches. Because humans as a species self-consciously exist across generations, behaviour and the way societies are organised could not be understood in isolation like a specimen from the natural world but must be understood in the context of history.

Modernity as a process or as an idea has underpinned and dominated the concerns of sociology since these pioneering insights. Broader questions about how society works have thus been asked by sociologists. How do people and structures respond to social and economic systems such as industrialisation, secularisation (that is, a growing absence of religiosity) and the progressive movement of people from rural to urban environments? Sociology grew up in the nineteenth century in the shadow of poverty and inequality, which persisted amid rapidly improving industry, science and technology, and gave rise to ideas that equality could level social difference, and promote progress. Theories of organic evolution (the notion that societies grow naturally) seemed initially to accompany early sociology when it could be defined narrowly as a 'science of man'.

From the formal recognition of the discipline in 1903 when the Sociological Society came into being and a Chair in the subject at the London School of Economics was created, sociology was marked out from other forms of social research or social work. Differences emerged between history and sociology, for example, which revolved around the following:

1 History is concerned with the unique and particular, while sociology is interested in the general (universal).
2 History is preoccupied with the refined use of evidence; sociology with the formulation of theories of society.
3 History is interested in change over time; sociology with questions of stability.
4 History deals with the past; sociology with the present.

Stated like this, the differences are oversimplified, whereas in practice the approaches can be complementary.

Some historians have feared that sociology would act as a substitute for historical theory, and that historians would simply adopt sociological theory without bothering to generate concepts for themselves. Gareth Stedman Jones as an historian of ideas and Raphael Samuel as a pioneer of 'history from below' were especially sensitive to this possibility and said so in an early edition of the *History Workshop Journal* (1976). About the same time in the mid-1970s when conventional approaches to history were being challenged and overtures were made to the social sciences, it looked as if historians would simply borrow concepts and theories from sociologists as a means of pursuing their research.

Sociology in the 1950s and 1960s had been dominated by the work of Talcott Parsons (1902–79). The essence of human behaviour was found in the social norms of individual behaviour and in the resultant order of the social system. The role here of functionalism – a term first tackled in Chapter 14 – is that social institutions such as the police or schools exist in order to maintain the social solidarity that Parson's described in his *The Social System* (1951) as homeostasis. The keyword here was 'maintain'. Systems existed, he argued, to reflect the shared norms of society and institutions mirror these general values. The meeting of needs in a society would ensure the survival of these institutions. There are a number of issues here that sociologists would identify. The claims made by Parsons were not particularly sensitive to parts of society not inclined to feel at one with the *conscience collective* – or shared moral beliefs. Gender and racial differences naturally come to mind, class and regional differences too are only dealt with in a blunt way. Nor then were graduations of power accounted for, indeed, Parsonian functionalism possessed an innate conservatism and resistance to social change.

As a wider critique of capitalist society and existing gender and race relations emerged in the 1960s, so too did a Marxist critique of functionalism. Sociology had long been interested in deviance but this now could coincide with an interest in the past. The Cambridge demographers interested in cliometrics were already looking at data over time, theorising about social processes and thinking sociologically about individuals and systems in the past (Abbott, 1991; also see Chapter 17). As seen already with the anxieties expressed by Stedman Jones and Samuel as representative samples of the Marxist-inspired new social history, the trick was to know how and to what extent historians could import theories derived from sociology. After all, the example of Parsons had not been propitious for historians.

Philip Abrams (1933–81) was perhaps the most vocal advocate of the hybrid approach taken by 'historical sociology', that is, a fusion of both disciplines that barely acknowledged that each had differing origins and aims. Citing the work of Immanuel Wallerstein, Michael Mann and others (scholars who used sociological modelling in their work), he believed that the disciplines of history and sociology had been coming together for at least three decades. Certainly, the relationship between sociology and history was a close one, even if historians seemed more wary than sociologists about how the two disciplines might work together.

History and sociology continue to enjoy a dialogue and have much in common. Yet there are dissident voices which remain sensitive to the differences. The sociologist John Goldthorpe, although or perhaps because he was first trained as an historian, has argued that sociologists are ill-placed to interpret primary sources, or what he seemingly dismisses as 'relics of the past'. Rather, sociologists should concentrate on constructing theoretical models and generating data in the present. Sociology should be 'historically minded' but sociology and history are fundamentally different 'intellectual enterprises' (Goldthorpe, 1991, 1994).

Historians have undoubtedly found it useful to use sociological constructs of power, authority, social stratification and legitimacy, but they are only constructs and as such need to be approached by historians with great caution. Some sociological approaches, as we have found when we have examined the causes of mutiny within wartime bureaucracies, are very useful to historians, but others need more qualification, as we shall now see as we turn to the themes of class, authority and the city.

Section 2

History and the problem of the sociological method in understanding class, authority and the city

'And fookin' amen to that' was a riposte from a member of the audience to 'an inordinately long, self-satisfied, godly and officious grace' from the president of the British mineworker's executive. According to the Marxist historian E. P. Thompson, the riposte represented the meeting of two contrasting working-class or plebeian cultures that developed sometime between 1870 and 1926 in the Deerness Valley, County Durham and doubtless elsewhere in the British coalfield (Thompson, 1976). The miner giving the grace was a 'devout Methodist' and as such represented respectability and anti-Communism and an acceptance of the conventions of society. The rather uncouth reply to the toast 'from a veteran class warrior and no respecter of persons' suggested a disputatious working-class culture more to Thompson's taste, that is, older, rougher, tougher and politically radical. In this sense the exchange may be seen as indicative of a culture and politics that had come to terms with capitalism by the end of the nineteenth century. Coal mining in North-East England was all-consuming well into the twentieth century: it dictated politics, culture, society in that area and impacted on the economy of a mighty empire. And yet the political allegiance of miners after 1870 was to Liberalism, and intrinsic to this non-revolutionary settlement for Thompson is Methodism, which as a form of Protestant dissent broke away from the Church of England at the end of the eighteenth century.

How class relationships at work can be understood in all their complexity from this single incident, however, is largely through sociological methodology. Thompson as a sophisticated proponent of the sociological approach claimed that 'there is no difference whatsoever in the methodology appropriate to the sociologist and to the social historian', but also warned of problems attached to the use of sociological methodology (Thompson, 1976). According to Thompson, there was 'a sociological itch' to generalise, to claim typicality in descriptions of phenomena when historians should be more inclined to find contrast and difference. To understand the development of miners' attitudes, working class culture and politics in the modern period, we must differentiate between the old plebeian culture (especially apparent among the radical Primitive Methodists who had merged with the Methodists in the 1930s), and those who had taken up positions of authority and trust on behalf of the miners. Drink, gambling, traditional fairs and feasts, sexual licence and profane song in this older culture, had given way to sobriety and conformity in the new. Sociology, according to Thompson, can help to understand this transition but only if deployed by the historian with subtlety and skill.

Care needs to be taken first to recognise that the old culture of a radical politics represented by Primitive Methodism had not completely disappeared, and that the existence of the drunkard, gambler, fornicator, blasphemer and layabout was worthy of comment. If historians uncritically adopt a sociological classification of people into types that takes no account of historical change, then they will not be able to adequately explain how 'fookin' amen' could have been so utterly offensive to a dominant Methodist respectability yet still represent a continuing or surviving counter-culture. It would be just plain rudeness and not historically significant at all. Alternatively, if we say that this is offensive to contemporaries but not representative of them in any way, then we merely parrot Methodism's own self-image, deploying an inflexible sociology to a situation that demands flexibility. Thompson urged us to register that both the 'officious, self-respecting, class-collaborationist Methodist lay preacher' and the 'irreverent blasphemer . . . class-conscious, self-disciplined secularist' are components of a common culture which have existed together for a long period. By keeping the polar extremes – collaborationist and respectable Methodism and cursing political radical – in *historical* view, we mitigate the tendencies in sociological methodology to favour one element of this common culture as 'typical' of the whole, so encouraging us to tell one half of the story at the expense of the other.

The example of the Durham miners suggested a community where class and culture were influenced by work, income and occupation but also a consciousness among miners that the sum of their existence was, in fact, working class. How then might we describe in sociological terms what it means to be 'working class'? One of the founding fathers of sociology, Max Weber, saw class as related to economic position, status to social prestige, and each related to political power. Weber was also been keen to focus on the meaning of social stratification, not through relationships unleashed by property relations but through the roles that individuals performed in society. Status, for example, can account for prestige, lifestyle, aspiration or deference in history. From this perspective, we can understand the deference or conservatism of the so-called blue-coated or newly affluent worker, or the uniformed working class, such as railway or postal workers, with their military sense of pride. These groups enjoyed a certain status and for that reason had a certain consciousness about their place in society, leading to a deference towards other status groups that in terms of income were, perhaps, a notch above them.

Marxists contend that class location is based objectively in property relations and what Marx called the forces of production. Forces in the marketplace thus determine the social standing of the proletariat or bourgeoisie. With class analysis used in this way, it is difficult to account for different cultures *within* the Durham miners, unless we say that one is a genuine expression of the working class and any other an expression of false consciousness. Thompson, however, rejected the idea of class as simply a structure that can be seen objectively, preferring instead to think of class as a subjective experience. It was not a 'thing' but a 'happening' that is realised in a 'relationship' with other classes, which most certainly cannot be found in passive sociological constructs such as occupation or status. Perhaps, as the historian Arthur Marwick commented, 'Class . . . is too serious a subject to leave to the social scientists' (Marwick, 2001, p. 15).

Let us take another concept developed by Weber as a means of exploring the potential of sociology. He claimed that charisma provides insights into how and why individuals influence history and is another example of the usefulness of sociological methodology to history, although it also serves a further warning of its inherent dangers. He saw charisma in individuals (a theological word derived from the Greek meaning 'gift of grace') as vital to the role of leadership in history. According to Weber's classic account, and to simplify, charisma is one of several ways that authority is manifested which tend to be associated with societies at different stages of economic, social and political development. These two are of interest to historians:

> ***Traditional authority*: Traditional forms of authority or authority built around the extraordinary personal gifts of a charismatic leader mean that leaders are obeyed because their followers believe in their special talents. The death of a leader who has personal gifts serves to invest posthumous authority in the office that he once occupied, thus enabling, according to Weber, 'traditional' authority to encompass the custom and ancient practice of any given society through 'clan' or 'institutional' charisma. Weber associates this 'ideal-typical' classification of power and authority with monarchical government of societies where no consensus existed as to the rules of procedure that should constitute society.**
>
> ***Legal-rational authority*: This is the most modern form of authority because it obeys formal rules and established procedures that are open to public scrutiny. Legal-rational authority is the typical authority associated with a modern society or bureaucracy. The authority of an office means that the personalities of the faceless or nameless bureaucrats that make that office function are quite irrelevant – they are still seen and accepted as legitimate because the office itself is seen as legitimate.**

These then are the basic ways of understanding charisma as it is conceived sociologically in the work of Weber and his followers. It has been especially tempting for historians concerned with how dictatorship works in a modern society to make use of these constructs, both as explaining the rise in the 1920s and 1930s of charismatic groups or charismatic individuals. Yet there remain problems in accepting these sociological approaches. How, as

Roger Eatwell (2006) asked, can individuals who rise at a time of crisis really attract a body of supporters unconcerned with anything else but the charisma of their leader? They would expect their charismatic leader to achieve and maintain superhuman feats of political mastery in an unstable environment and as historians we know just how unstable pre-war Germany or Italy or Spain was in the context of economic meltdown. Can charismatic authority invested in a single individual explain the anti-democratic nature of Nazi Germany or the Bolshevik Soviet Union, let alone the distinctly uncharismatic stuttering rhetoric of General Franco in Spain or Antonio Salazar in Portugal? Eatwell was also sceptical about explaining charisma as part of the psychology of a leader. Hannah Arendt, the German and Jewish political theorist, gave an example of how charisma can inform historical analysis:

> **The problem of Hitler's charisma is relatively easy to solve . . . it rested on the well-known experiential fact that Hitler must have realised early in his life, namely, that modern society in its desperate inability to form judgements will take every individual for what he considers himself and professes himself to be. . . . Extraordinary self-confidence and displays of self-confidence therefore inspire confidence in others; pretensions to genius waken the conviction in others that they are indeed dealing with a genius. . . . Hitler's real superiority consisted in the fact that under any and all circumstances he had an opinion.**
>
> (Cited in M. Canovan, 2004, p. 246)

This was in a society, pre-war German society, where no dominant opinion held sway and where equivocation had become the norm. Her *Totalitarianism* (Arendt, 1968) related how Hitler's 'extraordinary self-confidence' accounted for the support he enjoyed. More usual now, again according to Eatwell, is for historians to see the historic significance of the 'charismatic bond' which downplays the notion of a charismatic policy and to emphasise instead the relationship between leader and follower.

We have seen how, using concepts that originate with sociologists, historians have been able to understand how humans react in wartime bureaucracies, how class and social stratification explain cultures that essentially have common characteristics and, finally, how various notions of authority can unpick the legitimacy of political regimes. Turning now to the city, it is clear that historians and sociologists have long shared an interest in urban spaces. To Karl Marx and Emile Durkheim, two of the so-called 'founding fathers' of sociology, the city was a phenomenon that confirmed the massive changes that modern society was undergoing – although they each came to radically different conclusions about the significance and cause of the growth of urban spaces during industrialisation and its consequences for human existence. For Marx, the urban confirmed the inherent contradictions in capitalism, the most up-to-date place for the inequities of a system of exploitative production relationships and the resultant alienation (or separation) of the proletarian from the end product of his labour, losing humanity and becoming like a cog in a machine. For Emile Durkheim, however, the city suggested the disintegration of moral cohesion, the destruction of what he called the *conscience collective*. Durkheim conceived that societies were either 'mechanical' or 'organic'. A mechanical society is a society that is small and homogeneous with a simple division of labour; while an organic society is complex and has a developed legal system. He first identified them in *The Division of Labour in Society* (1893), and later in his *Rules of Sociological Method* (1938), and they are constructs with profound consequences for the urban historian. The remainder of the section, therefore, will concentrate on Durkheim, the adoption and development of his ideas by sociologists and the use historians have made of these ideas.

The testing ground for Durkheim's ideas was the so-called Chicago School, led from 1915 to 1935 by Robert E. Park, Roderick McKensie and Earnest W. Burgess. It was perhaps the first fully fledged sociology department, equipped to take on advanced projects such as social surveys and the census, as well as detailed investigations of topics including race and labour relations, and the ghetto. They elevated sociology to the level of an evidenced-based and peer-supported discipline by adopting a model of social change or evolution that was an admixture of Charles Darwin and Durkheim himself. The city, seen primarily as an ecological community, could adapt its environment to diverse human populations. As people flowed into the city (the population of Chicago in the 1840s was under 5,000, by 1930 it had risen to nearly three and a half million) its diverse population was in competition for the resources that would sustain life. In an urban environment, individuals have freedom and licence to pursue their goals, but this natural impulse to anarchy is pitted against a social need to exercise moral constraint. Society, in other words, seeks to preserve social solidarity through a *conscience collective*.

When the Chicago School represented the city using its now famous diagram of concentric circles (see diagram opposite), the land at the centre of the city was displayed as being used differently than the land on its outskirts. Different functional groups, therefore, occupy prime space, not haphazardly, but in a verifiable process that these new sociologists could observe and map. According to the Chicago School, urban change went through the following process as populations came and went:

> **disruption\change\destabilisation of the existing equilibrium\a renewed burst of competition either externally or internally prompted\new development\adaption to a 'higher' population\ new balance or equilibrium.**

With competition came dominance then succession then invasion; the different populations are re-sorted according to their functions and the zones reallocated with different demographic groups. Business tends to occupy the centre, and commuters serving the business centre occupy the outer circle, the suburbs. However, there is a 'transitional zone' that is in flux – occupied by failing business and reoccupied by those new to the city.

Sociologists by the 1950s (for reasons that do not concern us here) have largely abandoned a concept of the city as an eco-system. Yet sociological methodology remains useful to urban historians. If Chicago is swapped for London, we can see how during the 1880s the City and East End were transformed by the economic breakdown of small workshops at the inner perimeter, or the way that the 'transitional zone' took in new immigrants. Structural unemployment led, according to Gareth Stedman Jones in his *Outcast London* (1971), to social fears around the casualisation of the respectable poor and fears prompted by large-scale Jewish immigration from Russia and eastern Europe, and that these fears together found expression in contemporary social and scientific theories that were used to describe the poor.

Plate 9 brings this point to life and allows a sociological reading of this historical situation. Although historians dispute when and where they became prominent in the new shock cities of the nineteenth century – those industrial cities such as Leeds and Manchester

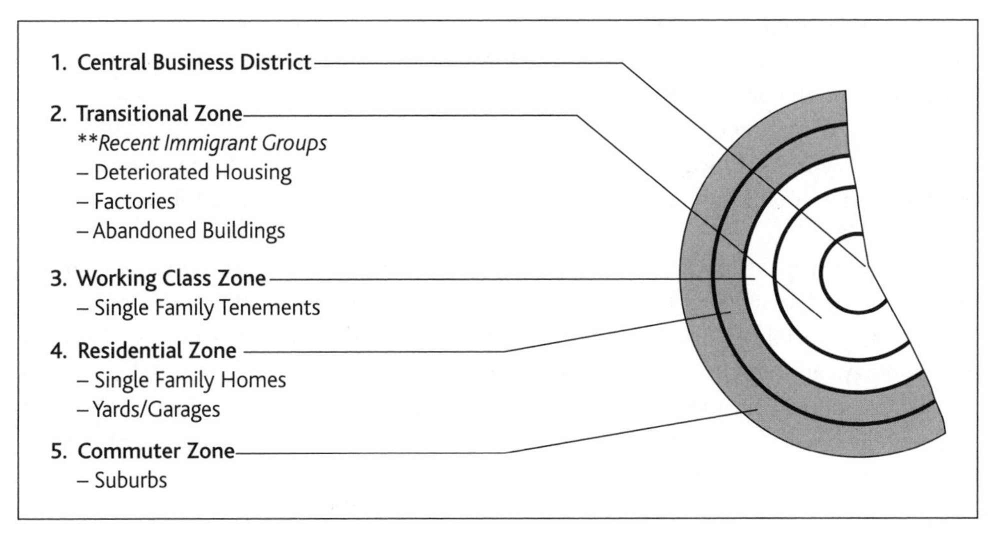

The concentric zone model

Source: Bruce Hoffman, courtesy of crimetheory.com.

that grew very quickly indeed, there is no doubt about the impact of the independent working-class neighbourhood on middle-class sensibilities and fears. Regardless of whether or not the Jewish or Irish immigrant occupied these neighbourhoods – as is doubtless the case in the example in Plate 9 from the *Illustrated London News* – there were profound implications for class relations and for the giving and receiving of poor relief. One might interpret this picture sociologically, revealing how sociological method can be used to the advantage of the urban historian. As these neighbourhoods became limited to the poor and working class, now living away from the gaze of their social 'betters', then so they became a social problem for a still Christianised middle class. How does one contact the poor in order to give charity? What happens when the poor themselves are not able to receive personally the necessary alms? Sociologically, these were dilemmas faced by *gesellschaft* communities that were characterised by a division of labour so advanced that quite literally people were thrown together as strangers. A *gemeinschaft* neighbourhood, on the other hand, according to the sociologist Ferdinand Tönnies (1855–1936), is a face to face community where the giver and receiver of philanthropy could in that very transaction maintain class and status relationships important to the social balance of society.

This is what Stedman Jones, following the anthropologist Marcel Mauss (1872–1950), called the 'deformation of the gift', and is a direct example of how an insight from a sociologist can provide stimuli for the historian with brilliant results. Without this gift relationship, the rich could not perform their Christian duty and the poor, correspondingly, could not be grateful, thereby breaking perhaps the most critical relationship in Victorian society. The very absence of a society where the poor were no longer under the moral gaze of the rich (because they lived in different neighbourhoods) meant that the rich could no longer scrutinise and manage the domestic lives of those less fortunate than themselves. The social crisis of the 1880s (unemployment, overcrowding, casualisation of the workforce) had thrown together the respectable working class with the 'residuum' or underclass, now perceived by modern Victorian science to be biologically incapable.

The subtitle of *Outcast London*, 'a study of the relationships between classes in Victorian society', refers to social relationships in the city. By concentrating on the structural breakdown of the inner parameter of London and observing the new relationships thrown up by casualisation, Stedman Jones, inadvertently perhaps, provided an interesting comparison with the Chicago School who were also seeking to understand how urban populations are established, migrate, are replaced or, in the case of 1880s London, admix to some extent.

This section began by looking at stratification among the Durham miners as a direct result of industrialisation and finished by looking at the effects of urbanisation. In each example we saw how sociology has provided insights for historians but also how sociological methodology can sometimes lay a trap for the unsuspecting. We have also seen how industrialisation and urbanisation, like the discipline of sociology itself, are direct results of a modernising process in society more generally. If this is true, then it is also true of religion in society and the gradual absence of religion.

Section 3

History, sociology and religion

Thirty-one million people in Britain and two and half billion people worldwide watched it live or on television; 580,000 condolence messages were sent electronically, countless and largely unrecorded ceremonies were held in Britain and abroad. All this surrounded the funeral of Diana, Princess of Wales in August 1997 and the extraordinary public outpouring of grief that followed her death. Flowers strewn along the way preceded her coffin with crying and wailing heard from the crowds that lined the route, expressions of emotion unthinkable when Sir Winston Churchill, a war hero after all, was buried in 1965. Perfect strangers left public notes to her around war memorials and other public places up and down the country. On these notes were references to a deity and afterlife that, if sociological research was to be believed, they should no longer have believed in or at least had been displaced.

According to many sociologists (and historians) religion, at least organised and conventional forms of religion, were in secular decline. Yet reactions to Diana's death displayed a religiosity or spirituality that sociologists thought abandoned long ago. By these accounts, modernity should have led us to a position where science and technology had made us rational with reasoned attitudes to death pointing us away from religion and religious tradition. Yet, when a seemingly beloved figure, well known and regarded by the general public, died violently in the prime of her life, then atheism and agnosticism were seemingly put aside. Older ideas of an afterlife and rituals of death revived, albeit adapted to modern circumstances. Of course, sociologists and historians alike have offered alternative explanations for this extraordinary reaction to the death of Diana. The dominant narrative of secularisation might, nevertheless, gives us pause to question an unfolding story of modernity that posits religion in a state of inexorable decline. We might ask how historical research can offer another narrative where instead of the decline of religious sensibilities, religion survives in many unexpected forms? Does sociology or history provide the most convincing explanation for this process? Is it a process at all?

Weber believed that religion served a function in giving meaning and shape to a society that was essentially meaningless and amorphous and where the fates of those that lived in pre-industrial societies tended to be arbitrary. He saw that its effects within the context of the modernising process – a growing rationality and bureaucratisation – had led to the decline of religion and, in his famous phrase, to the 'disenchantment of the world'. Likewise, Marx thought religion would fade away as science and technology came to determine contemporary material production, a process that had begun when the newly powerful bourgeoisie embraced materialism in the wake of the French Revolution. For Marx, atheism was a natural bedfellow of revolution and he equated it with a state of consciousness where social status and class power based on the idea of a natural hierarchy was challenged. Durkheim thought that as organic societies became more sophisticated, demands for social justice and new moral demands placed on the rational individual diminished the need for mystical explanations of the unknown. These assumptions – that secularisation is solely about a retreat from organised religion, that this retreat is progressive and ongoing, and that it is equated with living in an industrial society (the Chicago School certainly understood it as an obvious element of modern urban living) – form a thesis that until recently was broadly agreed by both sociologists and historians.

There is then a tension between sociological and historical models of secularisation. Sociology constructs theories but these may or may not have a universal application to real historical situations, and encourage generalisations concerning the individual and a 'process' that is analysed from the level of the institution, such as the church. Traditionally, sociological explanations have accepted the role of ideas, such as nineteenth-century critiques of the Bible, as a fundamental part of secularisation, but not necessarily examined the individual beliefs of, say, churchgoers. Historians also have tended to neglect this task, a point made by the sociologist Steve Bruce when he suggests that historians 'draw on often unstated and unexamined generalisations', uncritically adopting the work of sociologists when instead 'we have to build our general explanations of secularisation on a more detailed knowledge of religious belief and behaviour than we have at present' (Bruce, p. 6).

As sociologists have begun to question how modernisation and secularisation are related, so have historians refocused their research. Because sociologists have been more concerned with the institutional decline of religion, it has become rarer to find sociological studies concerned with either individual religious faith or social ritual. Hence the call by Bruce for historical studies that extend beyond religious structures such as the church. Religion has not disappeared in fact, rather it has transformed into other forms; similarly, religion has not declined, rather it has dispersed into areas where religious beliefs continue to matter but in ways that are not recognised. This shift in emphasis has created difficulties in defining what we mean by secularisation but, as this section will go on to prove, sociological approaches to secularisation (or the lack of secularisation), however defined, are invaluable for historians to understand and cultivate.

The accepted 'secularisation thesis', informed by sociological constructs, consists of a narrative of decline in religion and development of science in the nineteenth century.

Industrialisation and urbanisation led to a dominant rationalism and subservient religion that retreated to the periphery of *both* individual *and* national life. This process can be measured in the Victorian experience of religion when, for example, the observation of the Sabbath gave way to the 'English weekend', and Bible reading and daily family prayers were replaced by forms of secular entertainment (professional football and the like). In public life, by the close of the nineteenth century, national and local politics became based not on religious domination but on class, and concepts of Hell were redefined when a sense of inner-belief replaced Christianity as an institution. Finally, absolute truth and morality no longer took its cue from religion; instead, philosophical ideas were conceived in secular terms without recourse to the Divine.

Jose Harris's *Private Lives, Public Spirit: Britain 1870–1914* (1994) challenged these conclusions using close historical research, undermining previous sociological and historical work that assumed that the modern period was one of advancing secularisation. According to Harris, advancing notions of rationality did not produce a widespread anti-clericalism but instead natural and social sciences coexisted with Christian theology. Britain in the 1880s still had more clerics of differing kinds than any other European country beside Spain and Italy and while churches still maintained major welfarist and educational functions, many visiting foreigners noted that the country remained quite religious. This historical evidence, while surely still influenced by sociology and sociological modelling, was now beginning to suggest that in late nineteenth-century Britain secularisation was not a smooth process; something particularly true when historians look at how religiosity in the past has been measured by church attendance.

Far from bureaucracy or rationalisation crushing religion (especially if we are sceptical about church attendance as a sole indicator of religiosity), we find an increased sense of religious belonging, at least in London, by the close of the nineteenth century. Indeed, while 1880 was a low point for attendance, by the end of the century more people were active members of church denominations than at any time during Victoria's reign, including when the young lawyer Horace Mann conducted his religious census in 1851. In the same period, Roman Catholic membership doubled, attendance at Sunday school trebled and by 1906, membership of Christian associations such as the Bands of Hope, Boys' Brigade, Men's Societies, the Girls' Friendly Society and the Young Men's and Women's Associations ran into millions. Denominations of Christianity divided on gender, ethnic identity, region and class lines but females outnumbered males in every one of the Christian denominations. Remarkably, the imbalance, in favour of women, was the greatest where women had the least institutional power. Finally, thousands of new churches were built in this period dedicated to social welfare schemes: so too orphanages, industrial schools, soup kitchens, and clubs for women, men and the young (Harris, 1994).

Recent historiography suggests that working-class atheism was virtually unknown and that contemporary studies underestimated the extent of working-class piety. Outside London as many as 20 per cent of the working class may have attended church fairly regularly. Millions of children who attended Sunday Schools were overwhelmingly working class and respectable. Rites of passage were still observed by the working class: civil marriage declined from the 1860s but increased towards the end of the nineteenth century. 'Irregular liaisons' and 'common law' marriages were far less common than they had been at the beginning of the century. Similarly, 'shotgun weddings' (weddings prompted by pregnancy out of wedlock) were still popular up to 1914 and probably beyond. More than this, working people flocked to many of the newly invented religious ceremonies of the period, such as watch-night services, Mothering Sundays and harvest festivals. The elaborate pomp of working-class funerals (at a time when funerals in other classes were becoming simpler and more private) was conspicuous. Popular resistance to the spread of cremation and the universal fear of a pauper's grave – with its ideas of social stigma and fears of medical vivisection – suggest an interest in the resurrection of the body and the prospect of a life hereafter. By the 1900s, 'belief in hell-fire and everlasting judgement was probably stronger among working-class people who did not go to church than among middle-class people who did' (Harris, 1994, p. 00).

Moreover, the Labour movement was full of active Christians; a result of compulsory religious education after 1870, the first time that all the population were exposed to Christian teaching. Although women were missing from Church on a Sunday, they attended mothers' meetings on the Monday. Where working class men might avoid Matins and Eucharist, they might later attend a prayer meeting or discussion group. Harris also found that the backdrop to all this might have been industrialisation and urbanisation but in the foreground we can still find massive rallies attached to the movement for more ritual in Anglican worship, Bible study meetings, house churches and 'tea-and-experience meetings'.

Later, socialism brought Labour churches and hymns to humanism as temples of reason. After the First World War in 1918, there were sightings of ghosts at the Cenotaph as due homage was paid at the tomb of the Unknown Soldier. Spiritualism revived superstition amidst the grief of a generation that had fallen on Flanders Field; a belief that the spirits of the dead still walked amongst the living – a creed that famously accepted into its ranks the lapsed Catholic Sir Arthur Conan Doyle, creator of the arch-rationalist Sherlock Holmes. It wasn't until the 'swinging sixties', or so we are told by the historian Callum G. Brown (2000), that more secularisation was experienced than in all the previous decades put together. Declining rates of marriage and baptism were prompted by a new radicalism among women – but yet belief remained in mystic religions that originated from the East made popular by the Beatles and others.

Both sociologists and historians have been keen to stress the intellectual changes that occurred in the modernisation process. This includes that notion that human nature improved through evolution; that good can be conceived outside of religious categories; that hierarchy was not only organised through the accident of birth but by class, race, nationality and even merit; and that nature could be interpreted by scientific professionals as by clergymen. The main narrative is the seemingly inevitable rise of a secular society caused by the breakdown of a deferent society, criticism of the veracity of the Bible, the march of science, and the failure of religious, mainly Christian, institutions to respond to changes within society. Yet, as we have argued, the secularisation process that is described so well by sociological theory looks far more contingent and haphazard from an historical perspective when the actual evidence is confronted. Sociological approaches cannot explain in such detail how secularisation worked or even whether we should think of it as a process at all, especially as primary research suggests that it is an uneven historical experience. By pitting primary historical evidence against sociological theory, we are now in a position to explain the survival of religious forms unimagined by sociologists and in so doing place the public reaction to Diana's death in a longer and more convincing context.

In practice

The relationship between sociology and history is not unlike that between quarrelsome siblings. As recognisable disciplines, they were born and reached maturity at about the same time. And their interests are remarkably close. Social ordering and social order, bureaucracy, leisure, religion, war, the city, the family, electoral behaviour, to name a few, have attracted considerable attention from sociologists and historians. Their respective approaches to these matters have, however, been a source of friction, for the underlying premises contrast sharply. Sociologists are interested in identifying general patterns on the basis of which they can formulate universal laws of human behaviour. Historians, on the other hand, are rather more interested in explanations of the unique and the particular. Take, for example, the important phenomenon of human migration. Sociologists have studied different forms and experiences from which they have laid down laws which enable us to identify and explain their variety. In so doing, they have drawn distinctions between diasporas which have, say, been forced, such as the movement of those escaping persecution (for example, Huguenots, African slaves and Jews), and those which have been impelled by attempts to seek a better life (Asians and many Irish). Historians, on the other hand, look to understand the quite specific features and dynamics of these different diasporic experiences, and find the suggestion of any similarity between Huguenots and slaves rather unhelpful.

At times, however, historians have looked with envy on the ability of sociologists to play with theoretical toys. As we have seen, the development of history tended to eschew the idea of theory since it was believed that the use of theory would inevitably distort the historian's ability to deal with evidence objectively. With the recognition that history could never be totally objective because all history was informed consciously or otherwise by theoretical perspectives, historians looked more seriously at what theory had to offer. And there were many historians by now who were actually interested in going beyond the unique to identify universal or even regionalised patterns of human behaviour in the past on the basis of which laws could be formulated. Their own house had few theoretical toys to offer, and so they looked elsewhere. Anthropologists, economists and political scientists had their own, but the best ones were found in the possession of sociologists. Thus it was that historians enthusiastically took up the task of applying concepts such as class, bureaucracy, identity and social control – all of which had been developed by sociologists – to the historical record.

The results have been encouraging in that the scope of historical study has broadened into exciting new areas. Without this interest in sociology, historical work in areas such as the family and crime would not have happened. And yet, historians have to ensure that they simply do not take sociological concepts on board in an uncritical fashion. The relevance, meaning and therefore value of concepts can change from one historical period to another, and there is a real danger that universal theoretical categories mask the exceptional or particular in both the past and the present. We must therefore remain vigilant to avoid being too readily seduced by the attractions of our siblings' shiny toys.

Summary

The three sections of this chapter have said three things:

- Sociology as a discipline has a history of its own, and may be seen to use theory excessively and generate data in the present, but nevertheless has proved to be of distinct use to historians. Looking at how we might understand mutiny through sociological understandings of bureaucracy and authority, for example, we can see precisely why historians should be interested in sociology. On the one hand, if we use ideas from Max Weber about how individuals behave within a bureaucracy, then it is a small leap (one taken by Ashworth) to investigate the particular circumstances of, say, the French or Russian mutinies of 1917. From this model, we can discover similarities and differences between each when the danger might have been to miss patterns or join up historical dots when it was inappropriate so to do. Historians, on the other hand, who seek to go beyond sociological modelling because they are sceptical of its ability to provide explanations for particular historical phenomena, have sometimes missed a valuable insight.
- Looking at the plural working class cultures of the coalfields of North-East England, we found how useful sociological notions of social stratification are to the historian. We also discovered that sociology's tendency to generalise can pose a danger to the aims and objectives of an historian. While it can probably be agreed that modernity – social organisations changing rapidly in the face of industrialisation, secularisation and urbanisation – is the chief concern of sociologists, the use made of it by sociologists has limits. The methods derived from Marx, Durkheim and Weber can be useful but may tend towards generalisations such as 'the market' or 'bureaucracy' which can be hypothetical or too general for the historian concerned with the particular and the untypical. This said, Weber's constructs of authority and power, especially his notion of charisma, is useful to the historian if used with cautious imagination and confirms that historians can use sociological methods.
- Secularisation as a process has, until recently, been accepted by both sociologists and historians, although relatively recent research has cast doubt on the application of assumptions regarding the decline of religious affiliation, in whatever form. This research has emphasised surviving forms of religion and religiosity that no longer take conventional forms. Sociological models encourage generalisations based on theory and a 'process' but the historian would begin research from another place and would explain secularisation as an historical process in ways quite different from sociology.

Discussion document 1

Might the concerns expressed here by two sophisticated Marxist historians (at least at the time they were writing) be justified? Sociological theory, like theories borrowed from other related disciplines, may be useful but raises questions about the place of theory in history as a discipline and also the extent to which historians should construct their own theoretical framework.

There are in fact very good reasons why sociology should have appeared so attractive to British historians. Most obviously there was a complete vacuum of historical theory. Then, in the context of a narrowly political and constitutional historiography, it appeared as a progressive, even a subversive force, opening up new vistas of inquiry and directing the historian's gaze at hitherto untraveled terrain. It promised to restore meaning to history – pattern and structure in place of the increasing fragmentation of sub-disciplines. It encouraged historians in the use of comparative method, and instead of prohibiting reference to the present day (in the 1950s many university history courses still stuck fast at 1914) positively encouraged it. To the restless and discontented it offered a sudden release from the musty files of the underground search rooms. Instead of inching their way forward by painful degrees they were positively enjoined to take daring, high-fly leaps both in time and space; to dress up their findings in the language of social significance, modernize their footnotage and bring their work into line with the main thrust of theoretical debate.

We do not want to put a stop to the dialogue between history and sociology, but we think that the present relationship is an unhealthy one and that its terms should both be discussed and redefined. It leaves the historian in a position of abject dependency, craving recognition and taking theoretical propositions on trust. It does not engage the historian in the development of theoretical work, but simply in a passive acceptance of categories derived from elsewhere. According to some sociologists, this is as it should be: sociologists provide the empty conceptual boxes; it is the humble task of historians – if their services are admitted at all – to help to fill them. It is not in question that some of the problems and techniques pioneered by sociologically-minded historians have been useful and illuminating extensions to the scope of history. More doubtful are some of the sociological categories or concepts which have guided and channelled their enquiries – endowing certain types of data with an unargued importance, while filtering out others as irrelevant. For sociological findings are not easily separated from the classificatory and conceptual systems of which they are part. It is perhaps to avoid having to take on board such unwanted freightage that many historians have limited themselves to a more casual relationship with sociology. But the freedoms gained from this stratagem are really illusory. The historian who only occasionally resorts to sociology and forages for serviceable concepts, will just as surely end up trapped in a thicket of uncongenial and unbargained-for assumptions. Trying to evade these assumptions, lifting categories without working through the process of reasoning which has produced them, can only result in an unhappy electicism [sic].

Raphael Samuel and Gareth Stedman Jones, 'Sociology and history', *History Workshop Journal*, vol. 1, no. 1 (1976), pp. 6–8.

Discussion document 2

As this extract from the sociologically influenced Mass Observation movement in the 1920s and 1930s makes clear, class can be understood in its traditional Marxist concept as something that can be determined objectively through, say, income or occupation or it can be seen subjectively by, for instance, how a person may regard his or her place in the hierarchy. How does this extract describe class and social stratification?

Mass observation

We asked a local pub-goer (ex-policeman) to go round and ask a few chaps in the pubs he visited why they liked beer. This was done indirectly in the course of conservation. The following is his verbatim write-up of the results:

8.15pm. Man aged about 40 says 'I drink beer because I think it does me more good than doctor's medicine, it keeps my bowels in good working order.' This man was of the engineering type.

Navvy type of person aged about 35 says 'If I get three pints down me I can . . .' (What he said is the sort of thing considered 'unprintable.' It amounted to the fact that when he went home he was able to have sexual intercourse with his wife with the maximum of efficiency, and when he woke up in the morning he was able to repeat the process with the upmost satisfaction.)

A young man aged about 25, well dressed in the latest cut suit, says 'This stuff gives a good appetite and puts plenty of lead in my pencil.'

An aged coalbagger says 'Eh, lad, two or three pints every neet (night) and a pound o' chops and I could knock a bloody mon off a horse.'

A young man, a piecer, says 'I don't take too much, about a couple of gills every neet, it seems to put a bit of bant (energy) in thee for t' following day.'

A middle-aged man of about 40 of labouring type says 'What the bloody hell dost tha tak it for?' I said for my health, he said 'Th'art a – – a liar.' I paid for him a gill.

A man fairly well dressed looked to me like a lady killer says 'If tha comes in 'ere and pays for who tha fancies a couple of stouts tha's no need to get wed.'

A young man about 23 says 'I only drink this stuff because I come down to t' barracks about three times a week, if I weren't in the artillery I'd ne'er bother.'

A navvy type of man about 38 says 'This is a bloody habit with me an' I think if they stopped me tap I should bloody well snuff out tomorrow.'

A young man of shop assistant type about 25 says 'What can a chap do in a one-eyed hole like this, he'd go off his chump if there were no ale, pictures, and tarts.'

Geoffrey Smith, *The Pub and the People by Mass-Observation* (1987), pp. 46–7.

Further reading

* *essential*

* **Peter Burke**, *History and Social Theory* (2005).
An invaluable text for comparing the uses of social theory for historians. That this is a republication of a book whose title once explicitly mentioned sociology as a major concern is, perhaps, demonstration of the recent relevance sociology has for historians.

British Journal of Sociology, vol. 27, no. 3, Special Issue: History and Sociology (September, 1976).
This special edition of the major journal for sociologists has many articles worth consulting. It was also a symptom at its time of publication how sociology and sociological method was influencing social history of the time. It is certainly worth revisiting.

Peter Saunders, *Social Theory and the Urban Question* (1981).
An excellent but very theoretical account of Weber, Marx and Durkheim as social theorists, although as the title suggests its focus is very much centred on the urban.

* **S. J. D. Green**, *Religion in the Age of Decline: Organisation and Experience in Industrial Yorkshire 1870–1920* (1996).
A wonderful example of modern research on a common problem for sociologists and historians alike: secularisation. The introduction provides an invaluable summary and commentary on the historiographical debate on this subject.

Tony Ashworth, *Trench Warfare 1914–1918* (1980).
A solid and imaginative example of how sociological theory, particularly that derived from Weber, can be put to the service of the historian willing to bend theory to fact and not the other way around.

17 Economics

1 Economics, population and social change
2 Economic historians and the big historical questions
3 The business of business history

Introduction

Economic history has a massive influence on the wider discipline of history, even if it has become a little unfashionable in recent years. Marxist history has particularly benefited from a concentration on what it would call the 'economic base' of historical societies but more generally economic history has been sufficiently strong in the recent past to have maintained academic departments separate from 'straight' history and a number of dedicated professional journals. Economic history can reasonably claim to explain societies holistically while working on data (often by the application of the most up-to-date technology) which raise fresh questions about past societies. The opening section of the chapter examines how population data can unpick the shape of past societies; while the methods of economic history (with help from other disciplines such as archaeology) can add significantly to our historical knowledge. The second section focuses upon the contribution by economic historians to the understanding of wealth and poverty over centuries; in particular, we are concerned with the role of luxury and luxury goods in the modernising process and the way that historians have dealt with pessimistic and optimistic approaches to industrialisation; that is, economic understandings of industrialisation that argue whether the industrial revolution benefited the economic lives of contemporaries. The final section of the chapter switches attention to the role that business historians play in understanding past societies, defining and explaining the relationship of business history to economic history.

Section 1

Economics, population and social change

On the edge of a remote track, deep wooded until it branches out to reveal a vista of the Derbyshire countryside, is a field which contains a wall-bound graveyard containing just seven weather-beaten gravestones quite unattached to any church. The names on the stones are dated August 1666; all were victims of an outbreak of the bubonic plague in the village of Eyam. At least from the nineteenth century this outbreak has become notorious as the plague village par excellence. Here huge losses were suffered after the villagers decided in an act of heroic self-sacrifice that the plague would not spread beyond the village boundaries following the death of George Viccars, a journeyman tailor, in 1665. The story goes that the villagers quarantined themselves and thereby saved nearby communities from their own terrible fate. As a result, by spring of the next year, those residents of the secluded graves would be dead too. Not for the plague itself but for the response of the villagers, Eyam has become a cause célèbre for historians and the general public alike while its very topography is both a testimony to these events but also part of the evidence that may help explain them.

Economists and economic historians are not, contrary to popular belief, concerned simply with money. If they were, their interest would stop at the boundary to Eyam where villagers collected food and medicines, and where coins were left in shallow pools of vinegar to prevent the spread of the contagion. Rather, they are interested more generally with economic resources and in particular with their scarcity and distribution. It should be no surprise, therefore, that plague, pestilence and disease should be relevant topics for the economic historian as they touch on the elements that affected economic conditions in the past, whether it be the plague that first struck the Greeks in the centuries before Christ, the Great Famine of 1315–17, the Black Death of 1348–50 or the plagues of the seventeenth century to which we shall return in a moment. First, a little more should be said about what economic history is, why it is important and its principal concern for those historians working in the modern and medieval periods.

Economic history as a branch of history dates back to the social crisis of the 1880s and the need, particularly in London at the heart of the biggest and most important empire of the time, to understand a society where economic want existed for the many in the midst of economic plenty for a few. In order to address this issue and others like it, Arnold Toynbee (1852–83) flew the flag for economic history while Alfred Marshall (1842–1924) was perhaps the best-known exponent of the craft of modern economics. Around this time, the London School of Economics and Political Science (LSC) was founded in the 1890s and reflected, as the historian Christopher Dyer's *Making a Living in the Middle Ages* (2002) reminds us, the predominant contemporary interest in law, government and statecraft in the origins of the modern economy. In a sense economic history and economics became alternative ways of describing modernity and especially describing and explaining the roles of the ascendant middle classes. This section will attempt to draw the boundaries of these concerns and to offer some examples of how this approach works in historical practice when seeking to understand, for instance, medieval plagues and epidemics.

The production and distribution of resources in the past are thus the main concerns of the economic historian. Dyer goes further, however, for according to him the value of economic history derives not only from its ability to reveal the nature of societal resources, but because all social and cultural endeavours are built upon the economy:

> **It is the only branch of history which gives pride of place to the whole population, and through the study of the economy we can understand the everyday lives of working people. The economy was important. All other human endeavours depended on the production of food and other goods, which means that any investigation of non-material things must take into account the material base. Economic history is a unifying subject, not taking us into an obscure byway of the past, but acting as a crossroads from which we gain access to the history of the environment, culture, politics and thought.** (Dyer, 2002, p. 1)

This chapter started with the plague outbreak at Eyam in 1665, and how the episode has entered into popular imagination as an incidence of extraordinary self-sacrifice by a village community. Recent work by economic and demographic historians has, however, provided alternative scenarios. From the work of Leslie Bradley, Philip Race and Patrick Wallis, we now know that the mortality rates in Eyam were less extraordinary than had been believed by successive generations of historians and the general public alike. In many respects the Eyam story has been exposed for its mythic qualities. Bradley tells us that a 'very few' wealthy villagers fled at the outset of the epidemic, that those with sufficient wealth erected huts in nearby valleys to escape the plague, while some children of the better off were sent away only in June 1666 some eight months after the beginning of the epidemic when the mortality rates began to climb. Quarantine was not heroically self-imposed but enforced by the authorities as had been the case with other villages (Slack, 1985). It seems, therefore, that the circumstances surrounding the isolation of the village question the altruism of the villagers, while the motives of some of the village leaders have also been questioned. This and what follows, focuses on Eyam as a case study, an exemplar of how economic history can provide convincing explanations for historical problems in ways that are unique in method and approach.

This historiography of the Eyam plaque originated in 1977 when Bradley's important intervention questioned the 'evidence' about the plague. As we can see in Table 17.1, the source that originally set the tone for histories and commentaries on the plague was that of Anna Steward in 1810, although her account dates from 1765. Wallis argued that this description of the Eyam plague was set within the Romantic tropes of nationalist sentiment (the invention of the stiff-lipped Englishman), the value of strong leadership that partly characterised the Victorian age and the melodrama of romantic love that inculcates Victorian historical fiction and which was represented in art and so forth. If the history of epidemics and the tragedy of the Eyam plague are located chronologically in the seventeenth century, it was reinvented at a moment when cholera stalked Victorian centres of population. In this sense, Eyam is a Victorian phenomenon and is explained in narratives available and familiar to the Victorians but had been largely forgotten during most of the eighteenth century; indeed, as Table 17.1 suggests, from 1666 to 1790 there was very little

Table 17.1 Sources of information about the plague in Eyam

Original accounts

Sheffield Constables' Accounts, 1666
William Mompesson's three letters, 1666
Parish register, transcript from 1705

Subsequent accounts

Early eighteenth century

William Bagshaw, *De Spiritualibus Pecci*, 1702
Richard Mead, *Discourse*, 1722

Later eighteenth century

European Magazine, 1790
William Seward, *European Magazine*, 1793, repr. *Anecdotes*, 1795–7
Anna Seward, *Poetical Works*, 1810 (composed 1765)

Early to mid-nineteenth century

Holland, *Village of Eyam*, 1821
Rhodes, *Peak Scenery*, 1824
William and Mary Howitt, *Desolation of Eyam*, 1827
R. Ward, *Guide to the Peak*, 1827
Samuel Roberts, *Eyam*, 1834
William Adam, *Gem of the Peak*, 1838
Spencer T. Hall, *Peak and the Plain*, 1838
William Wood, *History and Antiquities of Eyam*, 1842
The Tale of Eyam, 1888

Late nineteenth and early twentieth century

History:
Charles Creighton, *History of Epidemics*, 1891

Guides:
J. M. J. Fletcher, *The Plague-Stricken Derbyshire Village*, 1924
Eyam and the Plague: A Guide, nd
Clarence Daniel, *History of Eyam*, 1932
W. R. B., 'William Mompesson', *Annals of Medical History*, 1939

Later twentieth century

Fictional accounts:
Marjorie Bowen, *God and the Wedding Dress*, 1938
Joyce Dennys, *Isolation at Eyam*, 1954
Don Taylor, *The Roses of Eyam*, 1970
Eyam: A Musical, 1995
Geraldine Brooks, *Year of Wonders*, 2002

Source: Reproduced from Patrick Wallis, 'A dreadful heritage: interpreting epidemic disease at Eyam, 1666–2000', *History Workshop Journal* (2006).

written about it. For Race, self-consciously building on the work of Bradley, the prime text was that of William Wood, which purported to summarise the available evidence up until that point.

Since Wood published his *History and Antiquities of Eyam* in 1842, other qualitative 'evidence' has continued to accumulate which has sought to understand the nature of the plague, its origins, and whether Viccars might or might not have been the first victim in Eyam of an epidemic that had travelled from London, or whether the plague was sourced locally. All this evidence is legitimate context for the economic historian to consider. But it is only context. Race, however, as someone who was concerned with quantitative evidence, looked instead to the evidence we find generated at the top of Table 17.1, that is, the newly available parish register of St Lawrence in Eyam which dates from 1630. It is especially valuable because it was annotated later in the seventeenth century with the names of the plague victims, giving a base line from which questions of demography (population), births, mortality and the lasting economic effects of the epidemic can be considered. From the perspective of an economic historian using a limited primary source from which vital statistics can be compared it can be discerned that no more than half of the population died (not the 259 of a total population of 330 suggested by accounts reported immediately after the event). Moreover, there was no serious demographic collapse in subsequent decades. There was severe mortality, however, which itself no doubt contributed to the accumulation of stories about the tragedy in the centuries since.

The problem of finding the exact circumstances of the causes and aftermath of plague in Eyam gives some sense of how economic historians go about their craft. By understanding approaches taken by economic historians to epidemics we can more readily appreciate the impact of demographics or population change on human societies. Take another example: the Black Death. Emanating from the Crimea in 1347 via Italy, economic historians and historical demographers have argued about the extent of the plague; with some estimates suggesting that half Europe's population was wiped out, others that the figure is nearer to one-fifth. On older historiography argued that the population fell because of the Black Death and other epidemics and then fell again. After 1430, it was further argued, the population began to rise. Data such as this only has a value to economic historians at the point when it explains related changes in economic activity. We know, for example, that prices rose as a result of the Black Death, and that food shortages ensued. In the longer term, the amount of productive land and labour fell and with it demand for goods and produce, thereby creating an economic downturn.

The relationship between population and economic activity was first investigated by the eighteenth-century political economist, Thomas Malthus (1766–1834), who in *An Essay on the Principles of Population* (1798) argued that population would rise inextricably but the means of maintaining that population would not keep up, leading in turn to an economic crisis. Under such circumstances, he continued, population increases should be prevented by powerful checks such as moral restraint; if these checks fail then economic failure and famine will ensue until a new balance is struck. Economic historians and demographers since Malthus have spent much time and effort investigating the relationship between population and economic activity. Perhaps the most dramatic intervention into this area of historical demography came from E. A. Wrigley and R. S. Schofield, who in their *The Population History of England, 1541–1871: A Reconstruction* (1989) measured fertility, mortality and migration as the essential components of population change, concluding that population growth led to a fall in real wages over this period.

Influential though the gloomy picture of Malthus has been, there are limits to its explanatory power. While the misery of the Black Death undoubtedly led to social tension which was linked to the 1381 Peasants' Revolt, for example, we know that there was no economic collapse or Malthusian crisis. Historians might agree with Malthus, however, to the extent that low marriage and fertility rates rather than mortality and migration were indeed the main constraint on population recovery. It is undeniable that cultivated land improved in quality and that new economic relations were born that culminated in the revolt. Equally, there is also no doubt that the 1348–50 outbreaks were indescribably severe and had economic ramifications of one sort or an other that lasted decades.

We would know nothing of this without economic history. The next section will underline this point by concentrating on how economic historians have approached important historical questions related to the decline of the Roman Empire, and the so-called standards of living debate which arose from attempts to assess the impact of the industrial revolution.

Section 2

Economic historians and the big historical questions

N. J. G. Pounds in his *Economic History of Medieval Europe* (1994) explained why the Roman Empire declined, a process which is often thought to signify the beginning of the Middle Ages, and how its slow downfall in the East culminated in the fall of Constantinople in 1453 when the Christian Byzantine Empire fell to the Muslim Ottomans. Pounds looked in places familiar to the economic historian in order to explain how this came about:

> **The facade of Roman civilization in the West, its towns, villas and roads, was created mainly in the first two centuries of the Empire, when the profits of imperialism made it possible to do so. It constituted, however, a superstructure which the later Empire found increasingly difficult to support. The barbarians did not overthrow the Empire in the West; they merely caused it to expend its scanty *resources* [our emphasis] in ways which it could not really afford. In other words, they made necessary high taxation for military ends.**
>
> (Pounds, 1994, p. 37)

Ultimately, Pounds argued that the western empire was dependent on its force of arms and that the shortage of recruits to the army explains why it was finally unable to maintain its imperial influence. But why were there shortages of manpower in the army? To answer this, he looked at demographic explanations that should, after the last section, be familiar. These explanations include a high death rate, low life expectancy (30 to 35 years) and disease such as the Black Death in 542–3 CE. Taxes that had to support the army were paid by four-fifths of the population, a 'venal and oppressive bureaucracy' made the task of collecting taxes more difficult, while a shortage of labour in what was an agricultural economy led to the abandonment of productive land when the principal source of state revenue was a land tax on small proprietors. For all the reasons mentioned, the tax take was reduced. As more slaves were used for productive purposes and barbarians recruited to the army had no loyalty to the empire, so the empire weakened.

Pounds highlighted the role of the 'frivolous and idle rich' in the decline of empire, which raises the question why frivolity, idleness or even decadence should be the business of the economic historian. Socially unequal societies demand that luxury goods be produced. This alone altered the economy of towns, and in the case of the Roman Empire compounded the problem of maintaining the strength of the army since it was the army that maintained the roads on which these goods were transported. When the strength of the army became compromised, luxury goods, enjoyed at the centre of the empire, could not be distributed to the provinces. The biggest impact on an economy distorted by luxury production and bedevilled by problems of distribution, however, derived from the avoidance of taxes by the senatorial class and their determination to abandon their social obligations.

This is an economic explanation which contained unstated assumptions about the loss of Roman power and the role of the barbarians in that loss, and implicitly raised the question as to whether barbarian influence constituted an 'overthrow'. That the barbarian or Germanic forces were to finally overrun the glory of Rome and that these forces were to somehow dominate the grandest of empires without the apparent use of undue violence has been perhaps the main unchallenged assumption of histories written on this subject. But Bryan Ward-Perkins in his *The Fall of Rome and the End of Civilization* (2005) has overturned decades of established historiography by suggesting that the massive change of late antiquity, the decline, fall, or crisis of the Roman Empire in the West, was not the result of gentle transformation or 'accommodation' of an organic and incremental kind but of invasion.

Ward-Perkins contended that economic explanations for the end of Roman power are not as convincing as those highlighting the economic ramifications caused by invasion. One commentator, Ward-Perkins reminded us, enterprisingly took evidence from written documents but also used tree-ring data to suggest that the obscuring of the sun in 536–7 CE caused by an asteroid strike had an adverse effect on crops and therefore on the economy. Similarly, as in the analysis of the same problem of Roman decline by Pounds, the Black Plague was cited as a negative impact on the economy and as a factor in the eventual collapse of the western empire (Ward-Perkins, 2005, p. 134). None of these more piecemeal explanations, however, can be compared to the shockwaves caused by invasion and the collapse of security for a sophisticated economy that required security to function as a coherent whole.

Ward-Perkins agreed that economic factors in the demise of the Roman Empire in the West were indeed important, but he pointed to a fundamental change in the economy of the ancient world which led to significant ruptures in all five of the Roman provinces (Ward-Perkins, 2005, p. 122). Central North Africa, the islands and coastal provinces of the Aegean, Britain and the Levant, which comprised a region that would include parts of modern day Egypt, Turkey, Israel and Syria, reacted differently to economic pressures and declined at different rates. For Ward-Perkins, however, the primary reasons for the ultimate decline were twofold: the problems of security hastened by invasion from the Vandals, Sueves and Alans when they crossed the Rhine into Gaul (Ward-Perkins, 2005, p. 2) and the excessively interdependent economic system whose lines of communication became stretched to breaking point under the pressures of conflict and invasion. All the provinces of the empire had relied on a complex and interlocking economy that had facilitated mass production and exchange, but under these new conditions, specialised trades that had once acted as the bedrock of the economy and which enjoined its various parts, now stood alone, quite unable to meet local needs. This caused privations in some areas, although in others (the Levant, for instance) prosperity stayed constant or even improved up until the seventh century.

In contrast to Pounds on the fall of Rome, economic historians have argued that well-being in the past was all about essentials (not luxuries) such as mass-produced soap made of vegetable oils. It was also about cheap, washable cotton, better nutrition, plus, of course, the application of science and knowledge to technology. All these factors (particularly the industrial use of soap) improved hygiene, transformed mortality rates and boosted demographic growth. Maintaining population levels and wealth, equality or inequality, diversity or uniformity, conflict or social peace, rested on whether or not the needs but also the expectations thrown up by the modern world could be met.

The nature of this relationship between poverty and wealth has long been of interest to thinkers beyond the realm of economic history. It was the radical Thomas Paine (1737–1809) who, as a veteran of both the eighteenth-century French and American Revolutions, first began to argue that inequality was neither natural nor was it divinely ordained and a result of sin, and in this he was joined by Enlightenment intellectuals, most notably Nicholas Condorcet (1743–93). As a result of the ideas unleashed by the eighteenth-century revolutions, poverty and understandings of poverty changed in the modern period, and with this transformation came the recognition that the state had a responsibility to provide welfare support to the disadvantaged.

The push to understand poverty as a societal problem and not as a problem of the flawed individual corrupting a hierarchy pre-ordained by God continued in the mid-nineteenth century with various forms of social and economic investigation that sought scientifically to ascertain the extent of poverty. These largely private initiatives from Henry Mayhew and Charles Booth to Benjamin Seebohm Rowntree (1871–1954), and the Institute of Community Studies in the 1960s, thereafter disappear into the corridors of state responsibility. While poverty remains today, western societies are better off now than only 60 years ago and it is this salutary fact that has shifted a collective focus away from poverty as the main cause of social conflict. This shift in perception and focus has occurred among economic historians too.

One such shift is from production to consumption. Where once economic historians (and others) focused on histories connected to issues around production, such as how skills developed in the industrial process promoted productivity, now they are equally concerned with how things were consumed – histories of shopping, advertising or fashion, for instance.

From histories of production and consumption come questions of how we earned our living in the past and the extent to which the industrial revolution improved standards of living. This, as shall be seen, has meant a wider, more holistic, cultural and social view of the industrial revolution, which has if anything challenged the centrality that it once occupied in interpretations of Europe's advance. Neil McKendrick and John Brewer have each drawn attention to the 'birth of the consumer society', inhabited by people who have both the desire and ability to consume. Advertising and selling, fashion and credit promoted a change of lifestyle (for some). This was to be a new world of 'things' and prosperity would come from self-indulgence. The result of this approach, according to the historian Maxine Berg, is that 'consumption has reshaped the grand narrative of the period, replacing the former narrative of the industrial revolution' (Berg, 2005, p. 27). This new narrative does not tackle the divisions and conflict thrown up by industrial production; indeed, it admits of no inherently antagonistic fissures.

Perspectives on luxury, like those on poverty, have changed significantly over time. Until Bernard Mandeville wrote his *Fable of the Bees* in 1714, it was widely held that if benefits to a life of luxury and idleness could arise from 'avarice, prodigality, pride, envy and vanity' they would be unquestionably immoral. After Mandeville and for that matter David Hume's oft-quoted 'ornaments and pleasures of life', set down in his essay *Of Luxury* published in 1752, but which acquired a new name, *Of Refinement in the Arts*, in 1760, the new consumer society or consumerism would become associated with words such as 'ingenuity', 'imitation', 'convenience', 'utility', 'taste and style', 'delight', and the desire for luxury considered necessary for economic growth.

This in a very small nutshell is the narrative within which economic historians have understood luxury, consumption and poverty. What impact has this thinking had on how economic historians have understood industrialisation and the standard of living? E. A. Wrigley, among other economic historians, has approached the question by investigating increases in productivity. He demonstrated that industries such as soap and paper manufacture, brewing and ship building grew to a considerable level of sophistication and productivity between say the 1760s–70s and the 1830s – the timespan which is normally allotted to the first industrial revolution. In addition to this there was, in some regions at least, a qualitative as well as quantitative change in the mode of industrial production – a decisive shift away from the methods and limitations of handicraft production towards larger units of production: towards bigger mills and factories, such as those found in the textile-producing areas of Lancashire and the West Riding of Yorkshire.

The approaches of economic historians are nicely illustrated by different perspectives on the revolutionary nature of the industrial revolution. The idea of an early start for English industrialisation is one made by many economic historians. Nick Crafts and C. K. Harley argued that the whole phenomenon was long and drawn out; but growth rates were too low to be honestly described as 'revolutionary'. Even if cotton had transformative power, the centres of production were too regionally localised, and more importantly the growth of this sector did not make up enough of the aggregate economy to justify the high level of overall growth in the British economy which earlier historians like T. S. Ashton, Phyllis Deane and W. A. Cole had suggested. The growth in the total volume of the economy owed much to agriculture and traditional industrial techniques. For example, even by the 1840s the majority of steam engines were still used only for the pumping of water. Accordingly, Crafts and Harley revised earlier growth figures downwards (see Table 17.2).

Maxine Berg and Pat Hudson insisted on a radical critique of Crafts and Harley and in so doing have reinvested the industrial revolution with something of its old significance. They argued that growth and productivity change have been underestimated; and that growth rates alone are an inadequate measure of change. In particular, Crafts and Harley have underestimated growing sections of the labour force such as women (the family economy)

Table 17.2 Annual percentage growth rates of industrial production.

Period	*Deane and Cole*	*Crafts*	*Harley*	*Jackson*
Early eighteenth century	0.74	0.70	–	–
Late eighteenth century	1.24	1.3	1.5	1.3
Early nineteenth century	4.4	2.8	3.0	2.9
Mid- to late nineteenth century	2.9	–	–	–

Source: Crafts and Harley (1992).

and the informal economy; the agrarian/industrial overlap where most people were still locked in the countryside with its seasonal employment, low wages and rural deprivation. There has been too much emphasis on finished goods, with the result that the products of some industries are underestimated, with undue emphasis on finished goods, while the service sector is all but ignored. Finally, by using 'official' national accounting systems as sources, the impact of the 'informal economy' (the so-called 'black market') on the formal economy was critically underestimated. Berg and Hudson put it this way:

> **It is time to move on from the macro accounting framework and to rebuild the national picture of economic and social change from new research at regional and local level. We need to adopt a broader concept of innovation, to insist on a greater awareness of female and child labour, and to recognise that the economic, social and cultural foundation of an industrial capitalist order rests on much more than conventional measures of industrial or economic performance. If this is done it should not be long before the notion of an industrial revolution, occurring in England in the late eighteenth century and early nineteenth century is fully rehabilitated.**
> (Berg and Hudson, 1992, p. 44)

What is the importance of this debate to our understanding of economic history? The period under review was a time of economic development – no matter how much or how little may be attributed to the industrial revolution – and it was also a period of rapid population growth and urbanisation. Taking these three things together – economic development, population growth, urbanisation – we have the makings of one of the great debates concerning the industrialising period, namely, that of whether the industrial revolution improved the standard of living for ordinary people. This debate has been of fundamental importance to economic history and brings together very many themes of this section and the last.

Optimists believed that real wages grew as a fairly immediate consequence of economic growth and industrialisation and in so doing they improved the lot of the majority very quickly. Much of their case was based on early work by influential economic historians such as Sir John Clapham (1873–1946) and T. S. Ashton (1889–1968). Clapham's *Economic History of Britain* (1926) looked at wages and prices and concluded that working-class living standards had improved. T. S. Ashton in the 1940s examined population, import and export prices, housing and diet. Poor conditions, he concluded, had existed but were balanced by the increased benefits of industrialisation. F. A. Hayek (1899–1992), the liberal economist, reinforced the optimists' case when he highlighted the relative merits of improving wages and prices in an industrialised capitalist economy in a debate that survived into the 1950s. The pessimists, including E. P. Thompson, Eric Hobsbawm and other members of the Communist Party Historians Group, believed that the rapidity of change, the rapaciousness of capitalism and the pace of urban growth led to desperate suffering at least in the short term. Even if manufacturing wages were good, they were not enjoyed by the majority who worked in dreadful conditions, for long hours and from very young ages (if the evidence and conclusions of the Factory Commission is to be believed).

To an extent the differences between the camps arose over the nature of the evidence used. Pessimists argued that optimists had measured working life using hard data such as incomes, food expenditure and so on, while the 'moral economy' of customs and culture provided a fuller and more meaningful context for assessing the impact of the industrial revolution. Pessimism about the effect on the masses could be found in ways that contemporaries described the industrial revolution in poems, novels and paintings. Because the pessimists used these more imaginative sources of evidence rather than the hard data more familiar to the economic historian, the sources themselves came under the microscope of R. M. Hartwell, W. H. Chaloner and W. W. Henderson, who all argued that much of the Marxist or pessimistic viewpoint was biased and ideological – a fruitless search for the missing revolution – without much attention paid to the integrity of the sources.

The ideological divide between 'pessimists' and 'optimists' has recently narrowed and there is recognition that there is 'no single, measurable "standard of living" in history'. (1997, p. 4) Indeed, Lindert and Williamson (1985) have argued that:

- real wages rose after 1820, but mostly among 'white-collar' workers;
- purchasing power increased in real terms – although the unskilled were worse off;
- the rich and the middle class got richer and so did the poor, although the relative difference between social extremes became greater.

Most historians now agree that real wages remained steady during the period between 1750 and 1815–20, but rose substantially up to 1850. It appears that the increase in the standard of living resulted from falling prices rather than rising wages. However, pessimists have been bolstered by the stature of the population (measured in height) which in the years 1825–60 declined, reflecting poor diet, environment and disease. Indeed, the relationship between nutrition, height and mortality rates has become a very live area in economic history; see, for instance, the work of Brian A'Hearn focused on Italy, or Roderick Floud *et al.*, *Height, Health and History* (1990).

Contemporary debates about luxury and poverty, and consumption and production, have their antecedence in those about the timing, extent and substance of the industrial revolution and the standard of living it produced. Much of the recent debate has centred on use of evidence which at best is incomplete and unreliable. Historically, statistics, which are the very lifeblood of economic history, existed at the micro level of the firm, not at the macro level of national economies. Some firms, for instance, whether large or small, were engaged with simple or complex technologies or technologies that were somewhere in-between. According to Howard Gospel, they required a certain skill set: they had to know where to source the raw materials required; how to shift their own product from one place to another; and how to communicate with other firms and their customers or potential customers. In aggregate, Gospel continued, the actions of the firm had implications for the economic fate of countries and continents. The study of this world is the domain of the business historian, to which we turn next.

Section 3

The business of business history

Hundreds of historians, artists and authors use the British Library every day, and few will give a thought to what stood on the site before the present library building. Just next door in St Pancras Station thousands of people pass through having travelled from all over Europe, perhaps visiting the shops and restaurants in the basement undercroft. Fewer still will ponder the existence of such a space, putting it down to clever design and the skill of the architect. However, what stood on both sites were conceived by individuals, but built by companies – in particular, a business called the Midland Railway. The Midland built an undercroft to St Pancras for the storage of beer from the Burton Brewery (a company) of Burton on Trent, while the site of the British Library was occupied by an enormous goods yard bringing a huge range of commodities into London for the consumption of its inhabitants and taking commodities away from London destined for the furthest corners of the Union and, indeed, the empire.

Let us think about this in more detail: how was bread brought to Manchester? From a farm (family owed business) to a railway (the London North Eastern Railway, joint stock limited liability company) via a road haulier (Carter Paterson, company) on to a miller/ baker (the Hovis company), then on to a shop (the Co-operative, a cooperative shop on a corner somewhere in rural or industrial Britain). Think about the variety of transactions involved and how goods were delivered to the consumer. All this involved business, to a varying degree, depending on the time and location under consideration.

The importance of business, of companies, in the industrial revolution that we outlined in the previous section should be recognised. This is not to say that business always delivered social goods or goods useful to society – it did not. But no one should deny its important role, alongside stable government, in delivering much higher standards of living cross the globe. Equally we ought not to dismiss the enterprise of business history itself; indeed, it might be argued that it is undeservedly neglected.

What is business history and what are its concerns? According to Edwin Hunt and James Murray in *A History of Business in Medieval Europe 1200–1550* (1999), business history is 'any activity involving exchange between two or more parties – in country or town, and on a local, regional, or international scale' (p. 1). Essentially, business history is concerned with how production and the delivery of goods and services was organised in the past; by an individual, a sole trader, a group of individuals, a partnership, or a joint stock limited liability concern – the modern company.

In Britain, the origins of the company lay in the organisation of universities and hospitals via a charter granted by the Crown, and it was not until the seventeenth century that they expanded into other areas, with joint stock companies gaining monopoly access to the slave trade in Spanish South America and in return acquiring government debt from which they could offer shares. The outcome of this particular type of company was the so-called

South Sea Bubble in 1720, which led to the banning of the corporate form until the nineteenth century in 1844 with the introduction of limited liability. Accordingly, in order to avoid the misuse of monopoly status, Britain's financial services expanded in more diverse ways and the railways and canals were organised by private Act of Parliament, as were many of the new utility industries such as gas, telephone, electricity and water. Indeed, most economic activity was concerned with the activity of the private firm, whether with limited liability or not.

So the difference between economic and business history is one of emphasis rather than substance. Steve Broadberry's study of British manufacturing productivity, *The Productivity Race: British Manufacturing Performance in International Perspective 1850–1990* (1997), for example, is widely regarded as an economic history but it also engaged with the performance of individual businesses. An important difference for the business historian is the role of the individual case study, whereas the economic historian is usually more concerned with industry wide analysis of business. Economic history is also concerned with much more than the business sector – after all the company as we know it is itself a relatively recent phenomena – and covers ancient, medieval and early modern forms of organising production.

Business history requires the macro theorising of the economist, sociologist and statistician but is combined with micro knowledge about accounting, finance, and commercial/business law. The history of business may not be just about the history of a particular business – often referred to by some economic historians in pejorative terms as an indulgence, an 'antiquarian' study – but may encompass the history of regulation, relations between government and business, the history of labour, of technology and the social history of the workplace.

The development of business history as an academic discipline began in the United States with N. S. B. Gras, *Business and Capitalism: an Introduction to Business History* (1939). This told the story of capitalism's development through the perspective of business organisation and its transactions with other producers and customers. Gras' scholarship provided the foundation for business history at the Harvard Business School and was followed later by Alfred Chandler's pioneering work, *Strategy and Structure: Chapters in the History of the Industrial Enterprise* (1962). This examined instances of business decision making in a historical context, but in a way that was intelligible to those studying organisations and management. Together with the business history curriculum at Harvard Business School, Chandler built on a tradition of case studies for teaching, thereby establishing business history in the United States.

In the United Kingdom, however, the interest in business history developed alongside the growing field of industrial archaeology. Britain in the 1950s was undergoing a period of change with many Victorian business premises, if not the businesses themselves, closing down, merging or moving to new locations. The preservation of business archives often went alongside the development of the textile or railway museum or the preservation of defunct office equipment now deposited at the Museum of London – all offering new opportunities for the researcher.

Business history remained marginalised within economic history until the late 1980s when economic history departments themselves began their long decline, and at the time of writing there are only two dedicated economic history departments: at Edinburgh and the

London School of Economics (LSE) in Britain; although more exist throughout the world, such as at the University of Barcelona or the Stockholm School of Economics, which has an Institute for Research in Economic History. To take Britain as an example, however, in 1978 the Business History Unit at LSE was established as a venue for the writing of histories commissioned by firms themselves, and the training of doctorates. Through its existence the Unit was headed by two of the most influential business historians – first Les Hannah, author of a commissioned history of Barclays Bank, *Barclays: The Business of Banking 1690–1996* (2001), and then Terry Gourvish, *British Railways 1948–73: A Business History* (1986) and *The Official History of Britain and the Channel Tunnel* (2006).

Has business/economic history had a massive impact on the wider history profession? Business historians are mainly found in business and management schools, but are increasingly being replaced by first social and then cultural historians in history departments (Chapter 9). Although the trend has moved decidedly away from economic and business history departments (there were perhaps 20 dedicated departments in the 1970s), humanities departments tend to be more generally interested in business 'studies'.

Yet even more recently, business history has struggled to become accepted by both the wider academic community of historians and scholars of management (xxx, 2007). However, some of the sub-branches have been notably successful. For example, the history of accounting has managed to break into the so-called mainstream accounting journals, with a mix of sophisticated methodology and archival analysis. Trevor Boyn's survey of recent scholarship in this field showed how theory and archival evidence have been used to explore the relationship between accounting and decision making in the running of business (Boyns, 2007). The relationship between history and management in business history has also been debated in the *Oxford Handbook of Business History* by Patrick Fredenson, and Lamoreaux, Raff and Temin (2009).

What is clear from this escalating interest is that business history uses archival evidence, and for the historian to make sense of this archive there must be an understanding of the archival material that remains. And to appreciate this material, the business historian needs to understand the variety of processes and procedures involved in management – accounting, law, finance, marketing, human resource management, strategy and technology. The best way to achieve this is to do what contemporaries would often have done – read a textbook from the time. So, for example, in order to put together data on profitability from internal company accounting information, it is necessary to understand what was meant by depreciation, costs, revenue and so on. The documents assume that the reader already understands what they contain – they were written for a well-qualified audience who understood the accounting practices of the day. There is much to learn from engineering texts and trade catalogues.

For example, students interested in how factories were organised, and the relationship between skill, technology and skill acquisition, might wish to examine how raw materials were moved to the workplace, around the factory and then distributed to customers. Two problems arise when using a company archive: either there may be a great deal of information concerning the plant, machinery or organisation of work, or you might have very little information at all. A text, such as the *Materials Handling Handbook*, published in 1958 by Ronald Press, provided extensive evidence of best practice in materials handling. Although this is an American publication, this was the practice that many British firms were aspiring to, and so is still useful. This might be supplemented by trade catalogues such as that produced by the firm Herbert Morris Ltd of Loughborough. In 1933 they published a trade catalogue-cum-textbook over an inch thick, full of pictures and technical specifications for a range of handling equipment. Both these publications would enable an understanding of the language and technical aspects of the processes, and render the archive more intelligible. Where there is little evidence, then these texts can fill in the gaps. Of course they may not be representative of specific firms, and like any evidence should be used with care. Similarly, the trade press is an excellent source of evidence both for the entire industry and for individual firms. For example, *Modern Transport*, first published in 1919 and lasting until 1963, is full of evidence from the shipping, railway and road haulage industries, including reports on financial performance, technical innovation and policy. These are questions and problems with which the historian of business must grapple.

All history reflects the concerns and issues of contemporary society, and economic/business history is no different. The perceived emergence of a knowledge- or information-driven economy has been examined by Joel Mokyr in *The Gifts of Athena: Historical Origins of the Knowledge Economy* (2002). Mokyr examined the increasing role of knowledge in the economy, noting the difference between knowledge required for doing (practical application) and that for understanding (learnt theory). In his later work, *The Enlightened Economy: An Economic History of Britain, 1700–1850* (2009), he explored the notion of an industrial enlightenment, examining how scientific method entered the workplace. Business records can be used to see how this worked on a firm-by-firm basis. By using internal company documents it is possible to examine the nature of the technology and the role of the individual in the design and manufacture of products. Josiah Wedgewood, Matthew Bolton and James Watt, for example, were all involved in the industrial enlightenment, and the records of their activity reside in archives. The records of companies such as Cowens and Sheldon, crane makers, and J. & E. Hall, engineers, contain information on production and engineering calculations that reveal how technical decisions were made and production organised. Most scholars would agree that the notion of a modern knowledge economy is overstated, and that, to a varying degree, the economy has always had a foundation in knowledge.

So business history has carved itself a valuable place within economic history. It has moved from a concern with the individual firm (such as the Midland Railway) to the role of business more generally, say in the so-called 'knowledge economy'. The key to its ascendency, perhaps, may have been a decline in labour history that dominated the field for decades but also the enterprise of business historians who have unearthed fresh archives.

In practice

In recent years there has been something of a reaction against the decisive influence that was once exerted by economics as an explanatory factor of historical change. Political, social and cultural historians have all responded by asserting the vital importance, even primacy, at least in Marxist terms, of 'superstructural' factors. Thus, for example, there are detailed studies of political movements, the role of sex in society, missionary work in the empire, and carnival which pay little if any regard to economics. At face value, this seems sound practice. It would be difficult, say, to explain the nature and chronology of missionary endeavour by relating it to economic change, for missionaries were not evidently motivated by economic considerations.

An historian does not have to be Marxist, however, in order to appreciate the importance of economics to any explanation of historical change. To say that how societies organise to sustain themselves, and to distribute their resources, impacts massively upon their structures and behaviours is so self-evident that one wonders how anyone could question the assertion. Economic historians take it as a given, and in this chapter we have looked at ways in which some have attempted to understand such dramatic events as epidemics, demographic change and the industrial revolution primarily as economic phenomena. We would wish to argue that without an awareness of the economic dynamics of such historical phenomena, our understanding of them would be compromised. The nature of human conflict and imperial expansion could just as easily have been investigated, for ultimately these too have been driven by struggles over limited resources.

As an adjunct to economic history, business history has in recent years reached a degree of maturity. Although most of the studies have been about individual companies or sectors of the economy, they have demonstrated the value of company archives to the historian. Such records can reveal a great deal about the nature of economic transactions, improvements in technology and therefore productivity, and relationships with other concerns. Together such studies help to build a more nuanced picture of the changing economic fortunes of the nation as a whole.

Having said that, there are perhaps limits to the approach that economic historians take in explaining human behaviour. Like missionaries, people do not always act consciously or unconsciously as economic agents, nor are they driven by economic considerations. It could well be argued, for example, that the industrial revolution was made possible by the dramatic shift in bourgeois ideology that took place during the civil war of the seventeenth century. The ideas about work, profit and private property which emerged were instrumental in encouraging entrepreneurial endeavour and hence industrialisation. As historians, therefore, we have to remain mindful of the role of economic forces, but at the same time recognise that they are not reflected linearly in how people act as historical agents.

Summary

The three sections of this chapter have said three things:

- The parameters of economic history are wide but its modern origins lay in the 1880s when social inequalities were startlingly obvious and there was a backdrop of economic decline. It is suggested that economic history deals not with money per se but with the distribution of resources. The Eyam plague is examined as a way of discussing what it is that economic historians do – both those historians that are concerned with a more 'number-crunching' approach and those content to use evidence that is more richly contextualised. The uses of quantitative and qualitative evidence are discussed, and questions about how wide the concerns of economic historians go are addressed. It is also an opportunity to explain the Marxist strand of economic history and to introduce an approach within economic history that looks at population, family fertility, migration patterns and so on. We then have a rounded way of explaining the phenomenon of the seventeenth-century plague at Eyam but also the approach to the economic history of epidemics more generally.
- Production and consumption, poverty and luxury have all played important roles in the debates within economic history, but now, it can be argued, this role has been challenged by a fresh historiography. Indeed, the growth of a luxury economy is traced through the way economic historians have explained the rise and fall of the Roman Empire and how both consumption and production as issues in the economy are still problems for the historian of industrialisation to understand. This section ends with a description of the 'optimist' versus 'pessimist' contribution to the so-called 'standard of living' debate and the way that economic historians of every kind have sought to explain and assess the industrial revolution, but also how this debate gives an insight into (1) the sources used by economic historians and (2) how they evaluate these sources.
- The growing importance of business history to economic history more generally and how it is derived from interests in the micro concerns of the firm as much as the aggregated and macro concerns of the national economy. It is explained that in the modern period at least, the history of the company is a history that by definition tends to be wide ranging: from the history of a corporation to the history of the so-called 'knowledge economy' where information and its distribution is now under the auspices of economic and business history. Finally, the growing importance of new archives to the writing of these histories is dissected as a way of extending the discussion throughout the chapter on sources and their uses.

Discussion document

This comes from a popular book on medieval Europe by a well-known and respected author. It weaves a secondary commentary with evidence gleaned from a noteworthy and colourful primary source. It attributes the spiritual revival at the end of the tenth century to economic factors. It goes on to look at the economic stagnation of the late thirteenth and early fourteenth centuries to the economic decline that arguably followed the Black Death and then the economic recovery that was to characterise the early modern and modern periods. It also says something interesting about the sources available to the economic historian working on this period.

A profound change took place in Europe in the later decades of the tenth century and the early years of the eleventh. There was a popular superstition that the Christian era would last for a thousand years. There is no evidence that such pious folklore inhibited economic life, but there nevertheless a burst of activity in the years which followed the year one thousand. Raoul Glaber [chronicler and monk who died around 1047] described the new spirit:

> So on the threshold of the aforesaid thousandth year . . . it befell almost throughout the world, but especially in Italy and Gaul, that the fabrics of churches were rebuilt, although many of these were seemly and needed no such care; but every nation of Christendom rivalled with the other, which should worship in the seemliest buildings. So it was as though the very world has shaken herself and cast off her old age, and were clothing herself everywhere in a white garment of churches.

No such spiritual revival can occur without an economic base. Churches were built from the profits of agriculture and trade, and monks were supported by the slender surplus produced by the peasant. The tenth century had seen the recovery of western and central Europe from the depredations of successive waves of invaders and the rebuilding of its decimated population. During the eleventh a surplus began to accrue. This was, in part, invested in stones and mortar; in part in the building of social and political institutions, and in part in an outward thrust, driving the Muslims from Spain and Italy, conquering parts of the Levant, and establishing an expanding frontier of settlement in central and eastern Europe.

The turning point in the European economy came at different times in different parts of the continent, and was earlier in Italy than in France, and earlier in much of France and the Rhineland than in the rest of Germany. The last areas to be touched by the expansive economy of the high Middle Ages were Scandinavia, east-central Europe and the interior of the Balkans. Almost everywhere, however, economic growth, whatever indices and measures we use, was apparent well before the year 1000. It was at this time that it became visible in the landscape of Burgundy, where the monk Glaber lived the greater part of his life.

It has come to be accepted that a period of economic stagnation followed the ending of the Empire in the west. This gave place in the tenth or eleventh century to one of growth, which lasted until the end of the thirteenth or early fourteenth century. On this there is complete agreement. There was some kind of economic decline in the middle years of the fourteenth century, associated in the common view, with the spread of the

Black Death. Sometime in the fourteenth century – the date is a matter of conjecture – the European economy again took an upward turn.

In modern times indicators of economic trends assume statistical form; they are indices of employment, investment, bank lending and business turnover, all of which are relatively easy to obtain. For the Middle Ages there are no statistical indicators, and very little evidence that lends itself to any form of qualitative analysis. One can point to five trends, none of them susceptible of precise measurement, which, nonetheless, in their own qualitative fashion do point to sustained economic growth. They are (1) the formation of a system of states with fixed seats of government and administrative institutions; (2) the growth of population; (3) the bringing of new land under cultivation and the creation of new rural settlements; (4) the expansion of trade and its increasing diversity; and (5) urbanisation.

N. J. G. Pounds, *An Economic History of Medieval Europe* (1994), pp. 91–2.

Further reading

* *essential*

Maxine Berg, *Luxury and Pleasure in Eighteenth Century Britain* (2005).
Berg makes an important intervention in economic debates by making the case for consumption (as well as production) as the main source of change, both industrial change and changes in the manners and mores of the urban middle class.

D. C. Coleman, *Myth, History and the Industrial Revolution* (1992).
Contains some excellent and important essays. Chief among them are 'Industrial growth and industrial revolutions', 'Gentlemen and players' and 'The uses and abuses of business history'.

Christopher Dyer, *Making a Living in the Middle Ages: The People of Britain 850–1520* (2009).
A survey of the economy of the centuries that spanned the Viking invasion to the Reformation. Its early reflection on approaches to the economic history of medieval Britain is invaluable.

Andrew Hinde, *England's Population* (2003).
Provides an excellent introduction to the demographic history of England. It not only uses sources but explains them and does so in the medieval and early modern periods up to the twentieth century.

David Landes, *The Wealth and Poverty of Nations* (1999).
A controversial book that brings the growth and importance of modernity and industrial development back to Europe, asserting that its advancement was ultimately down to its Protestantism, its climate and its approach to science. This book is especially interesting for us because it is an economic history that examines the importance of culture not simply economic data.

N. J. G. Pounds, *Economic History of Medieval Europe* (1994).
An excellent account of its subject area but also a very good example of how economic history approaches can assist historical understanding over a long period.

Gareth Stedman Jones, *An End to Poverty: An Historical Debate* (2004).
A comprehensive and penetrating analysis of the history of poverty from a very influential social historian. It examines closely historical debates about the economy and the role of poverty and the poor in it.

Bryan Ward-Perkins, *The Fall of Rome and the End of Civilization* (2005).
An extraordinary intervention on a well-worn area of historiography – the reasons that surround the decline of Rome in the West. Ward-Perkins takes a resolute approach that challenges historical conventions using economic history throughout.

* **E. A. Wrigley**, *Continuity, Chance and Change* (1990).
An amazing example of an informed scholar taking an argumentative stand and offering a provocative hypothesis. Since challenged by empirical research, it has remained an exemplar of how to frame the industrial revolution and is an invaluable spur to research for students.

For some excellent pamphlets written in the late 1980s to early 1990s in the ReFRESH series on the industrial revolution, women and the standard of living, go to the Economic History Society website, at www.ehs.org.uk/ehs/refresh/default.asp.

Part 6

SKILLS AND TECHNIQUES

18 Sources

1 Documents and their limits: form, tone, semantics
2 Reading early documents: palaeography and Latin
3 Fakes and forgeries: protocols and the Hitler Diaries
4 History and the Internet

Introduction

This chapter seeks to give some basic instruction on how to read primary sources (the limits of which shall be defined), how to confront the particular problems posed by reading old documents, and why fakes and forgeries remain a bugbear to both researchers and students of history. The initial section gives some indicators, tips and rules for the reading of diverse sets of evidence and, in particular, how to use a document in the light of these guidelines. A practical example from fifteenth-century Italy highlights how a document might be read and how historians can become adept at extracting information from a text that at first sight may appear limited and straightforward. The second section goes on to examine the techniques used to fathom difficult handwriting, how to identify one kind of 'hand' from another and how to transcribe handwriting of various different sorts. How an historian proceeds when confronted with a document in Latin is also considered. Fakes and forgeries have long perplexed the historian and it is important that we learn how to separate the authentic source from sources that are plainly, or otherwise, false. The case studies used here are unusual and untypical: the Protocols of the Learned Elders of Zion, which is commentary about a (non-existent) document that is supposed to chronicle the idea of a global Jewish conspiracy; and the so-called Hitler Diaries, which historians initially regarded as authentic but which also turned out to be fraudulent. Finally, there is a review of uses of the Internet for the historian, advice on how to use the Web in formal academic settings and some suggestions for using archives and digital resources online.

Section 1

Documents and their limits: form, tone, semantics

Both archaeologists and historians have long regarded human waste as an invaluable source. Forensic attention to excrement in the remains of the diets of past societies has proved to be as useful at piecing together the history of human communities as any reading of parchment, papyrus or paper-based documents. The balance of protein, especially the consumption of meat and different types of meat in the waste material of past societies, may help to unravel the wealth and belief systems of ancient peoples. Analysis of bones and the types of cooking implements used, for instance, suggest that the ancient peoples of Palestine, and before it Judea, probably avoided eating pig, earlier than any religious injunction that turned pork into a forbidden food. Even the modern world is open to this type of evidence. Avner Offer's *The First World War: An Agrarian Interpretation* (1989) examined the food shortages endured by Germany because of the allied blockade. He discovered that a diet rich in meat and animal fats was as important to international relations and warfare as diplomacy or the size of a navy. It seems that the population collectively lost half a million tons of body weight as the blockade on Germany took hold and so, as an American visitor to Germany put it at the time, 'Had the Germans been vegetarians, there would have been no problem'. Offer went on from work on the 'international food economy' to look at the historical relationship between obesity, affluence and market economies. By concentrating on diet, human excrement became one source every bit as important as a conventional document and, indeed, may be considered to be a document in and of itself.

A document usually means a primary source that can give us information about a person or a specific period. This might be an eye witness account of some sort: a government proclamation, a photograph, a diary, film or even a building, especially when buildings such as those planned by Hitler's architect, Albert Speer, are so very indicative of their times. Medievalists may as readily use place names as evidence of change or numismatics, the study of coins or medals, noting their design in order to, for example, determine the importance or even length of a reign. Even headgear or the symbolic wearing of 'a cap of liberty' can be considered as a source that can be read in different ways. Primary sources might equally constitute evidence that at first glance we might not imagine as evidence at all, revealing details about the past that the author of the document had not planned to divulge and informing many areas of historical study.

Take the so-called Babatha's documents, which were found in what became known as the Cave of Letters in 1961 by a volunteer on an archaeological expedition. Babatha was a Jewish woman who lived around 104 to 134 CE, and her papers have attracted historians working on many facets of historical interest. Two thousand years old and preserved by the perfect humidity of the desert areas around the Dead Sea, the archive of 35 scrolls reveal much about sales of property at the time, court business, marriage contracts, the relationship between Roman and local law, and so on. Petitions to court suggest much about the system of law and its apparent openness to women. We know that Babatha was married more than once, and that when her second husband owed her money she motioned to have his date groves in nearby En Gedi seized. From other documents, we may even learn how important or profitable it was to own date groves, as opposed to say land that grew olives, and thus learn something about the economy. It seems that Babatha even lent money to a daughter of her second husband who had children from another of his wives (polygamy was permitted in Judaism at that time), giving us a glimpse of marital and family relationships.

Now, if we can learn about legal, marital and gender relations from this astonishing find, we can also infer something from the way that the documents are presented: that they are recorded in a wide variety of languages suggests something about levels of education apparent at the time, at least among a section of the better heeled of Jewish society. We can't know, however, why these papayas were left undiscovered in a cave for 1800 years and why they were seemingly abandoned, although it seems almost certain that Babatha and her family were involved in the Jewish Bar-Kokhba Revolt of 132–135 CE against the Romans.

As well as the ability to come at a document from a number of angles, historical imagination and dogged determination are needed to squeeze the last drop of information from it. It was a great historian of modern France, Richard Cobb (1917–96), who in his *Modern French History in Britain* (1974) said that any historian needed above all else a 'willingness to listen to the wording of the document, to be governed by its every phrase and murmur . . . so as to hear what is actually being said, in what accent and in what tone' (Cobb, 1974, p. 14). If, for example, we came across a source that appears personal, one that addressed say a fellow politician by his or her first name but where the content is generally unremarkable, then, at first glance, it is unhelpful, even irrelevant. Two things could happen, however, that might prompt a change of mind. The discovery or rereading of another source or sources may suddenly give cause to rethink the subject matter of our letter. The very fact that these two politicians are writing to each other – regardless of the subject – may provide the evidence that we need to prove that they had confidence in the judgement and trustworthiness of the other, something not directly revealed in the text of the letter.

There is then method to working with historical documents. Mostly, this method consists of asking questions of the document. The National Archives at Kew has provided a useful guide to approaching documents, which it presents in the form of questions which need to be addressed of any source:

Identification

- **What type of document is it?**
- **Who produced it? Do you know anything about the author/creator?**
- **When was it written/produced?**
- **Why was it written/produced?**

Understanding

- **What are the key words and their meaning?**
- **What points or arguments are made?**
- **What values or attitudes does the content reflect?**
- **How does the content relate to a given historical situation?**
- **Are there any clues about the intended audience?**
- **How reliable is the source and does it have any limitations?**
- **How does it relate to other sources from this period? Does it share the same ideas, attitudes and arguments? How would you explain any differences between these sources?**

(www.nationalarchives.gov.uk/education/students/primary-sources.htm)

In order to apply this method to a source we need to establish two things. First, we need to be sure what, broadly speaking, the piece is about, and in order to do that the document should be read in its entirety. Second, we need to know the date of the piece. Is the dating historically significant? Who wrote the document? What was its intended audience? Now, taking each paragraph at a time, we will seek to draw conclusions from a document that may look complicated but can yield much. We have attempted to do just this with a fifteenth-century Italian source, reproduced in Jacob Marcus' *The Jew in the Medieval World* (1999), extracts from which follow.

The narrator of the document is Hakkym ben Jehiel Cohen Falcon, a Jewish innkeeper in the Italian city of Pavia. Falcon's wife left him and appealed to Christian neighbours for sanctuary. Because of this, she is suspected of sexual misconduct. It is not clear where the sexual misconduct is supposed to have happened but we do know that he is appealing to the Jewish authorities for permission to take her back as his wife within the context of *hallakha* or Jewish law. This case is especially important in Jewish law as Falcon is a Cohen (formally temple priests) and laws of purity and marriage are more extensive in his case than they would be in the cases of other Jews:

> **In order to relate everything that has happened to me I shall tell you in detail what my business is and I shan't hide a thing from you, sir. Now this is the matter concerning which I make inquiry of my master: . . .**

This appears immediately to be a petition of some sort and gives us some sense of to whom this is addressed. The language might suggest that the relationship between the petitioner, so to speak, and the petitioned, may be unequal. A little more preliminary research would also establish that the narrative is directed towards a Jewish court of three pious men and judges, called a Beth Din, and in particular towards the leading rabbinical authority in Italy, Rabbi Joseph Colon Trabotto (*c*.1420–80). Falcon establishes his own credentials and gives his version of the relationship he had with his wife:

> **For the past several years I have made my living as an innkeeper in Palvia, and this was my business up to the year 230 [sic] [1469] when my wife began to trouble me saying: 'You've got to leave this business', and she gave me some good reasons for it. After she had kept hammering away at me every day for about six months and I had paid no attention to her – I kept pushing her off – the quarrel between us regarding this affair reached its climax about the beginning of Adar 230 [February 1470]. While I was in the house teaching my daughter, my wife picked herself up right at noon, took all the silver vessels and her jewellery, and repaired to the house of a Gentile woman, a neighbour, to whom my wife went frequently. The woman used to sew linen clothes for me, for my household, and for the guests who used to come to my place. She was also my laundress.**

The use of the Hebrew, rather than Julian calendar, may be ostentatious, designed to make an impression on the rabbis, or a genuine sign of some separateness from the gentile community. We may need here to find out a little more about Palvia as a host for Jews at this time. Falcon has guests to his house and his clothes are repaired by a gentile. This may say something about lack of separateness from the majority community, his wealth (is it typical?) and his religious observance. A strict interpretation of Jewish law may prevent a gentile fixing the clothes of a pious Jew, although Falcon is perhaps self-consciously stressing linen and not clothes of mixed fibre. We may deduce that education is important in the world described here ('I was in the house teaching my daughter') and that women or girls have access to learning or, once again, this fact may have been inserted to impress the religious court. Might we also assume, given the audience, that he was teaching her the Torah or the Bible? If so, rabbinical teaching insists that nothing should interrupt the education of a child. He goes on:

> **My wife was in the house of this Gentile woman about half an hour before I inquired of my daughters where she had gone – for I was intent on teaching my daughter. Suddenly, however, my thoughts rose up and stirred me to ask my daughters: 'Girls, where is your mother?' They told me that she had gone outside and that my four year old little girl, holding her right hand, had gone with her. I thereupon went after her, seeing her in Jewish homes unsuccessfully, till my heart told me: 'Go to the house of the Gentile; perhaps she's staying there.' So I turned in her direction and came to the house of the Gentile but found the door locked. I knocked and the husband of the woman opened the door at once, but when he saw that it was I, the husband of the woman who had just come into his home, he was distressed and tried to close the door, but he couldn't, for I entered by force. When the auxiliary bishop, who was there, heard my voice, he said to me: 'Come on in and don't be afraid.'**

Like a good Jew, Falcon looked for his wife first in the homes of his fellow Jews and only then went to the Christian home. Were the Christians located in a different quarter? Would consulting contemporary maps help us here? That he entered by force is interesting and again may say something about his status, if not the status of Jews more generally. That an 'auxiliary bishop' was present tells us something but we really need to know more about the hierarchy of the church. 'Come on in and don't be afraid' suggests that Falcon may indeed have something to fear:

> **There were present there, in addition to the auxiliary, two citizens, the bishop's chaplain, and two Gentile women seated beside my wife, who was on a bench with her daughter in her arms. As I came into the house the auxiliary bishop said to me: 'Is this your wife?' and I answered: 'Yes my lord.'**

Who and what is the 'bishop's chaplain'? 'Yes my lord' sounds like deference. The narrative builds, although we must continue to remember the author of the narrative and those for whom it is intended to impress and for what reason. Now someone besides Falcon is afforded a voice:

> **'According to what we now observe,' he said, 'another spirit has clothed your wife, who wishes to change her religion; therefore are we come to encourage her to turn to the Christian religion if she has really set her heart on it. If not, we advise her to return to her people and to her God.'**

Some background is needed here on the sorry story of forcible conversions suffered by Jews in Christian Europe. To prevent a Jew from converting to Christianity was punishable by death. Before locating this exchange in that historiography, however, the last sentence uttered should give pause:

> **I then asked his permission to have an earnest talk with her in German, and he gave me permission to speak with her in any kindly way as long as I did not scold her. Now this is what I said to her: 'Why have you come here and why don't you return home?' To which she answered: 'I am going to stay here and I don't care to return, for I don't want to be mistress**

of a tavern.' 'Come on, come on back,' I said to her, 'I have already promised you, you can do whatever your heart desires in this matter.'

They spoke in German, why German? The Jewish community in Italy was almost alone in Europe in dating from before the destruction of the Second Temple in Jerusalem (70 CE) save for the Greek community who were decimated during the Second World War. The antiquity of the Jewish community in Italy meant that it predated the diaspora that went to Spain and Portugal (Sephardic) or Ashkenazi (German) who when expelled from England and then France headed further eastwards. Ashkenazim later joined these so-called *Italkim* or Italian Jews in the north of the country and, after the 1440s, were themselves joined by Sephardim who came to the south. This document dates from the 1460s and was situated in northern Italy. Rabbi Colon, for instance, was from a well-known French family and was Ashkenazi. Why then did Falcon converse in German, not even Yiddish it would seem? Certainly, it appears that it was a language understood by both himself and his wife but not by his Christian neighbours. Could Falcon have been a newcomer and might this have affected his status, both among Jews and gentiles? Why was his wife (who seems to lack a name) so against being mistress of a tavern? (Judaism makes no prohibition against alcoholic drink and its consumption is actually commanded during some festivals.) Now his wife was given a voice but (obviously) speaks through him:

'You can't fool me again', she responded. 'You've lied to me ten times and I don't trust you.' And as she was speaking to me after this fashion I said to her: 'Why have you your little daughter in your arms?' 'Take your daughter and go', she answered, and I took her in my arms. Then as I turned to go my way the auxiliary bishop said to me: 'Look here, Falcon, don't be disturbed about your wife. No pressure will be brought to bear on her. Nothing will be done in haste, but quietly, calmly, and with her consent. Before we make a decision in this matter we will place her in a cloistered spot, among virtuous nuns, where no man may enter. She'll have to stay there forty days until she completes the period of her isolation and reflection – for this practice has been established by the founder of Christianity that one may determine what is in the heart of those who came to change their religion, and so in order to prevent confusion to Christianity.'

The liberal tone of this exchange was striking, as was the overt reference to her being in the care of 'virtuous nuns'. There is a copious literature on this subject, but for now we press on with the narrative:

When I heard this as I turned homeward weeping as I went. My oldest daughter came out to meet me, and I told her all about the unseemly affair that had happened to me. She ran to her mother to find out what she had in mind. 'Go back to the house and don't be concerned, and don't bother about me', her mother told her. Whereupon the girl ran to a prominent Jewess and spoke to her. Behold, the entire conversation of this Jewess is recorded in a disposition that has been forwarded to you.

That the testimony of a 'prominent Jewess' was weighed in the balance may tell us something about the *matri*-focal nature of the community under review; it may be that the society was governed with the power of men but it was run with women very much in mind. That he left weeping may tell us something about contemporary notions of masculinity.

The source breaks out from the narrow concerns of inter-Jewish interest (important as these may be historically), and becomes a document more concerned with Jewish/Christian relations. By the bishop saying 'I'll cross-question her in the presence of witnesses, as is meant to be done in such a case' (p. 296) he is doing the work of the rabbis. Implicitly, even explicitly, he questions the wife regarding her sexual conduct since she left her husband, and with her answer, the *cohenim* laws of purity and propriety are satisfied. This may suggest some synergy between churchman and rabbinic Judaism, at least in their understanding of biblical text. At the very least it suggests a sympathy for Jewish sensibilities that were singularly absent across so much of the medieval period. It may be, moreover, a commentary on the social relationship of the communities in that particular place and in that particular time. This document may not be unique. Indeed, there are medieval sources that reveal Jews inviting Christians to celebrations such as a *bar mitzvah*, even if it attracted the opprobrium of the church itself.

Documents then can reveal much and can reveal different things depending on perspective and the questions that we ask of them. The document above is translated from Hebrew. It might have been Latin, if its origins were different. What do we do then with the problem of translation and what if we are presented with evidence that is so sparse and undemonstrative that the historian is left piecing together evidence like a parlour room detective? The next section will deal with these and other problems.

Section 2

Reading early documents: palaeography and Latin

In this section we outline the basics of palaeographical study, and explain why the skills are important in certain areas of historical research. Palaeography is the study of old handwriting and manuscripts. This may include handwriting (sometimes just called script or hand) used in the administration of business, church or the state, record keeping and correspondence of every sort from the twelfth century. It is particularly associated with a widely used term: 'documentary hand'. 'Documentary hand' is characterised by a style that is more steady and consistent and less, as it were, individual than handwriting was to become in the modern era. 'Book hand' refers to the handwriting of books and tends to be more formal, although as commentators have pointed out, the boundaries between the two styles became increasingly fluid as time went on. There is a third type of handwriting in documents that we associate with pre-modern manuscripts and that is 'Cursive', which is most often found in formal or official documents, while 'Diplomatic' refers to the study of the forms and conventions of a document.

The type of document and types of people that record and write documents changed over the centuries. Monastic chronicles dominate the twelfth century with annals written in localities recording invaluable local phenomena. These Chroniclers tackled subject matter that led us towards the more systematic study of history with Bede (see Chapter 7) as the most prominent example. The thirteenth century saw the blossoming of the state and with it a legal bureaucracy which has left us a richness of judicial records, chancery documents and records from royal interventions. In the fourteenth century, we must also take account of poems; in the fifteenth, increased correspondence. By the sixteenth century and the puritan revolution, we saw diaries used as individual confessions before God.

Throughout these centuries we witnessed what one historian, M. T. Clanchy, has called 'the growth of a literate mentality' (Clanchy, p. 2). According to his book, *From Memory to Written Record*, literacy levels 'grew out of bureaucracy, rather than from any abstract desire for education or literature' (p. 19). This process was prompted by the state – church, law, crown – ensuring that local communities gathered historical information when needed, not from the 'oral wisdom of their elders and remembrancers' (p. 3), but from books, charters and other written documents produced at that time and which are now treated as historical sources. These sources, however, present problems of comprehension, as we shall find out now by looking briefly at the art of palaeography and all that it involves.

The aim of palaeography is to learn the techniques of reading and interpreting documents from the antique and medieval periods. Perhaps the most comprehensive introduction for students is Raymond Clemens and Timothy Graham's *Introduction to Manuscripts* (2007), which dealt with a wide range of reading documents. This included the 'grammar' of medieval manuscripts, its genres, such as biblical and liturgical texts, and the tools needed to make sense of what it is they convey. Methods of how to read documents set out in the last section still apply but the search now is to find consistent characteristics in the writing itself, as much as the need to discover what is being said and to whom.

While there is a need to read and understand handwriting from these periods, *how* to read handwriting is another matter and requires training. There are excellent online courses, including 'Palaeography: reading old handwriting 1500–1800', available via the National Archives website, which is a series of practical tips on how to read and transcribe difficult handwriting, although palaeography is taught wherever postgraduates are studying medieval history. It is also true to say, however, that most undergraduates are not required to transcribe a document letter by letter, word by word in order to make it intelligible to the modern eye. This said, the exercise in its simplest form is a good instructor on the difficulties posed by reading old and unfamiliar language and gives a good idea of what it is that medievalists and others actually do. For example, *The Parliament Rolls of Medieval England, 1275–1504* (2008) provides the following extract, which is all but unreadable in its original form:

> **That it may please youre said wisedoms to praie the kyng our soveraigne lord to ordeigne, by auctorite of this present parliament, that the said acte and ordenaunce be and stonde god, vaileable and effectuell unto thende /of the seid .iiiij.\ yeres and from thende of the seid .iiij. yeres unto the ende and terme of .x. yeres then next ensuynge, at the reverence of God and in the way of charitite.**
> ***Responsio.***
>
> **Le roy de voet.**

Transcribed, however, it becomes:

> **May it please your said wisdoms to pray our sovereign lord the king to ordain, by authority of this present parliament, that the said act and ordinance shall remain and stand good, valid**

and effectual until the end of the said four years and from the end of the said four years until the end of the following ten years, at the reverence of God and in way of charity.
Answer.

The king wills it.

Dating is also a serious issue. As discussed in Chapter 2 in the context of the relationship of history to time, changes to the calendar in 1752 require us to recognise a break between the Old Style (OS) and New Style (NS) dating systems. In addition, there is the regnal dating of documents to consider; they neither conform to the old Julian calendar nor the new Gregorian, but to the length of a monarch's reign. Numbers or numerals change between the Roman and the English, while money and measurements have also undergone transformation. Before attempting to transcribe old documents, we must have a key at hand that can readily make the necessary calculations; for example, 40 perches equals 1 rood and 1 rood is 1 acre. *Car*, in the eleventh-century Domesday Book (commissioned in 1085 by William the Conqueror as a record of those English settlements that fell south of the Scottish border), has two meanings: *carucate*, a measure of land, and *caruca*, which refers to a plough team. A similar point can be made about money as it changes in value and denomination.

Dating is very closely allied to chronology. C. R. Cheney's *A Handbook of Dates for Students of British History* (2000) not only gave a guide to changes in the way time was measured (as described above) but also included a very useful list of popes, rulers, saints, festival days and so on. It is complemented nicely by Pryde and Greenway's *Handbook of British Chronology* (1986), which gave all offices in the state, church and aristocracy from the Middle Ages into modern times. These events are all reflected in the dating of documents which are needed for an effective reading of antique or medieval manuscripts. For example, in an apparently simple description of a day contained in a manuscript, we would be tempted to assume that a day is comprised simply of 24 hours – a unit of time that is surely shared by both the living and the dead. But this is not necessarily so. Cheney tells us that the Roman day was divided into two 12-hour fractions that would differ in length according to the season: from this we derive the seven 'canonical' hours adopted by the medieval church to mark its services: Matins, Prime, Terce, Sect, None, Vespers and Compline. A uniform length of day was not fully established until clocks with bells were displayed in churches and other public buildings sometime during the thirteenth century (Cheney, 2000, p. 16). Without this knowledge, at least some of what was read would make little or no sense to the historical researcher.

If transcribing this document into modern English does not seem challenging enough, there is the question of reading Latin documents in Latin. Eileen Gooder's book *Latin for Local History* (1978) is one of several excellent introductions to the subject. Tellingly the author labelled the Latin used in records 'the very stuff of history'. But it is 'stuff' that was shaped and altered by medieval lawyers and clerks and those that succeeded them across the centuries. Deeds, charters, manor and borough court records, estate accounts, church registers, chapter act books, sessions from justices of the peace and writs, all reveal the contours of the historical record and with the evolution of this record comes challenges for the historian. These challenges, however, are largely challenges regarding grammar. For example:

Consuetudo Waruuic fuit ut eunte rege per terram in expeditionem, decem burgenses de Waruuic pro omnibus aliis irent. Qui monitus non ibat, C solidos regi emendabat. Si vero paer mare contra hostes suos ibat rex, vel IIII batsueins vel IIII libras denariorum ei mittebant.

Note now that, in translation, the grammatical emphasis is all-important:

> **The custom of Warwick was that when the king went (ablative absolute: lit., the king going) by land on an expedition, ten burgesses of Warwick should go (*irent*: imperfect subjunctive after a command, 'custom' here implying an obligation) for all the others. (He) who did not go (imperfect of *eo*) when summoned, paid 100 shillings fine to the king. If however the king was going against his enemies by sea, they (i.e. the burgesses) sent him either 4 boatswains or 4 pounds of pennies.** (Cited in Gooder, 1978, pp. 68–9)

Abbreviations also pose problems. They are ubiquitous simply because they were inserted to save time and space. This means that the historian is faced with a language within a language that needs to be decoded. Here are some examples from the National Archives:

Abbreviations for prefixes:

ꝑ – 'per' or 'par' ꝑson – person or parson

ꝓ – 'pro' ꝓvide – provide

p̃ – 'pre' p̃sent – present

Abbreviation to denote a plural:

ꝭ – 'es', 'is' or 'ys' oatꝭ – oates

Abbreviations shown by superscript letters:

w^{t} – with

w^{ch} – which

M^{r} – Master (not 'Mister' at this time).

There are scholarly guides to assist in this task including Andriano Cappelli, *The Elements of Abbreviation in Medieval Latin Palaeography* (1982), Bernhard Bischoff, *Latin Palaeography: Antiquity and the Middle Ages* (1990) and C. T. Martin, *The Record Interpreter* (1976). How to fathom the meaning of arcane words; either the word is no longer in use or a regional dialect is masking its true denotation, basic meaning or true symbolic value. Squiggles and dashes in some documents pass for abbreviations. It seems that there are functional reasons for this. Speed may well have been of the essence and space and parchment could be expensive.

Medieval documents require knowledge of the workings of the scribes, as well as abbreviations used, place names, money, dating and chronology of major events. That it gives us as historians an unrivalled picture of life in the Middle Ages is beyond dispute but it is also a test of the skills needed to read any document before the seventeenth century, including knowledge of Latin. It may not be a challenge equal to the challenge posed by the Rosetta Stone and the need to revive a lost language but it is, nevertheless, representative of the tools required by medievalists and others whose everyday skills would necessarily include those outlined in this chapter. There is one other important skills set required by the historian and that is, as we are about to find out, to know when an historical document is a forgery or fake.

Section 3

Fakes and forgeries: protocols and the Hitler Diaries

The Last Days of Hitler (1947) was a unique book: combining scholarship and an historian's ability to interrogate a source. In 1945, a youthful Oxford historian, Hugh Trevor-Roper (1914–2003) served as a wartime intelligence officer in occupied Germany and from the confusion of war, the diaries of Goering's chief of staff, the Reich's Minister of Finance and that of Hitler's valet, came into his possession. Having completed his report to the British government on the demise of Hitler in November 1945, establishing seemingly beyond doubt that Hitler had died in his Berlin bunker, Major Trevor-Roper was informed that copies of Hitler's last will and testament were also to be retrieved, this time from an address near the Austrian border. A midnight raid, followed by the interrogation of a former German officer, led to a search party digging up a garden where the document was found hidden in a bottle. Such was the first draft of history written of this dreadful period of human history and such was it unconventionally researched. Yet, the story did not finish here. Speculation continued after Hitler's death that he might have left behind a diary – speculation that increased in the post-war period.

Germans could scarcely imagine how such a man lived and had come to power. Some longed, perhaps, for a return to those days. Perhaps Hitler had not died at all. Perhaps, like other Nazis, he had escaped or lived incognito, doing an ordinary job as a waiter or mechanic in a small border town somewhere in South America, perhaps. These imaginings and a need to know led in turn to possibly the greatest hoax ever perpetrated on a distinguished historian and emerged from a milieu where such a hoax might be believed. Hence the excitement when the German magazine *Stern* acquired Hitler's wartime diaries, which were said to have been rescued from a Luftwaffe transport plane that had crashed to the ground in flames in April 1945. They offered the material for sale in April 1988. Before the *Sunday Times* paid $4 million, however, the need was to authenticate the find, for someone to determine its provenance. Who better then Hugh Trevor-Roper, now ennobled as Lord Dacre, Master of a Cambridge college and a director of Rupert Murdoch's Times Newspapers. Dacre had misgivings. The script was suspect and, as it turned out, so was the paper it was written on. In any case, historians had discounted the possibility that Hitler wrote a diary, as he lacked both inspiration and purpose. Those close to him before and during the war had also generally discounted the fact. Eventually, the Hitler Diaries were exposed as an elaborate and expensive hoax. Before this, however, an initial, perhaps provisional, judgement by the historian and wartime intelligence officer, Lord Dacre, led to the unexpected declaration that the manuscript was genuine. The reputation of this brilliant post-war historian never really recovered. This section then will examine the importance that historians place on recognising sources that are illegitimate, that distort the historical record, whilst considering the importance of the Hitler Diaries and (as we shall see) the Protocols of the Learned Elders of Zion as examples of the importance of forgeries more generally.

There is no doubt that forgers and fakers have diverse motives: some do it for ideological reasons and some for monetary gain; others for the thrill of outwitting experts such as Trevor-Roper. The trade is certainly not a new one. Nineteenth-century scholarship was plagued by Shakespeare forgeries and, most recently perhaps, one enterprising soul added papers to the Himmler archive at the National Archives in Kew, hoping to suggest that the chief of the SS in Nazi Germany had been murdered by British intelligence. The most enduring and damaging of the forgeries was, however, the Protocols of Zion, which was said, indeed *is* said in some parts of the world, to prove that there is a Jewish conspiracy to dominate the world.

The historian Norman Cohn in his *Warrant for Genocide* (1967) traced the origins of the so-called Protocols. This was a document that appears to have been an invention of the early twentieth century. It purported to expose (although the original has, not unsurprisingly, never come to light) a Jewish plot to form a world government. The author of this pernicious fraud was reckoned to have been the Tsarist civil servant, one Serge Nilus. Most accounts have the elusive manuscript stolen by a woman from somewhere in France which was a 'Zionist headquarters' (which never existed). Alternatively, it is said that the Protocols had been read aloud at the First Zionist Congress held in Basel, Switzerland in 1897. Indeed, Hitler referred to the Protocols as the 'Basel' document and evoked the idea of a Jewish conspiracy at work in 1930s Germany.

Whenever we are confronted with manuscripts whose authenticity is in doubt, like the Hitler Diaries or the Protocols, historians are called upon to use their professional skills. Quite apart from technology that can confirm correct dating by testing the age of the paper or the veracity of say handwriting, we also need to establish provenance. In the case of the Hitler Diaries, it might indeed have been the handwriting or the age of the typewriter that first raised doubts; while eyewitnesses who claimed to have overheard Hitler's reaction to an aeroplane escaping the fall of Berlin with important cargo or even seen the 'plane plunge to the ground' may have initially made the find plausible. In either case, context is everything. As Hitler became such an enigmatic figure in post-war Germany and as his accomplices were spotted all over the world, often in the same place simultaneously, so the need to hear his voice again, to understand why Germany had acted as it had, increased. On the other hand, it raised the possibility among large numbers of former Nazis that were in senior positions in Germany during the post-war world, that the Third Reich may yet be realised.

Of course, in the case of the Diaries, the market could meet the need for sensational revelations, and by supplying newspaper and magazine articles that demand was duly met. When the time came, a forgery convinced those that wished to be convinced. In the instance of the Protocols, however, the motive was political, not economic. The Protocols emerged at a time of fearful change; first in the wake of revolutionary activity in Russia, then in the chaos of 1930s Germany. On each occasion, the modern world was encroaching on previously traditional societies and that modern world was nowhere better represented at its vanguard then by the cosmopolitan Jew. The Hitler Diaries and the Protocols each served the present.

The real origin of the Protocols, we are told by Cohn, was in fact an 1860s French satire that does not feature Jews at all. That it morphed and altered into a conspiracy theory illustrated the power of history and the force of historical mythology. Diverse countries such as Spain, Italy, Britain, Japan, Latin America (including Argentina, Brazil, Chile, Columbia and Paraguay), as well as Russia and Germany, have all produced copies of the Protocols. *The Times* in the 1920s argued that they were not forgeries at all and then later argued the other way. Henry Ford's *Dearborn Independent* published the Protocols in the same decade in a series entitled 'The international Jew: the world's foremost problem'. Republished in book form, they were said to have sold half a million copies. Now Islamic countries from Syria to Egypt to the Palestinian Authority publish copies. Cohn in his *Warrant of Genocide* saw the Holocaust and Nazism as the high point of a mythology about Jews that derived from the Christian apocalyptic tradition but which has mutated into Middle Eastern politics.

What then are the lessons of the Hitler Diaries and the Protocols? Clearly, the context of the forgery is crucial. For the Diaries this was all too apparent in the post-war world among a generation that borrowed their memories from the generation that preceded them. The thirst to understand the enormity of Hitler's crimes (or for some, achievements) among the public and the desire for historians to peek at evil was overwhelming, even to make money and further careers. Why conspiracy theories are promulgated is complex. People who feel marginal to power may, sociologically speaking, scapegoat people and groups who appear to be close to centres of power. We have not been especially interested in the sociology of fakes and forgeries in the course of this section. We have been concerned, however, to determine that authenticity of a source is of prime importance to historians. While the examples chosen here are extraordinary and far from typical – forged medieval title deeds would be singularly less rare in historical study – the principle that sources may not be authentic should nevertheless be borne in mind.

Section 4

History and the Internet

Many historians now make use of the Internet as a research, teaching or publishing tool. So extensive is this practice that, in ways we do not yet fully understand, the Net is transforming the practice of history. The practical consequences are obvious. The Internet contains an astounding amount and variety of sites containing historical information. So accessible are they, and so seemingly comprehensive, it might appear at first sight that it is possible to undertake and write up original research without leaving the comfort of your own room. No longer is it necessary to embark on weary treks in search of half-forgotten archives – a great relief, no doubt, to many of us who have found that the promise of the archive was only occasionally realised. In a similar way, many history students find it possible to write essays without consulting a single book from the library. The Internet is certainly one important way that the historian can access the very stuff of history, but rules and procedures still have to be applied.

Massive though the amount of information is, it is limited and has to be used with intelligence and discretion. Let us explore some of these issues using examples of some of the major types of sites containing historical materials. Many of the sites are merely historical commentaries written by people with differing levels of historical skill. *Wikipedia* is an obvious example, not least because it seems to be the resource most commonly used by students. This site contains entries covering a huge variety of historical topics, but at best they are skilful summaries; almost all are recycled, selective and partial accounts from other sources, and as such are poor substitutes for consulting the original primary and secondary materials. Indeed *Wikipedia*, for all its good intentions, should be treated with caution, effectively used only as a search engine if used at all. Essentially it is vital that any search of the Web follows contextual knowledge of a subject and does not precede it. It is vital too that Google is not the first site used to conduct a vague and ill-informed search, and *Wikipedia* likewise, although Google Scholar has something to recommend it.

Archives

Sites which give access to materials normally available only in libraries and archive collections are more valuable to historians. Publishers and libraries are for the moment very keen to make their materials available online, but again caution has to be exercised. Normally, only a tiny fraction of a library's archive has actually been digitised (in the case of the British Library, for example, less than 5 per cent). So what we have in most cases is at best a small window into a much larger resource. The Library of Congress American Memory website at www.memory.loc.gov/ammem, on the other hand, is an extraordinary collection of personal narratives and detailed background information providing a quite exceptional database for anyone interested in the history of North America. It should be required reading for every American citizen, and must be the envy of all modern historians.

For obvious reasons, most sites rather than choosing material randomly, choose to digitise particular archives created around a person or an historical episode. The historian can do no better than start with www.archive.org, a wonderful digital library of Internet sites created out of a dedication to provide universal access to all knowledge. It has not managed to achieve this yet, but what the site does include for the historian is an invaluable collection of official publications and books, mainly from the English-speaking world of the last two hundred years.

Funding bodies have been prepared to finance important initiatives to create online databases. One important recent example is *Proceedings of the Old Bailey, 1674–1913* at www.oldbaileyonline.org, which contains transcribed records of nearly 200,000 criminal trials held at London's most prominent criminal court. Helpfully, the website provides a contextual backdrop to the records, including headings such as gender, community histories of London's minorities, geographies of London and an architectural account of the Old Bailey courthouse. These sources unwittingly provide a collective biography of the thousands of men and women that went to trial at the Old Bailey, and the whole is fully searchable so that anyone can trace their criminal ancestors, determine, say, the numbers of people convicted of rioting between 1750 and 1800, or the numbers transported for petty theft, that went to trial or were executed at Tyburn.

Like the Old Bailey proceedings, the Charles Booth Online project is also fully searchable. Hosted and developed by the London School of Economics at www.booth.lse.ac.uk, it can display digital copies of the original survey notebooks, police notebooks, as well as the family papers of this late-Victorian philanthropist, social investigator, statistician and would-be sociologist.

For straightforward retrieval of archival material, the contemporary historian is immensely fortunate to draw upon websites that contain digitised versions of historic newspapers, historical images and video clips. Perhaps most prominent is *History Online* at http://historyonline.chadwyck.co.uk. International newspapers such as the *Wall Street Journal* and the *New York Times* are now available online, as are the national newspaper of record *The Times* and a local newspaper which, for example, catered for a specific community from the 1840s, the *Jewish Chronicle*. The Colindale Newspaper Library in London is an arm of the British Library and their collection of national and Sunday newspapers from the UK from 1801, provincial newspapers from the UK and Ireland, along with a collection of European newspapers from the seventeenth century, can be searched at www.bl.uk.

Finally, it is worth mentioning an example of the many online initiatives developed by enthusiastic amateurs. www.casebook.org is very much part of the industry that has arisen from the rather morbid interest in Jack the Ripper. But it contains a comprehensive collection of contemporary newspaper coverage, a photo archive and detailed factual information which is invaluable to anyone wishing to investigate the topic.

More specialist databases have become an important tool in historical research. Projects such as PASE (a prosopography of Anglo-Saxon England) and PBW (a prosopography of the Byzantine World), run by King's College, London and Cambridge University have attracted major funding. The former, we are told, at www.pase.ac.uk 'is a database which aims to cover all of the recorded inhabitants of England from the late sixth to the end of the eleventh century. It is based on a systematic examination of the available written sources for the period, including chronicles, saints' *Lives*, charters, *libri vitae*, inscriptions, and coins.' The latter at www.pbw.kcl.ac.uk/content/index.html is in its second phase with terminal dates of 1025–1102. The way that relational databases can be connected through online technology and promulgated to a global audience practically without limit, means that prosopography as an approach to generating historical evidence has found a new platform. Family and public historians (see Chapter 11) have certainly benefited but so have modern historians. The Clergy of England Database, involving King's London, Kent and Reading universities at www.theclergydatabase.org.uk documents the careers of every Church of England clergyman between 1540 and 1835. Happily, other such databases, including some interesting prosopographies of local individuals and groups such as a 'Survey of Scottish witchcraft, 1563–1736' or 'Mathematical women in the British Isles, 1878–1940', can be located at the *History Data Service* website http://hds.essex.ac.uk/history/data/prosopography.asp and is maintained by the University of Essex.

History on the Internet then provides us with quite staggering opportunities to research from the home or office. Before moving on to other categories of available online material, we should mention two major online archives devoted to visual and aural sources. One example is the so-called DIAMM project, which since 1998 has been concerned to obtain and digitise images of medieval polyphonic music; that is, to archive music taken from original music sheets. With an electronic archive of 14,000 images, the University of Oxford Music Faculty and the Bodleian Library manage this project that was originally a collaboration between Oxford and Royal Holloway London and can be found at www.diamm.ac.uk/index.html.

Another site dealing with images for the use of the historian is *Extending the Suffrage: The Digitisation of the Women's Library Suffrage Banners* at http://ahds.ac.uk/creating/case-studies/suffrage/index.htm, which details the banners used by this late nineteenth and twentieth century political movement in the marches and protests of both Suffragettes and Suffragists. Finally, the Web has also exploited the study of architecture and the built environment. *The Cistercians in Yorkshire* website focuses on Cistercian life in the great abbeys of the county. Run by the University of Sheffield at http://cistercians.shef.ac.uk the site uses multimedia movie facilities to great effect.

Finally, there are three other related developments. The Web has provided museums and libraries with a way to showcase online exhibitions. The British Library has brilliantly developed a 'turn page' facility. Exhibitions on the Online Gallery at www.bl.uk/onlinegallery/index.html, tackle subjects such as Magna Carta, Black Europeans, Music Manuscripts and historical texts from Bede and others. Similar claims of excellence can be made for other repositories, from the Imperial War Museum to the Smithsonian in Washington DC. Data has also been used very successfully online. *The History Data Service* at http://hds.essex.ac.uk/history/data/online.asp contains, for example, *The Online Historical Population Reports Collection*, *Enclosure Maps Database* and the *Contemporary and Historical Census Collection*. Finally, new Web-based technologies have transformed the way heritage is presented online. Virtual coliseums have been recreated from what we know about Rome and world heritage sites can now be explored via moving and roving cameras that take us into every corner. Even static cameras trained on an historic site such as the *Kotel* or 'wailing wall' in Jerusalem increase the range of resources available to an historian.

Archives with restricted access

Online archives have become commercial propositions in recent years. With the cooperation of libraries, a number of companies now supply extensive archival resources on particular themes for those wishing to subscribe. A few examples must suffice. Gale (www.gale.cengage.com) offers major collections including Sources in US History Online, which contains extensive materials on the Civil War, Slavery, the American Revolution, and struggles for voting rights for women. Adam Matthew Digital (www.amdigital.co.uk), for example, include in recent digitised archives, The First World War: personal narratives, Foreign Office India, Pakistan and Afghanistan, 1947–80, and Jewish Life in America, *c*.1654–1954. Although most of such collections are extensive, they do tend to draw selectively upon archives, and so while they might be wonderful resources for teaching and undergraduate work, more advanced research will require access to other sources. In addition, none of these collections is cheap, and so are beyond the means of most individuals. Institutional subscriptions are normally the only means of gaining access to them.

Limited access sites also include those containing valuable collections of journals. For example, www.jstor.org contains the contents of over a thousand journals, approximately 250 of which are classified as history, so providing a valuable service to those who do not have ready access to comprehensive collections of journals. In most cases, however, issues of the past three years are not included. Many journals are available online through subscription to individual publishers.

Most higher education institutions subscribe to such online resources. The major ones such as the Bodleian (www.oxlip-plus.bodleian.ox.ac.uk) make available to staff and students of the university numerous online resources including British Parliamentary Papers of the Nineteenth Century and American State Papers 1789–1838. Less advantaged institutions offer far fewer online resources.

Overall, therefore, there are considerable and rapidly growing numbers of resources available on the information highway which are of value to the historian. Having said that, they give access to only a tiny percentage of the archive material available, and access itself is very much determined by the institution to which you happen to belong. There is little doubt that such access has made historical research and teaching more convenient. It is now possible to consult relevant primary and secondary sources without leaving your desk. Has this led, however, to *better* research and teaching? Not necessarily. Most historians these days are under pressure to publish, and so have little time for critical reflection. Within such a climate, the temptation is to rely as much as possible on such ready sources, as a result of which the same bodies of knowledge tend to be recycled. And for some of the old fashioned amongst us, convenient though a computer is, it can never really substitute for the exhilaration of burrowing down into dusty archives and actually handling manuscripts and miscellaneous pieces of paper created by the heroes and villains of ages past.

Mark Poster has pointedly asked 'What is at stake in the alteration of material structure of cultural objects from the paper forms of manuscript and print to the digital form of computer files?' (Poster, 2003, p. 17). His answer to this important question is that the digitisation of sources such as texts, images and sounds presents several problems in defining the nature of historical truth. First, given that much of the information is put together by a variety of historians and amateur enthusiasts it is not always clear how much reliability can be placed on the individual sites. There is also the worry of the increasing concentration of archival material controlled by media companies which are able to restrict access. Second, digital sources are rather more prone than archival materials to alteration by their users. Texts can be rewritten and links made which potentially transform the original, so again throwing into doubt the authenticity of the materials. However, Poster noted that the excitement of working in a real as opposed to a virtual archive can seduce historians into the belief that here the truth is to be found. Digitisation debunks any such notions. Without the same intense emotional engagement, virtual archives can encourage more critical reflection on questions of reliability and authenticity.

In practice

As we have seen, since the nineteenth century there has been an important tradition of historical practice which places great stress upon the use of archival material (see Chapter 19). The principal object of the historian, it was argued, is to recreate past events through use of relevant sources, and a large part of the historian's craft derives from the skills and techniques he or she needs to accomplish this task. In this chapter we have attempted to examine some of the more practical aspects of working with archival materials.

The ability to read evidence is of paramount importance. As we approach a particular document or archive, we need to do so with a critical awareness. There are a number of questions that we need to have in mind about its production, authenticity, intended audience and so on, without which there is the danger we accept material at face value. In addition, and equally importantly, we need to be able to 'read' sources to reveal what they actually said. Documents may well have been intended to convey particular messages to an audience, but by reading beneath the lines, as it were, we can gain access to the hidden assumptions, to the ways of thinking of the author about the event being described, and hence the mind-set of people in similar positions in the past. Evidence submitted by a Jewish innkeeper in fifteenth-century Italy, for example, can, if properly read, reveal a great deal about his thinking on wider social matters relating to gender, religion and social exclusion.

Much of the older written material in particular is rather inaccessible to many of us who have grown up with standardised languages presented in readily recognisable printed forms. Ancient and medieval documents appear not only in languages that are unfamiliar, but are written in styles which are difficult to read. Handwriting at the best of times can be difficult to read, but when it is from a quite different age following very different conventions of spelling, grammar and style, and when as a means of shorthand uses abbreviations, then the task is one that can only be accomplished with the acquisition of special skills in reading.

In thinking about historical veracity, we should always be alert to the question of forgery. There have been notorious instances in the past of historical forgeries which have served to perpetuate particular myths with damaging consequences. Most of us are unlikely to encounter these forms of evidence. On the smaller scale, however, there is always the chance that we could come across letters, election leaflets, reported speeches which are not what they appear.

Finally, the nature of historical evidence has been transformed in recent years with the information revolution. The digitisation of archival material and historical commentary has greatly increased our access to evidence. Not only that, it has altered the nature of historical research, teaching and publishing but in ways that we do not yet fully understand. Despite the obvious advantages of ready access to knowledge, the use of the Internet has thrown into relief a host of questions about historical reliability, the control of information, plagiarism, and the logistics of research which we all need to be aware of when surfing.

Summary

The four sections of this chapter have suggested four things:

- The limits of how we define a document are wide. Examples were given of different primary sources and it was suggested that these sources were treated differently across periods. Sometimes the visual and the material come into view, although written documents are often privileged. Whatever the case, however, there are rules to follow in reading documents, in their identification and comprehension. An example from fifteenth-century Italy was examined in close detail in order to demonstrate, with some prior knowledge and historical imagination, what might be deduced from a single primary source.

- Different centuries have produced a range of different sources from the ecclesiastical record, to the judicial record, to the personal diary. Each period has thrown up challenges, however. Transcribing difficult handwriting is a practised art and is complicated by a need to understand, in many cases, Latin. Abbreviations, uses of chronology and a notion of how to measure changes to dating over time to understand how money or time is measured, also requires knowledge beyond that required by a modern historian.

- That documents are sometimes subject to forgery is not a new discovery. Examples of attempts to sabotage the archives go back into at least the nineteenth century. In the case of the Hitler Diaries in the 1980s, it was demonstrated how a post-war context could make a forgery financially rewarding. In the case of the Protocols, dating from around 1900, the motive is less clear and appears to be rather more ideologically or politically driven. It is a timely reminder that history is powerful enough to be considered worth falsifying and that the results of that falsification can matter.

- The digital revolution in humanities has facilitated a fundamentally different approach to historical knowledge and the acquisition of historical knowledge has been transformed. A whole world of online archives has been brought to life on the Internet with concomitant opportunities for the student to engage in study in areas and ways formerly beyond our wildest dreams. History on the Internet, however, also presents certain pitfalls for the historian unwilling to exercise caution in accessing the websites used and monitoring the veracity of the knowledge they present.

Discussion document

In many ways, the history of the sign and of symbols is connected to skills historians have acquired from social or cultural anthropology, a subject which was covered in Chapter 14. This said, the account here of early nineteenth-century radicalism focuses on an unlikely source – a cap. That this cap can be read mnemonically, as a shorthand for the radicalism of the French Revolution, does not take into account that it is potentially 'multi-vocal'; that is, it was also recognised by contemporaries as an emblem of national loyalty or of Englishness.

> There was another complication, however: the history of the sign – a history that came out most clearly at the trials following the Peterloo massacre. The mnemonic force of the cap of liberty was multivocal; what was being remembered was not as fixed as the *Times* portrayed. If the cap of liberty conjured only the horrors of the French Revolution for loyalists, its older – its classical and English – meanings came rushing forward as radicals moved into court-rooms to defend and accuse. Since the magistrates moved to disperse the meeting at St. Peter's Field before the speakers said anything of substance, the government had to prove that the meeting itself was illegal in form and intent. Lacking any evidence of inflammatory language the symbols themselves became all the more important in creating circumstances calculated to 'produce terror of immediate danger in the minds of the King's subjects'. Thus the meeting's banners and emblems, their inscriptions and meanings, became focal points of legal contention – central evidence of radical intent 'to alter the legal frame of the government of these realms, by force and threats'. But meanings were not so simple. In his opening address to the jury at York, Hunt drew attention to counter-meanings. The cap of liberty 'was an emblem of a most sacred nature. In ancient Rome if a slave had saved the life of a citizen, or had performed a service to the state, he received as a reward, his Freedom; and on his emancipation from Slavery, he had a Cap placed on his head as an emblem of his Liberty'. Hunt also pointed to the representation of the cap of liberty on the front of the town hall at York as evidence of the Englishness of the symbol.

J. A. Epstein, 'Understanding the Cap of Liberty: symbolic practice and social conflict in early nineteenth century England', *Past and Present*, cxx11 (1989), pp. 75–119.

Further reading

* *essential*

*** www.nationalarchives.gov.uk/education/students/primary.**
An award-winning website that relates in very simple terms the bare basics of indentifying and understanding a document. It uses some wonderful examples from the rich variety of the world's largest archive to illustrate these points.

*** www.nationalarchives.gov.uk/Palaeography/doc40/about.htm.**
Underlines the challenges and difficulties of reading old documents, difficulties raised during the chapter, and is a useful guide to approaching what for many is an unknown area of historical enquiry.

www.nationalarchives.gov.uk/Latin/advanced
www.nationalarchives.gov.uk/Latin/beginners
Both take the reader through the reading of Latin for the express purpose of understanding historical documents.

Eileen Gooder, *Latin for Local History* (1978).
A reliable source of information on its subject, especially for those that require instruction in Latin grammar. Simply laid out with some straightforward examples, it more than fulfils its purpose.

J. J. Bagley, *Historical Interpretations: Sources of Medieval History, 1066–1540* (1972).
Usefully takes the reader through centuries of accumulated sources, explaining in forensic detail the rise of this or that source from the eleventh to the sixteenth centuries.

M. T. Clanchy, *From Memory to Written Record: England 1066–1307* (2nd edition, 1993).
Deals with orality and literacy in the Middle Ages. It also deals comprehensively and imaginatively with the demise of record keeping via memory to the growth of local bureaucracies that fostered literary sources, especially in the affairs of state. First published in 1979, this edition takes in new research in these areas.

19 Archives

1 What is an archive?
2 'When we return as human beings again': archives and ashes
3 'Speaking for ourselves': state archives and community archives

Introduction

The idea of the archive is an ancient one and the archive itself is often a locus of power. Archives can take the form of a stone inscription, a clay tablet or perhaps even a recorded memory and need not simply comprise parchment and paper. This chapter moves beyond definitions and interpretations of the archive by examining how an archive is built and developed, the sheer variety of sources that can make up an archive, and how the archive can increase or recede in importance depending on the preoccupations and fashions of the day. This explored, the second section examines the preservation of an extensive archive of East European *shtetl* or small town Jewry through the YIVO, an institute for Jewish research. The mere existence of the YIVO archive allows, in a sense, a way of life to survive, even to live on, making it possible for historians to map the road to evil and back. This case study shows the possible extent of the archive but also the political nature and dimensions of archives more generally. Finally, by discussing The National Archives at Kew and the concept of community archives in the final section, we ask once again, not only what an archive is but also whom it should serve. In this way, the chapter finishes by moving away from an examination of the 'official' or national archives governed by agreed professional standards to the 'democratisation of the archive' and proposals for archives to be generated, not by the state, but by local associations and communities.

Section 1

What is an archive?

The Ark of the Covenant contained the Decalogue or the tablets on which was written the Ten Commandments. For the Israelites, it was part of their founding text. Made of acacia wood, lined inside and out with solid gold, richly decorated with gold cherubim, the Ark has been estimated by modern biblical scholars (assuming its actual existence) to have weighed close to ten tons. No wonder it needed oxen and cart to transport its contents from place to place.

Around 10,000 BCE David was crowned second king of the whole house of Israel, routing the Philistines in a series of battles, although his importance, if not his existence, is disputed by scholars. The Ark was the organising symbol of nationhood at the time of a new king, and therefore went ahead of a triumphant 30,000-strong army, dancing, according to biblical accounts, to the sounds of 'cypress wood instruments, with lyres, harps, timbrels, sistrums and cymbals'. When the oxen faltered and the Ark began to slip, a man who had been walking alongside the cart when it toppled stretched out an arm to steady it and God struck him dead for his trouble, at which point the music fell silent. Recognising and fearing its power, King David removed the 'archive', although eventually the Ark entered David's City to joy and more dancing before becoming the centrepiece in the 'holy of holies', before disappearing from history around the time of the destruction of the First Temple in 586 BCE.

The symbiotic relationship between power and the stewardship of an archive is explored throughout this chapter; this includes the power of the archive to influence society: determining the present by its governorship of the past. But also the power of archives to 'recover moments of inception: to find and possess all sorts of beginnings' as the historian Carolyn Steedman stated in her book *Dust* (2001, p. 5). First, however, to the problem of definition. Dictionary definitions of an archive will only get us so far. There is no need to go back into the mists of an Old Testament past to locate the origins of the word archive but instead look to the Greek meaning, which associates archive with a 'magisterial residence', 'a public office' and 'that which is old'. As John Burrow (1935–2009) has noted, the archive has been important to historians since Greek times, although Herodotus (see Chapter 6) as the 'father of history' tended to interrogate the keepers of the archive not the archive itself. Indeed the 'archive' in both the Egyptian and Greek civilisations is in origin a record (like the tablets of the Ten Commandments) 'inscribed on stones and clay tablets and, for most of the greatest matters, on the walls of temples, tombs and palaces' (p. 2). As such it was not casually put together as a set of dusty documents, instead it was chiselled in stone and built to last. The archive and the places where the archive might be kept can then be very eclectic and haphazard indeed. Whether historians recognise that the 'medieval tapestry' or the 'African body tattoo' is historical evidence, or regard the 'Victorian house museum' as an archival repository, really depends on the individual historian (Burton, 2006).

As a collection of documents or as inscriptions set in stone, an archive is synonymous with 'a place in which public records are kept', housed in a dedicated place and within the bureaucratic context of the modern state. The church had the responsibility and power of maintaining records up until the twelfth century or so. Whether the archive is kept by church or state, however, the keeping of an archive becomes both controversial and contested, inevitably the object of dispute (Brown and Davis-Brown, 1998). What might be contained in the archive? What ought to be omitted? What are the criteria for the selection of material? Who runs the repository in which it is kept and how?

Patrick Joyce is an historian known for his innovative histories and the use of sources that are anything but typical. He sees the built environment as a text, and asserts that buildings and urban space can be read like any book or manuscript (Joyce, 1999). In particular, Joyce is concerned with finding the 'liberal city', its municipal libraries and official repositories of historical meaning that resonate in his own life, providing some order and sense to the changing shape of these things in his own memory. The archive in his vision, therefore, need not be gathered together and locked away by the state in a gilded official building. According to Joyce, the archive is all around us – even the building itself should be considered part of the archive. Memory is part of the archive too; something that is stored away, consulted much later, and then reinterpreted in the light of present-day concerns or fashions. Buildings and landscapes are part of what might be described, more particularly, as an *unofficial* archive.

However, when an *official* archive is collected, catalogued and conserved according to the strict guidelines of the profession, it is done with due reference to agreed norms and guidelines. The archive is not, moreover, as it is persuasively argued by Burton, 'innocent':

> **For archives do not simply arrive or emerge fully formed; nor are they innocent of struggles for power in either their creation or their interpretative application. Though their own origins are often occluded and the exclusions in which they are promised often dimly understood, all archives came into being as used in history as a result of specific political, cultural, and socio-economic pressures – pressures which leave traces and which render archives themselves artefacts of history.** (Burton, 2005, p. 6)

The curators, archivists, librarians or directors of the grand institutions that keep our past in trust on behalf of the public sometimes keep our past from us, wielding significant power. The Browns argued that knowledge, power and discourse are related, an idea first popularised by the French philosopher, Michel Foucault (1926–84), who said that power resides in language, surveillance and examination. Put simply, whoever controls language controls the production and reception of knowledge, and therefore the 'discourse of the archive' describes the world. What may seem simply to be a pile of dusty documents, neutral, subject to open and objective scrutiny, is from this perspective part of a struggle for the power to describe and control the past and (therefore) the present. This is why the mobile archive of the biblical Ark has power and this is why it too is contested.

The Browns, like Patrick Joyce, open up the question of the relationship between the users and keepers of the unofficial archive, such as the community historians and archivists who are introduced in the last section of this chapter. These unofficial keepers of our memories are compared with the professional administration of the archive 'with its own pyramid of titles, powers, rights and duties' (Brown, 1998, p. 21). The hierarchies of the official archive, therefore, turn on controlling the ways in which the archive is both understood and described.

Nor does this process cease when the cataloguing of the archive is complete – meanings for Foucault are never static, they are always unstable and liable to change in accordance with present-day occupations. The archive, therefore, is anything but passive and harmless. According to Foucault, the archives are 'documents of exclusion' and 'monuments to particular configurations of power'. Or, as Antoinette Burton put it, 'they all have dynamic relationships, not just to the past and present, but to the fate of regimes, the physical relationship, the serendipity of bureaucrats, and the care and neglect of archivists as well' (Burton, 2005, p. 6). Archives can also be dangerous (Steedman, 2001).

The archive should be read in a way that recognises that it exists within levels of meaning. The meaning that scholars may place on the archive, however, is largely dependent on the process of creating and maintaining an archive. Elizabeth Bramm Dunn (2007) outlined in an admirably economic fashion the limits of archival practice. By the time historians have consulted the archive it has been collected in a way highly susceptible to chance or accident. Documents that survive, as it were, from the outside world are 'weeded', a process by which an archivist chooses to keep some material and exclude others. This highly subjective process will depend on arbitrary factors such as the collections policy of the repository in question, economic and staff factors, available storage space, personal interest of the archivist and so forth. Once the item is catalogued it is then stored on a closed shelf. Only at this point can the scholar take an educated guess as to the use of that document in relation to the research question he or she has posed.

The arbitrary nature of the archiving process provides historians with one of the most enduring pleasures of historical research: the fantasy of finding a preferably ancient document or collection that is as yet undiscovered. The frisson of having in one's hands a book whose pages are uncut gives the delightful and evocative sense of discovering hidden treasure, as yet apparently unseen, with its survival a matter of chance that makes the experience all the more remarkable. All this before historians 'read' levels of meaning into the document itself; tease out the tone and semantics of the language; second guess the intentions of the author.

The historian in conventional scientific approaches to evidence can 'peel away the fictive element of a document' in order to get at what is important (Hamilton, 2002). On the other hand, Natalie Zemon Davis confronted attempts by historians to either ignore what is obviously made up or embellished in an historical document, or, by the application of traditional method, to bypass what is truly important – in this case 'pardon tales' that in the sixteenth century provided mitigation for crimes such as murder and so forth. Instead, Zemon Davis argued for a reading of historical evidence that recognises narratives have elements of 'crafting' and by including the 'forming' and 'shaping' of narrative in an historical analysis, the very boundary of fact and fiction in the archive becomes part of how a document should be read:

> **I would like to take a different tack. I want to let the 'fictional' aspects of these documents be the center of analysis. By 'fictional' I do not mean their feigned elements, but rather, using the other and broader sense of the word *fingere* their forming, shaping, and molding elements: the crafting of the narrative.** (Zemon Davis, 1987, p. 3)

Or, as Raphael Samuel put it:

> **Now it is true that historians can never capture the reality of the past, but can only interpret it within the limits of the materials and of the conceptual tools to hand. Our knowledge of the past is mediated by the radical imperfection of the documents – the long silences, the huge absences; and it is crucially shaped by the preoccupations we bring to bear on them. What we have in the documents is not the past, but only the fugitive remains, flashing up at us, as the German Marxist Walter Benjamin put it, 'at a moment of danger'. They can be stored in files and indexed, but their original context and relationships are necessarily a matter of speculation. It is the historian who imposes discipline on the disorderly assemblage of material, marshalling and arranging to the scholarly conventions of the day. Transparency, however much the historian may strive for it, is evidently impossible when so many selectivities intervene. As it is a still life picture, some object will have been blown up out of all proportion, others reduced in scale, while the great majority will have been crowded out of the frame. Historians thus do not reflect the past – they signify and construct it; meaning is in the eye of the beholder.** (Samuel, 1980, pp. 162–75)

Archives, just by existing, create meanings that historians must unravel in response to the changing preoccupations of the present. That archives come in and out of our present day focus is useful for historians to understand but it is also especially significant because it reveals much about our present-day concerns.

This should convey a sense in which the archive is conceived differently over time; that the archive is not collated or read in a neutral way and, like the Ark and its contents discussed at the opening of this section, it is invested with both meaning and power. This will become clearer when we examine in the next section an archive that grew and moved with its subject matter.

Section 2

'When we return as human beings again': archives and ashes

Ashkenazi Jews once occupied the so-called 'Pale of Settlement', a huge strip of land that ran across the western borders of Russia and Central Europe. This land was put aside for Jewish occupation until the First World War and the Russian Revolution in 1917 threatened its borders. These communities had a distinctive way of life which remained more or less intact until the decimation wrought by the Nazi Holocaust. The archive of this vivid culture grew from the 1920s to the present day and contains the social memories and artefacts of European Jewry. It stands, perhaps, as an exemplar of a modern archive for its sheer diversity and exists as a remnant of a world now physically destroyed – or at least no longer existing in the form illuminated by the archive. The aim of this section is to chart why an archive such as this was begun; its changing content and the strategies used by its founding spirits to preserve it at all costs; and then using this to draw out how it is that archives more generally can preserve the 'figurative remains' of an entire way of life.

With the changing of national boundaries after the First World War (1914–18) and the trauma of the Bolshevik Revolution in 1917, Wilno in Poland became Vilnius in Lithuania, and so Polish Jews became Lithuanian Jews. They maintained their identities as Jews through religious practice, language, literature and culture. But as the modern world advanced with its opportunities and horrors, the *shtetlekh* (towns with a large Jewish population) lost their distinctiveness and coherence. This was part of the process later popularly dramatised by *Fiddler on the Roof*, a book by Joseph Stein set in Tsarist Russia during the pogroms of 1905, and based on a Yiddish story by Sholem Aleichem published as *Tevye and his Daughters* in 1894. That other great chronicler of the lost world of the *shtetl*, the painter Marc Chagall, inspired the metaphor of the survival of tradition amid danger, the fiddler balancing precariously on a roof.

The general recognition that this way of life faced rapid decline resulted in 1925 with the founding in Vilna of the YIVO Institute for Jewish Research, dedicated to the study and preservation of Yiddish and East European culture. Because the rabbinate and secular Jews (for different reasons, perhaps) believed that this rich culture was under threat, they cooperated in making sound recordings of the ancient prayers or collected archives connected to a disappearing art and literature. A network of volunteers (*Zamlers*) collected printed matter of all types. Young people were encouraged to write autobiographies and courses in Yiddish were organised for aspirant Jewish students. But the archive was also partly a response to an expression of national consciousness instilled by the great European powers at the Paris Conference in 1919, which, along with the gradually more persuasive arguments made by Zionists for a Jewish homeland, promoted the idea of the Jewish people as a unitary nation or people. The archive in this context had never been so important.

In 1940 the archive came under threat from Soviet occupation and between 1940 and August 1943 from Nazi domination. With occupation, YIVO headquarters became a Nazi depot for looted collections destined for destruction or, if there was some intrinsic value, for transport to the Fatherland. Under guard, Jews from the Vilna ghetto arrived at this depot each day to, as one witness put it, 'dig the graves for our souls'. Instead of doing the bidding of the Nazi destroyers, those volunteers, once so instrumental in creating the archive, transformed themselves into what became known in subsequent legend as the 'paper brigade'. These brave women and men smuggled out the precious contents of the archive page by page, secreting the fragments of a Jewish past in places where they hoped the Nazis would not look, or entrusting the archive to gentile Lithuanians. 'Our work is reaching its conclusion. Thousands of books are being dumped as trash and the Jewish books will be liquidated. Whatever part we can rescue, will be saved with God's help. We will find it when we return as human beings', recorded one diarist central to the rescue of this fascinating and extensive archive (Rose, 2008, p. 72). More of the dispersed archive came to light after the war: from Vilna itself, from Frankfurt-am-Main in Germany, from a village near Marseilles in France and from the recently-opened archives of the former Soviet Union. Now based in New York, the YIVO library contains more than 350,000 books in 12 languages and the archive amounts to over 22 million pages.

Only by going through the extensive YIVO archive do we get a sense of its true diversity and its use as a prompt to memory. It contains:

- visual records (photographs, paintings, maps, film);
- sound (interviews, music);

- material culture (objects such as postcards and greetings cards);
- manuscripts (private and public, individual and of organisations);
- electronic data (available on CD-ROM or online via the Web).

The visual material includes photographs from the Yiddish theatre and papers by prominent writers and artists. There are photographs of personalities and places and art produced by those in concentration camps during the Nazi era, especially art produced by children. This aspect is by no means exclusive to the YIVO archive; yet the YIVO archive is nonetheless comprehensive. Films came to the archive from the ghettos in Europe and as far afield as China. Sound recordings are varied: Yiddish and Hebrew music, both popular and liturgical; Holocaust era songs, choral and Hasidic song, children's and Klezmer (Ashkenazi Jewish music); radio programmes from the American Jewish radio stations; oral testimonies from the trade union movement and other leftist groups; orchestrations of all kinds. Private manuscript collections include those donated by prominent Zionists and communal leaders. Organisational records range from the American Jewish Committee (1918–70s) and the United Hebrew Trades (1899–1979) to the Workmen's Circle (1893–1972). Official records include those of Nazi Governmental Bodies and Institutions and the *Union Générale des Israelites de France*. Archivists add constantly to their collections, partly as opportunities present themselves but also in the light of present-day concerns. YIVO is no exception and so in 1992 it acquired the collection of the *Bund* or the Jewish Socialist Society founded in Geneva; their archive was transferred to Berlin in 1919, smuggled to France in 1933 and after a period of confiscation by the Germans, to New York in 1951. Somewhat akin to finding a branch of the Chartists in contemporary London, the *Bund* is listed still in the New York telephone directory.

The YIVO collection is especially interesting for a number of reasons. It gives account of how an archive builds layer upon layer, how parts of the archive become important in one historical moment, 'flashing up at a moment of danger', and then receding again to relative obscurity. The Holocaust remained relatively obscure, while its survivors maintained a silence in the years immediately following 1945, only coming into focus again in recent years with the breaking of this silence. The example of YIVO gives us a sense in which the archive can act as a compound to heal psychological wounds, to act almost as a surrogate for a culture and way of life now quite vanished.

But the archive has its limits. The *shtetl* way of life can be romanticised, of course, or framed in such a way that it seems almost impossible to reveal a picture that historians could regard as credible. The archive can assist in piecing together a lost civilisation or way of life, assisting in its romanticisation or, looking in retrospect, at the sheer poverty and discrimination suffered by Jews. The Jewish author, Theo Richmond, repopulated his parents' Polish *shtetl* by collecting testimonies from those that once lived and worked in Konin. Visiting Konin himself, the realisation dawned on Richmond that it only really existed through the oral history he had created, or in the local archives, but was most vivid in his own imagination. At its most basic, the archive is a work of the mind or, as time slips, of social memory – that is, memory becomes as important as a pile of dusty documents:

> **Every trace of Jewish life had been expunged, and only in the mind could that life be resurrected, perhaps more easily at a distance from this dismal place, which only seemed to deny its past. This was not the market square so many Koriners had described to me, crowded with people**

> **buying and selling and haggling, the fishmonger Bim-Bom scooping a wriggling carp from his barrel, shopkeepers leaning in doorways, porters and wheelbarrows, Aryeh-Leib going by with his milk churn, country women with eggs and home-made cheeses, *buba* [grandmother] Mindl selling vegetables fresh from Glinka, Zalman Ryczhe's gramophone horn booming from his tailor's workshop, Jews arguing over Judaism, Zionism, socialism, others hurrying to prayer, Simcha Sarna on his way to the Chevre Shas, the Lame Ryczke limping back to his *cheder*, peasants and pedlars, pots and pans, noise and chatter, and everywhere the lively, singsong cadences of Yiddish. . . . Only memory can keep that world alive.**
>
> (Richmond, 1995, p. 426)

Without the YIVO archive, we would know much less about the Jewish experience in eastern Europe and, perhaps, its aftershocks in the politics of Israel and the United States. In contrast, Sephardi Jews (that is, Jews who were originally expelled from Spain and Portugal and who largely resettled in the Arab countries of the Mediterranean rim) lived an equally vibrant cultural and religious life in Muslim lands, but were mostly expelled after the creation of the Jewish state. While there is now some effort by scholars and others to retrieve these experiences, for example by collecting popular songs and ballads that date back to life in medieval Spain, this lost world of Sephardi Jews will in all likelihood never achieve the vividness of accounts of European *shtetl* life. Even now the YIVO archive is being supplemented by a project whereby historians and linguists are literally going from town to town in Poland and elsewhere, interviewing the very last Jews that live there in isolation from a Jewish population that is now either dead or has made a new life in America, Israel or elsewhere.

In the next section, we will see how the archive is perhaps moving slowly away from its former role as bulwark to the nation or, as in the case of YIVO, as a solvent for an entire people. We ask how first the church and then the state assumed ownership of the archive, and then how the professional hierarchies that administer the archive responded to challenges from community historians that wished to become the stewards of their own past.

Section 3

'Speaking for ourselves': state archives and community archives

A reader at the National Archives of England and Wales at Kew might expect to consult any number of manuscripts and documents from a huge collection of state papers that stretch back over a thousand years: King Henry VIII's signature, perhaps, or the 1939 declaration of war on Germany. The Domesday Book that dates from the 1080s resides in a glass case, set back in a humidified space of its own, with a highly sophisticated alarm system and doors designed to trap any would-be thief inside the room – testimony to both the antiquity of the document but also to its status as a founding text of the modern British state. Only the *Magna Carta* of 1215 would come close to rivalling this symbol of national pride, whereas in Scotland the Act of Union signed by the Scots and the English in 1707, kept in Edinburgh, is conspicuously absent as a public exhibit – very different from the American Constitution or the Bill of Rights, which are widely accepted by the people of the United States as authentic primary documents of the founding of the state and a way of life.

Beer mats are part of this varied collection, originally submitted to the patent office and accordingly kept for posterity. E136\24\3\ is the classmark for a mummified rat which can be found on the miles of shelving (which increases at a rate of approximately one mile every year). Taking the mummified rat (as a symbol of the neglect of the national archives in past years) and the Domesday Book together for a moment, allows a comparison between the national records as they were once kept and the extraordinary lengths to which archivists and conservationists will now go in order to protect the national past.

The public educationalist and one-time reformer at what was then called the Public Record Office, Henry Cole (1808–82), or at least this is how the story is told, was so distressed in the 1830s about the condition of the national archive, he presented a rat to a Royal Commission called specifically to investigate the decay of the nation's records. He protested that rats had breached the state papers and as this particular rat had eaten so much of the archive, it too should now be part of state records. And so the rat was kept.

The veracity of this story is not an immediate concern. That the public archive was both neglected and widely distributed across the capital, however, is consistent with reports received in the seventeenth and eighteenth centuries – something graphically illustrated here:

> **[I]n 1709 the records of the Court of Wards were found to be in a house adjoining that of the royal fishmonger . . . near to Westminster Hall. The royal fishmonger, we are told, did as he pleased with the records, which were perishing rapidly. The records of the King's Bench were not far off, but equally under threat. They were stored above a place which had formally been a worsted shop, but was by 1709 partly a wash house and partly a stable 'which is a very Improper situation for records of such consequence'. By 1711 some attempts had been made to rescue both sets of records and the fishmonger's house has been organised as a record repository.** (Hallam, 1990, p. 33)

It would be a mistake then to overstate the continuity and consistency of care given by the state to the records of the state. A former Lord Chancellor, Lord Mackay of Clashfern, at a conference in 1988 to commemorate 150 years of the modern existence of the Public Record Office, rightly spoke about the importance of maintaining historical documents in the context of foreign invasion and the relative absence of internal strife. Starting his story in the early medieval period, he highlighted the 'rudimentary' archival 'principles and practices' that once existed, comparing them with the gradual development of modern archival practices:

> **Although we are today commemorating just 150 years of the records of the nation, the tradition of preserving our public records is a long one. Domesday Book has been carefully safeguarded for nine centuries. The systematic creation and preservation of records by the Exchequer and Chancery goes back some eight hundred years. And record repositories were established by the end of the thirteenth century in the Tower of London, the Exchequer at Westminster and at the House of Converts (*Domus Conversorum*) which was founded near the New Temple in 1232 for Jews who had converted to Christianity. The last of these repositories**

> **was used for the storage of the rolls of the Chancery, and from there, their custodian took his title of Keeper and Master of the Rolls, and the site its later name of the Rolls Estate.**
>
> (Mackay, 1990, p. 1)

No mention then of records kept with a less-than-diligent fishmonger, or of the rather more chequered history of the way in which records were kept in the Middle Ages.

Conservation has not always been the first priority of those charged with the maintenance of archives. Initially archives were in the hands of the church and local clerical offices. From approximately the ninth or tenth centuries, charters that pertained to monastic houses in Britain and elsewhere in Europe, gave way to the creation of cartularies. These cartularies are essentially transcribed copies of charters in the form of a codex or transcribed manuscript in a book or, more rarely, in the form of a roll. By the eleventh and twelfth centuries the transcriptions, which largely took place in Benedictine monasteries and other ecclesiastical institutions, increased in both number and importance. Patrick Geary (1994) persuasively argued that because of this process, the archive was transformed between the ninth and eleventh centuries. This transformation, he goes on, had a profound influence on the survival of historical evidence to the present day. Before 920, Britain had the largest collection of original charters in Europe – some 839 were extant in the monastery of St Gall alone. By the twelfth century, however, these archival riches had disappeared, the result of 'neglect', 'selection', 'transformation' and 'suppression', destroyed as a side-effect of the construction of the cartularies and the systematic and deliberate disposal of the original documents from which they had been copied. It appears that western churchmen 'used this raw material with great freedom, destroying, revising, recopying, and especially reorganizing. The result was a winnowing and restructuring process that provided the parameters within which subsequent generations could hope to understand the past' (Geary, 1994, p. 114). This process, it seems, was somewhat in advance of a properly organised royal chancery archive but appears to have coincided with the rise of a literate state.

Elizabeth Hallam (1990) took up the story in her essay 'Nine centuries of keeping public records' by outlining the emergence in 1100, or thereabouts, of the so-called 'pipe record' and with it a bureaucracy of state clerks. Later in the reign of Henry II the state archive was kept at Winchester but moved around in (taking us back to the very beginning of the chapter) 'arks' or 'hutches'. By 1200, the archive (now comprised of Royal Charters, Letters of Patent, Close Rolls, Fine Rolls, Inquisition Post Mortems and so on) saw an increase in bureaucratic support. Yet there was still no central repository and parts of the archive were in the hands and under the responsibility of an array of local officials, while the end of the century saw the compilation of lists of the contents of the archive which then and now are called 'Calendars'. Edward II, especially after the Templars were dissolved in 1312 (they apparently had been the main record keepers of the Exchequer), undertook a preliminary sorting of Exchequer records. This did not represent radical change, however, and the crisis of conservation witnessed at the fishmonger's in the early 1700s, and rather glossed over by Clashfern, began from about 1500 when government or state departments each kept their own records without bothering to transfer them to the so-called Treasury of Receipt. This trend had been apparent for some while and surprisingly it seems that the method of keeping government archives or records was widely known among the general populace.

So it was, in 1381, when disturbances began at the start of what is now known as the Peasants' Revolt, that the rebels knew enough about state records to identify state documents (especially documents that related to taxation) by the colour of their sealing wax:

> In both counties the Sheriff was captured on Monday 10 June . . . Sir John Sewale of Essex in his house in Great Coggeshall, Sir William Septvans of Kent when Canterbury Castle was successfully stormed. We learn that Sewale was abused, his clothing torn and his house pillaged, and that the rebels then removed 'all writs and sums of the lord King of the green wax or divers writs of the lord King and rolls of the same' and carried them to Chelmsford the next day where they were publicly burnt. Septvans was taken from Canterbury by Wat Tyler, John Hales of Malling, Ael (Ker) of Erith and many others to his Manor some two miles to the south of the city at Milton, where he was forced to hand over 'fifty rolls of the pleas of the county and the Crown', together with whatever royal writs were in his custody; these were taken back to Canterbury and burned there that same day. The desire to destroy documents sealed with green wax, for which we have evidence in Kent and Essex, reflects the fact that this was the colour used for documents issued from the Exchequer. For largely illiterate insurgents 'green wax' was an easy way of identifying documents that might concern taxation. It is clear that these simultaneous attacks on the Sheriffs of Essex and Kent represent a deliberate attempt to destroy the current records of the fiscal and judicial administration of the two Shires. They imply both careful planning and accurate knowledge of the Sheriffs' whereabouts and likely movements. (Brooks, 1985, p. 260)

It was not until the passing of successive parliamentary acts in the nineteenth century which centralised funding that professional state record keeping began to emerge. Legislation in 1838 established a need for an acquisitions policy and a central place of storage, while in 1879 problems caused by the accumulation of obsolete departmental records began to be addressed in systematic fashion. It was the explosion in paper records created by the First World War, however, that really gave momentum to the ongoing process of the late-Victorian professionalisation at the Public Record Office (PRO). The paper predicament grew until 1952/53 when the Grigg Committee tackled this problem but it coincided with a growing popularity in public records from the end of the First World War (Martin, 1990, p. 21).

Calendars and lists based on improving 'objective' standards could provide ever-greater access to the archive, while the 1910 Royal Commission on the Public Records led to the Deputy Keeper Reports which henceforth provided annually a comprehensive survey of archival practice. At the same time the by now formidable pyramid of postholders within the Public Record Office produced an increasing stream of publishing about the archive. This was not exactly new either: 'careful and critical' publications of archival documents appeared in the seventeenth century and in 1704 *Foedera* was one of the first official (or semi-official) publications of select documents, lists and indexes. By the twentieth century, however, these documents were still 'selected', with all the problems of subjectivity that this entails. By this time there were major figures working on the state archives. For example, James Gardiner at the PRO spent well over half a century working on a single publication. Or Henry Maxwell Lyte, who from 1886 organised Calendars that attempted a listing or cataloguing of documents in chronological order. He also was a long-standing servant of the PRO. Now the trend is towards placing documents online and a purpose-built repository stands on the edge of the Thames at Kew, while the PRO has been rebranded as The National Archives.

The professionalisation of The National Archives is not without significance for historians, even if the years of the decayed rat have lasted just as long as the years of what Lord

Clashfern liked to imagine as the glorious continuity of conservation and preservation of archives. To this extent then, a professional, state-run institution serving the citizenry is open to question, particularly as it should be apparent from previous sections that archives and the administration of archives cannot be neutral and free of bias.

The National Archives are reputed to be at the service of the citizenry but remain in the ownership and control of government. Permissive legislation in recent years has given the citizenry increased powers of access, of 'freedom of information', yet rules of privacy and secrecy continue to protect both private individuals and public bodies from embarrassment, with the release of documents in certain circumstances delayed by 30 years (from 1967), 50 years (from 1958) or even 100 years in some instances. As effectively the storehouse for government records, government has a proportionate say in what is kept and what is thrown away (typically 98 per cent of the total documentation produced every year by the state is destroyed). Government on a department by department basis can also call back documentation to the department for consultation. Yet we know from some examples of how states behave that they are not necessarily to be trusted in these areas:

> **Historians and other scholars are increasingly concerned to understand how knowledge is produced and, more specifically, how knowledge of the past is produced. Where previously historians 'mined' the archive for 'nuggets of fact' in a manner conscious of problems of bias in the record, today scholars pay greater attention to the particular processes by which the record was produced and subsequently shaped, both before its entry into the archive, and increasingly as part of the archival record. This approach draws attention to the way in which the record is altered over time, as well as the gaps and omissions in, and excisions from, the record. In South Africa historians have been cautious about relying exclusively on public and more specifically government records, because of their colonial and later apartheid biases. That the record is biased is widely recognised by researchers, but a great deal of work remains to develop our understanding of the circumstances of the creation of the archival record in general, and of specific collections in particular.** (Hamilton *et al.*, 2002, p. 9)

On the other hand, readers have become somewhat more sophisticated over the years. From the sixteenth century, antiquarians led enquiries into national records, as we discovered in Chapter 8, and from the 1960s more readers than ever had a university education, which coincides, it would seem, with a renewed interest in family history. In turn there have been more documents than ever to consult. Indeed, it has been suggested that more readers consulted the national records in the last six months of 1988 than in the whole of the nineteenth century.

In variance, perhaps, to its sharply hierarchical management structures, The National Archives seeks a role in the community beyond that of keepers of state records. In recent years there have been efforts, variously successful and variously supported within the institution, to reach out to localities and to local cultures which often reconstruct the past via a distinct 'sense of place'. Projects have focused for the most part on oral histories, cultural heritage and social memory, with the aim of enabling communities to respond to the challenges of change brought about by physical and economic regeneration. These community histories have generated community archives that not only consider the legacy of the past, but also assess the impact of regeneration in the places from which they come. Archives more generally, it has been argued in a number of reports commissioned by the government, are the mainstay of traditional scholarship, a vital resource of historical investigation. There is also a deep, popular interest in heritage, which was outlined in some detail in Chapter 11 on public history. This has encouraged increasing numbers of the public not only to use traditional archives but also to create their own, so expanding the sum of the nation's archival heritage. The overall aim of community archives is to improve the accessibility of archives for more diverse users and collections.

The Community Access to Archives Project (CAAP) in November 2003 was carried out in a partnership between The National Archives and a number of national and regional archive bodies. The idea was to encourage social inclusion and enable archives to reach new audiences. It endeavoured to connect archive users in the wider community to work with professionals, identifying sources required in order to develop educational and outreach opportunities, and to help foster a template for community involvement. Some regard this trend in professional/amateur collaboration and the new technologies of the 'information revolution' as a challenge to the whole notion of what an archive is, and the assumption of recent decades that it should be generated and kept centrally. The archives of the nation may well move from public institutions financed by the state to the archive accessed by and even controlled by local communities.

Events of recent years have transformed the ways in which the archive is conceived, created, managed and used. Conventionally thought as a repository of written, printed and visual records, the archive has tended to be financed, maintained and controlled by public institutions somewhat remote from the concerns of the public in general, cultural minorities in particular. The information revolution and the continued escalation of interest in various forms of public history, however, have provided conditions for a major reassessment of the ways in which archives relate to the communities which they are supposed to serve. It is now possible to transmit archival information with a speed and on a scale not previously possible. This is leading to a democratisation of the archive; not only are archives more accessible, but equally communities can actively contribute to them, even create their own.

Arguably, for the first time we thus have an opportunity through use of the archive to enhance community life. Imaginative archival work with local communities can help record hidden lives, excavate and preserve collective memories, and provide rich sources for its members to help make sense of their histories and hence their contemporary situations. Local history, family history and community history all stand to gain from this.

In its broadest sense, a community archive can celebrate and rebuild the sense of community in our lives today. Because of the new technologies available to us, an archive, not unlike the Ark of the Covenant, need not be tied to a particular location, nor does it have to conform to a particular format. Its creation, however, does have to involve communities, whether independently or in collaboration with a public archive service. In this respect, the notion of the archive has been transformed from its description in the first section – firmly tied to relationships of state power; identified with a particular community as we saw in the second section; to a definition of the archive apparently separate from the tussles of power and which emerges from communities themselves. This does not suggest for a moment that 'community archives' can replace 'national archives' but it might challenge archivists to reveal some of the 'mysteries' of their profession in order to create the kind of community based archive that quite simply we have not seen before. The alternative is to maintain a power structure that will inevitably persist when what remains of our past is in the exclusive care and ownership of a state, whether that state is at any one moment benign or belligerent.

In practice

An archive is generally thought of as a repository for materials of historic interest or social significance. Since the beginning of the nineteenth century when history emerged as a discipline, much intellectual, emotional and financial weight has been invested in the archive as a result of which it now stands as a store of pristine knowledge, sacred and inviolable. Such perspectives, however, have to be tempered by recognition that the archive does not create itself, but is shaped by the people who put it together and allow historians or the general public access to the materials. We therefore have to ask of any archive: Who are the collectors? What criteria do they use in collecting material? How is the archive controlled and maintained? Who act as the gatekeepers?

Archives are often put together through chance or accident. Documents which survive are those which an archivist has chosen to keep. That decision is a highly selective process which is determined by fairly arbitrary factors such as the collections policy, personal interest of the archivist, storage facilities and so on. And what is made available is strongly influenced by secrecy (against the national interest), privacy, preservation and decency.

Archives do not simply arrive or emerge fully formed. Nor are they immune to struggles for power in either their creation or use. Furthermore, their origins may not be that well known, and the gaps in knowledge only dimly understood. What is clear is that all archives came into being as a result of specific political, cultural and socio-economic processes, and these leave traces, rendering the archives themselves artefacts of history. And archives are never able to maintain their status as a pristine record of the past; as they are reshaped though cataloguing, classification and conservation, so they continue to create new meanings.

More recent thinking has opened up the boundaries of the archive. It is no longer thought to be exclusively a collection of printed and visual materials from the past. Take, for example, the city. From the early part of the nineteenth century when new forms of observation emerged, it seems that the street and the built environment generally became an archive, a repository of material that can be used a source of evidence.

One recent interesting development attendant on the extraordinary opportunities opened up by digital technologies has done much to challenge the orthodoxy of the archive in many ways. The notion of the community archive has attracted recent attention, and we believe it has some potential in opening up and democratising the archive. Thus, while the traditional archive is thought as a repository of textual records, financed and controlled by public institutions somewhat remote from the concerns of the public in general, cultural minorities in particular, the community archive – digital or otherwise – is created and maintained by communities themselves. There is a democratisation of the archives since they are more accessible, but equally communities create or contribute to archives on their own terms. Through the archive local communities can record hidden lives, excavate and preserve collective memories, and provide rich sources for its members to make sense of their own historical experiences.

Summary

The three sections of this chapter have said three things:

- Archives have traditionally been defined by sets of power relationships; most often in the modern period by the acquisition of the archive by the nation state. The archive is also acquired, maintained and read in ways more subjective than the professionalisation of the process might allow. This has led to a judgement about the archive that naturally questions its overall subjectivity and its ability to be a simple reflection of the society in which it is located. This has led to questions about the nature of the archive as a form of knowledge production. It has also prompted notions that the boundaries of the archive are very fluid with the archive seen as a partial survival of the past as well as a wholly owned subsidiary of the here and now.
- Archives can be varied and multi-layered and mean different things at different times. They can also, as in the case of the YIVO Jewish Research Institute, identify very closely with a particular subject; in this case collecting the last fragments of eastern European Jewry as they found ways of making sense of their lives and identities before many were murdered in the labour and death camps of the Nazi regime. While the archive that was surreptitiously collected proved to be very varied indeed, it nonetheless was an archive that was supplanted by the memories of those that survived. Its main function, however, was to rescue and then consolidate the narrative of a people or nation.
- The Public Record Office (now The National Archives) has gained over the centuries both influence and power over our national memory – this despite years when the archive was not gathered in one place and tended to be in poor shape. Yet, it has gathered to itself a good deal of expertise. Archives dominated by official approaches can by the application of new technologies also empower individuals and communities, opening up different types of archives and changing traditional approaches to the collection and maintenance of the archive. These so-called community archives open up distinct opportunities for the national archive to be more locally focused, and less beholden to the organised and professional systems that are charged with selecting the raw material today for the history that is likely to be written tomorrow.

Discussion document 1

Identifying and defining what it is an archive does in the wider society and culture is not simple. The differing viewpoints listed here represent a diversity of views that the historian would surely wish to bear in mind. The ramifications of choosing say (2) over (3) are fairly profound. In any case, these viewpoints are more than capable of prompting constructive debate.

> What then is the archive? The *Shorter Oxford English Dictionary* offers this derivation: Archives (1603); from the French *Archives*, from the Latin *archiva*; and from the Greek *archeia* meaning: magisterial residence, public office. The word is defined, then, as a place in which public records are kept. The *Petit Robert* gives the following. Archives from the low Latin *archivum*; the Greek *arkheion*: that which is old. The definition is much as in the *Shorter OED* above.

Irving Velody, 'The archive and the human sciences: notes towards a theory of the archive', in *History of the Human Sciences*, vol. 11, no. 4, 1998, pp. 1–16.

> An archive is a repository – that is, a place or space in which materials of historic interest or social significance are stored and ordered. A national archive is the storing and ordering place of the collective memory of that nation or people(s) . . . who controls, establishes and maintains the archive, and how do they do so? Which materials are preserved in the archive and which are excluded? As the documents and artefacts selected for the archive are ordered and classified, how do the schemas and structures applied include, exclude, foreground or marginalize those materials? Finally, to what extent do the logical hierarchies for classification and arrangement reflect social and political hierarchies?

Richard Harvey Brown and Beth Davis-Brown, 'The making of memory: the politics of archives, libraries and museums in the construction of national consciousness', in *History of the Human Sciences*, vol. 11, no. 4, 1998, pp. 17–32.

> But what is the archive? The work from which I draw these reflections on the archive concerns the city as an arena of liberalism. It is about the city, and the meanings and use of space. Therefore the street is my archive, the built environment is my archive. However, I walk now in the city that I wish to describe then. The person who walks in this city now is also the boy who once walked in the city then, in this case London. The archive, in my case the library, and especially the public library, certainly archives the street and the built environment, but of course it does not exhaust their meaning, which is produced out of the experience of these things, an experience refracted through memory, not least memories of class.

Patrick Joyce, 'The politics of the liberal archive', in *History of the Human Sciences*, vol. 12, no. 2, 1999, pp. 35–49.

> Surely, the storage and display of documents and other artefacts is not monopolized by the archive, and never has been. There have always been individuals who have spoken from outside such walls. But between these 'free' intellectuals and the knowledge workers who claim the titles of curator, archivist, librarian, or director that such institutions bestow, there runs a symbolic and material border, a line that divides the orthodox representatives of knowledge and memory from the non-orthodox and unauthorised speakers. This distinction, this boundary between institutional and freelance representatives, is but one instance of the power that is structured in and through the official knowledge discourse of the archive. Walking around and reading the door-plates we realize that every activity is part of a department with its own pyramid of titles, powers, rights and duties.

Richard Harvey Brown and Beth Davis-Brown, 'The making of memory: the politics of archives, libraries and museums in the construction of national consciousness', in *History of the Human Sciences*, vol. 11, no. 4, 1998, pp. 17–32.

Discussion document 2

It is by no means obvious that the archive is much more than a means of promulgating national consciousness and maintaining a subjective view of the past for posterity. Often, the archive is afforded grand surroundings and then that subjectivity is elevated to become itself an artefact of the nation, revered and preserved for future generations. This may be true of the archives collected in the Warsaw Ghetto by an underground group called *Oyneg Shabes*, whose 35,000 documents kept in tins and milk bottles were only retrieved in 1946, but rarely had so many been prepared to risk their lives so that they might be remembered.

> This collective effort brought together religious and secular Jews. Hebraists and Yiddishists, Zionists and Bundists. By documenting the creativity and resilience of Vilna Jewry in a time of crisis, these texts highlighted the emergence of a new Jewish community and new leaders who replaced older elites that had either fled Vilna or failed to meet the challenges of wartime leadership. Implicit in these texts was the conviction that Jewish national life had outgrown traditional frameworks. Jews in Eastern Europe were too diverse, energetic, and spontaneous to fit into the procrustean bed of traditional religion or the framework of narrow ideology. The key message of these texts was that the Jews were a people, not just a religious group. The first Vilna *Zamlburkh* appeared in 1916 at a time when Vilna was under German occupation and when Jews were fighting to secure recognition as a nationality. The stakes were high: recognition for Jewish schools, permission to run a separate Jewish network of relief organizations, equal treatment with the Poles. The *zamlibikher*, which at first glance seemed little more than a collection of miscellanea, in fact became a critical weapon of national self-defence . . .
>
> Determined to document the Jewish experience in the war, the Oyneg Shabes collected artefacts, texts, and testimonies that reflect on ongoing tension between prewar ideals and escalating chaos; between idealism and debasement; between continuity and rupture – material as disparate and varied as the experiences of the Jews who gathered and wrote them. There were outlines of studies that were never completed, sketches of projects cut short by the Great Deportation; fragments and pieces remain the only traces of individuals who vanished forever. Taken together, these materials tell a collective story of steady decline and unending humiliation, interspersed with many stories of quiet heroism and self-sacrifice. The postwar reader sees Polish Jewry disappearing in an ordeal where the todays were worse than the yesterdays but were still better than the tomorrows: from the siege of Warsaw to the early days of the occupation; from the imposition of the ghetto to the Great Deportation to the final months of the ghetto. It is a collective story composed of hundreds of smaller narratives, accounts of everyday horrors from different individual perspectives, yet illuminated by moments of reprieve, of dignity and courage.

Samuel D. Kassow, *Who Will Write Our History? Rediscovering a Hidden Archive from the Warsaw Ghetto* (London, 2007, pp. 10, 225).

Further reading

* *essential*

* **Antoinette Burton** (ed.), *Archive Stories, Fictions and the Writing of History* (2005).
This collection rejects the idea of the archive as static and objective, 'innocent of struggles for power in either their creation or their interpretative application'. Researchers expand on this theme by telling their stories of archives consulted in India, Australia and so on. The introduction by Burton is excellent.

Natalie Zemon Davis, *Fiction in the Archives: Pardon Tales and Their Tellers in Sixteenth-Century France* (1987).
Confronts the usual practice of historians to either ignore the fictive elements of an historical document or by the application of 'scientific' methodology peel away these stories to get at what is truly important – in this case 'pardon tales' that in the sixteenth century provided mitigation for crimes such as murder and so forth. Instead, it questions the boundary of fact and fiction in the archive.

Carolyn Hamilton *et al.* (eds), *Refiguring the Archive* (2002).
The result of a sustained project about archives and their uses, this collection contains papers presented at a conference on the subject. Its main concern is to both theorise the archive but also to interrogate the nature of the archive, especially the state archive of South Africa in the period after the colonial and apartheid eras.

* **G. H. Martin and Peter Spufford** (eds), *The Records of the Nation* (1990).
A reminder that The National Archives at Kew is not only the keeper of at least one nation's memory but also the centre of important scholarship. It tells the fascinating story of the world's largest continuously existing state archive and its conservation. Contains essays by G. H. Martin, Peter Spufford and Elizabeth M. Hallam.

20 Oral history

1 'Anthropologies of ourselves': urban, rural, foreign
2 Oral historiography
3 Interviewing techniques and the limits of memory: Arthur Harding and the East End underworld
4 The wider conceptual problem

Introduction

This chapter discusses the subject of oral history in terms of the opportunities it offers to the historian and in relation to the conceptual and methodological issues that it raises. In the first instance, this involves looking at the use made of oral history, not just in colleges and universities, but also in the wider community where it has found a home. Much of the ideological and political importance of oral history as a method can be understood by examining how it rose to its current popular status. To do this involves describing how it grew out of a background in social history and 'history from below' movements of the 1960s and 1970s. However, collecting and interpreting oral evidence has a much older history than this. Sociologists began using interviews and participant observation in urban settings as early as the 1920s and historians adopting such techniques were well aware of this. Finally, oral history is moved by an urgent sense of recovering a world of memory, the reflections of older people, that are about to be lost as they slip over the lip of memory into a forgotten obscurity. At a wider level, this informed the fear that whole cultures and sub-cultures might disappear. This thought alone opens up another lineage for oral history. While anthropologists and ethnographers had long used such techniques in their fieldwork in Africa, Asia and South America, the work of Jan Vansina in Africa most notably has had a somewhat different purpose. Taking both anthropology and history as his starting point, the aim was not to recover the memories of those who had participated in an historical event but to make use of African oral traditions that passed down stories from the past but which were then manifested as homilies or metaphors for current political or power relationships.

Section 1

'Anthropologies of ourselves': urban, rural, foreign

It is early in the morning. The date is 11 September 2001. Firefighters Alan Wallace and Mark Skipper wait on the heliport at the Pentagon for the arrival later that day of President George W. Bush. While waiting, they prepare fire truck 161. This is what happened next:

> **They had just pulled the foam truck out of the firehouse and were standing there when they looked up and saw the plane coming over the Navy Annex building.**
>
> **They turned and ran, and at the point of impact were partially shielded by their fire truck from the flying debris of shrapnel and flames. They were knocked to the ground by the concussion, were able to get up, go over to the fire truck, and initially they were able to get it started to call for help at Fort Myer. And then they had to put out parts of their uniform – their bunker gear was actually on fire, so the first thing they had to do was put out their own fire truck and their fire equipment and they tried to start the truck and move it, but they discovered that it wouldn't move.**
>
> **They got out and looked, and the whole back of the fire truck had melted. So they turned their attention to trying to rescue people from the building and went over and helped people escape from the building.** (http://americanhistory.si.edu/september11)

The highly dramatic terrorist attack on the United States in September 2001 was an occasion when an event of huge historic importance was recorded and where the spoken testimonies of witnesses instantly became primary sources. This evidence was then synthesised by oral historians into historical explanations of change and continuity over time. At no time has this process occurred on such a scale than in the period after the terrorist attacks on the United States in 2001.

This oral history project immediately raised a number of issues relating to intriguing problems of method, and opened up a universe of exciting possibilities amidst the debris of an extraordinary tragedy. As to the interview: which respondents to select? Which questions to ask? Which questions to leave out? How should a relaxed, non-threatening, environment for the interview be created? After the interviews are complete, there are problems and opportunities related to using and interpreting the material collected: how to transcribe the spoken word and turn it into text? How should the use of dialect terms be communicated and interpreted and how to use and importance of regional accents? What about non-verbal forms of communication like gesture? These are the standard questions associated with oral history. With the attacks on the Twin Towers in New York and the Pentagon in Washington, however, there was no time to consider such methodological niceties. Helena Wright, a Curator at the Smithsonian Institution at Washington responsible for collecting artefacts of national life, including oral testimonies, expressed the practically unique situation that a range of like organisations faced after that fateful day:

> **As historians we normally have a period of reflection when we evaluate what's happening. We're not really involved in current events – it's rather contradictory to what historians do.**

> **Usually some time elapses before we can evaluate and determine what's to be brought into a collection. So in that sense the immediacy of this situation [9/11] is quite unusual. It does feel different. There is a kind of rush to make sure that we actually do capture and acquire what we need to before it's either destroyed or disappears.**
>
> (http://americanhistory.si.edu/september11)

Within the limits necessarily set by living memory, oral history has allowed access to social groups and communities too often inadequately or even completely unrepresented by traditional archival sources. The financially impoverished, immigrant communities, benefit claimants and even children all have their faceless existences reflected in government statistics but these types of sources tell us little about the lived experience of such people. Thus oral history does not just have a sense of immediacy, it connects with neglected and under-represented groups, and by focusing on actually lived lives, illuminates them in completely new ways. It does not just discuss these individuals and groups as historical artefacts but gives expression to their own words and idioms, their dialects and folkways. Oral history, in very complex and problematic ways, gives them a historical voice.

Perhaps the most straightforward way of approaching the interaction of historians and interviewees, is to look at the work currently done by a range of recent oral history projects. This might give greater insight into how historians and community activists have used this method but also begin to allow an understanding of their motivations, their pre-suppositions and their ideological or political orientation. The three projects discussed in this section are:

- King's Cross Voices: King's Cross Oral History Project;
- East Midlands Oral History Archive: oral history of the village of Newton Burgoland;
- South African History [Oral History] Online.

Drawing on very different contexts, they typify a much wider range of similar projects undertaken in a huge variety of communities, speaking a wide range of languages in a large number of countries. Whilst being typical in this way, they are also quite different from each other and illustrate the diversity of contexts in which the contribution of oral history can be invaluable.

King's Cross Voices

The area of North London behind the great railway terminals of King's Cross, St Pancras and Euston is one that has undergone a number of transformations and the present moment is no exception. The demolition and clearing of redundant industrial sites, railway infrastructure and giant gasholders and the development of wasteland is accompanied by an anxiety that the formerly settled working-class community of the area known as Somers Town might itself be transformed. Inner-city regeneration may improve the urban infrastructure but it also comes with a cost in terms of human disruption. This reinforces a more general anxiety that, as older members of the community die, a world of memory, a record of lived human experience, is about to slip from sight into an unrecorded past. The King's Cross Oral History Project – a project run by community volunteers – addresses itself to that anxiety by attempting to record the voices of people who have lived in that area over a long period and in so doing provide a record of that history from a perspective that would otherwise be lost to us.

The stated aims of the King's Cross project are articulated on their website at www.kingscrossvoices.org.uk/default.asp:

- to create an accessible archive housing the recorded voices and transcripts of the people of King's Cross;
- to provide an educational resource for schools and the wider community;
- to develop publications, exhibitions and sound trails.

The motive of creating an archive of the voices of people who were long-term residents of the area is clear. They present their stories as people either born in or who migrated into that part of London. Likewise, it is a resource which is meant to feed back into the community itself: by reinforcing and validating the community's sense of self. At a wider level of historical interpretation, the project finally sets itself the task of interpreting and presenting this source material in publications and exhibitions to a wider public. To become, in effect, a part of the greater world of published history.

Using the actual material from this project, we can gain a sense of how social change in this area has impacted on the lives of ordinary individuals. From the testimony of Barbara Hughes, for example, we learn how she had been moved into social housing provided by the East End Dwelling Company, and how this recollection expressed a form of social solidarity but without being sentimental about traditional working-class community life. Rather, the force of her testimony illustrated the degree of regulation imposed upon tenants in this kind of accommodation:

> **Where we were was the East End Dwelling Company, it was meant to be for the working classes. You lived according to your block, to your station. We moved to Number 1 Midhope Buildings in 1954. That corner had been bombed, so it was then a very modern block, one of the better blocks. In Tonbridge and Hastings where lots of police officers lived, they didn't encourage people with children. There were sets of rules. I can remember moving in, and on my floor which overlooked what was then the café in Cromer Street and the Church, a very nice view, but it was the top floor, and me with two babies. I'd settled in for 2 or 3 days and there was a knock on the door. It was a very elderly neighbour who handed me a pummel stone and she expected me to clean – to do the stairs up, and the stairs down, and the loo, once a week. If someone couldn't do it for some reason, you'd do it for them. All very responsible. We also had those washing lines that went right across from one side to the other on pulleys.**
>
> (Barbara Hughes, King's Cross Voices, 2004, at www.kingscrossvoices.org.uk)

In a rather different vein, Reg Hopkins, who was born in the area, recalled the excitement of growing up near a major railway terminus in its heyday, communicating very directly its urgency, noise and colour:

> **It reminded me of a Turner painting. It was smoke and steam everywhere, great whooshes of steam would shoot forth. The station was so busy then as compared with now. Today it is all commuters. I don't say that it isn't busy today but then it was entirely different you know. If you went over to Platform 1 side, where the cab ranks is, there would be boxes of pigeons there. They were racing pigeons . . . It probably was the East End of London where there was this tradition of pigeon racing so they would be taken to King's Cross, loaded on the trains, off loaded at York, at Darlington, and fly back. And also the mail. It was very busy. Huge sacks of mail right the way along the platform. Trains would bring the mail in, the lorries would pick it up, the lorries would return with more sacks and load the trains and off they would go.**

It was an extremely busy station. It was the hustle and the bustle that made it very exciting wasn't it. You felt a sense of living there.

(Reg Hopkins, King's Cross Voices, 2004, at www.kingscrossvoices.org.uk)

Finally, and perhaps most poignantly, Norma Steel described hearing of the proposed redevelopment of the area in terms that almost turn the coming excavations into a metaphor for the destruction of the community she had spent years defending:

They [were] going to put the biggest hole Europe had ever seen in smack dab the middle of King's Cross. I just couldn't believe it! It was uncanny. It was absolutely devastating. After all the years of fighting for the community. It took a long time for the enormity of the project to sink in. Everything changed then. Everything changed.

(Norma Steel, King's Cross Voices, 2004, at www.kingscrossvoices.org.uk)

Oral History of Newton Burgoland

Oral history has very strong roots in accounting for change in rural society. Most villages have been undergoing a process of change over a very long period indeed and the rate at which they have changed has tended to increase with modern industrialisation and urbanisation. Many changed from being settled agricultural communities to smaller communities dependent on the commerce and industry located in their region (but not necessarily in the village itself). Some villages have become little more than residential dormitories for nearby towns which provide the main opportunities in employment, shopping, social life and so forth.

A project carried out by the East Midlands Oral History Archive on 'Growing up in a Leicestershire Village', which focused on Newton Burgoland, captured aspects of rural life by interviewing respondents who grew up in the village in the 1920s and 1930s. It offered a valuable insight into the character of village life in terms of social attitudes, infrastructure and amenities amongst many other things. The interviewees were not, nor are any of the interviews cited below dated but the following examples give a colourful sense of the role of religion in village life, education and schooling, and at the same time reveal a deeper substratum of meaning:

Religion

***Interviewee*: We had a Congregational Chapel and a Methodist. Eventually the Methodist was sold and the Congregational bought it for the village, for a hall.**

***EMOHA*: Could you tell me something about the differences between the two places of worship?**

***Interviewee*: Well, I think the Congregational were more, what should I say, free and easy really. The Methodists seemed very strict, it was really strict Methodist, and they didn't have any entertainment at all, where we had a marvellous choir mistress and organist who really had the children entertained the whole time, and we had wonderful concerts and outings and everything, and Sunday School anniversaries, of that was a very big day.**

(www.le.ac.uk/emoha/community/resources/county/newton/growingup.html)

Even this brief example on religious life provided insight into the diversity of religious experience of the village in the 1920s and 1930s – how, in particular, the very different social attitudes of Congregationalism and Methodism, as strands of nonconformity, shaped village life. This already suggests a great deal more than might have been surmised without oral history techniques to help provoke further questions about how divisions in the village as well as patterns of social solidarity worked in this rural community. Taking another example adds to the picture and emphasises the point:

Harvest and Beer

Interviewee: **At harvest time we used to, Mum used to make this beer in what we called a pancheon, stand it in the dairy, and at lunch we used to take it down to the fields to the men. We'd take it in bottles or in milk cans, anything like that, and then when we'd take our own lunch with us and we'd sit under the hedge on the sacks and have our lunch with the men down there. That was our life as children really, doin' that sort of thing.**

(www.le.ac.uk/emoha/community/resources/county/newton/growingup.html)

There is a great deal about the nature of labour in the village to be gleaned at a time of national economic downturn. The importance of harvest work is emphasised for one thing and the role that children played in taking food to the men while they were at work: men's work and children's work. Here is where the skills of reading documents and interviews overlap; much more can be wrung from this extract. The interviewee talked about making beer and feeding the working men but also revealed that making the beer was their mother's work, that the children spent time with male family members while eating with them. The sexual division of labour, the involvement of the whole family in the work process and the obligations of children were all evoked with a real immediacy in part because of the nature of the medium of oral history.

In another extract, an interviewee talked of school life and, after accounting for the structure of the school by age group, the authority of the headmaster, the heating of the school and the use of the school as a sort of community centre, there was a fascinating and revealing description of the toilet facilities:

School

EMOHA: **What sort of toilet facilities did they have at school?**

Interviewee: **They were in the school yard. There was a row of them. There was one kept locked for the staff. There was the girls' side and then there was a high wall and then there was the boys' side, and of course, they had the men come and empty the pans once a week.**

EMOHA: **When you say 'empty the pans' . . .**

Interviewee: **Never conscious of it being done but it was always done.**

EMOHA: **What sort of pans were these?**

Interviewee: **Well, they had metal pans into wooden seats, you see.**

EMOHA: **So, each toilet . . .**

Interviewee: **Had a wooden seat and metal pan.**

EMOHA: **Can you . . .**

Interviewee: **No chains or anything.**

EMOHA: **Can you remember what these were like to use?**

Interviewee: **Horrible. Well, I thought they were.**

EMOHA: **Was that very different from what you had at home? What sort of toilet did you have at home?**

Interviewee: **Oh no, we had the same thing at home! Oh yes. Lovely white seat because my sister and I used to scrub it.**

EMOHA: What happened to the pan at home?

Interviewee: My father emptied that. That went down the fields.

EMOHA: Did it?

Interviewee: Buried. So we never had an accumulation, it was always kept very nice.

EMOHA: So, the school ones weren't, you said they weren't, you didn't like using them?

Interviewee: I didn't like it but then I was a bit finicky anyway.

(www.le.ac.uk/emoha/community/resources/county/newton/growingup.html)

The structure of society and its relations with children are now known from the organisation of the school toilets. One was kept locked for the exclusive use of the staff while the boys and girls toilets were segregated. This is not very surprising and largely still pertains to this day. We also learnt that this village in the heart of England did not have flushing WCs either in the school or in the home of this respondent and that someone in the community had the job of emptying the facilities in the school. Beneath this something deeper can be glimpsed. The clear contrast between sanitation in the home and that in the school says much about how cleanliness and respectability might have been related. There is not much to go on here but there is a hint that might be pursued by further questioning. The interviewee did not just recall details about the school facilities but also made a statement about home and home life.

South African History Online

Oral history can retrieve histories of both urban and rural communities and give voice to people whose views and lives might otherwise go unrecorded. There is undoubtedly an ideological component to this act of retrieval but very often it lives in the background as an unstated assumption. This is not necessarily always the case. In South Africa, where the political turmoil and change of recent decades has operated alongside the legacy of the long-term exclusion of black people from all of the major political processes of national life, oral history has a particular immediacy. This context is not only inescapably political but it also makes clear how interviewees and oral history methods live alongside and complement other kinds of sources and techniques.

The South African History Online website, established in June 2000, has as its stated aim to 'break the silence on the historic and cultural achievements of the country's black communities'. To achieve this aim, whether it is an appropriate aim for the historian or not, will require more than just interviewing the urban and rural poor about the nature of their domestic and social lives. Reconstructing the history of the apartheid period in the light of the post-apartheid world in a way that gives a due account of the entire population is going to require every resource, method and conceptual framework that the historian can mobilise. But oral history is certainly part of that process.

At one level, the voice of the voiceless, the ordinary activist caught up in the sweep of extraordinary events can be heard. Here two women, Magdelene Matashdi Tsoane (MT) and Rahaba Mahlakedi Moedetsi (RM), were interviewed about their participation in an early great march against the apartheid regime in 1956:

_Q_: How did you feel as you were mixed according to race?

_RM_: I can say I was very happy to work with different people but the people I have enjoyed most were the Indians. I have many friends in India. People like Amina Cachalia were there.

MT: We also worked very closely with people like Lilian Ngoyi and many more. During the march we were together with Ma-Moeketsi and others. I was always with Ma-Moeketsi.

Q: Can you tell us a little bit about the South African Federation of Women?

RM: I am the one who was the member of that organization. I was working with many white women in this organization. We use to attend meetings in Johannesburg.

Q: Were you not afraid for your children during the 1956 March?

RM: No, we had our children on our backs during the March. Many women had their children with them during the March. Some were carrying the white children with them, those who were working for whites.

Q: Tell us about the songs you sung.

MT: We were singing the song, which says 'Verwoerd, the black people will kill you and we do not want Bantu Education'. And the song was saying: 'If you strike a woman, you strike a rock'.

(www.southafrica.info/public_services/citizens/education/sahistoryonline.htm)

We learn here about the importance of women in the history of the struggle against apartheid; about the use of children in marches (including white children) and demonstrations that would culminate in the horrors of the Sharpeville massacre on 21 July 1960 when 10 children were among the 69 people killed by the police. Song was clearly an important aspect of protest and, above all, the fact that the campaign was 'mixed according to race' – a fact that might be surprising to some. However, this image of inter-racial cooperation should not lull us into thinking that this campaign did not display the usual elements of factionalism and infighting.

This next voice was not that of an ordinary protester but that of Johnny Issel, a leader of the United Democratic Front in the Western Cape:

Q: Were there political factions in Cape Town at the time?

JI: Yes indeed . . . A number of political tendencies seemed to surface during 1980 when we saw an upsurge in mass action. The people were ready for direct political action against the state. A protracted bus boycott ensued. Communities were coming out in support of various worker struggles. Civic protests proliferated, like the one in Mitchells Plain against electricity penalties. With this surfaced a number of political groupings – all very eager to hoist their separate flags. There were three major groups on the left. One such group positioned itself at the leadership of the emerging independent trade union movement and held a critical position towards the ANC. Then there were the remnants of the old Unity Movement. Their base was within the non-racial sports movement, a few civic organisations and the municipal workers union. The largest, by far, were those who pledged allegiance to the Congress Movement. They were quite amorphous at the beginning but found greater cohesiveness . . .

. . . Whilst there was co-operation amongst these left groups on a number of campaigns, bitter tensions surfaced at the time of the UDF launch. [1983]

(www.southafrica.info/public_services/citizens/education/sahistoryonline.htm)

Recalling events that took place nearly three decades after the marches of 1956, Johnny Issels' voice was that of a campaign-hardened activist, operating at time when the prospect of success of the anti-apartheid movement must have seemed as distant as ever. In this context the tensions between different political interests within the broader campaign were all the more important and recalled by him in a level headed manner that illustrated this salutary fact without talking it up or, in any obvious way, speaking for his own faction in these debates.

The opening sections of this chapter have suggested a range of contexts within which oral history has made a valuable contribution to historical research. This is true in terms of its contribution to historical knowledge but also in terms of widening the range and nature of historical inquiry itself. Ranging from inner-city London, to rural Leicestershire and the political struggles of the South African anti-apartheid movement, oral history techniques can unearth what would remain unrecorded but can also allow space for the reflections of historical actors who have left a significant mark on the written record. In all of this, it should be allowed that oral history also has its limitations. In relation to the cases discussed above, for example, local authority and property developers' plans for the 'regeneration' of King's Cross should also be consulted, as should digests of social statistics like the government publication *Social Trends* to find out at what point running water and flushing toilets became commonplace in the villages of the English midlands. Most urgently, no historian would dream of building a history of modern South Africa on oral history sources alone. Oral history must be seen, therefore, in relation to its balance sheet of advantages offset against disadvantages. How to make such a calculation will be tackled in the next section.

Section 2

Oral historiography

It is difficult to say with any certainty when oral historiography began. We know from ancient times that some of the earliest historians relied upon the memories of people with whom they conversed (as seen in Chapter 6). In the modern era, folklorists, musicians and writers have a long history of interviewing ordinary people about their lives and cultures. Much of this was done in a haphazard fashion and little was recorded systematically. Arguably, therefore, the first work which we would recognise as oral history was conducted in the United States during the interwar years. Financed by funding provided by the federal government to relieve the effects of the depression, the Federal Writers Project embarked on an extraordinarily ambitious scheme to interview and record the experiences of thousands of ordinary working people. Most notable here were the interviews carried out with over 2,000 former slaves, which provided a unique insight into their lives (now available online as *Slave Narratives from the Federal Writers' Project, 1936–38*, www.memory.loc.gov). In some contrast, the first major academic research for the study of oral history, which recognised it as a discipline in its own right, was established at Columbia University in 1948. The moving spirit was Allan Nevins (1890–1971) and the project focused on producing an oral history of white male elites.

An early practitioner of a more popular oral history in Britain was George Ewart Evans (1909–88), who used interviews amongst other methods to recover the language and lore of ploughmen and agricultural labourers in East Anglia in the 1950s and 1960s, and had a keen antiquarian's eye for a world that was rapidly disappearing (see later). Another example of this approach was contained in *Akenfield* (1969). This account of class and status by the writer Ronald Blythe was set in a real-life, if tiny, English village in Suffolk and drew upon interviews conducted in late 1967. In a testimony from the local blacksmith, who was born in 1923 and recalled the financial hardship of the 1930s, there was a single paragraph which can be read as evidence of the way memory works. It shows how memories may sometimes be borrowed (he mentioned his grandfather), and the tendency for the brain to airbrush out the worst memories may be in evidence when he insisted that 'people were content', but it also suggested that the village worked on a strict hierarchy of patronage, with power and influence flowing downwards from the 'Big House':

> **This was the year [1930] my grandfather had to shut down the forge. He never went back to it. I used to walk by it, eying it and thinking. But nothing was rosy wherever you looked. Nearly everybody went out of business. Nothing was sold. People who had left school began to think about the Big House. You realized that it was there, with all the gardeners, grooms and maids and food. You have to face it, the Big House was then an asset to the village. It paid us to raise our hats, which is why we did it. I hear people run the gentry down now but they were better than the farmers in a crisis. Theirs was the only hand which fed us that we could see. So we bowed a bit; it cost nothing, even if it wasn't all courtesy. Nobody left, nobody went away. People were content. However hard up they were, they stayed content. The boys had the arse out of their trousers, no socks and the toes out of their boots. My brothers and myself were like this, yet so happy. I think other families were the same. The village kept close.**
>
> (Gregory Gladwel, aged 44, blacksmith, in Blyth, 1969, p. 126)

The gardener at the 'Big House' in the second of the direct quotations was only 39 when interviewed by Blyth and provides more information on class relationships within the community:

> **I went to his Lordship's when I was fourteen and stayed for fourteen years. There were seven gardeners and goodness knows how many servants in the house. It was a frightening experience for a boy. Lord and Ladyship were very, very Victorian and very domineering. It was 'swing your arms' every time they saw us. Ladyship would appear suddenly from nowhere when one of us boys were walking off to fetch something. 'Swing your arms!' she would shout. We wore green baize aprons and collars and ties, no matter how hot it was, and whatever we had to do had to be done on the dot. Nobody was allowed to smoke. A gardener was immediately sacked if he was caught smoking, no matter how long he worked there.**
>
> **We must never be seen from the house; it was forbidden. And if people were sitting on the terrace or on the lawn, and you had a great barrow-load of weeds, you might have to push it as much as a mile to keep out of view.**
>
> **If you were seen you were always told about it and warned, and as you walked away Ladyship would call after you, 'Swing your arms!' It was terrible. You felt like someone with a disease.**
>
> (Christopher Falconer, aged 39, gardener, in Blyth, p. 116)

Early examples of social history (see Chapter 9) also explored the lives of agricultural labourers, both male and female, industrial workers, car workers and political activists of very different persuasions through the techniques of oral history. They did so in a way that simultaneously mobilised social historians, sociologists, folklorists and emerging departments of cultural studies to create an awareness of the value of oral history. In *Fenwomen: A Portrait of Women in an English Village* (1975), for example, Mary Chamberlain retrieved the lives of East Anglian women and their world of work. Later, in *Poor Labouring Men* (1985), Alun

Howkins provided a similar account of male agricultural labourers. On the margins of the city of Oxford, the political lives of recently settled and sometimes turbulent quarry workers are recorded in the essay 'Quarry roughs' edited by Raphael Samuel in his *Village Life and Labour* (1975). In a large study that involved collaboration between British and Italian university departments, Paul Thompson and Luisa Passerini headed a project that excavated the lives of car workers in Coventry and Turin. Here oral history admirably transcended any parochial boundaries it may have been inclined to impose on itself by its efforts to engage with histories across national boundaries. Newer projects have often focused on the mobility of migrant groups rather than change in settled communities. In Cardiff, Wales, migration into the area now known simply as 'The Bay' and formerly as Butetown or, more notoriously, as Tiger Bay was typical of the use of oral history to trace the history of migrating communities or peoples.

Oral history developed in a similar fashion in a number of countries, and at the same time began to take on a new and more concrete institutional existence. The Oral History Association in the United States was founded in 1966 and the *Oral History Journal* began life in 1971. Courses about oral history or using oral history as a component method began to spring up in university departments across Britain and a number of other countries. In the United States, Eliot Wigginton's Foxfire Project was inspirational not just in its uses of oral historical methods but the place that it found in progressive education. Wigginton created a model of educational practice that was quite unlike any standard classroom approach, motivating students to interview members of the community in northern Georgia. Recipes, local folk remedies, traditions in music and dance, illuminated the unique and hitherto hidden culture of these Appalachian mountain people. In the wake of these developments, a number of reflexive studies emerged that discussed the methodology, techniques and historiography of oral history. The most notable of these was Paul Thompson's *The Voice of the Past: Oral History* (1978), which simultaneously argued the case for history written from oral testimony rather than from the more familiar document-based sources and for the potential of oral history methods to democratise history itself.

This all-too-brief survey should nevertheless complete a clear grasp of the chronology and character of this literature, allowing a return now to the political and ideological make-up of oral history. While it would be a mistake to see all of the writers in this field as belonging to one political camp, it is reasonable to suggest that oral historians were broadly socialist and feminist in this period and driven by a strong imperative to recover the experience of people neglected by the traditional historical canon and under-represented in printed archives. These people were largely poor and working class. The historians avoided sentimentalising their subject matter despite an obvious empathy, but they did remind us that oral history can fall prey to a sentimental over-identification with its subjects, both individually and as social groups. In fact, the noted Italian oral historian, Luisa Passerini, rightly suggested that oral history can easily move from this identification with the idea of representing the unrepresented into a vulgar populism that is itself a form of historical misrepresentation. As a left-wing historian, she recognised that oral history was not necessarily radical and warned historians not to fall into 'facile democratisation' and 'complacent populism', falsely romanticising the working class and presenting oral history as an unproblematic instrument of democratic scholarship.

Indeed oral histories need not be anymore 'democratic' than the subjects of oral history (Passerini, 1987). Speech and behaviour are constructed through culture and so oral history from this perspective is like storytelling and is simply another way of representing the self.

The evidence provided by oral history methods requires the same critical attention and evaluation as any other source material or history. Democratic intent does not of itself make good history: careful and critical historians can.

Even the most enthusiastic advocate of oral history would allow that it comes with a range of conceptual and methodological problems. Oral history concerns itself by definition with living memory which itself places inescapable temporal limits on its area of inquiry: at this time it would be difficult imagine a project centred on anything earlier than the 1920s or 1930s. Veracity and accuracy is another criticism often levelled at oral history. Memory is inherently selective, faulty, deluded and fraught with all sorts of problems as well as revealing and potentially informative. Psychologists, for example, now tell us that our autobiographical memories are used to construct our identities in the present but are played out in scenarios to test what our future reactions should be in similar circumstances. These are problems that are to some extent a product of the way that oral history developed in the later twentieth century.

The directness of the engagement between the historian/interviewer and the historical subject/interviewee means that the problem of interpreting evidence that can be seen in any historical engagement is especially urgent in the case of oral history. When an historical document is read, we are no more a blank sheet than the document itself. We bring our own knowledge, presuppositions and cultural belonging to the table – an issue of subjectivity that was confronted in the opening chapter of this book. Likewise, oral historians are actually an active part of the interviewing process, not just framing the questions but also playing a vital part in determining the nature of the moment.

Much of the practice of oral history is related to the techniques and complexities of actually interviewing people, in particular the forensic skills of constructing a table of questions that meet the needs of the research project and also allows the respondent the freedom to express themselves, introducing material of which the interviewer is otherwise unaware. Decisions have to be taken regarding the technicalities of the material and equipment: is the tape-recorder vital, or might the notebook be less intrusive and so more appropriate? How are the interviews to be transcribed in a way that allows a fuller understanding to emerge? These are technical problems that require a specific kind of training which is beyond our concerns. We wish, rather, to focus more specifically on the historiographical and conceptual issues associated with oral history.

Section 3

Interviewing techniques and the limits of memory: Arthur Harding and the East End underworld

As a pioneer in oral history techniques, Raphael Samuel developed oral history as a way of giving voice to the powerless but also as a device to retrieve historical detail that would otherwise stay beyond the reach of the historian. His interviews in the 1970s with Arthur

Harding (or Treserden to give him his real name) are no exception. Born in 1886, and brought up in the notorious neighbourhood of the Old Nichol in Bethnal Green, Harding appeared to offer a direct bridge back to the East End of the late nineteenth and early twentieth centuries.

He presented Samuel with a chance to talk to perhaps the last known survivor of a world we thought quite lost, as well as providing, as Samuel put it, a 'capital document' for future historians (Raphael Samuel Archive, Bishopsgate Institute). Harding first recorded his memories on paper. Harding's 400-page typescript arrived with Samuel via a mutual contact, Stan Newens (Newens, 2007). It focused mainly on Harding's life as a 'terror' in the East End, his stretches in jail (including a five-year term in Dartmoor), and his evidence to the Royal Commission on the Metropolitan Police in 1908 described him as 'the most slippery customer in Brick Lane' (Samuel, 1981). Fascinating as much of this material obviously was, Samuel believed that because it focused on Harding's criminal activities, the manuscript did not yield enough of Harding's life as a whole. More particularly, it said next to nothing about Harding's childhood in the Nichol. Samuel wished to develop the everyday aspects of Harding's life: his period as a cabinet maker, domestic life and child–parent relations, the informal networks of the underworld, the relationships between the English, Irish, Jews and what Harding called 'Half-Jews', and gambling, racing and street-trading. In contrast, Harding presented his autobiography as a life of crime but only in the important context of his 50 or so years of going straight.

The relationship between Harding and Samuel was always likely to be difficult. Politically, Harding was a Conservative voter – except in 1945 – and from a family of 'poor but loyal' Conservatives. He had spent a lifetime living on his wits and his physical courage. He even joined Mosley's Blackshirt's 'for the excitement', as he put it. Samuel, on the other hand, was a secular Jew brought up in the Communist party and intellectually steeped in its traditions. He gained a First Class degree at Oxford University and although later politically active with the New Left, lived to some extent a life of the mind. They had the East End in common (both saw it as their natural habitat) but generational chasms loomed large. Harding was born in 1886 and Samuel in 1934. By the time Harding was interviewed by Samuel he was old enough (and presumably harmless enough) to be known by the Mosleyites (see Chapter 11) with affection and perhaps with a patronising touch, as 'Uncle Arthur'.

Besides the wish to explain and vindicate his life, Harding wanted to expose what he regarded as the venal corruption of the Metropolitan Police. One in particular, Divisional Detective Inspector Wensley ('the Weasel'), presented as a villain in all but profession, pursued Harding through the back lanes and law courts of London. Harding's role was prominent. At one moment, he was at the heart of gangland London, fighting the Darby Sarbini gang or the Titanic Mob; in the next, he is championing the vulnerable (he was morally offended, for instance, at pimping and the women that suffered from it), a friend and respecter of the immigrant Jew and those physically weak or disabled. His appearances in the dock were always unfortunate accidents or deliberate efforts to put him away, but were testimony to Harding's verbal elegance, as well as a genuine autodidactic attitude to learning the law. He claimed never to have lied to the courts: a truthfulness which contrasted with Wensley's deliberate efforts to send him down.

Samuel's instinct as an oral historian was to let the subject speak for himself, running a danger that Harding's childhood and other areas of interest to the reading public would be neglected. Apparently, Harding even refused at first to focus on the criminal and sub-criminal characters of the East End: Long Hymie, Dodger Mullins, Darky the Coon and others, let alone the more mundane stuff of social history. Instead he lightened on extraneous events such as the Whitechapel murders and the Dockers' Strike, both of which date back to the 1880s. His evidence, given with no particular respect for structure or chronology, threatened to lead the reader into an unpromising labyrinth of characters and places. This apparent impasse called for a compromise. If the material was to be published and Harding's autobiography not to collapse into a biography authored by Samuel, something had to be done. A 'battle of wills', as Samuel was later to describe it, ensued:

> **We settled for a *de facto* compromise, in which each of us pursued our particular hobby-horse – the Jago in my case, Inspector Wensley in Arthur's – while the other waited patiently to return to the main point.** (Raphael Samuel Archive, Bishopsgate Institute)

To an extent then, both witness and inquisitor had tapered perspectives of the nature of the East End and drew upon the copious literature associated with the area, for Harding much of it sensational. For his part, Samuel self-consciously traced a journey from the slums described in the art and literature of the period, of social investigation and other social reportage, to the post-war slum clearances described in the sociology of that time. The end result was Samuel's *East End Underworld – Chapters in the Life of Arthur Harding* (1981).

Both interviewer and interviewee tended to draw upon popular constructions of the East End. Harding in particular looked for vindication and (in the style of the melodramas he watched at the Britannia theatre in Hoxton) for revenge. Samuel's first point of reference, on the other hand, was the slum literature of Arthur Morrison and others such as his *Child of the Jago*. Samuel was a pioneer in this hitherto little-known Booth archive at the London School of Economics. No doubt because of his own personal involvement, his knowledge of the tribal closeness of the East End described by the sociology of Young and Willmott (1957), Samuel complained that Harding was unable to separate narrative from analysis; unable it seemed to recall events without conceptualising and interpreting them, hypothesising or forever speculating on the motives of his enemies. Nor could Harding divorce his own memories from received views of the area. He continuously explained his experiences in clichés, drawing rather more on the 'darkest East End' representation made famous by late-Victorian social reportage, than that of the 'golden age' literature of East End writing that celebrates community solidarities. Biography is 'replete', Samuel observed, 'with cultural borrowings, drawing its categories from religious, political ideas and literary imaginings' (Raphael Samuel Archive, Bishopsgate Institute).

The real problem, however, was to agree the boundaries of oral history: to know whether these are the partially expunged memories and views of Harding or evidence crafted, shaped and even manipulated by a professional historian. Whether too, as there is such a confusion of images and messages about the East End, it was even possible to grasp a truthful, unsullied account by simply using oral history methods. Samuel recognised this tension in how the East End is characterised but also the tension between Harding and himself, both creatures of their time and each the instrument of their own memories where evidence derived by oral history methods is likely to say as much about the historian as the history.

Oral history has added a whole new dynamic to historical research and publication in relation to both method and subject matter but also comes packaged with problems peculiar to itself. The experience of *East End Underworld* revealed, in effect, a balance sheet of advantages and disadvantages. The rewards seem to far outweigh the methodological difficulties but there may be another perspective from which to view what we do with oral history and it is these we examine next.

Section 4

The wider conceptual problem

When one oral historian wanted to understand the circumstances of the Giriama revolt against the British in Kenya in 1914, he questioned members of the Mijikenda. Despite all historical or documentary evidence to the contrary, they insisted that the conflict was prompted by a rape. Structurally, there is an explanation for this. It seems that in the tradition of this particular culture, 'the idea of rape was a convenient abstraction denoting a serious social transgression which, when involving outsiders, was a legitimate cause for war' (Spear, 1981, p. 141). This explanation could be applied to all wars: as rape was the cause of one war it became the stock explanation for all wars.

This is an example of a strand of oral history that relies less on autobiographical memory and more on oral traditions that percolate down through the generations of preliterate societies. It is an approach that can be traced back to the early fieldwork of anthropologists and sociologists. Jan Vansina's *Oral Tradition as History* (1985) addressed the shortcomings of his own pioneering 1961 book and made a plea for the reconstruction of history using oral methods. It promoted a considerable debate about the merits of oral history and was couched in anthropological discourses (see Chapter 14). Within anthropology, functionalists were sceptical of oral history, believing that it could do little else but confirm present-day institutions, reflecting the social relations therein. Structuralists, on the other hand, argued that many preliterate societies constructed historical narratives which were transmitted in oral traditions in ways that allowed structural anthropologists to study societies, and (we might surmise) for historians to identify change. These oral traditions, which were 'largely composed of collages of universal symbols artfully constructed according to set patterns of thought to express essential human values', were therefore a vital element of the societies they studied (Spear, 1981, cf. p. 134).

Vansina later wrote *Living in Africa* (1994) with a developed knowledge that oral evidence was infused with structural conventions about the past that are accepted by members of the group, layered with mythology and laced with hearsay. The oral transmission of these 'unwritten documents', mediated through collective memory, was later re-explored by Vansina and others in *Oral Tradition: A Study in Historical Methodology* (2009). The purpose of his approach was to reconstruct knowledge by tapping into narratives that existed a priori in society and which were shared by members of a society regardless, for instance, of whether an event like the 1914 rebellion in Kenya was remembered by this or that individual giving testimony at any one time. Ethnographers, whether their subject area is the native cultures of modern Africa or the lives, narratives and rituals of western societies, use oral-based approaches in societies they study in order to gain insights into whole cultures, social lives and political practices. While Vansina and others do it by identifying the structural assumptions built into pre-literate society, European folk memory has been captured primarily by retrieving individual memories as a way of piecing together what psychologists call 'flashbulb memory'; that is, memories that are stirred by momentous social events such as the death of Princess Diana or the attacks on the United States in September 2001. It is to oral history as it has been applied to European narratives that we now turn.

Oral traditions speak to a deeper and more enduring human need that has been consistently present in western society since at least the transformations associated with large-scale industrialisation (and later de-industrialisation), urbanisation and migration. Most of us, at some point in our lives or in our relationship with older relatives, friends or neighbours have encountered the sensation of something passing from the world, and felt that their existence will pass from living memory and become a story told rather than a scene witnessed. In due course, even the story will be forgotten. This loss is apparent in individual lives but also in relation to change in the village, change in inner-city neighbourhoods, changing work-practices and relations, and in religious observance. This fear of loss can act as a powerful imperative to do something to preserve the past, and has two consequences for how oral history might be thought about. The first relates to the wider history which provides the context for oral testimory; the second is connected to the idea that people will 'do' oral history with or without the participation of the academy.

These are important sources of inspiration for all strands of oral history. It is interesting that for Ewart Evans, who we encountered in Section 2, the passing of folkways and traditional language acted as the mainspring that drove his research. He recognised a vocabulary used by East Anglian ploughmen who started work in the 1880s and 1890s that he had earlier found in medieval poetry. This, he knew, would not last. Once this was recognised, he became less insistent on finding academic antecedents, recognising instead another much older lineage behind the drive to record and recover a world that was about to disappear.

Ewart Evans was not the first to feel this and to act upon it. One point of origin for the study of oral history lies far outside of the formal field of historical inquiry and is deeply embedded in the history of literature and music as well as the scholarly practice of history. Collecting oral tradition and reproducing it in print for a wider audience became a particular enthusiasm in the German-speaking lands. Here it provided one of the many connections between the spirit of inquiry native to the European Enlightenment of the eighteenth century and the growing cultural nationalism of the later-eighteenth and nineteenth centuries often associated with romantic literature like that of Walter Scott in Scotland (see Chapter 3). Gotthold Ephraim Lessing (1729–81), for example, was a poet, philosopher and critic whose collection of stories entitled *Dschinnistan* (1786–9) used such folk tales alongside original stories. While there was an uncharacteristic emphasis on the triumph of reason over mysticism in these stories, they did help to legitimate the use of such folk tales in literature culture and the western art tradition. One of Lessing's tales concerns a magic zither that is considered one of a number of possible sources for Mozart's *Magic Flute* (1791).

Yet, it was the brothers Jakob Grimm (1785–1863) and Wilhelm Grimm (1786–1859) who did most to develop the art of collecting and whose names are best known beyond their native Germany. As leading academics, their first interest was in linguistics and philology (the relationship of languages and their histories), out of which their passion for collecting grew. Despite their popularity and the enduring place of 'Snow White and the Seven Dwarfs' and 'The Frog King' in our popular culture, their collecting was very much a function of their studies of language. They began collecting folk tales and legends in 1807 and rode the wave of enthusiasm for German folklore, publishing their *Children's and Household Tales* (1810) followed by another volume of 70 tales in 1814. They came with the scholarly apparatus and footnotes associated with serious folklore but also remained in more popular circulation. It is their method that is of primary interest to us. Their intention was to offer faithful renditions of folklore rather than adaptations intended for the print market. As with the Dane Hans Christian Anderson, the Grimm brothers expressed through their stories base national sentiments, and these stories represented a significant step towards modern folklore studies and ultimately towards the practice of oral history.

They were not alone in their endeavours. Klemens Brentano (1778–1842), also a novelist and poet, worked with his brother-in-law Ludwig Achim von Arnim (1781–1831) on a collection of folksongs, *Des Knaben Wunderhorn* (1805–8). Like the Grimms, they were rigorous in their approach and the collecting of folk song and music became another dimension to the systematic retrieval of the non-print worlds of the past. In Britain, a number of collectors started collecting folk song and dance. This was led by Cecil Sharp (1859–1924) who, upon returning from an attempt to develop a teaching and music career in Australia, encountered English folk music anew and particularly the almost-extinct practice of Morris dancing. He used the music he discovered in his own compositions, and retrieved and notated music and dance that would otherwise have been lost. The fact that Sharp frequently bowdlerised the lyrics of folksongs before publishing them or using them in teaching also raised an awareness of methodological problems associated with transcription as well as interpretation. In 1911 he founded the English Folk Dance Society, which went on in 1932 to merge with the Folk Song Society. Between 1916 and 1918 he travelled in the United States, contributing to the ongoing work of collecting and recording folk songs in the Appalachian Mountains.

Tracking the development of English and Scottish folk songs and the way in which they evolved over time as they migrated, along with the folk themselves, to North America was very much the concern of Francis James Child (1825–1896). Child made the return journey from his native United States, to study not only the folk song of his own land but their countries of origin. In this respect he pioneered the area developed by Sharp. Paralleling work going on in Denmark, he amassed a huge collection of songs (both tunes and words) and their historical lineage in his ten-volume *The English and Scottish Popular Ballad* (1882–98).

By the end of the early part of the twentieth century, folk songs were being widely collected. At one level this was an act of retrieval, undertaken for its own sake, but on another it was also being adapted in contemporary compositions. Lucy Broadwood (1858–1929), who followed her father John into collecting folk songs, was founder member and moving spirit of the Folk Song Society in England. In 1904, the English composer Ralph Vaughan Williams (1872–1958) was moved by the fear that the tradition of the English folk song would soon disappear and, worse still, disappear without trace. His method was simply to tramp the countryside talking to people, listening to them sing and transcribing and thus preserving what he heard. This was later incorporated into his music but the act of retrieval was done nonetheless and Vaughan Williams consciously saw it as contributing to the work of collectors like Broadwood.

The Hungarian composers Zotland Kodaly (1882–1967) and Bela Bartok (1881–1945) had a similar approach to their music. Here, in a way, is a return to the academic origins of the Grimm brothers because Kodaly's interest in folk tales and songs grew out of research for his doctorate on Hungarian folk song. Throughout 1905 he travelled through the Hungarian countryside recording songs and stories on phonograph cylinders. Out of his 1906 thesis came a hugely productive collaboration that made a major contribution to the rise of ethnomusicology. Kodaly met Bela Bartok (1881–1945) in 1908 with Kodaly initially acting as mentor to the older Bartok. Their own compositions were profoundly shaped by these researches but those researches were original and valuable in revealing the origins of Magyar folk music and its relationship with the gypsy music of the region.

Ethnomusicology and oral history are not the same. The early collectors of folk tales and songs did not always, if ever, use the kind of methodological discipline that we would expect of a modern historian. However, it can be seen that from the Grimms through to Child and then Kodaly and Bartok there was a growing awareness of the need to establish critical procedures and methods in the recording of the material collected. More than this though, through the rise of the practice of collecting folkways, including those who helped to popularise it even where they had no awareness of sound methods, there is still common ground with the inspirations behind oral history.

All this has two dimensions to consider. First, a world is constantly being lost as cultures change and as the memory of each generation passes from human recall. For Walter Scott it was the taming of the Scottish borders by the spread of modern commerce. For Vaughan Williams in England it was the loss of an oral tradition that had been overwhelmed by the tide of growing literacy. The anxiety was clear. If this is not recorded now, the world apparent to us now will be gone forever. The second area of common ground is that oral history tends to focus on the spoken, hence its name. This can lead to amnesia: to forget that which could as easily be called aural history. It is about hearing as well as speaking, and hearing is by no means restricted to hearing the spoken word alone.

With the sense of losing a part of the world as individual and social memories fade, comes an important motive for doing history by oral methods that in turn answers a deep human need. Either self-consciously in the manner of Scott in Scotland or through the Grimms as part of a rich lineage of folklore in Germany, or, through unselfconscious storytelling and ballad making, people have always done oral history. Now, in the age of the electronic recording, mass print culture and the Internet, and in the knowledge that academic historians, amateur historians and community groups have now practised oral history with great sophistication, people will carry on doing it using these more modern means. Putting the proverbial genie back in the bottle is not an option. It seems likely that a wide range of people will carry on interviewing and recording the memory of their villages and streets in the face of inexorable change, or recording the memories of 'the old country' before the tales of migration are lost. They will do this whether academic historians are paying attention or not. It would be better if attention is paid.

In practice

Oral history is a strand of historical inquiry that has grown in status in recent years, and although still regarded by more conventional historians with a degree of suspicion has also been responsible for innovative studies. Part of its appeal derives from its democratic impulses. Oral history has opened up opportunities for thousands of amateur historians in community groups and even schools to undertake research into aspects of the past. At its most basic level, you do not need to be a trained historian to pick up a tape recorder and interview elderly people about their past experiences. And oral history provides ordinary people who are largely absent from the historical record with the opportunity to speak for themselves. Without the work of oral historians, therefore, we would know much less about the lives and working conditions of the men and women who through their toil created the world as we know it.

There have been strands within what might loosely be described as oral history which have not addressed directly the experiences of the elderly trawled from their memories, but rather have striven to understand the role of storytelling, particularly in preliterate cultures. Folk tales and music constitute part of vital oral traditions. Their meanings may have been lost over time, but the stories have been resurrected and reconstructed by anthropologists and cultural historians to reveal the attitudes of the inhabitants of ancient societies to vital questions about life, death and change.

Not that oral history is without its difficulties, as conventional historians are quick to point out. For the most part, as a methodology it relies upon the memories of witnesses, and we know only too well how fickle, unreliable and selective these can be. In answer to this, we can say that oral historians are interested not only in the ability of people to recall factual information reliably, but also in how they interpreted the events which shaped their lives. It is clear also that recall of the past is shaped profoundly by the present. People interpret their lives through the prism of the here and now, and often attempt to reconstruct personal narratives as a means of making sense of, or celebrating them. The process of gathering information is also prone to influence from the presence of the interviewer. All memories are therefore recalled with a particular audience in mind, and responses to questions shaped by beliefs in what is required or expected of them. These sorts of criticisms do not necessarily compromise the promise of oral history, however, not least because they can also be levelled at other, more conventional sources. All documentary sources are written with a particular audience in mind, and equally importantly, also depend upon the memories of their authors.

Oral history thus continues to offer much in its ability to access the lives of ordinary people; over time, as it confronts and overcomes its most pressing theoretical and methodological problems, it may even become accepted as part of mainstream historiography.

Summary

The four sections of this chapter have said four things:

- Oral history is an invaluable tool for the historian and can be used in a variety of different situations to give us an invaluable view on the past. The subject area for these methodologies may differ – for example, urban change, rural social development or political transformation in South Africa. In all these instances, the need to contextualise findings derived from oral history remains paramount.
- Oral history exists within a wider context of myth, unreliable memory and competing narratives about the past, but this presents methodological problems. The development of oral history in its modern, western, guise is traced via its influence from attempts to retrieve a 'history from below' as the new social history developed in the 1960s. Oral history was seen as one way that a previous untold history could be pieced together using its methods.
- These methodological problems were played out in the chosen case study of an oral history from the 1980s, Raphael Samuel's *East End Underworld*. These were very clear when focusing on the detailed lives and preoccupations of historian and interviewee. In the case of Samuel and Harding it became clear that each was influenced by the historical context of the East End of London and its popular construction and came to the project with their own priorities and assumptions.
- The practice of oral history has existed in more anthropologically based oral methodologies in Africa and elsewhere that have at their centre a desire to understand the oral histories of preliterate societies. These societies tend to tell the lineage of their cultures collectively, handing down stories which then serve to make sense of their present and most certainly do not rely on living memory. It also exists in western cultures to provide a basic human need to retrieve memories from oblivion and this need has its origins in Enlightenment folklorist traditions.

Discussion document

Oral history comes in various guises and attempts to engage with a wide array of historical contexts; from the retrieval of those that were active in Italians fascism or those 'living the fishing' who followed the shoals of fish around the east coasts of Scotland and England. All, save the retrieval of ancestral stories handed down through generations in non-literate societies, rely on the recall of individual memory.

I remember it like it was yesterday. It's a warm and sunny English afternoon and I am playing outside in the garden. Suddenly a shiny silver aircraft appears in the clear blue sky. My mother picks me up and points to it; neighbours come out of their houses to watch. The aeroplane is Concorde, climbing out of Heathrow airport on one of its earliest flights.

I can play this memory over and over in my head as easily as watching a YouTube clip, and yet I know it almost certainly cannot be real. Even though Concorde could have passed over on test flights, I only lived there until 1971, when I was barely out of nappies. And Concorde was white, not silver.

Where does the mismatch between my memory and reality come from? 'We've known since the 1960s that memory isn't like a video recording – it's reconstructive,' says psychologist David Gallo of the University of Chicago. The collection of snapshots known as 'autobiographical memory' is not a true and accurate record of your past – it is more like a jumble of diary entries, photographs and newspaper clippings. 'Your memory is often based on what you've seen in a photograph or stories from parents or siblings rather than what you can actually recall,' says Kimberley Wade, a memory researcher at the University of Warwick in the UK.

In other words, one of the most important components of your self-identity – your autobiographical memory – is little more than an illusion . . .

Within days of 9/11, psychologists at the University of Illinois at Chicago asked nearly 700 people where they were, what they were doing, how they heard the news and who they were with at the time. A year later they asked them again. More than half of the participants had changed their story on at least one count – while still expressing supreme confidence that their memories were accurate.

Flashbulb memory is also highly suggestive. In 2002, psychologists from the University of Portsmouth in the UK went to a local shopping centre and asked people about their memories of the death of Diana, including whether they had seen 'the footage' of the actual crash. Nearly half said they had, despite the fact than no footage exists.

'Head full of half-truths', *New Scientist*, 14 May 2011.

Further reading

* *essential*

Robert Perks and Alistair Thompson (eds), *The Oral History Reader* (2nd edition, 2006).
Celebrates the establishment of oral history as an accepted part of the wider discipline; this impressive anthology takes in contributions from across the world. Of particular interest are the essays by Paul Thompson, Liusa Passarini, Joanna Bornat and Trevor Lummis.

* **Raphael Samuel**, *East End Underworld. Chapters in the Life of Arthur Harding* (1981).
An extraordinary example of the oral history method. Contentious in its planning and execution it nonetheless stands out as a model of interviewing technique. Unfortunately, this volume is now out of print but well worth consulting if possible.

Elizabeth Tonkin, *Narrating Our Pasts: The Social Construction of Oral History* (1992).
A complex argument, focused on the processes in which self-consciousness is constructed through a medley of social influences and which are understood through a multi-disciplinary approach.

Jan Vansina, *Oral Tradition as History* (1985).
Gives an insight into pioneering approaches in anthropological fieldwork as well as, for the oral historian, ideas on the importance of language, memory, performance and ritual.

Anthony Selden and Joanna Pappworth, *By Word of Mouth: Elite Oral History* (1983).
A guide to the study of elite oral history. This volume is especially notable because it is concerned with political power in socially high places.

Bibliography

The place of publication is London unless otherwise stated.

A' Hearn, Brian, Peracchi, Franco, Vecchi, Giovanni (2009) 'Height and the Normal Distribution: Evidence from Italian Military Data', *Demography* **46** (1) pp. 1–25.

Abbott, Andrew (1991) 'The Lost Synthesis', *Social Science History* **15** (2) pp. 201–38.

Abbott, Edith (1917) 'Charles Booth 1840–1916', *Journal of Political Economy* **25** (2) pp. 195–200.

Achinstein, Peter (ed.) (2004) *Science Rules: A Historical Introduction to Scientific Methods*, Baltimore: The John Hopkins University Press.

Adun, John W. (1981) 'Anthropology and History in the 1980s', *Journal of Interdisciplinary History*, XII:2 (Autumn), pp. 253–65.

Aldgate, Anthony (2007) *Britain Can Take It*, I. B. Tauris.

Alexander, Sally 'Women's Work in Nineteenth Century London' in Oakley, A. and Mitchell, T. (1976) *The Rights and Wrongs of Women*, Penguin.

—— (1994) *Becoming a Woman: And Other Essays in Nineteenth and Twentieth Century Feminist History*, Virago.

—— (1984) 'Women, Class and Sexual Differences in the 1830s and 1840s: Some Reflections on the Writing of a Feminist History', *History Workshop Journal* **17** (1) pp. 125–49.

Althusser, Louis (1962) *For Marx*, Allen Lane.

Amt, Emilie (ed.) (1993) *Women's Lives in Medieval Europe. A Sourcebook*, Routledge.

Anderson, Benedict (2006) [1983] *Imagined Communities: Reflection on the Origins and Spread of Nationalism*, Virago.

Anderson, Perry (1964) 'Origins of the Present Crisis' *New Left Review* **23** pp. 26–53.

Anon (1989) 'The Runes of Loki. A Mischievous Look at Wargamers', *Miniature Wargames* **71**.

Arendt, Hannah (2004) [1968] *The Origins of Totalitarianism*, New York: Schocken Books.

Ashworth, Tony (2000) [1980] *Trench Warfare 1914–1918: The Live and Let Live System*, Pan Books.

Avis, Paul (2002) *Christian Church: Theological Resources in Historical Perspective*, Edinburgh: T&T Clarke.

Azzam, Reem (1999) Modern Historical Methodology vs. Hadeeth Methodology, http://www.usc.edu/dept/MSA/fundamentals/hadithsunnah/historyandhadeeth/azzamcomparison.html.

Bacon, D. (2006) *Depoliticizing War*, http://dbacon.igc.org/Art/03PolWar.html.

Bagley, J. J. (1972) *Historical Interpretations: Sources of Medieval History, 1066–1540*, Devon: David & Charles.

Barbauld, Anna Laetitia (1825) 'On Monastic Institutions' in *The Works*, 2 vols., Longman.

Barnard, Alan and Spencer, Jonathan (eds) (2002) *Encyclopaedia of Social and Cultural Anthropology*, Routledge.

Barrow, J. W. (1981) *A Liberal Descent: Victorian Historians and the English Past*, Cambridge: Cambridge University Press.

Battuta, Ibn (2005) [1929] *Travels in Asia and Africa 1325–1354*, Routledge Curzon.

Bayly, C. A. (1989) *Imperial Meridian*, Longman.

—— (2004) *The Birth of the Modern World, 1780–1914*, Oxford: Blackwell.

Beard, Mary (1987) [1946] *Woman as a Force in History: A Study in Traditions and Realities*, New York: Persia Books.

Bede (2008) *The Ecclesiastical History of the English People*, Oxford: Oxford University Press.

Bennett, Judith M. (2006) *History Matters: Patriarchy and the Challenge of Feminism*, Pennsylvania: University of Pennsylvania Press.
—— (2008) 'Forgetting the Past', *Gender & History* **20** pp. 669–77.
Bentley, Michael (2005) *Modernizing England's Past: English Historiography in the Age of Modernism, 1870–1970*, Cambridge: Cambridge University Press.
Berg, Maxine (1992) 'Rehabilitating the Industrial Revolution' *Economic History Review* **XLV** (1) pp. 24–50.
—— (1994) *The Age of Manufactures: Industry, Innovation and Work in Britain*, Routledge.
—— (2007) *Luxury and Pleasure in Eighteenth Century Britain*, Oxford: Oxford University Press.
Berger, John (2008) [1973] *Ways of Seeing*, Harmondsworth: Penguin.
Berlin, Isaiah (1976) *Vico and Herder: Two Studies in The History of Ideas*, Chatto & Windus.
Berman, Marshall (1983) *All That is Solid Melts into Air: The Experience of Modernity*, Verso.
Bhabha, Homi (1994) *The Location of Culture*, Routledge.
Biagini, Eugenio F. and Reid, Alistair J. (1991) *Currents of Radicalism: Popular Radicalism, Organised Labour and Popular Politics 1850–1914*, Cambridge: Cambridge University Press.
Bischoff, Bernhard (1990) [1979] *Latin Palaeography: Antiquity and the Middle Ages*, Cambridge: Cambridge University Press.
Blaas, P. B. M. (1978) *Continuity and Anachronism: Parliamentary and Constitutional Development in Whig Historiography and the Anti-Whig Reaction*, Germany: Springer.
Black, Jeremy (2000) *Maps and Politics*, Chicago: Chicago University Press.
—— (2000) *Maps in History: Constructing Images of the Past*, Yale: Yale University Press.
Blythe, Ronald (1973) *Akenfield: Portrait of an English Village*, Harmondsworth: Penguin.
Bondanella, Peter E. (1973) *Machiavelli and the Art of Renaissance History*, Detroit: Wayne State University Press.
Booth, Charles (1989–1902) *Life and Labour of the People in London*, Macmillan.
Bourdieu, Pierre (1963) 'The Attitude of the Algerian Peasant Towards Time', J. Pitt-Rivers (ed.), *Mediterranean Countrymen: Essays on the Social Anthropology of the Mediterranean Paris*: Mouton **XXX** pp. 55–72.
Bowering, G. (1997) 'The Concept of Time in Islam', *Proceedings of the American Philosophical Society* **141** (1) pp. 55–66.
Boyns, Trevor (2007) 'Accounting, Information, and Communication Systems', Jones, Geoffrey and Zeitlin, Jonathan (eds), *The Oxford Handbook of Business History* pp. 447–469, Oxford: Oxford University Press.
Braudel, Fernand (1992) *The Mediterranean and the Mediterranean World in the Age of Philip II*, Harper Collins.
Briggs, Asa (1962) [1959] *Chartist Studies*, New York: St Martin's Press.
Broadberry, Steve (1997) *The Productivity Race: British Manufacturing Performance in International Perspective 1850–1990*, Cambridge: Cambridge University Press.
Brooks, Nicholas, (1985) 'The Organisation and Achievements of the Peasants of Kent and Essex in 1381', Hayr-Harting, H. and Moore, R. I. (eds), *Studies in Medieval History* presented to R. H. C. Davies, Hambledon.
Brown, Callum G. (2009) *The Death of Christian Britain: Understanding Secularisation 1800–2000*, Routledge.
Brown, Jonathan (1998) *Painting in Spain 1500–1700*, New Haven: Yale University Press.
Brown, Richard and Davis-Brown Beth (1998), 'The Making of Memory: The Politics of Archives, Libraries and Museums in the Construction of National Consciousness', *History of the Human Sciences* **11** (4) pp. 17–32.
Brown, Stuart *et al.* (1983) *Adam Smith's Wealth of Nations*, Milton Keynes: Open University.
Brownley, Martine Watson (1985) *Clarendon and The Rhetoric of Historical Form*, Pennsylvania: University of Pennsylvania Press.

Bruce, Steve (1992) *Religion and Modernization: Sociologists and Historians Debate the Secularization Thesis*, Oxford: Oxford University Press.
Burckhardt, Jacob (2002) *Civilization of the Renaissance in Italy*, New York: Modern House.
Burke, Peter(1985) *Vico*, Oxford: Oxford University Press.
—— (1997) *Varieties of Cultural History*, Cambridge: Cambridge University Press.
—— (2005) *History and Social Theory*, Cornell: Cornell University Press.
—— (2007) [2001] *Eyewitnessing: The Uses of Images as Historical Evidence*, Cornell: Cornell University Press.
—— (2008) *What is Cultural History?*, Cambridge: Cambridge University Press.
—— (2009) [1978] *Popular Culture in Early Modern Europe*, Fareham: Ashgate.
Burton, Antoinette (ed.) (2005) *Archive Stories: Fact, Fiction, and the Writing of History*, Durham: Duke University Press.
Butterfield, Herbert (1970) [1944] *The Englishman and his History*, New Haven: Archon Books.
—— (2005) [1931] *The Whig Interpretation of History*, Continuum.
Bynum, Caroline Walker (1984) *Jesus as Mother: Studies in the Spirituality of the Middle Ages*, Berkeley: University of California Press.
—— (1987) *Holy Feast and Holy Fast: The Religious Significance of Food to Medieval Women*, Berkeley: University of California Press.
Calder, Angus (1991) *Myth of the Blitz*, Pimlico.
Canovan, M. (2004) 'Hannah Arendt on Totalitarianism and Dictatorship', in Baehr, P. and Richter, M. (eds) *Dictatorship in History and Theory: Bonapartism, Caesarism, and Totalitarianism*, Cambridge: Cambridge University Press.
Cappelli, Andriano *et al.* (1982) *The Elements of Abbreviation in Medieval Latin Palaeography*, Kansas: University of Kansas Libraries.
Carr, E. H. (2001) [1961] *What is History?*, Basingstoke: Palgrave.
Chakrabarty, Dipesh (2000) *Provincializing Europe: Postcolonial Thought and Historical Difference*, New Jersey: Princeton University Press.
Chamberlain, Mary (1975) *Fenwomen: A Portrait of Women in an English Village*, Virago.
Chandler, Alfred (1990) [1962] *Strategy and Structure: Chapters in the History of the American Industrial Enterprise*, MIT.
Chandler, James (1999) *England in 1819: The Politics of Literary Culture and the Case of Romantic Historicism*, Chicago: University of Chicago Press.
Chase, Malcolm (2007) *Chartism: A New History*, Manchester: Manchester University Press.
Chaturvedi, Vinayak (ed.) (2000) *Mapping Subaltern Studies and the Postcolonial*, Verso.
Cheney, C. R. (2000) *A Handbook of Dates for British Students*, Cambridge: Cambridge University Press.
Childs, Peter and Williams, Patrick (1997) *An Introduction to Post-Colonial Theory*, Prentice Hall.
Clanchy, M. T. (1993) *From Memory to Written Record: England 1066–1307*, Oxford: Blackwells.
Clapham, John (1949) [1926] *Economic History of Britain*, Cambridge: Cambridge University Press.
Clark, Anna (1995) *The Struggle for the Breeches: Gender and the Making of the British Working Class*, Berkeley: University of California Press.
Clarke, Peter (2007) [1971] *Lancashire and the New Liberalism*, Cambridge: Cambridge University Press.
Clemens, Raymond and Graham, Timothy (2007) *Introduction to Manuscript Studies*, Ithaca: Cornell University Press.
Cobb, Richard C., (1974) *Modern French History in Britain*, Oxford: Oxford University Press.
Cobbett, William, Dyck, Ian (2001) *Rural Rides*, Harmondsworth: Penguin.
Cohn, B. (1980) 'History and Anthropology: The State of Play', *Comparative Studies in Society and History* **22** (2) pp. 198–222.
—— (1990) [1987] *Anthropologist Among the Historians and Other Essays*, Oxford: Oxford University Press.

Cohn, Norman (2005) [1967] *Warrant for Genocide: The Myth of the Jewish World Conspiracy and the Protocols of the Elders of Zion*, Serif.

Cole, G. D. H. [1941] (1989) *Chartist Portraits*, Cassell.

Cole, G. D. H. and Postgate, Raymond (1938) *The Common People 1746–1938*, Methuen.

Coleman, D. C. (1992) *Myth, History and the Industrial Revolution*, Hambledon.

Colish, Marcia L. (1997) *Medieval Foundations of the Western Intellectual Tradition, 400–1400*, New Haven: Yale University Press.

Colley, Linda (2004) [2002] *Captives: Britain, Empire and the World 1600–1850*, Pimlico.

—— (2009) *Britons: Forging the Nation 1707–1837*, New Haven: Yale University Press.

Collini, Stefan (1999) *English Pasts: Essays in History and Culture*, Oxford: Oxford University Press.

Conan Doyle, Arthur, 'The Man with the Twisted Lip', *The Strand Magazine*, London, December 1891, Vol. 2, No. 12.

Corfield, Penelope J. (2007) *Time and the Shape of History*, New Haven: Yale University Press.

Cosgrove, Denis E. (1999) *Mappings*, Reaktion.

Cowling, Maurice (1971) *Impact of Labour 1920–1924: The Beginning of Modern British Politics*, Cambridge: Cambridge University Press.

Crafts, N. F. R. and Harley, C. K. (1985) 'English Workers' Real Wages During the Industrial Revolution: Some Remaining Problems', *Journal of Economic History* **45** pp. 139–144.

—— (1992) 'Output Growth and the British Industrial Revolution: A Restatement of the Crafts-Harley View', *Economic History Review* **45** pp. 703–30.

Craig, David (2010) '"High Politics" and the "New Political History"', *Historical Journal* **53** pp. 453–75.

Crewe, Emma (2005) *Lords of Parliament: Manners, Rituals and Politics*, Manchester: Manchester University Press.

Daly, Mary (1979) *Gyn/Ecology*, The Women's Press.

Dangerfield, George (1997) [1935] *The Strange Death of Liberal England*, Stanford: Stanford University Press.

Darnton, Robert (2001) [1984] *The Great Cat Massacre: And Other Episodes of French Cultural History*, Harmondsworth: Penguin.

Davidoff, Leonore and Hall, Catherine (1987) *Family Fortunes: Men and Women of the English Middle Class 1780–1850*, Routledge.

Davis, David Brion (1988) [1966] *The Problem of Slavery in Western Culture*, Oxford: Oxford University Press.

Dawson, Graham (1994) *Soldier Heroes: British Adventure, Empire and the Imaginings of Masculinities*, Routledge.

De Beauvoir, Simone (2010) [1949] *The Second Sex*, Vintage.

Deliege, Robert (2004) *Lévi-Strauss Today*, Oxford: Oxford University Press.

Delogu, Paolo (2002) *An Introduction to Medieval History*, Duckworth.

Denikin, Anton (1975) *The Career of a Tsarist Officer: Memoirs, 1872–1916*, Minnesota: University of Minnesota Press.

Dennis, Richard (1991) 'History, Geography, and Historical Geography', *Social Science History* **15** (2) pp. 265–88.

Driver, Felix (2001) *Geography Militant: Geography, Exploration and Empire*, Oxford: Oxford University Press.

Duffy, Eamon (2005) [1992] *The Stripping of the Altars: Traditional Religion in England c.1400–c.1580*, New Haven: Yale University Press.

Dunn, Elizabeth Bramm (2007) 'Preserving or Distorting History? Scholars Reflect on Archival Repositories', *Historical Methods* **40** (4).

Dyer, Christopher (2009) *Making a Living in the Middle Ages: The People of Britain 850–1520*, New Haven: Yale University Press.

Eatwell, Roger (2006) 'Explaining Fascism and Ethnic Cleansing: The Three Dimensions of Charisma and the Four Dark Sides of Nationalism', *Political Studies Review* **4** pp. 263–278.

Echols, Alice (1989) *Daring to Be Bad: Radical Feminism in America 1967–1975*, Minnesota: University of Minnesota Press.

Eley, Geoff (2005) *A Crooked Line: From Cultural History to the History of Society*, Ann Arbor: University of Michigan Press.

Elsner, John and Cardinal, Roger (1994) *The Cultures of Collecting*, Reaktion Books.

Elton, G. E. R. (2002) [1967] *The Practice of History*, Oxford: Blackwell.

—— *Return to Essentials: Some Reflections on the Present State of Historical Study*, Cambridge: Cambridge University Press, 1991.

Englander, David and Oday, Rosemary (1983) *Mr Charles Booth's Inquiry: Life and Labour of the People in London Reconsidered*, Hambledon.

—— (eds) (1995) *Retrieved Riches: Social Investigation in Britain 1840–1914*, Aldershot: Ashgate.

Evans-Pritchard, E. E. (1971) *The Azande: History and Political Institutions*, Oxford: Clarendon Press.

Ferguson, Niall (ed.) (2011) [1997] *Virtual History: Alternatives and Counterfactuals*, Penguin.

—— (2011) *Civilization: The West and the Rest*, Allen Lane.

Ferguson, Wallace K. (1956) *The Renaissance*, New York: Holt.

—— (1981) [1948] *The Renaissance in Historical Thought: Five Centuries of Interpretation*, New York: AMS Press.

Fernández-Armesto, Felipe (1996) *Millennium*, Black Swan.

Figes, Orlando (1997) *A People's Tragedy: The Russian Revolution 1891–1924*, Pimlico.

Finn, Margot (1993) *After Chartism: Class and Nation in English Radical Politics, 1848–1874*, Cambridge: Cambridge University Press.

Fishman, William J. (1988) *East End 1888: Life in a London Borough Among the Labouring Poor*, Duckworth.

Fitzpatrick, Martin, Jones, Peter, Knellwolf, Christa and McCalman, Iain (eds) (2004) *The Enlightenment World*, Routledge.

Floud, Roderick *et al.* (1990) *Height, Health and History: Nutritional Status in the United Kingdom, 1750–1980*, Cambridge: Cambridge University Press.

Foucault, Michel (1995) [1977] *Discipline and Punish: Birth of the Prison*, New York: Vintage Books.

—— (2001) [1965] *Madness and Civilization: A History of Insanity in the Age of Reason*, Routledge.

—— (2002) [1972] *The Archaeology of Knowledge*, Routledge.

—— (2003) [1973] *The Birth of the Clinic: An Archaeology of Medical Perception*, Routledge.

Fredenson, Patrick (2009) 'Business History and History', in Jones, G. and Zeitlin, J. (eds) *Oxford Handbook of Business History*, Oxford: Oxford University Press.

Fukuyama, Francis (1992) *The End of History and the Last Man*, New York: Free Press.

Fulbrook, Mary (ed.) (1997) *German History Since 1800*, Arnold.

Fussner, Frank (1977) [1962] *The Historical Revolution: English Historical Writing and Thought, 1580–1640*, Westport, Conn: Greenwood Press.

Gallois, William (2007) *Time, Religion and History*, Harlow: Pearson Longman.

Gardiner, Samuel Rawson (1894) [1863] *History of England from the Accession of James I to the Outbreak of the Civil War 1603–1642*, Longmans Green & Co.

Geary, Patrick J. (1994) *Phantoms of Remembrance: Memory and Oblivion at the First Millennium*, Princeton: Princeton University Press.

Ghosh, Peter 'Whig Interpretation of History' in Boyd, K. (ed.) (1999) *Encyclopaedia of Historians and History Writing*, Fitzroy Dearborn.

Gibbon, Edward (1998) *The History of the Decline and Fall of the Roman Empire*, Lentin, D. and Norman, B. (eds), Ware: Wordsworth.

Ginzburg, Carlo (1983) *The Night Battles: Witchcraft and Agrarian Cults in the Sixteenth and Seventeenth Centuries*, Routledge & Kegan Paul.

—— (1990) *Myths, Emblems, Clues*, Hutchinson Radius.

—— (1992) [1980] *The Cheese and the Worms: The Cosmos of a Sixteenth-Century Miller*, Baltimore: Johns Hopkins University Press.

—— (2004) [1989] *Ecstasies: Deciphering the Witches' Sabbath*, Chicago: University of Chicago Press.

Given-Wilson, Christopher (2007) [2004], *Chronicles: The Writing of History in Medieval Britain*, Hambledon Continuum.

Glinert, Edward (2000) *A Literary Guide to London*, Penguin Books.

Goldthorpe, John H. (1991) 'The Uses of History in Sociology: Reflections on Some Recent Tendencies', *British Journal of Sociology* **42** (2) pp. 211–230.

—— (1994) 'The Uses of History in Sociology: A Reply', *British Journal of Sociology* **45** (1) pp. 55–77.

Gomery, Douglas and Allen, Robert Clyde (1993) [1985] *Film History: Theory and Practice*, Boston: McGraw-Hill.

Gooder, Eileen (1979) [1961], *Latin for Local History: An Introduction*, Longman.

Goody, Jack (1983) *The Development of the Family and Marriage in Europe*, Cambridge: Cambridge University Press.

Gospel, Howard *Skill Formation for British Industry: A Historical and Comparative Perspective* (forthcoming).

Gourvish, Terence Richard and Anson, Mike (2006) *The Official History of Britain and the Channel Tunnel*, Routledge.

Gourvish, Terence Richard and Blake, N. (1986) *British Railways 1948–73: A Business History*, Cambridge: Cambridge University Press.

Gras, Norman (1939) *Business and Capitalism: An Introduction to Business History*, New York: F. S. Crofts.

Graves, Robert and Unsworth, Barry (2006) *I, Claudius: From the Autobiography of Tiberius Claudius, Emperor of the Romans, born 10 BC, Murdered and Deified AD 54*, Penguin Classics.

Green, Abigail (2010) *Moses Montiefiore: Jewish Liberator, Imperial Hero*, Cambridge, Mass.; London: Belknap Press of Harvard University Press.

Green, Ewen Henry Harvey (ed.) (1997) *An Age of Transition: British Politics, 1880–1914*, Edinburgh: Edinburgh University Press.

Green, John Richard (1992) [1892–94] *A Short History of the English People*, Folio Society.

Green, Simon J. D. (1996) *Religion in the Age of Decline: Organisation and Experience in Industrial Yorkshire 1870–1920*, Cambridge: Cambridge University Press.

Groves, Reginald (1938) *But We Shall Rise Again: A Narrative History of Chartism*, Secker and Warburg.

Guha, Ranaji (1982) *Subaltern Studies: Writings on South Asian History and Society*, Oxford: Oxford University Press.

Gunaway, Bryan (2003) 'Review of Carolyn Steedman, Dust: The Archive and Cultural History', *H. Net Reviews in the Humanities & Social Sciences*.

Gunn, Simon (2006) *History and Cultural Theory*, Harlow: Pearson Longman.

Habermas, Jurgen (1987) [1972], *Knowledge and Human Interests*, Cambridge: Polity.

Hale, John Rigby (1967) *The Evolution of British Historiography From Bacon to Namier*, Macmillan.

Hall, Catherine (1992) 'The Tale of Samuel and Jemima: Gender and Working Class Culture in Nineteenth Century England', *White, Male and Middle-Class: Explorations in Feminism and History*, Cambridge: Polity.

Hallam, Elizabeth M. (1990) 'Nine Centuries of Keeping the Public Records', in Martin, Geoffrey Haward and Spufford, Peter (eds) *The Records of the Nation: The Public Record Office, 1838–1988: The British Record Society, 1888–1988*, Woodbridge: Boydell.

Hallam, Henry (1908) [1827] *Constitutional History of England from the Accession of Henry VII to the Death of George II* (2 vols), John Murray.

Hamblyn, Richard (2002) [2001] *The Invention of Clouds: How an Amateur Meteorologist Forged the Language of the Skies*, Picador.

Hamilton, Carolyn *et al.* (eds) (2002) *Refiguring the Archive*, Dordrecht, Netherlands: Kluwer Academic Publishers.

Hamish Fraser, W. (2010) *Chartism in Scotland*, Pontypool: Merlin Press.

Hammond, Barbara and Hammond (1947) [1934] *The Bleak Age*, West Drayton: Penguin Books.

—— (1962) [1930] *The Age of the Chartists, 1832–1852: A Study of Discontent*, Hamden, Conn.: Archon Books.

Hancock, David (1995) *Citizens of the World. London Merchants and the Integration of the British Atlantic Community, 1735–1785*, Cambridge: Cambridge University Press.

Hannah, Leslie and Ackrill, Margaret (2001) *Barclays: The Business of Banking 1690–1996*, Cambridge: Cambridge University Press.

Hareven, Tamara K. (1982) *Family Time and Historical Time: The Relationship between Family and Work in a New England Industrial Community*, Cambridge: Cambridge University Press.

Harper, Sue and Porter, Vincent (2003) *The Decline of Deference: British Cinema of the 1950s*, Oxford: Oxford University Press.

Harris, Jose (1994) *Private Lives, Public Spirit: Britain 1870–1914*, Harmondsworth: Penguin.

Harrison, Brian (1996) *The Transformation of British Politics, 1860–1995*, Oxford: Oxford University Press.

Harvey, David (1990) [1989] *The Condition of Postmodernity: An Enquiry into the Origins of Cultural Change*, Cambridge, MA; Oxford; Victoria: Blackwell Publishing.

Hartwell, Ronald Max (1972) [1965] *The Industrial Revolution in England*, Historical Association.

Haskell, Francis (1993) *History and its Images: Art and the Interpretation of the Past*, New Haven: Yale University Press.

Hauser, Arnold (1999) [1951] *Social History of Art, 1892–1978*, Routledge.

Held, David (*et al.*) (1999) *Global Transformations: Politics, Economics and Culture*, Cambridge: Polity Press.

Herodotus (2003) *The Histories*, Harmondsworth: Penguin.

Hill, Christopher (1991) [1972] *The World Turned Upside Down: Radical Ideas during the English Revolution*, Harmondsworth: Penguin.

Himmelfarb, Gertrude (2004) *The New History and the Old: Critical Essays and Reappraisals*, Cambridge, Mass.; London: Belknap.

Hinde, Andrew (2003) *England's Population: A History since the Domesday Survey*, Hodder Headline.

History and Sociology (1976) *British Journal of Sociology* **27** (3) pp. 295–412.

Hobsbawm, Eric and Ranger, Terence (1992) [1983] *The Invention of Tradition*, Cambridge: Cambridge University Press.

Hoffman, John and Graham, Paul (2006) *Introduction to Political Concepts*, Harlow: Pearson Education.

Hodgson, Marshall G. S. (1974) *Venture of Islam: Conscience and History in a World Civilization*, Chicago: University of Chicago Press.

—— and Burke, Edmund (1993) *Rethinking World History: Essays on Europe, Islam and World History*, Cambridge: Cambridge University Press.

Hornblower, Simon (ed.) (1994) *Greek Historiography*, Oxford: Clarendon Press.

Howkins, Alun (1985) *Poor Labouring Men: Rural Radicalism in Norfolk, 1872–1923*, Routledge & Kegan Paul.

Huizinga, John (2001) [1919] *The Waning of the Middle Ages*, S.l.: Benediction Classics.

Humphries, Jane (1977) 'Class Struggle and the Persistence of the Working Class Family', *Cambridge Journal of Economics* **47** (1).

Hunt, Edwin S. and Murray, James M. (1999) *A History of Business in Medieval Europe 1200–1550*, Cambridge: Cambridge University Press.

Hunt, Lynn (ed.) (1989) *The New Cultural History*, Berkeley: University of California Press.

Ife, B. W. (1985) *Reading and Fiction in Golden-Age Spain: A Platonist Critique and Some Picaresque Replies*, Cambridge: Cambridge University Press.

Iggers, Georg G., Wang, Q. Edward and Mukherjee, Supriya (2008) *A Global History of Modern Historiography*, Harlow: Pearson Longman.

Ignatieff, Michael (1994) [1984] *The Needs of Strangers*, Vintage.

Jacobs, Jane (1970) [1969] *The Economy of Cities*, New York: Vintage Books.

—— (1985) [1984] *Cities and the Wealth of Nations: Principles of Economic Life*, New York: Vintage Books.

—— (1994) [1993] *Systems of Survival: A Dialogue on the Moral Foundations of Commerce and Politics*, Hodder & Stoughton.

—— (2000) [1961] *The Death and Life of Great American Cities*, Pimlico.

—— (2000) *The Nature of Economies*, New York: Vintage Books.

—— (2004) *Dark Age Ahead*, New York: Random House.

Jenkins, Keith (1997) *The Postmodern History Reader*, Routledge.

Jordanova, Ludmilla (2006) [2000] *History in Practice*, Hodder Arnold.

Josephus (1981) [1959] *The Jewish War*, Harmondsworth: Penguin.

Joyce, Patrick (1994) *Democratic Subjects: The Self and the Social in Nineteenth-Century England*, Cambridge: Cambridge University Press.

—— (1999) 'The Politics of the Liberal Archive', *History of the Human Sciences*, **12** (2), pp. 35–49.

Kassow, Samuel D. (2009) [2007] *Who Will Write Our History? Rediscovering a Hidden Archive from the Warsaw Ghetto*, Harmondsworth: Penguin.

Kaye, Harvey J. (1995) [1984] *The British Marxist Historians: An Introductory Analysis*, Basingstoke: Macmillan Press.

Kean, Hilda, Martin, Paul and Morgan, Sally (eds) (2000) *Seeing History: Public History Now in Britain*, Francis Boutle.

Kekewich, Lucille (ed.) (2000) *The Impact of Humanism: A Cultural Enquiry*, New Haven: Yale University Press.

Kelley, Robert (1992) 'Public History: its Origins, Nature and Prospects', in Leffler, Phyllis K. and Brent, Joseph (eds) *Public History Readings*, Malabar, Fla.: Krieger Publishing.

Kelly, Joan (1984) *Women, History and Theory: The Essays of Joan Kelly*, Chicago: University of Chicago Press.

Kennan, George F. (1968) *Democracy and the Student Left*, Hutchinson.

Kern, Stephen (2003) [1983] *The Culture of Time and Space, 1880–1918*, Cambridge, Mass.: Harvard University Press.

Khaldi, Tarif (1994) *Arabic Historical Thought in the Classical Period*, New York: Cambridge University Press.

Kirby, Peter, (1997) 'The Standard of Living Debate and the Industrial Revolution', *Refresh* **25**.

Klingender, Francis and Elton, Arthur (1975) [1968] *Art and the Industrial Revolution*, St Albans, Herts: Paladin.

Kochan, Lionel (1977) *The Jew and his History*, Macmillan.

Ladurie, Emmanuelle Le Roy (1990) [1978] *Montaillou: Cathars and Catholics in a French village, 1294–1324*, Harmondsworth: Penguin.

—— (2003) [1980] *Carnival in Romans: Mayhem and Massacre in a French City*, Phoenix Press.

Lamoreaux, Raff *et al.*, 'Economic Theory and Business History', *Oxford Handbook of Business History* pp. 9–36, 37–66.

Landes, David (1999) [1998] *The Wealth and Poverty of Nations: Why Some are So Rich and Some So Poor*, Abacus.

Larner, Christina (1983) [1981] *Enemies of God: The Witch Hunt in Scotland*, Oxford: Blackwell.

Laslett, Peter (1971) [1965] *The World We Have Lost*, Methuen.

Laslett, Peter (ed.) with assistance from Wall, Richard (1972) *Household and Family in Past Time: Comparative Studies in the Size and Structure of the Domestic Group Over the Last Three Centuries in England, France, Serbia, Japan and Colonial North America, with Further Materials from Western Europe*, Cambridge: Cambridge University Press.

Lawrence, Jon (1998) *Speaking for the People: Party, Language and Popular Politics in England, 1867–1914*, Cambridge: Cambridge University Press.

Lawrence, Jon and Taylor, Miles (eds) (1997) *Party, State and Society: Electoral Behaviour in Britain since 1820*, Aldershot: Scolar Press.

Le Goff, Jacques (1980) *Time, Work and Culture in the Middle Ages*, Chicago: University of Chicago Press.

—— (2007) [2005] *The Birth of Europe*, Malden, MA; Oxford: Blackwell.

Lentin, Anthony *et al.* (1979) *Gibbon's The Decline and Fall of the Roman Empire*, Milton Keynes: Open University Press.

Lester, Alan (2001) *Imperial Networks: Creating Identities in Nineteenth-Century South Africa and Britain*, Routledge.

Levine, Joseph (1991) *Battle of the Books: History and Literature in the Augustan Age*, Ithaca: Cornell University Press.

Lévi-Strauss, Claude (1993–1994) [1958] *Structural Anthropology*, Harmondsworth: Penguin.

Levy, Fred Jacob (2004) [1967] *Tudor Historical Thought*, Toronto: University of Toronto Press.

Lindert, Peter H. and Williamson, Jeffrey G. (1985) 'English Workers' Real Wages: Reply to Crafts', *Journal of Economic History* **45** pp. 145–53.

Livingstone, David N. (1992) *The Geographical Tradition: Episodes in the History of a Contested Enterprise,* Oxford: Blackwell

Lowenthal, David (1985) *The Past is a Foreign Country*, Cambridge: Cambridge University Press.

—— (1998) [1996] *The Heritage Crusade and the Spoils of History*, Cambridge: Cambridge University Press.

Lüdtke, Alf *et al.* (1997) *Was bleibt von marxistischen Perspektiven in der Geschichtsforschung?*, Germany: Wallstein Verlay.

MacCalman, Iain (1988) *Underworld: Prophets, Revolutionaries and Pornographers in London, 1795–1840*, Cambridge: Cambridge University Press.

MacFarlane, Alan (1970) *The Family Life of Ralph Josselin: A Seventeenth-Century Clergyman. An Essay in Historical Anthropology*, New York, Norton.

—— (1973) *Times Literary Supplement*.

McCullin, Don (1994) *Sleeping With Ghosts*, Cape.

McC. Weis, Charles, Pottle, Frederick Albert (1971) *Boswell In Extremes, 1776–1778*, Heinemann.

McGinn, Bernard (1985) *The Calabrian Abbot: Joachim of Fiore in the History of Western Thought*, New York: Macmillan.

McKeon, Michael (1987) *The Origins of the English Novel, 1600–1740*, Baltimore: The John Hopkins University Press.

McNeill, William (1963) *The Rise of the West*, Chicago: Chicago University Press.

Malinowski, Bronislav (1929) *Sexual Life of Savages in North West Melanesia*, Routledge and Kegan Paul.

Mandler, Peter (1997) *The Fall and Rise of the Stately Home*, New Haven: Yale University Press.

—— (2002) *History and National Life*, Profile Books.

—— (2006) *The English National Character*, New Haven: Yale University Press.

Manning, Patrick (2003) *Navigating World History: Historians Create a Global Past*, Basingstoke: Palgrave.

Marchand, L. A. (1957) *Byron: A Biography, 3 vols.*, John Murray.

Marcus, Jacob, R. (1999) [1938] *The Jew in the Medieval World: A Sourcebook*, Cincinnati: Hebrew Union College Press.

Marincola, John (2000) *Herodotus, The Histories* (revised introduction and notes).

Marriott, John (2003) *The Other Empire: Metropolis, India and Progress in the Colonial Imagination*, Manchester: Manchester University Press.

Martin, C. T. (1976)[1910] *The Record Interpreter*, Dorking: Kohler and Coombes.

Martin, G. H. (1990) 'The Public Records in 1988', in Martin and Spufford (eds), *The Records of the Nation: The Public Record Office, 1838–1988*, Woodbridge: Boydell.

—— and Spufford, Peter (eds) (1990) *The Records of the Nation*, Woodbridge: Boydell.

Martin, Paul (1999) 'Look, See, Hear: A Remembrance with Approaches to Contemporary Public History at Ruskin', in Andrews, Geof, Kean, Hilda and Thompson, Jane (eds), *Ruskin College, Contesting*

Knowledge, Dissenting Politics, Lawrence & Wishart.
Marwick, Arthur (1998) *The Sixties: Cultural Revolution in Britain, France, Italy and the United States*, Oxford: Oxford University Press.
—— (2001) *The New Nature of History: Knowledge, Evidence, Language*, Basingstoke: Palgrave.
Marx, Karl (1990) [1886] *Capital: A Critical Analysis of Capital Production*, Chicago: Encyclopædia Britannica.
Marx, Karl and Engels, Frederick (2002) [1844] *The Communist Manifesto*, Harmondsworth, Penguin.
Meinecke, Friedrich (1946) *The German Catastrophe: Reflections and Recollections*, trans. Sidney B. Fay, Cambridge, Mass.: Harvard University Press.
Mellor, Ronald (1999) *The Roman Historians*, Routledge.
—— (ed.) (2004) *The Historians of Ancient Rome*, Routledge.
Merridale, Catherine (2001) *Night of Stone: Death and Memory in Russia*, New York: Viking.
Michie, Ranald (1992) *The City of London: Continuity and Change, 1850–1990*, Basingstoke: Macmillan.
Mighall, Robert *A Geography of Victorian Gothic Fiction: Mapping History's Nightmares*, Oxford: Oxford University Press.
Miller, Cecilia (1993) *Giambattista Vico: Imagination and Historical Knowledge*, Basingstoke: Macmillan.
Mokr, Joel (2002) *The Gifts of Athena: Historical Origins of the Knowledge Economy*, Woodstock: Princeton University Press.
—— (2009) *The Enlightened Economy: An Economic History of Britain, 1700–1850*, New Haven: Yale University Press.
Momigliano, Arnaldo (1990) *Classical Foundations of Modern Historiography*, Berkeley: California University Press.
Monmonier, Mark (1996) *How to Lie with Maps*, Chicago: University of Chicago Press.
Mumford, Lewis (1934) *Technics and Civilization*, Routledge.
—— (1938) *The Culture of Cities*, Secker & Warburg.
—— (1944) *The Condition of Man*, Secker & Warburg.
Muthu, Sankar (2003) *Enlightenment Against Empire*, Princeton: Princeton University Press.
Nead, Lynda (2000) *Victorian Babylon: People, Streets and Images in Nineteenth Century London*, New Haven, Yale University Press.
Newens, Stan (2007) 'The Genesis of East End Underworld: Chapters in the Life of Arthur Harding', *History Workshop Journal* **64** pp. 347–53.
Newton, Isaac (1999) *The Principia: Mathematical Principles of Natural Philosophy*, Cohen, Bernard and Whitman, Anne (trans.), Berkeley: California University Press.
Obeyesekere, Gananath (1997) *The Apotheosis of Captain Cook: European Mythmaking in the Pacific*, Princeton: Princeton University Press.
Offer, Avner (1989) *The First World War: An Agrarian Interpretation*, Oxford: Oxford University Press.
Oliver, W. H. (1979) *Prophets and Millennialists: The Uses of Biblical Prophecy in England from the 1790s to the 1840s*, Oxford: Oxford University Press.
The Parliament Rolls of Medieval England, 1275–1504 (2005) 16 vols., Woodbridge: Boydell Press.
Parsons, Talcott (1951) *The Social System*, Routledge and Kegan Paul.
Passerini, Luisa (1987) *Fascism in Popular Memory: The Cultural Experience of the Turin Working Class*, Cambridge: Cambridge University Press.
Perkin, Harold (1981) *The Structured Crowd*, Brighton: Harvester Press.
—— (1989) *The Rise of Professional Society*, Routledge.
Perks, Robert and Thompson, Alistair (eds) (2006) *The Oral History Reader*, Routledge.
Perry, Marvin and Schweitzer, Frederick M. (2002) *Antisemitism: Myth and Hate from Antiquity to the Present*, Basingstoke: Palgrave.
Pike, E. Royston (1966) *Human Documents of the Industrial Revolution in Britain*, Allen & Unwin.
Plumb, J. R. (1988) *The Making of an Historian. The Collected Essays of J. H. Plumb*, 3 vols., Brighton: Harvester Wheatsheaf.

—— (2003) [1969] *The Death of the Past*, Basingstoke: Palgrave.

Portelli, Alessandro (1991) *The Death of Luigi Trastulli and Other Stories*, Albany: State University of New York Press.

Porter, Roy (1995) *Enlightenment: Britain and the Creation of the Modern World*, Allen Lane.

Poster, Mark (2003) 'History in the Digital Domain', *Historian* **4** pp. 17–32.

Potts, Alex (1988) 'Picturing the Modern Metropolis: Images of London in the Nineteenth Century', *History Workshop Journal* **26** (1) pp. 28–56.

Pounds, N. J. G. (1994) [1974] *Economic History of Medieval Europe*, Longman.

Press, G. A. (1982) *The Development of the Idea of History in Antiquity*, Kingston, Ont.: McGill-Queen's University Press.

Pryde, E. B. and Greenway, D. E. (eds) (1986) [1941] *Handbook of British Chronology*, Cambridge: Cambridge University Press.

von Ranke, Leopold (1981) *The Secret of World History: Selected Writings on the Art and Science of History* (ed.) and trans. Roger Wines, New York: Fordham University Press.

Readman, Paul (2009) 'The State of Twentieth-Century British Political History', *Journal of Public Policy* **21** (3).

Reeder, David (1995) 'Representations of Metropolis: Descriptions of the Social Environment in Life and Labour', in Englander, David and O'Day, Rosemary (eds), *Retrieved Riches*.

Richmond, Theo (1995) *Konin: A Quest*, Cape.

Roberts, Elizabeth (1996) [1984] *A Woman's Place: An Oral History of Working Class Women*, Oxford: Blackwell.

—— (1995) *Women: Work 1840–1940*, Cambridge: Cambridge University.

Roberts, Stephen (2008) *The Chartist Prisoners*, Oxford: Peter Lang.

Robertson, E. W. (1872) *Historical Essays in Connexion with the Land and Church etc.*, Edinburgh: Edmonston and Doublas.

Robinson, Chase F. (2003) *Islamic Historiography*, Cambridge: Cambridge University Press.

Rohrbacher, David (2002) *The Historians of Late Antiquity*, Routledge.

Roper, Lyndal (1994) *Oedipus and the Devil: Witchcraft, Sexuality and Religion in Early Modern Europe*, Routledge.

Rose, Gillian and Ogborn, Miles (1988) 'Feminism and Historical Geography', *Journal of Historical Geography* **14** (4) pp. 405–9.

Rothstein, Theodore (1984) [1929] *From Chartism to Labourism*, Garland.

Rowbotham, Sheila (1973) *Hidden from History: 300 Years of Women's Oppression and the Fight Against It*, Pluto Press.

Royle, Edward (1996) [1980] *Chartism*, Longman.

Ryrie, Alex (2009) 'The Canon: The Stripping of the Altars: Traditional Religion in England, 1400–1580 By Eamon Duffy', *Times Higher Supplement*, 7 May 2009.

Sahlins, Marshall (1981) *Historical Metaphors and Mythical Realities: Structure in the Early History of the Sandwich Islands*, Michigan: Michigan University Press.

—— (1987) *Islands of History*, Chicago: University of Chicago Press.

—— (1995) *How 'Natives' Think: About Captain Cook, For Example*, Chicago: University of Chicago Press.

—— (2004) *Apologies to Thucydides: Understanding History and Culture and Vice-Versa*, Chicago: University of Chicago Press.

Said, Edward (1991) *Orientalism: Western Conceptions of the Orient*, Harmondsworth: Penguin.

Samuel, Raphael (1975) 'Quarry Roughs' in idem (ed.) *Village Life and Labour*, Routledge and Kegan Paul.

—— (1980) *East End Underworld: Chapters in the Life of Arthur Harding*, Routledge.

—— (1980) 'On the Methods of History Workshop: A Reply', *History Workshop Journal* **9** pp. 162–75.

—— (1994) *Theatres of Memory*, Verso.

Saunders, Peter (1981) *Social Theory and the Urban Question*, Hutchinson.

Savage, Mike and Miles, Andrew (1994) *The Remaking of the British Working Class, 1840–1940*,

Routledge.
Scarpino, Philip V. (1993) 'Some Thoughts on Defining, Evaluating, and Rewarding Public Scholarship', *Public Historian* **15** (2) pp. 55–61.
Schama, Simon (1987) *The Embarrassment of Riches: An Interpretation of Dutch Culture in the Golden Age*, New York: Knopf.
—— (1989) *Citizens: A Chronicle of the French Revolution*, Viking.
—— (1991) *Dead Certainties*, Granta.
—— (1995) *Landscape and Memory*, Harper Collins.
—— (2002) *A History of Britain*, 3 vols., BBC.
Schnepf, Ariane (2006) *Our Original Rights as a People*, Oxford: Peter Lang.
Scott, Joan W. (1986) 'Gender: A Useful Category of Historical Analysis', *American Historical Review* **91** (5) pp. 1053–1075.
—— (1999) *Gender and the Politics of History*, New York, Columbia University Press.
Scott, Sir Walter (1829) *The Antiquary*, Edinburgh: Robert Cadell.
Seeskin, Kenneth (2004) *Maimonides on the Origin of the World*, Cambridge: Cambridge University Press.
—— (2004) 'Maimonides Sense of History', *Jewish History* **18** pp. 125–8.
Selden, Anthony and Pappworth, Joanna (1983) *By Word of Mouth: Elite Oral History*, Methuen.
Sellar, W. C. and Yeatman, R. J. (1930)*1066 and All That*, Methuen.
Shiach, Morag (2004) *Modernism, Labour and Selfhood in British Literature and Culture, 1890–1930*, Cambridge: Cambridge University Press.
Sinha, Mrinalini (1995) *Colonial Masculinity: The 'Manly Englishman' and the 'Effeminate Bengali' in the Late Nineteenth Century*, Manchester: Manchester University Press.
Skinner, Quentin (1981) *Machiavelli*, Oxford: Oxford University Press.
Slack, Paul (1985) *The Impact of Plague in Tudor and Stuart England*, Routledge and Kegan Paul.
Smith, Adam (1977) [1772] *Wealth of Nations*, 2 vols., Everyman.
Sobel, Dava (1998) *Longitude*, New York: Walker.
Spear, Percival (1994) [1965] *A History of Modern India, 1740–1975*, Harmondsworth: Penguin.
Spear, Thomas (1981) 'Oral Tradition: Whose History?', Journal of Public History, **16**(3), July.
Spengler, Oswald (1922) *Decline of the West*, Allen & Unwin.
Spivak, Gyatri (2010) [1993] Rosalind C. Morris (ed.) *Can the Subaltern Speak?: Reflections on the History of an Idea*, New York; Chichester: Columbia University Press.
Stedman Jones, Gareth (1971) *Outcast London: A Study of the Relationship Between Classes in Victorian London*, Oxford: Clarendon Press.
—— (1983) 'Rethinking Chartism', in idem, *Languages of Class*, Cambridge: Cambridge University Press.
—— (2002) Introduction, *Communist Party Manifesto*, Harmondsworth, Penguin.
—— (2004) *An End to Poverty? An Historical Debate*, Profile Books.
Steedman, Carolyn (2001) *Dust*, Manchester: Manchester University Press.
Stiglmayr, Joseph (1909) 'Dionysius the Pseudo-Areopagite', *The Catholic Encyclopaedia*, vol. 5, New York: Robert Appleton Company, 1909. (Available on <http://www.newadvent.org/cathen/05013a.htm>.)
Stubbs, William (1873–78) *Constitutional History of England*, Oxford: Clarendon Press.
Suetonius (2003) *The Twelve Caesars*, Harmondsworth: Penguin.
Sureda, Joan (2008) *The Golden Age of Spain: Painting, Sculpture, Architecture*, New York: Vendome Press.
Sweet, Rosemary (2004) *Antiquaries*, Hambledon Press.
Tacitus (2008) *The Annals*, Oxford: Oxford University Press.
Tanner, Duncan (1990) *Political Change and the Labour Party, 1900–1918*, Cambridge: Cambridge University Press.
Taylor, Miles (1996) 'Rethinking the Chartists: Searching for Synthesis in the Historiography of Chartism', *Historical Journal* **39** pp. 479–95.
Tennyson, G. B. (1984) *A Carlyle Reader*, Cambridge: Cambridge University Press.
Thomas, Hugh (1979) *An Unfinished History of the World*, Hamish Hamilton.

Thomas, Keith (1971) *Religion and the Decline of Magic*, New York: Charles Scribner.
Thompson, Dorothy (1984) *The Chartists: Popular Politics in the Industrial Revolution*, Hounslow: Temple Smith.
Thompson, E. P. (1976) Pit-Men, Preachers and Politics: The Effects of Methodism in a Durham Mining Community by Robert Moore, *The British Journal of Sociology* **27** (3), Special Issue. History and Sociology pp. 387–402.
—— (1978) *The Poverty of Theory and other Essays*, Merlin Press.
—— (1991) 'The Moral Economy of the Crowd', in idem, *Customs in Common*, Merlin Press.
—— (1991) 'Rough Music', in *Customs in Common*.
—— (1991) 'Time, Work Discipline and Industrial Capitalism', in *Customs in Common*.
—— (1993) 'Theory and Evidence', *History Workshop Journal* **35** pp. 274–
Thompson, Paul (1978) *The Voice of the Past: Oral History*, Oxford: Oxford University Press.
Thucydides (1998) *The Peloponnesian War*, (eds) Blanco, Walter and Roberts, Jennifer, New York: Norton.
Tignor, Robert *et al.* (2008) *Worlds Together, Worlds Apart*, New York, Norton.
Tonkin, Elizabeth (1992) *Narrating Our Pasts: The Social Construction of Oral History*, Cambridge: Cambridge University Press.
Tosh, John (2002) *The Pursuit of History*, Longman.
—— (2005) *Manliness and Masculinities in Nineteenth Century Britain*, Harlow: Pearson.
Toynbee, Arnold (1933–61) *A Study of History*, 12 vols., Oxford: Oxford University Press.
Trouillot, Michel-Rolph (1995) *Silencing the Past: Power and the Production of History*, Boston, Mass.: Beacon Press.
Underdown, David (1971) *Pride's Purge: Politics in the Puritan Revolution*, Oxford: Oxford University Press.
—— (1985) *Revel, Riot and Rebellion*, Oxford: Oxford University Press.
Usher, Stephen (1985) *The Historians of Greece and Rome*, Hamish Hamilton.
Vansina, Jan (1985) *Oral Tradition as History*, Oxford: Oxford University Press.
—— (1994) *Living in Africa*, Wisconsin: University of Wisconsin.
—— (2009) [1961] *Oral Tradition: A Study in Historical Methodology*, New Brunswick: Transaction.
Velody, Irving (1998) 'The Archive and the Human Sciences: Notes Towards a Theory of the Archive', *History of the Human Sciences* **11** (4) pp. 1–16.
Vico, Giambattista (1999) [1744] *Principi di Scienza Nouva* (The New Science), (trans.) March, David, Harmondsworth: Penguin.
Wallas, Graham (1898) *The Life of Francis Place*, Longman.
Wallis, Patrick, 'A Dreadful Heritage: Interpreting Epidemic Disease at Eyam, 1666–2000', *History Workshop Journal* (2006) **61** (1) pp. 31–56.
Walton, Annette (2010) *Oxford Historian*, **VIII** 2010.
Ward-Perkins, Bryan (2005) *The Fall of Rome and the End of Civilization*, Oxford: Oxford University Press.
Weber, Eugen (1977) *Peasants into Frenchmen: The Modernization of Rural France*, Chatto and Windus.
Webster, Jim (1989) 'Storming the Bastille: 1789 and All That', *Miniature Wargames* **71**.
Wells, H. G. (1920) *The Outline of History*, Cassell.
—— (2005) *The Shape of Things to Come*, Harmondsworth: Penguin.
Wiesner, Merry (1993) *Women and Gender in Early Modern Europe*, Cambridge: Cambridge University Press.
Wilcox, D. J. (1987) *The Measure of Times Past: Pre-Newtonian Chronologies and the Rhetoric of Relative Time*, Chicago: University of Chicago Press.
Williams, Eric (1966) *Capitalism and Slavery*, Deutsch.
Williams, Francis (1947) *Fifty Years' March*, Odhams Press.
—— (1954) *The Magnificent Journey*, Odhams Press.
Williams, Raymond (2010) *Keywords: A Vocabulary of Culture and Society*, Fontana.
Williamson, Philip (2010) 'Maurice Cowling and Modern British Political History' in Robert Crowcroft

(ed.), *The Philosophy, Politics and Religion of British Democracy: Maurice Cowling and Conservatism* (2010).
Wilmer, E. (2000) Public History Resource Center, http://www.publichistory.org/what_is/definition.html.
Wilson, Adrian (1993) *Rethinking Social History: English Society 1570–1920 and its Interpretation*, Manchester: Manchester University Press.
Windscheffel, Alex (2007) *Popular Conservatism in Imperial London*, Royal Historical Society.
Wise, Sarah (2008) *The Blackest Streets: The Life and Death of a Victorian Slum*, Bodley Head.
Wolf, Eric (1997) *Europe and a People Without History*, Berkeley: University of California Press.
Wood, Marcus (2000) *Blind Memory: Visual Representations of Slavery in England and America, 1780–1865*, Manchester: Manchester University Press.
Woolf, D. R. (2000) *Reading History in Early Modern England*, Cambridge: Cambridge University Press.
Woolf, Virginia (2002) *Moments of Being*, (ed.) Schulkind, Jeanne, Pimlico Press.
Woolfson, Jonathan (ed.) (2005) *Renaissance Historiography*, Basingstoke: Macmillan.
Wright, Patrick (1998) *On Living in an Old Country: The National Past in Contemporary Britain*, Verso.
Wrigley, E. A. (1990) *Continuity, Chance and Change*, Cambridge: Cambridge University Press.
Wrigley, E. A. and Schofield, R. S. (1981) *The Population History of England, 1541–1871: A Reconstruction*, Edward Arnold.
Yonge, C. M. (1988) [1876] 'On Woman and the Church', cited in Moore, James (ed.) *Religion in Victorian Britain*, Manchester: Manchester University Press.
Young, Michael and Willmott, Peter (1957) *Family and Kinship in East London*, Routledge and Kegan Paul.
Young, Robert (1990) White Mythologies: Writing, History and the West, Routledge.
—— (2001) *Postcolonialism: An Historical Introduction*, Oxford: Oxford University Press.
Zemon Davis, Natalie (1987) *Fiction in the Archives: Pardon Tales and Their Tellers in Sixteenth-Century France*, Cambridge: Polity Press.
—— (2007) *Trickster Travels: A Sixteenth-Century Muslim between Worlds*, Faber.

Websites [online] (all addresses prefixed by http://www.)

ahds.ac.uk
Arts and Humanities Digital Service based at Essex University provides extensive information and guidance on digital resources. We have used the case study on suffrage (ahds.ac.uk/creating/case-studies/suffrage).

amdigital.co.uk
Contains details of the online resources made available by Adam Matthew Digital, an example of a commercial publisher in the field.

americanhistory.si.edu
National Museum of American History at the Smithsonian Institute, containing a large variety of online resources. We have used the case study of the attack on the Twin Towers (americanhistory.si.edu/september11).

archive.org
Internet archive containing a large library of online resources which are free to scholars and researchers.

bl.uk
Website of the British Library which provides access to the invaluable integrated catalogue of the materials held in their collections. We have used examples from their galleries (bl.uk/onlinegallery).

casebook.org
Contains a large variety of historical materials related to the Jack the Ripper murders.

cistercians.shef.ac.uk
Well designed and executed project at Sheffield University to investigate the lives and architecture of Cistercian monks in Yorkshire, England.

diamm.ac.uk
Digital Image Archive of Medieval Music is a free image library of European medieval polyphonic music created by a collaboration between Oxford University and Royal Holloway College, University of London.

hds.essex.ac.uk
Great Britain Historical Database Online provides access to a large collection of British statistics from the nineteenth and twentieth centuries put together by Essex University. We used prosopographical data found in hds.essex.ac.uk/history/data/prosopography.

history.ac.uk
The Institute for Historical Research (IHR) provides resources for historians, including an open-access library and major digital projects including British History Online and the Bibliography of British and Irish History. Among the most important of these is Connected Histories (www.connectedhistories.org.uk) featuring British History sources 1500–1900, the History SPOT (Seminar Podcasts and Online Training), which include podcasts of selected IHR seminars, with accompanying research materials and discussion facilities.

historyonline.chadwyck.co.uk
Another example of online databases created by a commercial publisher.

jstor.org
A large subscription based website providing access to past articles in over a thousand journals across the disciplines.

kingscrossvoices.org.uk
An online database compiled by a project to record the memories of people living in the King's Cross area of London.

le.ac.uk/emoha
The website of the East Midlands Oral History Archive hosted by Leicester University. The memories we accessed can be found at le.ac.uk/emoha/community/resources/county/newton/growingup.

memory.loc.gov/ammem
An outstanding archive put together by the American Memory Historical Collections of the Library of Congress. It includes the oral testimonies of former slaves created by the Federal Writers Project, 1936–38.

nationalarchives.gov.uk
One of the most important British databases compiled by The National Archives at Kew. Amongst the valuable services it offers are guidance for school children (nationalarchives.gov.uk/education/students/primary), help in deciphering historical handwritten documents (nationalarchives.gov.uk/Palaeography), and even the translation of documents in Latin (nationalarchives.gov.uk/Latin).

oldbaileyonline.org
A valuable online database of transcripts of trials held at the Old Bailey compiled by teams at the universities of Sheffield and Hertfordshire in the United Kingdom. It is fully searchable and contains authoritative background information.

oxlip-plus.bodleian.ox.ac.uk
Provides access to Oxford University's extensive online databases, most of which, however, are accessible only to its staff and students.

pase.ac.uk
The Prosopography of Anglo-Saxon England database, compiled by researchers at King's College, London and Cambridge University, provides information on all recorded inhabitants in England from the late sixth to the late eleventh centuries.

pbw.kcl.ac.uk
Prosopography of the Byzanytine World presents information on every individual mentioned in Byzantine textual sources over the period 642–1261.

publichistory.org
The Public History Resource Center is an American organisation that, in its own words, 'exists to support, promote, and disseminate the scholarly and professional work of public historians. The Resource Center provides a forum for research, scholarship, networking, and education in public history and seeks to broaden and deepen the general public's awareness of the field of public history in all its diversity and complexity'.

sahistoryonline.org.za
The South African History Online project was established in 2000 to break the silence which had afflicted histories of the country by creating a large online encyclopaedia of South African culture, politics and society.

theclergydatabase.org.uk
A searchable database of clerical careers in England and Wales over 1540–1835.

Index